The English Works of Giles Fletcher, the Elder

The English Works
of
Giles Fletcher, the Elder

Edited by

LLOYD E. BERRY

The University of Wisconsin Press

Madison, 1964

Published by the University of Wisconsin Press
430 Sterling Court, Madison 6, Wisconsin

Copyright © 1964 by the Regents of the
University of Wisconsin

Printed in The Netherlands
by N.V. Drukkerij G. J. Thieme
Nijmegen

Library of Congress Catalog Card Number 63-8437

TO

PETER G. PHIALAS

Preface

This critical edition of Giles Fletcher, the Elder, collects for the first time all his known English works: *Licia*, *Of the Russe Commonwealth*, *The Tartars or Ten Tribes*, and forty-one letters. I am hopeful that the biographical introduction, the introductions to the poetry and prose, and the explanatory notes will provide the reader with the material necessary for a proper evaluation of Fletcher as a typical man of the Renaissance—a statesman by profession and a man of letters by avocation.

Fletcher's sizable body of Latin verse I have decided to omit, believing its quantity far to exceed its quality. Much of the poetry was written either in Fletcher's schoolboy days at Eton or as occasional verse; and only the "De Literis Antiquæ Britanniæ," "Querela de obitu Clerj Haddonj," "Æcloga de contemptu ministrorum quj verbo diuino pascunt," and "Queræla Collegij Regalis sub D. P. B." have any appreciable literary or historical significance. These four poems have received attention by scholars, and I have edited them, along with "In nuptias clarissimj viri D. Edouardj Vere Comitis Oxoni, & Annæ Ceciliæ optimæ ac illustrissimæ fæminæ," in "Five Latin Poems by Giles Fletcher, the Elder," *Anglia*, LXXIX (1962), 338–77. The reader who is interested in Fletcher's Latin verse may care to consult Warren B. Austin, "Milton's *Lycidas* and Two Latin Elegies by Giles Fletcher, the Elder," *SP*, XLIV (1947), 41–55; Robert R. Raymo,

"Three New Latin Poems of Giles Fletcher the Elder," *MLN*, LXXI (1956), 399–401; and my "Three Poems by Giles Fletcher, the Elder, in *Poemata Varii Argumenti* (1678)," *N&Q*, n.s. VI (1959), 132–34; and "Giles Fletcher, the Elder: A Bibliography," *Transactions of the Cambridge Bibliographical Society*, III, part 3 (1961), 200–215.

In the course of the four years that have been devoted to this edition, I have incurred many debts which are my pleasure to acknowledge.

From 1957 to 1958 I held a University Scholarship and a Special First Year Graduate Scholarship at the University of North Carolina, and in 1958 I presented an edition of Fletcher's letters for the M.A. degree. From 1958 to 1960 I held a Marshall Scholarship to Magdalene College, Cambridge, and in 1960 I presented Fletcher's English works and biography for the Ph.D. degree. I am grateful indeed to the Marshall Aid Commemoration Commission, its Chairman, Lord Coleraine, its Executive Secretary, Dr. John F. Foster, and his assistant, Miss Mary Coppinger, for the personal interest each takes in the Marshall Scholars.

The following institutions, libraries, and persons have graciously permitted the use in this edition of material by or relating to Fletcher: King's College, Cambridge; Magdalene College, Cambridge; Trinity College, Cambridge; Queens' College, Cambridge; the University Archives, Cambridge; University Library, Cambridge; University College, Oxford; the Bodleian; the British Museum; the Public Record Office, London; Library of the Guildhall, London; Corporation of the City of London; His Grace the Archbishop of Canterbury and the Trustees of the Lambeth Palace Library; East Sussex Record Office; West Sussex Record Office; the Corporation of the City of Rye; the Parish Church of Cranbrook, Kent; the Parish Church of Watford, Hertfordshire; the Parish Church of St. Thomas the Apostle, London; the Parish Church of St. Luke's, Chelsea; the Parish Church of St. Olave, Hart Street, London; the Parish Church of Allhallows, London Wall, London; the Duke of Rutland; Lord Kenyon. I am especially grateful to the Marquis of Salisbury, who has permitted me to use freely his magnificent collection, and to his librarian, Miss Clare Talbot, who has answered patiently my numerous queries. In the United States, the University of Illinois, the Folger Shakespeare Library, the Henry E. Huntington Library, and the James Ford Bell Collection of the University of Minnesota have permitted the use of material in their libraries. For the reproductions of the title pages of *Licia*, *The Russe Commonwealth*, and *Israel Redux*, I am indebted to the Bodleian Library; for Fletcher's letter, to the Marquis of Salisbury.

My work has likewise profited by the suggestions of several persons. Dr. E. M. W. Tillyard and Dr. M. C. Bradbrook supervised my work at Cambridge, and each read parts of the edition. Mr. J. C. T. Oates and Mr. A. N. L. Munby made valuable comments on bibliographical matters. Mr. George Trapp, Senior Instructor in Russian for Service Courses in Cambridge University, assisted me with material relating to Fletcher in Russian and provided the translations from Russian sources which appear in this edition. My colleague, Professor G. Blakemore Evans, has kindly read all the introductory material. The faults that remain, I fear, are my own.

The editors of *The Journal of English and Germanic Philology*, *The Library*, *Notes and Queries* (and its publishers, the Oxford University Press), and *The Transactions of the Cambridge Bibliographical Society* have permitted me to use material from my articles in their journals.

But my deepest debt of gratitude is to Professor Peter G. Phialas, the only begetter of this work. He suggested that I edit Fletcher and patiently watched over the edition of the letters. His wise counsel and continuing friendship have meant much to me through the years.

I owe a great deal to my wife, who in 1957 admitted Fletcher as a guest in our house, and who has allowed him to remain these past years, even though he has at times been very trying indeed.

LLOYD E. BERRY

1 August 1961
University of Illinois
Urbana, Illinois

Contents

Abbreviations and Short Titles

Abbreviations and Short Titles

Grosart 1876   Alexander B. Grosart (ed.), *Poems by Giles Fletcher, LL.D.*, Manchester, 1876

Hakluyt   Richard Hakluyt, *The Principal Navigations, Voyages, Traffiques & Discoveries of the English Nation...*, 10 vols., London, 1927–28

Horsey   "The Travels of Jerome Horsey, Knt.," in *Russia at the Close of the Sixteenth Century*, edited by Edward A. Bond, London, 1856

JEGP   *Journal of English and Germanic Philology*

Kliuchevsky   V. O. Kluchevsky, *A History of Russia*, translated by C. J. Hogarth, 5 vols., London, 1911–31

L   Lee edition of *The Tartars or Ten Tribes*

Lansd.   Lansdowne MSS, British Museum

MLN   *Modern Language Notes*

MLR   *Modern Language Review*

MP   *Modern Philology*

N&Q   *Notes and Queries*

Notes on Russia   R. H. Major (ed. and trans.), *Notes Upon Russia: being a translation of the earliest account of that country, entitled* Rerum moscoviticarum commentarii, *by the Baron Sigismund von Herberstein*, 2 vols., London, 1851–52

OED   *Oxford English Dictionary*

PCC   Privy Council Cases

PRO   Public Records Office, London

RES   *Review of English Studies*

Seredonin   S. M. Seredonin, Сочиненіе Джильса Флетчера "Of the Russe common wealth," какъ историческій источникъ, St. Petersburg, 1891

SP   State Papers

SP   *Studies in Philology*

STC   Alfred W. Pollard and G. R. Redgrave, *A Short-Title Catalogue of Books Printed in England, Scotland, and Ireland and of English Books Printed Abroad, 1475–1640*, London, 1926

W Whiston edition of *The Tartars or Ten Tribes*

Wing Donald G. Wing, *A Short-Title Catalogue of Books Printed in England, Scotland, Ireland, Wales, and British America and of English Books Printed in Other Countries, 1641–1700*, 3 vols., New York, 1945–51

Transliteration

In the Introduction and Explanatory Notes to *The Russe Commonwealth*, names of Russian individuals are transliterated according to a modification of the Library of Congress system, with the exceptions that the final *-skii* is rendered *-sky* and the final *-yi* and *-ii* are rendered *-y* and *-i*, respectively. Russian place names are given in the form used in *Webster's Geographical Dictionary*.

General Introduction

The Life of
Giles Fletcher, the Elder

I

1546-1565

Richard Fletcher, the father of Giles, and the grandfather of three poets, John, Phineas, and Giles, was born in Yorkshire "honestis parentibus."[1] A. B. Grosart states that Ralph Thoresby, the antiquary, noted in his copy of Fuller's *Worthies* that Richard Fletcher, Bishop of London, was born at Great Liversedge; but he adds that Thoresby gave no authority for this information. Grosart suggests that Thoresby might have "confounded the son with the father."[2] As parish registers for the period

1. The best outline of Richard Fletcher's life is a plaque in the Cranbrook, Kent, Church, put there in 1589 by his sons, Richard and Giles. It reads as follows: "Richardvs Fletcher ex Eboracensi Provincia; Honestis Parentibvs natvs; a quibvs Cantabrigiam missvs, bonis artibvs, sese exercvit donec artivm magister factvs est; hinc Regnvm inevnte Edovardo VIᵒ, in sacrvm ministerivm assvmptvs est, a sanctissimo viro ac martyre, Nichilo Ridleio, Londinensi Episcopo (ex eorvm nvmero qvi tvm primo pro more ac ritvm ecclesiæ Reformatæ, sacris ordinibvs initiati svnt) in cvivs diocoesi verbi ministerio diligenter incvbvit, postea temporibvs Marianis cvm ferro et flamma evangelici peterentvr adversa mvlta et vincvla pertvlit: sed restitvto evangelio et ipse sacro mvneri restitvtvs est, et hvic ecclesiæ pastor designatvs anno Iᵒ serenissimæ principis Elizabethæ hic pvblice verbo: privatim vita, prædicando pavperibvs erogando: omnibvs consvlendo: (quantvm in ipso fvit,) interger ac bonis omnibvs charvs; cvm per XXVI annos et menses VII hvic ecclesiæ præfvisset tandem ex hac vita ad coelos demigravit anno ætatis qvarto svpra sexagesimvm filios svperstites reliqvit dvos qvos vidit altervm Theologiæ altervm legvm doctorem illvm capellanvm regivm decanvm Petribvrg nvnc Episcopvm Bristoll et Regiæ Maiestis, Eleemosynarivm svmmvm hvnc eidem Maiesti ad magnvm Rvssiæ, imperatorem legatvm. Obiit mvndo 12ᵒ die mensis Febrvarii anno 1585 vivit Deo ad æternitatem corpvs in area inferiori, svb proximo saxo reconditvr."

2. Grosart 1871, pp. 7–8.

are not extant in this area, I have been unable to discover any further information. There is an interesting mention of a Yorkshire Fletcher in the executors' accounts of the estate of Archbishop Thomas Savage: "Puero domini Roberti Flessher, meanti ad scholas Cant., xijd."[3] But as Savage died in 1507, it is obvious this boy could not be Richard,[4] although in due time Richard did go to Cambridge and eventually became a master of arts.[5]

After his graduation from Cambridge, there is a possibility that he traveled to Persia. Giles records this in *Licia*:

> I might have dyed, before my lyfe begunne,
> When as my father for his countries good,
> The Persians favour and the Sophy wonne:
> But yet with daunger, of his dearest blood.

> (Sonnet XXII)

But in the public records of this time there is no mention of Richard which would offer any corroborative evidence.

More definitely, after his graduation he married and settled in Watford, Hertfordshire. His wife's name, I believe, was Joan.[6] Their first child, Richard, was baptized on 28 September 1543. And three years later, on 26 November 1546, Giles was baptized.[7]

On 24 June 1550 Bishop Nicholas Ridley conferred Holy Orders on Richard Fletcher, John Foxe, and others "before the high altar at St. Paul's, according to the rite, manner, and form of the Church of England lately published and enjoined."[8] And on 9 November Bishop Ridley or-

3. *Testamenta Eboracensia, A Selection of Wills From the Registry at York*, IV, Surtees Society, LIII (1868), 307.

4. See Grosart 1871, p. 10.

5. Information from the plaque. Venn bases his information in *Alumni Cantabrigienses* on this.

6. As there is no mention of her in the church records of Cranbrook (where the family lived after 1559), it is possible that she had died before the family moved there. If this is the case, there is this possibility of identification: On 12 April 1557, Johan Fletcher was buried at Watford; and the only Fletchers in the register from 1540 to 1557 are the Richard Fletchers.

7. "Christnings 1546, November, 'Gyles son of Rychard Fletcher the 26 day.'" The Liber Protocollum of King's College, which records admissions, states that Fletcher was 17 when he was admitted. According to the baptismal date, Fletcher would have been 18. But there would be no reason to falsify the college entry, as no person was barred admittance until he had passed his twentieth birthday.

8. John Strype, *Ecclesiastical Memorials* (3 vols.; Oxford, 1822), II, 402.

dained Richard and others at Fulham.[9] It is probable that Fletcher and John Foxe were friends. Foxe mentions Fletcher twice in his *Actes and Monuments*, and Giles wrote a commendatory poem which appeared in the second and each succeeding edition of that work.

Richard's first living was Bishop's Stortford, to which he was collated on 19 June 1551; and on 7 February 1552 he was collated to the additional benefice of Ugley. Both parishes were in the jurisdiction of the Bishop of London, although Fletcher's patron at Bishop's Stortford was John Sherry, Archdeacon of Lewes, and his patron at Ugley was King Edward VI. Fletcher was a zealous Protestant, which proved unfortunate for him when Mary came to the throne. In 1553 she deprived Bishop Ridley of his bishopric, and two years later he was burned at the stake.[10] Fletcher did not suffer such adversity, but the plaque at Cranbrook states: "…postea temporibvs Marianis cvm ferro et flamma evangelici peterentvr adversa mvlta et vincvla pertvlit." On 18 April 1554 he resigned as vicar of Ugley; and on 23 February of the following year, he was deprived of the vicarage of Bishop's Stortford. Where he was from 1555 to 1559 can be only partly determined. In July 1555, he and his son Richard witnessed the martyrdom of Christopher Wade at Dartford, Kent.[11] And in June 1557, he and another man witnessed John Taylor, a cruel priest of Frittenden parish, accuse Edmund Allin and his wife before Sir John Baker of "exhorting and reading the Scriptures to the people." On 18 June, Allin and his wife, along with five others, were burned at Maidstone.[12]

According to the Cranbrook plaque, Richard was made pastor of Cranbrook church in the first year of Queen Elizabeth's reign. Archbishop Parker's register, however, records that Fletcher was collated to the vicarage of Cranbrook on 17 October 1561, upon the resignation of George Atkinson. So Fletcher was not, as has been supposed, the first Reformation vicar. The explanation could well be that he was assistant minister to Atkinson.

Cranbrook was Fletcher's home for the rest of his life. Edward Hasted

9. *Ibid.*, p. 403.

10. See *DNB*, and Charles Henry Cooper and Thompson Cooper (eds.), *Athenae Cantabrigienses* (3 vols.; Cambridge, 1858–1913), I, 135–38.

11. Josiah Pratt (ed.), *The Acts and Monuments of John Foxe* (8 vols.; London, 1877), VII, 319–21.

12. *Ibid.*, VIII, 321–22.

records that in 1648 the parsonage house consisted of "a hall, kitchen, buttery, milkhouse, with several rooms over them, an orchard, little garden, two great barns, one stable and fodder-house with several rooms over them."[13] Much, of course, can change in a hundred years; but it is possible that the parsonage was much like this when Richard and his family lived in it. Although on 17 May 1566 Richard was collated to the additional benefice of Smarden, a few miles away, the Cranbrook church records indicate that Fletcher considered Cranbrook his home.

The Cranbrook register records that a John Fletcher was buried on 14 October 1566, and there is no reason to doubt that he was Richard's son. From the Cranbrook plaque we know that two sons, Richard and Giles, survived their father; but no mention is made of daughters. Records indicate there were two—Priscilla, and one, whose Christian name is not recorded, who married Nathaniel Pownoll.[14] On 26 October 1573, Priscilla Fletcher married William Atkinson, a preacher.[15] Perhaps this Atkinson was the son of the George Atkinson who preceded Richard as vicar. Nothing further is known of this couple. And in his will dated 1593, Richard Fletcher, Bishop of London, bequeathed to "my sister Pownoll" twenty pounds. In a Chancery suit in 1600, she is referred to as the only aunt, an indication that Priscilla had died.[16] One of the Pownolls' children was Nathaniel, who was baptized in Cranbrook on 28 October 1584. He attended Christ Church College, Oxford, and died in 1610. Giles Fletcher, the younger, edited his prose treatise, *The Young Divine's Apologie*, in 1612.[17]

Giles Fletcher did not live long in Cranbrook, for he entered Eton College about 1561. Records of Eton are incomplete for this period, but Fletcher's name appears in the list of collegers for the year beginning September

---

13. *The History and Topographical Survey of the County of Kent* (4 vols.; Canterbury, 1790), III, 55.

14. A. B. Langdale, *Phineas Fletcher* (New York, 1937), p. 56, lists a third daughter, Phebe, but he simply did not read Phebe Fletcher's will carefully. In it she bequeathed a Bible to her cousin Priscilla and fifty pounds to her cousins of Cambridge, Phineas and Giles. So she must have been a daughter of a brother of Richard Fletcher, vicar. The Priscilla mentioned in her will was the daughter of Richard, Bishop of London.

15. A. B. Grosart (ed.), *The Poems of Phineas Fletcher* (4 vols.; n.p., 1869), I, xxvii–xxviii, says Atkinson was a physician; but this is clearly an error. The marriage entry is "Mr William Atkinson p̄chē."

16. C.2/F.6/63. Nathaniell Fletcher *v.* Giles Fletcher.

17. *STC* 20174

1563 and again in the list of January 1565. The only work that has survived from this period is the collection of Latin verses presented to Queen Elizabeth on her visit to Eton on 13 October 1563. Fletcher must have been considered one of the better versifiers at Eton, for he contributed eleven epigrams—more than twice as many as anyone else.

Sometime between 7 July and 15 August 1565, fellows from King's College came to Eton to examine and to determine the order of precedence of those collegers who would be entering King's the coming Michaelmas. This was the most important event of a colleger's life, because he would obtain a fellowship or a college position according to the order in which the examiners had placed him.[18]

II

1565-1581

On 27 August 1565, Fletcher was admitted as a scholar to King's College, along with his fellow Etonians Lakes, Fleminge, Hunte, Bond, and Dorington.[1] Three years later, on 28 August, Fletcher was made a fellow;[2] and in the academic year 1569–70 he proceeded to his B.A. degree and was eighth in the *Ordo senioritatis*.[3] Of the *Ordo senioritatis* Dr. Venn says: "There can be little doubt, that the original and dominant idea was simply that of assigning precedence."[4] But he adds:

> It is of course nearly certain that some notion of merit, in the sense of intellectual superiority, must have been recognised all along; at least so far as the men towards the top of the list are concerned.

18. James Heywood and Thomas Wright, *The Ancient Laws… for King's College, Cambridge, and… Eton College* (London, 1850), pp. 21–29.

1. King's College, Liber Protocollum, I, 206.

2. *Ibid.*, p. 213.

3. John Venn (ed.), *Grace Book Δ* (Cambridge, 1910), p. 233.

4. *Ibid.*, pp. x–xi.

Several considerations support this view. For instance, *examiners* were regularly appointed every year at the same time as the proctors; and it is difficult to imagine examiners making their order of precedence one in which "merit" was not recognised.[5]

A significant event in Fletcher's undergraduate career at King's was the expulsion of Philip Baker, the provost, in 1570. This was no sudden occurrence, for in 1565, several of the fellows appealed to the visitor, the Bishop of Lincoln, for removal of Baker as provost on the charges that he was a papist, that he failed to preach, that he failed to cause others to "divert" to the study of divinity, that he mismanaged college affairs, and that he threatened violence to some of the officers of the college.[6] Nothing seems to have come of this petition; but on 27 November 1569 the fellows again issued complaints, with twenty specific charges.[7] Baker fled from England to Louvain. On 22 February, he was formally deprived of the provostship, and on 19 March, upon the recommendations of the vice-provost and fellows,[8] of Walter Haddon,[9] and of Henry Knollys,[10] Roger Goad was elected provost. Fletcher did not sign any of the complaints against Baker, as he had been a fellow for only about a year and at the time of their presentation had not proceeded to his B.A.; but he did write two eclogues complaining of the state of the college under Baker— "Æcloga de contemptu ministrorum" and "Queræla Collegij Regalis sub D. P. B." Both of these poems can be dated about February 1570.[11] About this time, Fletcher wrote four other poems, one on the death of Bishop Edmund Bonner, who died in September 1569;[12] the other three,

---

5. *Ibid.*, pp. ix–x.

6. BM Lansd. MS 8, No. 53. Some of the documents pertaining to the college disputes of 1565, 1569, and 1576 are printed in James Heywood and Thomas Wright, *The Ancient Laws...for King's College, Cambridge...and Eton College* (London, 1850), pp. 208–50.

7. BM Harleian MS 7031, f. 5.

8. BM Lansd. MS 12, No. 39.

9. BM Lansd. MS 12, No. 52.

10. BM Lansd. MS 12, No. 51.

11. See my "Three Poems by Giles Fletcher, the Elder, in *Poemata Varii Argumenti* (1678)," *N&Q* n.s. VI (1959), 132–34.

12. *Ibid.*

epitaphs on the death of Bridget Butts, who died on 24 January 1570.[13]

In the following year Fletcher contributed verses to Nicholas Carr's edition of several of Demosthenes' orations, which he had translated from Greek into Latin. Carr had died on 2 November 1568, and the book was something of a memorial volume. William Dorington and Thomas Preston contributed memoirs of Carr, and a number of poems on the life and death of Carr were included. It is probable that Fletcher was a friend of Carr, for Greek was also Fletcher's field of study. In December 1571 or shortly thereafter, Fletcher wrote an eclogue celebrating the marriage of Edward de Vere, the Earl of Oxford, to Ann Cecil. About this time, too, he wrote his *De Literis Antiquæ Britanniæ*, which he subsequently revised about 1594.

On 22 March 1572 Fletcher became a lecturer in King's and held this position until 21 March of the following year,[14] when he became lecturer in Greek, a position which he held until Michaelmas term 1579. His duties seem to have been to deliver a lecture in the Greek language daily; for Goad, in a statement of what he had done to advance learning, said that "for the furtheraunce of Knowledge in the tongues ther is an ordinary greek lecture dayly reade vnto the Company."[15]

Fletcher commenced M.A. on 3 July 1573 and was twelfth in the *Ordo senioritatis*.[16] "The *Ordo*," Dr. Venn comments, "was quite as important for the M.A. as for the B.A.: in fact, of the two, the former is the more fully and regularly preserved."[17]

In the following summer the plague visited Cambridge, causing all university functions to be suspended. Most of the residents, C. H. Cooper states, retired to the country.[18] The commons books show that Fletcher left about 17 July and was not resident for the rest of the term; but as the commons books are missing for the next year, there is no way of determining

---

13. See R. R. Raymo, "Three New Latin Poems of Giles Fletcher the Elder," *MLN*, LXXI (1956) 399–401.

14. King's College, Mundum Books. These books record, among other things, the quarterly payments by the college to fellows for positions they held in the college. For example, Fletcher was paid 5s. per quarter as a lecturer and later 10s. per quarter as a lecturer in Greek.

15. BM Lansd. MS 23, No. 40.

16. *Grace Book Δ*, p. 262.

17. *Ibid.*, p. x.

18. Charles Henry Cooper, *Annals of Cambridge* (5 vols.; Cambridge, 1842), II, 321–22.

when he came back into residence. Cooper records that the plague lasted until 21 November.[19]

In 1576 King's College was again beset with strife between the fellows and the provost. Some of the younger fellows, including Fletcher, sent articles to the visitor, the Bishop of Lincoln, for the removal of Goad; and on 24 April the Bishop of Lincoln wrote to Lord Burghley:

My duetie consydered right honorable, forsomuch as diuers of the felowes of Kinges College in Cambridge haue ernestlie sued vnto me to signifie vnto your Lordship howe they haue dealte with me touch-inge redresse of certaine disorders in their howse: I am bolde to trouble you with thes letters. It maie please your Honour therfore to vnderstande that sens my late returne from London, diuers of that house haue complained vnto me of sundrie greate and enormious disorders, aswell touchinge the state of their howse, as certaine par-ticuler persons within the same: exhibitinge vnto me manie Articles drawen and set downe to that effecte for proof and redress wherof, the Bishop of Lincoln, for the time beinge, beinge ther vysitour, they haue ernestlie required at my handes a visitacion. The matters exhibited, when I ernestlie consydered of, the articles beinge true, as they ernestlie affirmed, I sawe they did touche the state of the howse verie neer, and therfore required speedie amendemente. Notwithstandinge mine aunswere to their requeste was, that al-thoughe I were their visitour by their Statutes apointed, yet had I no auctoritie extraordinarilie to visite, my visitacion beinge but a trien-nio ad trienium, and the time sens my last visitacion there, not yet elapsed: neither would I take vponn me to visite them extraordinarilie without auctoritie, least the same my proceadinge mighte be frustrate and to none effecte, as before time I haue had some cause to feare. And whenas by no meanes they coulde perswade me without law-full auctoritie by Statute to visite...they further requested my leaue with great importunitie...to seeke redresse of the higher auctoritie, wherevnto I in the ende accordinglie condescended.[20]

19. *Ibid.*, p. 324.
20. BM Lansd. MS 22, No. 89.

What was the cause of the rebellion? In a manuscript endorsed "Queries to bee put to those that articled against Dr. Goad the Provost," the first query is: "Seinge Mr. Fletcher hathe confessed at Dr. Wattes howse that the articles were brought vpp to make a showe to drawe on a Commission. Whether this devise grew from amongest them selues or was receyved abroad from any other?"[21] The articles have not survived, but we know that they were sixty-one in number;[22] however, in a note to Burghley, Goad summarizes the charges, the most serious charging him with:

1. Vsury, in havinge 400^{li} or 500^{li} of the Colledge monny at banke
2. Corruption and bribery
3. Clokinge of periury and vncleanes of lief not to be named
4. Takinge monny for my places at Eaton, and beinge a broker of sellinge places at Cambridge
5. Deludinge and glossinge with noble and honorable persons
6. Hinderinge and vtter clokinge of learninge contrary to myne othe
7. That I have very wyde back doores to loose and lewde lyvinge[23]

In defense of himself, Goad enumerated what he had done for the further-ance of learning in the college since becoming provost.[24] And in another manuscript he specifically answers twenty-five additional charges.[25]

Who were the fellows involved? Another of the "Queries" put to those concerned in the affair is: "Whether thei do not knowe that Mr Dunninge and Mr Lakys haue ben the cheif doers in their attemptes and provokers of others thervnto? or whether thei know any other more principall?"[26] These two seem to have been the leaders, and the other chief participants were Robert Liles, Robert Johnson, and Fletcher.

The course of events thus far follows almost exactly the action brought against the provost in 1569. But the results were far different. Burghley

21. BM Lansd. MS 23, No. 39.
22. BM Lansd. MS 23, No. 23. Robert Johnson, in this letter of submission, mentions that there were sixty-one articles.
23. BM Lansd. MS 23, No. 41.
24. BM Lansd. MS 23, No. 40.
25. BM Lansd. MS 23, No. 38.
26. BM Lansd. MS 23, No. 39.

decided in favor of Goad and took action swiftly. Dunning and Lakes were committed to the Gatehouse Prison, Westminster; and it is possible Fletcher was interned, as he was absent from college from 5 May to 2 June. All fellows involved had to submit to both Burghley and Goad. Fletcher wrote five letters of submission to Burghley and one to Goad.[27] The other four wrote some fifteen letters among them,[28] all between 22 and 28 May. But this was not enough. Burghley insisted that they make a public submission, which accordingly took place on 2 June:

> The Submission of Stephen Lakes and certein others within named, fellowes of the Kinges Colledge in Cambridge enioyned by the Right Honorable the Lord Treasurer of England to be pronounced by the said Lakes before the Provost of the same Colledge.
>
> I do acknowledge and confesse that I with others haue greately offended and iniured Mr Provost of this Colledge in indicting, wryting, exhibiting, and prosecuting dyvers vntrue, and sclaunderous articles against him, aswell to some of the Honorable Councell, and namely to the Right Honorable the Lord Burghley the head Chauncelour, as to others to the defaming of him, and impayring of his creditt, if the said Articles had conteyned truth. Wherein, I do lykewise acknowledge and confesse great rashnes in charging him with surmised matters, which I am not able to prove, beside the irreverent and odious termes in the same conteyned. For all which my doinge, I am now hartely sory, and wold be redie, if I knew how, to make any other satisfaction, to do it to my vttermost power. Wherefore before your Worships here, I promise hereafter by godes grace never to committ the lyke offence. But to lyve in this societie in duetifull obedience and quietnes withall others...so long as I shall lyve in this Colledge. And where I did ioyne and the wryting and prosecuting of the said complaintes Mr Robert Dunning, Gyles Fletcher, Robert Iohnson, and Robert Lylesse, which four persons haue also before your Right Honorable the Lord Burghley our

27. See Letters 1–6.
28. BM Lansd. MS 23, Nos. 18, 21–23, 25, 28–35, and 37.

Chauncelour and others confessed their faultes, I do with them, and for them here let this present promise to do our endevours to make amendes for the same, by our quyet lyving in this Colledge, and specially by our reverent behaviour towardes our provost in all causes reasonable.[29]

Dunning was expelled from the university;[30] and as no mention of Johnson occurs after this time, one can assume that he either was expelled or left on his own accord. Liles returned to college, but subsequently, in 1583, was expelled from the university when he libeled another fellow of King's.[31]

Peace again was restored to the college. Fletcher received commons from 2 June on, and continued as the lecturer in Greek. During 1576, also, he contributed to Foxe's *Actes and Monuments* the commendatory poem mentioned above,[32] and five poems to *Poematum Libri Duo*, a revised collection of Walter Haddon's poems. Haddon had died in January 1571, and to this volume of poems several elegies and eclogues were contributed in memory of him. One of Fletcher's poems is an eclogue on the death of Clere Haddon, Walter's son, who drowned in the Cam River only some four months after his father died.

In 1577 Fletcher became deputy public orator. One of his acts as orator has survived: on 14 September, on behalf of the university, he wrote to Thomas Wotton thanking him for a gift of books he had given to Cambridge.[33] And for the year 1577–78, Fletcher and Nicholas Athow were appointed examiners: "Conceditur 17 Januarii vt magister Egidius Fletcher et Nicholaus Athow sint vestra auctoritate examinatores..."[34]

In addition, Fletcher, from the time that he became fellow in 1568 until he became a senior fellow in 1578, served with the fellows in college as steward. This position rotated among the fellows each week; each fellow

29. BM Lansd. MS 23, No. 42.

30. Charles Henry Cooper and Thompson Cooper (eds.), *Athenae Cantabrigienses* (3 vols.; Cambridge, 1858–1913), I, 363.

31. BM Lansd. MS 39, No. 6.

32. See p. 5.

33. See Letter 7.

34. Venn, *Grace Book Δ*, p. 307.

held it about twice a year. The duties consisted mainly of recording which students would get full commons, which half-commons, and which were absent. The steward also listed the food purchased by the college for the week, and payments to servants of the college.[35]

In Michaelmas term 1578 Fletcher became one of the senior fellows. And in July of the following year he was one of the interrogators sent to examine those students at Eton who would be proceeding to King's the next Michaelmas.[36] By statute the examination had to take place between 7 July and 15 August; and the commons books indicate that Fletcher left college about 29 July. He did not return until about 20 October, well into the Michaelmas term. And this explains why it was not until Michaelmas that he claimed his expenses for the time at Eton: "Item. Magistro Fletcher pro conduct equi cum Interrogator Ætonam proficisteretur pro 10 diebus. Xˢ." [37] Most likely, after he performed his duties at Eton he visited his family in Cranbrook.

At some time between 1577 and 1579 Fletcher composed a poem on the coat-of-arms of Maximilian Brooke, the eldest son of Lord Cobham. Brooke was admitted to King's in June of 1577 but left the university without proceeding to a degree, and died sometime in 1583. Fletcher's poem does not mention Brooke's death, and it would be reasonable to assume that Fletcher wrote the poem at some time during, or immediately after, Brooke's residence at King's. Holinshed records that Fletcher "greatlie loued this gentleman."[38]

In 1579 Fletcher wrote a commendatory poem to be prefaced to Peter Baro's *In Jonam Prophetam Praelectiones*. Baro had been Lady Margaret's Professor of Divinity since 1574. Fletcher probably became friends with Baro when they both were lecturing in King's; for when Fletcher was giving his daily lecture in Greek, Baro was giving lectures in Hebrew and divinity.[39]

35. Heywood and Wright, *Ancient Laws for King's College*, pp. 73–74.
36. *Ibid.*, pp. 23–29. See p. 7 above.
37. King's College, Mundum Books.
38. Raphael Holinshed, *The Chronicles of England, Scotland, and Ireland* (3 vols.; London, 1587), III, sig. 7G5ᵛ.
39. BM Lansd. MS 23, No. 40.

14

For the year 1579–80, Fletcher was one of the bursars of the college. On 28 October 1579, he was diverted to the study of civil law.[40]

On 3 July 1580 Fletcher was appointed commissary to Dr. Richard Bridgewater, Chancellor of Ely;[41] and it is very likely that Fletcher owed his appointment to him. Fletcher's university career followed Bridgewater's almost exactly. Bridgewater was succeeded as lecturer in Greek by Fletcher; and both held the positions of bursar and dean of arts. Both studied civil law, and Fletcher was the deputy public orator when Bridgewater was the orator.

For the first two terms of the year 1580–81, Fletcher held the highest position he was to attain in King's, that of dean of arts. It was the dean's responsibility to maintain discipline among the scholars and to supervise their studies.[42] But since Fletcher was not in residence for most of this period it is unlikely that he performed many of the required duties. Fletcher had decided to marry, which meant that he would have to give up his fellowship. On 26 November he left Cambridge for Cranbrook; and on 16 January, in his father's church, he married Joan Sheafe. She was born on 19 December 1562, the daughter of Thomas and Mary Sheafe.[43] The Sheafes were influential clothiers in Cranbrook, and at his death Thomas was styled a yeoman.[44] He was also a churchwarden for many years.

Fletcher returned to Cambridge on 25 March, but he did not keep residence regularly. In fact, he was absent from 29 April to 30 June. On 23 June he received his Doctor of Civil Laws degree.[45] And on 5 July he was appointed to a commission to visit the church at Chichester: "...a Commission issued out dated at London July 5th from Aubrey and Clark for the Visiting of the Church of Chichester...was directed to Richard Bishop of

40. King's College, Liber Protocollum, II, 13.

41. William Stevenson, *Supplement to The History and Antiquities of the Conventual and Cathedral Church of Ely* (Norwich, 1817), p. 32.

42. Heywood and Wright, *Ancient Laws for King's College*, pp. 64–65.

43. A plaque placed in the church on the death of Mary Sheafe by her son Edmund reads: "Mary Sheafe, the wife of Thomas Sheafe, who lived together nere XLV years, and had issue between them IX sons and VI daughters, she a grave and charitable matron, dyed LXXIII years of Age, November, 1609. imposivit E S."

44. Cranbrook Churchwarden's Accounts. 1604, September 4. "Thomas Sheafe, Yeoman."

45. Venn, *Grace Book Δ*, p. 342.

15

the Diocese, and also Giles Fletcher, LL.D., Henry Blaxton, Daniel Gardiner, and William Cole, Masters of Art, and John Drury, Clerk, Bachelour of Laws."[46] Accordingly, Fletcher was absent from college from 15 to 28 July. He was back in residence the week beginning 29 July and remained in college until 29 September, when his name is dropped from the commons books.[47]

III

1582-1595

Joan Fletcher probably stayed in Cranbrook after her marriage, and when Giles returned from Cambridge in November, they settled in Cranbrook. For a short time now all the Fletcher family were reunited. Richard, who had been minister at Rye since he had left Corpus Christi College in 1574, became an assistant to his father in 1580 and continued as such until his appointment as Dean of Peterborough in November 1583.

The new year was good to Fletcher. On 8 April 1582 Giles and Joan's first child, Phineas, was baptized. During the early part of the year, Giles was made chancellor of the diocese of Sussex; and in May the mayor and jurats of Rye issued this proclamation:

> To all Christian people to whom these presents shall come we the Mayor and Iurats of the auncient towne of Rye in the countye of Sussex send greeting in our Lord god everlastinge.
>
> Forasmuch as it is the part of every Christian to giue a true and honest testimonye of those which deserue the same,
>
> Know ye that we the sayd Mayour and Iurates of Rye doe thus

46. John Strype, *The History of the Life and Acts of Edmund Grindal* (London, 1710), p. 267. The report of the commission is preserved at the West Sussex Record Office, Chichester, but it does not add anything to Fletcher's life. (EP I/18/16.)

47. In connection with this chapter see my "Phineas Fletcher's Account of His Father," *JEGP*, LX (1961), 258–67.

testifie concerning Mr Doctor Fletcher chauncellour of this Diocesse, that synce the time of his comming to the office of Chauncellorship he hath dealt very iustlie and vprightlie in the execution thereof, and never in any thinge iniustlie or corruptlie so farr as we know or ever hearde: And therfore as he hath desirved great loue and commendation among vs so we hartely desyre he may longe tyme abyde and contynew in this Diocesse to the glory of god and the benefitt of this countrye. In witnes wherof aswell the seale of office of Mairaltie within the said towne we haue hervnto put as also subscribed our names. Dated the xxixth of Maye in the xxiiijth yere &c.[1]

The only action by Fletcher as chancellor that has survived occurred on 8 March 1583, when he was involved in a controversy between William Jackson and Thomas Underdowne, and Henry Shales. Jackson exhibited twenty-eight articles against Shales, charging him with heresy, and Fletcher witnessed several of the articles.[2] Underdowne witnessed all the articles against Shales except one. On the same day, Shales wrote a letter charging Underdowne with advocating that anyone who had an inward persuasion and assurance that he was called by God might lawfully preach.[3] And on 18 April Shales answered each of the charges that had been levied against him,[4] apparently ending the controversy.

Fletcher was elected to the parliament which began on 23 November 1584, from Winchelsea, one of the Cinque Ports. It is probable that Lord Cobham, the Lord Warden of the Cinque Ports, was Fletcher's patron. Fletcher, it will be remembered, wrote a poem on the coat-of-arms of Maximilian Brooke, his eldest son.

Just before the parliament began, Joan Fletcher gave birth to a second child, Anne, who was baptized on 22 November in Cranbrook. It is likely that she did not join her husband in London until after the new year, as the parliament was adjourned for Christmas on 21 December and did not re-

1. Rye MS 12a/11.
2. SP 12/159, Nos. 14–15.
3. SP 12/159, No. 16.
4. SP 12/160, No. 12.

sume until 4 February. But from this time on, London was the Fletchers' home.

During the parliament of 1584–85, Fletcher served on three committees. The most important was called on 16 December to consider reforms of abuse in the Church of England: "to view over the said Petitions, and to reduce the contents of the same into some particular Heads or Articles, which being put in writing, might be imparted unto the Lords of the Upper House, and that request might thereupon be made to their Lordships to joyn with the House of Commons in such further course as should be meet."[5] The bill was drawn up, but when it came to the attention of the queen, she firmly ended further consideration of it, for she reminded the Commons that she had commanded them not to meddle with matters of the church, neither in reformation of religion nor of discipline, and that she would not receive any motion of innovation, nor alter or change any law whereby the religion or Church of England was established.[6]

Fletcher was also added to a committee on 26 February to consider a bill against "Idleness and Incontinent Life, and for the punishment of Rogues and Vagabonds."[7] A bill against unlawful marriages was sent by Dr. Fletcher to this committee.[8] There is no further reference to the first bill, but the latter was passed by Commons, only to die in Lords.[9]

And on 24 March, Fletcher was appointed to a committee to consider a bill for "suppressing of Pirates and Piracy,"[10] but as parliament was prorogued five days later, nothing came of the bill.

During the parliament, Fletcher seems to have come under the patronage of Sir Thomas Randolph and Sir Francis Walsingham. Fletcher accompanied Randolph to Scotland in 1586 and from there wrote Walsingham on two occasions,[11] in one letter begging him to be a means of securing some new

5. Sir Simonds D'Ewes, *The Journals of all the Parliaments During the Reign of Queen Elizabeth* (London, 1682), p. 340.

6. J. E. Neale, *Elizabeth I and Her Parliaments, 1584–1601* (London, 1957), p. 74. For a full account of this, see pp. 63–77.

7. D'Ewes, *Journals of the Parliaments*, p. 360.

8. *Ibid.*, p. 361.

9. Neale, *Elizabeth I and Her Parliaments*, p. 77.

10. D'Ewes, *Journals of the Parliaments*, p. 372.

11. See Letters 8 and 9.

18

employment.[12] Fletcher's selection for the mission to Russia in 1588 would also suggest the patronage of Randolph, who had been ambassador there himself.

In December 1585, the queen recommended Fletcher to the position of Remembrancer of the City of London:

> Right trustie and welbeloved, and trustie and welbeloved wee greete you well whereas in the late services divers waies supplied by our late lovinge subiect Thomas Norton deceased manie good offices were don in the name of that our Cittie to the verie good content-ment of vs and our Counsell whereby wee are moved to thinke that the Continuance of that service to be supplied by some trustie and sufficient man is a matter verie expedient bothe for vs and you: And vnderstandinge the same to be as yet vnfurnished wee have thought good to recommend vnto you for the same purpose, our wel-beloved subiecte Docter fletcher, as one whom for his learninge integretie and other Commendable partes wee iudge meete and sufficient to supplie the place of the said Norton, and further to serve for some other purposes which we esteeme verie expedient bothe for vs and for you we doe therefore verie earnestlie require you to make choice of him to that place wherein that he maie the better employ him self whollie to your and his contentacion ye shall doe verie well to allot vnto him some suche reasonable and sufficient stipend as shalbe requisite as well for the honor of that our Cittie, as for his better maynteinance with Credit in that place and service your readi-nes and Conformities herein to the performance of this our request (whereof we assure our self aforehand) wee will accept in right thank-full parte and acknowledge the same to your Comfortes hereafter, as of occasion may be offred. Seven [sic] vnder our signet at our manner of Richmond the xixth daie of December in the xxixth yere of our Raigne.[13]

On 19 January the mayor and aldermen replied to the queen:

12. Letter 9.
13. Corporation of London, Journal 22, f. 77ᵛ.

Most dread and gratious Soveraign may it please your Highnes to bee
advertised that vpon the receipt of your Maiesties Letters directed
vnto vs on the beehalf of Doctour Fletcher to be supplied into the service of our Citie lately perfourmed by Thomas Norton deceased wee
have proposed the same to our common Assemblie with all speedy
and duetifull regard of your Maiesties good pleasure. And according
to the contents of your Highnes sayed Letters wee proceeded foorthwith to the election of the sayed D. Fletcher as taking your Maiesties
good opinion and recommendation made of him to be meet and
sufficient direction for our iudgments thearin.[14]

On 21 January the request was considered favorably by the City's Common
Council;[15] on the twenty-sixth the Court of Aldermen confirmed the
appointment and took the opportunity to define the terms of the office.[16]
The tenure was for "so longe tyme as he shall well and honestlye vse and
behave hym selfe in the execucion" of the office. His duties were to write
letters for the City and to make a true copy of all letters sent and received
by the City; to attend the Lord Mayor and aldermen and to be ready at
all times to be employed in all messages, needs, services, and affairs of the
City as should be required. For this Fletcher was to receive fifty pounds
per year, paid quarterly. On the same day, Fletcher was admitted to the
freedom of the City by redemption in the Company of Haberdashers
without paying the usual fees.[17]

In February 1586, Fletcher was sent on his first mission as minister, as
an assistant to Sir Thomas Randolph, who was entrusted with negotiating
a league between James VI and Elizabeth. Before Fletcher left, however,
he probably went to Cranbrook, as his father died on 12 February and was
buried on the fourteenth.

Negotiations for this league had begun the previous May, when the
queen sent Edward Wotton to Scotland to urge James to enter into a joint

14. Corporation of London, Remembrancia I, 573.
15. Corporation of London, Journal 22, f. 77ᵛ.
16. Corporation of London, Repertory 21, ff. 384ᵛ–85.
17. *Ibid.*, f. 385.

league in defense of the Gospel. James was greatly interested in the league, but wanted a larger pension than the offered £5000, although he eventually agreed to this amount. Although all seemed to be going well, Burghley expressed doubt of the outcome, for Henry III of France had sent Baron d'Esneval to prevent its conclusion. But after Randolph's arrival, the negotiations proceeded quickly. In April Francis Miller was sent to the English court with the agreed-on league. James, however, insisted on two concessions for the alliance: (1) that he was to receive the £5000 pension, which the queen had reduced to £4000, and (2) that the queen would do nothing to bar his right to the succession to the English crown. The queen refused to yield to the first point. Nevertheless, because of Randolph's skill and the aid of the Master of Gray, James was persuaded to conclude the league, which was signed at Berwick on 5 July.[18]

Fletcher is not mentioned in any of the correspondence between the English and Scottish courts or emissaries, so it is reasonable to assume that he was not one of the principal agents for the queen. Probably he was an assistant to Randolph, having been chosen for his legal ability.

Sometime during this year, Giles, the younger, was born, although the precise date cannot be fixed.[19]

On 2 April 1587 the Privy Council directed Sir Thomas Puleston, Fletcher, and others to call the creditors of Thomas Charde, stationer, and to order them to give Charde ample time to pay debts of £1500. It was further ordered that neither Charde nor his sureties should be arrested for the debts and that Charde be permitted to travel for the recovery of his debts.[20] Charde, interestingly, is the person who published Fletcher's *Russe Commonwealth* in 1591.

On 4 May, Fletcher was one of the officials of the City of London ordered by the Court of Aldermen to appear at the Star Chamber on the following day to meet with the Privy Council concerning affairs of the City.[21]

---

18. Conyers Read, *Mr. Secretary Walsingham and the Policy of Queen Elizabeth* (3 vols., Oxford, 1925), II, 240–57.

19. A. B. Langdale, *Phineas Fletcher* (New York, 1937), pp. 12–13.

20. PC 2/14, p. 314. See my "Thomas Charde, Printer and Bookseller," *The Library*, 5th ser., XV (1960), 57–58.

21. Corporation of London, Repertory 21, f. 429ᵛ.

On the same day, Fletcher was ordered by the aldermen to go before the Privy Council to obtain warrants to remove all Irish beggars in the City of London, first to Bristol and then to Ireland.[22] The warrants must have been granted, for the aldermen issued orders on 9 May that the beggars should be so removed.[23]

Soon afterwards, Fletcher was sent on his first important mission as special agent for the queen, with Richard Saltonstall, the governor of the Merchants Adventurers, to negotiate with the senate of Hamburg for the restoration of trade rights to the Merchants Adventurers. This mission was unusually important for two reasons: it was the first positive negotiation since the expiration of the treaty between the Merchants Adventurers and Hamburg in 1577; and it was to mark the first time that a treaty would be signed with one of the Hanse towns without the consent of the rest of the League.

In the summer of 1585, representatives of the Hanse towns went to England to arrange terms for mutual trade and to try to obtain the restoration of the privileges of their confederacy. On 3 October at Nonesuch, Elizabeth proposed that if the Hanse towns would restore all the rights and privileges of which the English had recently been deprived, she would restore the rights which the Hanse towns had held at the beginning of her reign. The Hanses returned home, and a conference was held at Lübeck to discuss these proposals, but no general agreement was reached. On 14 December, the King of Denmark, Frederick II, wrote to Hamburg to urge that "in consideracion of this Cause you would shew your selfs forwarde and redie...and...gane the friendship and goodwill of that Queen and hir subiects, rather then by any vnkindnes giue hir occasion to Conceiue a hard opinion of you and moue hir displesur against you."[24] The Hamburghers decided to take independent action. On 6 March of the following year they sent a letter to the queen requesting that she would send ambassadors to treat for a new residence. On 9 March they sent a letter to the Merchants Adventurers asking them to send representatives to treat of the restoration

22. *Ibid.*
23. *Ibid.*, f. 430ᵛ.
24. SP 82/2, No. 30.

of trade. And toward the end of 1586, the Merchants Adventurers petitioned the queen, requesting her assistance in the negotiation.

> Therefore if it shall please her Maiestie by your honours advises that the said Merchantes shall withall convenient speede send their Commissioners in this behalfe. They humbly pray that they may haue with them lettres of commendacion and favour from her Maiestie vnto the Senate and Burghers of Hamburgh of suche effect as to your honourable wisdoomes in this case shall seeme meetest. And that they also may haue her Maiesties Commission vpon the said restitucion graunted as aforesaid (or if it be with somme smalle alteracion acceptable to the said Commissioners) that they may promise and assure to the Hamburghers the full performance of that offred by her Maiesties Commissioners at Nonsuch.[25]

In May of the following year accordingly, Fletcher, the agent of the queen, and Richard Saltonstall, the governor of the Merchants Adventurers, journeyed to negotiate with the senate of Hamburg, little suspecting that difficulties would arise. But from Saltonstall's and Fletcher's letters it is apparent that the Hamburgers were not agreed about the conditions of the establishment of trade.[26] They first insisted on the payment of tolls which they had established. Under protest, Fletcher and Saltonstall agreed to pay sixpence a cloth, but the next day the senate refused the offer. The senate then said that it would not negotiate until the queen granted it the privileges promised at Nonesuch; and finally it said it could not act independently of the rest of the Hanses, a complete reversal of its earlier attitude. Fletcher and Saltonstall, now beginning to doubt if a favorable treaty could be concluded, sent two of the Merchants Adventurers to nearby Stade to see what kind of treaty could be concluded there. They reported that the senate of Stade was very willing to make an agreement but insisted that negotiations with Hamburg be broken off first. This Fletcher and Saltonstall were hesitant to do, for they had six ships of goods and did not want to be left without some means of disposing of the merchandise. But after

25. SP 82/2, No. 52.
26. See Letters 10–13.

negotiating with Hamburg for two months to no effect, Fletcher and Saltonstall decided to conclude a treaty with Stade. They negotiated a ten-year treaty, on terms more favorable than those which had been offered by Hamburg. It was ratified by Elizabeth, and the consuls and senators of Stade acknowledged this ratification graciously.[27]

The reaction of the Hamburghers was immediate. On 7 November they sent a letter of protest to the queen and another to the Lord Chancellor, the Lord Treasurer, and the Secretary,[28] threatening that they would not tolerate the injury offered to their privileges by the new agreement with Stade. They added that they had been, and still were, willing to negotiate with the Merchants Adventurers. Fletcher and Saltonstall advised the queen that the treaty with Stade should not be revoked and explained the advantages of trade with Stade over trade with Hamburg.[29] The queen accordingly wrote to the senate of Hamburg, pointing out that they had refused to negotiate according to their promises.[30]

Fletcher and Saltonstall probably returned to England after concluding the treaty in October.[31] The Hamburghers, however, refused to recognize the treaty and carried through their threats of violence. They blocked the entrance to the Elbe, fired upon English ships, and forced the ships to discharge their cargo at Hamburg. The senate of Stade appealed to Emperor Rudolph II, who intervened and on 1 July 1588 issued a decree forbidding any interference in "free trade and traffique."[32] The matter was thus brought to a conclusion. Fletcher and Saltonstall had concluded a treaty that secured the rights of the Merchants Adventurers in the Hanse area for the next ten years, and they were fully aware of the significance of this treaty:

By this Residencie obtained at Stoad the late practise and confederacie

27. SP 82/2, No. 69
28. SP 82/2, Nos. 70 and 76.
29. See Letter 15.
30. SP 82/2, No. 79.
31. SP 15/30, No. 32. On 11 July, Thomas Egerton wrote Walsingham that the ship which took Fletcher and Saltonstall to Hamburg and was to bring them back again had been pressed into the queen's service by the Lord Admiral. He asked Walsingham to have the ship released, but there is no evidence whether it was or not.
32. SP 82/3, No. 7.

of the Hanse Townes hath ben disappointed, which was this: either to force hir Maiestie to a full restitution of all the Hanse Priviledges enioyed in England 200. years agoe and namely that of Vtrecht at xiiij^d a cloth, or ells to bannish the English commodities quite owt of Germanie. Which by the same means (vz by this residencie continued and strengthned at Stoad) may bee prevented and disappointed hearafter, and the Hanse Townes at least the Hamburghers reduced to more equall conditions.[33]

At some time during these negotiations Fletcher sent a petition to the queen requesting a license for the yearly buying and selling of four hundred sarplers of wool for a term of eight years, but there is no record whether he was awarded the license.[34]

While Fletcher was away on this mission, his wife and children returned to Cranbrook and stayed with her family. On 19 November a daughter, Elizabeth, was baptized.

In June 1588, Queen Elizabeth sent Fletcher as ambassador to Russia to treat especially concerning the English trade. But before he departed she made him a Master of Requests.[35]

At this time the privileges and prestige of the Russia Company had sunk to a new low level. In his report to Burghley upon his return, Fletcher

33. Letter 15.

34. Letters 16a and 16b.

35. There has been a great deal of confusion about this appointment. There is evidence for it in two letters of Queen Elizabeth dated 6 June 1588, one to Tsar Fedor and the other to Boris Godunov, in which she refers to Fletcher as "our master of requests." See also the letter from Elizabeth to Fedor dated 15 January 1589, pp. 26–27 below.

All available evidence suggests that this appointment was honorary and temporary. Fletcher wrote to Sir Robert Cecil on 7 July 1596 (Letter 22), requesting his mediation in his suit, which was specifically stated in two letters by Richard, his brother, to Lord Burghley and to Sir Robert Cecil on 17 May and 12 June, respectively, as being for Master of Requests in Extraordinary. Fletcher again unsuccessfully pleaded for this position in a letter to Cecil on 7 December 1600 (Letter 32). There is no mention in the Signet Office Docquet Books, Letters Patent, State Papers, or Privy Council Acts signifying that Fletcher ever became a Master of Request. The granting of this honorary title took place on two other occasions—once to Dr. Christopher Perkins on the eve of his mission to Denmark, and again to Dr. Daniel Dunn on the eve of his mission to Denmark. There is a useful account of the Court of Requests in W. B. J. Allsebrook, "The Court of Requests in the Reign of Elizabeth" (M. A. thesis, University of London, 1937).

says that when he arrived in Moscow, he found the privileges to be "of no account" and infringed in all parts.[36] Tsar Fedor was insisting on payment of arrears of customs duties and was levying half-customs on the company's goods. Rumors had been spread about that the Russia Company was in disfavor with Queen Elizabeth and that she would soon dissolve it, because she desired to see the trade laid open to all her subjects. This action, it was said, would increase her revenue and would also be advantageous to the Russians, because the other English merchants would be willing to pay full customs and could be treated as common men. In addition, Jerome Horsey had offended Boris Godunov, who was the one friend the English merchants had at court. Indeed, as early as 1587, Robert Peacock, the chief agent of the Russia Company in Russia, complained to Walsingham about Horsey's misconduct: "To tell of his disorderly behaviour here [Moscow] would be to enter into a sea that hath no bottom." Peacock urged Walsingham to call Horsey home and "to put him in hope of other employment."[37] Fletcher's mission was to restore good will between the English and Russian courts and to get a restoration of the Russia Company's privileges.

Fletcher was accompanied by Austin Folkes, who was to be the new chief agent for the company,[38] and he carried with him two letters from Elizabeth, one to Tsar Fedor and one to Boris Godunov, introducing him as ambassador and authorizing him to "conclude upon all matters and upon love and trade."[39] He landed at Colmogor on 17 September and arrived at Moscow on 25 November. He had his first audience with the tsar on 19 December.[40] Later in the year Tsar Fedor wrote Elizabeth, and on 15 January of the following year she answered, specifically stating the points for negotiation:

And before your majesty's letter came to us with your interpreter [Reginald Backman], we sent unto your majesty one of our masters of requests [Fletcher] to confer for our merchants about Anthony's

36. See Letter 17.
37. SP 91/1, No. 23.
38. A MS of Lord Kenyon: a newsletter, 1588.
39. Yury Tolstoi, *England and Russia, 1553–1593* (St. Petersburg, 1875), pp. 288–91, 294–95.
40. *Ibid.*, p. xlvii.

debt and also about the confirmation of the trade of the company according to your majesty's former letters of privilege, and we hope that you have afore this heard him with favor and we hope that this matter has been agreably settled. And we will again return Anthony Marsh to your majesty with your interpreter by our next ships, that he might declare before your counsellors what he said here that it is his special debt and that he has in Moscow and in other places of your kingdom wherewith to pay those debts, which are not paid.[41]

And on the same day she wrote to Godunov:

His highnes letters and scedule we thought good to send to our ambassador [Fletcher] to be showed by him to your honor for that we are of opinion yow are not acquainted with the matters that are conteyned in the same, and for that alsoe there shalbe noe doubt obiected of the true vnderstandinge and tranlacon of such thinge which his highnes hath written. Our said ambassador hath alsoe the coppie of our letter which we doe send to his highness; which coppie we have sent to our ambassador for further instruccons to solicite and treate vppon as his further commission from vs; who will at large acquaint your honor with the pointes of our letters.[42]

On 23 January, the Privy Council sent a letter to Fletcher informing him that William Trumbull, a merchant in Moscow, owed William Brooke, of London, £200; and they asked him to recover the £200 for Brooke, plus some reasonable sum for his having to wait three years for payment.[43]

Fletcher was not received in the manner generally accorded an ambassador. Indeed, Fletcher begins his report to Burghley by stating: "My whole intertainment from my first arrivall till towards the very end was such as if they had divised meanes of very purpose to shew their vtter disliking both of the trade of the Marchants, and of the whole English nation." All communications with the court, when he finally was admitted, were altered and falsified by the tsar's interpreter, on order of the chancellor, Andrei

41. *Ibid.*, pp. 311–12.
42. *Ibid.*, pp. 328–29.
43. PC 2/15, p. 391.

Shchelkalov, who had always been opposed to the English merchants. Fletcher was kept prisoner in his house and was not allowed to send any letters to England.

However, Fletcher by patience and forbearance effected the most favorable treaty the English had had since the privileges obtained by Sir Thomas Randolph in 1569.[44] Good will and friendship were restored between the tsar and Elizabeth. The most significant of the new privileges was that the Russia Company was to be no longer under the authority of Andrei Shchelkalov, but under Boris Godunov, who was favorably inclined to English merchants.[45] The only detail not resolved was how much of the debts owed by Antony Marsh, an agent, should be assumed by the Russia Company. The tsar demanded the full amount of 23,553 rubles, but the Company argued that the debts were incurred privately and it should not be held responsible. It now seemed that little could be accomplished in this matter, and on 22 April, Fletcher received permission to leave the court.

Before Fletcher left Moscow, however, two letters arrived from Queen Elizabeth, one to Fedor[46] and the other to Boris Godunov.[47] Fletcher tried to obtain another audience with the tsar but could not, so he sent the letters to Andrei Shchelkalov, and left Moscow on 6 May, taking Jerome Horsey with him. He had not reached Vologda when an order was given to detain him there, for Antony Marsh had arrived in Moscow. The whole matter of Marsh's debts was reviewed, and as a result the tsar, at Godunov's urging, reduced the amount claimed from the Company to 7,800 rubles. This news was communicated to Fletcher by the governor of the province, who also surrendered Marsh to him. Fletcher left Russia towards the end of July or the beginning of August,[48] with letters from Fedor[49] and from Godunov[50] to Queen Elizabeth. Both men urged her to give all English merchants the right to trade in Russia. Both assured her of their affection, and promised

44. T. S. Willan, *The Early History of the Russia Company* (Manchester, 1956), p. 107.
45. *Ibid.*, p. 176.
46. Tolstoi, *England and Russia*, pp. 298–312.
47. *Ibid.*, pp. 327–30.
48. *Ibid.*, pp. xlvii–xlix.
49. *Ibid.*, pp. 350–53. The letter was written in April 1589.
50. *Ibid.*, pp. 359–64. The letter was written in July 1589.

continued favor towards her merchants. On 1 April 1590 Elizabeth acknowledged receipt of these letters. She wrote to Godunov:

> Your princly letters we haue receaued by our embassador Gilles Fletcher and reed and overvewed them. The contents therof together with the reportt of our sayd embassador doth make vs wonder to hyer and see [sic] The sodden alteration of your princly regard towards vs professed in your former letters. The great indignities shewed vnto our princly highness by the gross vsag of our embassador with the hard dealings towards our merchants, doth make vs justly to suspect, that your princly effection towards vs is not as we desire.[51]

In August she again complained of Fletcher's treatment, requiring Fedor to give an explanation,[52] which he did;[53] and nothing further seems to have been said.

An anecdote concerning Fletcher on his return from Russia is recorded by Fuller:

> Returning home and being safely arrived at London, he sent for his intimate friend, Mr. Wayland,[54] Prebendary of St. Paul's, and Senior Fellow of Trinity Colledge in Cambridge (Tutor to my Father, from whose mouth I received this report), with whom he heartily expressed his thankfulnesse to God for his safe return from so great a danger; for the Poets cannot fansie Ulysses more glad to be come out of the *Den of Polyphemus*, then he was to be rid out of the power of such a *barbarious Prince*; who, counting himself by a proud and voluntary mistake, *Emperour of all Nations*, cared not for the *Law of all Nations*; and who was so habited in blood, that had he cut off this

---

51. *Ibid.*, p. 368.

52. SP 91/1, No. 64. See also Tolstoi, *England and Russia*, pp. 373–81; Edward A. Bond (ed.), *Russia at the Close of the Sixteenth Century* (London, 1856), pp. xcix–cvii.

53. SP 91/1, No. 82. See also Tolstoi, *England and Russia*, pp. 396–403; Bond, *Russia at the Close of the Sixteenth Century*, pp. cxi–cxix.

54. Henry Wayland (d. 1614). Admitted pensioner at Peterhouse, 1566; migrated to Trinity; scholar, 1568; B.A. 1569–70, M.A. 1573, B.D. 1584; fellow of Trinity, 1571; prebendary of St. Paul's, 1598; prebendary of Rochester, 1606–1614; rector of Ivychurch, 1589–1614. See John Venn and J. A. Venn, *Alumni Cantabrigienses* (Cambridge, 1927).

Embassador's head, he and his friends might have sought their own amends; but the question is, where he would have found it.[55]

On his return, Fletcher wrote two reports of his negotiations.[56] He likewise completed his *Russe Commonwealth* and presented it to the queen.

From London, Fletcher probably traveled to Cranbrook, for when he had departed for Russia, his wife and family had again moved to Cranbrook, as they had done when he had gone to Hamburg. He would then have seen for the first time his daughter Joan, who had been baptized on 22 December 1588, some six months after he had left for Russia.

On 11 January 1590, the Privy Council directed Fletcher and Ralph Rokeby to consider the complaint of the legatees of John Norden against William Trumbull for his refusal to pay the legatees certain sums due them.[57] In a letter to the Council, Fletcher and Rokeby recommended that a commission be established to examine those persons who were "factors" for Trumbull, and, having discovered what goods he had in England, to attach them by "due order of Law, towardes the satisfacion of these and other Legacies" owed by Trumbull.[58]

On 24 May, the Privy Council directed Fletcher and others to examine the complaint brought by George Leke that the senators of Hamburg had defrauded him of certain houses in Hamburg, as well as various sums of money owed to him by some of the burghers. Fletcher and the others were to investigate and report so that "such orders may be taken for the relief of the suppliant as shalbe thought requisit."[59]

More important, Fletcher himself appealed to the Privy Council, complaining that the Russia Company would not give him adequate recompense for his services in Russia. On 16 June, the Council directed Mr. William Wad and Mr. Thomas Aldersey to meet with Fletcher and representatives of the Russia Company to hear the charges made by Fletcher:

---

55. John Nichols (ed.), *The History of the Worthies of England Endeavoured by Thomas Fuller, D.D.* (London, 1811), p. 503.

56. Letters 17 and 18.

57. PC 2/16, p. 466.

58. See Letter 19.

59. PC 2/17, pp. 684–85.

Whereas we ar informed of some hard dealing offred vnto Doctor Fletcher by the Company of Marchantes trading to *Russia*, towching the recompenc of his late travill thither about their affaires. Wherin he alleageth their Consideracion for his paines taken to be so slendre as that he hath expended of his owne above all their allowances: and having intreated their further consideracions can receave no aunswer in any convenient manner. Forasmuch as we thinke yt very reasonable that hauing taken so longe and daungerous a Iorney about their affaires at their owne request, and so hapely preformed yt to their great benefit (as we are informed) being imployed also in the name of her Maiesties Embassadour for their behof, he should not in any wise be depriued of suche recompence as in equitie shalbe thought meet, and as to others in like case hath ben allowed. We have thought good to praie you to call the said Doctor vnto you with some two or three of the said Marchantes to peruse the peticion herwith sent you to heare the allegacions one bothe sides, and considering the demands to certyfie vs your opinions with all convenient speed, &c.[60]

Unfortunately, the results of this conference have not survived.

The summer brought tragedy to the Fletcher family: a daughter, Sara, who had been baptized on 28 June, died on 3 July.[61]

In the autumn, Fletcher turned his mind to literary pursuits. On 7 November he wrote to Lord Burghley, proposing to write a Latin history of the queen's time and requesting Burghley's patronage and also access to public documents, in order that his history might be a "storie" and not a "tale."[62] But since Fletcher did not obtain Burghley's patronage, he evidently abandoned this project; and he seems instead to have revised and expanded his *Russe Commonwealth*, which was then published in 1591.

On 10 January 1591, the Privy Council directed Fletcher and others to examine George Beesley, a seminary priest, and Robert Humberson, his familiar companion and confederate, and to obtain confessions from them.[63]

---

60. PC 2/17, p. 743.
61. The Parish Register of St. Thomas the Apostle, London.
62. See Letter 20.
63. PC 2/18, pp. 53–54.

A daughter, Judith, was baptized on 1 August.[64]

On 10 October, the Privy Council directed Fletcher to examine and take confessions of Eustace Whyte, a seminary priest, and Brian Lassy, a disperser and distributor of letters to papists, and instructed him that, should they not answer the questions put to them, they should be "put to the manacles and soche other tortures as are vsed in Bridewell."[65] According to Jardine, this is the first time the use of manacles as torture is mentioned; after this, however, it was frequent.[66]

In March 1592, the Lord Mayor of London called Fletcher and Sir George Barnes to his house to advise him in his conference with Edward Darcie, who had been granted letters patent for the "view, search and sealing of leather." The companies of the City of London objected to the patent, saying it was prejudicial to former patents granted to them.[67] An argument between Darcie and Barnes ensued, and Darcie assaulted Barnes. On 22 March, the Court of Aldermen made an official complaint of the matter to the Privy Council, stating that Fletcher was a witness to the affair.[68]

On 24 April, the Lord Mayor sent a letter by Fletcher to the Lord Treasurer, stating that the sum of money lent by several citizens of London to the queen was now past due and asking for repayment. Furthermore, he instructed Fletcher to remind Burghley of two suits the City had pending, one for a commission about the bounds between the City and the Tower of London, and the other for his warrant to the Attorney and Solicitor-General to sign the book of rules referring to the jurisdiction of the Thames.[69]

In 1594, the City of London decided to reward Fletcher for his "longe and faithfull service." On 29 July, the Court of Aldermen moved that the Common Council grant Fletcher the benefit of making three people free-

---

64. The Parish Register of St. Thomas the Apostle, London.

65. PC 2/19, p. 30.

66. David Jardine, *A Reading on the Use of Torture in the Criminal Law of England Previously to the Commonwealth* (London, 1837), p. 37.

67. Corporation of London, Remembrancia I, 628.

68. *Ibid.,* p. 651.

69. *Ibid.,* p. 658.

men by redemption,[70] but on 19 August the Common Council granted him instead an increase of fifty pounds yearly to his salary of fifty pounds.[71] Actually, this was a little less than the aldermen's proposal, the value of making a man free being about twenty pounds.[72]

On 30 May 1594, Fletcher, his wife, Joan, and their eldest child, Phineas, issued a bill of complaint in Chancery against John Hall.[73] Fletcher stated that Richard Fletcher, as Bishop of Worcester, possessed, among other lands, the Manor of Hynwich in the county of Worcester and also certain pasture lands on the banks of the Severn "vnder the Parke of Hallowe." Richard had leased these lands to the plaintiffs for the term of their lives and "the longest liver of them." But after they had taken possession, they discovered that the late bishop, Richard Pates, had made a long and unreasonable lease of this property, although he was fully aware of the statute which forbade the making of such a lease. Most of the lower part of the manuscript is torn away, but the request must have been for the Court to confirm the lease to Fletcher. John Hall answered that the matters in the complaint seemed to be "devysed and contryved" and asked for its dismissal. This was not done, as a commission was awarded to examine witnesses on the plaintiffs' behalf.[74] Nothing further is recorded about the case.

IV

1596-1611

In June 1596, Fletcher was brought into the celebrated affair of Buccleuch's rescue of Kinmont Willie at Carlisle.[1] The Duke of Buccleuch complained that Lord Scroope, the Warden of the West Marches, had taken

---

70. Corporation of London, Repertory 23, f. 264ᵛ.

71. Corporation of London, Journal 23, f. 301ᵛ.

72. I owe this information to Mr. M. J. Chandler, Assistant Keeper in the Corporation Records Office.

73. C.2/F.8/43.

74. C33/87, f. 319ᵛ.

1. For a concise account of the raid, see D. L. W. Tough, *The Last Years of a Frontier* (Oxford,

William Armstrong of Kinmont in violation of the "trew" which guaranteed the safety of all persons at the council meetings between the Scottish and English Wardens at the Border.[2] Since Scroope refused to release the prisoner, Buccleuch stormed Carlisle Castle and rescued "Willie." The Grame family was involved in this affair, and Scroope sent its six leaders to London to face charges of conspiracy in the plot, of blackmail, and of the murder of George Grame, alias Percivales Geordie.[3] On 11 June Scroope sent to the Privy Council depositions of witnesses that the Grames were guilty of blackmail.[4] These charges were denied by William Grame.[5] Scroope then sent additional proof against the Grames to Burghley and threatened to resign if severe punishment was not meeted out to them. Burghley directed Fletcher to interview the Grames and to obtain answers to the blackmail charges and also to inquire what lands they possessed in England.[6] On 3 July, Scroope wrote Lord Hunsdon, the Lord Chamberlain, enclosing articles of proceedings against John and Richard Grame for the murder of George Grame;[7] and on 10 July, John Grame protested his innocence to the Privy Council.[8] Again Burghley asked Fletcher to question the Grames, particularly John and Richard. The significance of Fletcher's reply is that he reveals that Burghley thought the Grames should be treated leniently.[9] But the problem was how to satisfy Scroope, since he still threatened to resign if the Grames were not severely punished.[10] On 31 July, articles of submission were proposed by the Privy Council and signed by the Grames, who thereby promised to be governed by the Lord Warden

---

1928), pp. 260–62; and for the ballad "Kinmont Willie" see any edition of Sir Walter Scott's *Minstrelsy of the Scottish Border*. Thomas Henderson's edition (London, 1931), pp. 179–90, has a good introduction; other sources are Thomas Hodgkin, *The Wardens of the Northern Marches* (London, 1908), pp. 31–32; P. Hume Brown, *History of Scotland*, (3 vols.; Cambridge, 1906), II, 222–23; and John Spottiswoode, *History of the Church of Scotland* (3 vols.; Edinburgh, 1851), III, 1–5.

2. Tough, *Last Years of a Frontier*, pp. 137–45; Hodgkin, *Wardens of the Northern Marches*, pp. 18–27.
3. SP 59/31, ff. 163, 175.
4. SP 59/31, f. 179.
5. SP 59/31, f. 193.
6. See Letter 21.
7. SP 59/31, f. 230.
8. SP 59/31, f. 236.
9. See Letter 23.
10. SP 59/31, ff. 283–84.

and according to Border law.[11] About 25 September the Grames returned to the North and proposed to submit themselves to Lord Scroope,[12] but because of disagreement over the wording of the submission[13] the ceremony did not take place until 21 January of the following year.[14]

On 20 August 1596, Queen Elizabeth issued a proclamation signifying her intention to appoint commissioners to restore justice to the Borders;[15] and on 2 October she appointed the Bishop of Durham, Sir William Bowes, Francis Slyngesby, and Clement Colmer commissioners.[16] One of the matters taken up by them on 17 February was a bill against Lord Scroope, charging him with illegal invasion of Liddesdale in August 1596; but the commission reported to the Privy Council that Scroope was warranted in his reprisal. The Privy Council, however, required the opinion of Drs. Caesar, Flude, Dunn, and Fletcher on the matter.[17] Their answer of 9 March concurred with that of the commission.[18]

The final mention of Fletcher in this Border affair occurs in a letter from the Bishop of Durham to Burghley on 2 March 1597, in which he states that if Sir William Bowes was unable to rejoin the commission, Burghley would send some "learned wise and expert civyle lawyer as I doe heare the Dean of Carlisle is, and as I thinke Mr. Doctor Fletcher to be."[19]

The summer of 1596 brought events that were to have far-reaching consequences for Fletcher. On 12 June his son Nehemias died,[20] and three

11. SP 59/31, ff. 285–86.
12. SP 59/32, f. 124.
13. SP 59/32, ff. 207–13, 219–21, 225–27.
14. SP 59/33, f. 38.
15. SP 59/32, ff. 51v–52.
16. SP 59/32, ff. 167–68.
17. SP 59/53, ff. 114–19.
18. See Letter 27.
19. SP 59/33, f. 201.
20. The Parish Register of St. Luke's, Chelsea. These are all the children I can identify, and for convenience it may be well to list them here:

1582, Apr. 8	Phineas	Cranbrook
1584, Nov. 22	Anne	Cranbrook
1585 or 1586	Giles	London (?)
1587, Nov. 19	Elizabeth d. 1593, Oct. 19	Cranbrook
1588, Dec. 22	Joan	Cranbrook

(continued on page 36)

days later, on 15 June, the sudden death of his brother, Richard, followed.[21] During that summer, too, he found a new patron. Both Walsingham and Randolph had died in 1590, and since that time Fletcher had unsuccessfully tried to obtain the Cecils' patronage. In November 1590 his appeal to Burghley for patronage of his proposed history of the queen's time was ignored; and in the following year the Russia Company requested Burghley to suppress Fletcher's *Russe Commonwealth*. When, in June 1596, the Cecils refused his appeal for the position of Master of Requests, Fletcher must have realized that he would not secure their patronage; and he seems to have turned to the Earl of Essex. Fletcher had three qualities which would particularly recommend him to Essex. He was a zealous Protestant, a man of letters, and Remembrancer of London—a position which had much influence over the people of the city. In a letter written in July from Essex to his secretary, Reynoldes, the first record of the relationship survives:

> Reynoldes, My other letter to you is to be looked on by my frendes as you shall haue occasion to shewe it them but this is for your owne eyes and after for the fire. You shall goe to Mr Caron and to Monseur la Fontanie [de la Fontaine] and tell them I am retorninge with this Armie, that is stronge riche and prowde, that they knowe the difference of perswading to leuie an Armie and of sollicitinge to vse an Armie alredie formed and disiplined besides the difference in the seruice of these 2 Armies wilbe as greate. Let them therefore make both themselues and their masters and see whether they can get this Armie to be kept together till we maie treate of conditiones for the seige of Callais or some suche like storie.... And yf it could be let falle to the Cittizens by Mr Dr. Fletcher howe fit this opportunitie werre for the makinge of Callais Englishe and that they would make

1590, June 28	Sara	d. 1590, July 3	London
1591, Aug. 1	Judith		London
1596, June 12	d. Nehemias		London

In a letter of appeal to the queen for the eight children of Richard Fletcher, Giles mentioned "having 9. poor Children of his own..." (see Letter 26a), but a search through all the registers of the parishes outside London where Fletcher was known to have lived and of all the extant registers of the parishes of the City of London (76 of 110) has not revealed any more children than those noted above.

21. See my "Biographical Notes on Richard Fletcher," *N&Q*, n.s. VII (1960), 378.

some offer to the Queen to that ende it would muche advance the busines. But he must doo as onlie sollicited by the occasion it self....[22]

In a postscript Essex adds that the letter should be shown to Anthony Bacon, "who in all these thinges is to me as the hande with which I write this"; and Bacon replies to Essex on 10 August:

> May it please your Lordship to be advertised that Mr Dr Fletcher immediatly after conference with me went to my Lord Treasurer and towld his Lordship that the Citty hauing vnderstood the returne of her Maiesties Army, desired that the setting out of 200 men which the Citty had agreed and dispatched yesterday morning might be stayde, and that in their place as many might be chosen out of the Army presently, and such greater nomber as her Maiestie should thinke requesite to send forth out of hand. He likewise intimated vnto his Lordship a generall concurrence of most earnest wishes of the Citizens, that her Maiestie would thinke of the recouery of Calis, wherevnto he perceaved a great readines in the Citty to contribute very largely to the vttermost of their ability.
>
> To the first pointe his Lordship gaue his consent, and writte this morning accordingly to my Lord Maior.
>
> To the second his answer was that he knew not how her Maiesty would be disposed, that it was a matter of great deliberation, that he could say nothing to it till he had knowne her Maiesties pleasure. Tomorrow or next day at the furthest, Mr Dr. Fletcher sayeth that the Maior and his Brethren will go and make a motion to the Lords of the Councell, and some dutifull offer. Thus your Lordship sees Mr Dr. Fletcher hath lost noe time since yesterday morning.[23]

Also in August, the Privy Council directed Fletcher and others to examine those players who had taken part in the "Isle of Dogs."[24]

22. Lambeth MS 658, f. 93.

23. Lambeth MS 658, f. 183.

24. PC 2/22, p. 346. C. H. Herford and Percy Simpson (*Ben Jonson* [11 vols.; Oxford, 1925–52], I, 217–18) reproduce the document from the Privy Council charging Fletcher and others to seek out and apprehend the actors in this play, and Thomas Nashe, the supposed author. Ronald B. McKerrow

General Introduction

The end of the summer of 1596 found Fletcher in financial difficulties as a result of the death of his brother. Not only did Richard Fletcher leave eight children without any provision, but he had been in debt to the queen for over £1400 for first fruits and tenths. Giles took his brother's children into his home even though he had nine of his own. And if that was not financial burden enough, Giles as executor of the estate was pressed by the Chancellor of the Exchequer for immediate payment of the debts owed to the queen. To secure her favor, Fletcher addressed to the queen two petitions entitled "Reasons to Move Hir Maiestie in Soom Commiseration Towardes the Orphanes of the Late Bishop of London"[25] and sent one to Anthony Bacon on 21 August with the request that he would ask Essex to intercede in his behalf. Bacon wrote the following day to Reynoldes:

> Good Mr Reynoldes. After I had receued yesterday the vnspeakeable comforte and ioy to inioy my Lords presence some time, my very good freind Mr Dr Fletcher verye devoted to my Lord sent me the inclosed and requested me to present and recommend it to his Lord-shipp and to craue the concurrence of his fauorable furtherance to her Maiestie whome my Lord Treasurer hath vndertaken to moue and dispose which I pray yow to make knowne to his Lordshipp from me at his first conuenient leisure....[26]

Bacon again mentions Fletcher's case in a letter to Reynoldes on 26 September: "The like fauour I must aske in the Orphanis behalf considering the Vncle Mr Dr Fletchers deuotion to his Lordship and the good vse maie be made thereof, accordinge to his Lordships occasions...."[27] In the margin Essex notes: "I will sollicite the Queen for them, and gett her to referr ther case to some counsaylor."

Nevertheless the case was not yet settled, for in a letter to Essex on 6 December Bacon says:

(*The Works of Thomas Nashe* [5 vols.; Oxford, 1958], V, 29–33) gives an account of Nashe's part in writing this play.

25. See Letters 24 and 25.
26. Lambeth MS 658, f. 141.
27. Lambeth MS 659, f. 91.

May it please your Lordship to giue me leaue to complaine of Sir John Fortescues hard dealing with Mr Dr Fletcher who relying vppon Sir Johnes promise both to Sir Gillie Merick and himselfe that your Lordships request should bee satisfied is now sodenilie fallen into the lurch to gether with his Creditors to their great discreditt processe being that day out against him whereof though Sir John will perhaps vppon your Lordships entreatie graunt out a supercedeis [supersedeas] yett is Dr Fletcher and his Sureties still in daunger to be scratched by the exchecker Clawes and so shallbe till the stallment of the late Bishops detes be obteined which therefore I am bould most humbly to recommend to your Lordships remembrance and honorable furtherance.[28]

And on the same day Essex sent this letter to Fortescue:

Sir, it pleased yow latelie at my request to promise respitt of Mr Dr Fletchers paymentes for the which I thought my selfe very much behoulden: Now therfore forasmuch as vnawares vnto yow processe is awarded against him and his sureties I am bould to intreat your fauour for the remedyeing thereof by the best and spediest course you can for that their credittes are very deeplie interessed and may be not a little preiudiced vnlesse some present order be taken for the graunting of a supercedeas. I pray yow to tender their reputation so much and for my sake to dispatch them which I will acknowledge withall thankfullness.[29]

Two days later Bacon wrote to Essex, complaining that the underofficers of the Exchequer were still pressing Fletcher for payment.[30] Fletcher again wrote a letter to the queen, pleading the case of the orphans, and this time he was successful.[31] On 27 April 1597 the queen directed the Exchequer to discharge Fletcher of the debt;[32] and on 9 July the discharge was issued.[33]

28. Lambeth MS 660, f. 100.
29. Lambeth MS 660, f. 186.
30. Lambeth MS 660, f. 95.
31. See Letter 26.
32. SP 13/33, No. 79.
33. SP 38/5. 9 July 1597.

While this correspondence was in progress, on 4 December 1596 the Privy Council directed Dr. Caesar and Dr. Herbert to confer with Fletcher, Dr. Perkins, and Dr. Dunn about a book on the Hanse towns that Mr. Beale had written and to certify whether they thought the book should be published or not.[34]

And on 23 May 1597, Fletcher was appointed Treasurer of St. Paul's by the queen.[35]

In May of the following year, Fletcher and five others[36] were sent to the United Provinces of the Netherlands to seek a residency for the Merchants Adventurers, since the company had been driven from Stade at the expiration of their ten years' treaty in 1597.

This was a particularly difficult time to have to deal with the United Provinces. The year 1598 was one of great importance to the Dutch Republic. Under the brilliant military direction of Prince Maurice of Nassau, the Dutch Republic was successful in defeating the Spanish troops which had been sent against it. The Dutch Republic, England, and France were in alliance against Spain; but in 1598, Spain determined to break up this alliance at almost any cost. Henry IV was eager to restore peace to France so that his country could recover from the disastrous civil Wars of Religion and the foreign wars, especially against Italy, which had left the government bankrupt and the people divided. Spain was prepared to offer an attractive treaty of peace to France and in April 1598 sent Richardot to negotiate with French representatives. When news of this possible peace reached the Dutch Republic, two embassies—one to France and another to England—were immediately dispatched to urge the maintenance of the league against Spain. Johan van Oldenbarneveldt and Admiral Justinus of Nassau, the two most prominent political leaders in the Republic, went to France. Admiral Duivenvoorde, who was highly respected by the English, was sent to Queen Elizabeth's court. In spite of the pleas of Oldenbarneveldt, a treaty was concluded with Spain on 2 May at Vervins under terms

34. PC 2/23, pp. 102–3.
35. SP 38/5. 23 May 1597.
36. SP 12/268, No. 5. The others employed in this mission were the governor of the Company, Alderman Richard Goddart, Alderman Thomas Bennett, Thomas Smith, and William Romney.

very favorable to the French. Having failed to prevent this treaty, Olden-barneveldt left immediately for England to try to preserve the defensive treaty between the Dutch Republic and England. Elizabeth was out of patience with the Republic. She had given aid to the Provinces for many years in their war with Spain, but they were no closer to a peace with Spain than when the rebellion began. Lord Burghley, Sir Robert Cecil, and Lord Buckhurst urged the Republic to negotiate immediately with Spain. Elizabeth said she would continue in the league only if the Republic would pay immediately the £1,400,000 owed to England, assume the whole cost of the garrisons in the cautionary towns, and give assurances that assistance would be forthcoming in case of an attack on England. On 31 May, accordingly, Oldenbarneveldt and Admiral Duivenvoorde returned to the Republic with these terms.[37]

This was the situation which Fletcher faced. In his first letter to Essex he comments that he had not had an audience with the States General concerning the affairs of the Merchants Adventurers because of "their great and waightie affayer, about which they have entred their consultacion," which was obviously the discussion of the terms set forth by Elizabeth.[38] At the end of the month Fletcher again wrote Essex telling him that he was having difficulties in negotiating with the States General.[39] On 14 July, however, an agreement was reached. The company's privileges were confirmed from 1587, an ordinance of the Earl of Leicester of 1586 was renewed, and, in exchange, the Dutch Republic was to enjoy the privileges granted to it in times past in England.[40] Fletcher had again successfully concluded a favorable trade agreement under adverse circumstances.

Fletcher must have returned to England soon after the treaty was signed, for he was involved in City business on 6 August. The queen and City owed Fabrico Palavicino some money, and he was now petitioning for repayment. The first petition went to Sir John Fortescue and another to the

---

37. For a full account see John Motley, *The United Netherlands* (4 vols.; London, 1904), III, Chapters 33–35.

38. See Letter 28.

39. See Letter 29.

40. SP 84/57, ff. 10–12ᵛ.

City magistrates, who forwarded it to the Privy Council by Fletcher.[41]

In 1599 and 1600, Fletcher was involved in three Chancery cases, all of which concern him as executor of his brother's estate. He issued a bill of complaint against Allen Henrye, who had been the attorney for Richard Fletcher in a suit against John and Barnard Hill. Judgment was awarded against the Hills, and they were instructed to discharge Richard Fletcher of all charges in connection with the suit. They evidently had not done so, as Henrye had entered a suit against Giles Fletcher, the executor. Fletcher asked the Court to stay Henrye's suit and to force the Hills to answer the present suit—i.e., why Henrye had not been paid. The Court directed Dr. Hunt, a master of the court, to consider the suit and to give his opinion.[42] He refused to act, and on 25 March 1600 Mr. Tyndall, another master of the court, was appointed to take his place.[43] Nothing further is recorded concerning the case.

Nathaniell Fletcher, Richard's eldest son, brought a bill of complaint against Giles, charging that he had obtained the executorship of Richard's estate by fraudulent means, that he had taken more than £500 in goods from the estate for his own use, that he refused to give an account of the estate, that by his mismanagement the estate was in debt to almost £2000— the greater part of which, Nathaniell says, could have been recovered had Fletcher made his best endeavor—and that he refused to pay the portion due each child as he came of age.[44] Nathaniell asked that the Court subpoena Giles to make him give a just account of the estate, to make Nathaniel Pownoll (husband of Giles and Richard's sister) guardian of the children who had not yet reached their majority and give him their portion of the estate for safekeeping, and finally to require Giles to give sufficient sureties for the right administration of the estate. Giles denied all allegations, and commented that they were more a libel than a complaint. On 30 January 1600, the Court ordered Dr. Carewe, a master of the court, to examine both the bill of complaint and the demurrer and to determine if the demurrer

---

41. Hatfield, Cecil Papers 78. 21.
42. C. 33/97, f. 94ᵛ.
43. C. 33/97, ff. 383ᵛ-4.
44. C.2/F.6/63.

was sufficient.[45] Nothing further is recorded concerning this case. Nathaniell Fletcher's bill of complaint is valuable, however, since it names all the children of Richard Fletcher.[46]

On 23 November 1599 Giles Fletcher issued a bill of complaint against Nathaniel Pownoll.[47] Fletcher says that the co-executor named in Richard's will, Francis James, being warned that the estate might not be in good financial condition, refused to act; and therefore he had had to assume the full responsibility of the executorship. And in connection with the settlement of the estate, he had asked John Lister, his faithful servant, and Nathaniel Pownoll to sell certain goods and to return the money to him. Fletcher says that Lister sold the goods entrusted to him and returned the money, but charges that Pownoll did not, keeping the money for his own use and refusing to give account of all he had taken. Fletcher therefore asks the Court to require Pownoll to declare what goods he had taken and what he had converted to his own use. Pownoll denied the charges and listed the items sold and the money each fetched, and asked that the bill of complaint be dismissed. No further mention of the case is recorded.

On 2 April 1600, the City of London granted Fletcher the benefit of a freeman;[48] and on 10 April, at the request of Fletcher, Thomas Burton was "admitted into the freedome and liberties of this Citty by redempcion in the Company of Poulters."[49]

In October, Fletcher petitioned the City that, because of "the infirmitie of his bodie and the vrgent occasion of busines other waies," Dr. Hawkins might become his assistant. The City agreed:

It is therevpon ordred and agreed by this Courte that the said Doctor Hawkyns shall in the absence of the said Doctor Fletcher assiste him in the service of this Citty monethlie or every fowerteene daies betweene them by turne for and during the pleasure of this Courte and the well deserving of the said Doctor Hawkyns and not otherwise.

45. C.33/97, f. 276v.
46. See my "Biographical Notes on Richard Fletcher," N&Q, n.s. VII (1960), 377–78.
47. C.2/F.3/63.
48. Corporation of London, Repertory 25, f. 66v.
49. Ibid., f. 70v.

Provyded alwayes that the said Doctor Fletcher shalbe ready at all tymes hereafter to serue and attende the service of this Citty in his owne person when he shalbe therevnto called by this Courte or sent for the Lord Maior for the tyme being.[50]

On 21 October King's College gave Fletcher a ten-year lease of Ringwood parsonage, one of the most lucrative of the college benefits.[51] It was renewed to Fletcher for another ten years on 4 July 1605.[52]

Fletcher and others were directed by the Privy Council on 31 January 1601 to settle a suit between Otwell Smith and Richard Kelley.[53] But probably Fletcher never served on this commission; and indeed this directive might well have been forgotten in the events which took place one week later—the day of Essex's rebellion. Essex's patronage, helpful in times past, now almost proved Fletcher's ruin.

On 13 February, Attorney General Coke noted that it would be necessary to examine Fletcher.[54] On the following day he was committed to the private custody of Alderman Hampson. He wrote letters to both Cecil and the Lord Mayor, protesting his innocence and begging them to be a means for his release, but to no avail.[55] And on 3 March, Fletcher sent his "confession" to the Privy Council. In it he states:

On Thursday or Fryday beefore the Earle of Essex his coomming into London in that tumultuous and seditious manner I mett with Maister Temple who tould mee that thear wear certein Iesuits and Seminary priests that lodged in divers places of the Citie, who had vowed to kill the Earle of Essex, and that they had divised and cast abroad certein Libels to make him odious to the people. Which beeing reported by him (as it seemed) in good sadnes I did then beeleeve, bycause it seemed not improbable, that beeing so followed by the militarie men and making profession of religion more then after an or-

50. *Ibid.*, ff. 157–57ᵛ.
51. King's College, Ledger Book, III, 19.
52. *Ibid.*, p. 132.
53. PC 2/26, p. 62.
54. SP 12/278, No. 58.
55. See Letters 33 and 34.

dinary manner, they might suppose that the sayed Earle stood in their way and might hinder their designes, if they intended any practise against hir Maiestie and the State. The end of his talk was that if I lighted vpon any of those Libels I would gett a copie and send it to him. Which (bycause it seemed to bee spoken in no ill meaning) I promised to doe.[56]

He further adds that on the day before the rebellion (Saturday), William Temple came to his house and told him a plot was laid by Sir Walter Raleigh to kill the Earl. The veracity of Fletcher's testimony is attested by the examinations of Thomas Smythe and William Temple. Smythe, in his examination on 13 February, said that four or five days before Essex's rebellion, Fletcher had told him that certain Jesuits had planned to murder Essex and that it would be well to see some of them.[57] Temple stated that on the Saturday before the rebellion Essex had urged him to tell Fletcher certain Jesuits had planned to kill him.[58] This does not completely tally with Fletcher's statement, but it is close enough to indicate that Fletcher was not taken into the confidence of the group planning the conspiracy. And indeed Fletcher makes this point in his "confession":

> As toutching his coomming into London in that tumultuous and seditious manner or any other his wicked designes the sayed Maister Temple didnot mention nor impart it to mee, neither did the Earle (as I am perswaded) ever thinck so ill of mee as to iudge mee a fitt man or safe for himself to impart with mee any suche vngodly practise knowing mee well that I would not indure to heer suche things, and not reveal them. The greatest matter I could suspect owt of these reports (which I see now to bee very fables and divised matters) was that soom great quarrell and open fray was lyke to break owt beetwixt the Earle and Sir Walter Raleigh.
>
> And as toutching Maister Temple in the reporting of these divises, I doe yet thinck (not knowing the contrary) that having been ever

56. See Letter 35.
57. SP 12/278, No. 59.
58. SP 12/281, No. 1.

accounted an honest man hee was deceived and abused by the Earle that he might deceive and abuse others.

Smythe and Temple also denied any foreknowledge of the rebellion; and the fact that all three were eventually acquitted of the charge of complicity further supports Fletcher's statement. More positive evidence of his innocence is that his positions of Remembrancer and of Treasurer of St. Paul's were not taken from him. Nevertheless, all suspicion had not been removed. Fletcher was not released from custody until some time between the fourteenth and twenty-first of March; and as late as May he was still under bond to appear before the Privy Council with two days' notice.

To add to his troubles, certain persons were petitioning Cecil for Fletcher's position of Remembrancer.[59] On 21 March Fletcher wrote to Cecil that he would like to give up the position if he were granted some other benefit; and at the same time he urged him to ignore the suits of those who were seeking his position.[60] By 5 April some arrangement was being made, as Fletcher says that Clement Edmondes and John Moore were "in hand to compound with mee for my Office."[61] But for some reason—perhaps the proper "benefice" could not be decided on—Fletcher did not give up his office. Instead, he urged that Clement Edmondes be made his assistant. This was agreed to; and on 5 May, Edmondes was sworn assistant to Fletcher as a probationer until Michaelmas.[62] On 1 October the appointment was confirmed and his salary set at half of Fletcher's, or fifty pounds.[63]

No doubt Fletcher thought Essex's patronage would ensure his future financially; but ironically enough, the opposite proved true. In his letter to Cecil on 14 March, Fletcher says: "My great charge and small revenue with the Executorship of my late Brother hath made my debt exceed my estate, beeing vndoon and woorse then nought by 500li." In November Fletcher wrote Cecil, trying once again to secure his favor, but he failed again.[64]

59. Hatfield, Cecil Papers 78. 21.
60. See Letter 37.
61. See Letter 38.
62. Corporation of London, Repertory 25, f. 228^v.
63. *Ibid.*, f. 282.
64. See Letter 40.

In 1605 Fletcher decided to resign as Remembrancer and submitted his resignation on 2 July:

Item this daye Gyles Fletcher Doctor of the Civill lawes, by a note in wryting written with his hand did thereby freely voluntarely and of his owne accord surrender resigne and give vp to this Court the place of Remembrancer of this Cittye and the stipend of a C^{li} by the yeare thereto perteyning and all his right and interest to the same of which surrender and resignacion this Court did accept and allowe. And therevppon it is ordered and agreed by this court that Mr Chamberlen shall in respect of the true and faithfull service of the said Mr Doctor heretofore by him done and performed in the service of this Cittye, geve vnto him out of the Chamber the somme of CC markes as of the free gift of this Court. And also acquite and discharge the sayd Mr Doctor of a Debt of XV^{li} by him owing to this Cittye by bond, and to deliver vnto him the sayd bond.[65]

And on the same day Clement Edmondes was sworn Remembrancer.[66]

In 1609 we have Fletcher's last extant letter, a significant document. I have elsewhere shown its importance in connection with Phineas' *Piscatorie Eclogs*.[67] But equally important, it shows that Fletcher was still in poor financial condition and still suffered from the consequences of his friendship with Essex.

In November 1610, Fletcher was employed by the Merchants Adventurers to meet with Dr. Jonas Charisius, the ambassador of the King of Denmark, concerning the possibilities of establishing trade at Krimp. A certain John Rolt had discussed the possibilities with the king without the company's permission. The difficulty that now faced the company was how to tell the king that they would consider Krimp only if the present negotiations with Stade failed. And it seems to have been Fletcher's task to do just this.[68]

Fletcher's health was now declining, and by February of the following year he was so weak that he could not write his will:

65. Corporation of London, Repertory 27, f. 40^v.
66. *Ibid.*, f. 41.
67. See my "Phineas Fletcher's Account of His Father," *JEGP*, LX (1961), 261–63.
68. BM MS Cott. Nero B.V. 333.

Memorandum that on the Eleaventh daye of Februarye one thowsand six hundred and tenne or theraboutes Giles Fletcher doctor of Lawe late of the parishe of Saincte Katherine Colman in the Citie of London deceased beyng of perfect mynde and memorye and having an Intent to make his last will did nuncupatively declare the same in manner and forme folowinge: or the like in effect viz: He gaue and bequeathed the residue of all his goodes and chattels (his debtes that he oughte beyng payed or deducted) vnto Johane Fletcher his wife or at least he declared his will in some other wordes of the like effect beyng then and there present William Webb John Lane and others.[69]

He quietly passed away on the eleventh of March.[70] Phineas records his last words in his own *Father's Testament*:

The great Legacy which I desire to confer upon you is that which my dying Father bequeathed unto me, and from him (through Gods grace) descended upon me, whose last, and parting words were these; *My Son had I followed the course of this World, and would either have given, or taken bribes, I might (happily) have made you rich, but now must leave you nothing but your education, which (I bless God) is such, as I am well assured you chuse rather that I should dye in peace, than your selves live in plenty. But know certainly, that I your weak, and dying Father leave you to an everliving, and All-sufficient Father, and in him a never fading inheritance; who will not suffer you to want any good thing, who hath been my God, and will be the God of my seed.*

   Thus he entred into peace, and slept in *Christ*; leaving behind the fragrant perfume of a good name, to all his acquaintance, leaving to us a prevalent example of an holy conversation, and that *goodly heritage where the lines are fallen to us in pleasant places*, (Psal. 16.6) and leaving us to his protection, who hath never failed us.[71]

And in the *Piscatorie Eclogs*, he also speaks of the death of Thelgon, who is his father:

69. PCC 22 Wood.
70. The Parish Register of St. Katherine Coleman, London.
71. Phineas Fletcher, *A Fathers Testament* (London, 1670), sigs. B[v]–B2[r].

48

Ah *Thelgon*, poorest, but the worthiest swain,
That ever grac't unworthy povertie!
How ever here thou liv'dst in joylesse pain,
Prest down with grief, and patient miserie;
Yet shalt thou live when thy proud enemie
    Shall rot, with scorn and base contempt opprest.
    Sure now in joy thou safe and glad doth rest,
Smil'st at those eager foes, which here thee so molest.

Thomalin, mourn not for him: he's sweetly sleeping
In *Neptunes* court, whom here he sought to please;
While humming rivers by his cabin creeping,
Rock soft his slumbering thoughts in quiet ease:
Mourn for thy self, here windes do never cease;
    Our dying life will better fit thy crying:
    He softly sleeps, and blest is quiet lying.
Who ever living dies, he better lives by dying.[72]

On 13 March, Joan Fletcher was granted the administration of her husband's will.[73] On 11 August, James I wrote the provost and fellows of King's College, requesting them to grant Joan Fletcher a ten-year extension of the Ringwood lease;[74] but this was not done, as King's College leased Ringwood to William Mendam on 16 July 1612.[75] On 14 August 1614, Joan Fletcher died.[76]

---

72. Frederick S. Boas (ed.), *The Poetical Works of Giles and Phineas Fletcher* (2 vols.; Cambridge 1909), II, 184.

73. PCC 22 Wood.

74. SP 38/10. 11 August 1611.

75. King's College, Ledger Book, III, 372.

76. The Parish Register of Allhallows, London Wall, London.

A Note on the Text

This edition presents a critical text of the English works of Giles Fletcher. The general procedures which have been the basis for this edition of *Licia*, *Of the Russe Commonwealth*, and *The Tartars or Ten Tribes* are outlined below. Of necessity, a somewhat different procedure has been followed in editing Fletcher's letters, which the reader will find outlined in the textual introduction to the Letters.

The copy text for each work is the first edition. Later editions have no textual authority, except for William Whiston's 1749 edition of *The Tartars or Ten Tribes*. Multiple copies of the edition chosen as copy text have been collated to determine if press variants exist; however, the press corrections I have found do not indicate authorial correction.

All other editions of Fletcher's works, including modern editions, have been collated. The substantive variants of the 1643 edition of the *Russe Commonwealth* and of Whiston's edition of *The Tartars or Ten Tribes* have been recorded; but only significant emendations of modern editors have been noted.

No substantive alteration has been made silently; however, some silent alteration of accidentals has been made. The long *f* is modernized throughout. The use of *vv* for *w* is ignored. Modern quotation marks replace the Renaissance practice of indicating quoted material by preceding each line

with an inverted comma. Obvious errors in punctuation have been corrected. All abbreviations are silently expanded, and, as a result of the ex-
pansion, the punctuation following the abbreviation is either omitted or
altered accordingly. Line numbers have been added for the text.

The Poems

Licia

Licia, or Poemes of Love, and *The Rising to the Crowne of Richard the Third* constitute all of Fletcher's poetical writings in English.[1] This volume was issued anonymously and without imprint, so that the problems of authorship and date are of great importance. Both introductory epistles to *Licia* are dated 1593; and in the textual introduction to *Licia*, I suggest reasons that would indicate that this is, in fact, the year of publication. Phineas Fletcher provides the proof of his father's authorship in the *Piscatorie Eclogs*, where Thelgon (Giles Fletcher), recalling a number of poems he has written, says: "And rais'd my rime to sing of *Richards* climbing." Alexander Dyce denied that this proved Fletcher's authorship of the sonnet sequence;[2] but Joseph Hunter[3] and A. B. Grosart[4] have defended Fletcher's authorship, and since Grosart's essay it has been taken as fact.

I

There is very little information in the sonnets that would indicate the date of their composition. The sonnet to the twin daughters of Lady

1. See my "Giles Fletcher, the Elder: A Bibliography," *Transactions of the Cambridge Bibliographical Society*, III, part 3 (1961), 200–215, for a bibliography of Fletcher's Latin poems.
2. In his edition of *The Works of Beaumont and Fletcher* (11 vols.; London, 1843–46), I, xv–xvi.
3. In *New Illustrations of the Life, Studies, and Writings of Shakespeare* (2 vols.; London, 1845), II, 77–78.
4. In his edition of *The Poems of Phineas Fletcher* (4 vols.; 1869), I, xlvii–l.

Molineux is not helpful, for the date of their birth is not known. But information in Sonnet XXII and the Dedicatory Epistle to Lady Molineux indicates that the sonnets were written sometime after 1591. The first eight lines of Sonnet XXII read:

> I might have dyed, before my lyfe begunne,
> When as my father for his countries good,
> The Persians favour and the Sophy wonne:
> But yet with daunger, of his dearest blood.
> Thy father (sweet) whome daunger did beset,
> Escaped all, and for no other end:
> But onely this, that you he might beget:
> Whom heavens decreed, into the world to send.

This sonnet alludes to Fletcher's trip to Russia. The daughter addressed is certainly Judith, who was baptized on 1 August 1591, although she was not the first child born to the Fletchers after his return from Russia. A daughter, Sara, was baptized on 28 June 1590, but she died shortly after birth and was buried on 3 July.

In the Dedicatory Epistle to Lady Molineux, Fletcher refers to "*Haringtons Ariosto*," and Harington's translation was first published in 1591.

II

The sources of *Licia* have been pointed out by Grosart,[5] Kastner,[6] Lee,[7] and in detail by Miss Scott.[8] Lee says of Fletcher's sources:

> His ideas are mainly borrowed from minor Latin poetry by Italian or French writers, of recent or contemporary date. He does not, however, disdain levying loans on Watson and Sidney, as well as on French and Italian sonneteers writing in their own tongue. Though his phrases are very often plagiarised, his adaptations are felicitous;

5. Grosart 1876, pp. 101–3.
6. L. E. Kastner, "The Elizabethan Sonneteers and the French Poets," *MLR*, III (1908), 276–77.
7. Sidney Lee (ed.), *Elizabethan Sonnets* (2 vols.; Westminster, 1904), I, lxxxii–lxxxv.
8. Janet G. Scott, *Les Sonnets Élisabéthains* (Paris, 1929), pp. 103–13, 312–14.

and, unlike Lodge and Daniel, he rarely descends to wholesale literal translation.[9]

Miss Scott has pointed out the extent of Fletcher's borrowing from the neo-Latinists, but her figures need a little revision.[10] Of the 54 sonnets, no less than 43 are "to the imitation of the best Latin Poets": Angerianus, 25; Gruterus, 7; Marullus, 4; Muretus, 2; Ronsard, 2; Secundus, 1; Melissus, 1; and Bonnefons, 1.[11]

Fletcher is generally consistent in his method of developing his sonnets from his sources. Miss Scott has justly observed that Fletcher usually begins his sonnet with one or two lines of literal translation from the source, but that from this point he becomes increasingly independent of his source and often develops his sonnet to a different conclusion.[12]

For example, Angerianus' "De Cæliæ furto" is the source for Sonnet IX.

Quum dormiret Amor, rapuit clam pulchra pharetram
Cælia; surrepta fleuit Amor pharetra.
Noli, Cypris ait, sic flere Cupido; pharetram
Pulchra tibi rapuit Cælia, restituet.
Non opus est illi calamis, non ignibus; vrit
Voce, manu, gressu, pectore, fronte, oculis.

Love was layd downe, all wearie fast asleepe,
Whereas my love his armour tooke away,
The boye awak'd, and straight began to weepe,
But stood amaz'd, and knew not what to say:
Weepe not, my boy, said Venus to her sonne,
Thy weapons, non can weild, but thou alone,
Lycia the faire, this harme to thee hath done,
I sawe her here, and presentlie was gone,

9. Lee, *Elizabethan Sonnets*, I, lxxxii–lxxxiii.

10. Janet G. Scott, "The Sources of Giles Fletcher's *Licia*," *MLR*, XX (1925), 187–88.

11. Miss Scott has likewise pointed out that Fletcher used the volume *Poetæ tres elegantissimi* (Paris, 1582), which contained the poems of Angerianus, Marullus, and Secundus.

12. There are, of course, exceptions. Sonnet II is a rather close translation from Angerianus, Sonnets XL and XLI from Gruterus, and Sonnet LII from Ronsard.

> She will restore them, for she hath no need,
> To take thy weapons, where thy valour lies,
> For men to wound, the Fates have her decreed,
> With favour, handes, with beautie, and with eies,
>   No, Venus no: she scornes them (credite me)
>   But robb'd thy sonne, that none might care for thee.

Sonnet XVI presents several interesting features. The sources are three "Basia" by Secundus.

Basium III

> "Da mihi suaviolum," dicebam "blanda puella!"
> Labasti labris mox mea labra tuis.
> Inde velut presso qui territus angue resultat,
> Ora repente meo vellis ab ore procul.
> Non hoc suaviolum dare, lux mea, sed dare tantum
> Est desiderium flebile suavioli.

Basium II

> Vicina quantum vitis lascivit in ulmo
> Et tortiles per ilicem
> Brachia proceram stringunt immensa corymbi:
> Tantum, Neaera, si queas
> In mea nexilibus proserpere colla lacertis!
> Tali, Nearea, si queam
> Candida perpetuum nexu tua colla ligare
> Iungens perenne basium!

Basium XIII

> Ergo age, labra meis innecte tenacia labris,
> Assidueque duos spiritus unus alat,
> Donec inexpleti post taedia sera furoris
> Vnica de gemino corpore vita fluet.

> Graunt fayrest kind, a kisse unto thy friend,
> A blush replyde, and yet a kisse I had:

It is not heaven, that can such nectar send,
Whereat my senses, all amaz'd, were glad.
This done, she fled, as one that was afrayde,
And I desyr'd to kisse, by kissing more,
My love she frown'd and I my kissing stayde,
Yet wisht to kisse her, as I did before:
Then as the vine, the propping elme doeth claspe,
Lothe to depart, till both together dye:
So folde me (sweete) untill my latest gaspe,
That in thy armes, to death, I kist, may lye.
    Thus whilest I live, for kisses I must call,
    Still kisse me, (sweete) or kisse me not at all.

Miss Scott has pointed out the similarity in sentiment of this poem to Sidney's Sonnet LXII and especially the last line of each poem. Sidney writes: "Dear! love me not that ye may love me more."[13] Another important point is demonstrated in the line "Then as the vine, the propping elme doeth claspe." Fletcher's line is certainly his rendering of the similar conceit in Secundus. But the ultimate source is Horace. Miss Lea has justly observed: "The exact source of each conceit, or even of each group of conceits, may as well be a matter of dispute as the pedigree of a mongrel, but the influence of Italy is omnipresent."[14]

As we have seen, Lee briefly mentions that Fletcher did not "disdain levying loans" on Watson. Professor Murphy has specified just what it seemed to him that Fletcher borrowed. He says: "Fletcher's Sonnet 3 uses the extended situation found in Watson's Number 42, and his "Charon" sonnet (Sonnet 41) is an adaptation of Watson's Number 49. The situations in these poems are not found in any of the other sonneteers, with one exception."[15] The fact that these situations are not found in any other sonnets is

13. Further parallels between Fletcher and Sidney are recorded in the explanatory notes; but it is unnecessary to list the other sonneteers' use of conceits found in Fletcher's sonnets, as this information is readily available in Miss Lisle C. John's The Elizabethan Sonnet Sequences (New York, 1938), pp. 195–200.

14. Kathleen M. Lea, "Conceits," MLR, XX (1925), 392.

15. William M. Murphy, "Thomas Watson's Hecatompathia [1582] and the Elizabethan Sonnet Sequence," JEGP, LVI (1957), 422.

of little significance, when one realizes that Fletcher's sources for his sonnets were Angerianus and Gruterus. A comparison of the relevant part of Watson's Sonnet XLIX with Fletcher's Sonnet XLI and Gruterus' poem in *Harmosynæ* will clearly demonstrate that Fletcher owes nothing to Watson. Watson XLIX reads:

> And yet she dread's, least when she partes from hence,
> Her Heates be such, that *Charon* will retire,
> And let her passe for prayer, nor for pence,
> For feare his with'red boat be set on fire;
>> So daung'rous are the flames of Mighty *Loue*
>> In *Stix* it selfe, in earth, or heau'n aboue.

Fletcher XLI:

> If (aged Charon), when my life shall end,
> I passe thy ferrye, and my wafftage pay,
> Thy oares shall fayle thy boate, and maste shall rend,
> And through the deepe, shall be a drye foote-way.
> For why my heart with sighs doth breath such flame,
> That ayre and water both incensed be.

Gruterus:

> Si cariose Charon, vbi pausam fecero vitæ,
> Debeo agi Eumenidum, te duce, per latices:
> Cymba tua interiit, tui et interire trientes.
> Mox pedi enim sicco per Styga semita erit.
> En quantis mea corda vomant incendia flammis.
> Aura et vt flagret proxima, et en, vt aqua.

Murphy also says: "Sonnet 28 in Fletcher's work, although an adaptation from Argeriano [*sic*], appropriates the exact wording of Watson's anaphora in Number 47."[16] This, of course, is so; but it is also the exact wording of Angerianus:

> Tempore tecta ruunt Prætoria, tempore vires,
> Tempore quæsitiæ debilitantur opes.

16. *Ibid.*, p. 421.

Tempore vernales flores, argentea et arent
Lilia; præfulgens tempore forma fluit.

Lee points out that Fletcher was indebted also to Sidney, and there can
be no doubt of this. Because of certain similarities between Sidney's sonnet
sequence and Fletcher's, Miss Scott has even suggested that *Astrophel and
Stella* might have inspired Fletcher to write his *Licia*.[17]

III

Fletcher's *Licia* has always been considered one of the most important
of the sonnet sequences, ironically, not for the sonnets, but for the two introductory epistles. Nevertheless, Fletcher's verse is not without merit, and
at least one sonnet will always be found in any anthology of sixteenth-
century poetry. Professor Lewis has commented: "There is some feeling for
nature in *Licia*, and some graceful fancy: no pathos and no exaltation."[18]
And it is a poem such as this we remember:

> In tyme the strong and statelie turrets fall,
> In tyme the Rose, and silver Lillies die,
> In tyme the Monarchs captives are and thrall,
> In tyme the sea, and rivers are made drie:
> The hardest flint, in tyme doth melt asunder,
> Still living fame, in tyme doth fade away,
> The mountaines proud, we see in tyme come under,
> And earth for age, we see in tyme decay:
> The sunne in tyme, forgets for to retire,
> From out the east, where he was woont to rise,
> The basest thoughtes, we see in time aspire,
> And greedie minds, in tyme do wealth dispise,
> > Thus all (sweet faire) in tyme must have an end:
> > Except thy beautie, vertues, and thy friend.[19]

---

17. *Les Sonnets Élisabéthains*, p. 105.
18. C. S. Lewis, *English Literature in the Sixteenth Century Excluding Drama* (Oxford, 1954), p. 494.
19. Sonnet XXVIII. Sonnets I, VI, IX, XXII, XXV, XXXVI, XLVII, and LII have all been cited
by various scholars for their poetic quality.

But what is the significance of the sonnet sequence as a whole? Miss Scott, I believe, provides the answer:

> La valeur de *Licia* est surtout dans la forme. Fletcher a un style assez clair, une langue pure et correcte sans trop de nouveautés. Il utilise très discrètement les mots composés, et presque tous sont des expressions avec "like", combinaison très anglaise....
>
> Comme Sidney, mais à un degré beaucoup moindre, Fletcher possède l'art d'écrire des conclusions épigrammatiques....
>
> Le sonnet anglais serait certainement moins complet, s'il ne possédait pas ces riens charmants. Fletcher est le premier et le dernier des sonnettistes élisabéthains à utiliser consciemment un fonds riche qui avait déjà fourni mainte pièce délicieuse en Italie et en France. Des poèmes anacréontiques, il est vrai, se rencontrent partout dans la poésie anglaise de la Renaissance, mais où les contemporains se contentent d'un ou deux sonnets sur l'*Amour anuité*, Fletcher en fait une vingtaine, introduisant des exploits de Cupidon inconnus aux autres sonnettistes élisabéthains.[20]

IV

In addition to the sonnets, Fletcher includes in *Licia* an ode; three elegies; a long poem, "A Lover's Maze"; and a translation of a passage in Lucian.

The ode, which immediately follows the sonnet sequence, tells of successful love—a contrast to the frustration recorded by the poet at times in his sonnets:

> Forget this fault, and love your frend,
> Which vowes his trueth unto the end.
> Content (she sayd) if this you keepe,
> Thus both did kisse, and both did weepe.
> For women, long they can not chyde,
> As I by proofe in this have tryde.

20. Scott, *Les Sonnets Élisabéthains*, pp. 112–13.

The three elegies are in some ways Fletcher's best poems. I can find no source for them, and it seems that for once Fletcher cast off the restraining bands of his Italian sources. In Elegy III Fletcher writes:

> No payne like this, to love and not enjoye,
> No griefe like this, to mourne, and not be heard.
> No time so long, as that which breed's annoy,
> No hell like this, to love and be deferd.

"A Lover's Maze" is without question Fletcher's poorest effort. The translation from Lucian, "A dialogue betwixt two Sea-nymphes, Doris and Galatea," is interesting because it is, in fact, a translation of Johannes Secundus' version of the dialogue of Lucian.[21] Secundus adds to Lucian's account, and Fletcher rather faithfully translates Secundus:

> Fortè deæ pelagi ludentes littore curuo,
> Captabant radios, auree Phoebe tuos.
> Hic Thetis, hic Melite, Spio, Panapeaque virgo,
> Cymodoce, Dorie, et Galatea fuit:
> Quum Doris ficto Caleteam molliter ore
> Risit, et arguto strinxit amara ioco.

Fletcher omits only the catalogue of the sea nymphs.

21. Dougall Crane, *Johannes Secundus, His Life, Work, and Influence on English Literature* (Leipzig, 1931), pp. 53–54.

The Rising to the Crowne of Richard the Third

I

The date of composition of *The Rising to the Crowne of Richard the Third* presents an interesting problem. In the *Piscatorie Eclogs*, Phineas Fletcher mentions several of his father's poems:

[1] I sang sad *Telethusa's* frustrate plaint,
And rustick *Daphnis* wrong, and magicks vain restraint:

[2] And then appeas'd young *Myrtilus*, repining
At generall contempt of shepherds life;

[3] And rais'd my rime to sing of *Richards* climbing;

[4] And taught our *Chame* to end the old-bred strife,
Mythicus claim to *Nicias* resigning:

$$(\text{I, ix–x, 6–7, 1–5})$$

The poem alluded to in [1] is Fletcher's "Queræla Collegij Regalis sub D. P. B." and the poem alluded to in [2] is "Æcloga de contemptu ministrorum." I have shown elsewhere that the date of composition of these poems is about February 1570.[1] The poem alluded to in [4] is *De Literis*

---

1. See my "Three Poems by Giles Fletcher, the Elder, in *Poemata Varii Argumenti* (1678)," *N&Q*, n.s. VI (1959), 132–34.

64

Antiquæ Britanniæ, which is extant in two versions; and the date of composition of the earlier is sometime before 1584.² The poem in [3] is *The Rising to the Crowne of Richard the Third*. Phineas' mention of these poems comes before the account of his father's diplomatic missions, which began in 1586. All this would suggest that *The Rising to the Crowne of Richard the Third* was likewise composed sometime between 1570 and 1586.

But there is evidence to suggest that the date of composition is no earlier than 1592. In the first six stanzas, Fletcher writes of the "falls" of women—Shore's wife, Rosamond, and Elstred. The story of Shore's wife appeared in both *A Mirror for Magistrates* (1563) and Anthony Chute's version (1593). The "falls" of Rosamond and Elstred are by Daniel and Lodge, respectively; and, significantly, each is appended to a sonnet sequence, which might have suggested a similar idea to Fletcher. This idea gains support from lines 31–36:

> Nor weepe I nowe, as children that have lost,
> But smyle to see the Poets of this age:
> Like silly boates in shallowe rivers tost,
> Loosing their paynes, and lacking still their wage.
> To write of women, and of womens falles,
> Who are too light, for to be fortunes balles.

This seems definitely to refer to Daniel and Lodge; and those who have written of Fletcher's poem cite this as evidence that it was composed in 1592 or 1593.³ But these first six stanzas are purely introductory and might well have been added when Fletcher decided to include the poem in his sonnet sequence. And this is exactly what I believe happened.⁴ The date of composition can be fixed with a little more precision, as Fletcher's source is Holinshed's account (1577) of Richard III. The date of composition would thus be sometime between 1577 and 1586.

2. See my "Phineas Fletcher's Account of His Father," *JEGP*, LX (1961), 259–60.
3. George B. Churchill, *Richard the Third Up to Shakespeare* (Berlin, 1900), pp. 529–30; Hallett Smith, *Elizabethan Poetry* (Cambridge, Mass., 1952), p. 110.
4. This naturally assumes that Phineas' account of his father is chronologically correct, but, in fact, there is one serious error in chronology—his father's mission to Scotland. I have shown at length why Phineas purposefully misplaced this. See my "Phineas Fletcher's Account of His Father," *JEGP*, LX (1961), 261–63.

II

Sir Thomas More's *The History of King Richard the Third* is the source of Fletcher's account; but Fletcher's knowledge of the work came from Holinshed. This is evident by Fletcher's allusion to Richard's winning of Buckingham:

> To match our children, I did him perswade,
> And Earle of *Herford* he him selfe be made.
>
> (ll. 239–40)

Holinshed includes this incident in his translation of More's Latin account, but Edward Hall omitted it from his *Chronicle*.[5]

How closely Fletcher used More's account can be seen by the following example:

> Friend and fo was much what indifferent, where his aduantage grew, he spared no mans death whose life withstoode his purpose. He slue with his owne hands king Henrie the sixt, being prisoner in the Tower, as men constantlie said...
>
> (Holinshed, *Chronicles*, III, 362)

> To gaine a kingdome still it me behoov'd:
> That all my lettes full soundlie were remoov'd.

> *Henrie* the sixt depriued of his crowne,
> Fame doeth report I put him to the death,
> Thus fortune smyl'd, though after she did frowne,
> A daggers stab men say, did stop his breath.
>
> (ll. 71–76)

Only once does Fletcher depart from the order of events as recorded by More. The two children were not murdered until after Richard's coronation, the point where Fletcher decided to end his account; so Fletcher has the children killed immediately after the younger boy was brought to London (ll. 233–34).

---

5. Raphael Holinshed, *Chronicles of England, Scotland, and Ireland* (6 vols.; London, 1807–8), III, 378. This was noticed by Churchill, *Richard the Third Up to Shakespeare*, p. 530.

Fletcher likewise alters one incident in the account. According to Fletcher, the Archbishop of York resolved to leave the Seal of England with the queen as a token of his fidelity, but "wiser thoughts" made him change his mind. In More's account, the Archbishop did leave the Seal, but on his return to the Council, he "secretly sent for the seale againe, and brought it with him after the customable maner" (Holinshed, *Chronicles*, III, 369).

Fletcher's debt to *A Mirror for Magistrates* is obvious. The 1559 edition had the accounts of Richard, Duke of York; King Henry the Sixth; George, Duke of Clarence; and King Edward the Fourth. The 1563 edition continued with the accounts of Anthony, Lord Rivers; Lord Hastings; Henry, Duke of Buckingham; Richard, Duke of Gloucester; and Shore's Wife.[6]

III

Fletcher's effort is very much in the tradition of *A Mirror for Magistrates*. And, indeed, one wonders if Fletcher did not decide to write his *Richard III* after reading the weak representation in the *Mirror*. Recall what Baldwin said in his "To the Reader" subjoined to the tragedy of Richard, Duke of Gloucester: "When I had read this, we had much talke about it. For it was thought not vehement ynough for so violent a man as kyng Rychard had bene. The matter was wel ynough lyked of sum, but the meeter was mysliked almost of all."[7] But one of the group pointed out to Baldwin: "Seyng than that kyng Rychard never kept measure in any of his doings, seing also he speaketh in Hel, whereas is no order: it were agaynst the *decorum* of his personage, to vse eyther good Meter or order." To forestall such criticism, Fletcher has Richard say:

> My verse is harsh, yet (reader) doe not frowne,
> I wore no garland but a golden Crowne.
>
> (ll. 281–82)

Fletcher's Richard does appear more "vehement," but little more than that can be said.

---

6. Lily B. Campbell (ed.), *A Mirror for Magistrates* (Cambridge, 1938), pp. 182–386.
7. *Ibid.*, p. 371.

The Text

There is only one edition of *Licia*, and it is indeed a very rare volume.

BIBLIOGRAPHICAL DESCRIPTION OF *Licia*

[within a frame of 4 woodcuts of female figures: 150 mm. × 106 mm. enclosing 104 mm. × 63 mm. the left side, rep. Humility, 102 mm. × 23 mm., a break of 4.5 mm. × 1.5 mm. 38 mm. from top on rt. mar.; the head, rep. Love, 106 mm. × 23 mm.; the rt. side, rep. Knowledge, 102 mm. × 23 mm.; the foot, rep. Patience, 99 mm. × 23 mm.; the head and foot figures face out] [rule] | LICIA, | [rule] | *or* | POEMES OF | *LOUE, IN HO-* | *nour of the admirable* | and singular vertues of his Lady, | *to the imitation of the best* | Latin Poets, and others. | [rule] *Whereunto is added the Rising to the* | Crowne of RICHARD | the third. | [rule] | *Auxit musarum numerum Sappho ad-* | *dit a musis.* | *Fælix si sævus, sic voluisset Amor.*

Special Title, sig. L^r: [within the frame of ornaments described above with these exceptions: the left and right side woodcuts have been transposed; the head and foot ornaments face in] THE RISING | TO THE CROWNE | of RICHARD the | third. | *VVritten by him selfe.* | [type orn. 31 mm. × 23 mm.].

68

Note: The Bodleian copy lacks this title page.

Col: 4⁰: A–M⁴ [fully signed except A A4 C4 G4 K2 L M4]; 48 leaves, pp. [10] 1–69 [3] 70–81 [misnumbering 47 as 32, 78 as 74; pp. 3, 15, 56, 68, 81 unnumbered].

Note: In the Huntington copy, M4 follows A1. This happened when the copy was rebound.

Contents: A1ʳ title page, A1ᵛ *Ad Amorem* and *Ad Lectorem*, A2ʳ–A3ᵛ THE EPISTLE DEDICATORIE, A4ʳ–Bᵛ TO THE READER, B2ʳ–H4ᵛ sonnets, Iʳ⁻ᵛ *AN ODE*, I2ʳ–I3ᵛ *A dialogue betwixt two Sea-nymphes*, I3ᵛ AD LECTOREM DISTICHON, I4ʳ–K2ʳ A LOVERS MAZE, K2ᵛ *AN ELEGIE*, K3ʳ⁻ᵛ *ELEGIE. II*, K4ʳ⁻ᵛ *ELEGIE. III*, Lʳ title page, Lᵛ blank, L2ʳ–M3ᵛ The Rising to the Crowne of Richard the Third, M4ʳ Errata, M4ᵛ blank.

CW: A2ᵛ no cw., Cᵛ Hard [Harde], D4ʳ Licia [Lycia], E2ʳ Seaven [Seven], I3ᵛ no cw., M2ᵛ Now [Nowe], M3ᵛ no cw.

Licia is conjectured by Pollard and Redgrave (*STC* 11055) to have been printed at Cambridge by John Legate in 1593; and on this evidence G. R. Barnes[1] entered the book under that year. But no proof has been hitherto offered to support this conjecture.

On the flyleaf of the Bodleian's copy of *Licia* appears this annotation:

The four figures surrounding this title page of *Licia* represent: Knowledge of God...Love of God...Patience...[and] Humility... and are part of a set of 22 used by Ihon Daye[2] in folios 41–51 of 'A

1. G. R. Barnes, *A List of Books Printed in Cambridge at the University Press, 1521–1800* (Cambridge, 1935), p. 8.

2. Each of the woodcuts measures 135 × 23 mm., and each consists of an upper compartment, the figure, and a lower compartment. The compartments each measure 15 × 20 mm. The four woodcuts used in *Licia* are: (1) Humility [within the upper compartment: Humilitie, | is tender har- | ted.] [within the lower compartment: Pride, despi- | seth his neigh- | bour.], (2) Love [within the upper compartment: Loue of God | is in spirite, and | truth.] [within the lower compartment: Idolatry, is | Spirituall adul- | tery.], (3) Knowledge [within the upper compartment: Knowledge of | God in Iesus | Christ is life.] [within the lower compartment: Mahomet, | and his Alco- | ron is perdition], (4) Patience [within the upper compartment: Patience, | ouercõmeth all | thinges.] [within the lower compartment: Wrath, | deuoureth it | selfe.].

Booke of Christian Prayers'...printed by him in 1578 and again in 1581. In 1590 an edition was printed by Richard Yardley and Peter Short, for the assignes of Richard Day when these 4 figures have evidently parted company with the rest of the set, and the printers were then necessitated to duplicate the use of Temperance, Chastitie, Measure and Industrie to make up the number.

Probably these four woodcuts were separated from the set after John Daye's death on 23 July 1584. An examination of all books printed at Cambridge from 1584 to 1594 reveals that they were acquired by the university's printer, Thomas Thomas; for the woodcut representing "Humilitie" appears as a head-piece on sig. B2^r in Whitaker's *Disputatio De Sacra Scriptura* (STC 25366), published on 2 May 1588. The upper and lower compartments of the woodcut have been cut away and all that remains is the figure as it appears on the title page of *Licia*.[3] Thomas died later in 1588, and on 2 November of the same year John Legate was appointed his successor. Dr. D. F. McKenzie has shown that Legate acquired all of Thomas' type and ornaments, among which one can assume were these four woodcuts.[4] The ornaments used as head- and tail-pieces in *Licia* offer additional proof that Legate printed the book; for of the eight varieties of ornaments used in *Licia*, five can be found in Thomas Bell's *Motives* (STC 1830), a quarto printed by Legate in 1593. In the following tabulation only the first occurrence of each ornament in *Licia* is listed.

	Fletcher's *Licia*	Bell's *Motives*
[woodcut]	A4^r	title page
[Bowes[5] no. 20]	B^v	¶¶3^v, V4^r
[type orn.]	B2^r	¶¶2^v, P4^v
[Bowes no. 14]	B2^v	G^v
[Bowes no. 29]	B4^v	A^r, B4^r

3. Why did Richard Daye, John Daye's son and successor in business, allow these four woodcuts to be separated from such a valuable set? A very probable answer is for some consideration of friendship. Both Thomas and Richard Daye proceeded to King's College in 1571 and were in residence together for over five years.

4. D. F. McKenzie, "Notes on Printing at Cambridge c. 1590," *Transactions of the Cambridge Bibliographical Society*, III, part 1 (1959), 96.

5. Robert Bowes, *Catalogue of Cambridge Books* (Cambridge, 1894), pp. xvi–xviii.

It seems very probable that *Licia* was printed in 1593. Fletcher dates "The Epistle Dedicatorie" 4 September 1593 and "To the Reader" 8 September 1593. And the fact that both Bell's *Motives* and Fletcher's *Licia* are printed on the same thin unwatermarked paper further suggests 1593 as the year of publication.

A fragment consisting of outer forme A (Bodl. Douce frag. e. 36) is generally referred to as a proof sheet; but it is equally possible that it is what R. B. McKerrow describes as a "rough pull."[6] There are three variants between this fragment and the extant copies. (1) The catchword on sig. A2v, "Now", is not present in the extant copies. (2) The woodcuts on the title page are arranged differently. In the fragment, the two vertical woodcuts are transposed, and the two horizontal woodcuts face in. The most likely explanation is that the rearrangement in the extant copies improves the aesthetic appearance of the page. In the fragment, the break in the woodcut representing "Humilitie" is more clearly noticeable, as it appears in the outer margin of the border; but by transposing the vertical woodcuts, the break appears in the inner margin. Furthermore, there is some aesthetic advantage in having the horizontal figures face out rather than in. And (3) in the process of rearranging these woodcuts, the line "the third" has slipped 3mm. to the left.

There is a late transcript of *Licia*, but it has no textual authority.[7]

Licia has been edited five times since 1593. A. B. Grosart edited *Licia* and *The Rising to the Crowne of Richard the Third* in 1871 and in revised form in 1876. His is the only edition which retains the original spelling, although the text suffers from the well-known limitations of Grosart as an editor. Edward Arber edited *Licia* and *The Rising to the Crowne of Richard the Third* in Volume VIII of *An English Garner* in 1896. There are numerous inaccuracies in the text, the two most flagrant being the omission of Sonnet XXIX and of line 48 of "An Ode." Also in 1896, Martha Crow edited

---

6. See McKerrow's definition of "rough pull" in *Introduction to Bibliography* (Oxford, 1928), p. 219.

7. BM Add. MS 25,477. It was purchased on 21 November 1863 at Sothebys, and is Lot 243 in the catalogue. It is part of the "Manuscripts and Transcripts written by or for the Rev. J. Hunter." The description of the manuscript in the BM Catalogue of Additional Manuscripts states that the paper is nineteenth century. Hunter refers to this transcript in his manuscript "Chorus Vatum Anglicanorum," f. 285v (BM Add. MS 24,487).

The Poems

Licia in *Elizabethan Sonnet Cycles*; but her text is unsatisfactory, not only because of the numerous inaccuracies, but also because she omits the poems *Ad Amorem* and *Ad Lectorem*, and "The Epistle Dedicatorie," "To the Reader," and *The Rising to the Crowne of Richard the Third*. *Licia*, but not *The Rising to the Crowne of Richard the Third*, appears in Volume II of Sidney Lee's *Elizabethan Sonnets*, 1904. The publisher's note states that the texts "are reprinted with very slight alterations" from Arber's *Garner* of 1896. This is the very truth; for all the errors of the 1896 edition are present in Lee's edition.

The present edition is based on a collation of all the extant copies of *Licia:* British Museum (L) (Huth 41), Bodleian (O) (Malone 325), and Huntington Library (CSmH). The collation reveals these press variants:

Outer forme B
    Corrected: O
    Uncorrected: L, CSmH
       B^r: Thus] Thue
Inner forme C
    Corrected: L, O
    Uncorrected: CSmH
       C^v: sonne] *om.*
Outer forme K
    Corrected: L, CSmH
    Uncorrected: O
       $K2^v$: sleepe] slaepe

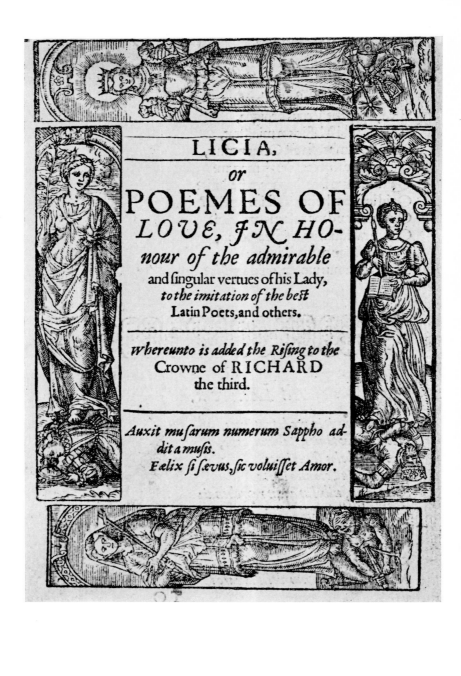

LICIA,

or

POEMES OF

LOVE, IN HO-
nour of the admirable
and singular vertues of his Lady,
to the imitation of the best
Latin Poets, and others.

whereunto is added the Rising to the
Crowne of RICHARD
the third.

Auxit musarum numerum Sappho ad-
dit a musis.
Fælix si sævus, sic voluisset Amor.

Ad Amorem.

Si Cœlum patria est puer beatum,
Si verò peperit Venus benigna,
Si Nectar tibi Massicum ministrat,
Si Sancta Ambrosia est Cibus petitus,
Quid noctes habitas, diesque mecum? 5
Quid Victum face supplicemque aduris?
Quid longam lachrimis sitim repellis?
Quid nostræ dape pasceris medullæ?
O verè rabidum genus færarum:
O domo stige patriaque digne: 10
Iam levis sumus umbra, quid lacessis?

Ad Lectorem.

Non Convitia, nec latrationes,
Nec Ronchos timeo, Calumniasvè,
Nec ullos obelos severiores.
Non quod judicio meo Poëta
Sim tantus, nihil ut queat reprehendi: 5
Sed quod judicio meo Poëta
Sim tam ridiculus, parùmque doctus,
Vt nullum fore judicem eruditum,
Meos carpere qui velit labores:
Nam quis Aethiopem velit lavare? 10

TO THE WOR-
thie, Kinde, Wise, and Vertuous
Ladie, the Ladie Mollineux; wife to the
Right Worshipfull Syr Richard
Mollineux Knight.

Howsoever in the settled opinions of some wise heads this trifling labor may easily incurre the suspicion of two evils, either to be of an idle subject, and so frivolous: or vainly handled, and so odious. Yet my resolute purpose was to proceed so farre, as
5 the indifferent Reader might thinke this small paines to be rather an effect then a cause of idlenesse; and howsoever Love in this age hath behaved himselfe in that loose manner, as it is counted a disgrace to give him but a kind looke; yet I take the passion in it selfe to be of that honour and credite, as it is the perfect resemblance of the great-
10 est happinesse, and rightlie valued at his just price, (in a minde that is syncerely and truly amorous) an affection of greatest vertue, and able of him selfe to æternize the meanest vassall. Concerning the handling of it, (especially in this age) men may wonder, if a Scholler, how I come by so much leasure: if otherwise, why a writer. Indeede
15 to say trueth, though I can not justly challenge the first name, yet I wish none to be writers, save onely such as knowe learning. And whereas my thoughtes and some reasons drew me rather to have dealt in causes of greater weight, yet the present jarre of this dis-agreeing age drive me into a fitte so melancholie, as I onely had

74

leasure to growe passionate. And I see not why upon our dissentions 20
I may not sit downe idle, forsake my study, and goe sing of love, as
well as our *Brownistes* forsake the Church, and write of malice.

And that this is a matter not so unfitte for a man, either that re-
specteth him selfe, or is a scholler. Peruse but the writings of former
times, and you shall see not onely others in other countryes, as 25
Italie, and *France*, men of learning and great partes to have written
Poems and Sonnets of Love; but even amongst us, men of best
nobilitie, and chiefest families, to be the greatest Schollers and most
renowmed in this kind. But two reasons hath made it a thing fool-
ishly odious in this age: the one, that so many base companions are 30
the greatest writers: the other, that our English *Genevian* puritie
hath quite debarred us of honest recreation; and yet the great pillar (as
they make him of that cause) hath shewed us as much witte and
learning in this kinde, as any other before or since. Furthermore
for all students I will say thus much, that the base conceit, which men 35
generally have of their wants, is such, as I scarce terme him a scholler,
that hath not all the accomplyments of a Gentleman, nor sufficiently
wise that will not take oportunitie in some sort to shew it. For I can
say thus much, that the Vniversitie wherein I lived, (and so I thinke
the other) hath so many wise, excellent, sufficient men, as setting their 40
learning aside, wherein they are most excellent, yet in all habilliments of a Gentleman they are equall to any besides. This woulde
that worthie *Sidney* oft confesse, and *Haringtons Ariosto* (which
Madame was respected so much by you) sheweth that his abode was
in Kinges Colledge. Yet nowe it is growen to this passe, that learning 45
is lightly respected, upon a perswasion, that it is to be found every
where, a thing untrue and unpossible.

Now in that I have written Love sonnets, if any man measure my
affection by my style, let him say, I am in Love; no greate matter,
for if our purest divines have not bene so, why are so manie married? 50
I mislike not that, nor I would not have them mislyke this. For a man
may be in loue and not marrie, and yet wise; but hee cannot marrie,
and not be in love, but be a mere foole. Nowe, for the manner; we

will dispute that in some other place; yet take this by the waie, though
I am so liberall to graunt thus much, a man may write of love, and
not bee in love, as well as of husbandrie, and not goe to plough:
or of witches and be none: or of holinesse and be flat prophane. But
(wise and kinde Ladie) not to trouble your eares with this idle discourse let this suffice I found favours undeserved in such manner as
my rude abilitie wantes meanes to make recompence, and therefore
in the meane time I request you to accept this. If I had not so woon-
dred at your admirable and rare vertues that my hearte was surcharg-
ed with the exceeding measure of your woorthinesse, I had not
written: you are happie everie way, and so reputed: live so, and I
wish so you may live long: excuse me, favour me, and if I live, for
I am loth to admire without thankefulnesse, ere long it shall be
knowne what favours I received from wise Sir *Richard*, to whome
in all kinde affectes I reste bound.

For the Reader, if he looke for my letters to crave his favour, he
is farre deceived: for if he mislike anie thing, I am sorie he tooke the
paines to reade, but if he doe, let him dispraise, I much care not:
for praise is not but as men please: and it is no chiefe felicitie, for I have
hearde some men and of late for Sermons at *Paules crosse* and for
other paines so commended by all (excepting some fewe Cynickes,
that commend none that do well) that you would have thought
England would haue striven for their spedie preferment, but lyke a
woonder it lasted but nine dayes, and all is quiet and forgotten: the
best is they are yong men and may live to be preferred at another
time: so what am I worse if men mislike and vse tearmes? I can say
as much by them. For our great men I am sure, they want leasure to
reade, and if they had, yet for the most part, the worse speake worst.
Well, let the Printer looke he grow not a begger by such bargaynes,
the Reader that he loose not his labour, and for mine that is past, and
who so wiselie after an afternoones sleepe gapes, and saith, Oh howe
yong men spend their time idlie: first, let him spende his tyme
better than to sleepe: Secondlie, he knowes not my age: I feared a
hot ague, and with Tasso I was content to let my wit blood. But

leaving these to their dogged humour, and wishing your Lady-
ship all happinesse, I humbly take my leave. From my chamber.
September 4. 1593.

90

To the Reader.

I had thought (curteous and gentle Reader) not to have troubled thy
patience with these lines; but that in the neglect thereof I shoulde either
scorne thee as careless of thine opinion (a thing savouring of a proud
humour) or dispaire to obtaine thy favor, which I am loth to conceive of
thy good nature. If I were knowne I would intreat in the best manner, and
speake for him, whome thou knewest: but beeing not knowne, thou speakest
not against me, and therefore I much care not; for this kinde of poetrie
wherein I wrote, I did it onelie to trie my humour: and for the matter of
love, it may bee I am so devoted to some one, into whose hands these may
light by chance, that she may say, which thou now saiest (that surelie he is
in love) which if she doe, then have I the full recompence of my labour, and
the Poems have dealt sufficientlie, for the discharge of their owne duetie.
This age is learnedlie wise, and faultles in this kind of making their wittes
knowne: thinking so baselie of our bare English (wherein thousandes have
traveilled with such ill lucke) that they deeme themselves barbarous, and
the Iland barren unlesse they have borrowed from Italie, Spaine, and
France their best and choicest conceites; for my owne parte, I am of this
mind that our nation is so exquisite (neither woulde I overweininglie seeme
to flatter our home-spunne stuffe, or diminish the credite of our brave tra-
veilers) that neither Italie, Spaine, nor France can goe beiond vs for exact

78

invention; for if anie thing be odious amongst vs, it is the exile of our olde maners: and some base-borne phrases stuft up with such newe tearmes as a man may sooner feele vs to flatter by our incrouching eloquence than sus- pect it from the eare. And for the matter of love, where everie man takes upon him to court exactlie, I could iustlie grace (if it be a grace to be excellent in that kinde) the Innes of Court, and some Gentlemen like students in both Vniversities, whose learning and bringing up together, with their fine natures makes so sweet a harmonie, as without partialitie, the most iniurious will preferre them before all others: and therefore they onelie are fittest to write of Love. For others for the moste parte are men of meane reach, whose imbased mindes praie uppon everie badde dish: men unfitte to knowe what love meanes; deluded fondlie with their owne conceit, misdeeming so divine a fancie, taking it to bee the contentment of themselves, the shame of others: the wrong of vertue: and the refiner of the tongue; boasting of some fewe favours. These and such like errours (errours hatefull to an upright minde) commonlie by learnlesse heades are reputed for loves kingdome. But vaine men naturallie led, deluded themselves, deceive others. For Love is a Goddesse (pardon me though I speake like a Poet) not respecting the con- tentment of him that loves but the vertues of the beloved, satisfied with woondering, fedde with admiration: respecting nothing but his Ladies woorthinesse: made as happie by love as by all favours chaste by honour, farre from violence: respecting but one, and that one in such kindnesse, honestie, trueth, constancie, and honour, as were all the world offered to make a change, yet the boote were too small, and therefore bootles. This is love, and farre more than this, which I knowe a vulgare head, a base minde, an ordinarie conceit, a common person will not, nor cannot have: thus doe I commende that love wherewith in these poemes I have honoured the woorthie LICIA. But the love wherewith Venus sonne hath injuriouslie made spoile of thousandes, is a cruell tyrant: occasion of sighes: oracle of lies: enemie of pittie: way of errour: shape of inconstancie: temple of trea- son: faith without assurance: monarch of tears: murtherer of ease: prison of heartes: monster of nature: poisoned honney: impudant courtizan: furious bastard: and in one word, not Love. Thus (Reader) take heede thou erre not, æsteeme Love as thou ought. If thou muse what my LICIA is, take

25

30

35

40

45

50

79

55 *her to be some* Diana, *at the least chaste, or some* Minerva, *no* Venus,
*fairer farre; it may be shee is Learnings image, or some heavenlie woonder,
which the precisest may not mislike: perhaps under that name I have
shadowed* Discipline. *It may be, I meane that kinde courtesie which I
found at the Patronesse of these Poems; it may bee some Colledge; it may*
60 *bee my conceit, and portende nothing: whatsoever it be, if thou like it, take
it, and thanke the worthie Ladie* MOLLINEVX, *for whose sake thou
hast it; worthie indeed, and so not onlie reputed by me in private affection
of thankefulnesse, but so equallie to be esteemed by all that knowe her. For
if I had not received of her and good* Sir RICHARD, *of kind and wise*
65 Master LEE, *of curteous* Master HOVGHTON, *all matchlesse, matched
in one kindred, those unrequitable favours, I had not thus idlely toyed.
If thou mislike it, yet she or they, or both, or divine* LICIA *shall patronize
it, or if none, I will and can doe it myselfe: yet I wish thy favour: do but
say thou art content, and I rest thine: if not farewel till we both meete.*
70 September 8. 1593.

TO LICIA THE WISE, KINDE,

Vertuous, and fayre.

Bright matchles starre, the honour of the skie,
From whose cleare shine, heavens vawt hath all his light,
I send these Poems to your gracefull eye:
Doe you but take them, and they have their right.
I build besides a Temple to your name,   5
Wherein my thoughtes shall daily sing your praise:
And will erect an aulter for the same,
Which shall your vertues, and your honour raise.
But heaven the Temple of your honour is,
Whose brasen toppes your worthie selfe made proude: 10
The ground an aulter, base for such a blisse
With pitie torne, because I sigh'd so loude.
    And since my skill no worship can impart,
    Make you an incense of my loving heart.

Sonnet. I.

Sadde all alone, not long I musing satte,
But that my thoughtes compell'd me to aspire,
A Laurell garland in my hande I gatte:
So the Muses I approch'd the nyer.
5   My sute was this, a Poet to become,
To drinke with them, and from the heavens be fedde:
Phæbus denyed, and sware there was no roome,
Such to be Poets as fonde fancie ledde:
With that I mourn'd; and sat me downe to weepe:
10   Venus she smil'd, and smyling to me saide,
Come drinke with me, and sitt thee still and sleepe:
This voyce I heard: and Venus I obayde.
    That poyson (sweete), hath done me all this wrong,
    For nowe of love, must needes be all my song.

Sonnet. II.

Wearie was love, and sought to take his rest,
He made his choice, uppon a virgins lappe:
And slylie crept, from thence unto her breast,
Where still he meant, to sport him in his happe.
5   The virgin frown'd, like Phœbus in a cloude,
Go packe sir boy, here is no roome for such,
My breast no wanton foolish boyes must shroude;
This saide, my Love did giue the wagge a tuch,
Then as the foot, that treads the stinging snake,
10   Hastes to be gone, for feare what may ensewe,
So love, my love, was forst for to forsak,
And for more speede, without his arrowes flewe.
    Pardon (he saide) for why you seem'd to me,
    My mother *Venus*, in her pride to be.

Sonnet. III.

The heavens beheld the beautie of my Queene,
And all amaz'd, to wonder thus began:
Why dotes not Ioue, as erst we all haue seene,
And shapes him selfe like to a seemely man?
Meane are the matches, which he sought before,   5
Like bloomelesse buddes, too base to make compare,
And she alone hath treasur'd beauties store:
In whome all giftes and princely graces are.
Cupid reply'd: I posted with the Sunne,
To viewe the maydes that liued in those dayes,   10
And none there was, that might not well be wonne:
But she, most hard, most cold, made of delayes.
    Heauens were deceiu'd, and wrong they doe esteeme,
    She hath no heat, although she liuing seeme.

Sonet. IIII.

Loue, and my loue, did range the forrest wilde,
Mounted alyke, upon swift coursers both:
Loue her encountred, though he was a childe,
Let's striue (saith he) whereat my loue was wroth,
And scorn'd the boy, and checkt him with a smile,   5
I mounted am, and armed with my speare,
Thou art too weake, thy selfe doe not beguile,
I could thee conquere, if I naked were:
With this loue wept, and then my loue reply'd:
Kisse me (sweet boy) so: weepe (my boy) no more;   10
Thus did my loue, and thus her force she try'd,
Loue was made yce, that fier was before.
    A kisse of hers, as I poore soule doe proove,
    Can make the hottest freese, and coldest loue.

Sonnet. V.

Love with her haire, my love by force hath ty'd,
To serve her lippes, her eies, her voice, her hand,
I smil'd for joy, when I the boye espy'd,
To lie inchain'd, and live at her commaund.
5   She if she looke, or kisse, or sing, or smile,
Cupid withall, doth smile, doth sing, doth kisse,
Lippes, handes, voice, eies, all hearts that may beguile,
Bicause she scornes, all hearts but onlie this.
Venus for this in pride began to frowne:
10   That Cupid borne a god, inthrald should be:
She in disdaine, her prettie sonne threwe downe,
And in his place, with love she chained me.
    So now (sweet love) though I my selfe be thrale,
    Not her a goddesse, but thy selfe I call.

Sonnet. VI.

My love amaz'd did blush her selfe to see,
Pictur'd by arte, all naked as she was:
How could the Painter, knowe so much by me,
Or Art effect, what he hath brought to passe?
5   It is not lyke, he naked me hath seene,
Or stoode so nigh, for to observe so much,
No, sweete; his eyes so nere have never bene,
Nor could his handes, by arte have cunning such:
I showed my heart, wherein you printed were,
10   You, naked you, as here you painted are,
In that (My Love) your picture I must weare,
And show't to all, unlesse you have more care:
    Then take my heart, and place it with your owne,
    So shall you naked never more be knowne.

Sonnet. VII.

Death in a rage, assulted once my heart,
With love of her, my love that doeth denie.
I scorn'd his force, and wisht him to depart,
I heartlesse was, and therefore could not die:
I live in her, in her I plac'd my life,   5
She guydes my soule, and her I honour must,
Nor is this life, but yet a living strife,
A thing unmeet, and yet a thing most just:
Cupid inrag'd, did flie to make me love,
My heart lay garded with those burning eies,   10
The sparkes whereof denyed him to remoove;
So conquerd now, he like a captive lies,
    Thus two at once by love were both undone:
    My heart not lov'd, and armlesse Venus sonne.

Sonet. VIII.

Harde are the rockes, the marble, and the steele,
The auncient oake, with wind, and weather tost,
But you my love, farre harder doe I feele,
Then flinte, or these, or is the winters frost.
My teares too weake, your heart they can not moove,   5
My sighes, that rocke, like wind it cannot rent,
Too Tyger-like you sweare, you cannot love:
But teares, and sighes, you fruitlesse backe have sent.
The frost too hard, not melted with my flame,
I Cynders am, and yet you feele no heate: 10
Surpasse not these (sweet love) for verie shame,
But let my teares, my vowes, my sighes, entreat,
    Then shall I say, as I by triall finde:
    These all are hard, but you (my love) are kind.

Sonnet. IX.

Love was layd downe, all wearie fast asleepe,
Whereas my love his armour tooke away,
The boye awak'd, and straight began to weepe,
But stood amaz'd, and knew not what to say:
5 Weepe not, my boy, said Venus to her sonne,
Thy weapons, non can weild, but thou alone,
Lycia the faire, this harme to thee hath done,
I sawe her here, and presentlie was gone,
She will restore them, for she hath no need,
10 To take thy weapons, where thy valour lies,
For men to wound, the Fates have her decreed,
With favour, handes, with beautie, and with eies,
 No, Venus no: she scornes them (credite me)
 But robb'd thy sonne, that none might care for thee.

Sonnet. X.

A paynter drew, the image of the boye,
Swift love, with winges all naked, and yet blind:
With bowe and arrowes, bent for to destroye,
I blam'd his skill, and fault I thus did fynde:
5 A needlesse taske, I see thy cunning take,
Misled by love, thy fancie thee betrayde,
Love is no boye, nor blinde, as men him make,
Nor weapons weares, whereof to be affrayde:
But if thou love, wilt paint with greatest skill,
10 A Love, a mayde, a goddesse, and a Queene:
Woonder, and viewe at Lycias picture still,
For other love, the world hath never seene;
 For she alone, all hope, all comfort gives:
 Mens hearts, soules all, led by her favour lives.

86

Sonnet. XI.

In Ida vale three Queenes the shepheard sawe,
Queenes of esteeme, divine, they were all three:
A sight of worth, but I a wonder sawe,
There vertues all in one alone to be.
Lycia the fayre, surpassing Venus pride,   5
(The matchlesse Queene commaunder of the goddes,
When drawen with doves, she in her pompe doeth ride)
Hath farre more beautie, and more grace by oddes.
Iuno Ioves wife, unmeete to make compare,
I graunt a goddesse, but not halfe so mylde: 10
Minerva wise, a vertue, but not rare.
Yet these are meane, if that my love but smyl'de.
    She them surpasseth, when their prides are full:
    As farre as they surpasse the meanest trull.

Sonnet. XII.

I wish sometimes, although a worthlesse thing,
Spurd by ambition, glad for to aspyre,
My selfe a Monarch, or some mightie King:
And then my thoughtes doe wish for to be hyer.
But when I view what windes the Cedars tosse,   5
What stormes men feele that covet for renowne,
I blame my selfe that I have wisht my losse,
And scorne a kingdome, though it give a crowne.
A' Licia thou, the wonder of my thought,
My heartes content, procurer of my blisse,   10
For whome a crowne, I doe esteme as nought,
And Asias wealth, too meane to buy a kisse;
    Kisse me sweete love, this favour doe for me:
    Then Crownes and Kingdomes shall I scorne for thee.

87

Sonnet. XIII.

Inamour'd Ioue, commaunding did intreat,
Cupid to wound my love which he deny'd,
And swore he could not, for she wanted heate,
And would not love, as he full oft had try'd.
5　Ioue in a rage, impatient this to heare,
Reply'd with threats: Ile make you to obey:
Whereat the boye did flie away for feare
To Lycias eyes, where safe intrench'd he lay:
Then Ioue, he scorn'd, and darde him to his face,
10　For now more safe than in the heavens he dwell'd,
Nor could Ioues wrath, doe wrong to such a place
Where grace and honour, have their kingdome helde.
　　Thus in the pride, and beautie of her eyes:
　　The seelie boye, the greatest god defies.

Sonnet. XIIII.

My love lay sleeping, where birdes musicke made,
Shutting her eies, disdainfull of the light,
The heat was great, but greater was the shade:
Which her defended from his burning sight:
5　This Cupid saw, and came a kisse to take:
Sucking sweet Nectar from her sugred breath:
She felt the touch, and blusht, and did awake,
Seeing t'was love which she did thinke was death:
She cut his winges, and caused him to stay,
10　Making a vowe, hee should not thence depart,
Vnlesse to her, the wanton boy could pay,
The truest, kindest and most loving heart:
　　His feathers still, she used for a fanne:
　　Till by exchange, my heart his feathers wan.

Sonnet. XV.

I stood amaz'd, and sawe my Licia shine,
Fairer then Phœbus, in his brightest pride,
Set foorth in colours, by a hand divine,
Where naught was wanting, but a soule to guide.
It was a picture, that I could descrye: 5
Yet made with arte, so as it seem'd to live,
Surpassing faire, and yet it had no eye:
Whereof my senses, could no reason give.
With that the Painter bidde me not to muse,
Her eyes are shut, but I deserve no blame.   10
For if she saw, in faith, it could not chuse:
But that the worke, had wholly beene a flame.
    Then burne me (sweete) with brightnesse of your eyes,
    That Phænix like, from thence I may arise.

Sonnet. XVI.

Graunt fayrest kind, a kisse unto thy friend,
A blush replyde, and yet a kisse I had:
It is not heaven, that can such nectar send,
Whereat my senses, all amaz'd, were glad.
This done, she fled, as one that was afrayde,   5
And I desyr'd to kisse, by kissing more,
My love she frown'd, and I my kissing stayde,
Yet wisht to kisse her, as I did before:
Then as the vine, the propping elme doeth claspe,
Lothe to depart, till both together dye: 10
So folde me (sweete) untill my latest gaspe,
That in thy armes, to death, I kist, may lye.
    Thus whilest I live, for kisses I must call,
    Still kisse me, (sweete) or kisse me not at all.

Sonnet. XVII.

As are the sandes (faire Licia) on the shore,
Or colourd floures, garlands of the spring,
Or as the frosts not seene, nor felt before,
Or as the fruites that Autume foorth doth bring,
5   As twinckling starres, the tinsell of the night,
Or as the fish that gallope in the seas,
As aires each part that still escapes our sight:
So are my sighes, controllers of my ease.
Yet these are such, as needes must have an end,
10   For things finite, none els hath nature done:
Onlie the sighes, which from my heart I send,
Will never cease, but where they first begunne.
       Accept them (sweete) as incense due to thee:
       For you immortall made them so to be.

Sonnet. XVIII.

I sweare (faire Licia) still for to be thine,
By heart, by eies, by what I held most deare,
Thou checkt mine oath, and said: these were not mine,
And that I had no right by them to sweare.
5   Then by my sighes, my passions, and my teares,
My vowes, my prayers, my sorrowe, and my love,
My griefe, my joy, my hope, and hopeles feares
My heart is thine, and never shall remoove.
These are not thine, though sent unto thy viewe,
10   All els I graunt, by right they are thine owne,
Let these suffice, that what I sweare is true,
And more than this, if that it could be known.
       So shall all these, though troubles ease my griefe:
       If that they serve, to worke in thee beliefe.

Sonnet. XIX.

That tyme (faire Licia) when I stole a kisse,
From of those lippes, where Cupid lovelie laide,
I quakt for colde, and found the cause was this,
My life which lov'd, for love behind me staid:
I sent my heart, my life for to recall: 5
But that was held, not able to returne,
And both detain'd as captives were in thrall,
And judg'd by her, that both by sighes should burne:
(Faire) burne them both, for that they were so bolde,
But let the altar be within thy heart: 10
And I shall live, because my lyfe you holde,
You that give lyfe, to everie living part,
    A flame I tooke, when as I stole the kisse:
    Take you my lyfe, yet can I live with this.

Sonnet. XX.

First did I feare, when first my love began,
Possest in fittes, by watchfull jealousie,
I sought to keepe, what I by favour wanne,
And brookt no partner in my love to be.
But Tyrant sicknesse, fedde upon my love,   5
And spred his ensignes, dy'd with colour white,
Then was suspition, glad for to remoove:
And loving much did feare to loose her quite.
Erect (faire sweet) the collours thou didst weare,
Dislodge thy griefes, the shortners of content: 10
For now of lyfe, not love, is all my feare,
Least lyfe, and love be both together spent.
    Live but (faire love) and banish thy disease:
    And love (kind heart) both when, and whom thou please.

Sonnet. XXI.

Lycia my love was sitting in a grove,
Tuning her smiles unto the chirping songs,
But straight she spy'd, where two together strove,
Ech one complaining of the others wrongs.
5   Cupid did crie, lamenting of the harme:
Ioves messenger, thou wrong'st me too too farre:
Vse thou thy rodde, relye upon thy charme:
Thinke not by speach, my force thou canst debarre.
A rodde (syr boy) were fitter for a childe,
10   My weapons oft, and tongue, and minde you tooke?
And in my wrong at my distresse thou smil'de,
And scorn'd to grace me with a loving looke.
     Speake you (sweet love) for you did all the wrong,
     That broke his arrowes, and did binde his tong.

Sonnet. XXII.

I might have dyed, before my lyfe begunne,
When as my father for his countries good,
The Persians favour and the Sophy wonne:
But yet with daunger, of his dearest blood.
5   Thy father (sweet) whome daunger did beset,
Escaped all, and for no other end:
But onely this, that you he might beget:
Whom heavens decreed, into the world to send.
Then father, thanke thy daughter for thy lyfe,
10   And Neptune praise, that yeelded so to thee,
To calme the tempest, when the stormes were ryfe,
And that thy daughter should a Venus be.
     I call thee Venus (sweet) but be not wroth,
     Thou art more chast, yet seas did favour both.

Sonnet. XXIII.

My love was maskt, and armed with a fanne,
To see the Sunne so carelesse of his light,
Which stood and gaz'd, and gazing, waxed wanne,
To see a starre, himselfe that was more bright.
Some did surmize, she hidde her from the sunne: 5
Of whome, in pride, she scorn'd for to be kist:
Or fear'd the harme, by him to others done,
But these the reason of this woonder mist.
Nor durst the Sunne, if that her face were bare,
In greatest pride, presume to take a kisse: 10
But she more kinde, did shew she had more care,
Then with her eyes, eclypse him of his blisse.
    Vnmaske you (sweet) and spare not, dimme the sunne:
    Your light's ynough, although that his were done.

Sonnet. XXIIII.

When as my love, lay sicklie in her bedde,
Pale death did poste, in hope to have a praie,
But she so spotlesse made him, that he fledde,
Vnmeet to die (he cry'd) and could not staie.
Backe he retyr'd, and thus the heavens he told,   5
All thinges that are, are subject unto me,
Both townes, and men, and what the world doth hold,
But let faire Licia still immortall be.
The heauens did graunt: a goddesse she was made,
Immortall, faire, unfit to suffer chaung,   10
So now she lives, and never more shall fade,
In earth a goddesse, what can be more strange?
    Then will I hope, a goddesse and so neare,
    She cannot chuse my sighes, and praiers but heare.

93

Sonnet. XXV.

Seven are the lights, that wander in the skies,
And at these seven, I wonder in my love,
To see the Moone, how pale she doeth arise,
Standing amaz'd, as though she durst not move:
So is my sweet, much paler than the snowe,
Constant her lookes, those lookes that cannot change,
Mercurie the next, a god sweet tong'd we know,
But her sweet voice, doth woonders speake more strange:
The rising Sunne doeth boast him of his pride,
And yet my love is farre more faire than he.
The warlike Mars, can weildles weapons guide,
But yet that god, is farre more weake than she.
The lovelie Venus, seemeth to be faire,
But at her best, my love is farre more bright;
Saturne for age, with groans doth dimme the aire;
Whereas my love, with smiles doth give it light.
    Gaze at her browes, where heaven ingrafted is:
    Then sigh, and sweare, there is no heaven but this.

Sonnet. XXVI.

I live (sweete love) whereas the gentle winde,
Murmures with sport, in midst of thickest bowes,
Where loving Wood-bine, doth the Harbour binde,
And chirping birdes doe eccho foorth my vowes:
Where strongest elme, can scarce support the vine,   5
And sweetest flowres enameld have the ground,
Where Muses dwell, and yet hereat repine:
That on the earth so rare a place was found.
But windes delight, I wish to be content:
I praise the Wood-bine, but I take no joye: 10
I moane the birdes, that musicke thus have spent:
As for the rest, they breede but mine annoye.
    Live thou (fayre Licia) in this place alone:
    Then shall I joye, though all of these were gone.

Sonnet. XXVII.

The Chrystal streames, wherein my love did swimme,
Melted in teares, as partners of my woe,
Her shine was such, as did the fountaine dimme:
The pearlike fountaine, whiter than the snowe,
Then lyke perfume, resolved with a heate,   5
The fountaine smoak'd, as if it thought to burne:
A woonder strange, to see the colde so great,
And yet the fountaine, into smoake to turne.
I searcht the cause, and found it to be this,
She toucht the water, and it burnt with love,   10
Now by her meanes, it purchast hath that blisse,
Which all diseases, quicklie can remoove.
    Then if by you, these streames thus blessed be:
    (Sweet) graunt me love, and be not woorse to me.

Sonnet. XXVIII.

In tyme the strong and statelie turrets fall,
In tyme the Rose, and silver Lillies die,
In tyme the Monarchs captives are and thrall,
In tyme the sea, and rivers are made drie:
The hardest flint, in tyme doth melt asunder,
Still living fame, in tyme doth fade away,
The mountaines proud, we see in tyme come under,
And earth for age, we see in tyme decay:
The sunne in tyme, forgets for to retire,
From out the east, where he was woont to rise,
The basest thoughtes, we see in time aspire,
And greedie minds, in tyme do wealth dispise,
    Thus all (sweet faire) in tyme must have an end:
    Except thy beautie, vertues, and thy friend.

Sonnet. XXIX.

Why dy'd I not when as I last did sleepe?
(O sleepe too short that shadowed foorth my deare)
Heavens heare my prayers, nor thus me waking keepe:
For this were heaven, if thus I sleeping weare.
For in that darke there shone a Princely light:
Two milke-white hilles, both full of Nectar sweete:
Her Ebon thighes, the wonder of my sight,
Where all my senses with their objectes meete:
I passe those sportes, in secret that are best,
Wherein my thoughtes did seeme alive to be;
We both did strive, and wearie both did rest:
I kist her still, and still she kissed me.
    Heavens let me sleepe, and shewes my senses feede:
    Or let me wake, and happie be indeede.

Sonnet. XXX.

When as my Lycia sayled in the seas,
Viewing with pride, god Neptunes stately crowne,
A calme she made, and brought the merchant ease,
The storme she stayed, and checkt him with a frowne.
Love at the stearne, sate smiling, and did sing: 5
To see howe seas, had learnd for to obey:
And balles of fire, into the waves did fling.
And still the boy, full wanton thus did say:
Both poles we burnt, whereon the world doeth turne,
The rownd of heaven, from earth unto the skies: 10
And nowe the seas we both intend to burne:
I with my bowe, and Licia with her eyes.
    Then since thy force, heavens, earth, nor seas can move,
    I conquer'd, yeeld; and doe confesse I love.

Sonnet. XXXI.

When as her lute is tuned to her voyce,
The aire growes proude, for honour of that sound;
And rockes doe leape, to shewe howe they rejoyce,
That in the earth, such Musicke should be found.
When as her haire, more worth, more pale, then golde,   5
Like silver threed, lies waffting in the ayre:
Diana like she lookes, but yet more bolde:
Cruell in chase, more chaste, and yet more fayre.
When as she smyles, the cloudes for envie breakes,
She Iove in pride encounters with a checke: 10
The Sunne doeth shine for joye when as she speakes:
Thus heaven, and earth doe homage at her becke.
    Yet all these graces blottes, not graces are:
    Yf you my love, of love doe take no care.

Sonnet. XXXII.

Yeares, months, daies, houres, in sighes I sadlie spend,
I blacke the night, wherein I sleeplesse tosse:
I love my griefs, yet wish them at an end,
Thus tymes expence, encreaseth but my losse.
5 I musing stand, and woonder at my love:
That in so faire, should be a heart of steele:
And then I thinke, my fancie to remove:
But then more painfull, I my passions feele.
Thus must I love (sweet faire) untill I die,
10 And your unkindnesse, doth my love encrease;
I conquerd am, I can it not denie:
My lyfe must end, yet shall my love not cease.
    Then heavens, make Licia faire, most kind to me:
    Or with my life, my loue may finisht be.

Sonnet. XXXIII.

I wrote my sighs, and sent them to my love,
I prais'd that faire, that none ynough could praise:
But plaintes, nor praises, could faire Lycia moove,
Above my reach, she did her vertues raise.
5 And thus reply'd: False Scrawle, untrue thou art,
To faine those sighes, that no where can be found:
For halfe those praises, came not from his hart:
Whose faith and love, as yet was never found.
Thy maisters lyfe, (false Scrawle) shall be thy doome:
10 Because he burnes, I judge thee to the flame:
Both your attempts, deserve no better roome,
Thus at her word, we ashes both became.
    Beleeve me (faire) and let my paper live:
    Or be not faire, and so me freedome give.

Sonnet. XXXIIII.

Pale are my lookes, forsaken of my lyfe,
Cynders my bones, consumed with thy flame,
Floodes are my teares, to end this burning stryfe,
And yet I sigh, for to increase the same.
I mourne alone, because alone I burne: 5
Who doubts of this, then let him learn to love,
Her lookes, colde yce into a flame can turne:
As I distressed in my selfe doe prove.
Respect (faire Licia) what my torments are,
Count but the tyth, both of my sighes and teares,   10
See how my love, doeth still increase my care,
And cares increase, my lyfe to nothing weares.
   Send but a sigh, my flame for to increase,
   Or lend a teare, and cause it so to cease.

Sonnet. XXXV.

When as I wish, faire Licia for a kisse:
From those sweet lippes, where Rose and Lillies strive,
Straight doe mine eies, repine at such a blisse,
And seeke my lippes, thereof for to deprive,
When as I seeke, to glut mine eies, by sight: 5
My lippes repine, and call mine eyes away:
Thus both contend, to have each others right:
And both conspire, to worke my full decay.
O force admyr'd, of beautie in her pride:
In whose each part, such strange effects there be,   10
That all my forces, in themselves devide:
And make my senses, plainlie disagree.
   If all were mine, this envie would be gone:
   Then graunt me all (faire sweet) or grant me none.

Sonnet. XXXVI.

Heare how my sighes, are ecchoed of the wind,
See how my teares, are pittied by the raine:
Feele what a flame, possessed hath my mind,
Taste but the griefe, which I possesse in vaine.
5 Then if my sighes, the blustering windes surpasse:
And watrie teares, the droppes of raine exceed,
And if no flame, like mine, nor is, nor was:
Nor griefe like that, wheron my soule doth feed:
Relent (faire Licia) when my sighes doe blowe,
10 Yeeld at my teares, that flint-like, droppes consume:
Accept the flame, that doth my incense showe,
Allowe the griefe, that is my hearts perfume.
  Thus sighes, and teares, flame, griefe, shall plead for me,
  So shall I pray, and you a goddesse be.

Sonnet. XXXVII.

I speake (faire Licia) what my torments be:
But then my speach, too partiall doe I finde:
For hardlie words, can with those thoughts agree:
Those thoughtes that swarme, in such a troubled mind.
5 Then doe I vowe, my tongue shall never speake:
Nor tell my griefe, that in my heart doth lie:
But cannon-like, I then surchardg'd, doe breake,
And so my silence, worse than speach I trie.
Thus speach, or none, they both doe breed my care.
10 I live dismayd, and kill my heart with griefe:
In all respectes, my case alyke doth fare:
To him that wants, and dare not aske reliefe.
  Then you (faire Licia) soveraigne of my heart:
  Read to your selfe, my anguish, and my smart.

Sonnet. XXXVIII.

Sweet, I protest, and seale it with an oath:
I never saw, that so my thoughtes did please:
And yet content displeas'd I see them wroth:
To love so much, and cannot have their ease.
I tolde my thoughts, my soveraigne made a pause,   5
Dispos'd to graunt, but willing to delay:
They then repin'd, for that they knewe no cause,
And swore they wisht, she flatlie would say nay.
Thus hath my love, my thoughts with treason fild:
And gainst my soveraigne, taught them to repine: 10
So thus my treason, all my thoughts hath kill'd,
And made faire Licia, say she is not mine.
　　But thoughts too rash, my heart doth now repent:
　　And as you please, they sweare, they are content.

Sonnet. XXXIX.

Faire matchlesse Nymph, respect but what I crave,
My thoughts are true, and honour is my love:
I fainting die, whome yet a smile might save:
You gave the wound, and çan the hurt remove.
Those eyes, like starres, that twinkle in the night,   5
And cheeks like rubies pale, in lilies dy'd,
Those Ebon hands, that darting have such might,
That in my soule, my loue and life devide.
Accept the passions, of a man possest:
Let Love be lov'd, and graunt me leave to live: 10
Disperse those clouds, that darkened have my rest:
And let your heaven, a sun-like smile but give.
　　Then shall I praise, that heaven for such a sunne,
　　That saved my life, when as my griefe begun

Sonnet. XL.

My griefe begunne (faire Saint) when first I saw,
Love in those eyes, sit ruling, with disdaine:
Whose sweet commandes, did keepe a world in awe:
And caus'd them serve, your favour to obtaine.
5 I stood as one enchaunted with a frowne,
Yet smilde to see, all creatures serue those eyes:
Where each with sighes, paid tribute to that crowne:
And thought them graced, by your dumme replyes.
But I, ambitious, could not be content:
10 Till that my service, more than sighes made knowne:
And for that end, my heart to you I sent:
To say, and sweare, that (faire) it is your owne.
   Then greater graces (Licia) doe impart:
   Not dumme replies, unto a speaking heart.

A SONNET MADE VPON THE TWO
Twinnes, daughters of the Ladie Mollineux, *both*
passing like, and exceeding faire.

Poets did faine, that heavens a Venus had:
Matchlesse her selfe, and Cupid was her sonne,
Men sew'd to these, and of their smiles were glad,
By whome so manie famous were undone.
Now Cupid mournes, that he hath lost his might: 5
And that these two, so comelie are to see:
And Venus frowns, because they have her right.
Yet both so like, that both shall blamelesse be.
With heavens two twinnes, for godhead these may strive
And rule a world, with least part of a frowne: 10
Fairer then these, two twinnes are not alive:
Both conquering Queenes, and both deserve a crowne.
    My thoughts presage, which tyme to come shall trie:
    That thousands conquerd, for their love shall die.

Sonnet. XLI.

If (aged Charon), when my life shall end,
I passe thy ferrye, and my wafftage pay,
Thy oares shall fayle thy boate, and maste shall rend,
And through the deepe, shall be a drye foote-way.
For why my heart with sighs doth breath such flame,
That ayre and water both incensed be.
The boundlesse Ocean from whose mouth they came,
For from my heate not heaven it selfe is free.
Then since to me thy losse can be no gaine:
Avoyd thy harme and flye what I foretell.
Make thou my love with me for to be slaine,
That I with her, and both with thee may dwel.
    Thy fact thus (Charon) both of us shall blesse:
    Thou save thy boat, and I my love possesse.

Sonnet. XLII.

For if alone thou thinke to waft my love,
Her cold is such as can the sea commaund.
And frosen Ice shall let thy boate to move,
Nor can thy forces rowe it from the land.
But if thou friendly both at once shalt take,
Thy selfe mayst rest for why my sighes will blowe.
Our colde and heate so sweete a thawe shall make,
As that thy boate without thy helpe shall rowe.
Then will I sitte and glut me on those eyes,
Wherewith my life, my eyes could never fill.
Thus from thy boate, that comfort shall arise,
The want whereof my life and hope did kill.
    Together plac'd so thou her skorne shalt crosse,
    Where if we part, thy boate must suffer losse.

Sonnet. XLIII.

Are those two starres, her eyes, my lifes light gone?
By which my soule was freed from all darke.
And am I left distres'd, to live alone?
Where none my teares and mournefull tale shall marke.
Ah Sunne, why shine thy lookes, thy lookes like gold,　5
When horseman brave thou risest in the East.
Ah Cynthia pale, to whome my griefes I told,
Why doe you both rejoyce both man and beast?
And I alone, alone that darke possesse
By Licias absence brighter then the Sunne,　　10
Whose smyling light did ease my sadde distresse
And broke the clowdes when teares like rayne begun.
　　Heavens graunt that light and so me waking keepe:
　　Or shut my eyes, and rocke me fast a-sleepe.

Sonnet. XLIIII.

Cruell fayre Love, I justly do complaine,
Of too much rigour, and thy heart unkind,
That for mine eyes, thou hast my bodie slaine,
And would not graunt, that I should favour find.
I look'd (fayre Love) and you my love lookt fayre,　5
I sigh'd for love, and you for sport did smyle.
Your smyles were such as did perfume the ayre,
And this perfumed did my heart beguyle,
Thus I confesse, the fault was in mine eyes,
Begun with sighes, and ended with a flame:　　10
I for your love, did all the world despise,
And in these poems, honour'd have your name.
　　Then let your love so with my fault dispense,
　　That all my parts feele not mine eyes offense.

105

Sonnet. XLV.

There shone a Comet, and it was full west.
My thoughts presaged, what it did portend:
I found it threatned, to my heart unrest,
And might in tyme, my joyes and comfort end.
5   I further sought, and found it was a Sunne:
Which day, nor night, did never use to set:
It constant stood, when heavens did restlesse run,
And did their vertues, and their forces let.
The world did muse, and wonder what it meant,
10   A Sunne to shine, and in the west to rise:
To search the trueth, I strength and spirits spent,
At length I found, it was my Licias eyes:
    Now never after, soule shall live in darke,
    That hath the hap, this westerne Sunne to marke.

Sonnet. XLVI.

If he be dead, in whome no hart remaines,
Or livelesse be, in whome no lyfe is found:
If he doe pyne that never comfort gaines,
And be distrest, that hath his deadlie wound,
5   Then must I dye whose heart els where is clad,
And livelesse passe the greedie wormes to feed:
Then must I pine, that never comfort had,
And be distrest, whose wound with teares doth bleed,
Which if I doe, why doe I not waxe cold?
10   Why rest I not lyke one that wants a hart?
Why moove I still, lyke him that lyfe doth hold?
And sense enjoy both of my joy and smart.
    Lyke Nyobe Queene, which made a stone, did weepe,
    Licia, my heart dead and alive doth keepe.

Sonnet. XLVII.

Lyke Memnons rocke toucht, with the rising Sunne,
Which yeelds a sownd, and ecchoes foorth a voice:
But when its drownde, in westerne seas is dunne,
And drousie lyke, leaves off to make a noise.
So I (my love) inlightned with your shyne,   5
A Poets skill within my soule I shroud,
Not rude lyke that, which finer wittes declyne,
But such as Muses to the best allowde.
But when your figure, and your shape is gone,
I speechlesse am, lyke as I was before: 10
Or if I write, my verse is fill'd with moane,
And blurd with teares, by falling in such store.
    Then muse not (Licia) if my Muse be slacke,
    For when I wrote, I did thy beautie lacke.

Sonnet. XLVIII.

I saw (sweet Licia) when the spydar ranne,
Within your house, to weave a woorthlesse web:
You present were, and feard her with your fanne,
So that amazed, speedilie she fled.
She in your house such sweete perfumes did smell,   5
And heard the Muses, with their notes refin'd:
Thus fill'd with envie, could no longer dwell,
But straight return'd, and at your house repin'd,
Then tell me (spidar) why of late I sawe
Thee loose thy poison, and thy bowels gone,   10
Did these enchaunt, and keepe thy limmes in awe,
And made thy forces, to be small or none?
    No, no, thou didst by chaunce my Licia see,
    Who for her looke, Minerva seem'd to thee.

Sonnet. XLIX.

If that I dye (fayre Lycia) with disdaine,
Or hartlesse live, surprised with thy wrong;
Then heavens and earth shall accent both my paine,
And curse the time so cruell, and so long.
5   If you be kinde (my Queene) as you are fayre,
And ayde my thoughtes, that still for conquest strive,
Then will I sing, and never more dispayre,
And praise your kindnesse, whylst I am alive.
Till then I pay the tribute of my teares,
10   To moove thy mercie and thy constant trueth.
Respect (fayre love) howe these with sorrowe weares
The truest heart: unlesse it finde some ruthe.
　　Then grace me (sweet) and with thy favour rayse me,
　　So shall I live, and all the world shall praise thee.

Sonnet. L.

A' Licia sigh, and say thou art my owne,
Nay be my owne, as you full oft have sayd.
So shall your trueth unto the world be knowne,
And I resolv'd, where now I am afrayd.
5   And if my tongue æternize can your prayse,
Or silly speech increase your worthy fame,
If ought I can, to heaven your worth can rayse,
The age to come, shall wonder at the same.
In this respect, your love (sweete love) I told,
10   My faith and trueth I vow'd should be for ever.
You were the cause, if that I was too bold,
Then pardon this my fault, or love me never.
　　But if you frowne, I wish that none beleeve me;
　　For slayne with sighes, Ile dye, before I greeve thee.

Sonnet. LI.

When first the Sunne, whome all my senses serve,
Began to shine upon this earthly round,
The heav'ns for her, all graces did reserve,
That Pandor-like, with all she might abound.
Apollo plac'd his brightnesse in her eyes,   5
His skill presaging, and his musicke sweete.
Mars gave his force, all force she now defyes.
Venus her smyles, wherewith she Mars did meete.
Python a voyce, Dyana made her chaste,
Ceres gave plentie: Cupid lent his bowe: 10
Thetis his feete: there Pallas wisdome plac't.
With these she Queene-like kept a world in awe.
   Yet all these honours deemed are but pelfe.
   For she is much more worthie of her selfe.

Sonnet. LII.

O sugred talke, wherewith my thoughtes doe live:
O browes loves Trophee, and my senses shine:
O charming smyles, that death or life can give:
O heavenly kisses from a mouth devine:
O wreaths too strong, and tramels made of hayre: 5
O pearles inclosed in an Ebon pale,
O Rose and Lillyes in a field most fayre,
Where modest whyte, doth make the red seeme pale.
O voyce whose accents live within my heart,
O heavenly hand that more then Atlas holds,   10
O sighes perfum'd, that can release my smart.
O happy they, whome in her armes she folds.
   Nowe if you aske where dwelleth all this blisse,
   Seeke out my love, and she will shew you this.

AN ODE.

Love I repent me that I thought,
My sighes, and languish, dearely bought,
For sighes and languish both did prove,
That he that languisht, sight for love.
5   Cruell rigour foe to state,
Lookes disdainfull, fraught with hate,
I did blame, but had no cause,
(Love hath eyes, but hath no lawes)
She was sadde, and could not chuse,
10 To see me sigh, and sitt, and muse.
We both did love, and both did doubt,
Least any should our love finde out.
Our heartes did speake by signes most hidden,
This meanes was left, all els forbidden.
15 I did frowne, her love to trye,
She did sigh, and straight did crye.
Both of us did signes beleeve,
Yet either grieved friend to greeve.
I did looke, and then did smyle;
20 She left sighing all that whyle.
Both were glad to see that change;
Things in love that are not strange.
Suspicion foolish foe to reason,
Caus'd me seeke, to finde some treason.
25 I did court another Dame,
(False in love it is a shame)
She was sorrie this to vewe,
Thinking faith was prov'd untrewe.
Then she swore, she would not love,
30 One whome false, she once did prove:
I did vowe I never ment,
From promise made, for to relent.

The more I said, the worse she thought,
My othes and vowes were dem'd as nought.
False (she sayde) howe can it be,   35
To court another, yet love me.
Crownes and Love no partners brooke,
If she be lyk'd, I am forsooke.
Farewell false, and love her still,
Your chaunce was good, but mine was ill.   40
No harme to you, but this I crave,
That your newe love, may you desave,
And jeast with you, as you have donne,
For light's the love, that's quickely wonne.
Kinde, and fayre-sweete, once beleeve me,   45
Ieast I did, but not to greeve thee.
Court I did, but did not love,
All my speach was you to prove.
Wordes and sighes, and what I spent,
(In shewe to her) to you were ment.   50
Fond I was your love to crosse,
(Ieasting love oft brings this losse.)
Forget this fault, and love your frend,
Which vowes his trueth unto the end.
Content (she sayd) if this you keepe,   55
Thus both did kisse, and both did weepe.
For women, long they can not chyde,
As I by proofe in this have tryde.

A dialogue betwixt two Sea-nymphes,
DORIS and GALATEA, concerning
Polyphemus; briefely translated
out of Lucian.

The Sea Nymphes late did play them on the shore,
And smyl'd to see such sport was new begunne:
A strife in love, the like not heard before,
Two Nymphes contend, which had the conquest wonne.
Doris the fayre, with *Galate* did chyd.
She lyk't her choyce, and to her taunts replyd.

Doris.

Thy love (fayre Nymph) that courts thee on this plaine,
As shepheards say, and all the world can tell,
Is that foule rude Sicilian Cyclop-swayne,
A shame (sweete Nymph) that he with thee should mell.

Galatea.

Smyle not (fayre *Doris*) though he foule doe seeme,
Let passe thy wordes that savour of disgrace,
He's worth my love, and so I him esteeme,
Renownd by birth, and comen of Neptunes race.
Neptune that doth the glassye Ocean tame,
Neptune, by birth from mighty Iove which came.

Doris.

I graunt an honour to be Neptunes chyld,
A grace to be so neere with Iove allyde.
But yet (sweete Nymph) with this be not beguyld,
Where natures graces are by lookes descryde.
So foule, so rough, so ugglye like a Clowne,
And worse then this, a Monster with one eye.
Foule is not graced, though it weare a Crowne,
But fayre is Bewtie, none can that denye.

Galatea.

Nor is he foule, or shapelesse as you say,   25
Or worse, for that he clownish seems to be,
Rough, Satyr-like, the better he will play,
And manly lookes the fitter are for me.
His frowning smyles are graced by his beard,
His eye-light Sunne-like, showded is in one.   30
This me contents, and others makes afeard,
He sees ynough, and therefore wanteth none.   With one eye.

Doris.

Nay then I see (sweete Nimph) thou art in love,
And loving, doates; and doating, doest commend.
Foule to be fayre, this oft doe lovers proove,   35
I wish him fayrer, or thy love an end.

Galatea.

Doris, I love not, yet I hardly beare,
Disgracefull tearms, which you have spoke in scorne.
You are not lov'd: and that's the cause I feare:
For why, my love, of Iove him selfe was borne.   40
Feeding his sheepe of late, amidst this plaine,
When as we Nymphes did sport us on this shore,
He skorn'd you all, my love for to obtaine;
That greev'd your hearts: I knew as much before.
Nay smyle not Nymphes, the trueth I onely tell,   45
For fewe can brooke, that others should excell.

Doris.

Should I envie that blinde did you that spite?
Or that your shape doeth pleease so foule a groome?
The shepheard thought of milke, you look'd so white,
The clowne did erre, and foolish was his doome,   50

113

Your looke was pale, and so his stomach fed,
But farre from faire, where white doth want his red.

Galatea.

Though pale my looke, yet he my love did crave,
And lovelie you, unlyk'd, unlov'd I view:
55 It's better farre one base, than none to have,
Your faire is foule, to whome there's none will sew:
My love doth tune his love unto his harpe,
His shape is rude, but yet his witt is sharpe.

Doris.

Leave off (sweet Nymph) to grace a woorthlesse clowne.
60 He itch'd with love, and then did sing or say,
The noise was such, as all the Nymphes did frowne,
And well suspected, that some Asse did bray.
The woods did chyde, to heare this uglie sound,
The prating Eccho scorn'd for to repeate,
65 This grislie voice did feare the hollow ground,
Whilst artlesse fingers did his harpstrings beat.
Two Bear-whelps in his armes this monster bore,
With these new puppies did this wanton play,
Their skinnes was rough, but yet your loves was more:
70 He fouler was and farre more fierce than they,
I cannot chuse (sweet Nymph) to thinke, but smyle,
That some of us, thou fearst, will thee beguyle.

Galatea.

Scorne not my love, untill it can be knowne,
That you have one that's better of your owne.

Doris.

75 I have no love, nor if I had, would boast,
Yet wo'd have bene, by such as well might speed:
But him to love, the shame of all the coast,
So uglie foule, as yet, I have no need.

Now thus we learne what foolish love can doe,
To thinke him faire, that's foule and uglie to. 80

To heare this talke I sate behinde an oake,
And mark'd their wordes to pend them as they spoke.

AD LECTOREM, DISTICHON
cujusdam de Autore.

Lascivi quæres fuerit cur carminis autor.
Carmine lascivus, mente pudicus erat.

A LOVERS MAZE.

Trewe are my thoughts, my thoughts that are untrue,
Blinde are my eies, my eyes that are not blinde:
New is my love, my love that is not newe,
Kind is that faire, that faire that is not kinde.
   Thus eyes, and thoughts, that fairest faire, my love, 5
   Blind, and untrue, unkind, unconstant prove.

True are my thoughts: because they never flitte.
Vntrew my thoughtes: because they me betraide.
Blinde are my eyes: because in cloudes I sitte,
Not blinde my eyes: because I lookes obeyed. 10
   Thus eyes, and thoughtes, my dearest faire may vewe:
   In sight, in love, nor blinde, nor yet untrew.

Newe is my love: because it never dies,
Olde is my love: because it ever lives.
Kinde is that faire: because it hate denyes, 15
Vnkinde that faire: because no hope it gives.
   Thus new my love, and still that faire unkinde:
   Renewes my love, and I no favour finde.

Sweete are my dreames, my dreames that are not sweet,
20   Long are the nightes, the nightes that are not long:
Meete are the panges, these panges that are unmeet:
Wrong'd is my heart, my heart that hath no wrong:
    Thus dreames, and night, my heart, my pangs, and all,
    In taste, in length, conspire to worke my fall.

25   Sweet are my dreames: because my love they showe.
Vnsweet my dreames: because but dreames they are.
Long are the nights: because no helpe I know,
Short are the nights because they end my care.
    Thus dreames, and nightes, wherein my love takes sport:
30   Are sweet, unsweet, are long, and yet too short.

Meet are my panges: because I was too bolde.
Vnmeet my panges; because I lov'd so well.
Wrong'd was my heart: because my griefe it tolde:
Not wrongd: for why? my griefe it could not tell.
35   Thus you my love, unkindlie cause this smart.
    That will not love, to ease my panges and heart.

Proude is her looke: her looke that is not proude,
Done are my dayes, my dayes that are not done,
Lowd are my sighes, my sighes that are not lowd,
40   Begun my death, my death not yet begunne.
    Thus looks, and dayes, and sighs, and death might move:
    So kind, so faire, to give consent to love.

Proud is her looke: because she scornes to see.
Not proud her looke: for none dare say so much.
45   Done are my dayes: because they haplesse be.
Not done my dayes: because I wish them such.
    Thus lookes, and dayes, increase this loving strife,
    Not proude, nor done, nor dead, nor giving life.

Loud are my sighes: because they pearce the skie.
50   Not loud my sighes: because they are not heard.

My death begunne: because I heartlesse crie.
But not begunne: because I am debard.
    Thus sighes, and death, my heart no comfort give:
    Both lyfe denie, and both do make me live.

Bold are her smiles, her smiles that are not bold   55
Wise are her wordes, those words that are not wise,
Cold are her lippes, those lippes that are not colde,
Ise are those hands, those handes that are not ise.
    Thus smiles, and wordes, her lippes, her hands, and she,
    Bold wise, cold ise, loves cruell torments be.   60

Bold are her smiles: because they anger slay.
Not bold her smiles: because they blush so oft.
Wise are her wordes: because they woonders say.
Not wise her wordes: because they are not soft.
    Thus smiles, and wordes, so cruell and so bold: 65
    So blushing wise, my thoughtes in prison hold.

Colde are her lippes, because they breath no heate.
Not colde her lippes: because my heart they burne.
Ise are her handes: because the snow's so great.
Not Ise her handes, that all to ashes turne.   70
    Thus lippes and handes, cold Ise my sorrowe bred,
    Hands warme-white-snow, and lippes, cold cherrie red.

Small was her wast, the wast that was not small:
Gold was her haire, the haire that was not gold,
Tall was her shape, the shape that was not tall,   75
Folding the armes, the armes that did not folde:
    Thus haire, and shape, those folding armes and wast:
    Did make me love, and loving made me waste.

Small was her wast, because I could it spanne,
Not small her wast: because she wasted all.   80
Gold was her haire: because a crowne it wanne,
Not gold her haire: because it was more pale.

Thus smallest waste, the greatest wast doth make:
And finest haire, most fast a lover take.

85 Tall was her shape: because she toucht the skie,
Not tall her shape: because she comelie was,
Folding her armes: because she hearts could tie.
Not folded armes: because all bands they passe.
    Thus shape, and armes, with love my heart did plie,
90   That hers I am, and must be till I die.

Sad was her joy, her joy that was not sadde,
Short was her staie, her staie that was not short:
Glad was her speach, her speach that was not glad:
Sporting those toyes, those toyes that were not sport:
95   Thus was my heart, with joy, speach, toyes, and stay,
    Possest with love, and so stollen quite away.

Sadde was her joy: because she did suspect.
Not sad her joy: because her joy she had.
Short was her staie: because to smal effect.
100 Long was her stay: because I was so sadde.
    Thus joy, and staie, both crost a lovers sporte,
    The one was sadde, the other too too short.

Glad was her speach: because shee spake her mind.
Not glad her speach: because affraid to speake.
105 Sporting her toyes: because my love was kinde.
Not toyes in sport: because my heart they breake.
    Thus speach, and toyes, my love began in jest:
    (Sweet) yeeld to love, and make thy servant blest.

Tred you the Maze (sweet love) that I have run:
110 Marke but the steppes, which I imprinted have:
End but your love, whereas my thoughtes begun,
So shall I joye, and you a servant have.
    If not (sweet loue) then this my sute denie:
    So shall you live, and so your servant die.

AN ELEGIE.

Downe in a bed, and on a bed of doune,
Love, she, and I to sleepe together lay:
She lyke a wanton kist me with a frowne,
Sleepe, sleepe, she saide, but meant to steale away:
    I could not choose, but kisse, but wake but smile,   5
    To see how she thought us two to beguile.

She faind a sleepe, I wakt her with a kisse:
A kisse to me she gave, to make me sleepe:
If I did wrong (sweete love) my fault was this,
In that I did not you, thus waking keepe,   10
    Then kisse me (sweet) that so I sleepe may take,
    Or let me kisse, to keepe you still awake.

The night drew on, and needs she must be gone:
She waked love, and bid him learne to waite:
She sigh'd, she said, to leave me there alone,   15
And bid love stay, but practise no deceit.
    Love wept for griefe, and sighing made great mone.
    And could not sleepe, nor staie, if she were gone.

Then staie (sweet love) a kisse with that I gave,
She could not staie: but gave my kisse againe: 20
A kisse was all that I could gett or crave,
And with a kisse, she bound me to remaine.
    A' Licia still, I in my dreames did crie,
    Come (Licia) come, or els my heart will die.

ELEGIE. II.

1 Distance of place, my love and me did part:
Yet both did sweare, we never would remove;
In signe thereof, I bid her take my heart:

Which did, and doth, and can not chuse but love.
5   Thus did we part, in hope to meete againe:
Where both did vow, most constant to remaine.

2 A She there was that past betwixt us both,
By whome ech knew how others cause did fare.
For men to trust, men in their love are loth:
10 Thus had we both of love, a lovers care.
   "Haply he seekes his sorrowes to renue,
   That for his love doth make another sue."

3 By her a kisse, a kisse to me she sent,
A kisse for price more worth then purest gold.
15 She gave it her, to me the kisse was ment,
A she to kisse, what harme if she were bold?
   Happy those lippes, that had so sweete a kisse;
   For heaven it selfe scarce yeeldes so sweete a blisse.

4 This modest she, blushing for shame of this,
20 Or loth to part from that she lik't so well,
Did play false play, and gave me not the kisse;
Yet my loves kindnesse could not chuse to tell.
   Then blame me not, that kissing sigh'd, and swore,
   I kist but her, whome you had kist before.

25   5 Sweete, love me more, and blame me not (sweet love)
I kist those lippes, yet harmlesse I doe vowe,
Scarse would my lippes, from off those lippes remoove,
For still me thought (sweet fayre) I kissed you.
   And thus kinde love, the summe of all my blisse,
30   Was both begunne, and ended in a kisse.

6 Then send me moe, but send them by your frend,
Kisse none but her, nor her, nor none at all.
Beware by whome such treasures you doe send,
I must them loose, except I for them call.

Yet love me (deare) and still still kissing be,   35
Both like and love, but none (sweete love) but me.

ELEGIE. III.

1 If sadde complaint would shewe a lovers payne,
Or teares expresse the torments of my hart,
If melting sighes would ruth and pitty gaine,
Or true Laments but ease a lovers smart,

2 Then should my plaints the thunders noyse surmount,   5
And teares like seas should flowe from out my eyes,
Then sighes like ayre should farre exceede all count,
And true laments with sorrow dimme the skyes.

3 But plaintes, and teares, laments, and sighes I spend,
Yet greater torments doe my heart destroy,   10
I could all these from out my heart still send,
If after these I might my love enjoy.

4 But heavens conspyre, and heavens I must obey,
That seeking love I still must want my ease.
"For greatest joyes are temperd with delay,   15
Things soone obtain'd do least of all us please."

5 My thoughtes repyne; and thinke the time too long,
My love impatient, wisheth to obtaine,
I blame the heavens, that do me all this wrong,
To make me lov'd, and will not ease my payne.   20

6 No payne like this, to love and not enjoye,
No griefe like this, to mourne, and not be heard.
No time so long, as that which breed's annoy,
No hell like this, to love and be deferd.

7 But heaven shall stand, and earth inconstant flye,   25
The Sunne shall freese, and Ice inconstant burne,

The mountaines flowe, and all the earth be drye,
Ear time shall force my loving thoughtes to turne.

8 Do you resolve (sweete love) to doe the same,
Say that you doe, and seale it with a kisse.
Then shall our truthes the heav'ns unkindnesse blame,
That can not hurt, yet shewes their spyte in this.

9 The sillye prentice bound for many yeeres,
Doeth hope that time his service will release.
The towne besieg'd that lives in midst of feares,
Doeth hope in time the cruell warres will cease.

10 The toyling plough-man sings in hope to reape;
The tossed barke expecteth for a shore;
The boy at schoole to be at play doeth leape,
And straight forgets the feare he had before.

11 If these by hope doe joye in their distresse,
And constant are, in hope to conquer tyme.
Then let not hope in us (sweete friend) be lesse,
And cause our love to wither in the Pryme.

Let us conspyre, and time will have an end,
So both of us in time shall have a frend.

FINIS.

THE RISING TO
the Crowne of RICHARD
the third. Written by him selfe.

The Stage is set, for Stately matter fitte,
Three partes are past, which Prince-like acted were,
To play the fourth, requires a Kingly witte,
Els shall my muse, their muses not come nere.
    Sorrow sit downe, and helpe my muse to sing,   5
    For weepe he may not, that was cal'd a King.

Shores wife, a subject, though a Princes mate,
Had little cause her fortune to lament.
Her birth was meane, and yet she liv'd with State,
The King was dead before her honour went.   10
    Shores wife might fall, and none can justly wonder,
    To see her fall, that useth to lye under.

Rosamond was fayre, and farre more fayre then she,
Her fall was great, and but a womans fall.
Tryfles are these, compare them but with me,   15
My fortunes farre, were higher then they all.
    I left this land, possest with Civill strife,
    And lost a Crowne, mine honour, and my life.

Elstred I pitie, for she was a Queene,
But for my selfe, to sigh I sorrow want,   20

Her fall was great, but greater falles have beene;
"Some falles they have, that use the Court to haunt."
 A toye did happen, and this Queene dismayd,
 But yet I see not why she was afrayd.

25 Fortune and I, (for so the match began)
Two games we play'd at tennyse for a Crowne;
I play'd right well, and so the first I wan:
She skorn'd the losse, whereat she straight did frowne.
 We play'd againe, and then I caught my fall,
30 *England* the Court, and *Richard* was the ball.

Nor weepe I nowe, as children that have lost,
But smyle to see the Poets of this age:
Like silly boates in shallowe rivers tost,
Loosing their paynes, and lacking still their wage.
35 To write of women, and of womens falles,
 Who are too light, for to be fortunes balles.

A King I was, and *Richard* was my name,
Borne to a Crowne, when first my life began.
My thoughtes ambitious, venterd for the same,
40 And from my nephewes I the kingdom wan.
 Nor doe I thinke that this my honour stayn'd,
 A Crowne I sought, and I a kingdome gayn'd.

Tyme-tyrant fate did fitte me for a Crowne,
My fathers fall did teach me to aspire;
45 He meant by force his brother to put downe,
That so himselfe might hap to rise the higher.
 And what he lost by fortune, I have wonne,
 A Duke the father, yet a king the sonne.

My father *Richard*, duke of *Yorke* was call'd,
50 Three sonnes he had, all matchlesse at that tyme;
I *Richard* yongest to them both was thrall'd,

Yet two of us unto the crowne did clyme.
   Edward and I this realme as kinges did holde,
   But *George* of *Clarence*, could not, though he would.

Sad Muse set downe in tearmes not heard before,   55
My sable fortune, and my mournfull tale:
Say what thou canst, and wish thou could say more,
My blisse was great, but greater was my bale.
   I rose with speed, and so did fall as fast,
   Great was my glorie, but it would not last.   60

My brother *George* did plot for to be king,
Sparkes of ambition did possesse us all:
His thoughtes were wise, but did no profite bring,
I fear'd his rising, and did make him fall.
   My reaching braine, did dout what might ensew,   65
   I scorn'd his lyfe, and so he found it trew.

My brother *George*, men say, was slaine by me,
A brothers part, to give his brother wine,
And for a crowne I would his butcher be,
(For crownes with blood the brighter they will shine)   70
   To gaine a kingdome still it me behoov'd:
   That all my lettes full soundlie were remoov'd.

Henrie the sixt depriued of his crowne,
Fame doeth report I put him to the death,
Thus fortune smyl'd, though after she did frowne,   75
A daggers stab men say, did stop his breath.
   I carelesse was both how, and who were slaine,
   So that thereby a kingdome I could gaine.

Clusters of grapes full rypened with the heat,
Nor smaller timber builded up on height,   80
Fall not so fast as persons that are great:
Loosing their honours, bruised with their weight.

125

But fewer means, the faster I did rise,
And to be king, I fortune did dispise.

85   My thoughts ambitious spread, began to flie,
And I a Crowne did followe with full wing,
My hope was small, but yet I meant to trie,
I had no right, yet long'd to be a king.
     Feare or suspect amaz'd me not at all,
90   If I were crost, the worst was but to fall.

The Lyon fearce dispoyled of his praie,
Runnes not with speed so fast as did my thought:
My doubtfull minde, forbad me long to stay:
For why a kingdome was the thing I sought.
95   Now was the tyme when this was to be done,
     Or blame my thoughts, because they it begun.

My brother dy'd, and left two Sonnes behind,
Both under age, unfitte to guyde the land,
This right fell out according to my minde,
100 For now these two were ruled with my hand.
     Englands great Lord the subjects did me call.
     And I was made protectour over all.

But as the Wolfe defends the harmelesse sheepe,
Whose bloodie mouth can hardlie bee content,
105 Vntill he spoile what he was set to keepe,
And sillie beast be all to peeces rent.
     So still a crowne did hammer in my head,
     Full of mistrust, till both these two were dead.

The elder sonne with speed to London came,
110 And walles forsooke where he had liv'd before:
London the place of greatest strength and fame,
The Ilands treasure and the English store.
     For him Lord *Rivers* was appoynted guyde,
     The Kings owne uncle by the mothers side.

Rivers was wyse, but him I could not brooke,   115
I well foresawe what harme there might ensew:
This to prevent with speed I counsell tooke,
And as I thought, so did I finde it trewe,
    For if that *Rivers* should obtaine his minde,
    My hearts desire, then hardlie could I finde.   120

Rivers and *Graie* of treason I accus'd,
And tolde the Prince, what both they did intend:
My tale was false, and I the king abus'd:
Thus both their lives unjustlie did I end.
    The King was yong, the greater was their griefe,   125
    And needs my words, did urge him to beleefe.

Not long this past, but hasting to the Queene,
A post wast sent to showe what did befall;
And who the actors of this fact had bene:
That Lord protector was the cause of all.   130
    The Queen amaz'd, did woonder at this newes,
    And skarse did think it, yet she could not choose.

Possest with feare, foure daughters and her sonne,
She thence convayd into a sacred place:
Supposing true, the harme but now begun,   135
And that I thought to murther all her race.
    She *Yorks* Archbishop did entreat for aide,
    Who in the Abbay not farre distant laide.

The Bishop came, and mourning found the Queene,
Who did lament the fortune of her sonne: 140
The realmes distresse, the lyke before not seene,
Her owne misfortune, and the state undone.
    Thus sigh'd the Queene, and wisht her state were lesse,
    And prayde that heavens would give the king successe.

My Lord (she said) my thoughts presage some ill,   145

And mournfull sorrowe seazeth on my heart:
This suddaine newes with griefe my soule doth fill,
And I for feare doe quake in everie part.
   In this distresse we cannot hope to live,
150   Except this sacred place some safetie give.

He then reply'd: dread Soveraigne, doe not faint,
A causelesse feare in wisdome do withstand:
Yeeld not to soone, with griefe to make complaint,
When no such cause approaching is at hand.
155   "For feeble minds through weaknes coyne new feares,
   When stronger hearts true griefe more wisely bears."

And if they crowne, some other, not your sonne,
A thing unlyke (yet feare what may befall)
Then shall the same, unto this child be done,
160 Whom brothers right by dew a king shall call:
   But tyrants force, will hardly be so bold:
   During the tyme, the other is in hold.

Then more advis'd, he told her what he thought,
She and her sonne some causes had to feare,
165 And *Englands* seale he therefore with him brought,
Which by his place he customd was to beare.
   Thus he resolv'd to leave the Seale behind,
   Till wiser thoughts straight altered had his mind.

The Bishop home returned in all haste,
170 And sadly sate, suspecting what might fall.
But then my comming made them all agast,
And for the Bishop I did straightway call.
   I knew his deede, and blam'd him to his face,
   And for the Seale, another had his place.

175 Thus tyrant hate possest me for a Crowne,
My minde the Anvill of a thousand harmes.

I rais'd my friendes, my foes I cast them downe.
This made the subjectes flocke to me in swarmes.
   My will was strong, I made it for a Lawe,
   "For basest mindes are ruled best by awe."   180

I cal'd the Counsell, and did straight perswade,
From mothers side to fetch the other Sonne.
My drift was further then they well could wade,
I gave them reasons why it must be donne.
   The King a play-mate wanted for his yeeres,   185
   And could not well be fitted with his Peeres.

The Cardnall went on message to the Queene,
And us'd perswasions for her other chyld,
He plainely sayd, her feare had causelesse bene,
Nor neede she dout by me to be beguyld,   190
   I was Protector chosen by consent,
   With counsell grave all treason to prevent.

And I protest (quoth Cardnall) on my life,
(For so indeede the Cardnall did suppose,)
Your Sonne with safetie shall cut off this strife,   195
And you, nor place, nor land, nor Sonne shall loose.
   Dread soveraigne graunt, and let your Sonne be free.
   If he have harme, then set the fault on me.

The Queene was mov'd, and quaking did reply,
A mothers love doeth breede a mothers feare,   200
And loth I am those mischiefes for to try,
With doutfull hazard of a thing so deare.
   I dout (my Lord) the neerest of his blood,
   In true intent scarce wisheth any good.

The lawes doe make my Sonne his mothers ward,   205
Religion bids I should not slacke my care,
And nature bindes mine owne for to regard,

These and his health (my Lord) good reasons are,
  To make my feare, no smaller then it is,
210 Whylst feare perswades what harme may come of this.

Yet take my sonne, and with my sonne take all;
Come kisse me (sonne) thy mothers last fare-well;
Thy yeeres (sweete boy) suspect not what may fall;
Nor can my tongue for teares thy fortune tell.
215 But hardly crownes their kindred will discerne,
  As you (sweete child) I feare yet long shall learne.

God blesse thee (sonne) and I my sonne thee blesse,
Thy mothers comfort, and thy brothers life.
Nay weepe not (sonne) God send thee good successe,
220 And safe defend thee from that tyrants knife.
  (Cardnal) farewell, be carefull of my sonne,
  For once I vow'd, this never to have done.

I and the counsell in Starre-chamber weare,
To whome the Cardnall did in haste resort;
225 Who brought the child, which ended all my feare,
The mothers care he briefely did report.
  I kist the child, and tooke it in my arme,
  Thus none did thinke I meant it any harme.

Then as the Wolfe halfe famisht for his pray,
230 Or hungrie Lyon that a lambe hath got;
My thirsty minde, I ment his blood should stay,
And yet the wisest not perceive my plot.
  To the Towre in haste I sent him to his brother,
  And there with speed, I both at once did smother.

235 Nowe two there was, but living in my way,
Buckingham and *Hastings* both to crosse my mind,
The one was headed straight without delay,
The other, favours did unto me bind.

To match our children, I did him perswade,
And Earle of *Herford* he him selfe be made.   240

Nowe as the Sea before a storme doeth swell,
Or fumes arise before we see the flame:
So whispering Brute began my drifts to tell,
And all Imparted unto babbling fame.
    I dem'd it danger, speech for to despice,   245
    For after this I knew a storme would rise.

Londons Lord Major, I used for my turne,
And caus'd him speake what treason had bene done,
I by these meanes the peoples hearts did turne,
And made them eye me as the rising Sunne.   250
    Thus whilest I ment the Iland to bring under,
    The peoples heads on newes I set to wonder.

Then at the crosse I caus'd a Doctor preach,
To tell the subjectes what I wisht them know;
The man was cunning, and had skill to teach,   255
Out of my braine I made his Sermon flow.
    Thus every where I did such notice give,
    As all did crie, Heavens let King Richard live.

So did I live, and called was a king,
Friendes swarm'd as fast, as Bees vnto the hive,   260
"Thus basest means the highest fortunes bring"
The crowne obtaind, did cause my thoughts revive.
    I scorn'd my friends, and those did most despyse,
    That were the means, by which I did aryse.

Blood and revenge did hammer in my head,   265
Vnquiet thoughts did gallop in my braine:
I had no rest till all my friends were dead,
Whose helpe I usde the kingdome to obtaine.
    My dearest friend, I thought not safe to trust,
    Nor skarse my selfe, but that perforce I must.   270

Nor speake I now, as if I did repent,
Vnlesse for this a crowne I bought so cheap.
For meaner things men wittes and lives have spent,
Which blood have sowne, and crowns could never reap.
275   Live *Richard* long, the honour of thy name,
    And scorne all such, as doe thy fortune blame.

Thus have I told, how I a crowne did win,
Which now torments me, that I cannot sleep
Where I doe end, my sorrow did begin,
280 Because I got which long I could not keep.
    My verse is harsh, yet (reader) doe not frowne,
    I wore no garland but a golden Crowne.

FINIS.

The Russe Commonwealth

The Russe Commonwealth

I

The date of composition of *The Russe Commonwealth* can be set within a period of three months. In the preface to the 1591 edition, Fletcher says:

> Most gracious Soueraigne, beeyng employed in your Maiesties seruice to the Emperour of *Russia*, I obserued the State, and manners of that Countrey. And hauing reduced the same into some order, by the way as I returned, I haue presumed to offer it in this smal Booke to your most excellent Maiestie.

Fletcher left Russia toward the end of July or the beginning of August, 1589,[1] but there is no record of exactly when he returned. His report to Lord Burghley of his negotiations in Russia is dated 21 September 1589. A source hitherto overlooked, however, provides a date for the completion of the manuscript. Hakluyt first printed *The Russe Commonwealth* in his 1598 edition; but in the first edition, 1589,[2] on sigs. 2Y4^{v}–2Y5^{v}, Hakluyt gives a list of twelve points of trade that Fletcher concluded on, and then states: "The said Ambassador *Giles Fletcher*, as I vnderstand, hath drawen a

1. See p. 28 above.
2. Hakluyt's edition can be more precisely dated, as he dates the dedication to Sir Francis Walsingham 17 November.

booke, intituled, *Of the Russe Common wealth*, containing:..." He then lists the chapters in the manuscripts, except for the chapter on the emperor's private behavior. He concludes with this statement: "The booke it selfe he [Fletcher] thought not good, for diuers considerations, to make publike at this time." *The Russe Commonwealth*, then, was actually written between August and November, 1589.

In the textual introduction to *The Russe Commonwealth*, it will be shown that the Queens' College, Cambridge, manuscript is the earliest extant version and that the University College, Oxford, manuscript and the James Ford Bell Collection, University of Minnesota, manuscript are successive revisions. Subsequently, extensive revisions and additions were made before *The Russe Commonwealth* was printed in 1591. There is no clue when the revisions in the James Ford Bell Collection manuscript were made; but there is evidence that the revisions in the 1591 edition were made in late 1590 or in 1591. In Chapter 18, line 19, Fletcher speaks of Ivan Vasil'evich's loss of territory in Lithuania "eight or nine yeares past," whereas the manuscripts have ".7. yeares since."

II

The three extant manuscripts and the 1591 edition offer an excellent opportunity to see the growth of a work through revisions and additions. The exact relationship of the manuscripts and the 1591 edition to each other is discussed in detail in the textual introduction to *The Russe Commonwealth*, but for convenience it might be well to state the relationship briefly here.

The Queens' College manuscript (A) is the earliest extant version and is probably a scribal copy of the original papers. The University College manuscript (B) is a scribal copy of a corrected version of the original version. The James Ford Bell Collection manuscript (C) probably represents the final stage of correction and revision before extensive revisions and additions were made in the manuscript from which the 1591 edition (D) was printed.

The additions in B, C, and D are certainly the most important of the revisions. A selection of forty-four of the more considerable additions will give an idea of their significance. Of the forty-four, there are two additions in B for a total of seven lines; there are twelve in C for a total of thirty-eight lines; and there are thirty in D for a total of six hundred and sixty-eight lines.

In B, the important addition is the anecdote that illustrates Tsar Ivan Vasil'evich's sovereignty over his people.

> To shewe his Soueraintie ouer the liues of his subiects, the late Emperour *Iuan Vasilowich* in his walkes or progresses, if hee had misliked the face or person of any man whom hee met by the way, or that looked vpon him, would command his head to be strook off. Which was presently done, and the head cast before him.
>
> (Ch. 7, ll. 63–68)

Most of the additions in C are of explanatory nature, providing further elucidation of a point already made. For example, A and B read: "The third *Tanais* or *Don* that taketh his head out of *Rezan Ozera*..."; C adds: "The third *Tanais* or *Don*, (the auncient bounder betwixt *Europe* and *Asia*) that taketh his head out of *Rezan Ozera*" (Ch. 2, ll. 89–90). In C, the story of Norgas, a Tartar captain who refused a present of pearls and other jewels because they had no practical value, is added. This type of addition is very interesting, as Fletcher mentions that he got the story from Pachymeres' *History of the Emperours of Constantinople*. And in D, further illustrations are taken from Laonicus Chalcocondylas. Most additions of this type are made in C and D and indicate that, after the original version had been written, Fletcher read certain accounts, especially of Turkey, and then, before the 1591 edition was published, expanded the sections which dealt with the neighbors of Russia.

Fletcher made another interesting addition in C. Speaking of the Samoyedes' religion, he records in A and B: "They acknowledge one God," but in C he adds: "I talked with certeine of them, and finde that they acknowledge one God" (Ch. 20, ll. 18–19). Although the following is not an addition, but a revision, the connection with the passage above is obvious: A and B read: "I talked with one of them at the Citie of *Vologda* by an interpreter. Thear was brought vnto him a *Russe* Testament..." C reads:

"I talked with one of them at the Citie of *Vologda*, where (to trie his skill) I offered him a *Russe* Testament..." (Ch. 21, ll. 432–33).

It has been stated that Fletcher knew Russian,[3] and no doubt he did; but in view of statements like these it is difficult to determine how proficient he really was.

The most extensive additions are in D. Chapters 4 (except for a short passage included elsewhere in the manuscripts), 5, and 6 are completely new. Also Chapters 18 through 20 are expanded, which further suggests that Fletcher's interest in the Tartars was developed after his return to England. The two stories from Chalcocondylas (Ch. 19. ll. 248–63, 289–318), have already been mentioned in connection with the additions in C. Chapter 18 is enlarged (lines 2–8, 124–33 are added). Chapters 19 and 20 are developed from one chapter in the manuscripts. Among the additions are discussions on the subtlety of the Tartar (Ch. 19, ll. 91–131), the Tartar religion (Ch. 19, ll. 173–90), the Tartars' physical characteristics (Ch. 19, ll. 276–87), the Samoyedes' religion (Chapter 20, lines 21–35 greatly expanded), and a discussion of the Lapps (Ch. 20, ll. 46–102).

Besides these long additions, there are additions similar to those in C. For example, Fletcher says that the tsar allows the dukes to extort, bribe, and rob the people in the provinces and then calls them to account for their misdeeds when they return to Moscow, and proceeds "to beat out of them all, or the most part of the bootie." And in D, Fletcher adds: "(as the honie from the Bee)" (Ch. 12, ll. 195–96). In another place, Fletcher speaks of one family of merchants who amassed a fortune worth over 300,000 rubles, and adds in D: "Which may partly be imputed to their dwellings far of from the eye of the Court, vz. in *Wichida*, a 1000. miles from *Mosko*, and more" (Ch. 13, ll. 78–80).

The order of certain passages is revised in B, C, and D. In A–C, lines 7–14 of Chapter 2 follow the sentence ending "mile" in line 77 of Chapter 1. But the change in D is certainly an improvement, as the passage fits much better into the discussion of "the soyle" of Russia. In A and B, lines 78–81 follow line 87 in Chapter 23, and here again the revision was an improvement, since the discussion of extreme unction is more appropriate to the dis-

3. Seredonin, p. 57.

cussion of the three sacraments of the church than to the discussion of the rebaptism of Christians who are not of the Greek church. And in D, in Chapter 19, lines 322–29, the order of discussion of the Chircasse and Nagay Tartar is the reversal of that in A–C. The change more effectively brings out the difference between the Chircasse and the rest of the Tartars. In C, lines 143–96 of Chapter 28 follow line 13; and this is rather puzzling, as the order does not make good sense. Perhaps the order is due to a copyist's error, although I think this is unlikely.

Besides the new additions, there are revisions of whole passages, phrases, and single words. Except for the group of progressive revisions—i.e., those revised in B, again in C, and again in D—there is no significant revision of this type in B, and there are more revisions in C than in D. For example, A and B read:

> This custome out of the great townes is therefore more certaine, and easie to be reckoned, because less they may not pay then is sett them down and rated preciselie for the Coustoom of the year, though they receave not so much, if...

C reads:

> This coustome out of the great townes is therefore more certaine, and easie to be reckoned, because it is set and rated precisely what they shal pay for the custome of the yeere. Which needes must bee paide into the saide office, though they receiue not so much. If...

(Ch. 12, ll. 72–76)

In speaking of the lack of courage in the Russian soldier, A and B read:

> Where as now he is farre meaner of courage and execution in any warlike service, which commeth partly of his servile condition, that will not suffer any great courage or valure to growe in him, though otherwise hee bee of a verie strong and fleshie bodye apt to bear owt anie labour.

C reads:

> Whereas now he is farre meaner of courage and execution in any warlike seruice. Which commeth partly of his seruile condition, that

139

will not suffer any great courage or valure to growe in him. Partly for lacke of due honour and reward, which he hath no great hope of, whatsoeuer seruice or execution he doe.

(Ch. 16, ll. 65–70)

In D, certain further revisions are made. A–C (with minor variants) read:

Their neighbours with whom they haue greatest dealings and intercourse, both in peace and warrs are the *Polonians* and *Sweadens* and *Tartars.*

D reads:

Their neighbours with whom they haue greatest dealings and intercourse, both in peace and warre, are first the *Tartar.* Secondly the *Polonian* whom the *Russe* calleth *Laches,* noting the first author or founder of the Nation, who was called *Laches* or *Leches,* whervnto is added *Po,* which signifieth *People,* and so is made *Polaches,* that is, the *People or posteritie of Laches:* which the *Latines* after their manner of writing call *Polanos.* The third are the *Swedens.*

(Ch. 19, ll. 1–8)

In a passage on the errors of the Russian doctrine, A–C read:

Concerning the divine nature and the three persons, in the one substance of God, they are free from the errours of *Arrius Macedonius, Marichie* and the rest.

D reads:

Concerning the diuine nature and the three persons, in the one substance of God, that the holy Ghost proceedeth from the Father onely, and not from the Sonne.

(Ch. 23, ll. 31–33)

There are also a number of progressive revisions of a passage first in C and then again in D. For example, where Fletcher speaks of the extortion and bribery of the dukes in the provinces, A and B read:

And therefore furnish themselves with all the spoile they can for the time of their gouernment, that they may have bothe to pay the other, and to reserve for them selves.

C reads:

And therefore they furnish themselves with all the spoile they can for the time of their gouernment, that they may have for both turnes, aswel for the Emperour, and the Lord of the *Chetfird*, as to reserve for them selves soom part of the spoile.

D reads:

And therefore they furnish themselues with all the spoile they can for the time of their gouernment, that they may haue for both turnes, aswel for the Emperour, and Lord of the *Chetfird*, as to reserue some good part for themselues.

(Ch. 10, ll. 96–99)

There is also an example of successive revision in B, C, and D. A reads:

As for Burghers or other to represent the communaltie, they have no place there: the people being of no better account with them then as servants or slaves that are to knowe nothing of publique matters and to have no parte in makinge but in obeyinge of lawes.

B reads:

As for Burghers or other to represent the communaltie, they have no place there: the people being of no better account with them then as servants or slaves that are to knowe nothing of publique matters, but to be vsed at pleasure.

C reads:

As for Burghers or other to represent the communaltie, they have no place there: the people being of no better account with them then as servants or bond slaves that are to obey, not to make lawes, nor to knowe any thing of publike matters before they are doon.

D reads as C, except that "doon" is changed to "concluded" (Ch. 8, ll. 6–10).

There are many examples of one-word revisions, and many times it is difficult to say whether the change is scribal or authorial. But in the following examples, I think there is no question that the revisions are authorial.

In the passage where Fletcher speaks of the feasts the Russians observe, A and B read, "The fourth, about Hallontide: which they keepe not of pollicie, but of meere devotion"; C reads, "The fourth, about Hallontide: which they keepe not of pollicie, but of meere superstition" (Ch. 25, ll. 115–17).

Fletcher speaks of the revenues of the tsar, among which is rent money. A–C read:

> Much of this surplusage that riseth out of the rent provision is emploied to the paiment of the wages of his houshold officers, which are very many both at home and abroad.

D reads:

> Much of this surplusage that riseth out of the rent prouision, is emploied to the paiment of the wages of his houshold officers, which are very many attending at home, and purueying abroad.
>
> (Ch. 12, ll. 38–41)

There are also many examples of factual correction, and the important point to note is that most revision of this type was made in B.

One of the most interesting types of revision is the toning-down of certain passages of criticism against Russia. For example, Fletcher speaks against the Russian clergy. A–C (with minor variants) read:

> To this purpose they have their deanes, and Archdeacons, after the order of the Popish Churches. And if it bee asked, what vse they have in their Churches of their Patriarch, Metropolites, Archbishopps &c. I can note nothing save that among so manie dead Idolls as they woorshipp, they may have soom a live to furnish their Church withall.

D reads: "They haue also their Deanes, and their Archdeacons" (Ch. 21, ll. 260–61).

Still another type of revision is cancellation. The cancellations take no particular pattern, and as might be expected occur mostly in C and D. For example, A and B (with minor variants) read:

> Their ordinarie lodging vpon benches at home, (when they are best interteined) prepareth them well to camp on the grownd, and their hard fare at home, to live hardlie in the feild, though the chief Captaines and other of account carry tents with them after the fashion of ours...

C reads:

> Though the chiefe Captaines and other of account carry tents with them after the fashion of ours...
>
> (Ch. 16, ll. 53–55)

There is an interesting example where a phrase is revised in C and then canceled in D. Fletcher is speaking of the officials of the Russian church. A and B read:

> They have also their assistants or several Counsels...of certeine Priests...residing within their cathedrall cities, to the number of four and twentie a piece, to whom thear is allotted owt of their livings the summe of fortie Rubbells.

C reads:

> They have also their assistants or severall Counsels...of certeine Priests...residing within their cathedrall cities, to the number of four and twentie a piece that resemble the ellders in the primitive Church to whome their is allotted owt of the Bishops livings the summ of 30. Rubbells a year.

D reads:

> They haue also their assistants or seuerall Counsels...of certeine

Priests...residing within their cathedrall cities, to the number of foure and twentie a piece.

(Ch. 21, ll. 224–27)

And finally, there are revisions where it is difficult to determine what improvement has been made. A–C read: "The Sergeants are many, and doe excell for their hard and cruell beehaviour over their prysoners." D reads: "The Sergeants are many, and excell for their hard and cruell dealing towards their prysoners" (Ch. 14, ll. 29–30).

III

In the preface to *The Russe Commonwealth*, Fletcher says:

Most gracious Soueraigne, beeyng employed in your Maiesties seruice to the Emperour of *Russia*, I obserued the State, and manners of that Countrey. And hauing reduced the same into some order, by the way as I returned, I haue presumed to offer it in this smal Booke to your most excellent Maiestie. My meaning was to note thinges for mine owne experience, of more importaunce then delight, and rather true then strange.

It would seem, then, that Fletcher derived his information from observation and from conversations with various people.[4] And yet there are several instances where Fletcher used material by other historians. He mentions the work of Cromer,[5] Berosus,[6] Saxo Grammaticus,[7] Bonfinius,[8] Pachymeres,[9] Chalcocondylas,[10] Gregoras,[11] and Strabo.[12] Josephus is mentioned only in the marginal notes.[13] But a closer examination of these works reveals that

4. Ch. 20, ll. 18–19; Ch. 21, ll. 432–34.
5. Ch. 21, l. 50.
6. Ch. 4, ll. 7–10.
7. Ch. 4, ll. 73–76.
8. Ch. 5, ll. 2–9.
9. Ch. 19, ll. 264–73.
10. Ch. 19, ll. 259–63, 290–318; Ch. 21, ll. 36–40.
11. Ch. 21, ll. 47–48.
12. Ch. 1, ll. 16–17.
13. Ch. 1, l. 26.

144

Fletcher used Cromer and Bonfinius more extensively than he acknowledged.[14]

The most significant point about these sources, however, is that they
were first used after *The Russe Commonwealth* had been written. Indeed,
except for two instances,[15] the material was first introduced in D. In other
words, the material was used either to enlarge upon a point already made
or as an illustration. When Fletcher uses material for illustration, he generally follows it closely; but when, for example, he uses Cromer's work for
his etymology of the words "Sclavi" and "Polanos," he gives only one
origin, whereas Cromer gives alternate origins.

> Slauorum autem etymologiam, uel à Slouo, quod uerbum et sermo-
> nem: uel à Slaua, quod famam siue gloriam genti significat, omnes
> deriuant:

> For the people called *Sclaui*, are knowen to haue had their beginning
> out of *Sarmatia*, and to haue termed themselues of their conquest
> *Sclauos*, (that is) famous or glorious, of the word *Sclaua*, which in the
> *Russe* and *Slauonian* tongue, signifieth as much as *Glory*, or *Fame*.
>
> (Ch. 13, ll. 133–37)

> Duplex autem nominis huius ratio assignatur: uel enim à Pole, quod
> et planiciem, et uenationem Slauis significat, Polanos et Polacos ap-
> pellari uolunt, propterea quòd et planam ferè apertamque regionem
> ij tenent, et apprimè tenentur uenandi studio: uel à conditore ac
> primo duce gentis Lecho siue Lacho, Polacos, quasi Polachos, hoc est,
> posteritatem Lachi, dici autumant.

> Secondly the *Polonian* whom the *Russe* calleth *Laches*, noting the first
> author or founder of the Nation, who was called *Laches* or *Leches*,
> whervnto is added *Po*, which signifieth *People*, and so is made *Pola-
> ches*, that is, the *People or posteritie of Laches*:
>
> (Ch. 19, ll. 3–6)

14. Cromer: Ch. 1, ll. 1–17, 25–34; Ch. 13, ll. 133–37; Ch. 19, ll. 3–7. Bonfinius: Ch. 19, ll.
95–119.

15. These first appeared in C: Ch. 19, ll. 264–73; Ch. 21, ll. 47–48.

Although it is quite possible that Fletcher had read Strabo and Josephus, his mention of them in *The Russe Commonwealth* by no means indicates that he knew these works, for in each case the immediate source for the discussion of Sarmatia is Martin Cromer, who also cites Strabo and Josephus. In fact, the marginal citations of Strabo are almost the same: Fletcher has "*Strabo* in his 7. booke of Geogr." Cromer has "*Strabo lib. 7. Geogr.*"

Fletcher also takes two incidents from Herodotus, concerning the Scythians,[16] and like the sources mentioned above, they first appeared in D.

IV

All the sources mentioned thus far are significant in separating Fletcher's work from that of others, but there is no indication that these sources had any influence on Fletcher's conception of Russia or his organization of *The Russe Commonwealth*. There are, however, two sources which can be classified as primary.

For all geographical descriptions in *The Russe Commonwealth*, Fletcher relied on Jenkinson's map of Russia, which was made in 1562.[17] Fletcher's three errors in hydrography offer certain proof that he used Jenkinson's map. (1) The source of the Don River according to Fletcher is the Rezan ozero, when in fact it is the Ivan ozero. (2) Fletcher's description of the course of the Onega River from Kargopol to Yama is imaginary. (3) Fletcher states that the Vychegda River rises in Permia.

Fletcher likewise made extensive use of the legends on Jenkinson's map. In speaking of the Samoyedes, Fletcher mentions the story of Zlata Baba and says that he has read this legend in some maps. Sigismund von Herberstein's map of 1549 has only the figure of Zlata Baba; and only Anton Wied's map of 1555 and Jenkinson's map have legends below the figure. Fletcher's further use of Jenkinson's map in *The Tartars or Ten Tribes* will be noted in the discussion of the sources of that work.

The most important consideration as to sources is the extent to which

16. Ch. 4, ll. 41–62; Ch. 19, ll. 251–52.

17. Jenkinson's map was published in Ortelius' *Theatrum Orbis Terrarum*, 1573 *et seq*. The map is conveniently reproduced in T. S. Willan's *The Early History of the Russia Company* (Manchester, 1956).

Fletcher depended on information given him by Jerome Horsey, who had lived in Russia for a great part of the time from 1573 to 1592. It will be remembered that Fletcher's mission to Russia was partly to pacify the tsar and Boris Godunov, whom Horsey had offended. Horsey returned to England with Fletcher, and as *The Russe Commonwealth* was written at this time, there was certainly an opportunity for Horsey to provide Fletcher with information.

In his *Travells*, Horsey speaks of the accounts of Russia "worthe the sight and readinge" and commends those by Hakluyt and Camden, but

> most by Doctor Flætcher, more scolastically—the originall natur and disposicion of the Russ people, the lawes, languages, goverment, discipline for their church and comonwealth, reveynes, comodities, climatt and sittuacion, wherof it most consists, and with whom they have most leag and comers—with all which I did furnish him—in a treatice of itself.[18]

Earlier in his work, Horsey writes of the coronation of the Tsar Fedor and says that he

> must referr the relacion therof to Mr. Hackluetts booke of Viages and Dr. Flætchers treatice, with other discourses of the state and government of this commonwælth, procured at my handes longe since...[19]

Joseph Hamel comments that Fletcher's work "was collected almost entirely from Horsey's notes."[20] He does not cite any evidence for this statement, and probably he is referring to the passages in Horsey just quoted. S. M. Seredonin discusses at length Horsey as a source for Fletcher's material and concludes:

> Of course, not knowing the notes which Horsey had and which he gave to Fletcher, we have no right to be definite as to the extent of Fletcher's dependency on Horsey; nevertheless, we consider it very probable that the chapters on the nobility, on regional government,

18. Edward A. Bond (ed.), *Russia at the Close of the Sixteenth Century* (London, 1856), p. 256.
19. *Ibid.*, p. 209.
20. *England and Russia* (London, 1854), p. 225.

on the Tsar's duma, revenue, the armed forces, and the Tsar's private life, i.e., the most interesting and important parts of the whole work, are a retelling of Horsey's information.[21]

Seredonin's opinion is based almost entirely on the assumption that Chapters 9–12, 15–17, and 26 contain "such information as an ambassador who had just arrived could not know."[22]

That Fletcher received information from Horsey I do not doubt, but Seredonin's opinion ignores the fact that Fletcher was in Russia for a year and that he did have some command of the Russian language[23] and could thus obtain on his own much of the information that Seredonin credits Horsey with. The corresponding passages in Horsey's *Travells* and Fletcher's *The Russe Commonwealth* have been noted in the explanatory notes, and on this basis (which is the only evidence available), I would suggest that Horsey provided the following information: the story of Maria (Ch. 5, ll. 77–90), the account of the Tartar tsar (Ch. 12, ll. 243–65), the Polish architect who was blinded by Ivan IV (Ch. 18, ll. 46–49), and the story of Mikola the Hermit (Ch. 21, ll. 494–514). And since Horsey had been at Fedor's coronation and also had had free access to his court, it is probable that he provided Fletcher with material for Chapters 6 and 26. Horsey comments that Kniaz Mstislavsky, whom Fletcher mentions in Chapter 9, was his chief informant about government affairs and that Mstislavsky even allowed him to see his personal diary. The fact that Horsey was an intimate friend of one of the most distinguished princes would suggest that he could well have provided Fletcher with information for Chapter 9, especially the account of the chief families of Russia.

Fletcher does not acknowledge Herberstein's account of Russia or any of the earlier English voyagers; and although corresponding passages have been noted in the explanatory notes, it seems unlikely that Fletcher was indebted to any of these accounts.

21. Seredonin, p. 67.
22. *Ibid.*, p. 68.
23. *Ibid.*, p. 57.

V

The *Russe Commonwealth* has long been recognized as the most important book on Russia by an Englishman in the sixteenth century.[24] S. M.
Seredonin has examined in detail *The Russe Commonwealth* as a source for
Russian history, and I have incorporated his findings in the explanatory
notes; although it should be pointed out that in many instances Fletcher's
statements must be accepted at face value, as there is no further evidence.

But besides its importance as an historical source, *The Russe Commonwealth* also influenced the Englishman's concept of Russia. Samuel Purchas
comments:

> *I thought good here to giue an account of my course. Hauing spent much
> time in that other* World, *so little known to* this (Tartaria *and* China)
> *that the parts least known might be made best known: I haue comme nearer
> home, to* Russia, *and her neighbours, the neerer, or* Chrim Tartars, *the*
> Samoyeds, *and others; whereof Doctor* Fletchers Story *being so elaborate
> (where, though the centre bee* Russia, *yet his circumference is more generall)
> and by men iudicious which haue in those parts enioyed most honourable
> employment, and exactest intelligence, commended; I haue giuen him the
> first place.*[25]

Milton in his *Brief History of Moscovia* comments: "1588. Dr. *Giles Fletcher*
went Ambassadour from the Queen to *Pheodor* then Emperour; whose
Relations being judicious and exact are best red entirely by themselves."[26]

Fletcher's description of Russia was also used in the literature of the
Renaissance. According to Professor Cawley, "But certainly the version
[of Russia] taken most account of then was Giles Fletcher's, the father of
the poets Giles and Phineas."[27] Those who certainly used Fletcher's *The*

24. Two recent authorities have made the following comments: "It was the best account of Russia
written by any sixteenth-century Englishman..."—T. S. Willan, *The Early History of the Russia Company*, p. 177; "*Of the Russe Commonwealth* provided Englishmen with a description of the country which
was not surpassed in many essentials till the eighteenth century..."—M. S. Anderson, *Britain's Discovery
of Russia, 1553–1815* (London, 1958), p. 12.

25. *Purchas His Pilgrimes* (London, 1625), sig. 2R3ʳ.

26. Frank Allen Patterson, *et al.* (eds.), *The Works of John Milton* (18 vols.; New York, 1931–38),
X, 378.

27. Robert Ralston Cawley, *The Voyagers and Elizabethan Drama* (Boston, 1938), p. 253.

Russe Commonwealth were Raleigh, Webster, Jonson, Beaumont and Fletcher, Dekker,[28] Phineas Fletcher, and Milton.[29] Others who may have derived their information on Russia from Fletcher are Browne, Burton, Bacon, Marston, Heywood, Spenser,[30] Massinger, and Shakespeare.[31]

VI

But there was one group of Elizabethans who did not like Fletcher's account of Russia—the merchants of the Russia Company. They wrote to Lord Burghley:

> The Companie of Marchauntes tradinge Muscouia havinge bene manie waies preiudiced by the errors which have bene Committed by her Maiesties subiectes imploied by the companie in those partes in givinge offence or some smale Color of offence to the g[ov]ernment of the state of the Countrie of Russia, doe greatelie feare that a booke latelie sett out by Mr Doctor Fletcher, dedicated to her Maiestie, intituled the Russe Common Wealthe, will turne the Companie to some greate displeasure with the Emperour and endaunger boeth theire people and goodes nowe remayninge there Except some good order be taken by your Lordships honorable Consideracion for the Callinge in of all the bookes that are printed, and some Cowrse holden therein, signifyinge her Maiesties dislike of the publishinge of the same. In which booke (besides the discowrse of the descripcion of the Countrie, the militarie government and forces thereof, the Emperoures Revenue, and howe yt ryseth which is offensive to the Russe that anie man should looke into) the person of the Emperour his father, his Brother and the Lord Boris Fedorowich the protector, and generallie the nature of the people, are towched in soe harde tearmes, as that the Companie doubt the revenge thereof will light on

28. See Robert Ralston Cawley, *Unpathed Waters* (Princeton, N. J., 1940), p. 225.

29. See my "Giles Fletcher, the Elder, and Milton's *Brief History of Moscovia*," *RES*, n.s. XI (1960), 150–56.

30. But Lois Whitney, "The Literature of Travel in the Faerie Queene," *MP*, XIX (1921), 147, thinks it unlikely that Spenser knew Fletcher's account.

31. All parallels are given in the explanatory notes.

theire people, and goodes remayninge in Russia, and vtterlie over-throwe the trade forever. Out of which booke for your Lordships readines, there is here vnder noted certen places offensive. Whereof the whole discowrse is full.

In the epistle dedicatorie of the booke he tearmeth the Russe govern-ment a straunge face of a tyrannycall state. [ll. 8–9]

fol 9 b. The intollerable exaccions of the Emperour vppon his sub-iectes maketh them carelesse to laye vp anie thinge, for that yf they have ought yt cawseth them to be spoiled not onlie of theire goodes but of theire lives. [Ch. 3, ll. 132–35]

fol 16. In shewinge the likelihoode of the ende of the whole race of the Emperour concluded in some one, two or some fewe of the bloud, he saieth there is noe hope of yssue in the Emperour by the Constitution of his bodie, and the barenes of his wief.

He noteth there the death of the Emperoures elder brother murthered by his father in his furie whose death was the murtheringe of the olde Emperour by extreame greefe. [Ch. 5, ll. 44–64]

fol 16: b. He noteth what practisinge there hath bene by such as aspire the succession to distroye the younger brother of the Emper-our that is yet livinge, beinge about Sixe yeares olde wherein he seemeth to ayme at Boris fedorowich.

He noteth in that younge infant an inclinacion to Crueltie resem-blinge his father, in delight of bloude, for that he beinge but Sixe yeares olde taketh pleasure to looke into the bleedinge throtes of beastes that are killed and to beate geese and hens with a staffe vntill they dye. [Ch. 5, ll. 65–77]

fol 20. a. The Russe government is plaine tirannycall, and exceadeth all iust measure without regard of Nobilitie or people givinge to the nobilitie a kinde of vniust and vnmeasured libertie, to exact on the baser sorte of people. [Ch. 7, ll. 5–17]

fol 21. b.   If the late Emperour in his progresse had mett a man whose person or face he had not liked, or yf he looked vppon him he would commaunde his heade to be stricken of and to be Cast before him.   [Ch. 7, ll. 63–68]

fol 26. b. 27. a.   The practise of the Godonoes to extinguishe the bloude Ryall who seeke to Cut of or keapt downe the best of the Nobilitie.   [Ch. 9, ll. 83–115]

fol 33. b.   That yt is to be merveled howe the Nobilitie and people will suffer themselues to be brought vnder suche oppression and slaverie.   [Ch. 10, ll. 145–48]

fol 34. b.   That the desperate state of thinges at home maketh the people to wishe for some forrein invasion.   [Ch. 10, ll. 187–91]

fol. 37. b.   That Boris Godonoe and the Empresse kindred accoumpt all that commeth to the Emperoures treasurie theire owne.

[Ch. 12, ll. 35–38]

fol 41. 42. 43. 44. 45.   Divers grosse practises of the Emperour to drawe the wealth of the land into his treasurie, which he Concludeth to be straunge kinde of extortions but that yt agreeth with the qualitie of the Emperour and the miserable subieccion of the poore Countrie.   [Ch. 12, ll. 178–336]

fol 53. a.   Theire onlie lawe is theire speakinge lawe that is the pleasure of the prince and Magistrates which sheweth the miserable condicion of the people against whose iniustice and extreame oppression they had neede to be armed with manie good lawes.

[Ch. 14, ll. 140–45]

fol 98. 99.   The practise of the Godones against the Emperoures brother to prove him not legittimate and to turne awaie the peoples likinge from him as next successor.   [Ch. 23, ll. 98–105]

fol 110.   The discripcion of the Emperour, viz meane of stature lowe and grosse, sallowe of Complexion enclyninge to dropsey hawcke nosed unsteadie in his pase by reason of the weaknes of his lymes heavie and vnactive commonlie smilinge, almost to a laughter for quallitie simple and slowe witted, but verie gentle and of an easie nature quiet mercifull &c.   [Ch. 26, ll. 124–32]

fol 116.   It is to be doubted whether is greater the Crueltie or the intemperauncie that is vsed in the Countrie, it is soe foull that is not to be named. The whole Countrie overfloweth with the synne of that kinde and noe mervell as havinge no law to restrayne whoredomes adulteries and like vncleanes of lief.

From the greatest to the smallest except some fewe that will scarcelie be founde the Russe nether beleeveth anie thinge that an other man speaketh nor speaketh anie thinge him self worthie to be beleaved.[32]

[Ch. 28, ll. 177–89]

It has been taken for granted that as a result of this petition Lord Burghley ordered *The Russe Commonwealth* to be suppressed, but there is no evidence in any official records that would corroborate such an assumption. But I have recently discovered a letter that clearly demonstrates that the Russia Company's petition was successful. On sig. A[r] of *The Russe Commonwealth* in Trinity College, Cambridge, a W. Dallye has written:

> To my worthy and ever honoured freind Mr Palmer Esquire secretary to the right honourable the Lord Keeper.
>
> I signified in Mr Hackeltes letter what is now really done by Mr Stirropp, who now by his soone preventeth what I premised. The booke was called in and rare, and therefore I pray you be carefull of it.
>
> Tuissimus
>
> W. Dallye

"The Lord Keeper" is probably Sir John Puckering, who was appointed to this position on 28 May 1592. "Mr Stirropp" refers to Thomas Stirropp, a

32. BM Lansd. MS 112, No. 39. The petition is not dated, but the statement that the book was "latelie sett out" would indicate 1591 or 1592.

bookseller in London, 1576–1600, and Warden of the Stationers Company, 1593–94; but the letter is too vague to say whether Thomas is the father or the son.[33] I have been unable to identify the other persons.

33. Ronald B. McKerrow (ed.), *Dictionary of Printers and Booksellers, 1557–1640* (London, 1910), p. 258.

The Text

The *Russe Commonwealth* was first published in 1591 and was subsequently reprinted in 1643. There are three manuscripts extant, each an earlier version than the 1591 edition. The work has been edited several times, first by Hakluyt in 1598 and most recently by Edward A. Bond for the Hakluyt Society in 1856. *The Russe Commonwealth* has been translated into French and Russian.

PRINTED EDITIONS

1591 EDITION

The Russe Commonwealth was printed in London by Thomas Dawson for Thomas Charde in 1591. It is not entered in the Stationers' Register. This edition is the only substantive printed text and is the basis for the present edition. [within a border of type orn.] OF | THE RVSSE | Common Wealth. | *or* | MANER OF GO- | uernement by the Russe | *Emperour,* (*commonly called the* | Emperour of *Moskouia*) with | *the manners, and fashions* | *of the people of that* | *Countrey.* | *** | The Contents are noted in the Ta- | ble, set downe before the be- | ginning of the Booke. | AT LONDON | Printed by T. D. for | *Thomas Charde.* | 1591.

Col: 8⁰: A⁴ B–P⁸ Q⁴ [$4 (–A2 A4 Q4) signed] 120 leaves. fol. [4] 1–116 [misnumbering 38 as 31, 58 as 54, 96 as 66].

Note: A1 is present only in O$_1$ (Bodleian); Trinity College, Cambridge; Lambeth Palace Library.

Contents: A1 blank except for the signature, A2^r title page, A2^v blank, A3^r–A4^r THE EPISTLE DEDICATORIE., A4^v table of contents, B^r–Q4^v OF THE RVSSE Common Wealth.

CW: B8^v shole, [shoale,], C4^v honses [houses], E8^v taries, [ted], M6^r marrie [marry], N5^r readie [ready], P2^r heathe- [heathenish].

The following copies have been collated: Cambridge (C) (L*. 16.42 [F]); Bodleian (O$_1$, Wood 455; O$_2$, F.12. Art. Seld.; O$_3$, Douce F.341); British Museum (L$_1$, C.114.a.6; L$_2$, G.7284); Trinity College, Cambridge (CT); Lambeth Palace Library (LLP); National Library of Scotland (EN); Folger Shakespeare Library (DFo); Huntington Library (CSmH); Yale University (CtY); University of Illinois (IU); Boston Public Library (MB); Harvard University (MH); New York Public Library (NN). This collation reveals these press variants:

Inner Forme B
    Corrected: DFo, O$_2$, O$_3$, CSmH, L$_2$, MH, NN, CtY, IU
    Uncorrected: O$_1$, C, L$_1$, EN, CT, LLP, MB
        B^v: *Boristhenes,* (as...reporteth)] *Boristhenes,* as...reporteth,
            Nouograd ve-] *Nouograd vr-*
        B3^v: desert] desart
            contei-] contai-
        B4^r: sommer] sommer in
            bee. And] bee: and
        B7^v: cõmoditie is of Wax, where- | of] commoditie is of
            Waxe, | wherof
        B8^r: *Rezan*] *Bezan*
    Outer Forme B
        Corrected: DFo, O$_1$, O$_2$, O$_3$, CSmH, C, L$_2$, MH, NN, CtY, IU
        Uncorrected: L$_1$, EN, CT, LLP, MB

B6^r: *Russe*] *Russes*
Outer Forme C
    Corrected: DFo, O$_2$, O$_3$, CSmH, L$_1$, L$_2$, EN, CT, MH, NN, CtY,
        IU, MB
    Uncorrected: O$_1$, C, LLP
        C7^v: perforce] perforee
Inner Forme F
    Corrected: DFo, O$_1$, O$_3$, C, L$_1$, L$_2$, EN, CT, LLP, MH, NN,
        CtY, IU, MB
    Uncorrected: O$_2$, CSmH
        F6^r: marks] markr
        F8^r: L.] L
Outer Forme P
    Corrected: O$_1$, O$_2$, O$_3$, CSmH, C, L$_1$, EN, CT, LLP, NN, CtY,
        IU, MB
    Uncorrected: DFo, L$_2$, MH
        P3^r: 26.] 22

1643, 1656, and 1657 editions

Wing lists three seventeenth-century editions. The first is that which is
referred to as the 1643 edition. This edition has only an engraved title page
without imprint, but in the lower right-hand corner appears "W. M. *fecit*.
1643." The second is the edition of 1656, represented by the Thomason
copy in the British Museum, and is dated by Thomason "1656, Oct. 13."
The third is the edition of 1657, with a printed title page in addition to the
engraved title page. It has the imprint: "London, | Printed by *Roger Daniel*
for *William* | *Hope* and *Edward Farnham* near | the Exchange. 1657."
    A collation of the copies of each supposed edition with particular note to
catchwords, running titles, spacing of type, and misprints, reveals that
there is in fact only one edition, and that in 1657 a new printed title page
was inserted. The Thomason copy belongs to the issue of 1643.

1643 EDITION

[engraved title page: Johnson, No. 92] THE | HISTORY of RUSSIA | or | The Goverment of the Emperovr | OF MUSCOVIA | with the manners & fashions of the | People of that Countrey. | *By G. Fletcher sometime fellow of Kings Colledge* | *in Cambridge, and employed in the Embassie thither.* | W. M. *fecit*. 1643.

Col: 12° ¶⁴ A–L¹² M⁸ [$5 (–M5) signed] 144 leaves, pp. [8] 1–280.
Notes: ¶1 is missing in all copies except O, L₁, and Folger Shakespeare Library. ¶ 2 has been pasted on paper and inserted in L₂. ¶ 2 engraved title page colored in by hand in L₁.

Contents: ¶ 1ʳ blank except for the signature, ¶ 1ᵛ blank, ¶ 2ʳ engraved title page, ¶ 2ᵛ blank, ¶ 3ʳ–¶ 4ᵛ table of contents, Aʳ–M8ᵛ text.

CW: A2ʳ be- [because], C4ᵛ ready [readie], D6ᵛ no cw, F3ᵛ *The* [*Their*], G6ᵛ our [out], I2ʳ sea [Sea], L6ʳ carry [carrie].

The following copies have been examined: British Museum (L₁, E. 1713 [Thomason copy]; L₂, 150.a.33); St. John's College, Cambridge; Balliol College, Oxford; Bibliothèque Nationale (M. 17482); Folger Shakespeare Library; University of Illinois; and a copy in the possession of the present editor. Wing records that a copy is in the Dulwich College Library, but the librarian informs me that the copy is no longer there.

1657 ISSUE

Engraved title page as 1643 edition.

THE | HISTORY | OF | RUSSIA, | OR | The Government of the | Emperour | OF | MUSCOVIA, | *with the manners and fashions* | *of the people of that Countrey.* | [rule] | By G. Fletcher sometimes | fellow of Kings Colledge in | Cambridge. | [rule] | London, | Printed by *Roger Daniel* for *William* | *Hope* and *Edward Farnham* near | the Exchange. 1657.

Col: 12°: ¶ 4 (¶⁴ + χ1) A–L¹² M⁸.

Contents: ¶ 1ʳ blank except for the signature, ¶ 1ᵛ blank, ¶ 2ʳ engraved title page, ¶ 2ᵛ blank, χ1ʳ printed title page, χ1ᵛ blank, ¶ 3ʳ–¶ 4ᵛ table of contents, Aʳ–M8ᵛ text.

Notes: ¶ 1 present only in University of Illinois copy. χ1 inserted before ¶ 2 in Bodleian and C₂. In C₁ and King's College copies, ¶ 2 has been cut and reversed so that the recto is blank and the verso is the engraved title page. C₁ and University of Illinois copies have the engraved title page colored in by hand. In C₂, ¶ 2 is torn away, but the edges show that the engraved title page was colored. In the Bodleian copy sigs. F12ʳ⁻ᵛ, G1ʳ–G12ᵛ are missing but supplied in manuscript in a nineteenth-century hand.

The following copies have been examined: Cambridge (C₁, Syn. 8.65.8; C₂, Syn. 8.65.9); King's College, Cambridge; University of Illinois; Bodleian (Wood 167[2]).

The date 1643 is the date William Marshall gives for making the engraved title page and is not necessarily the date of printing; but an examination of the other engravings Marshall made for Daniel (and for Thomas Buck and Daniel when they both were printers to Cambridge) does not reveal any case of dates different for the cutting of the engravings and the printed title page. This, then, suggests that the book was printed while Daniel was printer to Cambridge, and further evidence is offered by the type ornament (sig. Aʳ) and the woodcut (sig. M8ᵛ). The type ornament is used in M. Minucius Felix, *Octavius*, 1643 (Wing M 2198) on sigs. Aʳ (title page) and A2ʳ. It is also used in *Introductio ad Sapientiam*, 1643 (Wing I 282) on sigs. Aʳ (title page) and A2ʳ. The woodcut appears in J. Duport's *Tres Libri Solomonis*, 1646 (Wing D 2654) on sig. K7ʳ and in D. Stahl's *Axiomata Philosophica*, 3rd edn., 1645 (Wing S 5163) on sigs. ¶ 12ʳ and T12ʳ. Very interestingly, in the fourth edition, 1651 (Wing S 5164), printed by Daniel after he had gone to London, this woodcut has been replaced by a smaller, although similar, woodcut. This is not as significant as it might be, as I cannot find the woodcut in Fletcher's book used in any books of Legate (Daniel's successor at Cambridge) or of Daniel from 1650 to 1657.

To sum up, then, *The History of Russia* was printed by Roger Daniel at

Cambridge in 1643; and in 1657 (after he had removed to London) a printed title page was issued.

The 1643 edition is an unusually faithful reprint. The preface and all marginal notes are omitted, but other than that, there are only seventeen substantive variants. These are not significant, and there is no question that they are compositorial in nature.

MANUSCRIPTS

There are three manuscripts of *The Russe Commonwealth* extant: Queens' College, Cambridge; University College, Oxford; and James Ford Bell Collection, University of Minnesota.

QUEENS' COLLEGE MS 25

Measurement: 7 $^8/_{10}$ × 6 $^1/_{16}$ inches.

Foliation: 89 leaves. 5 preliminary leaves [leaves 4 and 5 numbered A$_1$, A$_2$ respectively], fols. 1–80, 4 leaves following text.

Watermarks: (1) a watermark very similar to the crest on the cover of the manuscript, used through leaf 12; (2) a watermark similar to Briquet No. 4113, except that there is a *fleur de lis* atop the bell, used through gathering ending leaf 28; (3) a watermark similar to Briquet No. 12660, used through gathering ending leaf 79; (4) a watermark similar to Briquet No. 1164, except that the scroll is blank, used the last gathering.

Contents: leaf 1 used as endpaper; leaf 2^r "Fletchers Commonwealth of Russia" in an eighteenth-century hand; leaf 2^v blank; leaf 3 blank; leaf 4^r has the following note in an eighteenth-century hand:

This belongs to ye Library of Queens College in Cambridge

The Author saith P. 74. y^t ye then Emperor's Name was Theodore Iuanowitz & y^t he was in ye fifth year of his Reign. He began to reign in 1584 says Puffendorf.[1] y^s therefore must be wrote in 1589

1. Samuel von Puffendorf, *An Introduction to the History of the Principal Kingdoms and States of Europe* (London, 1697), sig. Z8^v.

This Emperor died without Issue & was succeeded by his Brother
in Law Borise Godenove frequently mentioned

leaf 4ᵛ Fletcher's preface; leaf 5ʳ title page; leaf 5ᵛ table of contents; leaf
6 [fol. 1] through leaf 85ᵛ [fol. 79ᵛ] text; leaves 86 through 88 blank; leaf 89
used as endpaper.

Nature of MS: A presentation copy bound in vellum with a coat of
arms of Queen Elizabeth. Mr. H. M. Nixon, in a communication, says that
he has not seen this particular royal arms block before and suggests that it
was specifically cut for this manuscript, as it is a much more handsome piece
than the average trade job. The manuscript is in the secretary hand, but
there are three different scribes. This is the only manuscript with a preface,
which is in Fletcher's hand. Fols. 1 through 12 appear to be in a second hand,
and the rest of the text in a third. It is interesting that the change of scribe
coincides with the change of paper.

UNIVERSITY COLLEGE MS 144

Measurement: 8 9/16 × 6 9/16 inches.

Foliation: 112 leaves. 2 preliminary leaves, fols. 1–110.

Watermark: one used throughout, like Briquet No. 8079.

Contents: leaf 1 blank, leaf 2ʳ title page, leaf 2ᵛ table of contents, leaf 3
[fol. 1] through leaf 112 [fol. 110] text.

Nature of MS: A very neat scribal copy in the secretary hand. The
manuscript is bound in vellum.

JAMES FORD BELL COLLECTION MS

Measurement: 8 9/16 × 6 3/4 inches.

Foliation: 78 leaves. 3 preliminary leaves, fols. [1]–73, 1 leaf following
text.

Watermark: one used throughout, like Briquet No. 8079. It is interesting to note that the same paper was used in the University College manuscript.

Contents: leaf 1^r has the following notes in a seventeenth-century hand:

Mary Stradling

your servant

Mary S [crossed out]

Mary Strad [crossed out]

leaf 2 blank, leaf 3^r title page with the following annotation below it in a nineteenth-century hand:

> This book is printed with several alterations London, by Roger Daniel 1657. with this Title, The History of Russia or the Governm^t of the Emperor of Moscovia, with the manners & Fashions of the people of that Country. By G. Fletcher, sometimes Fellow of Kings College in Cambridge, who was employed in an Embassie thither. —in 12.mo—

> This book appears to be written in the year 1589
>
> pub 1591.

leaf 3^v table of contents, leaf 4 [fol. (1)] through leaf 77 [fol. 73] text, leaf 78 blank.

Nature of MS: A very neat scribal copy in the italic hand. This is the only manuscript that has marginal notes.

Relation of the manuscripts to each other and to the 1591 edition

Even a cursory look at the manuscripts and the 1591 edition will reveal that the manuscripts represent an earlier version. The 1591 edition has twenty-eight chapters, and each manuscript has only twenty-four. Chapters 4, 5, and 6 are not in the manuscripts, and Chapters 19 and 20 are developed from one chapter in the manuscript. The three manuscripts, however, are not scribal copies of the same manuscript. Each, in fact, represents a progressive stage of revision; and to determine their precise relationship, it is necessary to examine the variants between the manuscripts and the 1591 edition.

There are a total of 1945 substantive and semi-substantive variants among the manuscripts (A, B, and C) and the 1591 edition (D). This does not include the variants in the passages in the manuscripts that are canceled in D; but these variants are not significant and will not affect any conclusion about the relationship of the manuscripts and D. The following analysis of the variants will help to determine the genetic relationship of the manuscripts and D.

Table I demonstrates the relationship of the manuscripts to each other. A and B have a closer relationship than A and C; and B and C have a closer relationship than A and C.

Table I

	Agreements	Disagreements
A & B	1563	382
A & C	577	1368
B & C	668	1277

Table II demonstrates the relationship of the manuscripts to D. C has a closer relationship to D than does either A or B; and B has a closer relationship to D than does A.

Table II

	Agreements	Disagreements
A & D	144	1801
B & D	248	1697
C & D	1168	777

Table III confirms the results of Table II and demonstrates that, when only one manuscript agrees with D, the manuscript, except for twelve instances, is C. This is even more significant, as only two instances where D and A agree but differ from B and C could possibly be considered as authorial corrections;[2] and only one instance where D and B agree but differ from A and C could be so considered.[3]

Table III

D & A / B & C   6
D & B / A & C   6
D & C / A & B 963

Table IV lists the unique readings.

Table IV

Unique Readings
A — 161
B —   59
C —   78
D — 672

From this analysis, the texts can be put in the order A, B, C, D. And, more precisely, the relationship seems to be this: A and B are very closely related, but B cannot be a copy of either A or the lost original manuscript (α), as many of the variants cannot be scribal in nature. The variants, however, seem to be corrections rather than revisions, so that B is probably a scribal copy of a corrected version of α (β).[4] C probably represents the final stage of correction and revision of the manuscript (γ) before extensive revisions and additions were made in the manuscript (δ) from which D was printed. This relationship can be diagramed thus:

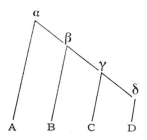

2. Ch. 3, l. 56 and Ch. 12, l. 129.
3. Ch. 12, l. 21.
4. E.g.: Ch. 2, ll. 24, 31, 82; Ch. 3, l. 17.

The literary importance of revisions made in the manuscripts and D has been discussed in the introduction to *The Russe Commonwealth*. The important consideration here is the textual significance of the manuscripts; and more especially the question of what readings, if any, should be admitted into the present edition.

If the relation of the manuscripts to D is as I have stated, then the instances wherein A and B agree but differ from C and D cannot have any inherent textual authority, as they represent readings discarded in the revised C and not re-introduced in D. Furthermore, except for the three cases noted, the readings paired D & A / B & C and D & B / A & C have no textual significance.

Our consideration is thus narrowed to the unique readings of the manuscripts and D. The unique readings of A, B, and C cannot have any inherent textual authority in emending D, so that the only group of variants that are significant are the unique readings of D. Of the 672 unique readings, all manuscripts differ from D with the same variant in 511 instances, and these would then seem to have special importance. But this is not so, as there is no exemplar of δ extant, where the major revisions and lengthy additions were made. Further, of the 511 variants in which all manuscripts agree, it should be noted that over 300 instances are additions in D. Therefore each of the remaining variants must be considered individually; however, as a general principle, unless there seemed good reason to prefer the manuscript reading, I have retained the reading of D, as being Fletcher's final intention. This means, then, that the manuscripts have little textual value to the present edition; and the only compensation is that a few of the emendations which they have suggested would have been impossible to make otherwise.

Certain procedures followed in the recording of the variants should be noted. When the manuscripts differ from D and there are variants among the manuscripts, I have, whenever possible, given only one textual note and enclosed the minor variants in brackets thus:

the... himselfe] their church, whear [Church. Whear (C)] the Friars take them privatlie into the [their (C)] monasterie church, and thear teach them how to beehave them selves (A–C).

If the notes state that all the manuscripts agree, it will be understood that this means substantively, and that there might be variants in the accidentals. For convenience, I have used the spellings and punctuation of A in recording the manuscript variants. Also, if the variant reading in the manuscript is abbreviated, it has been silently expanded in the notes. All substantive and semi-substantive variants among A–D have been recorded, except that I have not recorded the variants of the Table of Contents, the chapter headings, or running titles. I have not recorded the few instances where a word was canceled in the manuscript or crowded in between lines; they are neither significant nor numerous.

OTHER EDITIONS AND TRANSLATIONS

Richard Hakluyt was the first editor of *The Russe Commonwealth*. He mentions the work in the first edition of his *Voyages* in 1589, and the significance of this fact has been pointed out in the discussion of the dating of the manuscripts. He first included Fletcher's work in the edition of 1598, Vol. I, sigs. 2R3ʳ–2T3ʳ.[5] Hakluyt's edition is based on the 1591 edition of *The Russe Commonwealth* and has no textual authority. He omits almost every unfavorable comment on the Russian government, e.g., all of Chapters 5, 8–14, 21–26, and the Preface, and parts of Chapters 2, 3, 4, 15, 16, 18, 19, and 28.

Samuel Purchas included *The Russe Commonwealth* in his *Hakluytus Posthumus or Purchas His Pilgrimes*, 1625, Vol. III, sigs. 2N3ʳ–2R2ʳ. In a note on sig. 2N3ʳ, Purchas says: "I haue in some places contracted, in others mollified the biting or more bitter stile, which the Author vseth of the *Russian* Gouernment; that I might doe good at home, without harme abroad." Like Hakluyt, Purchas omits or rephrases certain parts of Fletcher's work, e.g., the Preface, Table of Contents, and parts of Chapters 6, 7, 9, 10, 12, 13, 14, 18, 19, 23, and 28. Still, Purchas gives a much more complete version than does Hakluyt.

John Harris epitomized Fletcher's account in his *Compleat Collection of*

---

5. Vol. I (1598), Vol. II (1599), Vol. III (1600). There is another issue of Volume I (1599), and as Fletcher's work is in this volume, both issues were examined, but there are no variants between the two issues insofar as Fletcher's work is concerned.

Voyages and Travels, 1705, Vol. I, sigs. 4F^v–4F4^v, 4G^r. All of Chapters 5, 10, 11, 16, 18, 26, and 27 and parts of the other chapters are omitted.

Edward A. Bond's edition of *The Russe Commonwealth* in 1856 was the first time that Fletcher's work had appeared in its entirety since 1591. Bond's edition is a reprint with modernization of punctuation and capitalization. He evidently did not know of the manuscripts of *The Russe Commonwealth*, as he did not mention them in his introduction.

There have been translations into French and Russian. Charles du Bouzet translated *The Russe Commonwealth* into French, *La Russie au XVIe Siècle par Giles Fletcher* (Leipzig et Paris: Librarie A. Franck, 1864). The translations into Russian have an interesting history. In 1848, O. M. Bodyansky, professor at Moscow University, published a translation which was immediately confiscated. Bodyansky was deprived of his professorship and was offered a professorship at Kazan University. He refused this and remained in Moscow in retirement.[6] After many years of government opposition, a translation by K. M. Obolensky was authorized and appeared in 1867. A second edition of this work appeared in 1905.

6. There is a full account of this in Obolensky's edition of 1905, pp. vii–xiv.

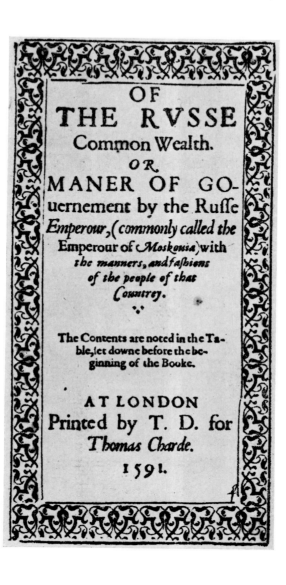

OF
THE RVSSE
Common Wealth.
OR
MANER OF GO-
uernement by the Ruſſe
Emperour, (commonly called the
Emperour of *Moskouia*) with
the manners, and faſhions
of the people of that
Countrey.

The Contents are noted in the Table, ſet downe before the beginning of the Booke.

AT LONDON
Printed by T. D. for
Thomas Charde.
1591.

To the Queenes
most *excellent Maiestie.*

Most gracious Soueraigne, beeyng employed in your Maiesties seruice to the Emperour of *Russia,* I obserued the
State, and manners of that Countrey. And hauing reduced the same
into some order, by the way as I returned, I haue presumed to offer
it in this smal Booke to your most excellent Maiestie. My meaning   5
was to note thinges for mine owne experience, of more importaunce then delight, and rather true then strange. In their maner of
gouernment, your Highnesse may see both: A true and strange face
of a *Tyrannical state,* (most vnlike to your own) without true knowledge of GOD, without written Lawe, without common iustice: 10
saue that which proceedeth from their *Speaking Lawe,* to wit, the
Magistrate who hath most neede of a Lawe, to restraine his owne
iniustice. The practise hereof as it is heauy, and grieuous to the
poore oppressed people, that liue within those Countreyes: so it
may giue iust cause to my selfe, and other your Maiesties faithfull   15
subiects, to acknowledge our happines on this behalfe, and to giue
God thankes for your Maiesties most Princelike, and gracious gouernment: as also to your Highnesse more ioy, and contentment in

your royall estate, in that you are a Prince of subiectes, not of slaues, that are kept within duetie by loue, not by feare. The Almightie stil blesse your Highnes with a most long, and happy reigne in this life, and with Christ Iesus in the life to come.

Your Maiesties most humble
subiect, and servant

G. Fletcher.

The sum of this discourse conteining the

1. Cosmographie of the Countrie.
- 1. The breadth and length of the Countrie, with the names of the Shires.
- 2. The Soyle and Clymate.
- 3. The natiue commodities of the Countrie.
- 4. The chiefe cities of Russia.

2. Pollicy.

1. The ordering of their State.
- 5. The house or stocke of the Russe Emperour.
- 6. The maner of inauguration of the Russe Emperours.
- 7. The forme or manner of their publique gouernment.
- 8. Their Parliamentes and manner of holding them.
- 9. The Russe Nobilitie, and meanes whereby it is kept in an vnder proportion agreeable to that State.
- 10. The manner of gouerning their Prouinces, or Shires.
- 11. The Emperours priuie Counsell.
- 12. The Emperours Customes and other Reuenues, and what they amount vnto, with the Sophismes practised for the encrease of them.
- 13. The Russe communaltie and their condition.

2. Their iudicial proceeding.
- 14. Their publique Iustice and manner of proceeding therein.

3. Their warlike prouisions.
- 15. The Emperours forces for his warres, with the officers and their Salaries.
- 16. Their manner of mustering, armour, prouision for vittaile, encamping, &c.
- 17. Their order in marching, charging, and their martiall discipline.
- 18. Their colonies and pollicie in mainteyning their purchases by conquest.
- 19. Their borderers, with whom they haue most to doo in warre and peace.
- 20. Of the Permians, Samoites, and Lappes.

4. Their Ecclesiastical State.
- 21. Their Church offices, and degrees.
- 22. Their Leiturgie or forme of Church seruice, with their manner of administring the Sacraments.
- 23. The doctrine of the Russe Church.
- 24. Their manner of solemnizing marriages.
- 25. The other Ceremonies of the Russe Church.

3. Oeconomie or priuat behauiour.
- 26. The Emperours domestique or priuate behauiour.
- 27. The Emperours houshold, and offices of his house.
- 28. The priuate behauiour, and manners of the Russe people

The description of the Countrie of Russia, with the breadth, length, and names of the Shires.
The I. Chapter.

The countrie of *Russia* was sometimes called *Sarmatia*. It chaunged the name (as some do suppose) for that it was parted into diuerse small, and yet absolute gouernments, not depending, nor being subiect the one to the other. For *Russe* in that tongue doth signifie asmuch as to parte, or diuide. The *Russe* reporteth that foure brethren, *Trubor*, *Rurico*, *Sinees*, and *Variuus*, diuided among them the North parts of the countrie. Likewise that the Southpartes were possessed by foure other, *Kio*, *Scieko*, *Cheranus*, and their sister *Libeda*: each calling his territorie after his owne name. Of this partition it was called *Russia*, about the yeare from Christ 860. As for the coniecture which I find in some Cosmographers, that the *Russe* nation borrowed the name of the people called *Roxellani*, and were the very same nation with them, it is without all good probabilitie: both in respect of the etymologie of the word (which is very far set) and especially for the seat and dwelling of that people, which was betwixt the two riuers of *Tanais* and *Boristhenes*, (as *Strabo* reporteth) quite an other way from the countrey of *Russia*.

Strabo in his 7. booke of Geogr.

When it bare the name of *Sarmatia*, it was diuided into two chiefe parts: the *White*, and the *Blacke*. The *White Sarmatia* was all that part that lieth towardes the North, and on the side of *Liefland*:

172

as the Prouinces now called *Duyna, Vagha, Vstick, Vologda, Cargapolia, Nouogradia*, &c: whereof *Nouograd velica* was the Metropolite, or chiefe cittie. *Blacke Sarmatia* was all that countrey that lieth Southward, towards the *Euxin*, or *Black Sea*: as the dukedome of *Volodemer* of *Mosko, Rezan*, &c. Some haue thought that the name of *Sarmatia* was first taken, from one *Sarmates*, whom *Moses* and *Iosephus* call *Asarmathes*, sonne to *Ioktan*, and nephew to *Heber*, of the posteritie of *Sem*. But this seemeth to be nothing but a coniecture taken out of the likenes of the name *Asarmathes*. For the dwelling of all *Ioktans* posteritie is described by *Moses*, to haue beene betwixt *Mescha* or *Masius* (an hill of the *Amonites*) and *Sephace*, neare to the riuer *Euphrates*. Which maketh it very vnlikely, that *Asarmathes* should plant any colonies so far off in the North and Northwest countries. It is bounded Northward by the *Lappes* and the North *Ocean*. On the Southside by the *Tartars*, called *Chrimes*. Eastward they haue the *Nagaian Tartar*, that possesseth all the countrie on the East side of *Volgha*, towards the *Caspian* sea. On the West and Southwest border lieth *Lituania, Liuonia* and *Polonia*.

The whole country being now reduced vnder the gouernment of one, conteyneth these chief Prouinces or Shires, *Volodemer*, (which beareth the first place in the Emperours stile, because their house came of the Dukes of that countrey) *Mosko, Nisnouogrod, Plesko, Smolensko, Nouogrod velica* (or *Nouogrod* of the low countrey) *Rostoue, Yaruslaue, Bealozera, Rezan, Duyna, Cargapolia, Meschora, Vagha, Vstuga Ghaletsa*. These are the naturall shires perteyning to *Russia*, but far greater and larger then the shires of England, though not so well peopled. The other countries or prouinces which the *Russe* Emperours haue gotten perforce added of late to their other dominion, are these which follow: *Twerra, Youghoria, Permia, Vadska, Boulghoria, Chernigo, Oudoria, Obdoria, Condora*, with a great part of *Siberia*: where the people though they be not natural *Russes*, yet obey the Emperour of *Russia*, and are ruled by the lawes of his countrie, paying customes and taxes, as his owne people doe. Besides these hee hath vnder him the kingdomes of *Cazan* and *Astracan*,

25

Gen. 10.
Ioseph. 1. I.
cap. 14.

30

The borders
of Russia.

The shires
of Russia.

45

The Pro-
uinces or
countries
got by con-
quest.

173

gotten by conquest not long since. As for all his possession in *Lituania* (to the number of 30. great townes and more,) with *Narue* and *Dorp* in *Liuonia*, they are quite gone, beyng surprised of late yeares by the kinges of *Poland* and *Sweden*. These Shires and Prouinces are reduced all into foure *Iurisdictions*, which they call

60 *Chetfyrds* (that is) *Tetrarchies*, or *Fourthparts*. Wherof we are to speake in the title or chapter, concerning the Prouinces, and their manner of gouernment.

The bredth and length of the coun- trie.   The whole countrie is of great length and breadth. From the North to the South (if you measure from *Cola* to *Astracan* which bendeth somewhat Eastwarde) it reacheth in length about 4260. verst, or miles. Notwithstanding the Emperour of *Russia* hath more territorie Northward, far beyond *Cola* vnto the riuer of *Tromschua*, that runneth a 1000. verst, welnie beyond *Pechinga*, neare to *Ward- house*, but not intire nor clearly limited, by reason of the kings of

70 *Sweden* and *Denmark*, that haue diuers townes there, aswell as the *Russe*, plotted togither the one with the other: euery one of them claiming the whole of those North parts as his owne right. The breadth (if you go from that part of his territorie that lieth farthest Westwarde on the *Narue* side, to the parts of *Siberia* eastward,

75 where the Emperour hath his garrisons) is 4400. verst or thereabouts. A verst (by their reckoning) is a 1000. pases, yet lesse by one quarter then an English mile. If the whole dominion of the *Russe* Emperour were all habitable, and peopled in all places, as it is in some, hee would either hardly hold it all within one regiment, or be ouer

80 mightie for all his neighbour Princes.

Of the Soyle and Climate.
The 2. Chapter.

The soyle of the countrie for the most part is of a sleight sandie moulde, yet very much different one place from an other, for the yeeld of such thinges as grow out of the earth. The countrie Northwards towards the partes of Saint *Nicolas* and *Cola*, and

Northeast towards *Siberia*, is all very barren, and full of desert 5
woods by reason of the clymat, and extremitie of the colde in winter
time. So likewise along the riuer *Volgha* betwixt the countries of
Cazan, and *Astracan*: where (notwithstanding the soyle is very
fruitefull) it is all vnhabited, sauing that vpon the riuer *Volgha* on
the west side, the Emperour hath some fewe castels with garrisons 10
in them. This hapneth by means of the *Chrim Tartar*, that will
neyther himselfe plant townes to dwell there, (liuing a wilde and
vagrant life) nor suffer the *Russe* (that is farre off with the strength
of his countrie) to people those partes. From *Vologda* (which lieth
almost 1700. verst from the porte of Saint *Nicholas*) downe towardes 15
Mosko, and so towardes the south parte that bordereth vpon the
Chrim, (which conteineth the like space of 1700. verst or there
abouts) is a very fruitfull and pleasant countrie, yeelding pasture,
and corne, with woods and waters in very great plentie. The like
is betwixt *Rezan* (that lieth southeast from *Mosko*) to *Nouograd* and 20
Vobsko, that reach farthest towards the northwest. So betwixt *Mosko*,
and *Smolensko* (that lieth southwest towards *Lituania*) is a very
fruitful and pleasant soile.

The whole countrie differeth very much from it selfe, by reason
of the yeare: so that a man would meruaile to see the great alteration 25
and difference betwixte the winter, and the sommer *Russia*. The
whole countrie in the winter lyeth vnder snow, which falleth
continually, and is sometime of a yarde or two thicke, but greater
towardes the north. The riuers and other waters are all frosen vp
a yarde or more thicke, how swifte or broade so euer they bee. And 30
this continueth commonly fiue moneths, vz. from the beginning of
Nouember till towardes the ende of March, what time the snow
beginneth to melte. So that it would breede a frost in a man to
looke abroad at that time, and see the winter face of that countrie.
The sharpenesse of the ayre you may iudge of by this: for that   The cold
water dropped downe or cast vp into the ayre, congealeth into Ise   of *Russia*.
before it come to the ground. In the extremitie of winter, if you
holde a pewter dishe or pot in your hand, or any other mettall

175

(except in some chamber where their warme stoaues bee) your
fingers will friese faste vnto it, and drawe of the skinne at the
parting. When you passe out of a warme roome into a colde, you
shall sensibly feele your breath to waxe starke, and euen stifeling
with the colde, as you draw it in and out. Diuers not onely that
trauell abroad, but in the very markets, and streats of their townes,
are mortally pinched and killed withall: so that you shall see many
drop downe in the streates, many trauellers brought into the townes
sitting dead and stiffe in their sleddes. Diuers lose their noses, the
tippes of their eares, and the bals of their cheekes, their toes, feete,
&c. Many times when the winter is very harde and extreame the
beares and woolfes issue by troupes out of the woodes driuen by
hunger, and enter the villages, tearing and rauening all they can
finde: so that the inhabitants are faine to flie for safegard of their
liues. And yet in the Sommer time you shall see such a new hew
and face of a countrie, the woods (for the most part which are all
of fir and birch) so fresh and so sweet, the pastures and medowes
so greene and well growen, (and that vpon the sudden) such varietie
of flowres, such noyse of birdes (specially of Nightingales, that
seeme to be more lowde and of a more variable note then in other
countries) that a man shall not lightly trauell in a more pleasant
countrie.

And this fresh and speedy grouth of the spring there, seemeth
to proceede from the benefite of the snow: which all the winter
time being spred ouer the whole countrie as a white robe, and
keeping it warme from the rigour of the frost, in the spring time
(when the sunne waxeth warme, and dissolueth it into water) doth
so throughly drench and soake the ground, that is somewhat of a
sleight and sandy mould, and then shineth so hotely vpon it againe,
that it draweth the hearbes and plants forth in great plenty and
varietie, in a very short time. As the winter exceedeth in colde, so
the sommer inclineth to ouer much heat, specially in the moneths
of Iune, Iuly, and August, being much warmer then the sommer
ayre in England.

176

The countrie throughout is very well watred with springs, riuers, and ozeracs, or lakes. Wherein the prouidence of God is to bee noted, for that much of the countrie beyng so farre inland, as that some parte lieth a 1000. miles and more euery way from any sea, yet it is serued with faire riuers, and that in very great number, that emptiyng themselues one into an other, runne all into the sea. Their lakes are many and large, some of 60. 80. 100. and 200. miles long, with breadth proportionate.

The chief riuers are these 1. *Volgha*, that hath his head or spring at the roote of an Aldertree, about 200. verst aboue *Yaruslaue*, and groweth so big by the encrease of other riuers by that time it commeth thither, that it is broad an English mile and more, and so runneth into the *Caspian* sea, about 2800. verst or miles of length.

The next is *Boristhenes* (now called *Neper*) that diuideth the countrie from *Lituania*, and falleth into the *Euxin* sea.

The third *Tanais* or *Don*, (the auncient bounder betwixt *Europe* and *Asia*) that taketh his head out of *Rezan Ozera*, and so running through the countrie of the *Chrim Tartar*, falleth into the great sea lake, or meare, (called *Mæotis*) by the Citie of *Azou*. By this riuer (as the *Russe* reporteth) you may passe from their citie *Mosko* to *Constantinople*, and so into all those partes of the world by water, drawing your boate (as their manner is) ouer a little *Isthmus* or narrow slippe of lande, a fewe versts ouerthwart. Which was proued not long since by an Ambassadour sent to *Constantinople*, who passed the riuer of *Moskua*, and so into an other called *Ocka*, whence he drew his boate ouer into *Tanais*, and thence passed the whole way by water.

The fourth is called *Duyna*, many hundred miles long, that falleth Northward into the Baye of Saint *Nicholas*, and hath great Alabaster rockes on the bankes towards the sea side.

The fifth *Duna*, that emptieth into the *Baltick* sea by the towne *Riga*.

The sixt *Onega*, that falleth into the Bay at *Solouetsko* 90. verst

177

from the port of Saint *Nicholas*. This riuer below the towne *Carga-polia* meeteth with the riuer *Volock*, that falleth into the *Finland* sea by the towne *Yama*. So that from the port of Saint *Nicholas* into the *Finland* sea, and so into the Sound, you may passe all by water, as hath bene tried by the *Russe*.

The seuenth *Suchana*, that floweth into *Duyna*, and so into the North sea.

The eight *Ocka*, that fetcheth his head from the borders of the *Chrim*, and streameth into *Volgha*.

The ninth *Moskua*, that runneth thorough the citie *Mosko*, and giueth it the name.

There is *Wichida* also a very large and long riuer that riseth out of *Permia*, and falleth into *Volgha*. All these are riuers of very large streames, the least to be compared to the *Thames* in bignesse, and in length farre more, besides diuers other. The Pole at *Mosko* is 55. degrees 10. minutes. At the porte of Saint *Nicholas* towards the North 63. degrees and 50 minutes.

The natiue commodities of the Countrie.
The 3. Chapter.

The fruites and graine of *Russia*.

For kindes of fruites, they haue Appels, Peares, plummes, cheries, redde and blacke, (but the blacke wild) a deene like a muske millian, but more sweete and pleasant, cucumbers and goords (which they call *Arbouse*) rasps, strawberies, and hurtilberies, with many other bearies in great quantitie in euery wood and hedge. Their kindes of graine are wheat, rie, barley, oates, pease, buckway, psnytha, that in taste is somewhat like to rice. Of all these graynes the countrie yeeldeth very sufficient with an ouerplus quantitie, so that wheate is solde sometime for two alteens or ten pence starling the *Chetfird*, which maketh almost three English bushels.

Their rye is sowed before the winter, all their other graine in the spring time, and for the most parte in May. The *Permians* and some other that dwell far north, and in desert places, are serued

178

from the partes that lye more Southward, and are forced to make
bread sometimes of a kinde of roote (called *Vaghnoy*) and of the
middle rine of the firre tree. If there be any dearth (as they accounted
this last yeare, *Anno* 1588. wheat and rye beyng at 13. *alteens*, or 5.
shillings 5. pence starling the *Chetfird*) the fault is rather in the
practise of their Nobilitie that vse to engrosse it, then in the countrie
it selfe.

The natiue commodities of the countrie (wherewith they serue
both their owne turnes, and sende much abroad to the great
enriching of the Emperour, and his people) are many and substantiall.
First, furres of all sortes. Wherein the prouidence of God is to be
noted, that prouideth a naturall remedie for them, to helpe the
naturall inconuenience of their countrie by the colde of the Clymat.
Their chiefe furres are these, *Blacke fox, Sables, Lusernes, Dunne fox,*
Martrones, Gurnestalles or Armins, Lasets or Miniuer, Beuer, Wuluerins,
the skin of a great water Ratte that smelleth naturally like muske, Calaber
or Gray squirrell, red squirrell, red, and white Foxe. Besides the great
quantitie spent within the countrie (the people beyng clad all in
furres the whole winter) there are transported out of the countrie
some yeares by the marchants of *Turkie, Persia, Bougharia, Georgia,*
Armenia, and some other of Christendome to the value of foure or
fiue hundred thousand rubbels, as I haue heard of the Marchants.
The best Sable furre groweth in the countrie of *Pechora, Momgosors-*
koy and *Obdorskoy,* the worser sort in *Siberia, Perm,* and other places.
The blacke fox and redde come out of *Siberia,* white and dun from
Pechora, whence also come the white wolfe, and white Beare skin.
The best Wuluerin also thence and from *Perm.* The best Martrons
are from *Syberia, Cadam, Morum, Perm,* and *Cazan.* Lyserns, Min-
euer, and Armins, the best ar out of *Gallets,* and *Ouglites,* many
from *Nouogrod,* and *Perm.* The Beauer of the best sort breedeth in
Murmonskey by *Cola.* Other common furres, and most of these
kindes grow in many, and some in all partes of the countrie.

The second commoditie is of Wax, whereof hath bene shipped
into forraine countries (as I haue heard it reported by those that

15

20

The chiefe
commodities
of the
countrie.
1. Furres.

25

30

35

40

45

2. Waxe.

179

best know it) the summe of 50000. pood yearlie, euery pood conteyning 40. pound, but now about 10000. pood a yeare.

3. Hony.   The third is their Hony, whereof besides an exceeding great quantitie spent in their ordinary drinks (which is *mead* of al sorts) and their other vses, some good quantitie is carried out of the countrie. The chiefe encrease of honie is in *Mordua* and *Cadam* neare to the *Cheremissen Tartar*: much out of *Seuerskoy, Rezan, Morum,*

55 *Cazan, Dorogobose,* and *Vasma.*

4. Tallow.   Fourthly, of Tallow they afoord a great waight for transportation: not only for that their countrie hath very much good ground apt for pasturage of cattaile, but also by reason of their many Lents and other fastes: and partly because their greater menne vse much waxe

60 for their lightes, the poorer and meaner sorte birch dried in their stoaues, and cut into long shiuers, which they call *Luchineos.* Of tallow there hath bene shipped out of the realme a fewe yeares since about a 100000. pood yearely, now not past 30000. or thereabouts. The best yeeld of tallow is in the parts and territories of *Smolensko,*

65 *Yaruslaue, Ouglits, Nouogrod,* and *Vologda, Otfer,* and *Gorodetskey.*

5. Hide.   An other principall commoditie is their Losh and Cowe hide. Their Losh or Buffe hide is very faire and large. Their bull and cowe hide (for oxen they make none, neyther yet weather) is of a small sise. There hath bene transported by Marchants strangers some

70 yeares, a 100000. hydes. Now it is decreased to a 30000. or thereabouts. Besides great store of goates skinnes, whereof great numbers are shipped out of the countrie. The largest kind of Losh or Buffe breedeth about *Rostoue, Wichida, Nouogrod, Morum,* and *Perm.* The lesser sorte within the kingdome of *Cazan.*

6. Trane oyle.   An other very great and principall commoditie is their *Trane oyle,* drawen out of the seal fish. Where it will not bee impertinent

The manner of hunting the Seal fish.   to shewe the manner of their hunting the seal, which they make this oyle of: which is in this sort. Towardes the ende of sommer (before the frost begin) they go downe with their boates into the

80 Bay of Saint *Nicholas,* to a cape called *Cusconesse* or *Foxnose,* where they leaue their boates till the next spring tide. When the sunne

180

waxeth warme towarde the spring, and yet the yse not melted within the Bay, they returne thither againe. Then drawing their boates ouer the sea yse, they vse them for houses to rest and lodge in. There are commonly about 17. or 18. fleete of them, of great large boates, which diuide themselues into diuers companies, fiue or six boates in a consort.

They that first finde the haunt, fire a beacon, which they carry with them for the nonce. Which being espied by the other companies, by such among them as are appoynted of purpose, they come altogither and compasse the seales round about in a ring, that lye sunning themselues togither vpon the yse, commonly foure or fiue thousand in a shoale, and so they inuade them euery man with his clubbe in his hand. If they hit them on the nose, they are soone killed. If on the sides or backe they beare out the blow, and many times so catche and holde downe the club with their teeth by main force, that the party is forced to cal for help to his fellowes.

The manner of the Seals is, when they see themselues beset, to gather all close together in a throng or plumpe, to sway downe the yse, and to break it (if they can) which so bendeth the yse, that many times it taketh the sea water vpon it, and maketh the hunters to wade a foot or more deepe. After the slaughter, when they haue killed what they can, they fall to sharing euery boate his part in equall portions: and so they flay them, taking from the body the skin, and the lard or fat withall that cleaueth to the skin. This they take with them, leauing the bodies behind, and so goe to shore. Where they digge pits in the ground of a fadome and an halfe deepe, or there about, and so taking the fat or larde off from the skinne, they throw it into the pit, and cast in among it hoat burning stones to melt it withall. The vppermost and purest is solde and vsed to oyle wooll for cloth, the grosser (that is of a red colour) they sell to make sope.

Likewise of *Ickary* or *Cauery*, a great quantitie is made vpon the riuer of *Volgha* out of the fish called *Bellougina*, the *Sturgeon*, the *Seueriga* and the *Sterledey*. Wherof the most part is shipped by

7. Ickary.

181

French and *Netherlandish* marchants for *Italy* and *Spaine*, some by English marchants.

8. Hempe and flaxe.

The next is of Flaxe and Hempe, whereof there hath bin shipped (as I haue heard marchants say) at the port of *Narue* a great part of a 100. ships smal and great yerely. Now, not past fiue. The reason of this abating and decrease of this and other commodities, that were wont to be transported in a greater quantitie, is the shutting vp of the port of the *Narue* towards the *Finland* sea, which now is in the hands and possession of the *Sweaden*. Likewise the stopping of the passage ouerland by the way of *Smolensko*, and *Plotsko*, by reason of their warres with the *Polonian*, which causeth the people to be lesse prouident in mainteining and gathering these and like commodities, for that they lack sales. Partly also for that the marchants and Mousicks (for so they cal the common sort of people) are very much discouraged by many heauy and intollerable exactions, that of late time haue bin imposed vpon them: no man accounting that which he hath to be sure his own. And therfore regard not to lay vp any thing, or to haue it before hand, for that it causeth them many times to be fleesed and spoiled not only of their goods, but also of their liues. For the grouth of flaxe the prouince of *Vobsko* and the countrey about is the chiefe and only place. For hemp *Smolensko*, *Dorogobose* and *Vasma*.

9. Salt.

The countrey besides maketh great store of salt. Their best salt is made at *Stararouse* in very great quantity, where they haue great store of salt wels, about 250. verst from the sea. At *Astracan* salt is made naturally by the sea water, that casteth it vp into great hils, and so it is digged down, and caried away by the marchants and other that wil fetch it from thence. They pay to the Emperor for acknowledgement or custome 3.d. *Russe* vpon euery hundred weight. Besides these two, they make salt in many other places of the Realme, as in *Perm*, *Wichida*, *Totma*, *Kenitsma*, *Solouetskey*, *Ocona*, *Bombasey*, and *Nonocks*, al out of salt pits, saue at *Solouetskey*, which lieth neere to the sea.

10. Tarre.

Likewise of tarre they make a great quantity out of their firre trees in the countrie of *Duyna* and *Smolensko*, whereof much is sent abroad. Besides these (which are all good and substantial commodities) they haue diuers other of smaller account, that are natural and proper to that countrey: as the fishe tooth (which they cal *Ribazuba* which is vsed both among themselues and the *Persians* and *Bougharians* that fetch it from thence for beads, kniues, and sword hafts of Noblemen, and gentlemen, and for diuers other vses. Some vse the powder of it against poyson, as the Vnicornes horne. The fish that weareth it is called a *Morse*, and is caught about *Pechora*. These fishe teeth some of them, are almost two foote of length, and weigh eleuen or twelue pound apiece.

    In the prouince of *Corelia*, and about the riuer *Duyna* towardes the North sea, there groweth a soft rocke which they call *Slude*. This they cut into pieces, and so teare it into thin flakes, which naturally it is apt for and so vse it for glasse-lanthorns and such like. It giueth both inwards and outwards a clearer light then glasse, and for this respect is better then either glasse or horne: for that it neither breaketh like glasse, nor yet will burne like the lanthorne. Saltpeter they make in many places, as at *Ouglites*, *Yaruslaue* and *Vstug*, and some small store of brimstone vpon the riuer *Volgha*, but want skill to refine it. Their iron is somewhat brittle, but a great weight of it is made in *Corelia*, *Cargapolia*, and *Vstug Thelesna*. Other myne they haue none growing within the Realme.

    Their beasts of strange kinds are the Losh, the Ollen, the wilde Horse, the Beare, the Woluering, or wood dogge, the Lyserne, the Beauer, the Sable, the Martron, the blacke and dunne Foxe, the white Beare towardes the Sea coast of *Pechora*, the Gurnstale, the Laset or Mineuer. They haue a kinde of Squirrel that hath growing on the pinion of the shoulder bone, a long tuft of haire, much like vnto feathers with a farre broader tayle then haue any other squirrels, which they moue and shake as they leape from tree to tree, much like vnto a wing. They skise a large space, and seeme for to flie withall, and therefore they call them *Letach Vechshe*, that is, the flying squirrels. Their hares and squirrels in Sommer are of the same

11. Ribazuba.

155

160

12. Slude.

165

13. Salt-peeter and brimstone.

14. Iron.

The strange beasts, fish, foule, &c. that breed in *Russia*.

180

185 colour with ours, in winter the Hare changeth her coate into milke white, the squirrell into gray, whereof commeth the *Calaber*.

They haue fallow Deere, the roe Bucke, and goates very great store. Their horses are but small, but very swift and harde. They trauell them vnshod both winter and Sommer, without all regard of pace. Their sheepe are but small and beare coorse, and harsh
190 wooll. Of foule, they haue diuers of the principall kindes: First, great store of Hawkes, the Eagle, the Gerfaulcon, the Slightfaulcon, the Goshawke, the Tassel, the Sparhawk, &c. But the principall hawke that breedeth in the countrey, is counted the Gerfaulcon.

Of other foules their principall kinds are the swanne tame and
195 wilde, (whereof they haue great store) the Storke, the Crane, the Tedder, of the colour of a Feasant, but farre bigger and liueth in the firre woods. Of Feasant and Partridge they haue very great plentie. An owle there is of a very great bignesse, more vglie to beholde then the owles of this countrey, with a broade face, and
200 eares much like vnto a man.

For fresh water fish besides the common sorts (as Carpe, Pikes, Pearch, Tench, Roach, &c.) they haue diuers kinds very good and delicate: as the *Bellouga*, or *Bellougina* of 4. or 5. elnes long, the *Ositrina* or *Sturgeon*, the *Seueriga*, and *Sterledy* somewhat in fashion
205 and taste like to the *Sturgeon*, but not so thicke nor long. These 4. kinds of fish breed in the *Volgha*, and are catched in great plenty, and serued thence into the whole Realme for a great food. Of the Roes of these foure kinds they make very great store of *Icary* or *Caueary* as was said before.

210 They haue besides these that breed in the *Volgha* a fish called the *Riba bela*, or white salmon, which they account more delicate then they do the redde salmon: wherof also they haue exceeding great plentie in the riuers northward, as in *Duyna* the riuer of *Cola*, &c. In the Ozera or lake neere a towne called *Perislaue*, not far from
215 the *Mosko*, they haue a small fish which they call the fresh herring, of the fashion, and somewhat of the taste of a Sea-hearing. Their chiefe townes for fish are, *Yaruslaue, Bealozera, Nouogrod, Astracan,*

and *Cazan*: which all yeeld a large custome to the Emperour euery yeere for their trades of fishing, which they practise in Sommer, but send it frozen in the Winter time into all partes of the Realme.　　220

The chiefe Cities of Russia.
The 4. Chapter.

The chiefe Cities of *Russia* are, *Mosko, Nouograd, Rostoue, Volodomer, Plesko, Smolensko, Iaruslaue, Perislaue, Nisnouograd, Vologda, Vstiuck, Golmigroe, Cazan, Astracan, Cargapolia, Columna.*

　　The citie of *Mosko* is supposed to be of great antiquitie, though *Mosko.* the first founder be vnknowen to the *Russe*. It seemeth to haue 　5 taken the name from the riuer that runeth on the one side of the town. *Berosus* the *Chaldean* in his 5. book telleth that *Nimrod* (whom other prophane stories cal *Saturn*) sent *Assyrius, Medus, Moscus*, and *Magog* into *Asia* to plant Colonies there, and that *Moscus* planted both in *Asia* and *Europe*. Which may make some probability, that 　10 the city, or rather the riuer whereon it is built, tooke the denomination from this *Moscus*: the rather bicause of the climate or situation, which is in the very farthest part and list of *Europe*, bordering vpon *Asia*. The citie was much enlarged by one *Euan* or *Iohn*, sonne to *Daniel*, that first changed his title of Duke into King: though that 　15 honour continued not to his posterity: the rather because he was inuested into it by the Popes Legate, who at that time was *Innocentius* the fourth about the yeere 1246. which was very much misliked by the *Russe* people, being then a part of the Easterne or Greeke Church. Since that time the name of this citie hath growen more famous, 　20 and better knowen to the worlde: insomuch that not onely the prouince, but the whole countrey of *Russia* is tearmed by some by the name of *Moscouia* the Metropolite citie. The forme of this citie is in a manner round with three strong walles, circuling the one within the other, and streets lying betweene, wherof the inmost 　25 wall, and the buildings closed within it (lying safest as the heart within the bodie, fenced and watred with the riuer *Moskua*, that

185

runneth close by it) is all accounted the Emperours castle. The number of houses (as I haue heard) through the whole citie (being reckoned by the Emperour a little before it was fired by the *Chrim*) was 41500. in all. Since the *Tartar* besieged and fired the town (which was in the yeare 1571.) there lieth waste of it a great breadth of ground, which before was well set and planted with buildings, specially that part on the south side of *Moskua*, built not long before by *Basilius* the Emperour for his garrison of souldiours, to whom he gaue priuiledge to drinke Mead, and Beer at the drye or prohibited times, when other *Russes* may drinke nothing but water, and for that cause called this newe citie by the name of *Naloi*, that is, *skinck or poure in.* So that now the Citie of *Mosko* is not much bigger then the citie of London. The next in greatnes, and in a manner as large, is the citie *Nouograde*: where was committed (as the *Russe* saith) the memorable warre so much spoke of in stories of the *Scythian* seruants, that tooke armes against their maisters: which they report in this sort: vz. That the *Boiarens* or Gentlemen of *Nouograde* and the territorie about (which onely are souldiers after the discipline of those countries) had warre with the *Tartars*. Which being well perfourmed and ended by them, they returned homewards. Where they vnderstood by the way that their *Cholopey* or bondslaues whome they left at home, had in their absence possessed their townes, lands, houses, wiues, and all. At which newes being somewhat amased, and yet disdayning the villanie of their seruants, they made the more speed home: and so not farre from *Nouograd* met them in warlike manner marching against them. Whereupon aduising what was best to bee done, they agreed all to set vpon them with no other shewe of weapon but with their horse whips (which as their manner is euery man rideth withall) to put them in remembrance of their seruile condition, thereby to terrifie them, and abate their courage. And so marching on and lashing altogither with their whips in their hands they gaue the onset. Which seemed so terrible in the eares of their villaines, and stroke such a sense into them of the smart of the whip which they had felt before, that they

Nouograd.

186

fled altogether like sheepe before the driuers. In memory of this victory the *Nouogradians* euer since haue stamped their coine (which they cal a *dingoe Nouogrodskoy* currant through al *Russia*) with the figure of a horseman shaking a whip a loft in his hand. These two cities exceed the rest in greatnes. For strength their chief townes are *Vobsko*, *Smolensko*, *Cazan* and *Astracan*, as liyng vpon the borders. But for situation *Iaruslaue* farre exceedeth the rest. For besides the commodities that the soyle yeeldeth of pasture and corne, it lieth vpon the famous riuer *Volgha*, and looketh ouer it from a high banke very faire and stately to behold: wherof the towne taketh the name. For *Iaruslaue* in that tongue signifieth as much as a faire or famous banke. In this towne (as may be ghessed by the name) dwelt the *Russe* king *Vlademir* sirnamed *Iaruslaue*, that married the daughter of *Harald* king of England, by mediation of *Sueno* the *Dane*, as is noted in the *Danish* storie about the yeare 1067.

The other townes haue nothing that is greatly memorable, saue many ruines within their walles. Which sheweth the decrease of the *Russe* people, vnder this gouernment. The streates of their cities and townes insteed of pauing, are planked with firre trees, plained and layed euen close the one to the other. Their houses are of wood without any lime or stone, built very close and warm with firre trees plained and piled one vpon an other. They are fastened together with dentes or notches at euery corner, and so clasped fast together. Betwixt the trees or timber they thrust in mosse (whereof they gather plentie in their woods) to keepe out the ayre. Euery house hath a paire of staiers that lead vp into the chambers out of the yarde or streat after the Scottish manner. This building seemeth farre better for their countrie, then that of stone and bricke: as being colder and more dampish then their woodden houses, specially of firre, that is a dry and warme wood. Whereof the prouidence of God hath giuen them such store, as that you may build a faire house for twentie or thirtie rubbels or little more, where wood is most scant. The greatest inconuenience of their woodden building is the aptnes for firing, which happeneth very

Iaruslaue.

The manner of *Russe* buylding.

65

70

75

80

85

90

95

187

oft and in very fearful sort, by reason of the drinesse and fatnesse of the firre, that being once fired, burneth like a torch, and is hardly quenched till all be burnt vp.

Of the house or stocke of the Russe Emperours.
The 5. Chapter.

The syrname of the imperiall house of *Russia,* is called *Beala.* It tooke the originall (as is supposed) from the Kinges of *Hungarie.* Which may seeme the more probable for that the *Hungarian* Kings many yeares agoe haue borne that name: as appeareth by *Bonfinius* and other stories written of that countrie. For about the yeare 1059. mention is made of one *Beæla* that succeeded his brother *Andreas,* who reduced the *Hungarians* to the Christian faith from whence they were fallen by atheisme and Turkish perswasion before. The second of that name was called *Beala the blinde,* after whom succeeded diuers of the same name.

That their auncestrie came not of the *Russe* nation, *Iuan Vasilowich* father to this Emperour would many times boast, disdaining (as should seeme) to haue his progenie deriued from the *Russe* bloud. As namely to an Englishman his goldsmith, that had receiued bullion of him to make certain plate: whom the Emperour commaunded to looke well to his waight. For my *Russes* (sayd he) are theeues all. Whereat the workeman looking vpon the Emperour, began to smile. The Emperour being of quicke conceipt, charged him to tell him what he smiled at. If your Maiestie will pardon me (quoth the goldsmith) I will tell you. Your highnesse said that the *Russes* were all theeues, and forgot in the meane while that your selfe was a *Russe.* I thought so (quoth the Emperour) but thou art deceiued. For I am no *Russe,* my auncestors were *Germanes* (for so they account of the *Hungarians* to be part of the *Germane* nation though in deed they come of the *Hunnes,* that inuaded those countries and rested in those parts of *Pannonia,* now called *Hungary.*

The house Beala not naturall Russe.

188

Chapter 5: The Imperial House

How they aspired to the Dukedome of *Volodemer* (which was their first degree, and ingrafting into *Russia*) and whether it were by conquest, or by marriage, or by what other meanes, I could not learne any certentie among them. That from these beginnings of a small Dukedome (that bare notwithstanding an absolute gouernment with it, as at that time did also the other Shires or Prouinces of *Russia*) this house of *Beala* spred it selfe foorth, and aspired by degrees to the monarchie of the whole countrie, is a thing well knowen, and of very late memorie. The chiefe of that house that aduanced the stocke, and enlarged their dominions, were the three last that raigned before this Emperour, to wit, *Iuan Basileus*, and *Iuan* father to the other that raigneth at this time. Wherof the first that tooke vnto him the name and title of Emperour, was *Basileus* father to *Iuan*, and grandfather to this man. For before that time they were contented to be called great Dukes of *Mosko*. What hath bene done by either of these three, and how much they haue added to their first estate by conquest or otherwise, may bee seene in the chapter of their colonies, or purchases perforce. For the continuance of the race, this house of *Beala* at this present is in like case as are many of the greatest houses of Christendome vz. the whole stocke and race concluded in one, two or some fewe of the bloud. For besides the Emperour that now is, who hath no childe (neither is like euer to haue for ought that may be coniectured by the constitution of his body, and the barennesse of his wife after so many yeares marriage) there is but one more vz. a child of sixe or seuen yeares old, in whom resteth all the hope of the succession, and the posteritie of that house. As for the other brother that was eldest of the three, and of the best towardnesse, he died of a blowe giuen him by his father vpon the head in his furie with his walking staffe, or (as some say) of a thrust with the prong of it driuen deepe into his head. That he meant him no such mortall harme when hee gaue him the blow, may appeare by his mourning and passion after his sonnes death, which neuer left him till it brought him to the graue. Wherein may be marked the iustice of God, that punished his

30

The aduancement of the house of *Beala*.

35

40

45

50

55

60

189

delight in shedding of bloud with this murder of his sonne by his owne hand, and so ended his dayes and tyrannie together, with the murdering of himselfe by extreame griefe, for this his vnhappie and vnnaturall fact.

65   The Emperours yonger brother of sixe or seuen years old (as was said before) is kept in a remote place from the *Mosko*, vnder the tuition of his mother and hir kinred of the house of the *Nagaies*: yet not safe (as I haue heard) from attempts of making away by practise of some that aspire to the succession, if this Emperour die
70 without any issue. The nurse that tasted before him of certaine meat (as I haue heard) died presently. That hee is naturall sonne to *Iuan Vasilowich*, the *Russe* people warrant it, by the Fathers qualitie that beginneth to appeare already in his tender yeares. He is delighted (they say) to see sheepe and other cattel killed, and to looke on
75 their throtes while they are bleeding (which commonly children are afraid to beholde) and to beate geese and hennes with a staffe till he see them lie dead. Besides these of the male kind, there is a widdow, that hath right in the succession, sister to the old Emperour, and aunt to this man, somtime wife to *Magnus* Duke of *Holst*,
80 brother to the king of *Denmarke*, by whom shee had one daughter. This woman since the death of hir husband hath bene allured again into *Russia*, by some that loue the succession better then hir selfe, which appeareth by the sequele. For hir selfe with hir daughter so soone as they were returned into *Russia* were thrust into a Nunnerie,
85 where hir daughter died this last yeare while I was in the countrie, of no naturall disease as was supposed. The mother remaineth still in the Nunnerie, where (as I haue heard) shee bewayleth hir selfe, and curseth the time when she returned into *Russia*, entised with the hope of marriage, and other fayre promises in the Emperours
90 name. Thus it standeth with the imperiall stock of *Russia* of the house of *Beala*, which is like to determine in those that now are, and to make a conuersion of the *Russe* estate. If it be into a gouernment of some better temper, and milder constitution, it will be happy for the poore people that are now oppressed with intollerable seruitude.

Of the manner of crowning or inauguration
of the Russe Emperours.
The 6. Chapter.

The solemnities vsed at the *Russe* Emperours coronation, are on this manner. In the great Church of *Precheste* (or our Lady) within the Emperours castle is erected a stage, whereon standeth a scrine that beareth vpon it the *Imperiall cappe* and robe of very riche stuffe. When the day of the Inauguration is come, there resorte thither, first the Patriarch with the Metropolitanes, Archbishops, Bishops, Abbots, and Priors, all richly clad in their Pontificalibus. Then enter the Deacons with the quier of singers. Who so soone as the Emperour setteth foote into the Church, beginne to sing: *Many yeares may liue noble Theodore Iuanowich &c:* Whereunto the Patriarch and Metropolite with the rest of the Cleargie, answere with a certaine Hymne, in forme of a prayer, singing it all together with a great noyse. The hymne beyng ended, the Patriarch with the Emperour mount vp the stage, where standeth a seat ready for the Emperour. Whereupon the Patriarch willeth him to sit downe, and then placing himselfe by him vpon an other seate prouided for that purpose, boweth downe his head towardes the ground, and sayeth this prayer: *Oh Lord God King of Kinges, Lord of Lordes, which by thy prophet Samuel diddest choose thy seruant Dauid, and annoint him for King ouer thy people Israell, heare now our prayers, and looke from thy sanctuarie vpon this thy seruant Theodore, whome thou hast chosen and exalted for King ouer these thy holy Nations, annoint him with the oyle of gladnesse, protect him by thy power, put vpon his head a crowne of golde and pretious stones, giue him length of dayes, place him in the seate of Iustice, strengthen his arme, make subiect vnto him all the barbarous nations. Lette thy feare bee in his whole heart, turne him from an euill faith, and from all errour, and shewe him the saluation of thy holy and vniuersall Church, that hee may iudge thy people with Iustice, and protect the children of the poore, and finally atteyne euerlasting lyfe.* This prayer hee speaketh with a lowe voyce, and then pro-

nounceth a lowde: *All prayse and power to God the Father, the Sonne, and the holy Ghost.* The prayer beyng ended, hee commaundeth certaine Abbots to reach the imperiall roabe and cappe: whiche is done verie decently, and with great solemnitie, the Patriarch withall
35 pronouncing alowde: *Peace be vnto all.* And so he beginneth an other praier to this effect: *Bowe your selues together with vs, and pray to him that reigneth ouer all. Preserue him (oh Lord) vnder thy holy protection, keepe him that hee may doo good and holy thinges, let iustice shine foorth in his dayes, that wee may liue quietly without strife and*
40 *malice.* This is pronounced somewhat softly by the Patriarch, whereto hee addeth againe alowd: *Thou art the King of the whole worlde, and the sauiour of our soules, to thee the Father, Sonne and Holy ghost, be all prayse for euer, and euer. Amen. Then putting on the roabe and the cappe, he blesseth the Emperour with the signe of the crosse:*
45 *saying withall, in the name of the Father, the Sonne, and the Holy ghost.* The like is done by the Metropolites, Archbishops, and Bishops: who all in their order come to the chaire, and one after an other blesse the Emperour with their two forefingers. Then is sayed by the Patriarch an other prayer, that beginneth: *O most holy virgin*
50 *mother of God, &c.* After which a Deacon pronounceth with an high lowde voice: *Many yeares to Noble Theodore, good, honourable, beloued of God, great Duke of Volodemer, of Mosko, Emperour, and Monarch of all Russia, &c.* Whereto the other Priestes and Deacons that stand somewhat farre of by the altar or table, answeare singing:
55 *Many yeares, many yeares, to the noble Theodore.* The same note is taken vp by the Priestes and Deacons, that are placed at the right and left side of the Church, and then all together, they chaunt and thunder out, singing: *Many yeares to the noble Theodore, good, honourable, beloued of God, great Duke of Volodemer, Mosko, Emperour*
60 *of all Russia, &c.* These solemnities beyng ended, first commeth the Patriarch with the Metropolites, Archbishops, and Bishops, then the Nobilitie, and the whole companie in their order, to doo homage to the Emperour, bending downe their heads and knocking them at his feete to the very ground.

192

Chapter 6: Coronation of the Emperor

The stile wherewith he is inuested
at his Coronation, runneth
after this manner.

Theodore Iuanowich, by the grace of God great Lord and Emperour 65
of all Russia, great Duke of Volodemer, Mosko, and Nouograd, King of
Cazan, King of Astracan, Lord of Plesko, and great duke of Smolensko,
of Twerria, Ioughoria, Permia, Vadska, Bulghoria, and others, Lord and
great duke of Nouograd of the Low countrie, of Chernigo, Rezan, Polotskoy,
Rostoue, Yaruslaueley, Bealozera, Liefland, Oudoria, Obdoria, and 70
Condensa, Commaunder of all Siberia, and of the North partes, and Lord
of many other Countries, &c.

This stile conteyneth in it all the Emperours Prouinces, and
setteth foorth his greatnesse. And therefore they haue a great delight
and pride in it, forcing not onely there owne people but also 75
straungers (that haue any matter to deliuer to the Emperour by
speach or writing) to repeate the whole forme from the beginning
to the end. Which breedeth much cauill, and sometimes quarrell
betwixt them and the *Tartar,* and Poland Ambassadours: who
refuse to call him *Czar,* that is Emperour, and to repeat the other 80
partes of his long stile. My selfe when I had audience of the Emperour,
thought good to salute him onely with thus much vz. *Emperour of*
all Russia, great Duke of Volodemer, Mosko and Nouograd, King of
Cazan, King of Astracan. The rest I omitted of purpose, because I
knew they gloried, to haue their stile appeare to bee of a larger 85
volume then the Queenes of England. But this was taken in so ill
part, that the Chauncellor (who then attended the Emperour, with
the rest of the Nobilitie) with a lowde chafing voice called still
vpon mee to say out the rest. Whereto I answered, that the Emperours stile was very long, and could not so well be remembered by 90
straungers, that I had repeated so much of it, as might shewe that
I gaue honour to the rest &c. But all would not serue till I commaunded my Interpreter to say it all out.

The State or forme of their Gouernment.
The 7. Chapter.

The manner of their gouernment is much after the Turkish fashion: which they seeme to imitate as neare as the countrie, and reach of their capacities in pollitique affayres will giue them leaue to doo.

The *Russe* gouernment tyrannicall. The State and forme of their gouernment is plaine tyrannical, as applying all to the behoofe of the Prince, and that after a most open and barbarous manner: as may appeare by the *Sophismata* or secretes of their gouernment afterwards set downe, aswell for the keeping of the Nobilitie and Commons in an vnder proportion, and far vneuen ballance in their seuerall degrees, as also in their impositions and exactions, wherein they exceede all iust measure without any regard of Nobilitie or people: farther then it giueth the Nobilitie a kinde of iniust and vnmeasured libertie, to commaund and exact vpon the commons and baser sort of people in all partes of the realme where so euer they come, specially in the place where their landes lye, or where they are appoynted by the Emperour to gouerne vnder him. Also to the Commons some small contentment, in that they passe ouer their landes by discent of inheritance to whither sonne they will: which commonly they doo after our *Gauill kinde*, and dispose of their goods by gifte or Testament without any controlment. Wherein notwithstanding both Nobilitie and Commons are but stoarers for the Prince, all running in the ende into the Emperours coffers: as may appeare by the practise of enriching his treasurie, and the manner of exactions set downe in the title of his customes, and reuenues.

Concerning the principall pointes and matters of State, wherein the Soueraintie consisteth (as the *making and annulling of publike Lawes, the making of Magistrates, power to make warre or league with any forraine State, to execute or to pardon life, with the right of appeale in all matters, both ciuill and criminall*) they doo so wholy and absolutely pertaine to the Emperour, and his Counsell vnder him, as that hee

194

may be saide to be both the Soueraine commaunder, and the executioner of all these. For as touching any Lawe or publique order of the Realme, it is euer determined of before any publique assemblie or Parliament bee summoned. Where besides his Councell, hee hath none other to consult with him of such matters as are concluded before hand, but onely a fewe Bishops, Abbots, and Friers: to no other end then to make aduantage of the peoples superstitions, euen against themselues, which thinke all to bee holy and iust, that passeth with consent of their Bishops and Cleargie men, whatsoeuer it be. For which purpose the Emperours are content to make much of the corrupt state of the Church, as now it is among them, and to nourish the same by extraordinarie fauours, and immunities to the Bishops seas, Abbeies and Frieries: as knowing superstition and false religion best to agree with a tyrannicall state, and to be a speciall meanes to vphold and mainteyne the same.

Secondly, as touching the publike offices and magistracies of the realme, there is none hereditarie, neither any so great nor so litle in that countrie, but the bestowing of it is done immediatly by the Emperour himself. Insomuch that the very Diacks or clearkes in euery head towne, are for the most part assigned by himselfe. Notwithstanding, the Emperour that now is (the better to entend his deuotions) referreth al such matters perteyning to the State, wholly to the ordering of his wiues brother, the Lord *Boris Federowich Godonoe.*

Thirdly, the like is to be said of the iurisdiction concerning matters iudiciall, specially such as concerne life and death. Wherein there is none that hath anie authoritie or publike iurisdiction that goeth by discent, or is held by charter, but all at the appoyntment and pleasure of the Emperour, and the same practised by the iudges with such awe and restraint, as that they dare not determine vpon anie speciall matter, but must referre the same wholly vp to the *Mosko* to the Emperours Councell. To shewe his Soueraintie ouer the liues of his subiects, the late Emperour *Iuan Vasilowich* in his walkes or progresses, if hee had misliked the face or person of any man whom hee met by the way, or that looked vpon him, would command his head to be strook off. Which was presently done, and the head cast before him.

Fourthly, for the soueraigne appeale, and giuing of pardons in criminall matters to such as are conuicted, it is wholly at the pleasure and grace of the Emperour. Wherin also the Empresse that nowe is, being a woman of great clemencie, and withall delighting to deale in publike affaires of the Realme, (the rather to supply the defect of her husband) doeth behaue her selfe after an absolute manner, giuing out pardon (specially on hir byrth day and other solemne times) in her owne name, by open proclamation, without any mention at all of the Emperour. Some there haue beene of late of the auncient Nobilitie, that haue held diuers prouinces by right of inheritaunce, with an absolute authoritie and iurisdiction ouer them, to order and determine all matters within their owne precinct without all appeale, or controlment of the Emperour. But this was all annulled and wrung cleane from them by *Iuan Vasilowich* father to this Emperour.

The manner of holding their Parliaments.
The 8. Chapter.

The States of Parlia-ment.

Their highest Court of publike consultation for matter of State, is called the *Zabore*, that is, the *Publike Assembly*. The states and degrees of persons that are present at their Parliaments, are these in order. 1. The Emperour himselfe. 2. Some of his Nobilitie about the number of twentie being all of his Councel. 3. Certain of the cleargy men, &c. about the same number. As for Burghers or other to represent the communaltie, they haue no place there: the people being of no better account with them then as seruants or bond slaues that are to obey, not to make lawes, nor to knowe any thing of publike matters before they are concluded.

The order of the summons or assembling.

The Court of Parliament (called *Zabore*) is held in this manner. The Emperour causeth to be summoned such of his Nobilitie as

196

himselfe thinketh meete, being (as was said) all of his Councell: together with the Patriarch, who calleth his Cleargie, to wit, the two Metropolites, the two Archbishops, with such Bishops, Abbots, [15] and Friers as are of best account and reputation among them. When they are all assembled at the Emperours court, the day is intimated when the session shal begin. Which commonly is vpon some friday, for the religion of that day.

When the day is come, the cleargie men assemble before at the [20] time and place appointed, which is called the *Stollie*. And when the Emperour commeth attended by his Nobilitie, they arise all, and meete him in an out roome, following their Patriarch, who blesseth the Emperor with his two forefingers, laying them on his forehead, and the sides of his face, and then kisseth him on the [25] right side of his brest. So they passe on into their Parliament house, where they sit in this order. The Emperor is enthronized on the one side of the chamber. In the next place not far from him at a smal square table (that giueth roome to twelue persons or thereabouts) sitteth the Patriarche with the Metropolites and Bishops, and [30] certeine of the principall Nobilitie of the Emperours Councel, together with two Diacks or Secretaries (called *Dumnoy dyakey*) that enact that which passeth. The rest place themselues on benches round about the roome, euery man in his ranck after his degree. Then is there propounded by one of the Secretaries (who represent- [35] eth the speaker) the cause of their assemblie, and the principall matters that they are to consider of. For to propound bils what euery man thinketh good for the publike benefite (as the maner is in England) the *Russe* Parliament alloweth no such custome, nor libertie to subiects. [40]

The poynts being opened, the Patriarch with his Cleargie men haue the prerogatiue to be first asked their vote, or opinion, what they thinke of the poyntes propounded by the Secretarie. Whereto they answere in order, according to their degrees, but al in one forme without any discourse: as hauing learned their lesson before, [45] that serueth their turnes at all Parliaments alike, whatsoeuer is

Their discourse at Parliament.

propounded. Commonly it is to this effect. *That the Emperour and his Councell are of great wisedome, and experience, touching the pollicies and publike affaires of the Realme, and farre better able to iudge what is*
50 *profitable for the common wealth, then they are, which attend vpon the seruice of God onlie, and matters of religion. And therefore it may please them to proceede. That insteede of their aduise, they will aide them with their prayers, as their dueties and vocations doe require, &c.* To this or like effect hauing made their answeres euery man in his course, vp
55 standeth some Abbot or Frier more bold then the rest (yet appointed before hand as a matter of forme) and desireth the Emperour it would please his Maiestie, to commaund to be deliuered vnto them what his Maiesties owne iudgement, and determinate pleasure is, as touching those matters propounded by his *Deiake.*

60 Whereto is replied by the saide Secretarie in the Emperours name. *That his Highnesse with those of his noble Councell, vpon good and sound aduise haue found the matters proposed to be verie good and necessarie for the common wealth of his Realme. Notwithstanding, forasmuch as they ar religious men, and know what is right, his Maiestie*
65 *requireth their godlie opinions, yea and their censures too, for the approuing or correcting of the saide propositions. And therefore desireth them againe to speake their mindes freely. And if they shal like to giue their consents, that then the matters may passe to a full conclusion.*

Hereunto when the Cleargie men haue giuen their consents
70 (which they vse to do without any great pausing) they take their leaues with blessing of the Emperour: who bringeth the Patriarch on his way so farre as the next roome, and so returneth to his seat, till all be made readie for his returne homeward. The actes that thus are passed by the *Zabore* or Parliament, the *Deiakeis* or Secre-
75 taries draw into a forme of proclamation, which they send abroad into euery Prouince, and head towne of the Realme, to be published there by the Dukes and *Diakeis*, or Secretaries of those places. The session of Parliament being fully ended, the Emperour inuiteth the Cleargie men to a solemne dinner. And so they depart euery man
80 to his home.

198

*Of the Nobilitie, and by what meanes it is
kept in an vnder proportion agreeable
to that State.*
The 9. Chapter.

The degrees of persons or estates of *Russia*, besides the soueraigne
State or Emperour himselfe, are these in their order. 1. The
Nobilitie which is of foure sortes. Whereof the chiefe for birth,
authoritie, and reuenue are called the *Vdelney Knazey*, that is, the
exempt or priuiledged Dukes. These held sometime a seuerall
iurisdiction, and absolute authoritie within their precincts, much
like vnto the States or Nobles of *Germany*. But afterwards (reseruing
their rights vpon composition) they yeelded themselues to this
house of *Beala*, when it began to waxe mightie, and to enlarge it
self by ouermatching their neighbours. Onely they were bound to
serue the Emperour in his warres with a certain number of horse.
But the late Emperour *Iuan Vasilowich* father to this prince, being
a man of high spirit, and subtill in his kind, meaning to reduce his
gouernment into a more strickt forme beganne by degrees to clip
of their greatnes, and to bring it downe to a lesser proportion: till
in the end he made them not onely his vassals, but his *Kolophey*,
that is, his very villains or bondslaues. For so they terme and
write themselues in anie publike instrument or priuate petition
which they make to the Emperour. So that now they holde their
authorities, landes, liues and all at the Emperours pleasure, as the
rest doe.

The meanes and practise whereby hee wrought this to effect
against those, and other of the Nobility (so well as I could note out
of the report of his doings) were these, and such like. First, he cast
priuate emulations among them about prerogatiue of their titles,
and dignities. Wherein hee vsed to set on the inferiours, to preferre
or equall themselues to those that were accounted to bee of the
nobler houses. Where he made his aduauntage of their malice and
contentions, the one against the other, by receiuing deuised matter,

30 and accusations of secrete practise and conspiracies to be intended against his person, and state. And so hauing singled out the greatest of them, and cut them off with the good liking of the rest, hee fell at last to open practise, by forcing of the other to yeeld their rights vnto him.

The faction of *Oppressini* and *Zempskey* deuised by the Emperour.

2. Hee deuided his subiectes into two partes or factions by a general schisme. The one part hee called the *Oppressini* or *Select men*. These were such of the Nobilitie and Gentrie as he tooke to his owne part, to protect and mainteyne them as his faithful subiects. The other hee called *Zemskey*, or the *Commons*. The *Zemskey* 40 conteyned the base and vulgar sort, with such Noblemen and Gentlemen as he meant to cut off, as suspected to mislike his gouernment, and to haue a meaning to practise against him. Wherein he prouided that the *Oppressini* for number and qualitie of valure, money, armour, &c: farre exceeded the other of the *Zemskey* side, 45 whom he put (as it were) from vnder his protection: so that if any of them were spoiled or killed by those of the *Oppressini* (which hee accounted of his owne part) there was no amendes to bee sought for by way of publike iustice, or by complaint to the Emperour.

50 The whole number of both partes was orderly registred and kept in a booke: so that euery man knewe who was a *Zemskey* man, and who of the *Oppressini*. And this libertie of the one part to spoyle and kill the other without anie helpe of Magistrate, or lawe (that continued seuen yeeres) enriched that side, and the 55 Emperours treasurie, and wrought that withall which hee intended by this practise, viz. to take out of the way such of the Nobilitie, as himselfe misliked: whereof were slayne within one weeke to the number of three hundred within the citie of *Mosko*. This tyrannicall practise of making a generall Schisme, and publike 60 diuision among the subiects of his whole Realme, proceeded (as should seeme) from an extreame doubt, and desperate feare, which hee had conceiued of most of his Nobilitie, and Gentlemen of his Realme, in his warres with the *Polonian* and *Chrim Tartar*. What

time hee grewe into a vehement suspition (conceiued of the ill
successe of his affayres) that they practised treason with the *Polonian*   65
and *Chrim.* Whereupon he executed some, and deuised this way to
be ridde of the rest.

   And this wicked pollicy and tyrannous practise (though now it
be ceassed) hath so troubled that countrey, and filled it so full of
grudge and mortall hatred euer since, that it wil not be quenched   70
(as it seemeth now) till it burne againe into a ciuill flame.

   3. Hauing thus pulled them and seased all their inheritaunce,
landes, priuiledges, &c. saue some verie small part which he left to
their name, hee gaue them other landes of the tenour of *Pomestnoy*
(as they call it) that are helde at the Emperours pleasure, lying farre   75
of in an other countrey, and so remoued them into other of his
Prouinces, where they might haue neyther fauour, nor authoritie,
not being natiue nor well knowen there. So that now these of the
chiefe Nobilitie (called *Vdelney Knazey*) are equalled with the rest:
saue that in the opinion and fauour of the people they are of more   80
account, and keepe stil the prerogatiue of their place in al their
publike meetings.

   Their practise to keepe downe these houses from rising againe
and recouering their dignities, are these, and such like. First, many
of their heires are kept vnmaried perforce, that the stocke may die   85
with them. Some are sent into *Siberia, Cazan* and *Astracan,* vnder
pretence of seruice, and there either made away, or else fast clapped
vp. Some are put into Abbeyes, and shire themselues Friers by
pretence of a vowe to be made voluntary, and of their owne accord,
but indeede forced vnto it by feare, vpon some pretensed crime   90
obiected against them. Where they are so garded by some of special
trust, and the Conuent it selfe (vpon whose head it standeth that
they make no escape) as that they haue no hope but to ende their
liues there. Of this kinde there are manie of verie great Nobilitie.
These and such like wayes begunne by the Emperour *Iuan Vasilowich*   95
are still practised by the *Godonoes,* who beyng aduaunced by the
mariage of the Empresse their kinsewoman, rule both the Emperour,

                                    201

and his Realme, (specially *Borris Federowich Godonoe*, brother to the Empresse) and endeauour by all meanes to cut of, or keepe downe all of the best and auncientest Nobilitie. Whereof diuers alreadie they haue taken away, whom they thought likeliest to make head against them and to hinder their purpose, as *Knez Andreas Guraken Bulgatkoue*, a man of great byrth and authoritie in the Countrey. The like they haue done with *Peeter Gollauni* (whom they put into a dungeon where he ended his life) with *Knez Vasilie Vrywich Golloohen*, with *Andrieu Iuanowich Suskoy* accounted among them for a man of a great wisedome. So this last yeere was killed in a Monasterie, (whither they had thrust him) on *Knez Iuan Petrowich Suskoy* a man of great valure, and seruice in that Countrey: who about fiue or sixe yeeres since, bare out the siege of the Citie *Vobsko* made by *Stepan Batore* King of *Polonia*, with a 100000. men, and repulsed him verie valiantly, with great honour to himselfe, and his countrey, and disgrace to the *Polonian*. Also *Micheta Romanowich* vnckle to the Emperour by the mothers side, was supposed to haue dyed of poyson, or some like practise.

Names of the greatest houses of the *Russe* Nobil- itie.

The names of these families of greatest Nobility are these in their order. The first is of *Knez Volodemer*, which resteth at this time in one daughter a widow, and without children (mentioned before) sometime wife to *Hartock Magnus* brother to the king of *Denmark*, now closed within a nunnery. The 2. *Knez Metheloskey* thrust into a Friery, and his only sonne kept from mariage, to decay the house. The 3. *Glimskoy*. But one left of his house, and he without children saue one daughter. The 4. *Suskoy*, wherof there are 4. brethren yong men, and vnmaried al. The 5. *Hubetskoy*. Of this house are 4. liuing. The 6. *Bulgaloy* now called *Guletchey* house, whereof are fiue liuing, but youths al. The 7. *Vorallinskoy*. Two left of that stock. The 8. *Odgoskey*. Two. The 9. *Tellerskoy*. One. The 10. *Taytoue*, three. These are the names of the chiefe families called *Vdelney Knazey*: that in effect haue lost all now, saue the very name it selfe, and fauour of the people, which is like one day to restore them againe, if any be left.

Chapter 9: The Nobility

The 2. degree of Nobility is of the *Boiarens*. These are such as
the Emperour honoureth (besides their nobility) with the title of
counsellers. The reuenue of these 2. sorts of their Nobles that riseth
out of their lands assigned them by the Emperour, and held at his
pleasure (for of their owne inheritaunce there is little left them, as
was said before) is about a thousand marks a yeere: besides pension
which they receiue of the Emperour for their seruice in his warres,
to the summe of 700. rubbels a yeere, and none aboue that summe.

But in this number the lorde *Borris Federowich Godenoe* is not to
be reckoned, that is like a *Transendent*, and in no such predicament
with the rest, being the Emperors brother in law, his protectour
for direction, for commaund and authority Emperour of *Russia*.
His yerely reuenue in land and pension, amounteth to the summe of
93700. rubbels and more, as appeareth by the particulars. He hath
of inheritance (which himselfe hath augmented in *Vasma Dorogobose*
sixe thousand rubbels a yeere. For his office of *Connick*, or Master
of the Horse 1200. rubbels, or markes, raised out of the *Conaslue
Sloboday*, or the liberties pertayning to that Office, which are
certeyne Landes and Townes neere about the *Mosko*. Besides, all
the meddowe and pasture grounde on both sides the banke of the
riuer *Mosko*, thirtie verst vp the streame, and fourtie verst down-
wards. For his pension of the Emperour (besides the other for his
office) 15000. rubbels. Out of the Prouince or Shire of *Vagha*, there
is giuen him for a peculiar exempted out of the *Chetfird* of *Posolskoy*
32000. rubbels, besides a rent of furres. Out of *Rezan* and *Seuer*,
(an other peculiar) 30000. rubbels. Out of *Otfer* and *Turiock* an
other exempt place 8000. rubbels. For rent of Bathstoaues and
Bathing houses without the walles of *Mosko* 1500. rubbels. Besides
his pomest, or lands which hee holdeth at the Emperours pleasure,
which farre exceedeth the proportion of land alloted to the rest
of the Nobility.

One other there is of the house of *Glinskoy* that dispendeth in
land and pension about 40000. rubbels yeerely. Which hee is
suffered to enioy because hee hath married *Borris* his wiues sister,

being himselfe verie simple, and almost a naturall. The ordering of him and his landes are committed to *Borris*.

In the third rank are the *Voyauodey* or such Nobles as are, or haue bin generals in the Emperours warres. Which deliuer the honour of their title to their posterities also: who take their place aboue the other Dukes and Nobles that are not of the two former sorts, vz. of the *Vdelney knazey*, nor of the *Boiarens*.

These three degrees of their Nobilitie (to wit) the *Vdelney knazey*, the *Boiarens*, and the *Voiauodey* haue the addition of *wich*, put vnto their sirname as *Borris Federowich*, &c: which is a note of honour that the rest may not vsurpe. And in case it be not added in the naming of them, they may sue the *Bestchest* or penaltie of dishonour vpon them, that otherwise shall terme them.

The fourth and lowest degree of Nobilitie with them, is of such as beare the name of *Knazey* or Dukes, but come of the yonger brothers of those chiefe houses, through many discents, and haue no inheritance of their owne, saue the bare name or title of Duke onely. For their order is to deliuer their names and titles of their dignities ouer to all their children alike, what soeuer else they leaue them. So that the sonnes of a *Voiauodey* or Generall in the field, are called *Voiauodey* though they neuer saw the field, and the sons of a *Knez* or Duke are called *Knazey*, though they haue not one groat of inheritance or liuelyhood to mainteine themselues withall. Of this sort there are so many that the plentie maketh them cheap: so that you shall see Dukes glad to serue a meane man for fiue or six rubbels or marks a yeare, and yet they will stand highly vpon their *Bestchest* or reputation of their Honours. And these are their seuerall degrees of Nobilitie.

The second degree of persons is of their *Sina Boiarskey*, or the sonnes of Gentlemen: which all are preferred, and hold that name by their seruice in the Emperours warres, being souldiers by their very stocke and birth. To which order are referred their Dyacks or Secretaries, that serue the Emperour in euery head towne, being ioyned in Commission with the Dukes of that place.

The last are their Commons, whom they call *Mousicks*. In which number they reckon their Marchants, and their common artificers. The very lowest and basest sort of this kind (which are held in no degree) are their countrie people whom they call *Christianeis*. Of the *Sina boiarskey* (which are all souldiers) we are to see in the description of their forces, and military prouisions. Concerning their *Mousicks*, what their condition and behauiour is, in the title or chapter *Of the common people*.

205

Of the gouernment of their Prouinces and Shires.
The 10. Chapter.

The whole countrie of *Russia* (as was said before) is diuided into foure parts, which they call *Chetfirds*, or *Tetrarchies*. Euery *Chetfird* conteineth diuers shires, and is annexed to a seuerall office, whereof it takes the name. The first *Chetfird* or *Tetrarchie* beareth the name of *Pososkoy Chetfird*, or the *Iurisdiction of the office of Ambassages*, and at this time is vnder the chiefe Secretarie and officer of the Ambassages called *Andreas Shalcaloue*. The standing fee or stipend that he receiueth yearely of the Emperour for this seruice, is 100. rubbels or markes.

The second is called the *Roseradney Chetfird*, because it is proper to the *Roserade* or high Constable. At this time it perteineth by vertue of office to *Basilie Shalcaloue*, brother to the Chancellor, but it is executed by one *Zapon Abramoue*. His pension is an hundred rubbels yearely.

10

The third is the *Chetfird* of *Pomestnoy*, as perteining to that office. This keepeth a Register of all lands giuen by the Emperour for seruice to his Noblemen, Gentlemen, and others, giueth out and taketh in all assurances for them. The officer at this time is called *Eleazar Wellusgine*. His stipend is 500. rubbels a yeare.

15

The fourth is called *Cassanskoy dworets*, as being appropriat to the office that hath the iurisdiction of the kingdomes of *Cazan* and

20

Astracan, with the other townes lying vpon the *Volgha*, now ordered by one *Druzhine Penteleoue*, a man of very speciall account among them, for his wisdome, and promptnes in matters of pollicie. His pension is 150. rubbels a yeare.

From these *Chetfirds* or *Tetrarchies* is exempted the Emperors inheritance or *Vochin* (as they cal it) for that it perteined from auncient time to the house of *Beala*, which is the sirname of the imperiall bloud. This standeth of 36. townes with their bounds or territories. Besides diuers peculiar iurisdictions, which ar likewise deducted out of those *Chetfirds*, as the Shire of *Vagha* (belonging to the Lord *Borrise Federowich Godonoe*) and such like.

These are the chiefe gouernours or officers of the Prouinces, not resident at their charge abroad, but attending the Emperour whether soeuer he goeth, and carriyng their offices about with them, which for the most part they hold at *Mosko*, as the Emperours chiefe seat.

The parts and practise of these foure offices, is to receiue all complaints and actions what soeuer, that are brought out of their seuerall *Chetfirds*, and quarters, and to informe them to the Emperours counsell. Likewise to send direction again to those that are vnder them in their said Prouinces, for all matters giuen in charge by the Emperour and his Counsell, to be done or put in execution within their precincts.

For the ordering of euery particular Prouince of these foure *Chetfirds*, there is appointed one of these Dukes, which were reckoned before in the lowest degree of their Nobilitie, which are resident in the head townes of the said Prouinces. Whereof euery one hath ioyned with him in Commission a Dyack or Secretarie to assist him, or rather to direct him. For in the executing of their commission, the Dyack doth all.

The parts of their Commission are these in effect. First to heare and determine in all ciuil matters within their precinct. To which purpose they haue vnder them certeine officers, as *Gubnoy Starets* or Coroners, who besides the triall of selfe murders, are to attach fellons: and the *Soudia* or vnder Iustices, who themselues also may

The Commission of the Dukes or Presidents of Shires.

heare and determine in all matters of the same nature, among the countrie people of their owne wardes or bayliwicks: but so that in case either partie dissent, they may appeale, and goe farther to the Duke and Dyack that reside within the head towne. From whom also they may remoue the matter to the higher court at *Mosko* of the Emperours Counsell, where lie all appeales. They haue vnder them also *Sotskoy Starets*, that is Aldermen, or Baliues of the hundreds.

Secondly in all criminall matters, as theft, murder, treason, &c. they haue authoritie to apprehend, to examine and to emprison the malefactor, and so hauing receiued perfect euidence and information of the cause, they are to send it ready drawen and orderly digested vp to the *Mosko*, to the officer of the *Chetfird*, whereunto that Prouince is annexed: by whom it is referred and propounded to the Emperours Counsell. But to determine in any matter criminall, or to doo execution vpon the partie offending, is more then their commission will allow them to doo.

Thirdly, if there be any publike seruice to be done within that Prouince, (as the publishing of any Law, or common order, by way of proclamation, collecting of taxes and impositions for the Emperour, moistering of Souldiers, and sending them forth at the day and to the place assigned by the Emperour or his Counsell) all these and such like perteyne to their charge.

These Dukes and Dyacks are appointed to their place by the Emperour himselfe, and are chaunged ordinarily at euery yeares end, except vpon some special liking or suit, the time be proroged for a yeare or two more. They are men of themselues of no credite, nor fauour with the people, where they gouerne, being neither borne, nor brought vp among them, nor yet hauing inheritance of their owne there, or els where. Onely of the Emperour they haue for that seruice an 100. markes a yeare, he that hath most, some fiftie, some but thirtie. Which maketh them more suspected and odious to the people, because being so bare, and comming fresh and hungrie vpon them lightly euery yeare, they rack and spoile them without all regard of iustice, or conscience. Which is easily

90 tollerated by the chiefe officers of the *Chetfirds*, to the end they may rob them againe and haue a better bootie when they call them to account: which commonly they doo at the end of their seruice, making an aduantage of their iniustice and oppression ouer the poore people. There are few of them but they come to the *Pudkey*

95 or whip when their time is ended, which themselues for the most parte doo make account of. And therefore they furnish themselues with all the spoile they can for the time of their gouernment, that they may haue for both turnes, aswel for the Emperour, and Lord of the *Chetfird*, as to reserue some good part for themselues.

100 They that are appointed to gouerne abroad, are men of this qualitie: saue that in the foure border townes that are of greatest importance, are set men of more speciall valure and trust two in euery towne. Wherof one is euer of the Emperours priuie counsell. These foure border townes are *Smolensko*, *Vobsko*, *Nouogrod*, and

105 *Cazan*, whereof three lie towards the *Polonian* and *Sweden*, one bordereth far of vpon the *Chrim Tartar*. These haue larger commission then the other Dukes of the Prouinces that I spake of before, and may doo execution in criminall matters. Which is thought behoofull for the Commonwelth: for incident occasions that may

110 happen vpon the borders, that are far of, and may not stay for direction, about euery occurrent and particular matter from the Emperour and his Counsell. They are chaunged euery yeare (except as before) and haue for their stipend 700. rubbels a yeare hee that hath most: some haue but 400. Many of these places that are of

115 greatest importance, and almost the whole countrie is managed at this time, by the *Godonoes* and their clients.

The citie of *Mosko* (that is the Emperours seat) is gouerned altogether by the Emperours Counsell. All matters there both ciuill and criminall, are heard and determined in the seuerall courtes, held

120 by some of the said Counsell, that reside there all the yeare long.

The Gouern-
ment of
Mosko.
Onely for their ordinary matters (as buildings, reparations, keeping of their streates decent and cleane, collections, leuying of taxes, impositions and such like) are appointed two Gentlemen, and

208

two Dyacks or Secretaries, who hold a court together for the ordering of such matters. This is called the *Zempskey* house. If any townes man suspect his seruant of theft or like matter, hither he may bring him to haue him examined vpon the *Pudkey*, or other torture. Besides these two Gentlemen, and Secretaries that order the whole Citie, there are *Starusts* or Aldermen for euerie seuerall companie. The Alderman hath his *Sotskey* or Constable, and the Constable hath certeine *Decetskeis* or Decurions vnder him, which haue the ouersight of ten housholds a peece, whereby euerie disorder is sooner spide, and the common seruice hath the quicker dispach. The whole number of Citizens poore and rich are reduced into companies. The chiefe officers (as the Dyacks and Gentlemen) are appointed by the Emperour himselfe, the *Starust* by the Gentlemen and Dyacks, the *Sotskoy* by the *Starust* or Alderman, and the *Decetskoies* by the Constables.

This manner of gouernment of their Prouinces and townes, if it were aswell set for the giuing of iustice indifferently to al sorts, as it is to preuent innouations, by keeping of the Nobilitie within order, and the commons in subiection, it might seeme in that kinde to bee no bad, nor vnpollitique way, for the conteyning of so large a Commonwealth, of that breadth and length as is the kingdome of *Russia*. But the oppression and slauerie is so open, and so great, that a man would maruell how the Nobilitie and people shoulde suffer themselues to bee brought vnder it, while they had any means to auoid and repulse it: or being so strengthned as it is at this present, how the Emperours themselues can be content to practise the same, with so open iniustice and oppression of their subiects, being themselues of a Christian profession.

By this it appeareth how harde a matter it were to alter the state of the *Russe* gouernment, as now it standeth. First, because they haue none of the Nobilitie able to make head. As for the Lords of the foure *Chetfirds* or *Tetrarchies* they are men of no Nobilitie, but Dyacks aduanced by the Emperour, depending on his fauour, and attending onely about his owne person. And for the Dukes that are

An harde matter to alter the State of Russia.

209

appointed to gouern vnder them, they are but men of a titular
dignitie (as was saied before) of no power, authoritie, nor credit,
160 saue that which they haue out of the office, for the time they enioy
it. Which doth purchase them no fauour, but rather hatred of the
people, for asmuch as they see that they are set ouer them, not so
much for any care to doo them right and iustice, as to keepe them
vnder in a miserable subiection, and to take the fliece from them,
165 not once in the yeare (as the owner from his sheepe) but to poule
and clip them all the yeare long. Besides the authority and rule
which they beare, is rent and diuided into many small pieces, being
diuers of them in euery great Shire, limited besides with a very
short time: which giueth them no scope to make any strength, nor
170 to contriue such an enterprise, if happily they intended any matter
of innouation. As for the common people (as may better appeare
in the description of their state and qualitie afterwardes set downe)
besides their want of armour and practise of warre (which they are
kept from of purpose) they are robbed continually both of their
175 harts and mony, (besides other means) somtimes by pretence of
some seruice to be done for the common defence, sometimes without
any shewe at all of any necessitie of Common-wealth or Prince. So
that there is no meanes either for Nobilitie, or people to attempt
any innouation, so long as the militarie forces of the Emperour
180 (which are the number of 80000. at the least in continuall pay) hold
themselues fast and sure vnto him, and to the present state. Which
needes they must doo beyng of the qualitie of Souldiours, and
enioying withal that free libertie of wronging and spoiling of the
commons at their pleasure, which is permitted them of purpose, to
185 make them haue a liking of the present state. As for the agreement
of the Souldiers and commons, it is a thing not to be feared, beyng
of so opposite and contrarie practise much one to the other. This
desperate state of things at home, maketh the people for the most
part to wishe for some forreine inuasion, which they suppose to bee
190 the onely meanes, to rid them of the heauy yoke of this tyrannous
gouernment.

210

Of the Emperours Counsell.
The 11. Chapter.

The Emperours of *Russia* giue the name of counsellour to diuers of their chiefe Nobilitie, rather for honors sake, then for any vse they make of them about their matters of state. These are called *Boiarens* without any addition, and may bee called Counsellors at large. For they are seldome or neuer called to any publique consultation. They which are of his speciall and priuie Counsell indeed (whom hee vseth daily and ordinarily for all publique matters perteining to the State) haue the addition of *Dumnoy*, and are named *Dumnoy boiaren*, or Lords of the Counsell, their office or sitting *Boarstua dumna.*

Their names at this present are these in their order. First, *Knez Feoder Iuanowich Methisloskey.* 2. *Knez Iuan Michailowich Glinskoy.* 3. *Knez Vasilie Iuanowich Suskoy Scopin.* (These three are accounted to bee of greater birth then wisedome taken in (as may seeme) for that ende, rather to furnish the place with their honours and presence, then with their aduise or counsell). 4. *Knez Vasilie Iuanowich Suskoy,* thought to be more wise then the other of his name. 5. *Knez Feoder Michailowich.* 6. *Knez Micheta Romanowich Trowbetskoy.* 7. *Knez Timophey Romanowich Trowbetskoy.* 8. *Knez Andriew Gregoriwich Curakine.* 9. *Knez Demetrie Iuanowich Forestine.* 10. *Knez Feoder Iuanowich Forestine.* 11. *Bodan Iuanowich Sabaroue.* 12. *Knez Iuan Vasilowich.* 13. *Knez Feoder Demetriwich Shestinoue.* 14. *Knez Feoder Michailowich Troyconioue.* 15. *Iuan Buterlyney.* 16. *Demetrie Iuanowich Godonoe.* 17. *Borrise Federowich Godonoe,* brother to the Empresse. 18. *Stephan Vasilowich Godonoe.* 19. *Gregorie Vasilowich Godonoe.* 20. *Iuan Vasilowich Godonoe.* 21. *Feoder Sheremitoue.* 22. *Andriew Petrowich Cleshenina.* 23. *Ignatie Petrowich Tatisloue.* 24. *Romain Michailowich Peua.* 25. *Demenshoy Iuanowich Cheremissen.* 26. *Romain Vasilowich Alferioue.* 27. *Andriew Shalcaloue.* 28. *Vasilie Shalcaloue.* 29. *Eleazar Wellusgin.* 30. *Drezheen Penteleoue.* 31. *Zapon Abramoue.*

211

The foure last of these are called *Dumnoy deiakey* or Lord Secretaries. These are all of the Emperours priuie counsell: though but fewe of them are called to any consultation, for that all matters are aduised and determined vpon by *Borris Federowich Godonoe* brother to the Empresse, with some fiue or sixe more whom it pleaseth him to call. If they come, they are rather to heare, then to giue counsel, and doo so demeane themselues. The matters occurrent which are of state done within the Realme, are infourmed them at their sittings by the Lordes of the foure *Chetfirds*, or *Tetrarchies*. Whereof mention is made in the Chapter concerning the *Gouernment of their Prouinces*. Who bring in all such letters as they receyue from the Dukes, Dyacks, Captaines, and other officers of the Cities, and Castels, perteyning to their seuerall quarter or *Chetfird*, with other aduertisements, and informe the Counsell of them.

The like is done by the chiefe officer of euery seuerall office of Record: who may come into the Counsell chamber, and informe them, as occasion incident to his office doth require. Besides matters of State, they consider of many priuate causes, informed by way of supplication in very great numbers. Whereof some they intertaine and determine, as the cause or meanes can procure fauour. Some they send to the offices whereto they perteyne by common course of Lawe. Their ordinarie dayes for their sitting, are mondaies, wensdaies, and fridayes. Their time of meeting is commonly seuen a clock in the morning. If there be any extraordinary occasion that requireth consultation on some other day, they haue warning by the Clarke of the counsell called *Dorofey Bushew*, who receiueth order from the *Roserad* or high Constable of the realme, to call them together at the time appointed.

Of the Emperours customes and
other Reuenues.
The 12. Chapter.

For the receyuing of customes, and other rentes belonging to the Crowne, there are appoynted diuers vnder officers, which deliuer ouer the same into the head treasurie. The first is the office of *Dwoertsoua* or Steward of the housholde. The second is the office of the *Chetfirds*: which I comprehend vnder one, though it bee diuided into foure seuerall partes, as was sayd before. The third is called *Bulsha prechode*, or the great Income.

As touching the first, which is the office of the Steward, it receyueth all the rents of the Emperours inheritance, or Crowne lande, whiche they call *Vochin*. The *Vochin* or Crowne lande conteyneth in it 36. townes with the territories or hundreds belonging vnto them. Whereof the chiefe that yeeld the greatest rents are these: *Alexandrisca, Corelska, Otfer, Slobodey, Danielska, Moisalskoy, Chara, Sametska, Strararouse, Bransoue*, &c. The inhabitants or tenants of these and the other townes, pay some rent money, some other rent dueties (called *Obrokey*) as certeine *Chetfirds*, or measures of graine, wheate, rye, barley, oates, &c. or of other victuall, as Oxen, Sheepe, Swannes, Geese, Hares, Hennes, wild fowle, Fish, Hay, Wood, Honie, &c. Some are bound to sowe for the Emperours prouision certaine Akers of ground, and to make the corne ready for his vse: hauing for it an allowance of certaine akers of ground for their owne proper vse.

This prouision for the houshold, specially of graine serued in by the Tenants, is a great deale more then is spent in his house, or in other allowance serued out in liuerie, or for the Emperours honour, called *Schalouaney*: for which vse there is bestowed very much both in graine, and other victuall. This surplus of prouision is sold by the Steward to the best hand, and runneth into the Emperours treasurie.

In the time of *Iuan Vasilowich*, father to this Emperour (who kept a more Princely and bountiful house then the Emperour now doth) this ouerplus of graine, and other incomes into the Stewardes office, yeelded to his treasurie not past 60. thousand rubbels yeerely, but riseth now by good husbanding of the Steward *Gregory Vasilowich Godonoe*, to 230. thousand rubbels a yere. And this by the meanes of the Empresse, and her kinred, specially *Borris Federowich Godonoe*, that account it al their owne that runneth into the Emperors treasurie. Much of this surplusage that riseth out of the rent prouision, is emploied to the paiment of the wages of his houshold officers, which are very many attending at home, and purueying abroad.

The second office of receipt called the *Chetfirds*, (being deuided into foure seuerall partes, as before was sayde) hath foure head officers: which besides the ordering and gouernment of the shires conteyned within their seuerall *Chetfirds*, haue this also as a part of their office, to receiue the *Tagla* and *Podat* belonging to the Emperour, that riseth out of the foure *Chetfirds* or Quarters. The *Tagla* is a yeerely rent or imposition raysed vpon euery *Wite* or measure of graine, that groweth within the land, gathered by sworne men, and brought into the office. The *Wite* conteyneth sixtie *Chetfirds*. Euery *Chetfird* is three bushelles English, or little lesse. The *Podat* is an ordinarie rent of money imposed vpon euerie soake, or Hundred within the whole Realme.

This *Tagla* and *Podat* bring in yeerely to the Offices of the *Chetfirdes* a greate summe of money: as may appeare by the particulars heere set downe. The towne and Prouince of *Vobsko* pay yeerely for *Tagla* and *Podat* about 18000. rubbels. *Nouogrod* 35000. rubbels. *Torshocke* and *Otfer* 8000. rubbels. *Razan* 30000. rubbels. *Morum* 12000. rubbels. *Colmigroe* and *Duyna* 8000. rubbels. *Vologda* 12000. rubbels. *Cazan* 18000. rubbels. *Vstiug* 30000. rubbels. *Rostoue* 50000. The citie of *Mosko* 40000. rubbels. *Sibierskoy* 20000. rubbels. *Castrome* 12000. rubbels. The totall amounteth to 400000. rubbels, or marks a yeere, which is brought in yeerely the first day of September, that is reckoned by them the first day of the yeere.

Chapter 12: The Emperor's Revenue

The thirde (that is called the *Bulsha Prechod*, or great Income) receyueth all the customes that are gathered out of all the principall townes and Cities within the whole Realme. Besides the fees and other dueties which rise out of diuers smaller Offices, which are all brought into this office of *Bulsha Prechod*. The townes of moste trade that doe yeelde greatest custome, are these heere sette downe. *Mosko, Smolensko, Vobsko, Nouogrod Velica, Strararouse, Torshocke, Otfer, Yaruslaue, Castrome, Nesua Nouogrod, Cazan, Vologda.* This custome out of the great townes is therefore more certaine, and easie to be reckoned, because it is set and rated precisely what they shal pay for the custome of the yeere. Which needes must bee paide into the saide office, though they receiue not so much. If it fal out to be more, it runneth al into the Emperours aduantage.

The custome at *Mosko* for euerie yeere, is 12000. rubbels. The custome of *Smolensko,* 8000. rubbels. *Vobsko* 12000. rubbels. *Nouogrod velica* 6000. rubbels. *Stararouse* by salt and other commodities 18000. rubbels. *Torshock* 800. rubbels. *Otfer* 700. rubbels. *Yaruslaue* 1200 rubbels. *Castrome* 1800. rubbels. *Nesna Nouogrod* 7000. rubbels. *Cazan* 11000. rubbels. *Vologda* 2000. rubbels. The custome of the rest that are townes of trade is sometimes more, sometimes lesse, as their traffike, and dealings with commodities too and fro, falleth out for the yeere.

This may bee saide for certaine, that the three tables of receipts belonging to this office of *Bulsha Prechod,* when they receiue lest, account for thus much, vz. The first table 160000. rubbels. The second table 90000. rubbels. The third 70000. rubbels. So that there commeth into the office of *Bulsha Prechod,* at the least reckoning (as appeareth by their bookes of customs) out of these and other townes, and maketh the summe of 340000. rubbels a yeere. Besides this custome out of the townes of trade, there is receiued by this office of *Bulsha Prechod,* the yeerely rent of the common Bathstoaues, and Cabacks or drinking houses, which pertein to the Emperour. Which (though it be vncertaine for the iust summe, yet because it is certaine and an ordinary matter, that the *Russe* wil bath himselfe

70

75

The office of *Bulcha Prechod* or great income.

The Emperours custome.

85

The whole receipt of the *Bulsha Prechod* or great income.

95

aswel within as without) yeeldeth a large rent to the Emperours treasurie.

There is besides, a certeine mulct or penaltie that groweth to the Emperour out of euery iudgement, or sentence that passeth in any of his courts of Record in all ciuill matters. This penaltie, or mulct is 20. *Dingoes* or pence vpon euery rubble or marke, and so ten in the hundred. Which is paide by the partie that is conuict by lawe. Hee hath besides for euery name conteyned in the writs that passe out of these courts, fiue *Alteens*. An *Alteen* is fiue pence sterling, or there abouts. This is made good out of the office, whence the writ is taken foorth. Thence it goeth to the office that keepeth the lesser seale, where it payeth as much more to the Emperours vse. This riseth commonly to 3000. rubbels a yeere, or thereabouts. Farther also out of the office of *Roisbonia*, where all fellonies are tried, is receiued for the Emperour the halfe part of fellons goodes, the other halfe goeth the one part to the informer, the other to the officers.

All this is brought into the office of *Bulsha Prechod*, or great income. Besides the ouerplus or remainder that is saued out of the land rents, allotted to diuers other offices: as namely to the office called *Roserade*, which hath landes and rentes assigned vnto it to pay the yeerely salaries of the souldiers, or horsemen, that are kept still in pay. Which in time of peace when they rest at home not employed in anie seruice, is commonly cut off and payde them by halfes, sometimes not the halfe: so that the remainder out of the *Roserade* Office that is layde into the Emperours treasurie, commeth for the most part euerie yeere to 250000. rubbels.

In like sort (though not so much) is brought in the surplus out of the *Strelletskoy* offices which hath proper lands for the payment of the *Strelsey* men or gunners, aswell those at *Mosko*, that are of the Emperors gard (12000. in ordinary pay) as on the borders, and other garrison townes and castels. Likewise out of the office of *Prechase*, *Shisiuoy Nemshoy* which hath set allowance of landes to mainteine the forreyne mercenarie souldiers, as *Poles*, *Sweadens*,

Doutches, Scots, &c. So out of the office of *Pusharskoy,* (which hath lands and rents allowed for the prouision of *munition, great Ordinance, powder, Shot, Salpeeter, Brimstone, Ledde,* and such like) there is left $\quad$ 135 somewhat at the yeres ende, that runneth into the treasurie. All these bring into the office of *Bulsha Prechod* that which remaineth in their hand at the yeeres end. Whence it is deliuered into the Emperours treasurie. So that the whole summe that groweth to this office of *Bulsha Prechod,* or the great income (as appeareth by the $\quad$ 140 bookes of the said office) amounteth to 800000. rubbels a yeere, or thereabouts.

$\quad$ All these offices, to wit, the office of the Steward, the foure *Chetfirds,* and the *Bulsha Prechod* deliuer in their receiptes to the head treasurie, that lyeth within the Emperours house or castle at the *Mosko.* Where lye all his moneyes, iewels, crownes, scepters, plate, and such like, the chests, hutches, and bagges beyng signed by the Emperours themselues with their owne seale. Though at this time the Lord *Borris Federowich Godonoe* his seale and ouersight supplieth for the Emperor, as in al other things. The vnder officer at this time $\quad$ 150 is one *Stepan Vasilowich Godonoe,* Coosin germane to the sayde *Borris,* who hath two Clearkes allowed to serue vnder him in the office.

The summe that groweth to the Emperoures treasurie in money onely, for euerie yeere.

1 *Out of the Stewards office aboue the expense of his house* 230000. *rubbels.*
2 *Out of the foure Chetfirds for soake and head money* 400000. *rubbels.*
3 *Out of the* Bulsha Precod *Office, or great incoome, for custome and other rents.* 800000 *rubbels.*

Summe 1430000 rubbles cleere, besides all charges for his house, and ordinary saleries of his souldiers otherwise discharged.

The Emperours treasure house within his castle of *Mosko.*

The summe of the Emperours rent money.

160

165

217

But besides this reuenue that is paid all in money into the Emperours treasurie he receiueth yeerely in furres, and other dueties to a great value out of *Siberia, Pechora, Permia,* and other places, which are solde or bartred away for other forreine commodities to the *Turkish, Persian, Armenian, Georgian* and *Bougharian* Marchants that trade within his countries, besides others of Christendome. What it maketh in the whole (though the value can not be set downe precisely, as being a thing casual as the commodity may be got) it may be gessed by that which was gathered the last yeere out of *Siberia* for the Emperours custome, vz. 466. timber of Sables, fiue timber of Martrones, 180. blacke Foxes, besides other commodities.

To these may bee added their seazures, and confiscations vpon such as are in displeasure, which riseth to a great summe. Besides other their extraordinary impositions, and exactions done vpon their officers, Monasteries, &c. not for any apparant necessity or vse of the Prince, or common wealth, but of will and custome: yet with some pretence of a *Scythian,* that is, grosse and barbarous pollicie (as may appeare) by these fewe *Sophismata,* or counterfeit pollicies, put in practise by the Emperours of *Russia,* all tending to this end to robbe their people, and to inrich their treasurie. To this purpose this byword was vsed by the late Emperour *Iuan Vasilowich: That his people were like to his beard. The oftner shauen, the thicker it would grow. Or like sheepe, that must needes be shorne once a yeere at the least: to keepe them from being ouerladen with their wooll.*

Meanes vsed to draw the wealth
of the land into the Emperours
Treasurie.

I

To preuent no extortions, exactions, or briberies whatsoeuer, done vpon the commons by their Dukes, Diacks, or other officers in their Prouinces: but to suffer them to go on till their time bee

expired, and to sucke themselues ful. Then to cal them to the
Praueush (or whippe) for their behauiour, and to beat out of them   195
all, or the most part of the bootie, (as the honie from the Bee) which
they haue wrung from the commons, and to turne it into the
Emperours treasurie, but neuer any thing backe againe to the right
owners, how great or euident soeuer the iniurie be. To this end the
needy Dukes, and Diacks, that are sent into their prouinces, serue   200
the turne very well, being chaunged so often (to wit) once a yeere:
where in respect of their owne, and the qualitie of the people (as
before was said) they might be continued for some longer time,
without all feare of inouation. For comming still fresh vpon the
commons, they sucke more egerly: like *Tiberius* the Emperours   205
flies, that came newe still vpon an olde sore. To whome hee was
wont to compare his *Prætors*, and other prouinciall officers.

2

To make of these officers (that haue robbed their people) sometimes a publike example, if any be more notorious then the rest:
that the Emperour may seem to mislike the oppressions done to his   210
people and transferre the fault to his ill officers.

As among diuers other, was done by the late Emperour *Iuan
Vasilowich* to a Diack in one of his Prouinces: that (besides many
other extortions, and briberies) had taken a goose ready drest full
of money. The man was brought to the market place in *Mosko*.   215
The Emperour himselfe present made an Oration. These good
people are they that would eate you vp like bread, &c. Then asked
hee his *Polachies* or executioners, who could cut vp a goose, and
commaunded one of them first to cut off his legges about the
middes of the shinne, then his armes aboue his elbowes (asking him   220
still if goose fleshe were good meate) in the ende to choppe off his
head: that he might haue the right fashion of a goose readie dressed.
This might seeme to haue beene a tollerable piece of iustice (as
iustice goeth in *Russia*) except his subtill end to couer his owne
oppressions.   225

219

3

To make an open shew of want, when anie great taxe, or imposition is towards. As was done by this Emperour *Theodore Iuanowich*, by the aduise of some about him at the beginning of his reigne: when being left very rich (as was thought) by his father, he sold most of his plate, and stamped some into coyne: that hee might seeme to want money. Whereupon presently out came a taxation.

4

To suffer their subiects to giue freely to the Monasteries (which for their superstition very many doe, specially in their last wils) and to lay vp their money and substance in them, to keepe it more safe. Which all is permitted them without any restraint, or prouiso, as was and is in some countries of christendome. Whereby their Monasteries grow to exceeding great wealth. This they do to haue the money of the Realme better stored together, and more ready for their hand, when they list to take it. Which manie times is done without anie noyse: the Fryers beeyng content rather to part from somewhat (as the encrease groweth) then to loose all at once. Which they were made to doubt of in the other Emperours dayes.

To this end *Iuan Vasilowich* late Emperour vsed a very strange practise, that few Princes would haue done in their greatest extremities. He resigned his kingdome to one *Velica Knez Simeon*, the Emperours sonne of *Cazan*: as though hee meant to draw himselfe from al publike doings to a quiet priuat life. Towards the end of the yeere, hee caused this newe King to call in all Charters graunted to Bishoprickes, and Monasteries, which they had enioyed manie hundred yeeres before. Which were all cancelled. This done (as in dislike of the fact and of the misgouernment of the newe King) hee resumed his scepter, and so was content (as in fauour to the Church and religious men) that they should renew their charters, and take them of himselfe: reseruing and annexing to the Crowne so much of their lands, as himselfe thought good.

A strange practise to get money.

220

By this practise hee wrung from the Bishoprickes, and Monasteries (besides the landes which he annexed to the Crowne) an huge masse of money. From some 40, from some 50, from some an hundred thousande rubbels. And this aswell for the increase of his treasurie, as to abate the ill opinion of his harde gouernment, by a shewe of woorse in an other man. Wherein his strange spirite is to bee noted: that beyng hated of his subiectes, (as himselfe knew wel inough) yet would venture such a practise, to set an other in his saddle, that might haue ridde away with his horse, while himselfe walked by on foote.

5

To sende their messengers into the Prouinces, or shires where the special commodities of their countrey grow, as furres, waxe, hony, &c. There to forestall and ingrosse somtime one whole commodity, sometime two, or more, taking them at smal prices what themselues list, and selling them againe at an excessiue rate to their own marchants, and to marchants strangers. If they refuse to buy them, then to force them vnto it.

The like is done when any commoditie eyther natiue, or forreine (as cloth of golde, broadecloth, &c). thus engrossed by the Emperour, and receiued into his treasurie, happeneth to decay, or marre by long lying, or some other casualtie. Which is forced vpon the Marchants to be bought by them at the Emperours price, whether they will or no. This last yeere of 1589. was engrossed all the waxe of the countrey: so that none might deale with that commoditie, but the Emperour onely.

6

To take vp and engrosse in like sort sometime forreine commodities (as silkes, cloth, ledde, pearle, &c. brought into his realm by *Turkish* marchants, *Armenians, Bougharians, Poles, English*, and other. And then to force his marchants to buy them of his officers at his owne price.

260

265

270

275

280

285

7

To make a Monopoly for the time of such commodities as are paid him for rent, or custom, and to inhanse the price of them, as furres, corn, wood, &c. What time none must sell of the same kind of commodity, til the Emperors be all sold. By this means hee 290 maketh of his rent, corn, and other prouision of victual (as before was said) about 200000. rubbels, or marks a yeere. Of his rent wood, hay, &c. 30000. rubbels, or thereabouts.

8

In euery great towne of his Realme he hath a *Caback* or drinking house, where is sold *aquavitæ* (which they cal *Russe wine*) mead, 295 *beere, &c.* Out of these hee receiueth rent that amounteth to a great summe of money. Some yeeld 800, some 900, some a 1000, some 2000 or 3000. rubbels a yere. Wherein besides the base, and dishonourable meanes to encrease his treasurie, many foule faultes are committed. The poore labouring man, and artificer, manie times 300 spendeth all from his wife and children. Some vse to lay in twentie, thirtie, fourtie rubbels, or more into the *Caback*, and vowe themselues to the pot, till all that be spent. And this (as he will say) for the honour of *Hospodare*, or the Emperour. You shall haue manie there that haue drunk all away to the verie skinne, and so walk naked 305 (whom they call *Naga*). While they are in the *Caback*, none may call them foorth whatsoeuer cause there be, because he hindereth the Emperours reuenue.

9

To cause some of his *Boiarens*, or *Nobles* of his court, (whom he vseth vpon trust) that haue houses in the *Mosko*, to faine them selues 310 robbed. Then to send for the *Zemskey* men, or Aldermen of the citie, and to commaund them to finde out the robberie. In default of not finding it, to praue or seasse the citie for their misgouernment in 8000. 9000. or 10000. rubbels at a time. This is many times practised.

In these exactions to shew their soueraigntie, sometime they vse *315* very plaine, and yet strange cauillations. As was that of *Iuan Vasilo-wich*, father to this Emperour, after this sort. He sent into *Permia* for certaine loads of *Cedar wood*, whereof hee knew that none grew in that Countrey. The inhabitants returned answere they could find none there. Whereupon hee seassed their Countrey in 12000. *320* rubbels, as if they concealed the commoditie of purpose. Againe he sent to the citie of *Mosko* to prouide for him a *Colpack*, or measure full of liue fleas for a medicine. They returned answere that the thing was impossible. And if they could get them, yet they could not measure them, for leaping out. Whereupon he praued, or beat *325* out of their shinnes 7000. rubbels for a mulct.

By like cauillation hee extorted from his Nobilitie 30000. rubbels, because he missed of his game, when he went a hunting for the Hare: as if their hunting and murdering of hares had bin the cause of it. Which the Nobilitie (as the manner is) praued presently *330* againe vpon the *Mousicks*, or common people of the Countrie. This may seeme a straunge kinde of extortion, by such pleasant cauils to fliese his poore subiectes in good sadnesse: but that it agreeth with the qualitie of those Emperours, and the miserable subiection of that poore Countrie. *These, and such like meanes are practised by* *335* *the Emperours of Russia, to encrease their Treasurie.*

Of the state of the Communaltie, or *vulgar sorte of people in the* *countrie of Russia.* ### The 13. Chapter.

The condition of the commons, and vulgar sort of people may partly be vnderstood by that which already hath bin said concerning the manner of their gouernment, and the state of the Nobilitie, with the ordering of their Prouinces, and chiefe townes of the land. And first touching their libertie how it standeth with them, it may appeare by this: that they are reckoned in no degree at all, nor haue any suffrage nor place in their *Zabore*, or high court of Parliament, where their lawes and publique orders are concluded vpon. Which commonly tend to the oppression of the commons.

10 For the other two degrees vz: of the Nobilitie, and Cleargie, whiche haue a vote in the Parliaments (though farre from that libertie that ought to bee in common consultations for the pubilique benefite, according to the measure and proportion of their degrees) are well contented that the whole burden shall light vpon the commons, so

15 they may ease their owne shoulders by laying all vpon them. Againe into what seruile condition their libertie is brought, not onely to the Prince, but to the Nobles, and Gentlemen of the Countrie (who themselues also are but seruile, specially of late yeares) it may farther appeare by their owne acknowledgments in

20 their supplications, and other writings to any of the Nobles or chiefe officers of the Emperours. Wherein they name and subscribe themselues *Kolophey*, that is, their villaines, or bondslaues: as they of the Nobilitie doo vnto the Emperour. This may truely be saide of them, that there is no seruant nor bondslaue more awed by his

25 Maister, nor kept downe in a more seruile subiection, then the poore people are, and that vniuersally, not only by the Emperour, but by his Nobilitie, chief officers, and souldiers. So that when a poore *Mousick* meeteth with any of them vpon the high way, he must turne himselfe about, as not daring to looke him on the face,

30 and fall down with knocking of his head to the very ground, as he doth vnto his Idoll.

Secondly concerning the landes, goods, and other possessions of the commons, they answere the name and lie common indeed without any fense against the rapine, and spoile, not onely of the

35 highest, but of his Nobilitie, officers, and souldiers. Besides the taxes, customes, seazures, and other publique exactions done vpon them by the Emperour, they are so racked and pulled by the Nobles, officers, and messengers sent abroad by the Emperour in his publique

224

affaires, specially in the *Yammes* (as they call them) and thorough
faire townes, that you shall haue many villages and townes of halfe   40
a mile, and a mile long, stande all vnhabited: the people being fled
all into other places by reason of the extreame vsage, and exactions
done vpon them. So that in the way towards *Mosko*, betwixt
Vologda and *Yaruslaueley* (which is two nineties after their reckoning,
litle more then an hundreth miles English) there are in sigt fiftie   45
Darieunes or villages at the least, some halfe a mile, some a mile
long that stand vacant and desolate with out any inhabitant. The
like is in all other places of the realme, as is said by those that haue
better trauelled the countrie then my selfe had time, or occasion to doo.

The great oppression ouer the poore Commons, maketh them   50
to haue no courage in following their trades: for that the more
they haue, the more daunger they are in, not onely of their goods,
but of their liues also. And if they haue any thing, they conceale
it all they can, somtimes conueying it into Monasteries, sometimes
hiding it vnder the ground, and in woods, as men are woont to   55
doo where they are in feare of forreine inuasion. In so much that
many times you shall see them afraid to be knowen to any *Boiaren*
or Gentleman of such commodities as they haue to sell. I haue
seene them sometimes when they haue layed open their commodities
for a liking (as their principall furres and such like) to looke still   60
behind them, and towards euery doore: as men in some feare, that
looked to be set vpon, and surprised by some enimie. Whereof
asking the cause, I found it to be this, that they haue doubted least
some Nobleman or *Sinaboiarskey* of the Emperour had bene in the
companie, and so layed a traine for them to pray vpon their   65
commodities perforce.

This maketh the people (though otherwise hardened to beare
any toile) to giue themselues much to idlenes and drinking: as
passing for no more, then from hand to mouth. And here of it
commeth that the commodities of *Russia* (as was said before) as   70
wax, tallow, hydes, flaxe, hempe, &c. grow and goe abroad in farre
lesse plentie then they were woont to doo: because the people

being oppressed and spoiled of their gettings, are discouraged from their laboures. Yet this one thing is much to be noted, that in all this oppression there were three brethren Marchants of late that traded together with one stocke in common, that were found to bee woorth 300000. rubbels in money, besides landes, cattels, and other commodities. Which may partly be imputed to their dwellings far of from the eye of the Court, vz. in *Wichida*, a 1000. miles from *Mosko*, and more. The same are said by those that knew them to haue set on worke all the yeare long ten thousand men in making of salt, carriages by cart, and boat, hewing of wood, and such like: besides 5000 bondslaues at the least, to inhabite and till their land.

They had also their physitions, surgeons, apothecaries, and all manner of artificers of *Doutches* and others, belonging vnto them. They are said to haue paied to the Emperour for custome to the sum of 23000. rubbels a yeare (for which cause they were suffered to enioy their trade) besides the mainteining of certeine garrisons on the borders of *Siberia*, which were neare vnto them. Wherin the Emperour was content to vse their purse, till such time as they had got ground in *Siberia*, and made it habitable, by burning, and cutting downe woods from *Wichida* to *Perm*, aboue a 1000 verst and then tooke it all away from them perforce.

But this in the end beying enuied, and disdained, as a matter not standing with their pollicie to haue any so great, specially a *Mousick*, the Emperour began first to pull from them by pieces, sometimes 20000 rubbels at a time, sometime more: till in the end their sonnes that now are, are well eased of their stocke, and haue but small parte of their fathers substance: the rest being drawen all into the Emperours treasurie. Their names were *Iacoue*, *Gregorie*, and *Simon* the sonnes of *Onyka*.

For the qualitie of their people otherwise, though there seemeth to be in them some aptnesse to receyue any art (as appeareth by the naturall wittes in the men, and very children) yet they excell in no kinde of common arte, much lesse in any learning, or litterall kinde of knowledge: which they are kept from of purpose, as they

226

are also from all militarie practise: that they may be fitter for the seruile condition, wherein now they are, and haue neyther reason, nor valure to attempt innouation. For this purpose also they are kept from traueling, that they may learne nothing, nor see the fashions of other Countries abroad. You shall seldome see a *Russe* a traueller, except he be with some Ambassadour, or that he make a scape out of his Countrie. Which hardly he can doo, by reason of the borders that are watched so narrowly, and the punishment for any such attempt, which is death if he be taken, and all his goods confiscate. Onely they learne to write, and to read, and that very few of them. Neither doo they suffer any straunger willingly to come into their realme out of any ciuill Countrie, for the same cause, farther then necessitie of vttering their commodities, and taking in of forreine doth enforce them to doo.

And therefore this yeare 1589. they consulted about the remouing of all Marchants straungers to the border townes, to abide and haue their residencie there, and to bee more wary in admitting other straungers hereafter into the Inland parts of the realm, for feare of infection with better manners and qualities, then they haue of their owne. For the same purpose also they are kept within the boundes of their degree by the lawes of their countrie: so that the sonne of a *Mousick*, artificer, or husbandman, is euer a *Mousick*, artificer, &c: and hath no means to aspire any higher: except hauing learned to write and read, he attaine to the preferment of a Priest, or Dyack. Their language is all one with the *Slauonian*, which is thought to haue bene deriued from the *Russe* tongue, rather then the *Russe* from the *Slauonian*. For the people called *Sclaui*, are knowen to haue had their beginning out of *Sarmatia*, and to haue termed themselues of their conquest *Sclauos*, (that is) famous or glorious, of the word *Sclaua*, which in the *Russe* and *Slauonian* tongue, signifieth as much as *Glory*, or *Fame*. Though afterwards being subdued and trod vpon by diuers nations, the *Italians* their neighbours haue turned the worde to a contrary signification, and terme euery seruant or peasant by the name of *Sclaue*, as did the *Romanes*

110

115

120

The ielousie of the Emperour concerning his state.

125

130

135

140

227

by the *Getes* and *Syrians*, for the same reason. The *Russe* character
or letter is no other then the *Greeke*, somewhat distorted.

Concerning their trades, diet, apparell, and such like, it is to be
noted in a seuerall chapter of their priuate behauiour. This order
145 that bindeth euery man to keepe his rancke, and seuerall degree,
wherin his forefathers liued before him, is more meet to keepe the
subiects in a seruile subiection, and so apt for this and like Common-
wealths, then to aduaunce any vertue, or to breed any rare or
excellent qualitie in Nobilitie or Commons: as hauing no farther
150 rewarde nor preferment, whereunto they may bend their endeuours,
and imploy themselues to aduaunce their estate, but rather procuring
more danger to themselues, the more they excell in any noble or
principall qualitie.

Of their publique Iustice, and manner
of proceeding in ciuill, and
criminall matters.
The 14. Chapter.

**Courts of
ciuill ius-
tice three.**

Their courts of ciuil iustice for matters of contract, and other
of like sort, are of three kinds, the one beyng subiect vnto
the other by way of appeale. The lowest Court (that seemeth to be
appointed for some ease to the subiects) is the office of the *Gubnoy*
5 *Starust*, that signifieth an Alderman, and of the *Sotskoy Starust*, or
Bailief of the soake or hundred, wherof I spake before in the
ordering of the Prouinces. These may ende matters among their
neighbours within their soke, or seuerall hundred, where they are
appointed vnder the Dukes and Diacks of the Prouinces, to whom
10 the parties may remoue their matter, if they cannot be agreed by
the said *Gubnoy*, or *Sotskoy Starust*.

**The Dukes
and Diacks
Court.**

The second is kept in the head townes of euery Prouince or
Shire, by the said Dukes and Diacks, that are deputies to the foure
Lords of the *Chetfirds* (as before was sayd). From these courts they
15 may appeale, and remoue their suites to the chiefe Court, that is

228

kept at the *Mosko*, where are resident the officers of the foure *Chetfirds*. These are the chiefe Iustices or Iudges, euery on of them in all ciuill matters that grow within their seuerall *Chetfird* or quarter, and may be either commenced originally before them, or prosequuted out of the inferiour Courts of the Shires by way of appeale.

Their commencing, and proceeding in ciuill actions is on this manner. First, the plaintife putteth vp his supplication, wherein hee declareth the effect of his cause, or wrong done vnto him. Whereupon is granted vnto him a *Wepis*, or warrant, which hee deliuereth to the *Præstaue*, or Sergeant, to doo the arrest vpon the partie whom hee meaneth to implead. Who vpon the arrest, is to put in sureties to answere the day appointed, or els standeth at the Sergeants deuotion, to be kept safe by such meanes as he thinketh good.

The Sergeants are many, and excell for their hard and cruell dealing towards their prysoners. Commonly they clappe irons vpon them, as many as they can beare, to wring out of them some larger fees. Though it bee but for sixe pence, you shall see them goe with chaynes on their legges, armes, and necke. When they come before the Iudge, the plaintife beginneth to declare his matter after the content of his supplication. As for Attourneis, Counsellours, Procuratours and Aduocates to plead their cause for them, they haue no such order, but euery man is to tell his owne tale, and plead for himselfe, so well as he can.

If they haue any witnesse, or other euidence, they produce it before the Iudge. If they haue none, or if the truth of the cause cannot so well bee decerned by the plea, or euidence on both partes: then the Iudge asketh eyther partie (which hee thinketh good, plaintife or defendant) whether hee will *kisse the Crosse*, vpon that which he auoucheth, or denieth. Hee that taketh the Crosse (being so offered by the Iudge) is accounted cleare, and carrieth away the matter. This ceremonie is not done within the Court or office, but the partie is carried to the Church by an officer, and there the ceremonie is done: the mony in the meane while hanging vpon a naile, or els lying at the idols feete, ready to be deliuered to the

50 partie, as soone as he hath kissed the Crosse before the said Idoll.

This kissing of the Crosse (called *Creustina chelouania*) is as their corporall oath, and accounted with them a very holy thing, which no man will dare to violate, or prophane with a false allegation.

Iudgement by lotte. If both parties offer to kisse the Crosse in a contradictorie matter, then they drawe lottes. The better lotte is supposed to haue the right, and beareth away the matter. So the partie conuicted is adiudged to pay the debt or penaltie whatsoeuer, and withall to pay the Emperours fees, which is twentie pence vpon euery marke, as before hath bene noted.

60 When the matter is thus ended, the partie conuicted is deliuered to the Sergeant, who hath a writte for his warrant out of the office, to carry him to the *Praueush* or Righter of Iustice, if presently hee pay not the monie, or content not the partie. This *Praueush* or Righter, is a place neare to the office: where such as haue sentence 65 passed against them, and refuse to pay that which is adiudged, are beaten with great cudgels on the shinnes, and calues of their legges. Euery forenoone from eight to eleuen, they are set on the *Praueush*, and beate in this sort till the monie be payd. The afternoone and night time, they are kepte in chaines by the Sergeant: except they 70 put in sufficient suerties for their apparance at the *Praueush* at the hower appointed. You shall see fortie or fiftie stand together on the *Praueush* all on a rowe, and their shinnes thus becudgelled, and bebasted euery morning with a piteous crie. If after a yeares standing on the *Praueush*, the partie will not, or lacke wherewithall to satisfie 75 his creditour, it is lawfull for him to sell his wife, and children, eyther out right, or for a certaine terme of yeares. And if the price of them doo not amount to the full payment, the creditour may take them to bee his bondslaues, for yeares or for euer, according as the value of the debt requireth.

80 Such kinde of suites as lacke direct euidence, or stande vpon coniectures and circumstances to bee waighed by the Iudge, drawe of great length, and yeeld great aduantage to the Iudge and officers. If the suite be vpon a bond, or bill, they haue for the moste parte

good and speedy iustice. Their bonds, or billes are drawn in a
very plaine sorte, after this tenour. *I Iuan Vasileo haue borrowed of*
Alphonasse Dementio, the summe of one hundred rubbles of going money
of Mosko, from the Kreshenea (or hallowing of the water) *vntill the*
Saburney voscreshenca (or Counsell Sunday) *without interest. And if*
this money rest vnpayed after that day, then hee shall giue interest vpon
the sayd money, after the common rate, as it goeth among the people,
vz. for euerie fiue the sixt rubbell. Vpon this there are witnesses, Micheta
Sydroueskoy, &c: Subscribed. This bill haue I written Gabriell Iacouelesui,
in the yeare 7096. The witnesses, and debter (if he can write) endorse
their names on the backe side of the bill. Other signing, or sealing
haue they none.

The forme of *Russe* bils or bonds.

90

95

When any is taken for a matter of crime (as treason, murder,
thefte, and such like) hee is first brought to the Duke, and Diack,
that are for the Prouince where the partie is attached, by whom
hee is examined. The manner of examination in such cases, is all
by torture, as scourging with whips, made of sinowes, or whitleather
(called the *Pudkey*) as bigge as a mans finger, which giueth a sore
lash, and entreth into the flesh, or by tying to a spit and rosting at
the fire, sometimes by breaking and wresting one of their ribbes
with a payre of hote tongues, or cutting their flesh vnder the nayles,
and such like.

Proceeding in criminall matters.

100

105

The examination thus taken withall the proofes, and euidences
that can bee alleadged against the partie, it is sent vp to the *Mosko*
to the Lord of the *Chetfird* or Fourthparte, vnder whom the Prouince
is, and by him is presented to the Counsell table, to bee read and
sentenced there, where onely iudgement is giuen in matter of life
and death, and that by euidence vpon information, though they
neuer sawe nor heard the partie, who is kept still in pryson where
the fact was committed, and neuer sent vp to the place where he
is tried. If they find the partie guiltie, they giue sentence of death
according to the qualitie of the fact: which is sent downe by the
Lord of the *Chetfird*, to the Duke and Diack to bee put in execution. The prisoner is carried to the place of execution with his

110

115

handes bounde, and a waxe candle burning helde betwixt his fingers.

Their capitall punishmentes are hanging, hedding, knocking on the head, drowning, putting vnder the yse, setting on a stake, and such like. But for the most part the prisoners that are condemned in Sommer, are kept for the winter, to be knockt in the head, and put vnder the yse. This is to bee vnderstood of common persons. For theft, and murder, if they be committed vpon a poore *Mousick* by one of Nobilitie are not lightly punished, nor yet is hee called to any account for it. Their reason is, because they are accounted their *Kolophey*, or bondslaues. If by some *Sinaboiarskey*, or Gentleman souldier, a murder or theft bee committed, peraduenture he shal be imprisoned at the Emperours pleasure. If the manner of the fact be verie notorious, he is whipped perchance, and this is commonly all the punishment that is inflicted vpon them.

If a man kill his owne seruant, little, or nothing is said vnto him, for the same reason: because hee is accounted to be his *Kolophey*, or bondslaue, and so to haue right ouer his verie head. The most is some small mulct to the Emperour, if the partie be rich: and so the quarell is made rather against the purse, then against the iniustice. They haue no written law, saue onely a smal booke that conteineth the time, and manner of their sitting, order in proceeding, and such other iudicial forms and circumstances, but nothing to direct them to giue sentence vpon right or wrong. Their onely lawe is their *Speaking Law*, that is, the pleasure of the Prince, and of his Magistrates and officers. Which sheweth the miserable condition of this poore people, that are forced to haue them for their law, and direction of iustice, against whose iniustice, and extreame oppression, they had neede to be armed with many good, and strong lawes.

Their forces for the warres, with the chief officers and their salaries.

The 15. Chapter.

The souldiers of *Russia* are called *Sinaboiarskey*, or the sons of Gentlemen: because they are all of that degree, by vertue of their millitary profession. For euery souldier in *Russia* is a gentleman, and none are gentlemen, but only the souldiers, that take it by discent from their ancestors: so that the sonne of a gentleman (which is borne a souldier) is euer a gentleman, and a souldier withal, and professeth nothing els but militarie matters. When they are of yeeres able to beare armes, they come to the office of *Roserade*, or great Constable, and there present themselues: who entreth their names, and allotteth them certeine lands to maintein their charges, for the most part the same that their fathers enioyed. For the lands assigned to mainteine the army, are euer certein, annexed to this office without improuing, or detracting one foot. But that if the Emperour haue sufficient in wages, the roomes being full so farre as the lande doeth extend already, they are manie times deferred, and haue nothing allowed them, except some one portion of the land be deuided into two. Which is a cause of great disorder within that countrie: when a souldier that hath many children, shal haue sometimes but one intertained in the Emperours pay. So that the rest hauing nothing, are forced to liue by vniust and wicked shiftes, that tend to the hurt and oppression of the *Mousick*, or common sort of people. This inconuenience groweth by mainteining his forces in a continual succession. The whole number of his souldiers in continual pay, is this. First, he hath of his *Dworaney*, that is, Pensioners, or Gard of his person, to the number of 15000. horsemen, with their captaines, and other officers, that are alwaies in a readines.

Of these 15000. horsemen, there are three sorts or degrees, which differ aswell in estimation, as in wages, one degree from another. The first sort of them is called *Dworaney Bulshey*, or the company of head Pensioners, that haue, some an hundred, some fourscore

Souldiers by birth and inheritance.

10

15

20

25

Degrees of horsemen.

30

233

1. *Prætoriani*
or such as
attend the
Emperours
person,
15000.

rubbels a yeere, and none vnder 70. The second sort are called *Seredney Dworaney*, or the middle ranke of Pensioners. These haue sixty, or fiftie rubbels by the yere, none vnder fourtie. The third and lowest sort are the *Dyta Boiarskey*, that is, the lowe Pensioners. Their salarie is thirty rubbels a yere for him that hath most, some haue but fiue and twentie, some twentie, none vnder twelue. Whereof the halfe part is paid them at the *Mosko*, the other halfe in the field by the generall, when they haue anie warres, and are imployed in seruice. When they receiue their whole pay, it amount-

40 eth to 55000. rubbels by the yeere.

And this is their wages, besides lands allotted to euery one of them, both to the greater and the lesse, according to their degrees. Whereof he that hath least, hath to yeeld him twentie rubbels, or marks by the yeere. Besides these 15000. horsemen, that are of better

45 choyce (as being the Emperors own gard when himself goeth to the warres, not vnlike the Romane souldiers called *Prætoriani*) are a 110. men of special account for their Nobilitie, and trust, which

Two other
troupes to
the number
of 65000.

are chosen by the Emperour, and haue their names registred, that find among them for the Emperours warres, to the number of 65000. horsemen, with all necessaries meet for the warres after the *Russe* manner.

To this end they haue yeerely allowance made by the Emperour for themselues, and their companies, to the summe of 40000. rubbels. And these 65000 are to repaire to the field euery yeere on

55 the borders towards the *Chrim Tartar*, (except they bee appoynted for some other seruice) whether there be warres with the *Tartars*, or not. This might seeme peraduenture somwhat dangerous for some state, to haue so great forces vnder the command of Noblemen to assemble euerie yeere to one certeine place. But the matter is so

60 vsed, as that no danger can grow to the Emperour, or his state by this meanes. 1. Because these noblemen are manie, to wit, an 110. in all, and changed by the Emperor so oft as he thinketh good. 2. Because they haue their liuings of the Emperour, being otherwise but of very small reuenue, and receiue this yeerely pay of 40000.

234

rubbels, when it is presently to be paide foorth againe to the   65
souldiers that are vnder them. 3. Because for the most part they
are about the Emperours person, being of his Councel, either
speciall, or at large. 4. They are rather as paymasters, then Captaines
to their companies, themselues not going forth ordinarily to the
warres, saue when some of them are appointed by speciall order   70
from the Emperour himselfe. So the whole number of horsemen   Horsemen in
that are euer in a readinesse, and in continuall pay, are 80000, a continuall
few more or lesse.   pay 80000.

If hee haue neede of a greater number (which seldome falleth
out) then he interteineth of those *Sinaboiarskey*, that are out of pay,   75
so many as hee needeth: and if yet hee want of his number, he
giueth charge to his Noblemen, that hold lands of him, to bring
into the fielde euery man a proportionable number of his seruaunts
(called *Kolophey*, such as till his lands) with their furniture, according
to the iust number that he intendeth to make. Which the seruice   80
being done, presently lay in their weapons, and returne to their
seruile occupations againe.

Of footmen that are in continuall pay, he hath to the number   Footmen in
of 12000. all Gunners, called *Strelsey*. Whereof 5000. are to attend continuall
about the Citie of *Mosko*, or any other place where the Emperour   pay 12000.
shall abide, and 2000. (which are called *Stremaney Stresley*, or
Gunners at the stirrop) about his owne person at the verie Court or
house where himselfe lodgeth. The rest are placed in his garrison
Townes, till there be occasion to haue them in the fielde, and
receiue for their salarie or stipend euery man seuen rubbels a yeere,   90
besides twelue measures a piece of Rye, and Oates. Of mercenarie
Souldiers, that are strangers (whom they call *Nimschoy*) they haue Strangers
at this time 4300. of *Polonians*: of *Chirchasses* (that are vnder the mercenaries
Polonians) about 4. thousand, whereof 3500 are abroad in his   in pay 4300.
garrisons: of *Doutches* and *Scots* about 150: of *Greekes*, *Turks*, *Danes*   95
and *Sweadens*, all in one band, an 100. or thereabouts. But these
they vse onely vpon the *Tartar* side, and against the *Siberians*: as
they doe the *Tartar* souldiers (whom they hire sometimes, but

onely for the present) on the other side against the *Polonian* and
Sweaden: thinking it best pollicie so to vse their seruice vpon the
contrary border.

The chiefe
captaines
or leaders.
1. The *Voi-
auod* or
Generall.

The chiefe Captaines or leaders of these forces, according to
their names, and degrees, are these which follow. First, the *Voyauodey
Bulshaia*, that is, the *Great Captaine*, or *Lieftenant* generall vnder the
Emperour. This commonly is one of the foure houses of the chiefe
Nobilitie of the lande: but so chosen otherwise, as that hee is of
small valure, or practise in martiall matters, beeyng thought to
serue that turne so much the better, if hee bring no other partes
with him saue the countenance of his Nobilitie, to bee liked of
by the souldiers for that, and nothing els. For in this poynt they
are very warie, that these two (to wit) nobilitie, and power meet
not both in one, specially if they see wisedome with all, or aptnesse
for pollicie.

Their great *Voiauod* or Generall at this present in their warres,
is commonly one of these foure: *Knez Feodor Iuanowich Methissoskey*,
Knez Iuan Michailowich Glinskoy, Cherechaskoy, and *Trowbetskoy*, all
of great Nobilitie, but of very simple qualitie otherwise: though
in *Glinskoy* (as they say) there is somewhat more then in the rest.

2. Liefeten-
ant generall.

To make vp this defect in the *Voiauod* or Generall, there is some
other ioyned with him as *Lieftenant Generall*, of farre lesse nobilitie,
but of more valure and experience in the warres then he, who
ordereth all things that the other countenanceth. At this time their
principall man, and most vsed in their warres, is one *Knez Demetrie
Iuanowich Forestine*, an auncient and expert captaine, and one that
hath done great seruice (as they say) against the *Tartar*, and *Polonian*.

3. Marshals
of the field
foure.

Next vnder the *Voiauod* and his *Lieftenant generall* are foure other
that haue the marshalling of the whole army, deuided among them,
and may be called the marshals of the field.

Euery man hath his quarter, or fourth part vnder him. Whereof
the first is called the *Praua Polskoy*, or right wing. The second is
the *Leuoy Polskoy*, or left wing. The third is *Rusnoy Polskoy*, or the
broken band, because out of this there are chosen to send abroade

236

vpon any sodaine exploit, or to make a rescue, or supply, as occasion
doth require. The fourth *Storeshouoy Polskoy*, or the warding bande.
Euery one of these foure Marshals haue two other vnder them
(eight in all) that twise euery weeke at the least must muster and
traine their seueral wings or bands, and hold and giue iustice for
all faultes, and disorders committed in the campe.

And these eight are commonly chosen out of the 110. (which
I spake of before) that receiue and deliuer the pay to the souldiers.
Vnder these eight are diuers other Captains, as the *Gullauoy*,
Captaines of thousands, fiue hundreds and 100. The *Petyde Setskoy*
or Captaines of fifties, and the *Decetskies* or Captaines of tennes.

Besides the *Voiauoda* or Generall of the Armie (spoken of before)
they haue two other that beare the name of *Voiauoda*: whereof one
is the Master of the great Ordinance (called *Naradna voiauoda*) who
hath diuers vnder Officers, necessarie for that seruice. The other is
called the *Voiauoda gulauoy*, or the walking Captaine, that hath
alowed him 1000. good horsemen of principall choyse, to range
and spie abroad, and hath the charge of the running Castle, which
we are to speake of in the Chapter folowing. All these Captaines,
and men of charge must once euery day resort to the *Bulsha voiauoda*,
or Generall of the Armie, to know his pleasure, and to informe him,
if there be any requisite matter perteining to their office.

Of their mustering, and leuying of forces,
manner of armour, and prouision
of victuall for the warres.
The 16. Chapter.

When warres are towards (which they fayle not of lightly
euery yeere with the *Tartar*, and manie times with the
Polonian and *Sweden*) the foure Lordes of the *Chetfirds* sende foorth
their summons in the Emperours name, to all the Dukes and Dyacks
of the Prouinces, to bee proclaymed in the head Townes of euery
Shire: that all the *Sinaboiarskey*, or sonnes of gentlemen make their

[marginal notes:]

Foure mar-
shals depu-
ties 8.

140
Fiue Coro-
nels vnder
Captaines.

Sixe Mas-
ters of the
Artillerie.

The walking
Captaine.

150

Their order
for mustering.

5

repaire to such a border where the seruice is to be done, at such a place, and by such a day, and there present them selues to such, and such Captaines. When they come to the place assigned them in the summons or proclamation, their names are taken by certaine Officers that haue Commission for that pourpose from the *Roserade*, or high Constable, as Clarkes of the Bandes.

If any make default and faile at the day, hee is mulcted, and punished very seuerely. As for the Generall and other chiefe Captaines, they are sent thither from the Emperours owne hande, with such Commission and charge as hee thinketh behoofull for the present seruice. When the souldiers are assembled, they are reduced into their Bands, and companies, vnder their seuerall Captaines of tennes, fifties, hundreds, thousands, &c. and these Bands into foure *Polskeis*, or Legions (but of farre greater numbers then the Romaine Legions were) vnder their foure great Leaders, which also haue the authoritie of Marshals of the fielde (as was sayd before).

Concerning their armour they are but slightly appointed. The common horseman hath nothing els but his bow in his case vnder his right arme, and his quiuer and sword hanging on the left side: except some fewe that beare a case of dagges, or a Iauelin, or short staffe along their horse side. The vnder captains wil haue commonly some piece of armour besides, as a shirt of male, or such like. The Generall with the other chiefe Captaines and men of Nobilitie, will haue their horse very richly furnished, their Saddles of cloth of golde, their Bridles faire bossed and tasselled with golde, and silke frindge, bestudded with Pearle and precious stones, themselues in very faire armour, which they call *Bullatnoy*, made of faire shinning steele, yet couered commonly with cloth of golde, and edged rounde with armin furre, his steele helmet on his head of a very great price, his sword bow and arrowes at his side, his speare in his hande, with an other faire helmet, and his *Shestapera*, or horsemans scepter carried before him. Their swordes, bowes, and arrowes are of the Turkish fashion. They practise like the *Tartar* to shoote forwards and backwards, as they flie and retire.

The horse-mans furniture.

238

The *Strelsey* or footeman hath nothing but his piece in his hande, his striking hatchet at his backe, and his sworde by his side. The stocke of his piece is not made calieuer wise, but with a plaine and straite stocke (somewhat like a fowling piece) the barrel is rudely and vnartificially made, very heauie, yet shooteth but a very small bullet. As for their prouision of victuall, the Emperour alloweth none, either for Captaine, or souldiour, neither prouideth any for them except peraduenture some corne for their money. Euery man is to bring sufficient for him selfe, to serue his turne for foure moneths, and if neede require to giue order for more to bee brought vnto him to the Campe from his tenant that tilleth his land, or some other place. One great helpe they haue, that for lodging and diet euery *Russe* is prepared to bee a souldiour beforehand. Though the chiefe Captaines and other of account carry tents with them after the fashion of ours, with some better prouision of victuall then the rest. They bring with them commonly into the Campe for victuall a kinde of dryed bread, (which they call *Sucharie*) with some store of meale, which they temper with water, and so make it into a ball, or small lumpe of dowe, called *Tollockno*. And this they eate raw in steade of bread. Their meate is bacon, or some other flesh or fish dryed, after the Dutch manner. If the *Russe* souldier were as hardy to execute an enterprise, as he is hard to beare out toyle and trauaile, or were otherwise as apt and wel trained for the warres, as he is indifferent for his lodging and dyet, hee would farre excell the souldiours of our partes. Whereas now he is farre meaner of courage and execution in any warlike seruice. Which commeth partly of his seruile condition, that will not suffer any great courage or valure to growe in him. Partly for lacke of due honour and reward, which he hath no great hope of, whatsoeuer seruice or execution he doe.

The footemans furniture.

45

Prouision of victuall.

50

55

60

65

70

239

Of their marching, charging, and other
Martiall discipline.
The 17. Chapter.

The Russe trusteth rather to his number, then to the valure of his souldiers, or good ordering of his forces. Their marching or leading is without all order, saue that the foure *Polskey* or Legions, (whereinto their armie is deuided) keepe themselues seueral vnder their ensignes, and so thrust all on together in a hurrey, as they are directed by their Generall. Their Ensigne is the image of Saint George. The *Bulsha Dworaney* or chiefe horsemen, haue euery man a small drumme of brasse at his saddle bowe, which hee striketh when hee giueth the charge, or onset.

They haue drummes besides of a huge bignesse, which they carry with them vpon a board layde on foure horses, that are sparred together with chaines, euery drumme hauing eight strikers, or drummers, besides trumpets and shawmes, which they sounde after a wilde manner, much different from ours. When they giue any charge, or make any inuasion, they make a great hallowe or shoute altogether, as loude as they can, which with the sound of their trumpets, shawmes, and drummes, maketh a confused and horrible noyse. So they set on first discharging their arrowes, then dealing with their swordes, which they vse in a brauerie to shake, and brandish ouer their heads, before they come to strokes.

Their footemen (because otherwise they want order in leading) are commonly placed in some ambush or place of aduantage, where they may most annoy the enemie, with least hurt to themselues. If it bee a set battell, or if any great inuasion be made vpon the *Russe* borders by the *Tartar*, they are set within the *running* or *mouing* Castle (called *Beza*, or *Gulay gorod*) which is caried about with them by the *Voiauoda gulauoy* (or the *walking General*) whom I spake of before. This walking or moouing Castle is so framed, that it may bee set vp in length (as occasion doeth require) the space of one, two, three, foure, fiue, sixe, or seuen miles: for so long it will

Margin notes:

Horsemens drummes.

The horse-mans man-ner of charging.

The foote-mans charge.

The walking Castle.

Line numbers: 5, 15, 20, 30

reach. It is nothing els but a double wall of wood to defende them on both sides behinde and before, with a space of three yardes or thereabouts betwixt the two sides: so that they may stande within it, and haue roome ynough to charge and discharge their pieces, and to vse their other weapons. It is closed at both endes, and made with loope holes on either side, to lay out the nose of their piece, or to push foorth any other weapon. It is carried with the Armie wheresoeuer it goeth, being taken into pieces, and so layed on cartes sparred together, and drawen by horse that are not seene, by reason that they are couered with their carriage as with a shelfe or penthouse. When it is brought to the place where it is to be vsed (which is deuised and chosen out before by the *walking voiauod*) it is planted so much as the present vse requireth, sometimes a mile long, sometimes two, sometimes three, or more: which is soone done without the helpe of any Carpenter, or instrument: because the timber is so framed to claspe together one piece within an other: as is easily vnderstood by those that know the manner of the *Russe* building.

In this Castle standeth their shotte well fenced for aduantage, specially against the *Tartar*, that bringeth no ordinance, nor other weapon into the field with him, saue his swoord, and bow and arrowes. They haue also within it diuers field pieces, which they vse as occasion doth require. Of pieces for the field they carry no great store, when they warre against the *Tartar*: but when they deale with the *Polonian* (of whose forces they make more account) they goe better furnished with al kind of munition, and other necessarie prouisions. It is thought that no Prince of Christendome hath better stoare of munition, then the *Russe* Emperour. And it may partly appeare by the Artillerie house at *Mosko*, where are of all sortes of great ordinance, all brasse pieces, very faire, to an exceeding great number.

The *Russe* souldier is thought to be better at his defence within some castle, or town, then hee is abroad at a set pitched field. Which is euer noted in the practise of his warres, and namely at the siege

35

40

45

50

55

60

65 of *Vobsko*, about eight yeares since: where hee repulsed the *Polonian* king *Stepan Batore*, with his whole armie of 100000. men, and forced him in the ende to giue ouer his siege, with the losse of many of his best Captaines and souldiers. But in a set field the *Russe* is noted to haue euer the worse of the *Polonian*, and *Sweden*.

Reward for valure. If any behaue himselfe more valiantly then the rest, or doo any speciall piece of seruice, the Emperour sendeth him a piece of golde, stamped with the Image of Saint George on horsebacke. Which they hang on their sleeues, and set in their caps. And this is accounted the greatest honour they can receiue, for any seruice they doo.

Of their Colonies, and mainteyning of their conquests, or purchases by force.
The 18. Chapter.

The *Russe* Emperours of late yeres haue verie muche enlarged their dominions, and territories. Their first conquest after the Dukedom of *Mosko* (for before that time they were but Dukes of *Volodomer*, as before as sayd) was the Citie, and Dukedome of

5 *Nouograd* on the West, and Northwest side: which was no small enlargement of their dominion, and strengthning to them for the winning of the rest. This was done by *Iuan* great grandfather to *Theodore* now Emperour, about the yeare 1480. The same began likewise to encroach vpon the countries of *Lituania*, and *Liuonia*,

10 but the conquest onely intended, and attempted by him vpon some parte of those countries, was pursued and performed by his sonne *Basileus*, who first wan the citie and dukedome of *Plesko*, afterwards the citie and dukedome of *Smolensko*, and many other faire towns, with a large territorie belonging vnto them, about the yeare 1514.

15 These victories against the *Lettoes* or *Lituanians* in the time of *Alexander* their Duke, he atchiued rather by aduantage of ciuill dissentions, and treasons among themselues, then by any great policie, or force of his owne. But all this was lost againe by his

sonne *Iuan Vasilowich*, about eight or nine yeares past, vpon composition with the *Polonian* king *Stepan Batore*: whereunto hee was forced by the aduantages which the *Pole* had then of him, by reason of the foile he had giuen him before, and the disquietnes of his owne state at home. Onely the *Russe* Emperour, at this time hath left him on that side his countrie, the cities of *Smolensko*, *Vitobsko*, *Cheringo* and *Bealagorod* in *Lituania*. In *Liuonia*, not a towne, nor one foote of ground.

When *Basileus* first conquered those countries, he suffered the natiues to keepe their possessions, and to inhabite all their townes, onely paying him a tribute, vnder the gouernment of his *Russe* Captaines. But by their conspiracies and attempts not long after, he was taught to deale more surely with them. And so comming vpon them the second time, hee killed and carried away with him, three partes of foure, which hee gaue or solde to the *Tartars* that serued him in those warres, and in steede of them placed there his *Russes*, so many as might ouermatch the rest, with certaine garrisons of strength besides. Wherein notwithstanding this ouersight was committed, for that taking away with him the vpland, or countrie people (that should haue tilled the ground, and might easily haue bene kept in order without any daunger, by other good pollicies) he was driuen afterwards many yeares together, to vittaile the countrie (specially the great townes) out of his owne countrie of *Russia*, the soile lying there in the meane while wast, and vntilled.

The like fell out at the port of *Narue* in *Liefland*, where his sonne *Iuan Vasilowich* deuised to build a towne, and a castle on the other side the riuer, (called *Iuangorod*) to keepe the towne, and countrie in subiection. The Castle he caused to be so built, and fortified, that it was thought to be inuincible. And when it was finished, for reward to the Architect (that was a *Polonian*) he put out both his eyes, to make him vnable to build the like againe. But hauing left the natiues all within their owne countrie, without abating their number or strength, the towne and castle not long after was betrayed, and surrendred againe to the king of *Sweden*.

Lituania.

Narue.

243

On the Southest side, they haue got the kingdomes of *Cazan*, and *Astracan*. These were wonne from the *Tartar*, by the late Emperour *Iuan Vasilowich*, father to the Emperour that now is: the one about 35. the other about 33. yeares agoe. Northward out of the countrie of *Siberia*, he hath layed vnto his realme, a great breadth and length of ground, from *Wichida* to the riuer of *Obba*, about a 1000. miles space: so that hee is bold to write himselfe now, *The great Commaunder of Siberia*.

Permia and *Pechora*.

The countries likewise of *Permia*, and *Pechora*, are a diuers people and language from the *Russe*, ouercome not long since, and that rather by threatning, and shaking of the sword, then by any actuall force: as being a weake and naked people, without meanes to resist.

Meanes of holding his chiefe townes.

That which the *Russe* hath in his present possession, hee keepeth on this sorte. In his foure chiefe border townes of *Vobsko*, *Smolensko*, *Astracan*, and *Cazan*, he hath certeine of his Counsell not of greatest nobilitie, but of greatest trust, which haue more authoritie within their precincts (for the countenauncing and strengthning of their gouernment there) then the other Dukes that are set to gouerne in other places, as was noted before, in the manner of ordering their Prouinces. These hee chaungeth sometime euery yeare, sometime euery second or third yeare, but exceedeth not that time, except vpon very speciall trust, and good liking of the partie, and his seruice: least by enlarging of their time, they might grow into some familiaritie with the enimie (as some haue done) being so farre out of sight.

The townes besides are very strongly fenced with trenches, castels, and store of munition, and haue garrisons within them, to the number of two or three thousand a piece. They are stoared with vittaile if any siege should come vpon them, for the space of two or three yeares before hande. The foure Castels of *Smolensko*, *Vobsko*, *Cazan* and *Astracan*, he hath made very strong to beare out any siege: so that it is thought that those townes are impregnable.

As for the countries of *Pechora* and *Permia*, and that part of

244

Siberia, which he hath now vnder him, they are kept by as easie meanes, as they were first got. vz. rather by shewing, then by vsing of armes. First, hee hath stoared the Countrie with as manie *Russes* as there are natiues, and hath there some fewe souldiers in garrison, inough to keepe them vnder. Secondly, his officers and Magistrates there, are of his owne *Russe* people, and hee chaungeth them very often, vz. euery yeare twise or thrise: notwithstanding there bee no great feare of any innouation. Thirdly, he deuideth them into many small gouernments, like a staffe broke in many small pieces: so that they haue no strength beyng seuered, which was but litle neyther when they were all in one. Fourthly, hee prouideth that the people of the Countrie haue neither armour, nor monie, beyng taxed and pilled so often as hee thinketh good: without any means to shake of that yoke, or to relieue themselues.

In *Siberia* (where he goeth on in pursuing his conquest) he hath diuers castles and garrisons, to the number of six thousand souldiers of *Russes*, and *Polonians*, and sendeth many new supplies thither, to plant and to inhabite, as he winneth ground. At this time besides he hath gotten the kings brother of *Siberia*, allured by certeine of his Captaines, to leaue his owne countrie by offers of great intertainement, and pleasanter life with the *Russe* Emperour, then he had in *Siberia*. He was brought in this laste yeare, and is now with the Emperour at *Mosko* well interteyned.

This may be sayd of the *Russe* practize, wheresoeuer he ruleth, either by right of inheritance, or by conquest. First, he berieueth the countrie of armour and other means of defence, which he permitteth to none, but to his *Boiarskeis* onely. Secondly, he robbeth them continually of their monie, and commodities, and leaueth them bare with nothing but their bodies, and liues, within certeine yeares compasse. Thirdly, he renteth and deuideth his territories into many small pieces by seuerall gouernments: so that none hath much vnder him to make any strength, though he had other oportunities. Fourthly, he gouerneth his Countries by men of small reputation, and no power of themselues, and straungers in those

Meanes of holding the countries of *Pechora*, *Permia*, and *Siberia*.

95

100

105

110

115

120

245

places where their gouernment lieth. Fiftly, he chaungeth his gouernours once a yeare ordinarily, that there grow no great liking nor intiernesse betwixt the people and them, nor acquaintance with the enemy, if they lie towards the borders. Sixtly, he appointeth in
125 one and the same place aduersarie gouernours, the one to bee as Controller of the other, as the Dukes and Diacks: where (by meanes of their enuies and emulations) there is lesse hurt to bee feared by their agreement, and himselfe is better infourmed what is done amisse. Seuenthly, he sendeth many times into euery Prouince
130 secrete messengers of speciall trust about him, as intelligences, to prie and harken out what is doing, and what is a misse there. And this is ordinary, though it be sodaine, and vnknowen what time they will come.

Of the Tartars, and other borderers to the Countrie of Russia, with whome they haue most to doo in warre, and peace.
The 19. Chapter.

Their neighbours with whom they haue greatest dealings and intercourse, both in peace and warre, are first the *Tartar.*
The *Polo-nians* called *Laches* by the *Russe.* Secondly the *Polonian* whom the *Russe* calleth *Laches*, noting the first author or founder of the Nation, who was called *Laches* or *Leches*, wherunto is added *Po*, which signifieth *People*, and so is made *Polaches*, that is, the *People or posteritie of Laches*: which the *Latines* after their manner of writing call *Polanos.* The third are the *Swedens.* The *Polonians* and *Swedens* are better knowen to these partes of *Europe* then are the *Tartars*, that are farther of from vs
10 (as being of *Asia*) and diuided into many tribes, different both in
The *Chrim Tartar.* name, and gouernment one from another. The greatest and mightiest of them is the *Chrim Tartar*, (whom some call the *Great Cham*) that lieth South, and Southeastward from *Russia*, and doth most annoy the Countrie by often inuasions, commonly once euery yeare,
15 sometimes entring very farre within the inland parts. In the yeare

246

1571. he came as farre as the citie of *Mosko*, with an armie of 200000. men, without any battaile, or resistance at all, for that the *Russe* Emperour (then *Iuan Vasilowich*) leading foorth his armie to encounter with him, marched a wrong way: but as it was thought of very purpose, as not daring to aduenture the fielde, by reason that hee doubted his nobilitie, and chiefe Captaines, of a meaning to betray him to the *Tartar*.

The citie he tooke not, but fired the Subburbs, which by reason of the building (which is all of wood without any stone, brick, or lime, saue certein out roomes) kindled so quickly, and went on with such rage, as that it consumed the greatest part of the citie almost within the space of foure houres, being of 30. miles or more of compasse. Then might you haue seene a lamentable spectacle: besides the huge and mighty flame of the citie all on light fire, the people burning in their houses and streates, but most of all of such as laboured to passe out of the gates farthest from the enemie, where meeting together in a mightie throng, and so pressing euery man to preuent another, wedged themselues so fast within the gate, and streates neare vnto it, as that three ranks walked one vpon the others head, the vppermost treading downe those that were lower: so that there perished at that time (as was sayd) by the fire and the presse, the number of 800000 people, or more.

The *Chrim* thus hauing fired the Citie, and fedde his eyes with the sight of it all on a light flame, returned with his armie, and sent to the *Russe* Emperour a knife (as was sayd) to sticke himselfe withall: obbraiding this losse, and his desperate case, as not daring either to meet his enimy in the fielde, nor to trust his friends, or subiects at home. The principall cause of this continual quarell, betwixt the *Russe* and the *Chrim*, is for the right of certeine border parts claimed by the *Tartar*, but possessed by the *Russe*. The *Tartar* alleageth that besides *Astracan*, and *Cazan* (that are the ancient possession of the East *Tartar*) the whole countrie from his bounds North and Westward, so farre as the citie of *Mosko*, and *Mosko* it selfe, perteineth to his right. Which seemeth to haue bene true by

The firing of *Mosko* by the *Chrim Tartar*, in the yeare 1571.

Homage done
by the *Russe*
to the *Chrim*
Tartar.

the report of the *Russes* themselues, that tell of a certeine homage that was done by the *Russe* Emperour euery yeare, to the Great *Chrim* or *Cham*, the *Russe* Emperour standing on foote and feeding the *Chrims* horse, (himselfe sitting on his back) with oates out of his owne cap, in stead of a boule or maunger, and that within the

55 castle of *Mosko*. And this homage (they say) was done til the time of *Basileus* grandfather to this man. Who surprising the *Chrim* Emperor by a stratagem, done by one of his Nobilitie (called *Iuan Demetrowich Belschey*) was content with this raunsome, vz: with the chaunging of this homage into a tribute of furres: which afterwards

60 also was denied to be paied by this Emperours father.

Hereupon they continue the quarrell, the *Russe* defending his countrie, and that which he hath wonne, the *Chrim Tartar* inuading him once or twise euery yeare, sometime about Whitsontide, but oftener in Haruest. What time if the great *Cham* or *Chrim* come in

65 his owne person, he bringeth with him a great armie of 100000. or 200000. men. Otherwise they make shorte, and sudden roads into the countrie with lesser numbers, running about the list of the border as wild geese flie, inuading and retiring where they see aduantage.

The manner
of the *Tar-*
tars fight,
and armour.

Their common practise (being very populous) is to make diuers armies, and so drawing the *Russe* to one, or two places of the frontiers, to inuade at some other place, that is left without defence. Their manner of fight, or ordering of their forces, is much after the *Russe* manner (spoken of before) saue that they are all horsemen,

75 and carrie nothing els but a bow, a sheafe of arrowes, and a falcon sword after the *Turkish* fashion. They are very expert horsmen, and vse to shoot as readily backward, as forward. Some wil haue a horsmans staffe like to a bore speare, besides their other weapons. The common souldier hath no other armour then his ordinary

80 apparel, vz: a blacke sheeps skin with the wooll side outward in the day time, and inward in the night time, with a cap of the same. But their *Morseys* or Noblemen imitate the *Turke* both in apparel, and armour. When they are to passe ouer a riuer with their armie,

they tie three or foure horses together, and taking long poles or
pieces of wood, bind them fast to the tails of their horse: so sitting
on the poles they driue their horse ouer. At handie strokes (when
they come to ioyne battaile) they are accounted farre better men
then the *Russe* people, fearse by nature, but more hardie and blouddy
by continuall practise of warre: as men knowing no artes of peace,
nor any ciuill practise.

    Yet their subtiltie is more then may seeme to agree with their
barbarous condition. By reason they are practised to inuade continually, and to robbe their neighbours that border about them, they
are very pregnant, and ready witted to deuise stratageams vpon
the suddaine for their better aduantage. As in their warre against
Beala the fourth king of *Hungarie*, whome they inuaded with
500000. men, and obteined against him a great victorie. Where
among other, hauing slaine his Chauncellor, called *Nicholas Schinick*,
they founde about him the Kings priuie seale. Whereupon they
deuised presently to counterfait letters in the Kings name, to the
cities and townes next about the place, where the field was fought:
with charge that in no case they should conuey themselues, and
their goods out of their dwellings, where they might abide safely
without all feare of daunger, and not leaue the countrie desolate to
the possession of so vile and barbarous an enimie, as was the *Tartar*
nation, terming themselues in all reprochfull manner. For notwithstanding he had lost his carriages, with some fewe straglers that had
marched disorderly, yet hee doubted not but to recouer that losse,
with the accesse of a notable victorie, if the sauage *Tartar* durst abide
him in the fielde. To this purpose hauing written their letters in the
Polish character, by certaine young men whom they tooke in the
field, and signed them with the Kings seale, they dispatched them
foorth to all the quarters of *Hungarie*, that lay neare about the place.
Whereupon the *Vngarians*, that were now flying away with their
goods, wiues, and children, vpon the rumour of the Kings ouerthrow,
taking comfort of these counterfait letters, stayed at home. And so
were made a pray, being surprised on the suddaine by this huge

The subtil-
tie of the
Tartar.

85

90

95

100

105

110

115

number of these *Tartars*, that had compassed them about before they were aware.

120   When they besiege a towne or fort, they offer much parle, and sende many flattering messages to perswade a surrendry: promising all things that the inhabitants will require: but beyng once possessed of the place, they vse all manner of hostilitie, and crueltie. This they doo vppon a rule they haue, vz: that Iustice is to be practised but

125   towardes their owne. They encounter not lightly, but they haue some ambush, wherevnto hauing once shewed themselues, and made some short conflict, they retire, as repulsed for feare, and so draw the enimie into it if they can. But the *Russe* being wel acquainted with their practise, is more warie of them. When they come a

130   rouing with some small number, they set on horsebacke counterfait shapes of men, that their number may seeme greater.

     When they make any onset, their manner is to make a great shoote, crying all out together *Olla Billa, Olla Billa, God helpe vs, God helpe vs*. They contemne death so much, as that they chuse

135   rather to die, then to yeeld to their enimie, and are seene when they are slaine to bite the very weapon, when they are past striking, or helping of themselues. Wherein appeareth how different the *Tartar* is in his desperate courage from the *Russe*, and *Turke*. For the *Russe* Souldier if he begin once to retire putteth all his safety in his speedie

140   flight. And if once he be taken by his enemie, he neyther defendeth himselfe, nor intreateth for his life, as reckoning straight to die. The *Turke* commonly when he is past hope of escaping, falleth to intreatie, and casteth awaie his weapon, offereth both his handes, and holdeth them vp, as it were to be tyed: hoping to saue his life,

145   by offering himselfe bondslaue.

     The chiefe bootie the *Tartars* seeke for in all their warres, is to get store of captiues, specially yong boyes, and girls, whom they sell to the *Turkes*, or other their neighbors. To this purpose they take with them great baskets made like bakers panniers to carrie

150   them tenderly, and if any of them happen to tyer, or to be sicke on the way, they dash him against the ground, or some tree, and so

250

leaue him dead. The souldiers are not troubled with keeping the captiues, and the other bootie, for hindering the execution of their warres, but they haue certein bands that intend nothing els, appointed of purpose to receiue, and keepe the captiues and the other praye.

The *Russe* borders (being vsed to their inuasions lightly euery yeere in the sommer) keepe fewe other cattel on the border parts, saue swine onely, which the *Tartar* will not touch, nor driue away with him: for that he is of the *Turkish* religion, and will eate no swines flesh. Of Christ our Sauiour they confesse asmuch as doeth the *Turke* in his Alkaron, vz. that hee came of the Angell *Gabriel*, and the virgin *Marie*, that hee was a great Prophet, and shalbe the Iudge of the world at the last day. In other matters likewise, they are much ordered after the manner and direction of the *Turke*: hauing felt the *Turkish* forces when hee wonne from them *Azou*, and *Caffa*, with some other townes about the *Euxine*, or *Blacke sea*, that were before tributaries to the *Chrim Tartar*. So that now the Emperour of the *Chrims* for the most part is chosen some one of the Nobilitie whom the *Turke* doeth commend: whereby it is brought nowe to that passe, that the *Chrim Tartar* giueth to the *Turke* the tenth part of the spoyle, which hee getteth in his warres against the Christians.

Herein they differ from the *Turkish* religion, for that they haue certeine idole puppets made of silke, or like stuffe, of the fashion of a man, which they fasten to the doore of their walking houses, to be as *Ianusses* or keepers of their house. And these idols are made not by all, but by certeine religious women, which they haue among them for that, and like vses. They haue besides the image of their King or great *Cham*, of an huge bignes which they erect at euery stage: when the army marcheth: and this euery one must bend and bowe vnto as hee passeth by it, bee he *Tartar*, or stranger. They are much giuen to witchcraft, and ominous coniectures, vpon euery accident which they heare, or see.

In making of mariages they haue no regard of alliance or consanguinitie. Onely with his mother, sister, and daughter a man

155

The *Tartar* religion.

160

165

170

175

180

185

may not marrie, and though hee take the woman into his house, and accompany with her, yet hee accounteth her not for his wife, till he haue a childe by her. Then he beginneth to take a dowrie of her friendes of horse, sheepe, kyne, &c. If she be barren after a certeine time, he turneth her home againe.

Vnder the Emperour they haue certeine Dukes, whome they call *Morseis* or *Diuoymorseis*: that rule ouer a certeine number of 10000. 20000. or 40000. a piece, which they call *hoords*. When the Emperour hath any vse of them to serue in his warres, they are bound to come, and to bring with them their souldiers to a certeine nomber, euery man with his two horses at the least, the one to ride on, the other to kill, when it commeth to his turne to haue his horse eaten. For

their chiefe vittaile is horse flesh, which they eate without bread, or any other thing with it. So that if a *Tartar* be taken by a *Russe,* he shall be sure lightly to finde a horse legge, or some other part of him at his saddle bow.

This last yeere when I was at the *Mosko*, came in one *Kiriach Morsey*, nephewe to the Emperour of the *Chrims* that now is (whose father was Emperour before) accompanied with 300. *Tartars,* and his two wiues, whereof one was his brothers widdow. Where being intertained in very good sort after the *Russe* manner, hee had sent vnto his lodging for his welcome, to bee made ready for his supper and his companies, two very large and fatte horses, ready flawed in a sledde. They preferre it before other flesh, because the meate is stronger (as they say) then beefe, mutton, and such like. And yet (which is marueile) though they serue all as horsemen in the warres, and eate all of horseflesh, there are brought yeerely to the *Mosko* to be exchanged for other commodities 30. or 40. thousand *Tartar* horse, which they call *Cones*. They keepe also great heards of kine, and stockes of blacke sheepe, rather for the skins and milke (which they carry with them in great bottels) then for the vse of the flesh, though sometimes they eate of it. Some vse they haue of ryse, figs, and other fruites. They drinke milke or warme blood, and for the most part carde them both together. They vse sometimes as they

traueile by the way, to let their horse blood in a vain, and to drinke
it warme, as it commeth from his body.

Townes they plant none, nor other standing buildings, but haue
walking houses which the Latines call *Veij*, built vpon wheeles like
a shepheards cottage. These they drawe with them withersoeuer
they goe, driuing their cattaile with them. And when they come
to their stage or standing place, they plant their cart houses very
orderly in a ranke: and so make the forme of streetes, and of a large
towne. And this is the manner of the Emperour himselfe, who hath
no other seat of his Empire but an *Agora*, or towne of wood, that
moueth with him whithersoeuer hee goeth. As for the fixed and
standing building vsed in other countreys, they say they are vnwhol-
some and vnpleasant.

They beginne to mooue their houses and cattaile in the spring
time from the South part of their Countrey towards the North
parts. And so driuing on til they haue grased all vp to the farthest
part Northwarde, they returne backe againe towardes their South
countrey (where they continue all the winter) by ten or twelue
miles a stage: in the meane while the grasse being sprung vp againe,
to serue for their cattaile as they returne. From the border of the
Shalcan towards the *Caspian* sea, to the *Russe* frontiers, they haue
a goodly Countrey, specially on the South and Southeast partes,
but lost for lacke of tillage.

Of money they haue no vse at all, and therefore preferre brasse
and steele before other mettals, specially bullate, which they vse
for swords, kniues, and other necessaries. As for golde and siluer
they neglect it of very purpose, (as they doe all tillage of their
ground) to be more free for their wandring kinde of life, and to
keepe their Countrey lesse subiect to inuasions. Which giueth them
great aduantage against all their neighbors, euer inuading, and neuer
being inuaded. Such as haue taken vpon them to inuade their
Countrey (as of olde time *Cyrus* and *Darius Hystaspis*, on the East
and Southeast side) haue done it with very ill successe: as we find
in the stories written of those times. For their manner is when any

will inuade them, to allure and drawe them on by flying and
255 reculing (as if they were afraide) till they haue drawen them some
good way within their countrey. Then when they beginne to want
vittaile and other necessaries (as needs they must where nothing is
to bee had) to stoppe vp the passages, and inclose them with
multitudes. By which stratagem (as we reade in *Laonicus Chalcacon-*
260 *dylas* in his *Turkish* storie) they had welnigh surprised the great and
huge armie of *Tamerlan*, but that hee retyred with all speede hee
coulde, towardes the riuer *Tanais*, or *Don*, not without great losse
of his men, and carriages.

In the storie of *Pachymerius* the *Greeke* (which he wrote of the
265 Emperours of *Constantinople* from the beginning of the reigne of
Michael Palæologus to the time of *Andronicus* the elder) I remember
hee telleth to the same pourpose of one *Nogas* a *Tartarian* captaine
vnder *Cazan* the Emperour of the East *Tartars* (of whome the Citie
and kingdome of *Cazan* may seeme to haue taken the denomination)
270 who refused a present of Pearle and other iewels sent vnto him
from *Michael Palæologus*: asking withall, for what vse they serued,
and whither they were good to keepe away sicknesse, death, or
other misfortunes of this life, or no. So that it seemeth they haue,
euer or long time bene of that minde to value things no further,
275 then by the vse, and necessitie for which they serue.

For person and complexion they haue broad and flatte visages,
of a tanned colour into yellowe and blacke, fearse and cruell lookes,
thin haired vpon the vpper lippe, and pitte of the chinne, light and
nimble bodied, with short legges, as if they were made naturally
280 for horsemen: whereto they practise themselues from their childe-
hood, seldome going afoote about any businesse. Their speach is
very suddaine and loude, speaking as it were out of a deepe hollowe
throate. When they sing you woulde thinke a kowe lowed, or
some great bandogge howled. Their greatest exercise is shooting,
285 wherein they traine vp their children from their very infancie, not
suffering them to eate, til they haue shot neere the marke within
a certein scantling. They are the very same that sometimes were

called *Scythæ Nomades,* or the *Scythian Shepheards,* by the *Greeks*
and *Latines.* Some thinke that the *Turkes* tooke their beginning
from the nation of the *Chrim Tartars.* Of which opinion is *Laonicus* 290
Chalcocondylas the *Greeke* Historiographer, in his first booke of his
Turkish storie. Wherein hee followeth diuers very probable coniectures: The first taken from the very name it selfe, for that the
worde *Turke* signifieth a shepheard, or one that foloweth a vagrant,
and wilde kinde of life. By which name these *Scythian Tartars* haue 295
euer bene noted, being called by the *Greekes* σχύθαι νόμαδες or
the *Scythian* shepheards. His second reason, because the *Turks* (in
his time) that dwelt in *Asia the lesse,* to wit, in *Lydia, Coria, Phrygia,*
and *Cappadocia,* spake the very same language that these *Tartars* did,
that dwelt betwixt the riuer *Tanais* or *Don,* and the countrey of 300
Sarmatia, which (as is well knowen) are these *Tartars* called *Chrims.*
At this time also the whole nation of the *Turkes* differ not much
in their common speach from the *Tartar* language. Thirdly because
the *Turke* and the *Chrim Tartar* agree so well together, aswell in
religion, as in matter of traffique neuer inuading, or iniurying one 305
another: saue that the *Turke* (since *Laonicus* his time) hath encroached
vpon some Townes vpon the *Euxin* sea, that before perteined to the
Chrim Tartar. Fourthly, because *Ortogules* sonne to *Oguzalpes,* and
father to *Otoman* the first of name of the *Turkish* nation, made his
first roads out of those partes of *Asia,* vpon the next borderers, till 310
he came towardes the countreys about the hill *Taurus,* where hee
ouercame the *Greeks* that inhabited there: and so enlarged the name
and territorie of the *Turkish* nation, til he came to *Eubea* and *Attica,*
and other partes of *Greece.* This is the opinion of *Laonicus,* who
liued among the *Turks* in the time of *Amurat* the sixt *Turkish* 315
Emperour, about the yeere 1400. when the memorie of their
originall was more freshe and therefore the likelier hee was to hit
the trueth.

   There are diuers other *Tartars* that border vpon *Russia,* as the
Nagaies, the *Cheremissens,* the *Mordwites,* the *Chircasses,* and the 320
Shalcans, which all differ in name more then in regiment, or other

condition, from the *Chrim Tartar* except the *Chircasses* that border Southwest, towardes *Lituania*, and are farre more ciuil then the rest of the *Tartars*, of a comely person, and of a stately behauiour, as applying themselues to the fashion of the *Polonian*. Some of them haue subiected themselues to the kings of *Poland*, and professe Christianitie. The *Nagay* lyeth Eastwarde, and is reckoned for the best man of warre among all the *Tartars*, but verie sauage, and cruell aboue all the rest. The *Cheremissin Tartar*, that lieth betwixt the *Russe* and the *Nagay*, are of two sorts, the *Lugauoy* (that is of the valley) and the *Nagornay*, or of the hillie countrey. These haue much troubled the Emperours of *Russia*. And therfore they are content now to buy peace of them, vnder pretence of giuing a yeerely pension of *Russe* commodities, to their *Morseis*, or *Diuoymorseis*, that are chiefe of their tribes. For which also they are bound to serue them in their wars, vnder certeine conditions. They are saide to be iust and true in their dealings: and for that cause they hate the *Russe* people, whom they account to be double, and false in all their dealing. And therfore the common sort are very vnwilling to keep agreement with them, but that they are kept in order by their *Morseis*, or Dukes for their pensions sake.

The most rude and barbarous is counted the *Mordwit Tartar*, that hath many self fashions, and strange kinds of behauiour, differing from the rest. For his religion, thogh he acknowlege one god, yet his maner is to worship for god, that liuing thing, that he first meeteth in the morning, and to sweare by it al that whole day whether it be horse, dogge, catte, or whatsoeuer els it be. When his friend dieth, he killeth his best horse, and hauing flayed off the skin he carrieth it on high vpon a long pole, before the corpes to the place of buriall. This hee doeth (as the *Russe* sayeth) that his friend may haue a good horse to carie him to heauen: but it is likelier to declare his loue towardes his dead friende, in that hee will haue to die with him the best thing that hee hath.

Next to the kingdome of *Astracan*, that is the farthest part Southeastward of the *Russe* dominion, lyeth the *Shalcan*, and the

256

countrey of *Media*: whither the *Russe* marchants trade for raw silks, syndon, saphion, skins, and other commodities. The chiefe townes of *Media* where the *Russe* tradeth, are, *Derbent* (built by *Alexander* the great, as the inhabitauntes saye) and *Zamachie* where the staple is kept for rawe silkes. Their manner is in the Spring time to reuiue the silke-wormes (that lye dead all the Winter) by laying them in the warme sunne, and (to hasten their quickening that they may sooner goe to worke) to put them into bags, and so to hang them vnder their childrens armes. As for the worme called *Chriuisin* (as we call it *chrymson*) that maketh coloured silke, it is bred not in *Media*, but in *Assyria*. This trade to *Derbent* and *Samachie* for rawe silkes, and other commodities, of that countrey, as also into *Persia*, and *Bougharia*, downe the riuer *Volgha*, and through the *Caspian* sea, is permitted aswell to the English, as to the *Russe* marchants, by the Emperours last Graunt at my being there. Which hee accounteth for a very speciall fauour, and might prooue in deede very beneficiall to our English marchants, if the trade were wel, and orderly vsed.

The whole nation of the *Tartars* are vtterly voyde of all learning, and without written Lawe. Yet certeine rules they haue which they holde by tradition, common to all the *Hoords* for the practise of their life. Which are of this sort. First, *To obey their Emperour and other Magistrates, whatsoeuer they commaunde about the publique seruice.* 2. *Except for the publique behoofe, euery man to be free and out of controlement.* 3. *No priuate man to possesse any lands, but the whole countrey to be as a common.* 4. *To neglect all daintinesse and varietie of meates, and to content themselues with that which commeth next to hand, for more hardnesse, and readinesse in the executing of their affaires.* 5. *To weare any base attire, and to patch their clothes, whether there bee anie neede or not: that when there is neede, it bee no shame to weare a patcht coate.* 6. *To take, or steale from anie stranger whatsoeuer they can gette, as beeyng enemies to all men, saue to such as will subiect themselues to them.* 7. *Towardes their owne hoorde and nation to be true in word, and deede.* 8. *To suffer no stranger to come within the Realme. If any doe,*

390   *the same to bee bondslaue to him that first taketh him, except such marchants and other as haue the Tartar Bull, or pastport about them.*

Of the Permians, Samoites, *and* Lappes.
The 20. Chapter.

The *Permians* and *Samoits* that lye from *Russia*, north and Northeast, are thought likewise to haue taken their beginning from the *Tartar* kind. And it may partly be gessed by the fashion of their countenance, as hauing all broade, and flat faces, as the

The Permians.   *Tartars* haue, except the *Chirchasses*. The *Permians* are accounted for a very ancient people. They are now subiect to the *Russe*. They liue by hunting, and trading with their furres, as doth also the

The Samoites.   *Samoyt*, that dwelleth more towardes the North sea. The *Samoyt* hath his name (as the *Russe* saith) of eating himselfe: as if in times

10   past, they liued as the Cannibals, eating one another. Which they make more probable, because at this time they eat all kind of raw flesh, whatsoeuer it bee, euen the very carion that lieth in the ditch. But as the *Samoits* themselues wil say, they were called *Samoie*, that is of themselues, as though they were *Indigenæ*, or people bredde

15   vpon that very soyle, that neuer changed their seat from one place to another, as most nations haue done. They are subiect at this time to the Emperour of *Russia*.

The Samoites religion.   I talked with certeine of them, and finde that they acknowledge one God: but represent him by such things as they haue most vse

20   and good by. And therfore they worship the Sun, the Ollen, the

Slata Baba or the golden Hag.   Losh, and such like. As for the storie of *Slata Baba*, or the *Golden hagge*, (which I haue read in some mappes, and descriptions of these countries, to bee an idole after the forme of an olde woman) that being demaunded by the Priest, giueth them certeyne Oracles,

25   concerning the successe, and euent of thinges, I founde it to bee but a verye fable. Onelie in the Prouince of *Obdoria* vpon the Sea side, neare to the mouth of the great riuer *Obba*, there is a rocke, which naturally (beeing somewhat helped by imagination) may seeme to

258

beare the shape of a ragged woman, with a child in her armes (as the rock by the North cape the shape of a Frier) where the *Obdorian Samoites* vse much to resort, by reason of the commoditie of the place for fishing: and there sometime (as their manner is) conceiue, and practise their sorceries, and ominous coniecturings about the good, or bad speed of their iourneies, fishings, huntings, and such like.

They are clad in Seale skins, with the hearie side outwards downe as low as the knees, with their breeches and netherstocks of the same, both men and women. They are all blacke haired, naturally beardlesse. And therefore the men are hardly discerned from the women by their looks: saue that the women weare a lock of haire down along both their eares. They liue in a maner a wilde and a sauage life, rouing stil from one place of the countrey to another, without anie propertie of house or land more to one then to an other. Their leader or director in euery companie, is their *Papa* or Priest.

On the North side of *Russia* next to *Corelia*, lieth the countrey of *Lappia*, which reacheth in length from the farthest poynt North-ward, (towardes the Northcape) to the farthest part Southeast (which the *Russe* calleth *Sweetnesse* or Holie nose, the English men *Capegrace*) about 345. verst or miles. From *Sweetnesse* to *Candelox* by the way of *Versega* (which measureth the breadth of that countrey) is 90. miles or thereabouts. The whole countrey in a manner is eyther lakes, or mountaines, which towardes the Sea side are called *Tondro*, because they are all of hard and craggy rocke, but the inland partes are well furnished with woods, that growe on the hilles sides, the lakes lying betweene. Their diet is very bare and simple. Bread they haue none, but feed onely vpon fish and fowle. They are subiect to the Emperour of *Russia*, and the two kings of *Sweden*, and *Denmark*: which all exact tribute and custome of them (as was said before) but the Emperour of *Russia* beareth the greatest hand ouer them, and exact of them farre more then the rest. The opinion is that they were first termed *Lappes* of their briefe and

30

35
The *Samoits* habite and behauiour.

40

45
The *Lappes*.

50

55

60

259

short speach. The *Russe* deuideth the whole nation of the *Lappes*
into two sorts. The one they call *Nowremanskoy Lapary*, that is, the
65 *Noruegian Lappes*: because they be of the *Danish* religion. For the
Danes and *Noruegians* they account for one people. The other that
haue no religion at all, but liue as brute and Heathenish people,
without God in the world, they call *Dikoy Lopary*, or the wild
Lappes.

70   The whole nation is vtterly vnlearned, hauing not so much as
the vse of any Alphabet, or letter among them. For practise of
witchcraft and sorcery, they passe all nations in the world. Though
for the enchaunting of shippes that saile along their coast (as I haue
heard it reported) and their giuing of winds good to their friends,
75 and contrary to other, whom they meane to hurt by tying of certein
knots vpon a rope (somewhat like to the tale of *Æolus* his windbag)
is a very fable, deuised (as may seeme) by themselues, to terrifie
sailers for comming neare their coast. Their weapons are the long
bow, and handgunne, wherein they excell, aswell for quicknes to
80 charge and discharge, as for nearnesse at the marke, by reason of
their continuall practise (wherto they are forced) of shooting at
wild fowle. Their manner is in Sommer time to come downe in
great companies to the sea side, to *Wardhuyse, Cola, Kegor*, and the
bay of *Vedagoba*, and there to fish for Codd, Salmon, and But-fish,
85 which they sell to the *Russes, Danes*, and *Noruegians*, and now of
late to the English men that trade thither with cloth, which they
exchaunge with the *Lappes* and *Corelians* for their fish, oile, and
furres, whereof also they haue some store. They hold their mart at
Cola on Saint *Peters* day: what time the Captain of *Wardhuyse* (that
90 is resiant there for the king of *Denmarke*) must be present, or at
least send his deputie to set prices vpon their stockfish, traine oile,
furres, and other commodities: as also the *Russe* Emperours customer,
or tribute taker, to receiue his custome, which is euer payed before
any thing can be bought, or sold. When their fishing is done, their
95 manner is to drawe their carbasses, or boates on shoare, and there
to leaue them with the keele turned vpwardes, till the next spring

260

tide. Their trauaile too and fro is vpon sleds, drawen by the Olen deer: which they vse to turne a grasing all the Sommer time, in an iland called *Kilden* (of a very good soile compared with other partes of that countrie) and towards the winter time, when the snow 100 beginneth to fall, they fetch them home again, for the vse of their sledde.

Of their Ecclesiasticall state, with their Church offices.
The 21. Chapter.

Concerning the gouernement of their Churche, it is framed altogether after the manner of the Greek: as being a part of that Church, and neuer acknowledging the iurisdiction of the Latine Church, vsurped by the Pope. That I may keepe a better measure in describing their ceremonies, then they in the vsing them (wherein 5 they are infinite) I will note briefly: First, what Ecclesiasticall degrees, or offices they haue with the iurisdiction, and practise of them. Secondly, what doctrine they holde in matter of religion. Thirdly, what leiturgie, or forme of seruice they vse in their Churches, with the manner of their administring the Sacraments. 10 Fourthly, what other straunge ceremonies, and superstitious deuotions are vsed among them.

Their offices, or degrees of Churchmen, are as many in number, and the same in a manner both in name and degree, that were in the Westerne churches. First they haue their *Patriarch*, then their Metropolites, their *Archbishops*, their *Vladikey* or *Bishops*, their *Protopapes* or *Archpriests*, their *Papes* or *Priests*, their *Deacons*, *Friers*, *Monkes*, *Nunnes*, and *Eremites*.

Their *Patriarch*, or chiefe directer in matter of religion vntill this last yeare, was of the citie of *Constantinople* (whom they called the *Patriarch* of *Sio*) because being driuen by the *Turke* out of *Constantinople* (the seate of his Empire) he remoued to the Ile *Sio*, sometimes called *Chio*, and there placed his Patriarchiall sea. So

The church officers.

15

The Patriarch.

261

that the Emperours, and clergie of *Russia*, were wont yearelye to send gifts thither, and to acknowledge a spirituall kind of homage, and subiection due to him, and to that Church. Which custome they haue held (as it seemeth) euer since they professed the Christian religion. Which how long it hath bene I could not well learne, for that they haue no storie, or monument of antiquitie (that I could heare of) to shewe what hath bene done in times past within their countrie, concerning either Church, or common wealth matters. Onely I heare a report among them, that about three hundred yeares since, there was a marriage betwixt the Emperour of *Constantinople*, and the kings daughter of that countrie: who at the first denied to ioyne his daughter in marriage with the *Greeke* Emperour, because he was of the Christian religion. Which agreeth well with that I finde in the storie of *Laonicus Chalcacondylas* concerning Turkish affaires in his fourth booke: where hee speaketh of such a marriage betwixt *Iohn* the Greeke Emperour, and the Kings daughter of *Sarmatia*. And this argueth out of their owne report, that at that time they had not receyued the Christian religion: as also that they were conuerted to the faith, and withall peruerted at the very same time, receyuing the doctrine of the gospell, corrupted with superstitions euen at the first when they tooke it from the *Greeke* Church, which it selfe then was degenerate, and corrupted with many superstitions, and fowle errours, both in doctrine and discipline: as may appeare by the story of *Nicephorus Gregoras*, in his 8. and 9. bookes. But as touching the time of their conuersion to the christian faith, I suppose rather that it is mistaken by the *Russe*, for that which I find in the *Polonian* storie the second booke the third chapter: where is said that about the yeare 990. *Vlodomirus* Duke of *Russia*, married one *Anne* sister to *Basilius*, and *Constantinus* brothers, and Emperours of *Constantinople*. Wherupon the *Russe* receiued the faith and profession of Christ. Which though it be somewhat more auncient then the time noted before out of the *Russe* report, yet it falleth out al to one reckoning, touching this point, vz: in what truth and sinceritie of doctrine the *Russe* receiued the first stampe

262

of religion: for asmuch as the *Greeke* church at that time also was many waies infected with errour, and superstition.

At my being there, the yere 1588. came vnto the *Mosko* the *Patriarch* of *Constantinople*, or *Sio*, called *Hieronomo* being banished (as some said) by the *Turke*, as some other reported by the *Greeke* clergie depriued. The Emperour being giuen altogether to superstitious deuotions, gaue him great intertainment. Before his comming to *Mosko*, he had bene in *Italy* with the Pope, as was reported ther by some of his company. His arrand was to consult with the Emperour concerning these points. First about a league to passe betwixt him and the king of *Spaine*, as the meetest Prince to ioyne with him in opposition against the *Turke*. To which purpose also Ambassages had passed betwixt the *Russe* and the *Persian*. Likewise from the *Georgians* to the Emperour of *Russia*, to ioyne league together, for the inuading of the *Turke* on all sides of his dominions: taking the aduantage of the simple qualitie of the *Turke* that now is. This treatie was helped forward by the Emperours Ambassadour of Almaine, sent at the same time to solicite an inuasion vpon the parts of *Polonia*, that lie towards *Rusland*, and to borrow mony of the *Russe* Emperour, to pursue the warre for his brother *Maximilian*, against the *Swedens* son now king of *Poland*. But this consultation concerning a league betwixt the *Russe* and the *Spaniard*, (which was in some forwardnes at my comming to *Mosko*, and already one appointed for Ambassage into *Spaine*) was marred by means of the ouerthrow giuen to the *Spanish* king by her Maiestie, the Queene of England, this last yeare. Which made the *Russe* Emperour and his Counsell, to giue a sadder countenance to the English Ambassadour at that time: for that they were disappointed of so good a policie, as was this coniunction supposed to bee betwixt them and the *Spanish*.

His second purpose (whereto the first serued as an introduction) was in reuenge of the Turke and the Greeke cleargie, that had thrust him from his seat, to treate with them about the reducing of the *Russe* church vnder the Pope of Rome. Wherein it may seeme that comming lately from Rome, he was set on by the Pope, who hath

The translation of the Patriarchicall sea from *Constantinople* or *Sio*, to *Mosko*.

70

75

80

85

90

263

attempted the same many times before, though all in vaine: and namely in the time of the late Emperour *Iuan Vasilowich*, by one *Anthony* his Legate. But thought this belike a farre better meanes

95 to obteine his purpose by treatie and mediation of their owne Patriarch. But this not succeeding, the Patriarch fell to a third point of treatie, concerning the resignation of his Patriarchship, and translation of the Sea from *Constantinople*, or *Sio*, to the citie of *Mosko*. Which was so well liked, and intertained by the Emperour

100 (as a matter of high religion, and pollicie) that no other treatie (specially of forrein Ambassages) could be heard, or regarded, till that matter was concluded.

The reasons wherewith the Patriarch perswaded the translating of his Sea to the citie of *Mosko*, were these in effect. First, for that

105 the Sea of the Patriarch was vnder the *Turk* that is enemie to the faith. And therefore to bee remoued into some other countrie of Christian profession. Secondly, because the *Russe* church was the only naturall daughter of the Greeke at this time, and holdeth the same doctrine and ceremonies with it: the rest being all subiect to

110 the Turke, and fallen away from the right profession. Wherein the subtill Greeke to make the better market of his broken ware, aduaunced the honour that would growe to the Emperour, and his countrie: to haue the Patriarches seat, translated into the chief citie, and seat of his Empire. As for the right of translating the sea,

115 and appointing his successour, hee made no doubt of it, but that it perteyned wholy to himselfe.

The Patri-
archship of
*Constanti-
nople* trans-
lated to
Mosko.
So the Emperour, and his Counsell, with the principall of his cleargie being assembled at the *Mosko*, it was determined that the *Metropolite* of *Mosko*, should become Patriarch of the whole Greeke Church, and haue the same full authoritie, and iurisdiction that perteined before to the Patriarch of *Constantinople*, or *Sio*. And that it might bee done with more order, and solemnitie, the 25. of *Ianuary*, 1588. the Greeke Patriarch accompanied with the *Russe* Cleargie, went to the great Church of *Precheste*, or our Ladie,

125 within the Emperours castle (hauing first wandred thorough the

264

whole citie in manner of a procession, and blessing the people with his two fingers) where hee made an Oration, and deliuered his resignation in an instrument of writing, and so laied downe his Patriarchicall staffe. Which was presently receiued by the Metropolite of *Mosko*, and diuers other ceremonies vsed about the inauguration of this new Patriarch.   130

The day was held very solemne by the people of the citie, who were commaunded to forbeare their workes, and to attend this solemnitie. The *Greeke* Patriarch that day was honoured with rich presents sent him from the Emperour and Empresse, of plate, cloth   135 of gold, furres, &c: carried with great pompe thorough the streats of *Mosko* and at his departing receiued many giftes more, both from the Emperour, Nobilitie, and Cleargie. Thus the Patriarchship of *Constantinople*, or *Sio*, (which hath continued since the Counsell of *Nice*) is now translated to *Mosko*, or they made beleeue that   140 they haue a Patriarch with the same right and authoritie that the other had. Wherin the subtil *Greeke* hath made good aduantage of their superstition, and is now gone away with a rich bootie into *Poland*, whither their Patriarchship be currant or not.

The matter is not vnlike to make some schisme betwixt the   145 *Greeke* and *Russe* Church, if the *Russe* holde this Patriarchship that he hath so well payed for, and the Greekes elect an other withall, as likely they will, whither this man were banished by the Turke, or depriued by order of his owne Cleargie. Which might happen to giue aduantage to the Pope, and to bring ouer the *Russe* Church   150 to the sea of Rome (to which end peraduenture he deuised this stratageam, and cast in this matter of schisme among them) but that the Emperours of *Russia* know well enough, by the example of other christian Princes, what inconuenience would grow to their state and countrie, by subiecting themselues to the Romish sea. To   155 which ende the late Emperour *Iuan Vasilowich* was very inquisitiue of the Popes authority ouer the Princes of christendome, and sent one of very purpose to Rome, to behold the order, and behauior of his court.

160   With this Patriarch *Hieronimo* was driuen out at the same time by the great Turke, one *Demetrio* Archbishop of *Larissa*: who is now in England, and pretendeth the same cause of their banishment by the Turke (to wit) their not admitting of the Popes new Kalender, for the alteration of the yeare. Which how vnlikely it is, may

165 appeare by these circumstances. First, because there is no such affection, nor friendlie respect, betwixt the Pope and the Turke, as that he should banish a subiect for not obeying the Popes ordinance, specially in a matter of some sequele for the alteration of times within his owne countries. Secondly, for that he maketh no such

170 scruple in deducting of times, and keeping of a iust and precise account from the incarnation of Christ: whom he doth not acknowledge otherwise then I noted before. Thirdly, for that the said Patriarch is now at *Naples* in *Italy*, where it may be ghessed he would not haue gone within the Popes reach, and so neare to his

175 nose, if he had bene banished for opposing himselfe against the Popes decree.

The Patriarches iurisdiction.

    This office of Patriarchship now translated to *Mosko*, beareth a superiour authoritie ouer all the Churches, not onely of *Russia*, and other the Emperours dominions, but thorough out all the

180 churches of Christendome that were before vnder the Patriarch of *Constantinople*, or *Sio*: or at least the *Russe* Patriarch imagineth himselfe to haue the same authoritie. Hee hath vnder him as his proper diocesse the Prouince of *Mosko*, besides other peculiars. His court, or office is kept at the *Mosko*.

The Metropolites.

    Before the creation of this new Patriarch, they had but one *Metropolite*, that was called the *Metropolite* of *Mosko*. Now for more state to their Church, and newe Patriarch, they haue two Metropolites, the one of *Nouogrod velica*, the other of *Rostoue*. Their office is to receiue of the Patriarch such Ecclesiasticall orders, as he

190 thinketh good, and to deliuer the charge of them ouer to the Archbishops: besides the ordering of their owne diocesse.

Archbishops.

    Their Archbishops are foure: of *Smolensko*, *Cazan*, *Vobsko*, and *Vologda*. The partes of their office is all one with the Metropolits:

saue that they haue an vnder iurisdiction, as Suffraganes to the Metropolites, and superiours to the Bishops. The next are the *Vladikeis*, or Bishops, that are but sixe in all: of *Crutitska*, of *Rezan*, of *Otfer* and *Torshock*, of *Collomenska*, of *Volodemer*, of *Susdalla*. These haue euery one a very large diocesse: as diuiding the rest of the whole countrie among them.

195
Bishops.

The matters perteyning to the Ecclesiasticall iurisdiction, of the Metropolites, Archbishops, and Bishops, are the same in a manner that are vsed by the Cleargie in other partes of Christendome. For besides their authoritie ouer the Cleargie, and ordering such matters as are meare Ecclesiasticall, their iurisdiction extendeth to all testamentarie causes, matters of marriage, and diuorcementes, some pleas of iniuries, &c. To which purpose also they haue their Officials, or Commissaries (which they call *Boiaren Vladitskey*) that are Laymen of the degree of Dukes, or Gentlemen, that keepe their Courtes and execute their iurisdiction. Which besides their other oppressions ouer the common people, raigne ouer the Priestes: as the Dukes and Diacks doo ouer the poore people, within their precincts. As for the Archbishop or Bishop himselfe, he beareth no sway in deciding those causes, that are brought into his Court. But if hee would moderate any matter, hee must doo it by intreatie with his Gentleman officiall. The reason is, because these *Boiarskey*, or Gentlemen officials, are not appointed by the Bishops, but by the Emperour himselfe, or his Counsell, and are to giue account of their doings to none but to them. If the Bishoppe can intreat at his admission to haue the choice of his owne officiall, it is accounted for a speciall great fauour. But to speake it as it is, the Cleargie of *Russia*, aswell concerning their landes and reuenues, as their authoritie and iurisdiction, are altogether ordered and ouer ruled by the Emperour, and his Counsell, and haue so much, and no more of both as their pleasure doth permit them. They haue also their assistants or seuerall Counsels (as they call them) of certeine Priests that are of their diocese, residing within their cathedrall cities, to the number of foure and twentie a piece. These aduise with

Ecclesiasti-
call iuris-
diction.

205
Their Gen-
tlemen com-
missaries.

210

215

220

225

them about the speciall and necessarie matters belonging to their charge.

The church reuenues. Concerning their rentes and reuenues to mainteyne their dignities, it is somewhat large. The Patriarches yearely rents out of his landes (besides other fees) is about 3000. rubbels, or markes. The Metropolites and Archbishops about 2500. The Bishops some a 1000. some 800. some 500. &c. They haue had some of them (as I haue heard say) ten or twelue thousand rubbels a yeare: as had the Metropolite of *Nouograde*.

The habite of their clergy men. Their habite or apparell (when they shewe themselues in their Pontificalibus after their solemnest manner) is a miter on their heades, after the popish fashion, sette with pearle and pretious stone, a cope on their backes, commonly of cloth of golde, embrodered with pearle, and a Crosiers staffe in their handes, layed ouer all with plate of siluer double guilt, with a crosse or sheepheardes crooke at the vpper ende of it. Their ordinarie habite otherwise when they ride or goe abroad, is a hood on their heads of blacke colour, that hangeth downe their backes, and standeth out like a bongrace before. Their vpper garment (which they call *Reis*) is a gowne or mantell of blacke Damaske, with many listes or gardes of white Sattin layed vpon it, euerie garde about two fingers broad, and their Crosiers staffe carried before them. Themselues followe after, blessing the people with their two forefingers, with a marueilous grace.

The election of Bishops. The election, and appointing of the Bishops and the rest, perteyneth wholy to the Emperour himselfe. They are chosen euer out of the Monasteries: so that there is no Bishop, Archbishop, nor Metropolite, but hath bene a Monke, or Frier before. And by that reason they are, and must all bee vnmaried men, for their vow of chastitie when they were first shorne. When the Emperour hath appointed whom hee thinketh good, he is inuested in the Cathedrall church of his dioces, with many ceremonies, much after the manner of the Popish inauguration. They haue also their Deanes, and their Archdeacons.

268

As for preaching the worde of God, or any teaching, or exhorting such as are vnder them, they neyther vse it, nor haue any skill of it: the whole Cleargie beyng vtterlie vnlearned bothe for other knowledge, and in the word of God. Onely their manner is twise euery yeere, vz. the first of September (which is the first day of their yere) and on Saint *Iohn* Baptists day, to make an ordinarie speach to the people, euery Metropolite, Archbishop, and Bishop, in his Cathedrall Church, to this or like effect: That if anie be in malice towardes his neighbour, hee shall leaue off his malice: if any haue thought of treason or rebellion against his Prince, he beware of such practise: if he haue not kept his fasts, and vowes, nor done his other dueties to the holie Church, he shal amend that fault, &c. And this is a matter of forme with them, vttered in as many words, and no more, in a manner then I haue heere set downe. Yet the matter is done with that grace and solemnitie, in a pulpit of purpose set vp for this one Acte, as if he were to discourse at large of the whole substance of diuinitie. At the *Mosko* the Emperour himselfe is euer present at this solemne exhortation.

As themselues are voyde of all maner of learning, so are they warie to keepe out all meanes that might bring any in: as fearing to haue their ignorance, and vngodlinesse discouered. To that purpose they haue perswaded the Emperours, that it would breed innouation, and so danger to their state, to haue anie noueltie of learning come within the Realme. Wherein they say but trueth, for that a man of spirit and vnderstanding, helped by learning and liberal education, can hardly indure a tyrannicall gouernment. Some yeres past in the other Emperors time, there came a Presse and Letters out of *Polonia*, to the citie of *Mosko*, where a printing house was set vp, with great liking and allowance of the Emperour himselfe. But not long after, the house was set on fire in the night time, and the presse and letters quite burnt vp, as was thought by the procurement of the Cleargy men.

Their Priestes (whom they call *Papaes*) are made by the Bishops, without any great triall for worthinesse of giftes, before they admit

270

275

280

285

290

Priests.
295

269

them, or ceremonies in their admission: saue that their heades are shorne (not shauen for that they like not) about an hand bredth or more in the crowne, and that place annoynted with oyle by the Bishop: who in his admission putteth vpon the priest, first his surplesse, and then setteth a white crosse on his brest of silke, or some other matter, which he is to weare eight dayes, and no more: and so giueth him authoritie to say and sing in the Church, and to administer the Sacraments.

They are men vtterly vnlearned, which is no marueile, forasmuch as their makers, the Bishops themselues (as before was saide) are cleere of that qualitie, and make no farther vse at al of any kind of learning, no not of the scriptures themselues, saue to reade and to sing them. Their ordinary charge and function is to say the Leiturgie, to administer the Sacraments after their maner, to keepe and deck their idoles, and to doe the other ceremonies vsuall in their Churches. Their number is great, because their townes are parted into many smal parishes, without any descretion for deuiding them into competent numbers of housholds, and people for a iust congregation: as the manner in all places where the meanes is neglected, for increasing of knowledge, and instruction towardes God. Which cannot well be had, where by means of an vnequall partition of the people, and parishes, there followeth a want and vnequalitie of stipend for a sufficient ministerie.

The *Russe* Priests can marry but once.

For their priests, it is lawful to marrie for the first time. But if the first wife dye, a second hee cannot take, but hee must loose his Priesthood, and his liuing withall. The reason they make out of that place of Saint *Paul* to *Timothie* 1. 3. 2. not well vnderstood, thinking that to bee spoken of diuers wiues successiuely, that the Apostle speaketh of at one and the same time. If he will needs marry againe after his first wife is dead, hee is no longer called *Papa*, but *Rospapa*, or *Priest quondam*. This maketh the Priestes to make much of their wiues, who are accounted as the matrones, and of best reputation among the women of the parish.

For the stipend of the Priest, their manner is not to pay him

any tenthes of corne, or ought els: but he must stand at the deuotion 330
of the people of his parish, and make vp the incommes towards
his maintenance, so wel as he can, by offerings, shriftes, marriages,
burials, dirges, and prayers for the dead and the liuing (which they
call *Molitua*). For besides their publike seruice within their Churches,
their manner is for euery priuate man to haue a prayer saide for 335
him by the Priest, vpon any occasion of businesse whatsoeuer,
whether he ride, goe, saile, plough, or whatsoeuer els he doeth.
Which is not framed accor ding to the occasion of his businesse,
but at randome, being some of their ordinarie and vsuall Church-
prayers. And this is thought to be more holy, and effectuall, if it 340
be repeated by the Priests mouth, rather then by his owne. They
haue a custome besides to solemnize the Saints day, that is patrone
to their Church once euery yeere. What time al their neighbours
of their countrey, and parishes about, come in to haue prayers
saide to that Saint for themselues, and their friendes: and so make 345
an offering to the Priest for his paines. This offering may yeeld
them some ten poundes a yeere, more or lesse, as the patrone, or
Saint of that Church is of credite, and estimation among them.
The manner is on this day (which they keep anniuersarie) for the
priest, to hire diuers of his neighbour priestes to helpe him: as 350
hauing more dishes to dresse for the Saint, then he can wel turne
his hand vnto. They vse besides to visite their parishioners houses,
with holy water, and perfume, commonly once a quarter: and so
hauing sprinckled, and besensed the good man and his wife, with
the rest of their houshold, and houshold-stuffe, they receiue some   The priests
deuotion more or lesse, as the man is of abilitie. This and the rest   maintenance.
laid altogether, may make vp for the priest towardes his main-
tenaunce, about thirtie or fourtie rubbels a yere: wherof he payeth
the tenth part to the Bishop of the Dioces.

The *Papa* or Priest is knowen by his long tufts of haire, hanging   The priests
downe by his eares, his gowne with a broad cape, and a walking   attire.
staffe in his hand. For the rest of his habite, he is apparelled like
the common sort. When he saith the Leiturgie or seruice, within

the Church, he hath on him his surplesse, and sometimes his coape,
if the day be more solemne. They haue besides their *Papaes* or
Priestes, their *Churnapapaes* (as they call them) that is, *Blacke Priestes*:
that may keepe their Benefices, though they bee admitted Friers
withall within some Monasterie. They seeme to bee the verie same
that were called Regular Priestes in the Popish Church. Vnder the
Priest, is a Deacon in euery Church, that doeth nothing but the
office of a parish Clearke. As for their *Protopapaes*, or Archepriestes,
and their Archdeacons (that are next in election to be their *Protopopas*)
they serue onely in the cathedral Churches.

Friers.   Of Friers they haue an infinit rabble farre greater then in any
other countrey, where popery is professed. Euery city, and good
part of the countrey, swarmeth ful of them. For they haue wrought
(as the popish Friers did by their superstition and hypocrisie) that
if any part of the Realme bee better and sweeter then other, there
standeth a Friery, or a monastery dedicated to some Saint.

The number of them is so much the greater, not onely for that
it is augmented by the superstition of the countrey, but because
the Fryers life is the safest from the oppressions, and exactions,
that fall vpon the Commons. Which causeth many to put on the
Fryers weede, as the best armour to beare off such blowes. Besides
such as are voluntarie, there are diuers that are forced to shire
themselues Fryers, vpon some displeasure. These are for the most
part of the chiefe Nobility. Diuers take the Monasteries as a place
of Sanctuary, and there become Friers, to auoyde some punishment,
that they had deserued by the lawes of the Realme. For if hee gette
a Monastery ouer his head, and there put on a coole before hee
be attached, it is a protection to him for euer against any law, for
what crime soeuer: except it be for treason. But this *Prouiso* goeth
withal, that no man commeth there, (except such as are commanded
by the Emperour to be receiued) but hee giueth them lands, or
bringeth his stock with him, and putteth it into the common
Treasurie. Some bring a 1000 rubbels, and some more. None is
admitted vnder 3. or 4. hundred.

Chapter 21: The Russian Church

Their manner
of shiring
Friers.

The manner of their admission is after this sort. First, the Abbot strippeth him of all his secular or ordinarie apparell. Then hee putteth vpon him next to his skinne, a white flannel shirt, with a long garment ouer it down to the ground, girded vnto him with a broade leather belt. His vppermost garment is a weede of *Garras*, or *Say*, for colour and fashion, much like to the vpper weed of a Chimney-sweeper. Then is his crown shorne a hand breadth, or more close to the very skinne, and these, or like wordes pronounced by the Abbot, whiles hee clippeth his haire: *As these haires are clipped of, and taken from thy head: so now we take thee, and separate thee cleane from the worlde, and worldly thinges, &c.* This done, hee annoynteth his crowne with oyle, and putteth on his coole: and so taketh him in among the Fraternitie. They vowe perpetuall chastitie, and abstinence from flesh.

Besides their landes, (that are verie great) they are the greatest marchants in the whole countrey, and deale for all manner of commodities. Some of their monasteries dispend in landes, one thousande, or two thousande rubbels a yeere. There is one Abbey called *Troits*, that hath in lands and fees, the summe of 100000. rubbels, or marks a yeere. It is built in maner of a Castle, walled rounde about, with great ordinance planted on the wall, and conteineth within it a large bredth of grounde, and great varietie of building. There are of Friers within it, (besides their officers, and other seruants) about 700. The Empresse that now is, hath many vowes to *Saint Sergius*, that is patrone there: to intreat him to make her fruitful, as hauing no children by the Emperour her husband. Lightly euery yeere she goeth on pilgrimage to him from the *Mosko*, on foote, about 80. English miles, with fiue or sixe thousand women attending vpon her, all in blewe liueries, and foure thousand souldiers for her garde. But *Saint Sergius* hath not yet heard her prayers, though (they say) he hath a speciall gift and facultie that way.

What learning there is among their Fryers, may be knowen by their Bishops, that are the choyce men out of all their monasteries.

The Friers
learning.

I talked with one of them at the Citie of *Vologda*, where (to trie his skill) I offered him a *Russe* Testament, and turned him to the first Chapter of Saint *Mathewes* Gospel. Where hee beganne to

435 reade in verie good order. I asked him first what part of scripture it was, that hee had read? Hee answered, that hee coulde not well tell. Howe manie Euangelistes there were in the newe Testament? Hee sayde he knew not. Howe manie Apostles there were? Hee thought there were twelue. Howe he shoulde be saued? Whereunto

440 he answeared mee with a piece of *Russe* doctrine, that hee knew not whether he shoulde bee saued, or no: but if God woulde *Poshallouate* him, or gratifie him so much, as to saue him, so it was, hee would be glad of it: if not, what remedie. I asked him, why he shoare himselfe a Fryer? He answered, because he would eat his

445 bread with peace. This is the learning of the Friers of *Russia*, which though it be not to bee measured by one, yet partly it may bee gessed by the ignorance of this man, what is in the rest.

Nunneries.
They haue also many Nunneries, whereof some may admitte none but Noblemens widowes, and daughters, when the Emperour

450 meaneth to keepe them vnmarried, from continuing the blood or stocke, which he would haue extinguished. To speak of the life of their Friers, and Nunnes, it needes not, to those that know the hypocrisie, and vncleannesse of that Cloyster-broode. The *Russe* himselfe (though otherwise addicted to all superstition) speaketh so

455 fowlly of it, that it must needes gaine silence of any modest man.

Eremites.
Besides these, they haue certeyne *Eremites*, (whome they call *Holy men*) that are like to those *Gymnosophists*, for their life and behauiour: though farre vnlike for their knowledge, and learning. They vse to go starke naked, saue a clout about their middle, with

460 their haire hanging long, and wildely about their shoulders, and many of them with an iron coller, or chaine about their neckes, or middes, euen in the very extremity of winter. These they take as Prophets, and men of great holines, giuing them a liberty to speak what they list, without any controulment, thogh it be of

465 the very highest himselfe. So that if he reproue any openly, in

274

what sort soeuer, they answere nothing, but that it is *Po græcum*, that is, for their sinnes. And if anie of them take some piece of sale ware from anie mans shop, as he passeth by, to giue where he list, hee thinketh himselfe much beloued of God, and much beholding to the holy man, for taking it in that sort. 470

Of this kinde there are not many, because it is a very harde and colde profession, to goe naked in *Russia*, specially in Winter. Among other at this time, they haue one at *Mosko*, that walketh naked about the streetes, and inueyeth commonly against the state, and gouernment, especially against the *Godonoes*, that are thought 475 at this time to bee great oppressours of that Common wealth. An other there was, that dyed not many yeeres agoe (whome they *Basileo* the called *Basileo*) that would take vpon him to reproue the olde *Eremite.* Emperour, for all his crueltie, and oppressions, done towards his people. His body they haue translated of late into a sumptuous 480 Church, neere the Emperours house in *Mosko*, and haue canonized him for a Saint. Many miracles he doth there (for so the Friers make the people to beleeue) and manie offrings are made vnto him, not only by the people, but by the chiefe Nobilitie, and the Emperour, and Empresse themselues, which visite that Church with 485 great deuotion. But this last yeere, at my beeing at *Mosko*, this Saint had ill lucke, in working his miracles. For a lame man that had his limmes restored (as it was pretended by him) was charged by a woman that was familiar with him (being then fallen out) that hee halted but in the day time, and coulde leape merily when 490 he came home at night. And that hee had intended this matter sixe yeeres before. Now he is put into a Monastery, and there rayleth vpon the Fryers, that hyred him to haue this counterfaite miracle, practised vpon him. Besides this disgrace, a little before my comming from thence, there were eyght slaine within his 495 Church by fire in a thunder. Which caused his belles (that were tingling before all day and night long as in triumph of the miracles wrought by *Basileo* their Saint) to ring somewhat softlier, and hath wrought no little discredite to this Miracle-worker. There was

Nicôla the Eremite.

another of great account at *Plesko*, (called *Nichôla* of *Plesko*) that did much good, when this Emperours father came to sack the towne, vpon suspition of their reuolting and rebellion against him. The Emperour, after hee had saluted the *Eremite*, at his lodging, sent him a reward. And the *Holy man* to requite the Emperour, sent him a piece of rawe fleshe, beyng then their Lent time. Which the Emperour seeing, bid one to tell him, that hee marueiled that the *Holy man* woulde offer him flesh to eat in the Lent, when it was forbidden by order of holie Church. And doth *Euasko*, (which is as much to saye, as *Iacke*) thinke (quoth *Nicôla*) that it is vnlawfull to eate a piece of beasts flesh in Lent and not to eate vp so much mans flesh, as hee hath done already. So threatning the Emperour with a prophecy of some hard aduenture to come vpon him, except hee left murdering of his people, and departed the towne: he saued a great many mens liues at that time.

This maketh the people to like very well of them, because they are as *Pasquils*, to note their great mens faults, that no man els dare speake of. Yet it falleth out sometime, that for this rude libertie, which they take vpon them, after a counterfeite maner, by imitation of Prophets, they are made away in secret: as was one or two of them, in the last Emperours time, for beyng ouer bolde in speaking against his gouernment.

Of their Leiturgie, or forme of *Church-seruice,* and their manner of administring the Sacraments. The 22. Chapter.

Their morning Seruice.

Their morning seruice they call *Zautrana*, that is, mattins. It is done in this order. The Priest entereth into the Church, with his Deacon, following him. And when hee is come to the middle of the Church, he beginneth to say with a loude voyce: *Blasslauey Vladika* (that is) *Blesse vs heauenly Pastor*: meaning, of Christ. Then he addeth, *In the name of the Father, and of the Sonne, and of the holy*

276

Ghost, one very God in Trinitie: and Aspody Pomeluy, or, *Lorde haue mercy vpon vs, Lorde haue mercie vpon vs, Lorde haue mercie vpon vs*: repeated three times. This done, hee marcheth on towardes the Chauncell, or *Sanctum Sanctorum*, (as they vse to call it) and so entreth into the *Scharsuey Dwere*, or the heauenly doore: which no man may enter into, but the Priest only. Where standing at the altar, or table (set neere to the vpper wall of the chauncell) hee sayeth the Lordes prayer, and then againe *Aspody Pomeluy*, or *Lord haue mercie vpon vs, Lorde haue mercie vpon vs, &c*: pronounced twelue times. Then *praysed be the Trinitie, the Father, the Sonne, and holie Ghost, for euer and euer*. Wherto the Deacons, and people say, *Amen*. Next after, the Priest addeth the Psalmes for that day, and beginneth with *O come let vs worshippe, and fall downe before the Lorde, &c*. and therewithall himselfe, with the Deacons, and people, all turne themselues towardes their Idoles, or Images, that hang on the wall and crossing themselues, bowe downe three times, knocking their heades to the verie ground. After this, he readeth the ten commandements, and *Athanasius* Creed, out of the Seruice booke.

This being done, the Deacon that standeth without the heauenly doore, or chauncel, readeth a piece of a Legend, out of a written booke, (for they haue it not in print) of some Saints life, miracles, &c. This is diuided into manie partes, for euerie day in the yeere, and is read by them with a playne singing note, not vnlike to the Popish tune, when they soung their Gospels. After all this (which reacheth to an houre, and an halfe, or two houres of length) hee addeth certeyne sette Collectes, or prayers vpon that which hee hath read out of the Legend before: and so endeth his Seruice. All this while stand burning before their Idoles, a great many of waxe candles, (wherof some are of the bignesse of a mans wast) vowed, or enioyned by penance, vpon the people of the parish.

About 9. of the clock in the morning, they haue an other seruice, called *Obeidna*, (or Compline) much after the order of the Popish Seruice, that bare that name. If it bee some high, or Festiuall day, they furnish their Seruice beside, with *Blessed bee the Lorde God of*

277

Israel, &c. and *We prayse thee O God, &c*: sung with a more solemne, and curious note.

Their Eue-
ning seruice.

Their Euening seruice, is called *Vecherna*, where the Priest beginneth with *Blaslauey Vladika*, as hee did in the morning, and with the Psalmes appointed for the *Vecherna*. Which beyng read, hee singeth, *My soule doeth magnifie the Lorde, &c.* And then the Priest, Deacons, and people, all with one voice sing, *Aspody pomelui,* or *Lord haue mercie vpon vs*, thirty times together. Whereunto the boyes that are in the Church, answere all with one voyce, rowling it vp so fast, as their lippes can goe: *Verij, Verij, Verij, Verij,* or *Prayse, Prayse, Prayse, &c.* thirty times together, with a very straunge noyse. Then is read by the priest, and vpon the holidaies sung, the first Psalme: *Blessed is the man, &c.* And in the end of it, is added *Alleluia* repeated ten times. The next in order is some part of the gospell read by the Priest, which hee endeth with *Alleluia* repeated three times. And so hauing said a collect in remembrance of the Saint of that day, he endeth his euening seruice. All this while the Priest standeth aboue at the altar or high table, within the Chancel, or *Sanctum Sanctorum*, whence he neuer moueth al the seruice time. The Deacon, or Deacons (which are many in their cathedrall Churches) stand without the chancell by the *Scharsuey dwere*, or heauenly doore: for within they may not be seene all the seruice time, though otherwise their office is to sweepe, and keepe it, and to set vp the waxe candels before their Idols. The people stand together the whole seruice time in the body of the Church, and some in the church porch, for piew, or seate they haue none within their churches.

The manner of
the *Russe*
baptisme.

The Sacrament of baptisme they administer after this manner. The child is brought vnto the Church (and this is done within eight daies after it is borne) if it bee the childe of some Nobleman, it is brought with great pomp in a rich sled or wagon, with chaires and cushions of cloth of gold, and such like sumptuous shew of their best furniture. When they are come to the Church, the Priest standeth ready to receiue the child within the church porch, with his tub of water by him. And then beginneth to declare vnto them, that they haue brought a little Infidell to be made a Christian, &c. This ended, he teacheth the witnesses (that are two or three) in a certeine set forme out of his booke, what their dutie is in bringing vp the childe after hee is baptised, vz. That he must be taught to know God, and Christ the Sauiour. And because God is of great maiestie, and wee must not presume to come vnto him without mediatours (as the manner is when wee make any suit to an Emperour, or great Prince) therefore they must teach him what Saints are the best, and chiefe mediatours, &c. This done, he commandeth the diuell in the name of God after a coniuring manner, to come out of the water: and so after certeine praiers he plungeth the childe thrise ouer head, and eares. For this they holde to be a point necessary, that no part of the childe be vndipped in the water.

The words that beare with them the forme of baptisme vttered by the Priest, when he dippeth in the childe, are the very same that are prescribed in the gospell, and vsed by vs, vz: *In the name of the Father, and of the Sonne, and of the Ghost.* For that they should altar the forme of the words, and say *by the holy Ghost,* (as I haue heard that they did) folowing certein heretikes of the Greeke church, I found to be vntrue, aswell by report of them that haue bin often at their baptismes, as by their booke of *Leiturgie* it selfe, wherein the order of baptisme is precisely set downe.

When the childe is baptized, the Priest laieth oile and salt tempred together vpon the forehead, and both sides of his face, and then vppon his mouth, drawing it along with his finger ouer the childes lippes (as did the Popish priestes) saying withall certeine prayers to this effect: that God will make him a good Christian, &c. All this is done in the Church porch. Then is the childe (as being now made a Christian, and meet to be receiued within the church dore) carried into the church, the Priest going before, and there he is presented to the chiefe Idoll of the Church, being layd on a cushion before the feete of the image, by it (as by the mediatour) to bee commended vnto God. If the child be sick, or weake (spe-

cially in the winter) they vse to make the water luke warme. After
110 baptisme the manner is to cut of the haire from the childes head,
and hauing wrapped it within a piece of wax to lay it vp, as a
relique, or monument in a secret place of the church.

    This is the manner of their baptisme, which they account to be
the best and perfectest form. As they doo all other parts of their
115 religion, receiued (as they say) by tradition from the best church,
meaning the Greeke. And therfore they will take great paynes to
make a proselite, or conuert, either of an infidell, or of a forrein
Christian, by rebaptizing him after the *Russe* manner. When they
take any *Tartar* prisoner, commonly they will offer him life, with
120 condition to be baptized. And yet they perswade very few of them
to redeeme their life so: because of the naturall hatred the *Tartar*
beareth to the *Russe*, and the opinion he hath of his falshood, and
iniustice. The yere after *Mosko* was fired by the *Chrim Tartar*, there
was taken a *Diuoymorsey*, one of the chiefe in that exploit with 300.
125 *Tartars* more: who had all their liues offered them, if they would
be baptized after the *Russe* manner. Which they refused all to doo,
with many reproches against those that perswaded them. And so
beyng carried to the riuer *Mosko* (that runneth through the citie)
they were all baptized after a violent manner: being thrust downe
130 with a knock on the head into the water, through an hole made
Rebaptizing. in the yse for that purpose. Of *Lieflanders* that are captiues, there
are many that take on them this second *Russe* baptisme to get
more libertie, and somwhat besides towards their liuing, which
the Emperour ordinarily vseth to giue them.

    Of Englishmen since they frequented the countrie there was
135 neuer any found, that so much forgot God, his faith, and countrie,
as that he would bee content to be baptized *Russe*, for any respect
of feare, preferment, or other meanes whatsoeuer: saue onely
Richard Relph, that following before an vngodly trade, by keeping
140 a *Caback* (against the order of the countrie) and being put of from
that trade, and spoiled by the Emperours officers of that which he
had, entred himself this last yeare into the *Russe* profession: and

280

so was rebaptised, liuing now asmuch an idolater, as before he was
a rioter, and vnthrifty person.

Such as thus receiue the *Russe* baptisme, are first carried into
some Monasterie to be instructed there in the doctrine and ceremonies
of the church. Where they vse these ceremonies. First, they put
him into a new and fresh suite of apparell, made after the *Russe*
fashion, and set a coronet or (in Sommer) a garland vpon his head.
Then they annoint his head with oile, and put a waxe candle light
into his hand: and so pray ouer him foure times a day, the space
of seuen daies. All this while he is to abstaine from flesh, and white
meats. The seuen daies being ended, he is purified and washed in
a bathstoue, and so the eight day hee is brought into the church,
where he is taught by the Friers how to behaue himselfe in presence
of their idols, by ducking downe, knocking of the head, crossing
himself, and such like gestures, which are the greatest part of the
Russe religion.

The sacrament of the Lordes supper they receiue but once a
yeare, in their great Lent time, a litle before Easter. Three at the
most are admitted at one time, and neuer aboue. The manner of
their communicating, is thus. First they confesse themselues of all
their sins to the Priest, whom they call their ghostly father. Then
they come to the Church, and are called vp to the Communion
table, that standeth like an altar, a little remoued from the vpper
end of the Church, after the Doutch maner. Here first they are
asked of the Priest whither they be cleane or no, that is, whither
they haue neuer a sinne behind that they left vnconfessed. If they
answere, *No*, they are taken to the table. Where the Priest beginneth
with certeine vsuall prayers, the communicants standing in the
meane while with their armes foulded one within an other, like
penitentiaries, or mourners. When these prayers are ended, the
Priest taketh a spoone, and filleth it full of claret wine. Then he
putteth into it a small piece of bread, and tempereth them both
together: and so deliuereth them in the spoone to the Communicants,
that stande in order, speaking the vsuall wordes of the Sacrament.

Marginal notes:
- 145
- 150
- 155
- The administring of the Lords supper.
- 165
- 170
- 175

Eat this &c. Drinke this &c. both at one time without any pause.

After that he deliuereth them againe bread by it self, and then wine carded together with a little warme water, to represent blood
180 more rightly (as they thinke) and the water withall, that flowed out of the side of Christ. Whiles this is in doing the communicants vnfold their armes. And then foulding them againe, follow the Priest thrise round about the communion table, and so returne to their places againe. Where hauing said certeine other prayers, he
185 dismisseth the communicants, with charge to bee meary, and to cheere vp themselues for the seuen daies next following. Which being ended, he enioyneth them to fast for it as long time after. Which they vse to obserue with very great deuotion, eating nothing els but bread and salt, except a little cabbage, and some
190 other hearbe or roote, with water or quasse mead for their drinke.

This is their manner of administring the Sacraments. Wherein what they differ from the institution of Christ, and what ceremonies they haue added of their owne, or rather borrowed of the Greekes, may easily be noted.

Of the doctrine of the Russe church, and what errours it holdeth.
The 23. Chapter.

The *Russe* errours. 1. Their disallowing of certeine parts of the Canonicall scriptures.

Their chiefest errours in matter of faith I find to be these. First, concerning the word of God it self, they will not read publiquely certeine bookes of the Canonicall scripture, as the bookes of *Moses*: specially the foure last, *Exodus, Leuiticus, Numeri,* and *Deuteronomie,* which they say are al made disauthentique, and put out of vse by the comming of Christ: as not able to discerne the difference betwixt the morall, and the ceremoniall law. The bookes of the prophets they allow of, but read them not publikely in their churches for the same reason: because they were but directers vnto Christ,
10 and proper (as they say) to the nation of the Iewes. Onely the booke of Psalmes they haue in great estimation and sing and say

282

them dayly in their Churches. Of the new Testament they allow, and read all, except the *Reuelation*: which therefore they read not (though they allow it) because they vnderstand it not, neither haue the like occasion, to know the fulfilling of the prophecies conteyned within it, concerning especially the apostasie of the Antichristian Church, as haue the Westerne Churches. Notwithstanding they haue had their Antichrists of the Greeke Church, any may finde their owne falling of, and the punishments for it by the Turkish inuasion in the prophecies of that Booke.

Secondly (which is the fountain of the rest of al their corruptions, both in doctrine and ceremonies) they holde with the Papistes, that their church *Traditions* are of equall authoritie with the written worde of God. Wherein they prefer themselues before other churches: affirming that they haue the true and right traditions deliuered by the Apostles to the Greeke church, and so vnto them.

3. That the church (meaning the Greeke and specially the Patriarch and his Synod, as the head of the rest) haue a soueraigne authoritie to interpret the Scriptures, and that all are bound to holde that interpretation as sound, and authentique.

4. Concerning the diuine nature and the three persons, in the one substance of God, that the holy Ghost proceedeth from the Father onely, and not from the Sonne.

5. About the office of Christ, they holde many fowle errours, and the same almost as doth the Popish church: namely that hee is the sole mediatour of redemption, but not of intercession. Their chiefe reason (if they bee talked withall) for defence of this errour, is that vnapt and foolish comparison, betwixt God and a Monarch or Prince of this world, that must bee sued vnto by Mediatours about him: wherein they giue speciall preferment to some aboue others, as to the blessed *Virgin* whom they call *Precheste*, or vndefiled, and Saint *Nicôlas*, whom they call *Scora pomosnick*, or the *Speedy helper*, and say that he hath 300. angels of the chiefest appointed by God to attend vpon him. This hath brought them to an horrible excesse of idolatry, after the grossest and prophanest manner,

15

20

2. Traditions equall to the holy Scripture.

25

3. The Church to haue soueraigne authoritie in interpreting the Scriptures.
4. The holy Ghost to proceed from the Father onely.
5. Christ not sole mediator of intercession.

40

45

283

giuing vnto their images al religious worship of praier, thanksgiuing, offerings, and adoration with prostrating and knocking their heads to the ground before them as to God himself. Which because they doo to the picture, not to the portraiture of the Saint, they say they worship not an idol, but the Saint in his image and so offend not God: forgetting the commandement of God, that forbiddeth to make the image or likenes of any thing, for any religious worship, or vse whatsoeuer. Their church walles are very full of them, richly hanged and set forth with pearle and stone vpon the smooth table. Though some also they haue embossed, that stick from the board almost an inch outwards. They call them *Chudouodites*, or their miracle workers: and when they prouide them to set vp in their Churches, in no case they may say that they haue bought the image, but exchaunged monie for it.

6. Iustifi-
cation by
workes.

6. For the means of iustification, they agree with the Papists, that it is not by faith only apprehending Christ, but by their works also. And that *Opus operatum*, or the worke for the worke sake, must needes please God. And therefore they are all in their numbers of praiers, fastes, vowes, and offrings to saints, almes deeds, crossings and such like, and carrie their numbring beads about with them continually, aswel the Emperour and his Nobilitie as the common people, not only in the church, but in all other publike places, specially at any set or solemne meeting, as in their fastes, lawe courts, common consultations, intertainement of Ambassadours, and such like.

7. Saluation
vncerteine.

7. They say with the Papists that no man can be assured of his saluation, till the last sentence be passed at the day of iudgement.

8. Auricular
confession.

8. They vse auricular confession, and thinke that they are purged by the very action from so many sinnes, as they confesse by name, and in particular to the Priest.

9. Three
Sacraments.

9. They hold three sacramentes, of *Baptisme*, the *Lords supper*, and *the last annoiling*, or *vnction*. Yet concerning their Sacrament of extreame vnction, they holde it not so necessarie to saluation

284

as they do baptisme, but thinke it a great curse and punishment of
God, if any die with out it.

10. They thinke there is a necessitie of baptisme, and that all
are condemned that die without it.

11. They rebaptise as many Christians (not being of the Greek
church) as they conuert to their *Russe* profession: because they
are diuided from the true Church, which is the Greeke, as they
say.

12. They make a difference of meates and drinks, accounting
the vse of one, to be more holy then of an other. And therefore
in their set fastes they forbeare to eate fleshe, and white meats (as
we call them) after the manner of the Popish superstition: which
they obserue so strictly, and with such blinde deuotion, as that they
will rather die, then eat one bit of flesh, egges, or such like, for the
health of their bodies in their extreme sicknesse.

13. They hold marriage to be vnlawfull for all the Clergie
men, except the priests only, and for them also after the first wife,
as was said before. Neither doo they well allow of it in Lay men
after the second marriage. Which is a pretence now vsed against
the Emperours only brother, a child of six yeres old. Who therefore
is not praied for in their churches (as their manner is otherwise
for the Princes bloud) because hee was borne of the sixt marriage,
and so not legitimate. This charge was giuen to the priests by the
Emperour himselfe, by procurement of the *Godonoes*: who make
him beleeue that it is a good pollicie to turne away the liking of
the people from the next successour.

Many other false opinions they haue in matter of religion. But
these are the chiefe, which they holde partly by meanes of their
traditions (which they haue receiued from the Greeke church) but
specially by ignorance of the holy Scriptures. Which notwithstanding they haue in the *Polonian* tongue, (that is all one with
theirs some few wordes excepted) yet fewe of them read them with
that godly care which they ought to doo: neither haue they (if
they would) bookes sufficient of the old and new Testament for

80

10. All dam-
ned that die
without
baptisme.
11. Ana-
baptisme.

12. Difference
of meates.

90

13. Marriage
for some
persons vn-
lawfull.

100

105

110

285

the common people, but of their Leiturgie onely, or booke of
115   common seruice, whereof there are great numbers.

    All this mischief commeth from the clergie, who being ignorant
and godlesse themselues, are very warie to keepe the people likewise
in their ignorance and blindnesse, for their liuing and bellies sake:
partly also from the manner of gouernment setled among them:
120   which the Emperours (whom it specially behoueth) list not to haue
chaunged by any innouation, but to retaine that religion that best
agreeth with it. Which notwithstanding it is not to be doubted,
but that hauing the word of God in some sort (though without
the ordinarie meanes to attaine to a true sense and vnderstanding
125   of it) God hath also his number among them. As may partly appeare
by that which a *Russe* at *Mosko* said in secret to one of my seruaunts,
speaking against their images and other superstitions: That God had
giuen vnto England light to day, and might giue it to morrow
(if he pleased) to them.

130   As for any inquisition or proceeding against men for matter of
religion, I could heare of none: saue a few yeares since against one
man and his wife, who were kept in a close prison the space of
28. yeares, till they were ouer growen into a deformed fashion, for
their hayre, nailes, collour of countenance, and such like, and in
135   the end were burned at *Mosko*, in a small house set on fire. The
cause was kepte secrete, but like it was for some part of truth in
matter of religion: though the people were made to beleeue by
the Priests and Friers, that they held some great, and damnable
heresie.

Of the manner of solemnizing their Marriages.
The 24. Chapter.

The manner of making and solemnizing their marriages is
different from the maner of other countries. The man (though
he neuer saw the woman before) is not permitted to haue any
sight of hir al the time of his woing: which he doth not by himself,

but by his mother or some other ancient woman of his kin, or 5
acquaintance. When the liking is taken (aswell by the parents as
by the parties themselues, for without the knowledge and consent
of the parents, the contract is not lawful) the fathers on both sides,
or such as are to them in steede of fathers, with their other chiefe
friends, haue a meeting and conference about the dowrie, which 10
is comonly very large after the abilitie of the parents: so that you
shal haue a market man (as they call them) giue a 1000. rubbels,
or more with his daughter.

As for the man it is neuer required of him, nor standeth with
their custome to make any iointer in recompence of the dowrie.
But in case he haue a child by his wife, she enioieth a thirde deale
after his disease. If hee haue two children by hir or more, shee is
to haue a courtesie more, at the discretion of the husband. If the
husband depart without issue by his wife, shee is returned home
to hir friends without any thing at al, saue only hir dowrie: if the 20
husband leaue so much behind him in goods. When the agreement
is made concerning the dowrie, they signe bonds one to the other,
aswell for the paiment of the dowrie, as the performing of the
mariage by a certein day. If the woman were neuer married before,
hir father and friends are bound besides to assure hir a maiden. 25
Which breedeth many brabbels and quarrels at Law, if the man
take any conceipt concerning the behauiour, and honestie of his
wife.

The manner
of indow-
ment for
wiues.

Thus the contract being made, the parties begin to send tokens
the one to the other, the woman first, then afterwards the man, 30
but yet see not one an other till the marriage be solemnized. On
the eaue before the marriage day, the bride is carried in a *Collimago*,
or coach, or in a sledde (if it be winter) to the bridegromes house,
with hir marriage apparell and bedstead with hir, which they are
to lie in. For this is euer prouided by the Bride, and is commonly 35
very faire, with much cost bestowed vpon it. Here she is accompaned
all that night by hir mother, and other women: but not welcommed,
nor once seene by the Bridegrome himselfe.

When the time is come to haue the marriage solemnized, the Bride hath put vpon her a kind of hood, made of fine knitworke, or lawne, that couereth her head, and all her body downe to the middle. And so accompanied with her friends, and the bridegroome with his, they goe to Church all on horsebacke, though the Church bee neere hande, and themselues but of very meane degree. The

45   wordes of contract, and other ceremonies in solemnizing the marriage, are much after the order, and with the same wordes that are vsed with vs: with a ring also giuen to the Bride. Which beeing put on, and the wordes of contract pronounced: the Brides hand is deliuered into the hand of the Bridegroome, which standeth

50   al this while on the one side of the altar or table, and the Bride on the other. So the marriage knot beeing knitte by the Priest, the Bride commeth to the Bridegroome (standing at the end of the altar or table) and falleth downe at his feete, knocking her head vpon his shooe, in token of her subiection, and obedience.

55   And the Bridegroome againe casteth the lappe of his gowne, or vpper garment, ouer the Bride, in token of his duetie to protect, and cherish her.

Then the Bridegroome, and Bride, standing both together at the tables ende, commeth first the father, and the other friends of

60   the Bride, and bowe themselues downe low to the Bridegroome: and so likewise his friends bow themselues to the Bride, in token of affinity and loue, euer after betwixt the two kinreds. And withall, the father of the Bridegroome offreth to the priest, a loafe of bread, who deliuereth it straight again to the father, and other friends

65   of the Bride, with attestation before God and their idols, that hee deliuer the dowry wholly and truely at the day appointed, and hold loue euer after, one kinred with another. Wherupon they break the loaf into pieces, and eate of it, to testifie their true and sincere meanings, for performing of that charge, and thenceforth

70   to become as grains of one loafe, or men of one table.

These ceremonies being ended, the Bridegroome taketh the Bride by the hand, and so they goe on together, with their friendes

288

after them, towardes the Church porche. Where meete them certein with pots, and cups in their handes, with meade and *Russe* wine. Whereof the Bridegroome taketh first a charke, or little cuppe full in his hand, and drinketh to the Bride: who opening her hood, or vale below, and putting the cup to her mouth vnderneath it (for beeing seene of the Bridegroome) pleadgeth him agayne. Thus returning altogether from the Church, the Bridegroome goeth not home to his owne, but to his fathers house, and she likewise to hers, where either intertayn their friends apart. At the entring into the house, they vse to fling corne out of the windowes, vpon the Bridegroome, and Bride, in token of plentie, and fruitfulnes to bee with them euer after.

When the Euening is come, the Bride is brought to the Bridegrooms fathers house, and there lodgeth that night, with her vale or couer still ouer her head. All that night she may not speak one word (for that charge she receiueth by tradition from her mother, and other matrones her friendes) that the Bridegroome must neither heare, nor see her, till the day after the marriage. Neither three dayes after, may shee bee hearde to speake, saue certeyne fewe wordes at the table, in a set forme with great manners, and reuerence to the Bridegroome. If she behaue her selfe otherwise, it is a great preiudice to her credite, and life euer after: and will highly be disliked of the Bridegroome himselfe.

After the third day, they depart to their owne, and make a feast to both their friends together. The marriage day, and the whole time of their festiuall, the Bridegroome hath the honour to bee called *Moloday Knez*, or yong Duke, and the Bride *Moloday Knezay*, or young Dutchesse.

In liuing with their wiues, they shewe themselues to be but of a barbarous condition: vsing them as seruaunts, rather then wiues. Except the Noble-women, which are, or seeme to be of more estimation with their husbands, then the rest of meaner sort. They haue this fowle abuse, contrary to good order, and the worde of God it selfe, that vpon dislike of his wife, or other cause whatsoeuer,

289

the man may goe into a Monasterie, and shire himselfe a Frier, by pretence of deuotion: and so leaue his wife to shift for her selfe so well as she can.

Of the other Ceremonies of the Russe Church.
The 25. Chapter.

The other ceremonies of their Churche, are manie in number: especially, the abuse about the signe of the Crosse, which they set vp in their high wayes, in the tops of their Churches, and in euery doore of their houses, signing themselues continually with it,

5 on their foreheads, and brests, with great deuotion, as they will seeme by their outward gesture. Which were lesse offence, if they gaue not withall, that religious reuerence and woorship vnto it, which is due to God onely, and vsed the dumbe shewe, and signing of it insteede of thanksgiuing, and of all other dueties which they

10 owe vnto God. When they rise in the morning, they goe commonly in the sight of some steeple, that hath a crosse on the toppe: and so bowing themselues towardes the crosse, signe themselues withal on their foreheads, and brests. And this is their thanksgiuing to God for their nightes rest, without any word speaking, except

15 peraduenture they say, *Aspody Pomeluy*, or, *Lorde haue mercie vpon vs*. When they sitte downe to meate, and rise againe from it, the thanksgiuing to God, is the crossing of their foreheads and brests. Except it be some few that adde peraduenture, a worde or two of some ordinarie prayer, impertinent to that purpose. When they

20 are to giue an oath for the deciding of anie controuersie at Lawe, they doe it by swearing by the Crosse, and kissing the feet of it, making it as God, whose name onely is to bee vsed in such triall of iustice. When they enter into any house (where euer there is an idole hanging on the wall) they signe themselues with the crosse,

25 and bow themselues to it. When they begin any work, bee it little, or much they arme them selues first with the signe of the crosse. And this commonly is all their prayer to God, for good

speede of their businesse. And thus they serue God with crosses, after a crosse and vaine maner: not vnderstanding what the crosse of Christ is, nor the power of it. And yet they thinke all strangers Christians, to be no better then Turkes, in comparison of themselues (and so they wil say) because they bow not themselues, when they meete with the crosse, nor signe themselues with it, as the *Russe* maner is.

They haue holie water in like vse, and estimation, as the Popish Church hath. But herein they exceede them, in that they doe not onely hallow their holie water stockes, and tubbes ful of water, but all the riuers of the countrey once euery yeere. At *Mosko* it is done with great pompe, and solemnitie: the Emperour himselfe being present at it, with all his Nobility, marching through the streets towards the riuer of *Moskua*, in manner of procession, in this order as followeth. First goe two Deacons, with banners in their hands, the one of *Precheste* (or our Ladie) the other of *Saint Michael*, fighting with his dragon. Then follow after, the rest of the Deacons, and the priests of *Mosko*, two and two in a ranke, with coaps on their backs, and their idols at their brests, carried with girdles or slinges, made fast about their necks. Next the priests come their Bishops in their pontificalibus: then the Friers, Monks, and Abbots: and after, the Patriarch, in very rich attire, with a ball, or sphere on the top of his myter, to signifie his vniuersalitie ouer that Church. Last commeth the Emperor with all his nobility. The whole traine is of a mile long, or more. When they are come to the riuer, a great hole is made in the yse, where the market is kept, of a rod and a halfe broad, with a stage round about it to keepe off the presse. Then beginneth the Patriarch to say certaine praiers, and coniureth the diuel to come out of the water: and so casting in salt, and censing it with frankincense, maketh the whole riuer to become holy water. The morning before, all the people of *Mosko* vse to make crosses of chawlke ouer euerie doore, and window of their houses: least the Diuell beyng coniured out of the water, shoulde flye into their houses.

Holy water.

Hallowing of riuers.

291

When the ceremonies are ended, you shal see the black Gard of the Emperours house, and then the rest of the Towne, with their pailes and buckets, to take off the hallowed water for drinke, and other vses. You shall also see the women dippe in their children ouer head and eares, and many men and women leape into it, some naked, some with their clothes on, when some man woulde thinke his finger woulde freese off, if hee should but dippe it into the water. When the men haue done, they bring their horse to the riuer, to drinke of the sanctified water: and so make them as holie as a horse. Their set day for this solemne action of hallowing their riuers, is that we cal *Twelfthday*. The like is done by other Bishops, in al parts of the Realme.

Drinking of holy water. Their maner is also to giue it to their sick, in their greatest extremitie: thinking that it will eyther recouer them, or sanctifie them to God. Whereby they kill many, through their vnreasonable superstition, as did the *Lord Borris* his onely sonne, at my beyng at the *Mosko*: whom he killed (as was said by the phisitions) by powring into him, colde holie water, and presenting him naked into the Church, to their Saynt *Basileo*, in the colde of the Winter, in an extremitie of sicknesse.

They haue an image of Christ, which they call *Neruchi*, (which signifieth as much as *Made without hands*) for so their priests, and superstition withal, perswadeth them it was. This in their processions, they carry about with them on high vpon a pole, enclosed within a Pixe, made like a lanthorn, and doe reuerence to it, as to a great mysterie.

Brewing with holy water. At euery brewing, their maner is likewise, to bring a dish of their woort to the Priest, within the Church: which beyng hallowed by him, is powred into the brewing, and so giueth it such a vertue, as when they drink of it, they are seldome sober. The like they doe with the first fruites of the corne in Haruest.

Palmsunday. They haue an other ceremonie on Palmsunday of auncient tradition: what time the Patriarch rideth through the *Mosko*, the Emperour himself holding his horse bridle, and the people crying

Hosanna, and spreding their vpper garmentes vnder his horse feete. The Emperour hath of the Patriarch for his good seruice of that day 200. rubbels of standing pension. Another pageant they haue much like to this, the weeke before the natiuitie of Christ: when euery Bishop in his Cathedral Church, setteth forth a shew of the three children in the Ouen. Where the Angell is made to come flying from the roofe of the Church, with great admiration of the lookers on, and many terrible flashes of fire, are made with rosen, and gun-powder, by the *Chaldeans* (as they call them) that run about the towne all the twelue dayes, disguised in their plaiers coats, and make much good sport for the honour of the Bishops pageant. At the *Mosko*, the Emperour himselfe, and the Empresse neuer faile to be at it, though it be but the same matter plaid euery yeere, without any new inuention at all. 100 105

Besides their fastes on Wednesdayes, and Fridayes throughout the whole yeere, (the one because they say Christ was solde on the Wednesday, the other because he suffered on the Friday) they haue foure great Fastes, or Lentes euery yeere. The first, (which they call their great Lent) is at the same time with ours. The second, about Midsommer. The third, in Haruest time. The fourth, about Hallontide: which they keepe not of pollicie, but of meere superstition. In their great Lent for the first weeke, they eate nothing but bread and salt, and drinke nothing but water, neither meddle with anie matter of their vocation, but intende their shriuing, and fasting only. They haue also 3. *Vigils*, or *Wakes* in their great Lent, which they cal *Stoiania*: and the last Friday their great *Vigil*, as they cal it. What time the whole parish must bee present in the Church, and watch from nine a clocke in the Euening, til sixe in the morning, all the while standing, saue when they fall downe, and knock their heads to their idoles, which must be an hundred and seuentie times, iust through the whole night. *Fasts.* 115 *Vigils.* 125

About their burials also, they haue manie superstitious and prophane ceremonies: as putting within the finger of the corpes, a letter to Saint *Nicôlas*: whome they make their chiefe mediatour, *Burials.*

293

130 and as it were, the porter of heauen gates, as the Papistes doe their *Peter.*

In Winter time, when all is couered with snow, and the ground so hard frozen, as that no spade, nor pikeaxe can enter, their manner is not to burie their dead, but to keepe the bodies (so many as die 135 all the Winter time) in an house, in the suburbs, or outparts of the towne, which they call *Bohsedom,* that is, *Gods house*: where the dead bodies are pyled vp together, like billets on a woodstack, as hard with the frost as a very stone, till the Springtide come, and resolueth the frost: what time euery man taketh his dead friend, 140 and committeth him to the ground.

Moneths mindes.   They haue besides their yeeres and moneths mindes, for their friendes departed. What time they haue praiers saide ouer the graue by the Priest: who hath a penie ordinarie for his paines. When any dieth, they haue ordinary women mourners, that come to lament 145 for the dead party: and stand howling ouer the bodie, after a prophane, and heathenish manner (sometimes in the house, somtimes bringing the bodie into the backside, asking him what hee wanted, and what he meant to die. They bury their dead, as the party vsed to goe, with coate, hose, bootes, hat, and the rest of his apparell.

150   Many other vaine and superstitious ceremonies they haue, which were long and tedious to report. By these it may appeare, how farre they are fallen from the true knowledge, and practise of Christian religion: hauing exchanged the worde of God, for their vaine traditions, and brought al to external, and ridiculous 155 ceremonies, without any regard of spirite and trueth, which God requireth in his true worship.

Of the Emperours domestike or priuate behauiour.
The 26. Chapter.

The Emperours priuate behauiour, so much as may bee, or is meete to bee known, is after this maner. Hee riseth commonly about 4. a clock in the morning. After his apparrelling, and washing,

in commeth his ghostly father, or priest of his chamber, which is
named in their tongue, *Otetz Duhouna,* with his crosse in his hand, 5
wherwith he blesseth him, laying it first on his forehead, then vpon
his cheekes, or sides of his face, and then offreth him the ende of
it to kisse. This done, the Clearke of the crosse (called *Chresby
Doyack Profery*) bringeth into his chamber, a painted image, representing the Saint for that day. For euery day with them hath 10
his seuerall Saint, as it were the patrone for that day. This he placeth
among the rest of his image gods, wherewithall his chamber is
decked, as thicke almost as the wall can beare, with lampes and
waxe candles burning before them. They are very costly and
gorgeously decked with pearle, and precious stone. This image 15
being placed before him, the Emperour beginneth to crosse himselfe
after the *Russe* manner, first on the forehead, then on both sides
of his breaste, with *Aspody Pomeluy, Pomeluy mena hospody, sacroy
mena gresnick Syhodestua*: which is as much to say, as, *Helpe me O
Lorde my God, Lorde comfort me, defende and keepe me a sinner from* 20
doing euill, &c. This hee directeth towardes the image, or Saynt for
that day, whom hee nameth in his prayer, together with our Lady
(whom they call *Precheste*) *Saint Nicholas,* or some other, to whome
he beareth most deuotion, bowing himself prostrate vnto them,
with knocking his head to the verie ground. Thus he continueth 25
the space of a quarter of an houre, or thereabouts.

His priuate
prayer.

    Then commeth againe the ghostly father, or chamber priest,
with a siluer bowle full of holy water, which they call in *Russe,*
Sweta Voda, and a sprinkle of Basill (as they call it) in his hand:
and so al to besprinckleth first the image gods, and then the Em- 30
perour. This holy water is brought fresh euery day from the
Monasteries, farre and neere, sent to the Emperour from the Abbot
or Prior, in the name of the Saint, that is patrone of that Monastery,
as a speciall token of good wil from him.

    These deuotions being ended, he sendeth in to the Empresse, to 35
aske whether she hath rested in health, &c. And after a little pawse
goeth himselfe to salute her in a middle roome betwixt both their

chambers. The Empresse lieth apart from him, and keepeth not one chamber, nor table with the Emperour ordinarily, saue vpon the eaue of their Lentes, or common Fastes: what time she is his ordinarie ghest at bedde and boorde. After their meeting in the morning, they goe together to their priuate Churche or Chappell, where is sayde, or soung a morning Seruice (called *Zautrana*) of an houre long or thereabouts. From the Church hee returneth home, and sitteth him downe in a great chamber, to be seene and saluted by his Nobilitie, such as are in fauour about the Court. If hee haue to say to anie of them, or they to him, then is the time. And this is ordinarie, except his health, or some other occasion alter the custome.

The Emperour giueth presence euery morning.

About nine in the morning, he goeth to another Church within his Castle: where is soung by Priests, and Choristers, the high Seruice (called *Obeadna* or *Complin*) which commonly lasteth two houres: the Emperour in the meane time, talking commonly with some of his Councell, Nobilitie, or captaines, which haue to say to him, or he to them. And the Councell likewise conferre together among themselues, as if they were in their councell house. This ended, he returneth home, and recreateth himselfe vntill it be dinner time.

The Emperours seruice at his Table.

He is serued at his table on this manner. First, euery dish (as it is deliuered at the dresser) is tasted by the Cooke, in the presence of the high Stewarde, or his Deputie. And so is receyued by the Gentlemen wayters (called *Shilshey*) and by them carried vp to the Emperours table, the high Stewarde or his Deputie going before. There it is receiued by the Sewer (called *Erastnoy*) who giueth a taste of euerie dishe to the Taster, and so placeth it before the Emperour. The number of his dishes for his ordinarie seruice, is about seuenty: dressed somwhat grosely, with much garlicke, and salt, much after the Doutch manner. When hee exceedeth vpon some occasion of the day, or entertainment of some Ambassador, he hath many more dishes. The seruice is sent vp by 2. dishes at a time, or three at the most that he may eate it warme, first the baked, then the rost meats, and last the brothes. In his dyning chamber is an other table: where sit the chiefe of his Nobilitie that are about his Court, and his ghostly father, or Chapleine. On the one side of the chamber standeth a cubbard or table of plate, very fayre and riche with a great cesterne of Copper by it, full of yse and snow, wherein stande the pottes that serue for that meale. The taster holdeth the cup that he drinketh in all dinner time and deliuereth it vnto him with a say, when hee calleth for it. The manner is to make many dishes out of the seruice after it is set on the table, and to send them to such Noblemen and officers, as the Emperour liketh best. And this is counted a great fauour, and honour.

After dinner hee layeth him downe to reste, where commonly hee taketh three houres sleepe, except he employ one of the houres to bathing, or boxing. And this custome for sleeping after dinner, is an ordinary matter with him, as withall the *Russes*. After his sleepe, he goeth to euensong (called *Vechurna*) and thence returning, for the most parte recreateth himself with the Empresse till supper time, with iesters, and dwarfes, men and women, that tumble before him, and sing many songs after the *Russe* manner. This is his common recreation betwixt meales, that hee moste delightes in. On other speciall recreation is the fight with wilde Beares, which are caught in pittes, or nets, and are kepte in barred cages for that purpose, against the Emperour be disposed to see the pastime. The fight with the Beare is on this sort. The man is turned into a circle walled round about, where he is to quite himselfe so well as he can: for there is no way to flie out. When the Beare is turned loose he commeth vpon him with open mouth. If at the first pushe hee misse his aime, so that the Beare come within him, hee is in great daunger. But the wilde Beare being very fearse, hath this qualitie, that giueth aduantage to the Hunter. His manner is when he assaileth a man, to rise vp right on his two hinder legges, and so to come roaring with open mouth vpon him. And if the Hunter then can pushe right into the very brest of him betwixt his forelegges (as

75

80

85

90

95

100

105

297

commonly hee will not misse) resting the other ende of their boarespeare at the side of his foote, and so keeping the pike still towards the face of the Beare, he speedeth him commonly at one blow. But many times these Hunters come short, and are either slaine, or miserably torne with the teeth and talents of the fierce beast. If the partie quite himselfe well in this fight with the Beare, he is carried to drinke at the Emperours seller doore: where he drinketh himselfe drunke for the honor of *Hospodare.* And this is his rewarde for aduenturing his life, for the Emperours pleasure. To maintain this pastime the Emperor hath certein huntsmen that are appointed for that purpose to take the wild Beare. This is his recreation commonly on the holy daies. Somtimes he spendeth his time in looking vpon his goldsmiths, and Iewellers, tailers, embroderers, painters, and such like, and so goeth to his supper. When it draweth towards bed time, his priest saieth certein praiers: and then the Emperour blesseth and crosseth himselfe, as in the morning for a quarter of an houre or thereaboutes, and so goeth to his bedde.

The Emperour that now is (called *Theodore Iuanowich*) is for his person of a meane stature, somewhat lowe and grosse, of a sallowe complexion, and inclining to the dropsie, hawke nosed, vnsteady in his pase by reason of some weakenes of his lims, heauie and vnactiue, yet commonly smiling almost to a laughter. For qualitie otherwise, simple and slowe witted, but verie gentle, and of an easie nature, quiet, mercifull, of no martiall disposition, nor greatly apt for matter of pollicie, very superstitious, and infinite that way. Besides his priuate deuotions at home, he goeth euery weeke commonly on pilgrimage to some Monasterie, or other that is nearest hand. He is of 34. yeares old, or thereaboutes, and hath reigned almost the space of sixe yeares.

Of the Emperours priuate, or householde Officers.
The 27. Chapter.

The chiefe officers of the Emperours houshold, ar these which follow. The first is the office of the *Boiaren Conesheua*, or maister of the Horse. Which conteineth no more then is expressed by the name, that is, to be ouerseer of the Horse, and not *Magister equitum*, or Master of the Horsemen. For he appointeth other for that seruice, as occasion dothe require (as before was said). He that beareth that office at this time, is *Borris Federowich Godonoe*, brother to the Empresse. Of Horse for seruice in his warres (besides other for his ordinary vses) he hath to the number of 10000. which are kept about *Mosko*.

The next is the Lord Stewarde of his houshold at this time, one *Gregorie Vasilowich Godonoe*. The third is his Treasurer, that keepeth all his monies, iewels, plate, &c: now called *Stepan Vasilowich Godonoe*. The fourth his Controller, now *Andreas Petrowich Clesinine*. The fift his Chamberlaine. He that attendeth that office at this time, is called *Estoma Bisabroza Pastelnischay*. The sixt his Tasters, now *Theodore Alexandrowich*, and *Iuan Vasilowich Godonoe*. The seuenth his Harbengers, which are three Noble men, and diuers other Gentlemen that doo the office vnder them. These are his ordinarie officers, and offices of the chiefest account.

Of Gentlemen beside that wait about his chamber, and person (called *Shilsey Strapsey*) there are two hundred, all Noblemens sonnes. His ordinary Garde is 2000. Hagbutters ready with their pieces charged, and their match lighted, with other necessarie furniture, continually day and night: which come not within the house, but wait without in the court or yard, where the Emperour is abiding. In the night time there lodgeth next to his bedchamber the chiefe Chamberlaine, with one or two more of best trust about him. A second chamber of, there lodge sixe other of like account, for their trust and faithfulnesse. In the third chamber lie certeine young Gentlemen, of these two hundred, called *Shilsey Strapsey*,

Maister of the Horse.

5

10

The Lord Steward.
The Lord Tresurer.
Controller.
Chamberlaine.
Tasters.
Harbengers.

20

Gentlemen of the chamber.
The Gard.

25

30

299

Grooms.

that take their turnes by forties euery night. There are Grooms besides that watch in their course, and lie at euery gate and doore of the Court, called *Estopnick*.

35

The Hagbutters or Gunners, whereof there are two thousand (as was said before) watch about the Emperours lodging, or bed chamber by course two hundred and fiftie euery night, and two hundred and fiftie more in the Court yarde, and about the Treasure house. His court or house at the *Mosko* is made Castle wise, walled

40

about with great store of faire ordinance planted vpon the wall, and conteyneth a great breadth of ground within it, with many dwelling houses. Which are appointed for such as are knowen to be sure, and trustie to the Emperour.

Of the priuate behauiour, or qualitie
of the Russe people.
The 28. Chapter.

Constitution
of their
bodies.

The priuate behauiour and qualitie of the *Russe* people, may partly be vnderstood by that whiche hath beene said concerning the publique state and vsage of the countrie. As touching the naturall habite of their bodies, they are for the most parte of a large

5

sise, and of very fleshly bodies: accounting it a grace to bee somewhat grosse and burley, and therefore they nourish and spread their beardes, to haue them long and broad. But for the most part they are very vnweldy and vnactiue withall. Which may bee thought to come partly of the climate, and the numbnes which they get

10

by the cold in winter, and partly of their diet that standeth most of rootes, onions, garlike, cabbage, and such like things that breed grosse humors, which they vse to eate alone, and with their other meates.

Their diet.

Their diet is rather much, then curious. At their meales they

15

beginne commonly with a *Chark* or small cuppe of *Aqua vitæ*, (which they call *Russe* wine) and then drinke not till towardes the ende of their meales, taking it in largely, and all together, with

300

kissing one another, at euery pledge. And therefore after dinner there is no talking with them, but euery man goeth to his bench to take his afternoones sleepe, which is as ordinary with them as their nightes reste. When they exceede, and haue varietie of dishes, the first are their baked meates (for roste meates they vse little) and then their broathes, or pottage. To drinke drunke, is an ordinary matter with them euery day in the weeke. Their common drinke is *Mead*, the poorer sort vse water, and a thinne drinke called *Quasse*, which is nothing els (as wee say) but water turned out of his wittes, with a little branne meashed with it.

This diet would breede in them many diseases, but that they vse bathstoues, or hote houses in steede of all Phisicke, commonly twise or thrise euery weeke. All the winter time, and almost the whole Sommer, they heat there *Peaches*, which are made lyke the *Germane* bathstoaues, and their *Potlads* like ouens, that so warme the house, that a straunger at the first shall hardly like of it. These two extremities, specially in the winter of heat within their houses, and of extreame colde without, together with their diet, maketh them of a darke, and sallow complexion, their skinnes beyng tanned and parched both with colde and with heate: specially the women, that for the greater parte are of farre worse complexions, then the men. Whereof the cause I take to bee their keeping within the hote houses, and busying themselues about the heating, and vsing of their bathstoues, and peaches.

The *Russe* because that hee is vsed to both these extremities of heat and of cold, can beare them both a great deale more patiently, then straungers can doo. You shal see them sometimes (to season their bodies) come out of their bathstoues all on a froth, and fuming as hote almost as a pigge at a spitte, and presently to leape into the riuer starke naked, or to powre colde water all ouer their bodies, and that in the coldest of all the winter time. The women to mende the bad hue of their skinnes, vse to paint their faces with white and redde colours, so visibly, that euery man may perceyue it. Which is made no matter, because it is common, and liked well by their

20

25

30

35

40

45

50

301

husbandes: who make their wiues and daughters an ordinarie
allowance to buy them colours to paint their faces withall, and
delight themselues much to see them of fowle women to become
such faire images. This parcheth the skinne, and helpeth to deforme
them when their painting is of.

They apparell themselues after the Greeke manner. The Noblemans attire is on this fashion. First a *Taffia*, or little night cappe on
his head, that couereth little more then his crowne, commonlie
verie riche wrought of silke and gold thread, and set with pearle
and pretious stone. His head he keepeth shauen close to the very
skin, except he be in some displeasure with the Emperour. Then
hee suffereth his haire to growe and hang downe vpon his shoulders,
couering his face as vgly and deformedly as he can. Ouer the *Taffia*
he weareth a wide cap of black Foxe (which they account for the
best furre) with a *Tiara* or long bonnet put within it, standing vp
like a *Persian* or *Babilonian* hat. About his neck (which is seene al
bare) is a coller set with pearle and pretious stone, about three or
foure fingers broad. Next ouer his shirt, (which is curiously wrought,
because he strippeth himselfe vnto it in the Sommer time, while
he is within the house) is a *Shepon*, or light garment of silke, made
downe to the knees, buttoned before: and then a *Caftan* or a close
coat buttoned, and girt to him with a *Persian* girdle, whereat he
hanges his kniues and spoone. This commonly is of cloth of gold,
and hangeth downe as low as his ankles. Ouer that he weareth a
lose garment of some rich silke, furred and faced about with some
gold lace, called a *Ferris*. An other ouer that of chamlet, or like
stuffe called an *Alkaben*, sleeued and hanging low, and the cape
commonly brooched, and set all with pearle. When hee goeth
abroad, he casteth ouer all these (which are but sleight though they
seeme to be many) an other garment called an *Honoratkey*, like to
the *Alkaben*, saue that it is made without a coller for the neck. And
this is commonly of fine cloth, or Camels haire. His buskins (which
he weareth in stead of hose, with linnen folles vnder them in steed
of boot hose) are made of a *Persian* leather called *Saphian*, embrodered

302

with pearle. His vpper stockes commonly are of cloth of gold. When he goeth abroad, he mounteth on horsebacke, though it be but to the next doore: which is the manner also of the *Boiarskey*, or Gentlemen.

The *Boiarskey* or Gentlemans attire is of the same fashion, but differeth in stuffe: and yet he will haue his *Caftan* or vndercoat sometimes of cloth of gold, the rest of cloth, or silke.

The Gentle-
mans apparell.

The Noble woman (called *Chyna Boiarshena*) weareth on hir head, first a caull of some soft silke (which is commonly redde) and ouer it a fruntlet, called *Obrosa* of white colour. Ouer that hir cap (made after the coife fashion of cloth of gold) called *Shapka Zempska*, edged with some riche furre, and set with pearle and stone. Though they haue of late begonne to disdaine embrodering with pearle about their cappes, because the Diacks, and some Marchants wiues haue taken vp the fashion. In their eares they weare earerings (which they call *Sargee*) of two inches or more compasse, the matter of gold set with Rubies, or Saphires, or some like pretious stone. In Sommer they goe often with kerchieffes of fine white lawne, or Cambricke, fastned vnder the chinne, with two long tassels pendent. The kerchiefe spotted and set thicke with rich pearle. When they ride or goe abroad in raynie weather, they weare white hattes with coloured bands (called *Stapa Zemskoy*). About their necks they were collers of three or foure fingers broad, set with riche pearle and pretious stone. Their vpper garment is a loose gowne called *Oposhen* commonly of skarlet, with wide loose sleeues, hanging downe to the ground buttened before with great gold buttons, or at least siluer and guilt nigh as bigge as a walnut. Which hath hanging ouer it fastned vnder the cappe, a large broad cape of some riche furre, that hangeth downe almost to the middes of their backes. Next vnder the *Oposken* or vpper garment, they weare another called a *Leitnick* that is made close before with great wide sleeues, the cuffe or half sleeue vp to the elbowes, commonly of cloth of golde: and vnder that a *Ferris Zemskoy*, which hangeth loose buttoned throughout to the very foote. On the hand wrests

The Noble
womans attire.

95

100

105

110

115

120 they weare very faire braselets, about two fingers broad of pearle and pretious stone. They go all in buskins of white, yellow, blew, or some other coloured leather, embrodered with pearle. This is the attire of the Noblewoman of *Russia*, when shee maketh the best shew of hir selfe. The Gentlewomans apparell may differ in 125 the stuffe, but is all one for the making or fashion.

The *Mousicks* or common mans attire.

As for the poore *Mousick* and his wife they go poorely cladde. The man with his *Odnoratkey*, or loose gowne to the small of the legge, tyed together with a lace before, of course white or blew cloth, with some *Shube* or long wastcoat of furre, or of sheepskinne 130 vnder it, and his furred cappe, and buskins. The poorer sort ot them haue their *Odnoratkey*, or vpper garment, made of Kowes haire. This is their winter habite. In the sommer time, commonly they weare nothing but their shirts on their backes, and buskins on their legges. The woman goeth in a redde or blew gowne, when 135 she maketh the best shew, and with some warme *Shube* of furre vnder it in the winter time. But in the Sommer, nothing but her two shirts (for so they call them) one ouer the other, whether they be within doores, or without. On their heades, they weare caps of some coloured stuffe, many of veluet, or of cloth of golde: but 140 for the most part kerchiefes. Without earings of siluer or some other mettall, and her crosse about her necke, you shal see no *Russe* woman, be shee wife, or maide.

Their wits and capac- ities.

As touching their behauiour, and quality otherwise, they are of reasonable capacities, if they had those means that some other nations haue to traine vp their wittes in good nurture, and learning. Which they might borrowe of the *Polonians*, and other their neighbours, but that they refuse it of a very self pride, as accounting their owne fashions to be far the best. Partly also (as I said before) for that their manner of bringing vp (voide of all good learning, 150 and ciuill behauiour) is thought by their gouernours most agreable to that State, and their manner of gouernment. Which the people would hardely beare, if they were once ciuilled, and brought to more vnderstanding of God, and good policie. This causeth the

Emperours to keep out al meanes of making it better, and to be
very warie for excluding of all peregrinitie, that might alter their
fashions. Which were lesse to bee disliked, if it set not a print into
the very mindes of his people. For as themselues are verie hardlie
and cruellie dealte withall by their chiefe Magistrates, and other
superiours, so are they as cruell one against an other, specially ouer
their inferiours, and such as are vnder them. So that the basest and
wretchedest *Christianoe* (as they call him) that stoupeth and croucheth
like a dogge to the Gentleman, and licketh vp the dust that lieth
at his feete, is an intollerable tyrant, where he hath the aduantage.
By this meanes the whole Countrie is filled with rapine, and murder.
They make no account of the life of a man. You shall haue a man
robbed sometime in the very streats of their townes, if hee goe late
in the euening: and yet no man to come forth out of his doores
to rescue him, though hee heare him crie out. I will not speake of
the straungenesse of the murders, and other cruelties committed
among them, that would scarsly bee beleeued to bee done among
men, specially such as professe themselues Christians.

155

160

Crueltie of
the *Russe*
people.

170

The number of their vagrant and begging poore is almost
infinite: that are so pinched with famine and extreame neede, as
that they begge after a violent and desperate manner, with *giue mee
and cut mee, giue mee and kill mee,* and such like phrases. Whereby
it may bee gheassed, what they are towardes straungers, that are
so vnnaturall and cruell towardes their owne. And yet it may bee
doubted whither is the greater, the crueltie or intemperancie that
is vsed in that countrie. I will not speake of it, because it is so foule
and not to bee named. The whole countrie ouerfloweth with all
sinne of that kinde. And no marueile, as hauing no lawe to restraine
whoredomes, adulteries, and like vncleannesse of life.

175

Intemper-
ancie.

180

As for the truth of his word, the *Russe* for the most part maketh
small regard of it, so he may gaine by a lie, and breache of his
promise. And it may be saide truely (as they know best that haue
traded most with them) that from the great to the small (except
some fewe that will scarcely be founde) the *Russe* neither beleeueth

185

any thing that an other man speaketh, nor speaketh any thing himselfe worthie to be beleeued. These qualities make them very

190 odious to all their neighbours, specially to the *Tartars*, that account themselues to be honest and iust, in comparison of the *Russe*. It is supposed by some that doe well consider of the state of both countries, that the offence they take at the *Russe* gouernment, and their maner of behauiour, hath beene a great cause to keepe the *Tartar*

195 still Heathenish, and to mislike (as he doeth) of the Christian profession.

FINIS.

The Tartars or Ten Tribes

The Tartars or Ten Tribes

I

It is difficult to be precise as to the date of composition of *The Tartars or Ten Tribes*. The work was first published by Samuel Lee as a part of *Israel Redux* in 1677, some sixty-six years after Fletcher's death. But there are two statements by Fletcher that help in determining a date. He says (ll. 91–94): "But that the *Tartars* are the *Israelites*, who were transported into *Media*, and the other 2 adjoyning Countries, you shall hear such reasons as I observed, when I remained among the *Russes*, their next Neighbours, some years ago…" And toward the end of the work, he refers to Thomas Brightman's *Apocalypsis Apocalypseos*, which was published posthumously in 1609. Brightman's preface is dated 25 February 1607, only five months before his death.

The first statement would suggest a date rather remote from 1589, and the second would more specifically suggest a date sometime after 1609. So unless Fletcher read Brightman's commentary in manuscript, the date of composition of *The Tartars or Ten Tribes* can be fixed as sometime between 1609 and Fletcher's death in March 1611.

II

Fletcher's statement cited above indicates that he obtained his information from conversation with persons in Russia. And there is nothing in

309

Fletcher's work that would suggest that he knew the writings of Rabbi Benjamin of Tudela,[1] Guillaume Postel,[2] or Giovanni Botero,[3] each of whom had advanced the idea that the Tartars were the Ten Lost Tribes of Israel. Of contemporary writers on the subject, Fletcher mentions only Philippe du Plessis-Mornay, but his statement indicates that he was not familiar with Du Plessis-Mornay's book.[4]

For geographical information Fletcher used Strabo, Ptolemy,[5] and especially Jenkinson's map of Russia. Jenkinson has this legend:

> Shamareandia olim totius Tartariæ metropolis fuit, at nunc ruinis deformis iacet, vna cum multis antiquitatis vestigijs. Hic conditus est Tamerlanes ille, qui olim Turcarum Imperatorem Bayasitem captum aureis catenis vinctum, circumtulit.

Which Fletcher renders:

> Their Metropolis or chief City (though now deformed with many Ruins) is *Samarchian*, which hath many Monuments of that Nation (as they report who have been there) where the great *Tamerlain*, who led about in a Golden Chain the Turkish Emperor called *Bajazet*, had his Seat and place of residence.
>
> (ll. 158–62)

Concerning Corazen, Jenkinson has: "Corasaum parua, à Rege Persico adiuuantibus Tartaris 1558 expugnata fuit." Fletcher has: "They have *Corazen* the great and the less, whereof the less was surprised not long agoe, and taken from them…" (ll. 180–81).

Fletcher quotes (ll. 256–76) two passages from Chalcocondylas which he had previously used in *The Russe Commonwealth* (Ch. 19, ll. 219–318).

---

1. *The Travels of Rabbi Benjamin of Tudela (A.D. 1160–73)*, in Thomas Wright (ed.), *Early Travels in Palestine* (London, 1848), p. 110.

2. *Des Histoires Orientales et Principalement des Turkes* (Paris, 1575), sigs. C^v–C3^r.

3. *Relations of the Most Famous Kingdomes of the World* (London, 1630), sig. 2M^r. This was first published in England in 1601.

4. See the explanatory note to ll. 85–90.

5. See the explanatory note to l. 112.

III

The basis for Fletcher's speculation that the Tartars are the Ten Lost Tribes of Israel can be found in 2 Kings xvii.6; Isaiah xxvii.13; Revelation xvi.12; and more specifically in the apocryphal book of Esdras, where the account is more detailed:

And whereas thou sawest that hee gathered another peaceable multitude vnto him;
Those are the ten tribes, which were caried away prisoners out of their owne land, in the time of Osea the king, whom Salmanasar the king of Assyria ledde away captiue, and hee caried them ouer the waters, and so came they into another land.

But they tooke this counsaile amongst themselues, that they would leaue the multitude of the heathen, and goe foorth into a further countrey, where neuer mankind dwelt,

That they might there keepe their statutes, which they neuer kept in their owne land.

And they entred into Euphrates by the narrow passages of the Riuer.

For the most high then shewed signes for them, and held still the flood, till they were passed ouer.

For through that countrey there was a great way to goe; namely, of a yeere and a halfe: and the same region is called Arsareth.

Then dwelt they there vntill the latter time; and now when they shall begin to come,

The highest shall stay the springs of the streame againe, that they may go through: therefore sawest thou the multitude with peace.
2 Esdras xiii.39–47

Josephus also mentioned that the Ten Tribes were beyond the Euphrates:

But the Israelite nation as a whole remained in the country. In this way has it come about that there are two tribes in Asia and Europe subject to the Romans, while until now there have been ten tribes beyond the Euphrates—countless myriads whose number cannot be ascertained.[6]

IV

In 1614, Edward Brerewood's *Enquiries Touching the Diversity of Languages, and Religions* was published, and in it he refutes the idea that the Tartars are the Ten Lost Tribes.[7] Brerewood specifically answers the three arguments generally advanced in support of the notion: (1) that "Tartari" signifies "remainders," (2) that the Tartars have always embraced circumcision, and (3) the authority of Esdras.

William Whiston (1667–1572) advanced the idea that the Tartars were the Ten Lost Tribes, but it seems that he worked out his own theory independently of Fletcher's account.[8]

---

6. Josephus, *Jewish Antiquities*, XI. v. 2 ([Loeb Classical Library; 7 vols.; London, 1926–43] VI, 376–79).

7. The book also appeared in Purchas' *Pilgrimes*. See the 1905–7 edition (20 vols.; Glasgow), I, 326–36.

8. He summarizes his conclusions in his *Memoirs* (London, 1749), sigs. 2Q^r–2Q^v .

The Text

The *Tartars or Ten Tribes* was first published by Samuel Lee in 1677 and subsequently by William Whiston in 1749.

LEE EDITION, 1677

Israel Redux: | OR THE | Restauration of *ISRAEL,* | Exhibited in Two short Treatises. | The First contains an Essay upon some pro- | bable grounds, that the present *Tartars* | near the *Caspian* Sea, are the Posterity of | the ten Tribes of *Israel.* | [rule] | By *Giles Fletcher* LL.D. | [rule] | The Second, a dissertation concerning their | ancient and successive state, with some Scrip- | ture Evidences of their future Conversion, | and Establishment in their own Land. | [rule] | by *S. L.* | [rule] | Isa. 11. 11. | *The Lord shall set his hand again, the second time, to* | *recover the remnant of his People &c, v. 12.* *and shall* | *assemble the Out-casts of* Israel, *and gather together the dis-* | *persed of* Judah *from the four Corners of the Earth.* | Jer. 33. 7. | *I will cause the Captivity of* Judah, *and the Captivity of* | Israel *to return, and I will build them as at the first.* | *LONDON,* | Printed by *S. Streater,* for *John Hancock* at the | three Bibles in *Popes-head* Alley in *Cornhill.* 1677.

Special Title, sig. F10ʳ: Ἐπεὶσαγμα, | OR A | SUPERADDITION | to the former | Dissertation. [BL] | Containing a Discourse of | the grand Charter

313

of the Donati- | on of the Land of *Canaan* to *Is-* | *rael*. | Together with a short Natural Hi- | story of the Animals, Vegetables, and Minerals, found in that Country, and | of its present Fertility. | No less useful, than delightful. | [rule] | *Ezek.* 47. 14. | *And ye* [the 12 Tribes of Israel | v. 13.] *shall inherit the Land:* | *Concerning which I lifted up my* | *Hand to give it to your Fathers.* | [rule] | LONDON, Printed *Anno Domini* 1677.

Col: 12⁰: A–L¹² [$5 (–A I5 K3) signed; misprinting A4 as A5, B4 as B5, B5 as B7, D4 as D5, E4 as E5, E5 as E7] 132 leaves, pp. [6] 1–131 [misprinting 36–37 as 34–35] [2] 1–124 [misprinting 21 as 19, 98–99 as 99–98, 109 as 119; p. 1 unnumbered].

Contents: A1ʳ title page, A1ᵛ blank, A2ʳ–A3ᵛ THE PREFACE, A4ʳ–B5ᵛ THE TARTARS OR, TEN TRIBES, B6ʳ–F9ʳ The ten Tribes, F9ᵛ blank, F10ʳ title page, F10ᵛ blank, F11ʳ–L12ᵛ THE LAND OF PROMISE.

CW: A4ᵛ call- [ed], A8ʳ af- [ter], B4ᵛ Coun- [try], C5ʳ main [mained], Eᵛ there- [fore], F6ʳ The [*The*], H2ᵛ then [thcn], K6ᵛ tion [tions,], L11ʳ they [*they*].

Note: This work is entered in the Term Catalogue, Hilary Term, 1679, February 18:

> Israel *redux*, or The restoration of the Jews, exhibited in Two Treatises. The First contains an Essay, upon some probable grounds, that the present Tartars, near the Caspian sea, are the posterity of the ten Tribes of *Israel*. By Giles Fletcher, LL.D. The Second, a dissertation concerning their ancient and successive state; with some Scripture evidences of their future conversion and establishment in their own Land. By Sam. Lee. In Twelves. Price, bound, 2s. 6d. Printed for John Hancock at the Three Bibles in *Pope's Head Alley*. [Arber, I, 342–43.]

WHISTON EDITION, 1749

MEMOIRS | OF THE | Life and Writings | OF | Mr. *WILLIAM WHIS-*

TON. | CONTAINING, | MEMOIRS of several of his Friends also. | [rule] | Written by himself. | [rule] | *Ne quid falsi dicere audeat:* | *Ne quid veri non audeat:* | [rule] | *Who art thou that thou shouldst be afraid of a Man that shall die,* | *and of the Son of Man which shall be made as Grass? and* | *forgettest the Lord thy Maker, that hath stretched forth the* | *Heavens, and laid the Foundations of the Earth.* Is. li. 13, 14. | *Thou shalt not accept Persons when thou reprovest for Sins;* | *but do* | *as* Elijah *and* Michaiah *did to* Ahab; *and* Ebedmelech *the* | Ethiopian *did to* Zedekiah; *and* Nathan *to* David; *and* John | *to* Herod. Constitut. VII. 10. | *Them that sin rebuke before all, that others also may fear.* | 1 Tim. v. 20. | *Thou shalt not hate thy Brother in thine Heart. Thou shalt in* | *any wise rebuke thy Neighbour, and not suffer Sin upon him.* | Levit. xix. 17. | [double rule] | LONDON: | Printed for the Author, and Sold by Mr. Whiston, in *Fleet-* | *street*; and Mr. Bishop, in *Little Turn-Stile, Holborn.* 1749. | (Price in Sheets Six Shillings.).

Special Title, sig. χ1ʳ: After Page 368. | [line of type orn.] | MEMOIRS | OF THE | Life and Writings | of | Mr. *WILLIAM WHISTON.* | [rule] | Part II. | [rule] | [line of type orn.].

Col: 8⁰: *vol. 1* [A] B–Z⁸ 2A⁸: *vol. 2* χ1 2B–2U⁸ 2X⁶ [$4 (–N4 O4 2K4 2U3 2U4) signed; misprinting E3 as E2] 345 leaves. *vol. 1* pp. [2] 1–368; *vol. 2* pp. [2] 369–662 [663–684] [p. 87 unnumbered].

Contents: vol. 1 [A]ʳ title page, [A]ᵛ motto in Greek, Bʳ–2A8ᵛ Memoirs; *vol. 2* χ1ʳ half-title page, χ1ᵛ blank, 2Bʳ–2S6ᵛ Memoirs, 2S7ʳ–2U3ᵛ Addenda & Emendanda, 2U4ʳ–2X6ᵛ Indices.

Note: Fletcher's work is printed on sigs. 2O8ʳ–2P8ᵛ.

CW: T8ᵛ *tome* [*Epitome*], U8ʳ Directors, [Directors;], 2A8ᵛ no cw., 2C4ʳ "undue ["*undue*], 2F8ʳ which ["which], 2Hʳ rable [mirable], 2Q7ᵛ (2.) [(12.)].

In the preface to his edition, Lee states that he obtained the manuscript of this work from Dr. Fletcher's grandson, Phineas, together "with his kind leave to pass it into Publick Light." In his preface, Whiston comments:

I therefore here insert this small Paper, which I have long had in my Custody, but which has been very little known by the learned hitherto[;] it was found in MS in Sir *Francis Nethersole's* Study, (who had been an Ambassador himself) at *Polesworth, Warwickshire*, after his Death, in *Charles* the IId Time, *tho' I find it is in print, and preserved in the* Bodleian *Library*.[1]

Whiston's son, John, issued a second edition of the *Memoirs* in 1753; but it has no textual authority whatsoever.

It is evident that two manuscripts are involved. The ownership of the manuscript used by Lee can be reconstructed with little difficulty. Phineas, Giles's son, evidently fell heir to his father's manuscripts, for in 1633 he published the *De Literis Antiquæ Britanniæ*, and we can assume that he also possessed this manuscript. Upon his death in 1650, the manuscript passed to Phineas, his eldest living child (an older son had died in 1638); and in 1677 Phineas gave the manuscript to Lee. The Whiston manuscript presents more difficulty. Sir Francis Nethersole (1587–1659) was a scholar, fellow, and tutor of Trinity College, Cambridge, and very likely acquired his copy of the manuscript through his friendship with Giles, the younger. Nethersole, it will be remembered, contributed two commendatory poems to Giles's *Christs Victorie, and Triumph*. However, I have not been able to discover what happened to the manuscript after Nethersole's death and exactly when Whiston acquired it.

The relation of the two manuscripts seems to be that the Nethersole manuscript is a scribal copy of the Fletcher family manuscript. There is the possibility that the two manuscripts could both be copies of some third manuscript, but there is no evidence to support this theory. The fact that there are a great many variants is not significant; most of them can be accounted for as either the personal vagaries of the copyist or, more likely, the differences in compositorial orthography, since over seventy years separate the two editions. For example, there are twelve variants in the use of "who" and "what," sixteen variants in the use of "-s" and "-eth" as the ending of the third person singular of the present indicative, twenty-six

1. Sig. Qq^r; "*tho'*... *Library*" added in the "addenda & Emendanda," sig. Uu2^r.

variants in number, and seven transpositions. Many of the variants are omissions of words such as *the, a, that, who, why,* and *which* in one edition or the other.

The most significant variants are certain omissions in Whiston's edition, all of which tend to indicate that Whiston edited the text in these instances. The most conclusive instances of this are the following examples. Where Lee has "agoe, and taken from them" (see l. 181), Whiston has "ago (—*deest nonnihil,* I guess by the *Russe*)." Lee has "divided by their Tribes at this day, as anciently they were called" (see ll. 8–9); Whiston, "divided at this day."[2]

A collation of the following copies of Lee's edition reveals no press variants: Cambridge (5.47.112); Bodleian (Z.122 Th.); British Museum (860.6.4); King's College, Cambridge, 2 copies; Huntington Library; Harvard University; John Carter Brown Library; Yale University; Columbia University; American Antiquarian Society.

A collation of the following copies of Whiston's edition (1749) reveals no press variants: Cambridge (1.48.25[2]); British Museum (L_1, G.1358–60; L_2, 275.h.24–5); King's College, Cambridge, 3 copies.

The present edition is based on Lee's text, but certain readings from Whiston's edition have been admitted. There has been no edition of *The Tartars or Ten Tribes* since Whiston's.

2. The other examples: ll. 67, 105–6, 223–24.

Israel Redux:

OR THE

Restauration of ISRAEL,

Exhibited in Two short Treatises.

The First contains an Essay upon some probable grounds, that the present *Tartars* near the *Caspian* Sea, are the Posterity of the ten Tribes of *Israel*.

By *Giles Fletcher* LL. D.

The Second, a dissertation concerning their ancient and successive state, with some Scripture Evidences of their future Conversion, and Establishment in their own Land.

By *S. L.*

Isa. 11. 11.

The Lord shall set his hand again, the second time, to recover the remnant of his People &c, v. 12. and shall assemble the out-casts of Israel, *and gather together the dispersed of* Judah *from the four Corners of the Earth.*

Jer. 33. 7.

I will cause the Captivity of Judah, *and the Captivity of* Israel *to return, and I will build them as at the first.*

LONDON,

Printed by *S. Streater,* for *John Hancock* at the three Bibles in *Popes-head* Alley in *Cornhill.* 1677.

That the Tartars *are the Ten Tribes, who were carried*
Captives, and transplanted by the ASSYRIANS.

What is become of those Ten Tribes, who were subdued and carried Captives by the *Assyrians*; and whether they live and hold together as a People apart, or by themselves, or are confused with other Nations, and where they are, is often questioned by Divines, but not resolved, for ought I know, with any reasonable probability. 5 That they have lost their name, and the distinction of their Tribes, is more then probable; for that no Nation of the World are called *Israel*, and so divided by their Tribes at this day, as anciently they were called. Neither was there cause why the distinction of their Tribes should be continued, seeing that the end for which this 10 people are dispersed by God himself, is fully passed, and accomplished long agoe.

For that men might know where to look for that blessed Seed, it pleased God to Elect one Nation of all the World, and out of that Nation one tribe or kindred, and out of that Tribe, one house 15 or family, whereof the *Messias* should be born, teaching in the Flesh; who being now come, there is no cause why the distinction of their Tribes should still continue. Onely the *Jews* or Tribe of *Judah* retain their name, but are so commixed with that of *Benjamin*, as that they are, and long have been called by one name; so that 20 neither the *Benjamites*, nor the *Jews* can tell of whether Tribe they came. But that these *Israelitish* ten Tribes are somewhere extant, and by Gods Providence, as a People kept intirely and unconfused with other Nations, is plain by this.

The 10
Tribes pre-
served by
God uncon-
fused with
other Nations.

For that they were not quite destroyed, no, nor dispeopled, but onely captived and transplanted by the *Assyrians*; and because all *Israel* (whereby is meant the whole Nation) shall be called *to the acknowledgment of Jesus Christ* to be the *Messias*, so long expected, and yet refused by that People when he came.

Which General Calling cannot be true, except those Tribes be still continuing and somewhere extant in the World, to be conjoyned and re-united into one Nation, as once they were.

As for those other 2 Tribes, to wit, of *Judah* and the other of *Benjamin*, which for their notable infidelity and contempt of Gods Son, are made a spectacle to the World, and plagued by God with this so horrible a desolation and dispersion through the World, it is well known both where they are, and how they live, not distinguisht by their Tribes, nor yet united into one Polity or Community amongst themselves, but diffused (though not confused) and dispersed in small numbers here and there, deprived of all, save their name, which they retain (and that rather for a reproach, than for an honor, and estimation in those places where they live) that they may be known by other Nations to be that People, whom God hath punisht and rejected for that sin, in so rejecting the Son of God, but will receive and call again for his own mercy and promise sake. A thing exemplary to the World, as well of the rigour and severity of Gods Justice, which he would have observed and marked by all, but especially by the Christian States wherein they live, least for the like infidelity and contempt, they procure unto themselves the like Judgment; and also that of his infinite mercy in preserving that People from commixture, and confusion with other Nations; that the truth and certainty of his Word may so be known, when they shall be called to the publick knowledge and profession of Jesus Christ, as by his Apostle he hath foretold, and will perform in due time.

Romans 11. 22.

320

But these other Tribes, whereof we speak, which were not 55
massacred nor extirped, but transplanted by the *Assyrians*, where
now they are; and how they have lived ever since, and whether
they be a several People, or else commixed with other Nations, is
no where mentioned either in Heathen or Sacred Story, for ought
I know; yet it is not hard to find them out, if we enquire and seek 60
for them, where it is likely that they are to be found. And truly
the likeliest place to find them in, is it not in, or near those Colonies,
where they were planted at the first?

And what I pray you, if we should seek them among the *Tartars*,
who are esteemed to be the most vile and barbarous Nation of all 65
the World? You will say, perhaps, a thing unworthy and un-
beseeming that great mercy of God, which he vouchsafed to that
People, when they were yet his own peculiar; an holy Nation
elected by God, out of all the Nations in the World; as if it could
not stand with that most holy and perfect Justice, so to abase a 70
wicked People, and so rebellious against their God, as were these
Israelites, though he cast them down from the highest Heaven, to
the lowest Center of dishonour, even *ad Tartaros*, whereby you
know, in the Poets phrase, is meant the place of the damned souls,
and Hell it self, in resemblance, as may be thought, of like disorder 75
and confusion of both the places.

As for the conjecture of some Divines, that they are the People
called *Alani*, it is not only an improbable, but a very absurd and
gross Opinion. These *Alani*, as all men know, being a People not
of *Asia*, but of *Europe*, by their other name called *Triballi*, and this 80
their passage and expedition through one Country into another,
which was to be made through so many great Nations, both of
the upper and lower *Asia*, being impossible, at least unlikely to be
passed over by all Stories, which since have written in every Age.
Onely I hear the same affirmed by that Learned *French*-man, *Philip* 85
Morney Lord of *Plessey*, whom I name for honour's sake, as for
his Learning, and Nobilitie, thrice Renowned; but not confirmed
by any reason, save that which he draws from the Notation of the

word; for that *Tartar* in the *Syrian* Tongue signifies *Remnants* or

90
Remainders.

The Tartars, the 10 *Tribes, or the Israelites.*

But that the *Tartars* are the *Israelites*, who were transported into *Media*, and the other 2 adjoyning Countries, you shall hear such reasons as I observed, when I remained among the *Russes*, their next Neighbours, some years ago, which if they be

95
not demonstrative, yet to me seem so probable, as that I my self am now perswaded, and fully settled in that Opinion, that they are the natural and true Off-spring and Posterity of those *Israelites*.

1. *From the Place.*

My First Reason is, From the Place; the place whither they were transported by the *Assyrians*, and there planted; as is the manner of great Conquerors, when they aspire unto a great Monarchy, to abate the spirits of such a People as may be dangerous to their States, and likely otherwise to make revolt, as were the *Israelites*, who could not endure a foreign Prince to break their

2 *Reg.* 17.
strength by dividing them into many parts.

The Place, I say, where they were transplanted, were the Cities and Parts of *Media*, then a Province, and in subjection to the *Assyrians*, where they placed the greatest number, (as by the Story may be gathered) the rest in *Harak*, and by the River *Haborus*,

110
whereof the one is part of *Chaldaran*, the other a River of *Mesopotamia*, with a Town adjoyning of the same name. The Country

Ptolomeus.
of *Media* (as it is described by Cosmographers, but more especially by our Merchants and other Travellers, who have been there) lyeth about the *Caspian* Sea, which the *Russe* calls the *Bachualensky*, and

115
(by taking away the first syllable for shortness sake, wherewith the *Sclavone* and the *Russe* tongues are much delighted) *Chualensky-More*. All which Country lying upon the North-east, or Northern side of the *Caspian*, and *Chualensky* to the *Siberian* and *Northern* Sea, which contains in it a large Territory by the description of

120
Cosmographers, and the report of such as have been there, is now possessed and inhabited by the *Tartars*; and by the consent of all Stories, which since have written of the *Assyrian* and *Persian*

322

Monarchies, have so continued since *Cyrus's* time; who after he
had obtained the Monarchy, did first invade those *Scythian* Shepherds,
or *Tartar* people, 200 years or thereabouts, after the *Israelites* deporta- 125
tion, who were grown by that time into a great and mighty
people.

For we may not think, neither is it likely, that the *Assyrians*,
who were the Monarchs of all the East, would place a conquered
and captive People in the fairest Cities of all *Media*, and pleasantest 130
places of that Country, which lye on the South and South-west
part of the *Bachualensky*, or *Caspian* Sea, which by the report of
all stories, and Travellers who have been there, is one of the sweetest
and fertilest Countrys of all the World, and best replenished with
all things necessary, and delightful, but in the remote and barren 135
places of that Country, which were beyond the *Caspian* Sea, upon
the North and North-East Parts, where these *Tartar* People have
had their dwelling and habitations ever since. As for those other
2 Colonies of the *Israelites*, which were placed in *Harak* and *Habore*,
they bordered both upon the *Medians*. So that all these Tribes 140
might easily meet and joyn together, when opportunity serves their
turns, which happened unto them not long after, when all these
Provinces of *Media*, *Chaldaran*, and *Mesopotamia*, with their Gov-
ernors, *Merodack*, *Baladan* and *Dejoces*, by a defection fell away
from the *Assyrians* in the 10th year of *Esar-haddon*. And, that these 145
Tribes did (not long after) reunite themselves, and joyn together in
one Nation, as they were before, being induced partly by their
own desires, as disdaining ever to live commixt with other people,
and partly forced by the violence of the *Medians*, who expelled
them thence, being but strangers, and thrust upon them by the 150
Assyrians, shall appear plainly by that which followeth.

A Second Reason is, From the names and appellations of their
Cities and greater Towns, which are scituated upon the East and
North-East side of the *Bachualensky*, or *Caspian* Sea.

These *Tartar* Cities which yet are extant, have many of them 155
the same names, as had those ancient Towns and Cities, which

*From the
Appellation
of the* Tartar
Cities.

were inhabited by the *Israelites*, while they enjoyed their own Country. Their Metropolis or chief City (though now deformed with many Ruins) is *Samarchian*, which hath many Monuments
160 of that Nation (as they report who have been there) where the great *Tamerlain*, who led about in a Golden Chain the Turkish Emperor called *Bajazet*, had his Seat and place of residence. And how little differing is *Samarchian* from *Samaria*, the chief City of these *Israelites*, and their Seat, and Chamber of their Kings? onely
165 differing in termination, a thing usual in proper names of Men or Citys, when they are pronounced in divers languages. For what differs the name of *Londres*, as it is termined by the *French*, from this of *London*; or the Town of *Antwerp*, from that of *Anverse*; or *Edenborough*, from *Edenburgum*? The same difference may be
170 observed in the proper names of men and women, both in the front and first sylable, and termination of the name. For what consonance hath *Maria*, or *Marianne* with that *Miriam* of the *Hebrews*? or the *English James*, with the *Scottish Jamy*, with the *French Jaimes*, or the *Latine Jacob*? and yet these names are all one.
175 They have besides, the Mount *Tabor*, a great Town and well fenced with a strong Fort, scituate upon a high Hill, nothing differing in form or name from the Mount *Tabor* of the *Israelites*, so often mentioned in the Scriptures. They have a City called *Jericho*, seated upon the River *Ardoce*, near the *Caspian*, upon the North and North-
180 East. They have *Corazen* the great and the less, whereof the less was surprised not long agoe, and taken from them, upon whose Country the *Tartar* People sometimes encroach, and he on theirs. This univocation of *Tartar* Cities with those of *Israel*, concurring with the former reason, from the Place or Country, whither they
185 were sometime transplanted by the *Assyrians*, doth plainly shew, that the *Israelitish* People have been there, and given the names unto these Cities, as the manner is in all places, for the remembrance of their Countrys and dwelling places from whence they came, or of the Planters, or first Founders of the Colonies; as of *Galatia*
190 by the *Gaules*, and the Tyre of *Africk*, from that of *Phœnice*; the

like is used in New Colonies, as *Nova Francia, Nova Hispanica, Nova Britannica,* Saint *Domingo, Carthagena,* and other like.

These Tartar Cities are inhabited by so many as are sufficient to defend them from the Hostility of the *Persians,* and other Borderers. But the greater part which are commonly called Σκύθαι νόμαδες or *Scythian* Shepherds, do seldome come within any City, or standing houses, unless it be in Winter-time, but abide in Tents, or walking-houses, which the *Latine* writers call *Veij,* which are built and carried upon wheels, like Carts and Waggons. Their manner is in Summertime, when grass is grown and fit for Pasturage, with their herds and flocks to march Northward, and North-West from the South-East parts, where they continue all the Winter, not all together, but in their Hoords, and several Armies, under the conduct and directions of their *Morsoyes,* and *Divoi-Morsoyes,* which are their Princes and Vicegerents under the great *Cham,* their Emperor, and graze along by the way as they go, until they come to the next stage or resting place, where they plant their *Veij,* or Waggon-houses, and so make a form of a great City with many Streets, there continuing till their Cattle have grazed up all. Thus they proceed by small Stages till they arrive at the farthest point towards the North, and then return towards the South, and South-East parts another way, where their Cattel have fresh Pasturage. And so retiring by short Journeys, by the end of Summer they arrive again into the South-East Countrys near the *Caspian,* in a more mild and temperate Climate, where they continue all the Winter, within their Cities or Cart-houses, set together in form and fashion of a Town, as before was said.

My Third Reason is from the distinction of their Tribes, (which by the *Tartar* are called *Hoords*) which being united in one Government, and communicable in all things else, yet may not unite nor mixe together by inter-marriage, but keep apart to avoid confusion of Kinreds, except it be for defence or publick benefit of the whole, they unite themselves and joyn together as one People. And this division of the Nation into Tribes, and without

The manner of dwelling and living of the Tartars.

200

205

210

215

3. *From the distinction of their* Tribes.

225 commixtion of their Kinreds, which was no where else used by any Nation, save the *Israelites*, is still observed and continued among the *Tartars* most religiously.

4. From the number of their Tribes. A Fourth Reason is from the number of their Tribes, which are 10 in all, neither more nor less, as were the *Israelites*.

Their names are these.

1. The *Chrime-Tartars*, which most infesteth the *Russe* Borders, for which respect the chief leaders of this Tribe, whom they call *Morsoyes*, or *Divoi-Morsoyes* receive their pension from the *Russe*, not to invade or hurt their Country. 2. The Second is the *Cheremissim*.

235 3. The Third is the *Morduit-Tartar*. 4. The Fourth is the *Nagay*; whereof the one is the warlikest People, the other is the cruellest, and most barbarous of all the rest. 5. The Fifth is the *Sebair*, whence the *Siberes*, or *Siberians*, who dwell by the River *Obba*, derive their Pedigree, and are therefore reckoned and numbred to this Tribe.

240 6. The sixth is the *Mecrite-Hoord*. 7. The seventh is the *Shalcan*. 8. The eighth is the *Chercassey*; the most civil *Tartar* of all the rest, of a comely person, and much affected to be like the *Lachish* or *Polonian*, in his habit, gesture, and whole behaviour; by means whereof some number of them have of late received the Christian faith. 9. The ninth is the *Cassach*. 10. The tenth and last is called

245 *Turkestan*, which imports as much as *Herdman Tartar* by an ἐξοχὴ because this *Hoord* is the greatest Herd-master and Cattle-breeder

The Turks *a Tribe of the* Tartar *Nation.* above all the rest; from whom the *Turks* had their begining, as saith the *Russe*. And that this is true besides the report of the *Russe* People, and other Borderers, who have best cause to know their Pedigree, it is the opinion of all the Historians, who lived about the time when the *Turkish* Nation invaded the upper *Asia*, and began to grow a great and mighty Monarchy. Among the rest, it shall not be idle nor impertinent to report here what *Leanicus*

Leanicus Chalcodon. *in his* Turkish History *written in* Greek. *Chalcocondilos* the *Athenian* briefly writes in the beginning of his Story, touching the Origine of the *Turks*. "It is thought (said he) that the *Turkish* Nation derive their Pedigree from the *Scythians* who are commonly called the *Tartarians*; very probably because they differ very little in tongue or manners. That the *Tartar* People have sundry times invaded *Asia* at what time the *Parthians* held 260 the Monarchy of the East, first the upper, and then the lower; as *Phrygia*, *Lydia*, and *Cappadocia*, it is well known to the inhabitants of those Countries; and truly even at this day, you may see a number of such people, dispersed abroad here and there throughout all *Asia*, who in their diet and whole behaviour resemble the *Scythian* 265 or *Tartar* People." And a little after; "It is very manifest, that the *Tartars* who now inhabit a part of *Europe* towards the East (whereby he means the *Chrime-Tartars*) have a resemblance every way with the *Turkish* Nation, which are of *Asia*, daily bartering and commercing with them, in diet, habit, and whole behaviour like the 270 *Turk*; and no marvel is it, because the *Scythians* or *Tartar* People were sometimes Lords, both of higher and lower *Asia*. The name of *Turk* whereby is signified a Herd-man, or one who liveth a wild life among Beasts and Cattel, doth likewise argue the very same, that the *Turkish* Nation have their beginning from the *Tartars* 275 or *Scythian* Shepherds." Thus far *Leonicus Chalcocondilos* in his story written in *Greek*, where he begins with the *Oguzians* the *Turkish* Emperors, afterwards called the *Othomanides*, about the year of Christ 1294. But to return, These *Scythian* Shepherds now called *Tartars*, (as by all Stories both *Greek* and *Latine* doth appear) have 280 contained themselves in those Countrys, betwixt the *Caspian* and *Northern* Seas, since *Cyrus's* time, when for their Victory against so great and mighty a Monarch, they began to be first known and famous with other Nations.

How long before, it is not recorded by any Story; but they 285 inhabited not that Country which is now possessed by the *Tartar*, till after the *Israelites* deportation into *Media*, which was 240 years or thereabouts, before *Cyrus* his time, as may be collected from the best and ancientest stories.

Fifthly, They affirm as they receive it by Tradition from their *5. From the* Ancestors, that they had their Origine from the *Israelites*, who *testimony of* were transplanted near the *Caspian* or *Hircan* Sea; by which tradition, *the* Tartars.

327

as by the stories of those times, it is reported that the great *Tamerlain* would boast himself, that he was descended from the Tribe of *Dan*.

Sixthly, Though the *Tartar* language be yet unknown, because they live as a savage people, without society or commerce with other Nations, suffering none to come within them, yet it is reported and conjectured by some words of the *Tartar* language, which I have heard repeated by the *Russes*, that they have many *Hebrew* and *Chaldee* words; whereof also this may be an argument that the *Turkish* is a dialect little differing from the *Scythian* or *Tartar* tongue; but the *Turkish* language though it be mingled with much *Arabick*, and some *Greek*, hath great consonance with the *Hebrew*, as by learned Travellers is observed.

Seventhly, They are circumcised, as were the *Israelitish* and *Jewish* people.

The last reason (which I alledge to give occasion to our Divines to consider better of that place) is taken out of the 16th Chapter of the *Apocalypse*, where the Angel of the sixth Vial is commanded to prepare the passage for the Kings of the East, by drying up the River *Euphrates*, which by all Interpreters of that place is understood of the *Jews* calling from their dispersion among the *Gentiles*, to their ancient dwelling-place, and Native Country, there to profess the true knowledge of God in Christ. Which (as I take it) cannot be meant of the Tribe of *Judah*, for the exceptions which may be forced from the very place and text it self.

1. Because the Tribe of *Judah*, and the remainder of that of *Benjamin*, which were dispeopled and carried Captive by the *Romans*, have their being, and are dispersed not in the East or North-East Country, from whence the passage towards *Syria* and *Palæstine*, lyes over the River *Euphrates*, but in these Western and Southern parts of *Asia*, *Africa* and *Europe*, where ever since they have continued in that exiled and servile state; from whence the passage towards *Syria* or *Palæstine* lyes not over the River *Euphrates*, but is far wide and distant from it towards the East and North-East.

328

2. Because the persons there mentioned, who are to pass over the River *Euphrates*, are called Kings; which being taken for spiritual Kings, as they intend it, is but a forced Exposition, the whole number of faithful Christians, in this sence being Kings alike; neither is it agreable with the meaning of that place, which speaks plainly of such Kings as are to lead some great Army over the River *Euphrates*, but being literally understood of Kings indeed, can no way suit with the *Jewish* Tribes, which have no Kings, but are all a poor and servile people to the Towns and Countrys where they dwell. The place therefore is literally understood of these *Israelitish* 10 Tribes, which we affirm to be the *Tartars*.

1. Because these 10 Tribes or Hoords of *Tartars*, from the Isle of *Patmos*, where *John* wrote, are an Oriental, or Eastern people on the East and North-East of the *Caspian*, which cannot be said of the *Jewish* Tribe, or that of *Benjamin*, as now they dwell in the higher parts of *Asia*, *Africa*, and *Europe*, which lye South and South-West towards *Euphrates*.

2. From the scituation of the place, for that the *Tartars* whom we suppose to be the *Israelites*, can no way pass out of the Countrys where they now dwell, towards *Judea* and *Palæstine*, (which lyes South ward from the *Caspian* or *Hircan* Sea) but over the River *Euphrates*, which lyes a cross, and intermiddle betwixt these 2 Countrys.

3. Because the title and name of Kings in the plural number, agrees properly with the *Tartars*, who have many Kings, to wit, as many as they have Tribes, 10 in all; every *Morsoy* or *Divoi-Morsoy* (beside their Emperor the great *Cham*, whom they esteem above the dignity of a King) being a Prince or Sovereign Lord over all his Tribes. To which purpose the famed *Esdras* (whom I alledge not as authentick to confirm matters of faith and doctrine, but to illustrate as a story, this holy prophecy, which is more obscurely here set down by the Apostle) infereth the Angel thus expounding his Night-vision of things to come in the latter time. "That which thou sawest, to wit the man (who is there called the

330

335

340

345

350

355

360

Son of God) to gather to him another multitude of more peaceable and quiet people, are the ten Tribes who were carried Captives out of their Land in the time of *Oseas* King of *Israel,* whom *Salmanasser* King of *Assur* carried beyond the River *Euphrates,* so were they brought to another Land. But they took this counsel among themselves, that they would leave the multitude of the Heathen, and go into a farther Country, where never man had dwelt before;" (whereby it seems that he means the Country which lyes betwixt the *Bacualensky,* and Northern Seas, which is possessed by the *Tartars.*) And a little after, (*v. 46*). "Then dwelt they there till the latter time, but when they shall come forth again, the most High shall hold fast the springs of the River, (to wit, *Euphrates*) that they may pass through, therefore sawest thou the multitude peaceably." Where he tells that this return of the holy people over *Euphrates* towards their Country, in the latter times is meant of the *Israelitish* 10 Tribes, who were carried Captive by the *Assyrians,* who, after the manner of that people, would live alone, not commixed with other Nations, and therefore brake out of the Colonies where they were placed by the *Assyrians,* and went from thence to a remote and inward Country, (as is *Tartaria*) from the society of other men; which cannot be said of the *Jewish* Tribes, who notwithstanding by the example of those other Tribes shall be encouraged to joyn together, and to march likewise out of the places where now they are, towards the Country of *Judea,* without any impeachment, or resistance of other Nations. As for the manner of their passing over the said River, whether it shall be actual drying of the River, or a removing of all impediments, which may stop or hinder their speedy passage in this their expedition towards their Country, I will not argue it at this time. That it shall be an actual exiccation of the River, with no less miracle, then the drying up of the Red Sea, or River *Jordan,* when they passed towards the Land of *Canaan,* that so this work of God, which shall be famous in all the World, even the restoring of this people, may be observed by other Nations, with great reason and probability is affirmed by *Thomas Brightman,*

330

the last interpreter of that Book, whom God endued with special 395
gifts, and great brightness after his name, for the full clearing and
exposition of that Prophecy; above all that hitherto have written
of it.

FINIS.

The Letters

The Text

The letters are arranged in chronological order. At the left margin at
the beginning of each letter appears the number assigned to the
letter by the editor; following the number, the names of the correspondents;
and on the same line at the right margin, the date of the letter. In several instances the date assigned by the editor differs from that of the manuscripts,
in which case the reason for the date is stated in the textual notes. At the
left margin of the second line, the provenance of the letter is given. If a
letter exists in an additional manuscript or if the letter has been printed,
this information is recorded in the textual notes.

No substantive change has been made silently, and, except as noted
below, no change in punctuation has been made silently. With regard to
accidentals, the editor has adopted a more liberal procedure. All abbreviations have been expanded silently, and in so doing, the spellings that Fletcher
most commonly used have been adopted. Only when there is the possibility of ambiguity has the abbreviation been recorded in the textual
notes. Some editors have equated the symbol "ϱ" with "es", which does
not seem to be correct.[1] On several occasions Fletcher writes "merchantϱ",
but when he writes the word out he never writes "merchantes";

1. S. A. Tannenbaum, *Handwriting of the Renaissance* (New York, 1930), p. 73, agrees with the
editor's opinion.

therefore, this symbol is interpreted as Fletcher generally wrote the word.

Certain changes have been made silently in the punctuation. The punctuation following an abbreviated word has been either omitted or changed when the word is expanded. Fletcher several times, but not commonly, omits the period at the end of a sentence, and this has been added. Also, Fletcher uses a period within the sentence where the comma is required, and this has been amended. All extraneous marks, such as meaningless virgules or decorative flourishes at the end of the line, have been disregarded.

The letters are presented in a form as close to the original as possible but certain normalization has had to be made. The text of the letters is given in roman, regardless of whether the original was in the secretary hand or italic. The very few, and insignificant, canceled words are not recorded. All notes by the recipients of the letters have been ignored, as the notations are only summaries of points Fletcher has made. Unless stated otherwise, all Fletcher's letters are holograph.

My humble duety to yr Lp. remembred. Beeing enlarged by yr Lp. good & speciall meanes (wch I will ever remember with all thankfullnes & humble duety) I fynd divers suiters for my poor office towards the Citie. Among other ther of on wch is seen attending in yr Lp. lodging to procure favour & commendation from yr Lp. to my L. Maior & Court of Aldermen. I have been bould to acquaint yr Lp. wth my great regard & poor estate. I have served the Citie in this painfull place now these 15 yeers or thereabouts. & have gott nothing by my great paines but a poor estate. And therefore desire to give it over vpon condition of som benefitt towards relief of my wantes. Wherin I should the place none shalbee found more devoted & ever ready to doe yr Lp. all faithfull service then my self as so mean a place can make able to requite a person of so honourable sort. My humble sut is that you wilbee pleased not to regard the vncharitable sut of suche as seek to deprive a poor distressed man of that little reste, God hath given me & vnder yr Lp to advaunce themselves. And so most humbly praying yr Lp. in yr Christian wisdom to consider how assured & everlasting love is procured by clement dealing I humbly take my leave. The 21 of March, 1600.

yr Lp. most humble & bounden.

Fletcher.

1 FLETCHER, LILES, AND JOHNSON TO LORD BURGHLEY
[BM Lansd. MS 23, No. 19]   22 May 1576

Wee moste humblie beseach your Lordshipp, to bee our good Lord and
to heare our humble submission. Wee acknowledge our vndiscrete, and
vnreverente dealinge vnto your Lordship, and howe our dutie to the
Colledge ought not to have made vs so farr forgett our dutie to the Provoste.
But wee proteste before god, that verie Conscience moved vs to com-   5
plaine and to him wee referr the truth, and doe moste humblie submitt
vs to your Authoritie; for the faults in manner wee have but two thinges
in this poincte, our Lyvinge and our Honestie. To confesse generallie were
to resiste our owne Conscience. To Lease our Colledg is to vndoe our
selves. Wee are poore, and simple, your Lordship is noble, and wise, to   10
considre the truth, and to respecte our Calamitie. And if it shall please your
Lordship to deale mercifullie with vs, and our Colledge, wee truste it shall
not repente your Lordship to have sett vp Maister Provosts credite without
our vtter shame, and vndoinge; if yowe shall deale otherwise, our onlie
comforte is that wee hope god which knowith our hartes and seeth our   15
Calamitie in his good tyme will reveale our innocencye to your Lordshipp.

Your Honours moste Humble Oratours
GILES FLETCHER
ROBERT LILES
ROBERT IHONSON

Endorsement: 22. Maij. / Fletcher. / Lilesse / Johnson / Their first submissio

The Letters

2 FLETCHER TO LORD BURGHLEY   22 May 1576
[BM Lansd. MS 23, No. 20]

In most humble wise submitting my self before yowr Honour I acknowledg and confesse that I have verye vndiscreatlye and contrary to my
dutye and that good perswasion whiche I had of Maister Provost whome
I iudge to be the servaunt of god accompanied those whiche have exhibited
5   Articles against him tending to his discreadit and have my self very vnad-
visely healped forward that matter. In the which I see and confesse after
due examining the most part to be verye false tempered with vnseemlye
and odious woords, others light and frivolous, for the most part not toutching him but to be referred to others whome they concern. Whiche not-
10   withstanding I had never assented vnto if certaine abuses wherewith I
found my self grieved had not moved me therevnto. In this also confessing
and acknowledging my fault that being grieved therewith I deferred not
those abuses vnto him who I am perswaded would have punished them as
the qualitie of the fault deserved. For the whiche as well as for the rest in
15   most humble wise I crave pardon referring the reformation therof wholy
to yowr most honourable consideration whiche can far better iudg of thes
matters then we owr selves.

GILES FLETCHER.

Endorsement: 22. Maij. 1576 / Giles Fletcher.

3 FLETCHER TO LORD BURGHLEY   22 May 1576
[BM Lansd. MS 23, No. 24]

Testor Deum optimum maximum teque simul (illustrissime Domine)
cuius iudicium summopere reuereor, me nihil aliud in hac causa, spectasse,
præter domesticam pacem, vtilitatemque communem. Quod siquis sit cuj
domestica dissidia, hæque lites Academicæ summopere displiceant, is ego
5   sum (honoratissime Domine) quem et ipsa natura ad pacem composuit,
et hæc studia in quibus et sj non æqué proficiam, delectarj tamen maiorem

338

in modum soleo, á contentionibus semper auocârunt. De Præposito nostro sané optimo viro, et (sj seipso vsus esset) moderatissimo homine meum iudicium quale semper, et quám singulare fuerit, pluribus dicerem, sj vel ej ex meo iudicio aliquid possit ornamentj accedere nec id antea mea per- petua obseruantia declarâsset. Quare siquid iniqué, siquid petulanter, ac contumeliosé dictum sit, (fateor autem esse quam plurima) id non solúm non consentiente me, sed et inuito, ac repugnante factum esse profiteor. A quo tamen cum nulla priuatim iniuria lacessitus sim, inepté fecisse videor, quj illius gratiam collectam plurimis officijs temeré, ac imprudenter effuderim.

Dicam (honoratissime Domine) fretus tua prudentia, et æquitate. Habet nostra familia pulcherrimum florem optimæ iuuentutis. Vidj hanc ego pessimis exemplis deprauarj, nullis præmijs incendj ad studia, multorum debilitarj industriam, et grauioribus supplicijs vexarj, alijs contra impuni- tatem concedj, quj nec ita literis, nec industria, nec probitate commendan- tur. Ignosce mihj (honoratissime Domine ac optime) sj cum domesticæ dignitatj consulerem, eodem æstu paulo etiam longiús abreptus sum, quám, aut mea natura, aut consyderatj hominis ratio postulabat. Ego, sj meo insti- tuto vtj licuisset, accusassem neminem, tuum auxilium implorassem, quod se neminj solet occludere. Quod et nunc etiam vehementius imploro. Nihil habet aut fortuna tua maius quám vt possis, nec natura melius quám vt velis, quam plurimis prodesse. Id autem decernere quantum, et cuius modj sit, tuæ prudentiæ est, et æquitatis.

Tuæ Dignitatis humillimus supplex
ÆGIDIUS FLETCHER.

Endorsement: 22. Maij. 1576. / Ægidius Fletcher.

4 FLETCHER TO ROGER GOAD   23 May 1576
   [BM Lansd. MS 23, No. 26]

Ornatissimo viro Magistro Goado Præposito Collegij Regalis.

Meum iudicium de te quale semper, et quám singulare fuerit (vir ornatissime) pluribus apud te testatum facerem, nisj tibj suspectum esse

possit hijs temporibus, idque mea perpetua obseruantia, ac plurimijs ser-
mones de te non antea declarâssent. Adductus sum et priuato officio,
5 et exemplo domestico, quod in te huiusmodj semper fuit ac optimj
hominis esse debebat, et cum reliquis virtutibus instructj, tum hjs ornamen-
tis inprimis ornatj, quibus doctj homines ad honores commendantur, et id
sané vehementer lætabar, nobis ad domesticam commoditatem etiam foris
ornamentum accedere. Accessit enim et illa pietatis existimatio, integritatis-
10 que tuæ, quæ reliquum amorem mirabiliter accendit. Quæ tametsj ad totius
familiæ dignitatem spectarent, mihj tamen etiam priuatam visa sunt ad te
colendum, propriamque causam attulisse. Nam illud indignum est cuj
vniuersj plurimum debeant, eidem nolle et singulos quam plurimum
debere, idque optimis rationibus, sj possint, minoribus, sj id assequj neque-
15 ant, ostendere. Quæ cum omnia certissimé iudicarem, inconstanter fecisse
videor, quj nunc eius existimationj labem asperserim, aut ab alijs violarj
eandem passus sum, de quo ipse tam officiosé prius, ac honorificé cogitarem,
et hanc gratiam optimj hominis collectam plurimis officijs temeré, ac imprudenter effuderim. Sed ignosce mihj per humanitatem tuam, quj non tam
20 voluntate, quám errore lapsus sum, patere me vel in hac causa defensionem
adhibere, in qua tamen culpam libentissimé agnosco. Nunquam ego te
quem omnibus rebus ornatissimum esse cupio nunquam ego dignitatem
tuam, sed eorum importunitatem accusandam putauj, quj domesticam
pacem perturbant, quj sj tuam authoritatem, sequutj fuisset (cuj omnia
25 officia et priuatim et publicé debebant) nunquam res nostræ tantis, tamque
duiturnis incendijs deflagrâssent. Incredibile (inquis), quod tamen vel cons-
cientia teste sanctissimé profiteor. Ac mihj quidem illud diuino beneficio
accidisse visum est, vt hæc causa quæ a nostris satis odiose iactata est contrá
dignitatem tuam, tandem ad honoratissimum Burliensem deueniret, quem
30 huius lumen ac ornamentum Rei publicæ omnes agnoscunt. Nam nec tibj
ad existimationem quicquam potuit optatuis accidere, quám a tanto viro
hanc causam intelligj quj tuam innocentiam suo possit iudicio probare,
quod omnes æquissimum esse cognoscunt: nec nobis ad reliquam vitam
vtilius, quam deprehendj ab eius prudentia, quj nostram temeritatem suo
35 iudicio possit, ac authoritate refellere. Neque enim tam nobis graue viderj
debet repræhendj a sapientibus viris et quj reliquos dignitate antecellunt,

quanquam est illud quidem peracerbum hominj pudentj, quám eorum consilio, prudentia, humanitate recrearj. Sed quid facio. Mihj institutum fuit, id breuiter confiterj apud te, in quo iam grauiter offenderim. Quod sané libentissime facio. Sed vt hoc committere fuit leuitatis nostræ, ita remittere prudentiæ ac humanitatis tuæ. Agnoscimus totam hanc causam temere á nobis ac imprudenter susceptam multa iniqua, dura odiosa esse, ac non ferenda. In hijs adolescentiam nostram vix iustam excusationem adferre. Sed hæc suscipere imprudentiæ fuit, temeritatis defendere, agnoscere autem quod et temoré susceperis, et pertinaciter defenderis, melioris con-silij, ac voluntatis.

40

45

ÆGIDIUS FLETCHER

Endorsement: 23. Maij. 1576 / Mr Fletcher. / His submission to y^e / Provost.

5 FLETCHER TO LORD BURGHLEY   23 May 1576
[BM Lansd. MS 23, No. 27]

Honoratissimo Domino Domino Burghleiensj Angliæ Thesaurario et Cantabrigiensis Academiæ Cancellario dignissimo.

Honoratissime Domine, quj audet apud te pluribus agere, is prudentiam tuam ignorat, quj non audet æquitatem. Quare cum Dignitas tua petitionem nostram humanissimé susceperit, in qua Collegij nostrj statum explicauimus, ad officij nostrj summam pertinere putauimus, humillimas gratias Digni-tatj tuæ offerre. Atque vt Dignitas tua intelligat, quanto studio expectemus, quid sibj in hoc negotio statuendum existimet, et erroris in hac causa nostrj, petitionisque rationem breuiter demonstrandam suscepimus, vt quod Dig-nitatj tuæ visum fuerit, id nobis approbandum reseruemus. Cum nobis liberum esset impetrata venia ad Dignitatem vestram prouocare, causam nostram in iustas, ac humanissimas Dignitatis tuæ manus tradidimus. In hunc finem singulas sociorum nostrorum querælas tabulis, et confusé conscriptas adduximus: vt sj Dignitas tua argumenta flagitaret, ex illis quod nobis idoneum, ac opportunum videretur, peteremus. Has tabulas ex nobis vnus repugnantibus nobis tanquam querælæ nostræ capita imprudenter

5

10

341

15 exhibuit. Quo ita perculsj, et exanimatj sumus cum primum in conspectum
Dignitatis tuæ prodiremus, vt cogitata nobis hac de re excusatio in mentem
non veniret. Itaque temeritatem nostram, ac stuporem agnoscimus, sum-
masque Deo laudes, tuæque Dignitatj gratiam habemus, quod et prudentiæ
tuæ iudicio, et exemplj honore iam primum intelligimus, quis rerus fructus
20 sit literarum nostrarum, teque maiorem in modum obsecramus né Dignitas
tua quamuis id iusté facere possit, inopem nostram, et afflictam causam hoc
imprudentiæ pondere opprimat, atque obruat. Quod ad Collegij nostrj
detrimenta attinet, petimus ab Honore tuo et publicé vniuersj, et ego
priuatim, vt hoc audiat, atque cognoscat: præmia non doctrinæ sed partibus
25 decernj, neminem esse quj in vlla arte gradum susceperit, quosdam ita
indoctos esse, ac nullius diligentiæ, vt nullam spem in constitutis Collegij
rebus habere possint, eosdem omnibus locis Rei publicæ ita ineptos ac
imparatos, vt nihil sibj præter domesticum otium proponant, honestos ac
probatos adolescentes excludere, quj in eorum loca meliorj cum spe succe-
30 derent, omnes nobis ad Collegij commoda aditus esse præclusos, cum nos
ante hæc tempora eorum vtilitatibus nunquam repugnaremus, ex nobis
aliquos esse quj supplicijs semper afflictj, ac vexatj sint, quj eorum partibus
adhærerent, querentibus ac reclamantibus nobis solutas esse, atque dimissos.
De hijs collegij nostrj detrimentis necessitate, ac religione adductj ad Digni-
35 tatem tuam querelam afferimus, non vt accusatores, sed vt supplices, neque
tam cupimus vt ista puniantur, quám vt corrigantur: et idcircó Dignitatj
tuæ humillimé supplicamus, né hanc occasionem negligas, qua secundus
collegij nostrj fundator nomineris. Quod ad nos attinet quemadmodum nihil aliud quærimus nisj vt ordinum concordia, et literarum studia in Collegio
40 nostro restituantur, ita paratj sumus ad Dignitatis tuæ decreta humillimé
accipienda, neque dubitamus quin Deus miserijs nostris commotus Episco-
patem authoritatem ideo abrogarj passus sit, vt tandem calamitates nostræ
singularj sapientia et authoritate tua lenatæ sisterentur.

Endorsement: 23. Maij. 1576. | Mr Fletcher | to my L.

6 FLETCHER TO LORD BURGHLEY   28 May 1576

[BM Lansd. MS 23, No. 36]

Honoratissimo Domino Domino Burghlæio Angliæ Thesaurario et Cantabrigiensis Academiæ Cancellario dignissimo

Magnum beneficium ac plané diuinum accepimus á te (illustrissime Burghliensis) quod non vnius epistolæ gratias, sed perpetuæ memoriæ honorem desyderat. Sed vicit officium et Collegij studium, vt Dignitatj tuæ per literas significarem, hoc illustre beneficium erga nos, et Collegium nostrum, quám gratis animis prosequamur. Cum enim omnj ex parte et   5 imprudentia nostra, et aduersariorum authoritate, et tua iusta offensione premeremur, singularis tua et incredibilis mansuetudo et nos afflictos excitauit, et peccantes tulit, et errantes correxit. Miserum veró collegium perpetuis discordijs distractum, et literarum luce priuatum, hoc tuo Iudicio ità reuixit, vt omnem salutem Honorj se tuo debere cognoscat. Quod non   10 nobis solúm ad rem præclarum, sed reliquis etiam ad exemplum fore confidimus. Nam et adolescentes nostrj hac re cognita, et audita seueritate tua, cauebunt, atque circumspicient, et seniores æquitatem tuam videntes, ac verentes prudentiam, multó consyderatiús de se, ac suis officijs cogitabunt. Quód ad nos ipsos attinet, etsj necesse est vt quám moderatissimé in collegio   15 viuamus, ne rumores illos confirmemus quj ad Academiam de nostra infamia multj et certissimj perferuntur: gratissimum tamen nobis est, quód ex nostro dedecore Magistrj Præpositj multo clariorem existimationem interpretantur, et quód multa nobis relinquuntur officiorum genera, quibus et Iudicij tuj fructus, et humanitatis suæ gratiam mereamur. Oramus itàque   20 (clarissime Domin[e]] vt cum tu solus sis quj Collegium nostrum constituere possis, tuam solúm prudentiam audias, et honorificentissimum Magistro Præposito decretum existimes, sj tuis decretis paruerit: oramus (inquam) per Deum immortalem vt hoc beneficium re clarissimum, authoritate tua firmissimum facias. Nos quod gratos homines decet, incredibilem istam   25 munificentiam et studiosé accipimus, et moderaté temperabimus, et

343

gratias Deo á quo res ipsa nata est, referendas relinquemus. Nostram summam gratitudinem ingratam agnoscimus.

> Dignitatj tuæ humillimé deditus.
> ÆGIDIUS FLETCHER.

Endorsement: 28 Maij. 1576 | Ægidius Fletcher.

7 FLETCHER TO THOMAS WOTTON   14 September 1577
[Cambridge Epistolæ Academiæ MS ii, f. 455]

Magistro Woottono

Quanto studio litteras et Academiam nostram complexus es (ornatissime Woottone) antea nobis cognitum fuit quam tibj priuatim aliquid debere cæperamus. Itaque cum Dominus Pickarnigus vir omnibus rebus ornatus, et qui ad reliquam ornamenta quæ in eo maxima plurimaque fuerunt, etiam
5 amorem erga litteras singularem adiunxerat, (cuius item tu viuj præstantia, nos mortuj beneficentia perfruimur) in nos beneficium conferret, minus miratj sumus, te hac mente, qui et litteras amares, et ipse parte non nihil potes in hoc genere, id semper egisse, vt hoc beneficum ad nos integrum posset et quam amplissmum accedere. Hanc in te voluntatem diligere iam
10 antea cæperamus, nunc autem plane beneficium agnoscrimus quj cum rem optima fide administrares, id nobis perfecistj, vt non tuis magis quam nostris rationibus prospicere videreris; nunc etiam (quod nostro commodo fierj potuit) rem integram nobis confeceris.

Itaque eadem opera perfecistj, vt et fidem tuam erga splendidissimum
15 hominem iam mortuum, et erga Academiam singulare studium et beneuolentiam omnes cognoscerent. Hoc nos itaque accipimus (ornatissime Wottone) vt quod illius beneficium est, hoc tamen tuum esse non nihil fateamur. Cuj si reliquum adieceris, incredibile est nos tibj et Academiam nostram quantopere deuinxeris. Woottonus patruus tuus cum adhuc in
20 viuis esset, is fuit vt neminj vnquam ex suo ordine Res publica magis deberet. Fuit enim et fide singularj (id quod sæpius ac in maximis rebus

344

perspectum est) prudentia autem tanta quanta esse potuit in eo homine, cuj
ad reliquam doctrinam etiam rerum forensium vsus accesserat, quem ille ex
maximis plurimisque negotijs collegerat. Sed hæc aliena fortassis ab eo quod
volumus ac postulamus. Hunc accepimus cum e vita discederet, te eundem 25
et fortunarum suarum hæredem reliquisse quem suj nominis ac præstantiæ
iam antea habebat. In hijs autem et librorum tantam copiam quantam
verisimile est eam sibj cum ad prudentiæ studium tum ad reliquam delec-
tationem comparasse, qui se ab ineunte ætate litteris tradiderat. Vides iam
(optime Woottone) quid postulemus. Ex hijs aliquot sj in Academiam 30
conferas, incredibile est quantus nobis ad reliquum officium ac obseruantiam
cumulus accedet. Praesertim signi ex historijs sint, nam hoc genere et ipse
abundauit, quod et ipsius prudentia ac vitæ ratio postulabat. Nemo enim
πολιτιχωτερος habitus est. Sed nolumus tuæ beneficentiæ modum statuere,
nec hoc pluribus a te beneficium contendere. Nemo est qui honesta tibj 35
persuadere posset melius, aut eadem facilius impetrare quam voluntas tua.
Intelligis nullum beneficium esse quod in Academiam melius posset aptiusque
conferrj. Auget praeterea quod et tuum sit, acolim illius virj, cuius adhuc vel
ipsam memoriam deligimus, quem etiam mortuum idem velle putamus,
et sj sentire posset hoc tuo beneficio maiorem in modum delectarj. Nisi 40
forte hoc parum modeste postulare videmur abs eo cuj nunc etiam plurimum
debemus. Sed vide (optime Woottone) quam non liceat tibj semel impune
gratiam praestare; praesertim in litteras et Academiam. Ecquid putas Academiam (quæ tamen verecunda esse solet in postulandis beneficijs aut gratia
prouocanda nisj cum valde necesse est) adducj potuisse, vt hoc munus a te 45
postularet, nisj tua gratia ac humanitas, quam iam experta est ad hoc
invitasset? Nostj eam fortunam esse Academiæ vt eidem necesse sit quam-
plurimis debere. Debere autem neminj malit ex tuo ordine quam tibj: cuj
et iam plurimum debere cepit, et quem propter tuam ac familiæ dignitatem
et amorem erga hæc studia sua obseruantia dignissimum esse arbitratur. 50
Da nobis et hoc (ornatissime Woottone) volumus. Musas nostras et Academiam quæ tuorum beneficijs iam ornatur, etiam tuo non minus beneficio
ornarj; cum et æque abs te amarj certiss[imum esse.] Hoc a te et nos singuli
postulamus et Musæ nostræ Academicæ post[ula]nt. Nostrum erit (id quod
gratos homines decebit) et nominis vestrj et huius beneficij perpetuiam 55

345

memoriam diligenter conseuare. Bene Vale. Cantabrigia. 18º Calendæ.
Septembres. 1577.

Tuæ [dignitatj deditissimj] Procancellarius
[et reliquus] senatus Cantabrigiensis.
ÆGIDI[US] FLETCHER subscripsit

8 FLETCHER TO SIR FRANCIS WALSINGHAM   13 March 1586
[BM Cott. MS Calig. C. viii., f. 298]

Right Honourable. I doubt not but my Lord Ambassadour hath certified your Honour of all the important matter of his negotiation. With
soom lesser accidents not impertinent to bee knowen to your Honour I
thought good to furnish my duety of writing at this time whearin if I mis-
take my self in making that a duety which is but your Honours trouble it
may please you to pardon mee. After the second Audience which was the 3.
of Marche it pleased the King to appoint his Secretarie to repair to my Lord
abowt conference vpon the Articles of the Confederation, who after expectation of .5. dayes cam to him beeing stayed by occasion of his fathers sicknes
with whome hee had ben the mean while. It pleased my Lord Ambassadour
to have mee present at their conference. Whear after soom forspeache had
by my Lord to very good pourpose concerning the mutuall care and forwardnes that ought to bee hear on their parts for the perfecting of the
League aswell as hath ben by your Honours thear and more specially on the
Secretaries part both in regard of his duety to the King and of his former
offices and indevours towards the effecting of this matter hee answeared
with very good termes that both hee had ben and wouldbee as forward in
this action as any man in Scotland, adding his reasons withall (to make
credit of his single meaning) gods glory, the strengthning of his Church,
the common good of both Realms &c. In the perusing of the Articles hee
lyked all save twoe, the one that concerneth the aydes to bee sent by hir
Maiestie into Scotland in case of need &c. Whearin hee would have
the pay and charges to coom from the Queen. The other the Article concerning the Borders in which hee required soom alteration the Bigons

to bee from the Kinges coronation. Which beeing replyed vnto by my   25
Lord Ambassadour hee rested content and satisfied with the whole, only
making an addition of Ireland to be comprised with England in the last
article.

And whearas the French Ambassadour hear is sayed to cast in soom
matter of delay (if hee can) to keep of the conclusion for the League, vz   30
that the King hear would forbear to give his assent till suche time as the
Frenche King may bee certified of the confederation and the message retourned hee declared farther that the day before his comming to my Lord,
the French Ambassadour had sent for him and intreated his favour and
assistaunce with the King to perswade this dilatory matter. Which as hee   35
sayed hee refused to doe, adding a reason that inasmuche as the League
betwixt Fraunce and Scotland hath equall respects and standeth all vpon
reciproque tearms (except in a fiew points) and yet the French King had
concluded a League with the Queen of England withowt his Maisties consent or intimation made to him hee had now the lyke libertie and equitie   40
on his side to confederate with England withowt any intelligence made to
the King of Fraunce. This I thought good to make knowen to your Honour
for that the common opinion hear is (and so peradventure is notified to your
Honour) that the Secretary runneth a French course which can not stand
with these protestations nor other apparaunces nor with events hithertoe,   45
except hee should bee thought to temporize and to bee carried with the
stream of the Kinges forwardnes and inclination in this matter and so to
bend whear hee can not resist, which wear hard to thinck of him withowt
soom good apparaunces.

The cause of this iealousie had of the Secretarie (if it please you I may   50
sett down my coniecture) is this. Your Honour knoweth what particulars
ly betwixt the Secretarie and the Maister Gray, who as hee is indeed so hee
would appear and bee knowen to bee very well affectionate towards the
effectuating of the League. Which office hee thincketh peradventure wilbee
held of better reputation and desert in England if it appear to bee wrought   55
with soom contention and opposition. Which beeing derived vpon the other
hee gaineth both wayes more thancks and better acceptation of his own
offices and displeasure towards the other, whome for the privat differences

347

betwixt them (which ar noted hear to bee very great and dieply setled) hee
60 couldbe content peradventure to have in disfavour in England. Which I
write not to detract from the Maister Grayes deserts (to whome this cause
is very muche beholding) but to offer soom circumstaunces to your Honour to
make your iudgment of the other, who must either mean good faith or els
bee very subtill and dishonourable bearing suche contradiction within him
65 self.

   If it might please your Honour to thinck vpon soom good means for the
according them again whither by letters or otherwise it wear a good part of
recompence to them both for their service in this matter. It is muche to bee
feared least their falling asunder and following after particularities (if it goe
70 on as it hath begoon) will breed soom niew faction and disturbaunce hear,
and overthrow both their privat and the publique again.

   Concerning the principall matter I will not presume to write any thing
to your Honour specially my Lord Ambassadour writing at suche length.

   Of whome I may bee bold to say so muche to your Honour as my self
75 and the res[t] with him may take to vs for a good example that on the way
hee neglected him self and the health of his body to hasten his iourney
beeing muche troubled as well with infirmitie of his body as with the hard
season and sharpnes of the weather. And what dilegence and carefullnes hee
hath perfourmed since his arrivall hither your Honour perceiveth by the
80 effects. The Lord Allmightie bless your Honour with every good thing
both of this lyfe and of the lyfe to coom. From Edenborough the 13 of
March 1586.

Your Honours most humble
G. FLETCHER.

9 FLETCHER TO SIR FRANCIS WALSINGHAM 17 May 1586
[SP 52/39, No. 84]

   My humble duetie remembred. Right honourable knowing your good
care for the Church of god at home I thought you couldbee content to hear
how thinges stand with it hear. And thearfore have noted to your Honour

what hath passed hithertoe in their generall Assemblie begoon hear the xth
of this present if peradventure your Honour may fynd leysure to peruse it. 5

It pleased my Lord Ambassadour at his last writing to conferre with mee
about my abode in this countrey after his retourn for suche service as should-
bee thought meet. Hee wished mee to advise well vpon it. Which my self
have doon *pro et contra* according to my reason. And bycause I kniew it to
coom from his very good affection (whearof I have had good experience 10
both in this iourney and before) I referred my self to him again so far foorth
as that (if hee so pleased) hee might make mention hearof to your Honour
who can far best iudge whither I bee meet for that service or that for mee.
For my self I am not desirous to follow any ambitious course, yet having
strove with the woorld now soom good time to attain to soomwhat whear- 15
with to sett my self forward in the course of my profession and yet destitute of means I wouldbee very glad to bee employed (specially by your
Honour to whome I have vowed my service and my self) in soom honest
service, that exceedeth not the measure and proportion of my mean qualitie.
Whearof your Honour can far better iudge then I of my self. To whome 20
wholy I referre my self both in this and what so ells to bee commaunded and
disposed of after your good pleasure.

The Lord allmightie increase your Honour with all his good blessinges.
From Edenborough the 17th of May. 1586.

Your Honours most humble
G. FLETCHER.

Endorsement: 17 May 1586 / ffrom Doctor ffletcher.

10 FLETCHER AND SALTONSTALL TO THE MERCHANTS
ADVENTURERS   19 June 1587
[SP 82/2, No. 58]

Right woorshipfull Sir and Sirs after our very hartie commendacions,
yt may please yow to vnderstand that we arrived here the 3 of this Instant,
and vpon Monday folowinge we sent to Heer Harman Watkins, vpperst

349

Boroughmaister, that it would please him to apointe a tyme when we might
haue Audience, which he sent vs answere should be vpon Wednesday in the
same weeke, at which tyme he sent one of the Lords of this towne, and
a secretary for vs, who brought vs to the towne house, where we found the
whole senatt Assembled, vnto whom after some speeches vsed, we delivered
her Maiesties lettres, my Lords of the Councell with the companies, which
donn the vpperst Boroughmaister required of vs to put in writinge briefelye
our demaund, which we did that afternoone and sent it him, afterwardes
we vnderstood they had apointed fyve comissioners to treate with vs, to
wit, Heer William Milner a Doctor of the Civill lawe, and recorder of this
towne, Heer Doctor Newbo, Heer Iohn Schult, Heer Iohn Brand, and
Heer Dirck van Holt, with whom we haue had fowre severall meetings;
and first the matter they entred into with vs, was for the dischardge of our
six ships what tolle we should pay inward and outward, and libertie to buy
and sell with forreiners, aswell as townesmen wherein hath benn much said
on both sides, for they stood stifelye vpon the tolles latelye set vp, and said
their owne Burghers did pay it and the straungers pay doble and no reason
why we should be freer then their owne Cittizens, to the which was answered as much as was needfull and in fine it was concluded vnder protestacion to pay vj^d vpon a cloth for these six ships, but the next day they fell
from that agreement havinge the advantage vpon vs everye way, first our
shippes comminge before any agreement made was very hurtfull. Second
the Alderman of the Stilliard hath written the worst he can against vs,
sayenge that this openinge and relentynge to the Hanse townes was not
vpon any good will borne to them, but vpon a complaint made in England
by the gentlemen and clothiers for lacke of vent of their clothes, and for
feare of a rebellion the Queene was forced to do it. Also they of Lubecke
write to this towne, with most slaunderous wordes against vs willinge them
of this towne not to deale with vs. Also our owne contriemen which be
here as enterloopers and Staplers have declared to the Senatt (as we are
informed) that her Maiestie hath set all men at libertie in England to shipp
clothes whether they will, and that if the senate will hold of from any agreement with vs that they and others her Maiesties subiectes that are not free of
the company of Merchants Adventurers will bringe them clothes enowe.

The Prince of Parma hath sent an ambassadour hether, whose commission was (as we are informed) to will them of this towne not to graunte vs any priviledges, but to Ioyne with the rest of the Hanse townes, and to sue to the emperour to get our cloth banished the empire, vntill the Queene of England had graunted to them their old priviledges for nowe was it tyme so to do, and the Kinge of Spayne would Ioyne with them, which priviledges the Queene should be forced to graunt them, or the people would rebell. Also the Lordes of this towne laid before vs, that the Queene had dissolved our company and brought foorth the proclamacion latelye set out in England. Lastly that the Hanses were not permitted to buy in Blackewell Hall, but at the signe of the George in Westminster, with a nomber of other matters to longe to recite. All which so farre as we can learne were written over by the Alderman of the Stilliard, for a frend of this towne sent vs word that if the Queenes Maiestie knewe what the alderman had written, she would banish him out of England. But truelye we are very sory that the proclamacion was set fourth, for that sheweth our weaknes at home and geveth a great advantage to the enemye. All which matters conscidered we are in doubt to obteyne our old priviledges, for although we haue alledged not onelye to the comissioners but also severally to the fowre Boroughmaisters so much as in reason ought to suffice them, and haue made divers frendes yet can we litle prevaile. And the cause that the Boroughmaisters will not performe that which was agreed vpon by the commissioners as they say that certen of the Burghers would not confirme the same. Wherevpon they determine to call the whole Burghers of this towne together againe and to propound the matter to them agayne whose answer we do daylye exspect which once receaved we will fourthwith advertise your Worships thereof. And thus we comit you to the tuition of the almightie. Hambrough the xixth day of Iune 1587.

> Your Worships very lovinge frendes
> RICHARD SALTONSTALL governour
> GILES FLETCHER.

Direct: To the right woorshipfull the deputie and Assistentes of the felowship of Merchants Adventurers of England in London.

The Letters

11 FLETCHER AND SALTONSTALL TO THE MERCHANTS
   ADVENTURERS   29 June 1587
   [SP 82/2, No. 60]

Right woorshipfull Sir and Sirs, after our very hartie commendacions
may it please you to vnderstand, that our last was the xixth of this instant by
one Flint a Goldsmith of London, who went from hence in a Hoy of this
towne and therein we writt yow how farre we had proceaded with the
5 Senate of this towne, and of our agreement with their Comissioners which
they broake of from, excusinge them selves vpon their Burghers, but as we
vnderstand the same came vpon the Ambassadour of the Prince of Parma,
and of certeine Sclaunderous lettres written by the Alderman of the Stilliard
and the Senate of Lubeck. Wherevpon we sent two of our company to
10 Stoed, to know if we might be receaved there and in what order they would
vse vs: whom they found very friendlye and willinge therevnto, and offred
to clere vs from the Hamburghers for any demaundes of toll for our goodes
in the River, and for the tolle there they would vse vs and the straungers
that should deale with vs Frendlye. But they would not enter into capitula-
15 cion with vs vntill we were whollye broake of from Hambrough. Whose
answere beinge had, we sent to the Senate of this towne to haue Audience,
which they graunted to vs the next day where we laid before them the
effect of their lettres written to our company in August last, the Fredome
and priviledges her Maiestie had graunted them in England, the agreement
20 which we made with their comissioners, which if they would not performe
we desired to departe freelye with our shipps and goodes, and to seeke some
other place for the vent of our commodities, and that forasmuch as they
had receaved at her Maiesties handes all that which was graunted to their
Ambassadours the third of October 1585: vpon condition that we should
25 be restored to our old priviledges which we were sent to demaund, the
which if they refused and denyed vs, we protested that we had fulfilled our
comission, and must make report to her Maiestie of their deniall, wherein
her Maiestie should haue iust cause to complayne, first to themselves, after
to the Emperour the Kinge of Denmarke, as also to all other princes her
30 neighbours and confederates. Wherevpon they desired vs to go aparte,

352

which we did, and after they had consulted therevpon, they sent the recorder of their towne, Heere Iohn Schult, and Heer Direck van Holt, who vsed
some speeches to haue brought vs vp to an higher tolle, which we in no wise
would consent vnto, which they perceavinge that by no entreatie they
could bringe vs any higher, we concluded once agayne vnder protestacion   35
for vj^d a cloth for all theis clothes in theis six ships, and for as many as should
come duringe this treatie, which beinge so donn and concluded, we prayed
we might haue it vnder their Handes in writinge, who said they would
shew the Senate thereof, which they did, who said they must first call the
Burghers together and haue their consent therevnto, which they would do   40
eyther that afternoone or the next day at the furthest, and that donn they
would send it vs, which seinge we could not get the same by no meanes in
writinge, we were forced to haue patience and departed; the same day at
noone they sent vs xx pottes of wine and the musitions of the towne to
reioyce vs withall.   45

Since which tyme the commons of this towne haue mett, and haue
concluded that they and we shall pay presentlye iijs. luips for the tolle of
the towne, and iiijs. luips for the boy and Beacon mony, and iiijs. luips of
everye hundreth marks, of wares outwardes with condition that the same
shalbe without preiudice of the treatie now in hand. In which treatie if it be   50
agreed to pay lesse tolle then is beforesaid then to haue so much restored
agayne, for at this tyme the Senate sayth they cannot helpe it. Vpon this
report we haue taken tyme to answere and haue called some of the auncien-
tes of the company together, who like not to pay this great tolle, but would
rather go to Stoed, yf we may haue their reasonable conditions: wherevpon   55
we haue sent three merchants of our company to treate with them and
minde if we cannot get some further mittigacion of the Bacon and Boy
mony to dischardge our ships at Stoed, where we hope to find good sales
desiringe your Worships to be a meane to the Lords of her Maiesties privey
counsaill, to stay the common subiect that he send no wollen clothe for this   60
Towne, vntill we haue concluded with the maiestrates of this towne, for
otherwise it will hinder our proceadinges very much.

Since the writinge hereof, one of the three merchants of our company
that were sent to Stoed is returned who hath spoken with the Lords of that

65 towne who saye they are willinge to receave vs and our goodes but they will neyther answer our lettres nor articles which we sent vnto them but say when we are whollye broken of with Hambrough and come downe thether with our shipps, then they will enter into capitulacion with vs but not before. Wherevpon we consideringe the vncertentie to procead vpon such a

70 waightie cause vpon bare wordes, do not thincke it good to departe from hence with theis shipps, but if we cannot get any rebatment of the vijs. luips, which the Lords and the Burghers haue agreed vpon, then to pay it vnder protestacion that the same shalbe no preiudice to vs nor to the treatie, that we haue in hand, for the Maisters of our six ships do complayne very

75 much of longe lienge and demaund allowance, and we feare our clothes havinge benn so longe laden as they haue benn, haue taken harme so that of necessitie we shalbe forced to dischardge our goodes here for this tyme hopinge your Worships will procure her Maiesties lettres to the Lords of this towne for the helpe of this toll, and that they will graunt vs the rest of

80 our old priviledges. Wherein we stand in some doubt for that they haue the advantadge of vs now divers wayes by the proceadinges in England. Wherefore we pray your Worships let vs haue your opinions and counsaill how the state of our company standeth since we came from home and if by your good meanes there be any hope to restrayne the common subiect it would

85 be a good helpe to our proceadinges here for then we might be the bolder to stand with them in other pointes.

Maister Rawleyes licence hath benn a great lett to bringe downe the tolle here, for they say his licence for overlengthes, is contrarye to the decree made at Nonesuch the third of October 1585 wherefore except that

90 licence be called in we doubt the toll here will hardlye be brought downe.

Therefore least we should not agre here it were good that the companye continue some trade at Embden, which not onelye would content the Erle and townesman there, but also draw these people to be the willinger to yeld. Thus &c.

Your very lovinge friendes
RICHARD SALTONSTALL
G. FLETCHER

Direct: To the Woorshipfull the Deputie and Assistents of the company of
  Merchants Adventurers of England rezident in London.

12 FLETCHER AND SALTONSTALL TO SIR FRANCIS
  WALSINGHAM   1 August 1587
  [SP 82/2, No. 62]

My humble duetie remembred. Right honourable this bearer Maister
Tirrell beeing in these parts about the matter of religion cam vnto vs freely
of him se[lf] confessed his name, his profession, his fault, vs that after soom
favours received in England (beeing once in hand beefore) hee had broken
away and revolted again, that since that time hee had growen dayly into a   5
greater dislyke of him self and of Popery, aswell of the lyfe and doctrine of
that part, that hee pourposed and had fully resolved to retourn home lyke
the lost sheep, and to offer him self to your Honours whatsoever cam of it
either to punishment or to compassion and mercy.

  I have conferred with him in privat abowt the means of his conversion   10
to feal what soundnes might bee in it, and of certain doubtes which hee
seemed simply to propound as desirous to bee resolved in them, though for
the grosse partes of Poperie hee seemeth to have vtterly renounced them.
And I fynd (to my vnderstanding) that his conversion and farther desire to
bee informed in the truth is not in hypocrisie but in very truth. Which by-   15
sides other reasons his tears have perswaded mee, which I have seen him
shedd many and in the very bitter and passionat sort. This I thought good to
signifie to your Honour that it may please you the rather to bee induced according to your Christian wisdoom and discretion to bee a means for him
that beeing on the way to god or rather allready coom home hee may bee   20
drawen forward with love and compassion rather then beaten back again
with rigour and hard dealing, specially that hee may have free accesse to the
hearing of the woord and conference with soom of the godlier and sounder
sort, which him self desireth. Which I leave to your Honours good and
godly discretion.   25
  For our proceedings in our treatie hear at Hamburgh wee fynd aswell by

the Hamburghers as by other of the Hanse Townes whome wee have tried
of late that they ar all in confederacie not to yeld to any priviledges on their
parts towardes vs till hir Maiestie have perfourmed hir decree or promise
of Nonesuch. Which they alleadg not to bee doon as yet forasmuch as
divers niew impositions ar not yet remitted which by information from the
Alderman of the Stilliard they recite in particular as that of Sir Walter
Rawleys Licence, the graunt to Maister Beal for Steel, a niew exaction (as
they say) by the Coustomer of Hull &c. Whearunto wee answear them that
hir Maiestie allready having delt so largely and Princelyke with them in
graunting them so much as they have cause to bee thanckfull it is very vnreasonable they should stand in these termes and require all and more of hir
beefore them selves have perfourmed any on thing on their parts again,
specially seeing it had ben their parts to have yelded first to hir beefore any
thing graunted on hir part to them. Notwithstanding shee hath had that
farther regard to sat[isfie] them in all reasonable sort (as appeareth by a
clause of hir decree) as shee promiseth to referre it to a Commission to bee
considered vpon if the[re] bee any farther grievaunces or demaunds on their
parts. But fynding them not satisfied with this and lyke reasons, wee ar
forced now to drive it (all wee can) to a conditionall conclusion, vz. they
to ratifie our former priviledges for a cer[tain] time. In the mean while
wee tell them hir Maiestie may bee pleased to consider of their farther
grievaunces concerning these particulars, not by our means (which can not
nor dare not vndertake any such matter) but solicited (if they thinck good)
by their own Letters. And in case hir Highnes graunt not to such their
demaunds or otherwise satisfie them not within that time limited in this
conditionall contract then them selves to resume and frustrat their Priviledges so graunted for the Residencie of the Companie of the Marchants Adventurers. This wee thinck good (as the case standeth) to Labour and effect
the best that wee can, that having to serve our tournes for a time (vz a year
or twoe) in the mean while wee may hope for soom better events and lyke
advauntage to fall owt on our parts which they have now on theirs, which
they thinck good pollicie to make their best of. The reason that moveth
those of Hamburgh to stand wholy now vpon the consent of the rest of the
Hanses (contrary to the promise of their Letters) is the present doubt and

356

fear they have of the King of Denmark who will not bee intreated to remitt
or compound for matters beetwixt them withowt flatt resigning to him
their criminall iurisdiction and best part of their territorie. And thearfore of
late hath sent back their Commissioners (which they sent to him to treat
abowt the redeeming of this claim with a large annuitie or ells present pay   65
of a great soom of money) with nothing ells but absolute threatnings if they
yeld not owt of hand. And hath given order withall for the building of a
Castell in Holst at the mouth of their River to check and intercept their
trade to and froe, farther hath sent foorth of the Sound about xij. dayes
since eight tall shippes very well appointed, which they fear much hear to   70
bee sent against them. But I willbee bolld to signifie to your Honour what
my opinion is, that they ar sent for Scotland with the Kinges daughter. My
presumptions ar these. 1. Bycause I hear of certain that wear at the Danish
Court when the Scottish Ambassadour departed thence of late that the
marriage is agreed vpon and concluded, notwithstanding the report cast   75
abroad hear that the treaty brake of bycause the Scottish King will not
render the Orcades, which seemeth nothing ells but a very cloak to cast
over the Lady to convey hir in more secreat. 2. The Danish shippes sett
foorth with the Scottish all in on day the on in the fornoon the other in the
after noon. 3. The wynd not serving them they wear forced to ride about   80
this coast, the Scottish barks abowt the Holy Iland, the Danish fower
within the Emmes, and fower within the Weaser not farr of the one from
the other, and so with soom dissimulation kept companie togither. 4. Certain of them went vp into the Weaser (whear they did nothing apparant)
near to the Bishop of Bream who is nephiew to the King, as may bee sup-   85
posed that the Lady beeing a boord might have better opportunitie to re-
fresh hir self on Land. 5. The wynd comming about and serving their
tournes I hear it reported that they wear mett all sailing togither the day
beefore the date of this Letter towards the Northwest. These coniectures I
have ben bolld to sett down to your Honour notwithstanding I doubt not   90
of your Honours better intelligence in this and lyke matters. This perplexitie
they stand in with the King of Denmark maketh the Hamburghers to ioign
fast now with the other Haunse Townes specially their nearest neighbours
as Lubeck and Bream and Lunebrugh, which ar the better content to com-

95 bine them selves with Hamburgh for that they doubt their own case if so
strong and absolute a neighbour as the King of Denmark should coom so
near to them and bee possessed of on of their chief and principall Townes.
Our common Letter sent of late by the way of Middelburgh wee hope
your Honour hath received. Wee humbly beeseach you (if it may bee and
100 your Honour thinck it good) to favour our petition made thear for the
helping of this treatie. And thus humbly craving pardon for so muche
le[ngth] I leave your Honour to all the good blessings of allmightie god.
From H[am]burgh the first of August 1587.

> Your Honours most humble
> G. FLETCHER
> RICHARD SALTONSTALL

Wee ar promised a copie of the Alderman of the Stilliards letter, which
wee will send to your Honour god willing by the next passage.

Address: To the right Honourable S^r / ffrauncis Walsingham prin- / cipall
Secretarie to hir / Matie

Endorsement: 1 August 1587 / ffrom Mr Saltonstall / and Mr Docto^r ffletcher /
at Hambroughe

13 FLETCHER AND SALTONSTALL TO THE MERCHANTS
ADVENTURERS   5 August 1587
[SP 84/17, ff. 35–36]

Right woorshipfull. The iiijth of this present we came to a village called
Loy where accordinge to apointment mett with vs the Burghmaister and
one other of the Senate of Stoade in the name of their whole Senate with
whom we had conference to this effect. We propounded to them 3 pointes.
5 The first whether they would interteyne the residence of the company with
the same priviledges and conditions in all pointes absolutelye and fullye
which they enioyed at Hambrough in their late residence there. The second
whether they could and would contract this league and societie of commerce
with the company without consent of the rest of the Hanses Speciallye the

358

towne of Breame with which they are ioyned in a speciall confederacie. 10
Thirdlye whether they could vndertake to free the company of the toale
claymed by the Hamburghers for Beacon and Boy guilt as they call it of so
many as passe with merchandize within the River of Elue wherein Hambrough challengeth a prerogative. To the first they answered vs that the
Senate had alredye determined to receave the company with full graunt of 15
all the priviledges which they enioyed at Hambrough at their last residence
there without any exception. To the second that they might and would enter
and determine this contract with vs without askinge advise or consent of
any of the other Hanses, and namelye of Breame. To the third that their
senate would assure all merchants that brought trade to them of free pas- 20
sadge in and out of the River without imposition or molestacion from any
which they said they had in commission to answere vs onelye in generall
termes and not in particuler as naminge of Hambrough which they could
not do in equitie and common humanitie till such tyme as we had broken of
wholly with Hambrough. We vrged this point as farre as in reason we could, 25
vz that we demaunded not of them whether they would but whether they
might or could clear vs of this niew tolle imposed vpon the River by the
Hamburghers. But could not obteyne further answere from them forasmuch as it exceeded their commission as they said. So requiringe of them to
commend that point togeather with our reasons to the Senates consultacion 30
and to send vs their resolucion with convenient spede we departed for that
tyme. This we thought good to signifie to your Worships that yow may
the better consider and resolue whether yow thincke good to send more
cloth for this River or no which for our owne partes we thincke would not
be inconvenient for that in the meane while we hope god willinge to make 35
full dispatch with the Hamburghers one way or other and in case we grow
with them to a friendlye conclusion then that supplie of cloth to be vented
there, if otherwise at Stoade who by this gratificacion or hope of sale of
cloth with them will the rather be induced to all good conditions and
frendlye dealinge with vs. How we stand with the Hamburghers we signi- 40
fied to you in our last. The men are variable and subtile and at this tyme the
more shiftinge by reason they are so much feared and perplexed by the
Kinge of Denmarke. Yet now againe they geve vs great hopes of a finall and

frendlye conclusion for the conditionall contract which we vrge now vpon
45   them accordinge to the content of her Maiesties decree of Nonesuch which
they seeme willinge to yeld vnto and to graunt the contract accordinge to
the forme and conditon of that decree or promise made to them. But we
dare assure our selves nothinge they have deceaved so oft, and therefore we
deale with them as men vse to do with them they trust not. We earnestlye
50   expect and desire your answere. And thus &c. the 5th of August 1587.

> Your Worships very lovinge friendes
> RICHARD SALTONSTALL
> G. FLETCHER

For this conditionall contract which we perswade with them now we
55   are in great doubt that the tolles will not be driven downe lower then
where it standeth now, vz vij stivers vpon a cloth except Maister Rawleyes
imposition be released which they vrge very much and challenge by her
Maiesties decree of Nonesuch to be remitted to them. Wherein also we
desire your playne resolucion in case the tolle of vij stivers will not be
60   abated but with that condition, whether we shall agree to that tolle or no.
Thus agayne we comit you to god.

Endorsement: 5th August 1587 / A Coppie Mr Salton- / stall and Doctor
fflet- / chers letter to the Com- / panie of marchantes / adventurers.

14 FLETCHER AND SALTONSTALL TO THE PRIVY COUNCIL
COUNCIL   27 December 1587
[SP 82/2, No. 80]

*Reasons of our not acceptance of the decree or last answear of the Senat of
Hamburgh given vs for a Vale.*

1. Bycause it conteineth no on matter answearable to the petition of hir
Maiesties Letters sent and delivered them by vs, nor to our Commission
received from the Companie of the Marchants Adventurers.
Our commission was to treat for the reniewing of the former Residencie
5   at Hamburgh vpon the same or vpon equall conditions: Their Decree or

last Answear conteineth a flatt deniall and totall refusall to contract at this time for any residencie vpon any articles or conditions whatsoever. Again, our commission was to treat for the Companie of the Marchants Adventurers only and to gett this place reserved only for them: Which was allso the effect of hir Maiesties and your Honours Letters written to the Senat: Their Decree setts all open to the common Marchant and to so many as will come, quite contrary and oppositt to the charge and meaning of our commission &c.

2. Bycause the sayed Answear requireth of vs vnreasonable matter, vz. that wee should beecoom suiters to hir Maiestie and your Honours for the taking away of all impositions and grievances comprised in a book, late sent them by the Alderman of the Stilliard which is in effect a full restitution of all the Hanse Priviledges in England and namely the Accord of Vtrecht at xiiij^d a cloth. Which in case wee should have vndertaken or any wayes approved (which needs wee must have doon by making acceptance of this Decree) wee had good cause to doubt how it might bee taken by hir Maiestie and your Honours beeing a matter of so auncient controversie and so preiudiciall to hir Maiesties Coustomes.

3. In respect of the ends they had in making this Decree which wear twoe principall. 1. To gratifie the King of Spain and Duke of Parma who laboured it with them by Ambassage and Letters to reiect hir Maiesties petition and to make no contract with the English Nation. 2. That within the time prescribed in their Decree they might see the events and successe of matters now in hand beetwixt hir Maiestie and the King of Spain and thearafter to frame their determination either by refusing or accepting the contract vpon what conditions them selves thought good. In which respect, to have rested vpon this answear of their Decree had ben nothing ells but to have applied our selves to their advauntage. And these to bee their ends wee ar well assured vpon sufficient ground.

4. Bycause their sayed Decree conteineth an vntrue accusation against hir Maiestie and your Honours, vz. that hir Maiesties and your Honours Letters sent them by vs ar obscure and contein only a shew of certain generall matter to bee doon for the Hanses, but specifie nothing in particular. Whearas the sayed Letters contein a recitall and promise in particular of all

40 such pointes to be perfourmed by hir Highnes as wear promised to the Hanse Legates in hir Maiesties Rescript or answear of Nonsuch. Which bycause it conteineth a secreat accusation of indirect and subtill dealing and so toutcheth your Honours (which wee ought to defend by all good means wee can) wee thought it not our part to approve the sayed Decree by our
45 acceptance of it.

5. Bycause their sayed Answear conteineth divers other vntruthes and plain contradictions to their own Letters aswell to hir Maiestie as to the Governour and Companie of the Merchants Adventurers the 19 of August 1586, namely Their Letters say they can and will contract for residencie with
50 the English Marchants Adventurers withowt the consent of the rest of the Hanse Townes as beefore they have doon: Their Decree sayeth they must and will have regard to the rest of the Hanse Townes and doe nothing in this matter withowt their consent. Again, Their Letters say they willbee content to accept of that hir Maiestie promised them at Nonesuch, vz of so much as
55 they enioyed at the beeginning of hir Highnes reign: Their Decree claimeth a full restitution of all the Hanse priviledges. Their Letters promise to yeld first and to restore the former residencie of the Merchants Adventurers: Their Decree requireth hir Maiestie first to yeld and to remove all the grievances complained of by the Alderman of the Stilliard &c.
60 Which vntruthes and contradictions wee might seem to have approved by making acceptance of their Decree.

Endorsement: Reasons of o^r not accepting y^e / decree or last answear given / vs by y^e Senat of H$\tilde{a}$burgh. / 27 Deceb^r 1587.

15 FLETCHER AND SALTONSTALL TO THE PRIVY COUNCIL   27 December 1587
[SP 82/2, No. 81]

Reasons for the continuance and strengthning of the Residencie of the Merchants Adventurers at Stoad.

1. Bycause by this Residencie obtained at Stoad the late practise and confederacie of the Hanse Townes hath ben disappointed, which was this:

either to force hir Maiestie to a full restitution of all the Hanse Priviledges
enioyed in England 200. years agoe and namely that of Vtrecht at xiiij^d a
cloth, or ells to bannish the English commodities quite owt of Germanie.   5
Which by the same means (vz by this residencie continued and strengthned
at Stoad) may bee prevented and disappointed hearafter, and the Hanse
Townes at least the Hamburghers reduced to more equall conditions. Otherwise if wee fall of from Stoad it must neads follow, either that hir Maiestie
must neads fall into the olld controversie and importunitie of the Hanse   10
Townes, or the Companie of Marchants Adventurers into the hard conditions and hands of the Hamburghers, or ells bee content to goe quite owt of
Germanie.

That the Hanse Townes wear thus confederat togither and ment to
prosequute this pourpose to effect taking their advauntage of the time and   15
extremities they thought our Countrey to stand in for lack of place to vent
the commoditie in and other consequences that might follow vpon it, is
apparant by these: 1. By relation of divers best affected to the Companie
and the Nation. 2. By the common Letters of the rest of the Hanse Townes
to the Town of Stoad to the same effect, whearin they expostulat the dis-   20
appointing of this pourpose &c. 3. By certain propositions delivered in
writing by the Commissioners of Hamburgh to the Senat of Stoad to
dissolve this contract. Whearin the same is alleadged for a reason. 4. By
their Decree given vs for a vale whearin they require all the grievaunces to
bee taken away that have ben imposed vpon the Hanse Townes since the   25
accord of Vtrecht &c.

2. The conveniencie of the place in the iudgment of Marchants both our
own and forrein aswell or better seated then that of Hamburgh to bring in
and carry owt all kynd of marchandise by sea or by Land. Proof hearof the
late mart thear which beeing the first in that place exceeded the best they   30
had these xxtie years by report of ther Marchants in other places.

3. In regard of hir Maiesties honour, who hath voutchsafed to confirm
this contract made with Stoad by hir Letters to the Senat and Communitie
of that Town. And thearfore can not yeld to give hir consent for the dis-
solving of this contract withowt soom note of dishonour, except they of   35
Stoad depart from it first, or at least give their consent to have it dissolved.

363

4. The great discredit that would grow to the Companie of the Marchants Adventurers that ar noted allready with often flieting from on place to an other, and so the lesse account made to intertain their residencie in those parts.

Who in case they should deceive Stoad and break of their contract for residencie thear might never look for the lyke friendship and intertainment hearafter in any Town of Germanie, in case they should bee driven to the lyke extremitie. Which consequence soomwhat allso toucheth the state of the Realm.

5. The qualitie and disposition of both places towards the Companie and towards the whole Nation, and so the better vsage and safetie of their goods and persons that shall reside thear. The Stoders farre better conditioned and better affected towards the Nation and Companie then the Hamburghers bee.

And that the Hamburghers for the generallitie of them aswell Senat as Burghers (if they bee not plain enimies) yet ar but hard and subtill friends towards this Realm thear is too much and too evident demonstration of it, first vpon this ground, bycause they ar Spanish and thearfore no friends to England at this time. And that they make more account of the Spanish part and preferre that friendship beefore this with England it is apparant by these. 1. The reiecting hir Maiesties petition on the beehalf of the Companie of the Marchants Adventurers at the request of the King of Spain and Duke of Parma and that at such a time when they supposed they might most hurt and preiudice the Realm. And that this is true it is apparant by these proofes. The confession of divers of their Senat to vs that the Ambassage from the King of Spain or Duke of Parma and certain Letters writt from soom principall men of that part wear the cause of our casting of and reiecting hir Maiesties petition. The propositions communicated in writing by the Commissioners of Hamburgh to the Senat of Stoad whearin they professe this to bee their motive and end, and vse the same reason (vz. the power and authoritie of the King of Spain) to disswade and terrifie the Stoders from this contract. The relation of a Burgher of Groninghen who certified vs of the Hamburghers Letters to Verdugo Captain thear to that effect: vz that they had satisfied the King of Spaines request by casting of the English &c.

2. By their common reioicing when any niews commeth of losse or disadvauntage to England or good successe for Spain, as at the losse of Scluse, the report of Sir Francis Drake hurt, and part of his fleet surprised by the Spanish, the safe arrivall of the Spanish fleet from the Indies &c. What time the Senat sent for him that brought the niews to their Roathowse to relate it to them with great reioicing &c.

3. By their late fleet of x. shippes bought by the King of Spaines factour and sent towards Spain with men, vittail, armour and engin to furnish the enimie. By the way divers of the shippes entred Stoad, professed them selves to serve the King of Spain, quarelled and fought with the English marchants, vttred many despiteful woordes against the whole Nation.

This fleet beeing stayed as wee vnderstand in the West countrey (and so the enimie disappointed of that furniture) would have occasioned the Hamburghers to have seased vpon the English goods at Hamburgh for recompence with advauntage in case our residencie had ben planted thear.

6. In respect of the conditions farre better and more equall at Stoad then could or can bee hoped for at Hamburgh. As the free exercise of religion with a Preacher and administration of the sacraments. Coustoom of on stiver on a cloth whear Hamburgh requireth fower. A convenient howse free &c.

7. For that the rest of the Hanse Townes ar lesse discontented with this residencie at Stoad then if it wear retourned and planted at Hamburgh as appeareth in the Lubeckers Letters to the Senat of Stoad, to that effect: vz That they ought all to refuse this residencie of the English Marchants but yet can better affoord it to the Town of Stoad then to Hamburgh if it wear to be received by eyther of them.

Endorsement: Reasons for the continuance / of the Residencie of the / Marchants Adventurers / at Stoad. / 27 Decembr. 1587.

16a FLETCHER TO THE QUEEN   1587
    [Hatfield, Cecil Papers 186. 42]

May it please your most excellent Maiestie of your free and naturall disposition towards the relieving of your poor subiects, as allso in regard of

365

twoe severall Leases intended to bee made to your subiect Giles Fletcher by
the Kinges Colledg in Cambridg whearof your poor subiect was then made
5 frustrate by reason the same wear otherwise bestowed by means of your
Highnes Letters of commendation directed to the sayed Colledg whearby
your sayed poor subiect having then put foorth him self from the sayed
Colledg vpon hope and full assurance (as hee then thought) of on of the
sayed Leases, hath since that time ben very muche distressed and is growen
10 into debt: in consideration whearof may it please your most excellent Maiestie to graunt to your sayed poor subiect your Highnes Licence for the yearly
buyeng and selling of 400. sarpler of wooll within your Realm for the space
and term of eight years. For which your Maiesties most gratious bountie
as allso for all other the great and manifold blessings of Allmightie god
15 powred on this Realm by means of your Maiesties most happy government
your sayed poor subiect shalbee ever most bounden to pray for your Highnes most long and happy reign and after this lyfe your everlasting happines
in the Kingdoom of Christ.

Endorsement: Peticion to the Queen / Giles Fletcher

16b FLETCHER TO THE QUEEN   1587
    [Hatfield, Cecil Papers 186. 43]

Reasons to induce hir Maiestie to favour my suit for the Lease &c.

1. The respect of twoe Leases in the bestowing of the Kinges Colledg
of Cambridg (whearof I was Fellow) commaunded away from mee by
hir Maiestie the one about vij years since to Maister Middellmoor the other
of late called Samford Courtney to my Lady Cobham either of them farre
5 better value then this I sue for.

2. To remember to hir Maiestie my attendaunce doon hir Ambassadour
in Scotland, and my employment now to Hamborough.

3. To signifie to hir Highnes my readines with soom aptnes to write
a storie in Latin of things doon in hir Maiesties reign if I had soom compe-

366

tencie of living whearby I might better spare time to bee employed in this   10
busines.

4. If hir Maiestie answear that shee hath of late commended mee to a
place in the Citie to signifie to hir my great thanckfulnes for it and withall
the smallnes of the stipend beeing but L^{li} a year towardes my charges which
must needs bee far greater. And that the missing of those Leases by hir   15
Maiesties meãns and my service in Scotland have brought mee into soom
debt which can not bee eased but by soom extraordinarie means.

Endorsement: Reasons to induce hir Matie / to favour D. Fletchers / suit.

17 FLETCHER TO LORD BURGHLEY   21 September 1589
    [BM Lansd. MS 60, No. 59]

                                1 *My intertainment.*
                                2 *The causes of my hard intertainment.*
The summe of my Negotiation.   3 *What is doon and brought to effect.*
                                4 *What could not bee obteined on the beehalf*
                                    of the marchants.

                    .1. *My intertainment.*

My whole intertainment from my first arrivall till towards the very end
was such as if they had divised meanes of very purpose to shew their vtter
disliking both of the trade of the Marchants, and of the whole English
nation.

1. At my arriving at the *Mosko* thear was no man to bidd mee well-   5
coom, not so much as to conduct mee vpp to my lodging.

2. After I had stayed two or three dayes, to see if anie wellcoom or
other message would coom from the Emperour, or the Lord *Boris Federowich Godonove*, I sent my Interpreter to the saied Lord *Boris*, to desier him
to bee a meanes for audience to the Emperour, that having doon my Am-   10
bassage to the Emperour, I might doe my message, and deliver my Lettres
likewise to him. My Interpriter having attended him two or three dayes,

withowt speaking with him, was commaunded by the Chauncellour to coom no more at the Court, nor to the howse of the saied Lord *Boris*.

15   3. The Counsell was commaunded, not to conferr with mee, nor I to send to anie of them.

    4. When I had audience of the Emperour, in the verie entrance of my speach, I was cavilled withall by the Chauncellour, bycawse I saied not forth the Emperours whole stile, which of purpose I forbare to doe, bycawse I

20 would not make his stile of two ellnes, and your Highnes stile of a span long, having repeated the first and principall parts of it, and giving him the titles of great *Lord, Duke and Emperour of all Russia, King of Cazan, King of Astracan* &c. I answeared him that the Emperour was a mightie Prince, and had manie Countries which straungers could not, nor wear not bound to know,

25 that I repeated the principall of his stile, to shew my honour to the rest. But it would not serve till all was repeated.

    5. The Presents sent by your Highnes to the Emperour, and delivered to him in his own presence, wear the day following retourned to mee, and very contemptouslie cast down beefore mee.

30   6. My articles of petition delivered by woord of mouth, and afterwards by writing, with all other writings wear altered and falsified by the Emperours Interpriter, by meanes of the Chauncellour *Andreas Shalcalove*, speciallie whear it concerned him self, manie things wear putt in, and manie things strook owt, which being complained of and the points noted would

35 not bee redressed.

    7. I was placed in an howse verie vnhandsoom, and vnholsoom, of purpose (as it seemed) to doe mee disgrace, and to hurt my health, whear I was kept as prisoner, not as an Ambassadour.

    8. I was not suffred to send anie Lettre into England by the winter way

40 to signifie of my proceedings, not so much as of my health though I desired it earnestlie.

    9. My allowance for vittail was so bare and so base, as I could not have accepted it but to avoide cavillation, that I beegan to contend with them abowt so mean a matter.

45   10. At my retourn, at *Vologda*, open proclamacion was made by the Duke and Diake thear, by order from the Chauncellour *Andreas Shalcalove*,

that no man should hier owt horse or boat to anie Englishman: which bredd an opinion in the people thear, that thear was great matter of disliking from the Emperour towards the English nation, which was a cawse of great daunger towards mee and my Companie, and of the firing of the English howse at *Colmigore* (as appeared by the sequeal) whear the Companie of the English Marchants lost to the valiew of 6. or 7. thowsand Marks.

These parts of hard interteinment wear offred mee by the Chaunncellour *Andreas Shalcalove*, who is allso the Officer for Ambassages, of verie purpose (as it seemed) to move mee to impatience, that hee might have wearwith to disturb this busines. And thearfore I determined with my self to vse all moderation, so farr as might stand with your Highnes honour, that if other meanes of faier treatie prevailed not with them, I might make soom advantage of my hard interteinment towards the end of my negotiation, by layeng it all in on dish beefore them, and applieng it to your Highnes dishonour (as indeed it was) which beeing doon in as earnest and vehement manner as I could divise with discreation, brought them to soom remorse of their former dealings, and so to yeild divers points, and in a manner all that I intreated of them, in recompence of their hard interteinment given mee beefore, whearof they desired mee to make the best to your Highnes at my retourn home.

2. The causes of my hard intertainment.

.I.

Since the loss of the *Narve*, the Russ hath divised by all meanes hee could to dissolve the trade that way (whearbie hee thincketh the enimie is enritched) and to bring it over to the Port of Saint Nicholas. This had been doon long since in the other Emperours time, but for a speciall affection hee bare towards your Highnes, which staied him from that which otherwise hee intended. This purpose of reducing the whole trade from the Narve to the Port of Saint Nicholas, they suppose to bee hindred speciallie and onlie by the Coompanie of the English Marchants, and their privileadged trade, beeing assured by the Hanses, Neitherlanders, and Frenchmen that if the Companie of the English Marchants wear cast of, and their Privileadge dissolved, they should presentlie have a famous and notable trade at their saied Port of Saint Nicholas, which should much encrease the Emperours Coustoom. Vpon hope whearof, they have built a Town and Castle abowt

80 xxx miles within the river that falleth into the bay or road of Saint Nicholas. And this is the cheefe grownd of their dislike towards the Companie of the English Marchants and their privileadged trade.

.2.

It was informed to the Emperour and his Counsell, by Lettres and mes-sage owt of England, that the saied Companie was vtterlie disliked by your

85 Highnes, by your Counsell, by all the Marchants of England, speciallie of late, having reduced them selves to the nomber of xij, and so beeing now more notable Monopoliers then they wear beefore, that in case they wear cast of, they showld have a farr greater trade of English Marchants, of 20. 30. or 40. sail a year, which would bee content to pay whole Coustoom, and

90 to bee vsed as common men, that on man would trade for asmuch as the whole Companie now doth, that your Highnes would like it better to have the Companie disolved, and the trade laied open for all your subiects alike, then to have anie Privileadge confirmed to the saied Companie at this time, for that it would increase your Maiesties Coustoom hear, as it doth the

95 Emperours thear. As for your Highnes Lettres written at this time on the Companies beehalf, it was informed that the same wear gott by great im-portunitie, that your Highness sett your hand to manie things which yow never read over, and for my self that I was sent but as a messinger not as an Ambassadour, that I never spake with your Highnes.

.3.

I found the Lord *Boris Federowich Godonove* so displeased with the Com-

100 panie, that no reason nor intreatie would reconcile him. The matters that greived him I found to bee these. 1. That Hierom Horsey was so chased away by the Companie (as hee was informed) being sent as a messinger from him with Lettres and Presents to your Highnes. In which respect (hee

105 thincketh) hee should have been forborn at that time, for his sake and ac-counteth it his dishonour that hee was retourned in that sort. 2. For that hee was not provided of certein particulars, which hee sent for to the Companie,

as horse, armour, pearle &c. 3. For that his late Present sent to your Highnes
by Hierom Horsey was dishonoured and disgraced by the saied Companie,
by whose meanes (as hee is vntrulie informed) it was divided into two parts, 110
the on from the Emperour (who sent then no Present) the other from him
self, whearby the grace and honour of his present was defaced as hee
thought.

·4·

When I arrived at the *Mosko*, I found a League in hand beetwixt the
Emperour and the King of *Spain*, about an opposicion against the Turk. To 115
which purpose an Ambassadour was appointed to goe into Spain, on Peter
Ragon a Slavonian and the Emperours Interpreter. This League was sett
forward by the Patriarch of *Constantinople*, who beeing banished by the
Turk, had been with the Pope and was sent by him to the Emperour of
Russia, aswell to treat abowt this niew League beetwixt him and the 120
Spanish King as to reduce the Russ from vnder the Greek to the Latine
Church. For the effecting whearof, hee thought their own Patriarch (beeing
thus banished and discontented) to bee the likeliest meanes. This treatie of
League with the Spaniard, was a cawse of more sadd countenance towards
mee at my first arrivall. But after your Highnes victorie against the King 125
of Spain was well known thear, (which I vnderstood by Lettres sent mee by
Sir *Francis Drake* which I cawsed to bee translated into the Russ toongue
togeather with your Highnes Oration made to the Armie in *Essex*) all this
conceipt of a Spanish League vanished away.

·5·

I found at the *Mosko* an other Ambassadour sent from the Emperour of 130
Almaign, to treat of a confeaderacie with the Russ Emperour against the
Polonian, that is over mightie for the Russ, by the access of *Sweaden*. This
Ambassadour (as if hee had been sent for nothing ells) inveighed against the
doings of England, made small account of the Spanish defeat, assuring them,
that the King of Spain would sett on again, and make a conquest of your 135
Highnes Realmes. These and like suggestions made them woorse affected
then otherwise they would have been, and bycawse they wear desirous to

conclude this league with the Emperour of Allmain, having for that purpose
sent vnto him for this Ambassage, they wear the more willing to gratifie
his Ambassadour with my hard intertainment.

.I.

To the First I answeared them that to perform this divise was a matter
impossible, that the Marchants that vse to trade by the way of the Sound,
would never bee brought to leave a knowne safe, and speedie trade, for so
long, tedious, and daungerous a course, as lieth by the way of Saint Nicholas. That in case your Highnes wear, and the Companie of Marchants so
requited for their discoverie, and other desert, having served the Emperour
so manie yeares with necessarie commodities for his warrs &c (when the
other way by the Narve was quite shutt vpp) and thus dishonoured by
reiecting your petition and Presents, and they should assure them selves
neither to have the English nor anie other Marchant to trade that way to the
Port of Saint Nicholas. That your Highnes both could and would provide
for your own honour, and good of your Marchants, by stopping that way,
and not suffer them thus to bee spoiled both of their privileadge and goods.
And this they might consider, what inconveinence it would grow vnto, if
(the Narve passage being shutt vpp by the Sweaden) the other way allso by
the Port of Saint Nicholas wear debarred from them, so that they showld
have no way to vent their own commodities nor to receive in forreign,
speciallie powder, saltpeeter, brimstone, lead &c necessarie for the Emperours warrs. With these and like pointes, I did what I could to beat them
from that grownd.

.2.

To the 2. I assured them that I receaved my charge and instructions from
your Maiestie, that your Highnes had a speciall care what was doon at this
time on the beehalf of your Marchants, whom yow accounted not as Mousickes or base people (as they termed them) but as verie speciall and necessarie
members of your common wealth. And thearfore made your suit to the
Emperour at this time, as a full experiment of his good will and affection
towards your Maiestie. And as for the increasing of your Highnes Cous-

toom, yow made more account of your Honour and continuing of the graunt made to the Companie of your Marchants by your Maiestie and your predicessors, for the incouragement of your subiects to the like enterprises for discovering of niew trades &c. then yow did of the enlarging of your Coustoomes, or anie matter of commoditie whatsoever. That your Highnes Coustoom could no whitt bee increased by this meanes forasmuch as the whole Countrey of *Russia* was not able to receave so much of English commodities, as wear now brought in yearlie by the saied Companie of Marchants, their lead, copper, and other commodities lyeng still vpon their Agents hand, and they never vttering past 130. or 140. clothes yearlie, whearas other English Marchants in on small Towne of *Germanie* vent 60. or 80. thowsand Clothes yearlie.

·3·

To the 3. To remove that conceipt owt of the Lord *Boris* I assured him of your Highnes verie speciall affection and great good opinion of him, that your Highnes thought your self allreadie greatlie beeholding to him, that yow desired to bee beeholding to none but to him for this good tourn towards your Marchants. That your Highnes beeing the best and thanck-fullest Prince in the world would not bee vnmindfull of his good desert, whearof yow had given mee a charge to assure him in your name. As for the Companie of Marchants, they should and would bee readie to make him amendes if they had given him anie iust cawse of offence &c.

3. *What is effected in this busines.*

Concerning the matter of League and friendshipp beetwixt your High-nes and the Emperour: it is receaved in verie kinde sort, and profession made of like good will and other correspondencie as was beefore beetwixt your Highnes and the Emperours Father.

1. Thear is remitted of the debt made by on Anthonie Marshe claimed from the Companie amounting to the summe of twentie-three thowsand fyve hundred fiftie and three Marks: two partes of three with an overplus, so that thear remaineth to bee paied by the Marchants but 7800 Marks.

373

2. Thear is remitted them bysides at this tyme by the Emperour the sume of 1840 Rubbells or Marks, claimed, and exacted beefore of the Agent for Coustoom of the last year.

3. Farther thear is remitted by the Emperour 300 Marks claimed for rent for their howse at the Mosko.

4. Concerning their Privileadge of trade (which I found to bee of no account at my cooming thither) but infringed in all the principall pointes of it (coustoom, howserent &c beeing claimed of them) thear is graunted in effect all that I required on the beehalf of the Companie, save that half Coustoom is claimed hearafter. This beeing doon they promise a continuance of the Privileadge for ever withowt anie revocation. The additionalls now made to the former Privileadge are these.

That the Companie shall trade freelie down the river *Volgha* into *Media*, *Persia*, *Bougharia* &c and no stranger shalbee permitted trade that way but they.

That present paiment shalbee made to the Agent hearafter for all commodities that are taken of the Companie for the Emperours vse by his Treasurers and other Officers.

That a great charge shalbee given to all the Emperours Officers, that no exaction bee made hearafter vpon the Companie, contrarie to their Privileadge.

That (to prevent all inconvenience that may happen hearafter) none shalbee accounted to bee of the Companie, or for their affaiers in that Countrey, but such as shalbee enregistred by the Agent in writing in the Office of the Treasurie, and this is to bee added as an article to the Privileadge.

That such as are so inregistred, and their names stroken owt afterwards by the Agent, shall no longer bee reputed for the Companies servants, or to have to doe in their affaiers.

That no Englishman hearafter shalbee sett on the pudkey, or otherwise tormented, for anie suspition of cryme whatsoever, but onlie safe kept till hir Maiestie bee informed and the truth of the cawse throwghlie knowne.

That all commodities shalbee transported free, save wax to bee bartred for saltpeeter, powder and brimstone.

374

That the Companie of English Marchants shall not bee hearafter vnder the Office of *Andreas Shalcan*, but pertein to the Office of the Treasurie, so that they may appeal to the Lord *Boris Federowich Godonove* if they thinck they have wrong.

That the Privileadg graunted to the Companie with these addicions, shalbee proclaimed and made knowne to all the Emperours authorized people.

235

4. *What is not graunted on the Marchants beehalf.*

Bysides the 7800. Marks, which ar exacted of the Companie of Marchants, thear is deteined allso from the saied Companie, the summe of 11000 marks or thearabowtes, which was seazed on and taken away perforce (by *Andreas Shalcalove* Chauncellour to the Emperour) owt of the hands of on *Anthonie Marsh*. The cawse of this iniust deteinment is this. The Chauncellour this last year, had his goods confiscat (to the valiew of 60000. Marks in money bysides other stuff and commodities) in the Emperours name, but indeed to the vse of the Lord *Boris* and other of the *Godonoves* that vse the Emperours authoritie at their pleasure. Among which goods was the saied summe of 11000 Rubbells belonging to Anthonie Marsh. Which beeing once possessed by the said Lord *Boris* and other of his name, not as Marshes goods, but as the Chauncellours due to the Emperour by confiscation could not bee recovered from their hands, the Chauncellour denieng that ever hee receaved anie such goods. Notwithstanding the evident prooves alleadged by mee to the contrarie.

240

245

250

Endorsement: 1589 | A brief of this negotia- | tion in Moscovia | Mr D. Fletcher | receaved 21 Septeb.

18 FLETCHER TO THE QUEEN   1589
   [BM Lansd. MS 52, No. 37]

Means of Decay of the Russe trade.

I.

 The desier the Russ hath to draw a greater trade to the port of Saint Nicolas:
beeing the better and surer way to vent his own commodities, and to bring
in forrein, then the other wayes by the Narve and Riga, that ar many times
stopped vp by reason of the warres with the Polonian and Sweden. This ma-
5 keth them discontent with our English Marchants and their trade thear:
which beeing very small (viz but of 5. or 6. sail a year) keepeth other from
trading that way. Whearas they ar made assured by French, Netherlandish
and other English Marchants that they shall have great numbers and a
flourishing trade at that port to the enhaunsing of their commodities and the
10 Emperours coustooms, if they will cast of the English Company and their
priviledged trade.

2.

 The keeping of their trade and staple at Mosko. Whearby grow these incon-
veniences. 1. A great expense by their travail and carriages to and fro by
land from the sea side to Mosko which is 1500. verst or miles. 2. An expense
15 of houskeeping at five places, viz at Mosko, Yaruslave, Vologda, Colmigroe, and Saint Nicolas. 3. Their commodities ar ever ready at hand for the
Emperour and his Nobilitie lyeng within the eye and reach of the Court.
By this means much is taken vpon trust by the Emperour and his Nobilitie
(which may not bee denied them) and so it beecommeth desperate debt. 4.
20 Their whole stock is still in daunger to bee pulled and seazed on vpon every
pretence and picked matter by the Emperour and his Officers. Which cannot bee helped so long as the trade is helld at Mosko: considering the nature
of the Russ which cannot forbear to spoil and fliece strangers now and then
(as hee doeth his own people) if hee suppose they gain by his Countrey.
25 This hath caused all other Marchants strangers to give over that trade save
two only: Whearof the one also (beeing a Netherlander) beecam banckrupt

this last year, the other (a Frenchman) beeing spoiled by them at my beeing thear, cam away the last year and hath given over that trade. As for our Marchants priviledges (which they wear suffred to enioy when the discovery was first made, and when the olld Emperour was in a dotage about a marriage in England &c) they must not look that they will protect them hearafter against these seazures and spoiles the Russe having no respect of honour and credit in respect of his profit.

3.

Their servants which (though honest beefore) ar made ill by these means. 1. The profannes of that Countrey and liberty they have to all kynd of syn. Whearby it commeth to pass that many of them (beeing vnmarried men) fall to ryott, whoredoom &c: which draweth one expenses: so having not of their own they spend of the Companies. Of this sort they have had to many (as they know). 2. Lack of good discipline among them selves, specially of a preacher to keap them in knowledg and fear of God, and in a conscience of their service towards their Maisters. 3. Their wages and allowance is very small, or (if they bee apprentizes) nothing at all: beeing debarred bysides of all trade for themselves. This maketh them practise other means to mend their estates, first by imbezeling and drawing from the Company, and then following a privat trade for themselves. Whearby divers of them grow ritch and their Maisters poor. Which they make less conscience of, bycause they say they spend their time in so barbarous a Countrey whear they ar made vnfit for all other trades, and service in other countries abroad. 4. Certein of their servants that have soom better conceipt of themselves grow into acquaintance with Noblemen of the Court to countenance their dealinges after they ar entred into a privat trade and other disorders. This friendship of great persons in the Russ Court is very dear and hath cost the Company many a thowsand pownd: having gained nothing by it but the protection of their own lewd servants against themselves.

4.

Privat trade by certein of the Company that have their factours thear vpon the common charge. Who bysides their inland trade buyeng at one part of the

377

Countrey and selling at the other (as if they wear Russe Marchants to the great dislyke of the Russ) bring in and ship over commodities in Flemmish bottoms at Saint Nicolas, Riga and Narve. Which hindereth muche the common trade and profit of the Company.

Means to please the Russe Emperour for the Marchants beehalf.

1. If the Queen seem willing to ioign with him for drawing a greater trade to the Port of Saint Nicolas from the other wayes of Narve and Riga. 2. If hir Highnes Letters, treaties, and presents sent to him bee so ordered as that they seem indeed to coom from hir self and hir good affection, and not from the Marchants (as hee is perswaded still they doe) and thearfore reiecteth them, and little regardeth the treaties doon in hir name, bycause (as hee sayeth) they coom but from the *Mousicks*. 3. If hir Maiestie (when occasion doeth requier) offer hirself ready to mediat beetwixt him and the Polonian and Sweden, whome the Russ ever feareth bycause hee is ever invaded by them, and not they by him. And thearfore is glad to procure his peace by any means with them: the rather bycause hee never wanteth an enimie on the other side viz. the *Tartar*.

Remedyes.

I.

The remedy for this is to give the Russ soom better contentment by enlarging the English trade at the port of Saint Nicolas so much as may bee. This may bee doon by refourming the trade after the manner of the Adventurers vz: Every man to trade for him self vnder a governours deputy that is to attend and follow their busines on the other side. 2. The number of the Russe Company to bee enlarged, and young men suffred to trade aswell as the rest. This manner of trading after the order of the Adventurers, and drawing a greater trade to the port of Saint Nicolas, is lyke to prove much better for the Generallitie of the Company, for common wealth, and the Queens coustooms then that which now is, whear all trade togither in one common stock. If it bee obiected that the Russe countrey will bear no such enlargement of trade, nor vent greater quantitie of our English commodities then

378

now it doeth (which is but 1500 English clothes a year, with soom propor-   85
tionate quantitie of tin, lead, brimston &c:). It is answeared by the opinion
of soom of good experience, that the trade by Saint Nicolas hath ben stinted
of late, and restrained of pourpose, and by very practise for the benefit of
soom fiew and that the sayed trade will vtter far greater quantities then now
it doeth, whatsoever is pretended; if the way by Saint Nicolas wear ons   90
well inured and frequented in manner (as beefore is noted), specially when
troubles grow on the Narve side.

2.

The remedy. To draw their trade and staple from Mosko, and other inland parts
to the sea side, whear they shall bee farther of from the ey and reach of the Court.
This will avoyd the seasures doon vpon every pretence and cavillation and   95
takings vp vpon trust by the Emperour and his Nobles. Which is the speciall means that vndoeth our Marchants trade: the rather when every man
dealeth severally for himself with his own stock, which will not bee so
ready for the Russ to commaund as when all was in the hand and ordering
of one Agent. 2. By this means allso the inland privat trades practised by   100
certein of the Company to the hurt of the Generallitie, will bee prevented,
when they ar restrained all to one remote place from the inland parts. 3.
The charge of houskeeping and houserents at those 5. severall places will
bee cutt of. 4. The charge and trouble of traveiling to and fro with their
commodities and carriages (viz. 1500. miles within land) will bee eased. 5.   105
The Russe commodities (that our Marchants trade for) will bee easier provided towards the sea coast then in the inland parts. And as toutching the
lykelyhood of obteining the Emperours favour for the removing their
trade from Mosko towards the sea side thear ar these reasons to induce it.
1. The pollicie of the Russ to remove strangers out of the inland parts,   110
specially from Mosko (the Emperours seat) towards the outparts of the
Countrey for bringing in novelties, and breeding conceipts in their peoples
heads by their beehaviour and reports of the governments and fashions of
other Countries. To this pourpose the Emperours Counsell consulted at my
beeing thear, and conferred with mee abowt the removing of our Marchants   115
trade from Mosko to Archangell, that lyeth 30. miles from the port of

Saint Nicolas vpon the river Duyna, to feell how it would bee taken if it wear forced by the Emperour. 2. The desier the Russ hath to draw trade to the port of Saint Nicolas for the reasons mencioned beefore. 3. The necessitie of our English commodities will draw the Russe Marchants to follow the Mart or staple whearsoever it bee specially at Saint Nicolas for the commoditie of that port. 4. The whole inland trade will then bee the Russe Marchants. Wheareas beefore our English Marchants (that kept residence at Mosko, and other inland parts) had trade within land and delt with Bougharians, Medians, Turks &c: aswell as the Natives. Which the Russe Marchants very much envyed and mislyked. 5. The Emperour and his Counsells lyking will force the Marchants to frequent that trade though themselves should mislyke it.

3.

Remedy for this. viz: 1. By removing their trade from Mosko, and by severall trading (noted beefore). Whear every man followeth his busines by himself or his factour. Hearby their servants ill dealing will bee prevented, and if the servant prove ill and vnthriftie, it hurteth but his Maister. 2. If they continew their trade (as they doe) by common servants, to allow them better wages, and to give them more contentment by permitting them to have a peculium to a certein stint, and to trade with it for bettering their own estates. This will give their servants better contentment when they see soom care had of them and their own estate to mend aswell as the Companies. 3. To have a preacher thear resident with them that they may learn to know God and so their dueties towards their Maisters. Which will easier bee graunted if the trade bee removed towards the sea side. If they obiect they have no great number of servants thear that should need a preacher (as was answeared mee when I propounded that matter to them at my gooing over) it may bee answeared that if they have never so fiew in that Countrey (whear they want all good means of instruction towards God) the Company ought in Christian duety to provide that means for them. The preacher (bysides that vse of him) might earn his stipend by advise with their Agent abowt their affaires beeing a man of soom iudgement and discretion.

4.

This inconvenience is prevented. By removing the trade to the coast, and observing the order mencioned beefore, as the Adventurers doe.

Means to terrifie the Russ and keep him in order.

1. By threatning to stoppe the way to the port of Saint Nicolas. Which   150
(howsoever it can bee doon) the Russ is perswaded hir Maiestie can doe it.
2. If hir Highnes shew any correspondence with the Polonian, Sweden, and
Turk, and that shee hath means to incite them &c. 3. If the Russ practise any
seazure or violence vpon our Marchants goods (as was lykely beefore my
comming thither) revenge may bee made at Pechora by the sea side vpon   155
the Mart thear. Which is helld yearly abowt Midsommer. Whear ar marted
of furres of all sortes to the value of 100000^{li} yearly: Which may bee surprised by a fiew sail and a small company well appointed comming on a
soodain, the Russ having no means to forsee or prevent it.

Endorsement: Means of decay & reme- / dies for ye Russe trade.

19 FLETCHER AND ROKEBY TO THE PRIVY COUNCIL   6 February 1590
[SP 12/230, No. 63]

Our humble dutie remembred. According to the direction of your
Honours lettres, wee have perused the peticion made to your Honours by
the Legataries of on Iohn Norden deceased, soomtime Agent to the English
Marchants trading into *Russia.* And as touching the informacion given vnto
your Honours by the saied Legataries concerning certein Legacies due vnto   5
them by the last will of the saied Norden, which they say are deteined from
them by on William Trumbull his Executor now resiant in *Mosko:* wee
fynd the same to bee very true, aswell by the confession of the saied Trumbull made to on of vs at his beeing in that Countrey, as by a noat of his estate vnder his own hand, whearin hee acknowledgeth the saied Legacies as   10
due to bee paied by him to the saied pore men, amounting in all to the summe

381

of fifteen hundreth powndes. And wheareas it pleaseth your Honours
to requier our opinions, what way wee thinck best for the recovering of the
Legacies towardes the releef of these pore men, it may please you to vnder-
15 stand that wee fynd the saied Trumbull to have dealt very subtillie, for that
having first recovered all the goodes of the saied Norden into his own handes, hee refused to take vpon him the Executorshipp, and perswaded the
saied Legataries, to take owt an Administracion in their own names, and to
administer the saied goodes, according to the tenour of the saied *will*, which
20 can bee of no force now to releeve the saied Legataries: forasmuch as
Trumbull is possessed of Nordens whole estate, beeing in so farr a Countrey,
and owt of reach of Law, and the propertie of the saied goodes altered long
agoe. And thearfore wee can thinck of no other way for the releeving of the
pore men, but by a speciall Commission to bee directed from your Honours,
25 for the examining of such persons vpon their oathes, as are thought by
them to bee factors for Trumbull, and to have large parcells of his goodes
within the Realm, which beeing once found owt, may afterwardes bee
attached by due order of Law, towardes the satisfacion of these and other
Legacies, due to bee paied by the saied Trumbull, which wee finde to bee
30 many and to very godly vses, to the summe of 4500^{li} or thearabouts, as
appearith by the *will*. And thus leaving to your wisdooms, the farther
consideracion of the whole matter: wee committ your Honours to the
goodnes of the Allmighty. At London the 6. of February 1589.

Your Honours most humble.
R. ROKEBY
G. FLETCHER.

Address: To the right honourable the / Lordes and others of hir Maties /
    Privie Counsell.

Endorsement: 6th ffebru: 1589 / ffrom Mr Rookeby and M^r / Doctor Fletcher.

20 FLETCHER TO LORD BURGHLEY   7 November 1590
   [BM Lansd. MS 65, No. 59]

My humble duety remembred. I acquainted your Honour with my
pourpose to make triall of my self for writing a Latin storie of hir Maiesties
time. Your Lordship knoweth what is needfull to make a storie not a tale,
bysides *res gestae* to have *consilia rerum gestarum*. Whearin I shall fynd great
defect except your Honour voutchsafe mee your help for instructions. I   5
desire not the very *arcana* (which ar best when they ar secreatst) but so
muche as shalbee necessary to explain and iustifie the actions. To which
pourpose I have sett down a brief of the first book and extracted owt of it
the pointes to bee instructed in. Which I mean to observe in the course of
the whole for beeing over troublesoom to your Honour and to note only   10
so muche at once as may serve for on book. Except it please your Lordship
to give order to Maister Mainard that I may see at once so muche as I need.
Whear allso I am most humbly to intreat your Lordship that it may bee
doon vnder your patronage. Your Honour knoweth what it is to write a
storie specially *de præsentibus* and how hard it is to please truth and the ac-   15
tours. If the idea and generall scope tend to the honour of hir Maiesties
government I hope it wilbee borne withall if I tell truth in occurrent matters.
For the rest I am to speak honour of that which deserveth it and truth of all.
Which wilbee doon with better discretion if I may have your Honours
direction in soom niecer points. As in the first book whither I shall deal   20
with iustifieng the marriage beetwixt King Henry and hir Maiesties mother
in soom larger discourse. Which I would thinck better rather to passe by
withowt any toutch for making a doubt whear the matter is sound and of so
great sequeal but for the open and scurrilous sclaunders of the Popish part
allready in print in large discourses whearof soom of late have written with   25
more venom then the rest. Which may bear credit hearafter if the truth bee
not knowen by soom other discourse of better spirit and credit then theirs.
   As also whither I wear better to beegin the storie with hir Maiesties time
(toutching only King Edward and Queen Maries time) as I have sett down
in this brief, or whither I shall beegin whear Polydor endeth, vz at the 30th   30
year of King Henrie the 8. whear hee concludeth with Catharin Dowagers

383

letter written to him at hir death, or ells with the Kings marriage with
Queen Anne, whear occasion is offred in both places to make narration and
discourse of the lawfullnes of that marriage in the very entrance of the
35   storie. Your Honour knoweth Polydores deserts, his stile soomwhat harsh
and vneaven and the matter not very iudiciall, which both I would avoyd.
I have enfolded hearwithall these scribled papers that contein a beeginning
of the storie at King Edwards time, which I toutch very briefly to make an
introduction to hir Maiesties reign. If I fetch the beeginning from King
40   Henryes marriage with hir Maiesties Mother (which will make the fuller
storie) all this of King Edward and Queen Marie is to bee amplified more
at large. These scriblings I am bold to offer to your Honours iudgment that
you may censure the stile which wilbee more eaven and historicall when it
commeth to the full narration. If your Honour allowe it and will voutchsafe
45   mee your help and patronage God willing I mean to proceed. Thus humbly
I take my leave. 7th of November 1590.

Your Honours most humble
G. FLETCHER.

Summa Librj primj, quj res gestas complectitur anno primo
ELIZABETHÆ.

1. *Generis*. Natus ex Iana Semoria cuius Pater ex equestrj Ordine
&c:

1. Narratio   2. *Actionum*. 1. *Religiosarum.* Romanj Pontificis authoritatem, ac
brevis   ritus reiccit. 2. *Politici*. Initio imperij fœdus contraxit cum vicinis
5   Principibus, quj tum opibus ac potentiâ præcipuj habebantur. Vbj
pacta explicanda de Bolloignia restituenda, &c: Domj summa cum
moderatione Rem publicam tractabat. Egit de matrimonio contra-
1. EDOVAR-   hendo cum Maria Scota. Finis quó duo regna coniungeret. Bellum
DUS   Musculburgense &c:
10   *Ab adiunctis*. 1. *Naturæ*. excellens ingenium. 2. *Artis*. industria
singularis, præclara institutio. Vnde linguarum varietas, Græcæ,
Latinæ, Gallicæ, Italicæ, Peritia philosophandj, equitandj, iaculandj,
concinendj &c: 3. *Morum*: maiestas, moderatio, modestia, clementia.

384

Vbj de Iohanna Boucher, iustitia. Vbj narratio de aulico ministro &c: gravitas, suavitas. 4. *Politicj*. Peritia tractandæ Rei publicæ. Quód Regij Senatus consulta corrigeret, Legationibus per se responderet, &c: Arculam habebat in qua Regij Senatus consulta seposita fuerunt, &c: Tres libros assidué secum circumferre solebat divinj, Patrij iuris, historiam Regum Anglorum. 5. *Religiosarum*: Assiduitas legendj, dicendj, agendj aliquid, quod ipsius pietatem testatam faceret. Rogatus a Carolo Quinto vt Mariæ Sororj facultatem concederet vtendj Romanos ritus, id constanter et cum lachrymis pernegavit. Ipsius precatio cum é vita excederet. 6. *Tempus*. Regnavit annis 6. mensibus 5.

Generis. Nata ex Catharina Arragonia quacum Henricus Pater matrimonium contraxit intercedete Pontificis Romanj.

Actionum. 1. *Religiosarum*. Pontificiam authoritatem ac ritus revocavit. Cives 500. flammis vivos absumpsit. *Politicj*. Nuptiæ cum Philippo Hispano, quj potentior &c: Vnde Rei publicæ periculum, ipsj mæror ac solitudo.

Ab adiunctis: Pudica benifica ergá suos. Odium erga Evangelicos, Hos præsertim quorum operâ vsus est Henricus Pater in divortio faciendo, &c: *Tempus*. regnavit annis 5. menses 4.

1. *Generis*. Nata ex Anna Bolleinia quæ ex nobilj familia &c: Vbj primó tractandum: Henricj matrimonium legitimum fuisse cum Anna Boleinia. Ratio. Quod divortium cum Catharina recté ac ordine factum fuerit, ergo &c: Probatio antecedentis. Quod iure divino perpetuum est ac perenne, id tollj non potest, aut mutarj á Pontifice Romanj. Nequis fratris vxorem sibj matrimonio adiungat, perennis ac perpetua lex est ex iure divino, ergo &c: Integrum argumentum probetur, et amplificetur. Maior. axioma theologicum. Minoris probatio. 1. Quód haec læx moralis sit moribus ac naturæ á deo tradita, ergo &c: 2. Quod Canones ipsj, ac ius Pontificium non permittunt ea mutarj a Pontificis Romanj quæ plané adversantur iurj divino. 3. Consensus Academiarum. 4. Testimonium Hispanorum á quibus Catharina oriunda: quj cum ageretur de matrimonio

Marginal notes:

2. Demonstratio seu iudicium

20

25

1. Narratio

2. MARIA

30

2. Demonstratio

35

40

1. Narratio

45

contrahendo inter Carolum Quintum et Mariam principem regnante Henrico Rege, id plané detestatj sunt, hac ipsa ratione adductj, quód hanc pater ex fratris vxore susceperat. 5. Testimonium Gallorum, quj hanc ipsam ob causam Delphinj coniugium cum Maria aversatj sunt &c: 2. Refutatio maledictorum contra Annam Boleiniam. 1. Ab adiunctis contrarijs, summâ pudicitiâ ac religione. 2. Temporum descriptio, quæ eiusmodj fuerunt vt nec Pontificijs nec Evangelicis tutum esset: cum reiecta authoritate Romanj Pontificis, ritus tamen ac religio Romana pœne integra permaneret. Hinc (quód inclinante re Pontificia Anna Boleinia Regem assiduè incitaret contra Pontificios) calumnia conficta &c: 3. Quæ sibj postremo imprecata est, cum securj feriretur. 3. Conclusio. Querela contrá tam proiectam licentiam maledicendj, præsertim eorum quj publica maledicta contra principes proijciunt.

2. *Inaugurationis.* 1. Tempus: qua ætate cum regnare cæperit. 2. Locus: Westmonasterij. 3. Personæ: Episcopus Carliensis nequid ipse Pontificij haberent, quod contra obijcerent &c: 4. Modus: Sella curulj per vrbem invecta, pompa applausus, publica lætitia. Describendus ritus, ac modus inaugurationis, iusiurandum &c:

3. Politicων: quæ initió adhibita sunt ad regnum confirmandum. 1. Portus omnes ac aditus maritimj ad tempus interclusj. 2. Legationes missæ, vel acceptæ ab ijs Principibus quj in proximo constitutj fuerunt, quique opibus ac potentia præcipuj habebantur. Ratio in genere quod plurima domj immutanda, et in Re publica et in re religionis, ergo foris omnia priús pacanda. Ratio sigillatim. Cum Gallo, quod Philippum sequuta Maria cum eodem bellum gesserat, &c: Cum Hispano. Quod á Philippo Elizabetha gratiam acceperat regnante Maria. Quod videbatur Philippus velle vasa, suppellectilem ornamenta, pecunias privatas Mariæ sibj vendicare iure matrimonij, etiam Elizabethæ nuptias appetere. Cúm Scota. Quód tum Gallis fœderata. Guisianis consilijs vteretur &c. Legatio: Gustabj Sueviensis. Vbj notandum quantum Elizabethæ res initio adiuverit, quod principes vicinj sibj spem facerint, eius nuptijs perfruendj, quæ tum

HENRICO
8º TRES
LIBERJ
FUÊRE

3. ELIZA-
BETHA

386

princeps adolescens regno, opibus, forma florebat &c: Hac singulæ   80
legationes explicandæ, quæ capita fæderum ac pactionum &c:

4. *Religionis* immutatæ. Vbj duo explicanda. 1. Deliberatio de
religione immutanda. *Contrarij.* 1. A Consequentia: Quod omnis
mutatio cum periculo coniuncta præsertim in re religionis. 2. Quód
videbatur Pontifex Romanj velle omnia humana, et divina permis-   85
cere, quo se vlciscj possit &c: 3. Quod principes vicinj religione
dissentirent. Vnde perpetuæ simultates, præsertim incitante Pontifice
Romanj. 4. Quód domj plurimj essent ex primario ordine quj
Pontificæ religionj adhærebant. Vnde periculum de domestico
tumultu præsertim si primis comitijs pacuniæ in subsidium exige-   90
rentur. 5. De Hibernia periculum, ne ab officio descicent præsertim
incitantibus ijs quj ex sacro ordine Romanæ religionj se penitus
addixerant. *Refutatus*: Primæ rationis. Nisi prudens ratio incatur de
periculis avercendis. Vbj thesis tractanda: In sacris promovendis
divina consilia sequenda esse, non humana. 2. Pontificiæ minæ ac   95
fulmina contemnenda si domj et foris omnia prius pacentur. 3.
Cum vicinis principibus qui religione dissentiunt fædera prius
ineunda. Interim portus ac fines regnj præsidijs communtj. 4. Hij
ad tempus suspensj inter spem ac metum. Interim hij paulatim
abdicatj magistrata qui Pontificæ religionj favebant. In singulis   100
provincijs publica munera ac magistratus hijs demandatj qui et
religionj et principj studebant. *Conclusio.* quod freta divino præsidio
in religione restituenda, hijsque consilijs vsa periculum contempserit,
ac pro nihilo duceret. 5. *Modus.* Res dilata ad tempus semestre
donec omnia constituta et donij et foris. Deinde ad publica commitia   105
relata. Vbj explicanda publica disceptatio de re religionis.

5. *Bellum.* Lethense gestum cum Gallis quj in Scotia consederant.
Vbj primo causæ explicandæ quó Mariæ Scotæ aditum præmunirent
&c: 2. Modus bellj gerendj per Graium Wiltonium, quj eó missus
est cum 10000 armatorum. 3. Legatio per Gulielmum Cecilium   110
Equitem, et capita conventionis &c.

387

The Letters

King Edwards time

The Ambassage to the French King in the beeginning of King Edwards time with the Articles of treatie agreed vpon for the restoaring of Bolloign.

If your Honour know any memorable thing toutching the privat qualitie and beehaviour of King Edward.

The Queens time

5   The Ambassage to the King of Fraunce in the beeginning of hir Maiesties time with the articles treated and concluded vpon.

The Ambassages to the Kinges of Spain, Queen of Scotts, King of Denmark with the articles &c.

The propositions made by Iohn Duke of Finland toutching the marriage
10   beetwixt Erick his brother and hir Maiestie.

The articles of pacification treated and agreed vpon with the Frenchmen at Lieth in Scotland by your Honour then Ambassadour.

Doubts to bee resolved in

Whither King Phillip at his beeing hear made request to bee crowned King of England and whither thear wear any consultation toutching that
15   matter.

Whither hee made any motion of a marriage with the Queens Maiestie after the decease of Queen Marie.

Whither the Pope sent any Legat to the Queen at the beeginning of hir reign, how far hee cam and what hee had to treat of.

20   Whither any charge was given for shutting vp the Ports and havens through the Realm presently vpon the death of Queen Marie.

Address: To the right honourable / my very good L. the / L. high Treasurer of / England.

Endorsement: 7. Noveb. 1590 / Doctor fletcher to my L.

21 FLETCHER TO LORD BURGHLEY   30 June 1596
[SP 59/31, f. 212]

My humble duety to your Lordship remembred. I have talked with the
Graymes and have taken their answear, the effect whearof is, That they wear
drawen into the Patronage of the Tenants of Leonard Coast by the old
Lord Scroop in default of their Landlord Maister Christopher Dacres. And
as toutching the Blackmaile (which as they define it is nothing ells but a   5
protection money, or a reward *pro clientela*) they vtterly denye that they
received any save onlie in satisfaction of such sooms of money as they have
laied out for redemption of the Tenants goods, with their own consents.
Which could not bee recovered by any other mean for want of a warden
of the middle marshes on the Scottish side. For the other complaint of   10
abetting or receiving the Scottishmen that harried the Tenants, they protesting great earnest (and it seemeth trulie) that they ar innocent thearin, in
puting the matter to a false suggestion by Iefferie Bell and Rowland Robson
whome they affirm to bee men of verie bad qualitie, fiet to bee suborned
for very small reward. I have sent to your Lordship their answears at large,   15
if it please you to bee troubled with the perusing. I have likewise inquired of
every one of them what Landes they hold of the Queens Maiestie according
to the Direction of your Lordships lettre, and find that none of them save
onlie Richard Grayme holdeth land of the Queen within the Barronye of
Gilsland. Hee that holdeth land of the Barrony of Burgh is another Richard   20
Grayme. Thear ar many of them of the same forename. And if their distinction had been sett down in the note, and the place of their dwelling, they
could have answered (they saie) for most of the rest what lands they hold
in either of the Barronies. They humblie crave your Lordships good favour
for their dismission or triall, the rather for that since their coming hither,   25
their Tenants (they saie) have been harried and spoiled by the Scottish men.
They promise to praie for your good Lordship, and when occasion shall
serve that your Lordship shall hear of their good service on the Borders.
I note in them soom splene towards the Lord Scroop as if they had received
soom wronge from his Lordship by this accusation. Whearin if your Lord-   30
ship beestow vpon them soom grave admonition after your wisedoom,

389

when they shalbee discharged, it maie doo them soom good for the observing their duety towards his Lordship when they ar retourned. And so most
humblie I take my leave. From London the Last of Iune 1596.

Your Lordships most humble

Address: To the right honourable / my very good L: the L: / High Treasurer
of / England

Endorsement: Vlt. Iunij 1596 / Mr D. Fletcher to / my l. / wth ye Greames
awnsweares.

22 FLETCHER TO SIR ROBERT CECIL   7 July 1596
[Hatfield, Cecil Papers 42. 12]

Right honourable among other your Honours devoted poor friends I
am to gratulate to you the title of that whearof you had the employment
and substance beefore. And I most hartilie pray God who hath given you this
honour and wisedoom withall to perfourm the dueties of so high a calling,
5   to give you the direction of his holy Spirite that it may ever sort to your
Honours own coomfort, the good of this Realm and the high satisfaction of
hir most excellent Maiestie who hath graced you the more in this preferment
for that shee hath doon it with so long deliberation and good experience,
which sheweth the choise to have proceeded not from affection only, but
10   from the iudgment of so wise a Prince.
    Hearof I am bould to advertize your Honour as on that converseth both
with the popular and with other sorts of iudgment and qualitie that thear is
a great expectation of your Honours proceedings who have made theise
beginnings, and given suche experiment in your younger years of so great
15   sufficiencie to discharge your dueties of so honourable a calling. My self
rest wholy at your Honours disposition in all poor service I am able to doo.
Toutching my suit I am not importune, and yet desirous to owe this benefit
to the honourable mediation of my Lord your father, and of your self
vpon whome I rest. The lesse my desert is towards your Honour the greater
20   my obligacion and thankfullnes shalbee, which I will ever owe and by

390

Gods grace perfourm to the vttermost I can. And so humblie I take my leave. From London the vijth of Iuly 1596.

Your Honours ever to bee Commaunded

G. FLETCHER.

Address: To the right honourable S^r / Robert Cecill Knight on / of hir Maties most honourable / Privie Counsell.

Endorsement: 7 Iuly 1596. / Dr. ffletcher to my M^r.

23 FLETCHER TO LORD BURGHLEY   16 July 1596
[SP 59/31, f. 246]

My humble duety to your Lordship remembred. I have extracted so muche owt of the writinges sent by your Lordship as concerneth the six Graimes. Whearof two ar touched Richard and Iohn. They have sett down their answears, and protest for their innocencie of partaking the murder doon vpon George Graime. How trulie it cannot appeer by theise bare ac-   5
cusations and answears. Which forasmuch as they ar of matters doon long agoe and in so remote a place, vnder correction, it may seem not vnmeet to referre them for triall for this and other matters whear with they ar charged to the next Assizes to bee held at Carleil about the beginning of the next moneth. Whearby your Lordship may bee well eased of this trouble in   10
perusing theise verball accusations and answears, and my Lord Scroop of that envie and offence which might bee conceived against him by the Graimes if the matter should bee remitted to his Lordship and hee proceed as their Iudge. Whear in case they shalbee fownd guiltie of theise crymes which ar now revived against them (as themselves doo pretend) by par-   15
tialitie and mallice of soom of that Countrey with whome they have feed, they maie afterwards have favour shewed vnto them (if it shalbee thought meet) from hir Highnes clemency and gratious pardon. Which maie make them more modest and bee a bond to them to keep them in good order and obedience hearafter. Which agreeth with that which your Lordship (I re-   20
member) did gravely advise, not to have them made desperate beeing so great a number, and so able to doo muche good or hurt on the borders, and

391

yet to keep them in awe and good order, that they may doe their duety to my Lord Scroop and the rest. With whome it wear good that they wear
25 reconciled. The means whearof your Lordship for your wisedoom can best prescribe. And so craving pardon for my rash boldnes in vttering to your Lordship my fond opinion, I humblie take my leave. From London the xvjth of Iuly 1596.

> Your Lordships most humble
> G. FLETCHER.

Address: To the right honourable / my very good L: the L: / High Treasurer of Eng- / land.

Endorsement: 16. Iuly 1596. / Mr D. Fletcher. / wth the Graimes aunsweres / touchinge ye Enditemt℮.

24 FLETCHER TO THE QUEEN   21 August 1596
[Lambeth MS 658, f. 193]

Reasons to moue her Maiesty in some commiseration towards the Orphanes of the late Bisshopp of London.

1 He was translated from Worcester Bisshoprick to the Sea of London within two yeares and so entered into new first fruites beefore he had fully paid the ould. By which meanes hir Maiesties good and gratious meaning for his preferment was rather turned to his great hinderance
5 and diminution of his worldly Estate hauing paid within 3 yeares or not much more into her Highnes Exchequer for his first fruites, Tenthes and Subsidies the some of 1458li.

2 He bestowed in allowances and gratifications to diuers attendants about her Maiesty since his preferment to the Sea of London the some of
10 3100li or thereabouts without any regarde made to him selfe as appeareth by his note of particulers which was giuen by him for the most parte of it by her Highnes direction and spetiall appointment.

3 Finding the building and mansion howses of the Sea of London greatly decayed and in a manner ruinate hee hath bestowed great somes of
15 mony vppon reperations, namelye vppon the bishops houses at Wick-

392

ham, Hadham, London and Fulham where he bestowed extraordinary
charges as in respect of his owne dutie and necessary vse so in speciall
regard of her Highnes liking and good contentment hoping one day
as himselfe would say after the end and pacefication of her Highnes
displeasure and the recouery of her gratious fauour which of all worldly   20
thinges he most desired to see her Maiesty in his house at Fulham.

4 He employed himselfe and his whole reuenew in hospitality and all
   other duties of his vocation as for conscience sake so with a speciall
   regard of her Maiesties liking and to prouoke her Highnes reconciliation
   and fauour towards him.
                                                                           25
5 He hath satisfied the errour of his late marriage with his vntimely and
   vnloked for death which proceded spetially from the conceipt of her
   Highnes displeasure and indignation conceuied against him bearing a
   most louing and reuerent affeccion towards her Maiesty as euer poore
   subiect towards hir Prince which may moue her Maiesties royall harte   30
   in some compassion towards his poore and fatherles children. He hath
   left behinde him 8 poore children whereof diuers are very yong, his
   dettes due to the Queens Maiesty and to other creditours are 1400^li or
   thereaboutes, his whole state is but one house wherein the widow claymeth hir thirds, his plate valewed at 400^li, his other stuffe at 500^li.   35

Endorsement: D^r ffletcher / Bishop of Londons reasons to haue / his debt
stalled ye 21th of / August 1596.

25a FLETCHER TO THE QUEEN   1596 or 1597
   [Hatfield, Cecil Papers 58. 23]

*Reasons to move hir Maiestie in soom commiseration towardes the Orphanes of
the late Bishop of London.*

1 Hee was translated from Woorcester Bishoprick to the Sea of London
   within two years, and so entred into niew first fruits beefore hee had
   fully paied the old. By which means hir Maiesties good and gratious
   meaning for his preferment was rather tourned to his great hinderance
   and diminution of his worldly estate, having paied within three years   5

or not much more into hir Highnes Exchequer for his first fruits, Tenthes and Subsedes the soom of 1458^{li}.

2 Hee bestowed in allowances and gratifications to divers attendants about hir Maiestie since his preferment to the Sea of London the soom of 3100^{li} or thearabouts without any regards made to himself, as appeereth by his note of particulars, which was given by him for the most part of it by hir Highnes direction and speciall appointment.

3 Finding the buildings and mansion howses of the Sea of London greatly decayed and in a manner ruinate, hee hath beestowed great sooms of money vpon Reparations, namely vpon the Bishops houses at Wickham, Hadham, London, and Fulham, whear hee beestowed extraordinary charges, as in respect of his own duety and necessary vse, so in speciall regard of hir Highnes liking and good contentment, hoping on day (as himself would saye) after the end and pacification of hir Highnes displeasure and the recovery of hir gratious favour (which of all worldly things hee most desired) to see hir Maiestie in his house at Fulham.

Hee employed himself and his whole revenue in hospitality and all other dueties of his vocation as for conscience sake so with a speciall regard of hir Maiesties liking and to provoke her Highnes reconciliation and favour towards him.

5 Hee hath satisfied the errour of his late marriage with his vntimely and vnlooked for death, which proceeded specially from the conceipt of hir Highnes displeasure and indignation conceived against him, bearing a most loving and reverent affection towards hir Maiestie as ever poor Subiect towards his Prince, which may move hir Maiesties Royall hart in soom compassion towards his poor and Fatherles children.

6 Hee hath left beehind him eight poor Children, whearof divers ar very young. His debts due to the Queens Maiestie and to other Creditors ar 1400^{li} or thearabouts, his whole state is but on house whearin the widdowe claymeth hir thirds, his Plate valiewed at 400^{li}, his other stuff at 500^{li}, or thearabouts. Which beeing all sould and the debts paied thear wilbee very little or nothing at all left for the mainteynance and education of his poor Children except it please hir most gratious Maiestie to have soom regard and commiseration of their poor estate.

394

They humbly pray to have remitted 300^{li} of hir Maiesties debt and soom   40
competent tyme to paie the rest after the rate of 150^{li} the year.

Endorsement: 1597 / Bishope of Londons / note concerning / orphanes.

25b FLETCHER TO THE QUEEN   1596 or 1597
[Hatfield, Cecil Papers 205. 111]

The suit of the poor Orphanes of the late Bishopp of London

The whole soom due to hir Maiestie was_____ 1360^{li} or thearabouts
Thear is already paied into the Exchequer_____ 460^{li}
Thear remayneth to bee paied_____. 900^{li}
Whearof shalbee paied at the beginning of Tearm__ 300^{li}

The remainder of which is 600^{li} they humbly pray may bee paied into the   5
Exchequer by 150^{li} the Year. And the howse at Chelsey to bee mortgaged
for the payment. Soe the whole debt shalbee cleered within fower years.

Endorsement: Y^e Orphans of y^e B. of / London.

26a FLETCHER TO THE QUEEN   1596 or 1597
[SP 12/259, No. 47]

To move hir Maiestie in compassion towards the poor Orphanes of the
late Bishop of London.

1 Hee served hir Maiestie as Chaplain and Almner the space of 18. years.
2 His on offence may bee satisfied with the service and dueties of soe many
   years, and with his vntymely death, which followed as an effect of his
   vnhappie marriage.
3 If the rest of the debt bee exacted of the Executour it must bee raised   5
   by extent of his howse at Chelsey, which is the only mean left to relieve
   his poor Children beeing viij. in number and soom of them infants.
4 What a discredit it would bee to the Church of England for a Bishopps
   Children to goe a begging, which must needs followe if hir Maiestie
   bee not gratious vnto them in remitting that which remayneth of hir   10

debt: their vnkle (who may not forsake them though it bee to his
vndooing) having 9. poor Children of his own, and his poor estate
hardlie sufficient to maintein his own charge.

   5 Hee griew into debt by no other means then by his preferrments, whearby he was kept in contynuall payments of first Fruits, and Tenthes,
having paied into the Exchequer within 3. years the soom of 3000^{li} or
thearabouts. Whearby his poor Children have more cause to flie to hir
Maiesties gratious favour, which by accident contrary to hir Maiesties
gratious meaning was a speciall cause of his vndooing.

   6 Hee made gratifications out of London Bishoprick to divers of the
Court by hir Highnes appointment to the soom of 2000^{li} or thearabouts,
as appeereth by particulars, which was an other means of diminishing
his estate.

Endorsement: ffor the poor Orphanes of / the late Bishop of London

26b FLETCHER TO THE QUEEN   1596 or 1597
     [SP 12/259, No. 47, 1]

Gratifications made by the late Bishop of London at hir Highnes commendation.

To my Lady Stafford out of Padington	800^{li}
To Maister Darcy out of Witham	200^{li}
To Sir Edward Denny out of Starford	500^{li}
For the Office of Registership	600^{li}
Summ	2100^{li}

27 CAESAR, DUNN, FLETCHER, AND LLOYD   9 March 1597
   TO SIR ROBERT CECIL
   [SP 59/33, f. 218]

   Our humble dueties to your Honour premissed. Wee have according to
your letter mett together, And have pervsed the Scottish Commissioners

bill against the Lord Scroope, and the answers made by the English Commissioners therevnto, and the questions also therevpon made by your Honour. It maie please your Honour therefore to be advertised, that the cir- 5
cumstances of the Lord Scroops fact therein mentioned, being admitted
to be true, as likewise the complaynt made of the missedemeanours of the
keeper of Lidesdale, and his people first complayned of to the King, then
signified to her Maiestie, And furder her Maiestie demaunding redresse
against the King, and no redresse being made, and herevppon insuing that 10
fact, sayed to have bene don by the said Lord Scroope in Lydesdale: Wee
are of opinion, that the said fact is iustifiable by lawe, as a Reprisall; Wherevnto wee are induced by these growndes of the Civill lawe insuing.

Vt Represaliæ licite concedantur, duo requiruntur: Superioris authoritas, et
iusta concedendj causa. 15

Superior concedens talis esse debet. Qui non agnoscit superiorem nisi liberam
habeat facultatem concedendj represalias a superiori suo sibi concessam, vel
nisj facultas suj superioris, sine magna difficultate haberi non possit.

Et generaliter dicj potest, iustam causam esse represalias concedendj, quando
Princeps, et dominus iniuriam facientis requisitus iustitiam ministrare recusa- 20
verit neglexerit, vel plus iusto distulerit.

Your Honours humblie at commaundement.
IUL. CÆSAR.
DANIEL DUN.
IO. LLOYD.
G. FLETCHER.

Address: To the right honorable S^r / Robert Cecill Knight / principall
secretarie to / the Queenes most / excellent Ma:^{tie}

Endorsement: 9 Mar: 1596 / Do: Cesar. / Do: Dun. / Do: ffletcher / Do:
Lloyd. / to my M^r / Their opinion of the / Scottishe Com^{rs} byll / against
ye L. Scroope

The Letters

My honourable good Lord. Wee ar heer attending on the States
Generall of the United Provinces toutching the affayers of the Marchants
Adventurers, but have had no audience by reason of their great and waightie
affayer, about which they have entred their consultacion, Grave Maurice
5 beeing present heer at the *Haghe*. The peace (as wee hear) beetwixt the twoo
Kinges was proclaymed at Antwerp and other great Townes of Flanders
and Brabant vpon Soonday last with great solemnitie and complements of
ioy. I will not presume to meddell with this great and important cause that
is now in hand, but advertize your Lordship of the disposicion which I
10 observe in this people and soom of the States with whome I have con-
fered. They seem not so much to fear this treatie and conclusion of peace
beetwixt the 2. Kinges, as they doo the allurements and invitacions whearby
her Maiestie might bee induced to incline vnto it, which they suppose to
bee a Catholique devise to disioygn the Nacions. At Bruxells of late (as I
15 hear them report) was a dumb shew, whearin wear represented the French
King and Cardinall, who after long warrs fell to a treatie and conference of
peace. Whiles they ar conferring and readie to signe, in coometh a Ladie,
and conveys her self beehind the French King, and thear at his back pryeth
and lysteneth what they say and doo, expressing withall many perturbacions
20 vpon the Conceipt of that which shee heares, soomtyme frowning, and
soomtime flattering, and plucking the French King by the sleeve of his coat.
In the mean while one of the Minions beeginneth to chafe, and to enquire
what shee is that presumes so neer. Wheareto it is gestured shee is the Queen
of England. So they whisper and laugh at the Conceipt. With that, thear
25 coom in 4. or 5. fellowes apparrelled lyke Boores, and beegin soomwhat
rudely to presse to the place, and to interrupt the treatie. Whearvpon the
Cardinall inquires what they ar, and they ar described to bee Boores of
Holland. Whearat the king laughes, and derides the rudenes of the poor men.
But the Cardinall gestureth that hee will hang them all vp, so soon as hee
30 hath doon with his greate buisines. So it may seem wee ar mocked by them
whiles wee treat with them toutching this peace.

Whiles I desire to pick an occasion to wryte to your Lordship in testifi-
cacion of my humble Dutie, I am bould to report this poor *Satyr* to your
Lordship having no better nor greater niewes. And so humbly craving pardon I take my leave. From the Haghe the 2. of Iune 1598.   35

Your Lordships most humble

G. FLETCHER.

Address: To the Right hono^rable my / very good L. the Earle of / Essex.
Endorsement: Dr. Fletcher 2 Iune 98 / at ye Hag[h]e

29 FLETCHER TO THE EARL OF ESSEX   29 June 1598
   [Hatfield, Cecil Papers 62. 6]

My honourable good Lord. I may seem more officious then well
advised to trouble your Lordship with the advertizement of our mean
affayres. But bycause your Lordship hath voutchsafed alreadie to take soom
paynes for the advancing of this buisines toutching the Marchant Adventurers trade within these Countries, I suppose your Lordship with lyke   5
patience can bee content to hear the successe. Wee have long attended the
States Generall of these provinces, with such publique and private solicita-
cion as wee thought meet. But toutching the chief and principall point of
our negotiacion, and which concerneth not this Companie only of Marchants Adventurers, but the whole Realm, from whence is drawn so great a 10
substance by this exacion to inritch these Countries, wee can obtein no
remission, but a moderacion; which wee doubt will prove very moderat,
or none at all. For which respect I am bould again to intreat your Lordship
that forasmuch as soom one or twoo (as is heer reported) ar to bee sent
foorthwith from the States Generall to the Queens Maiestie about the great 15
affayr that is now in hand: your Lordship wilbee pleased to take knowledge
of our hard handling and discontentment, and to lett them know what
expectacion her Highnes hath of their friendly dealing towards her Marchants.

Toutching the affayres of these Countries I doubt not but that your   20
Lordship hath intelligence from the very fountain. And thearfore I should

but abuse your Lordships time to report vnto you the resolucion of the
States Generall, with the Commissioners of the severall provinces and chief
Townes in their late Assembly held at the Haghe. The effect whearof is,
25 never hearafter to submitt themselves to the King of Spain vpon any condicion. But in case it please him to beecoom their Scarm-heir, in lyke sort
as is the Emperour to the States of Germanie, leaving vnto them the whole
authoritie and absolute government of these Countries in that forme as
it is now sett, they wilbee content to yeeld vnto him a large pension, such
30 as may well beeseem a King. Since our coomming hither, I have welnigh
travailed through these whole Countries, and have observed their strength
of shipping, which farr exceedeth the great opinion which I had beefore.
One thing I gather out of many particular observacions, that beeing an
Oligarchie (as your Lordship knowth) of a fiew persons, and of degree but
35 equall to those over whome they rule, they ar much subiect to many
schisms and emulacions among themselves, and discontentment of their
provinces and common people, who repine much at their great burdens, and
ar distracted with many sects and opinions in religion, specially fower,
the least whearof (toutching number, as I observed both in their Cities and
40 smaller Townes) is the profession of that religion that is authorized. And
thearfore in case they have not soom Superiour (though no Commaunder,
yet an Admonisher and Moderatour) to rectifie their affayres, and to keep
their provinces and States Generall in good correspondence one with the
other, it may bee feared they cannot long continue their State, but it will
45 decline to one Superiour, or to divers Cantons and Divisions, as beefore it
was. But I presume too much to babble thus to your good Lordship of
these affayres. And thearfore craving your Lordships pardon, with remembrance of my humble dutie, I take my leave. From the Haghe, the 29. of
Iune. 1598.

>Your Lordships most humble
>G. FLETCHER.

Address: To the Right honoᵣable / my verie good L. the / Earle of Essex.
Endorsement: Dr. Fletcher / 29 Iune 98 / at yᵉ Haghe.

400

30 FLETCHER TO SIR ROBERT CECIL   31 August 1598
[SP 12/268, No. 36]

My humble dutie remembred to your Honour. I have enquired for the
ground of the niews of the *Edict* published by the Cardinall, whearof I
advertized your Honour the last day. And I fynd that the report came first
from twoo Marchants of *Camphere* in *Zealand*, that came hither on Saturs-
day. Who affirm to our Marchants that they saw the *Edict* and read it in   5
print. I have seen divers lettres sent to our Marchants from the other syde,
to the same effect, which I have perused, and send to your Honour a note
extracted out of one of them, whearwith the rest doo concurr, with a
Copie of the Articles now agreed vpon beetwixt the Cardinall (beefore his
goeing into Spain) and the States of the Provinces. And so humbly I take   10
my leave. From London this last day of *August*. 1598.

                              Your Honours most humble
                                   G. FLETCHER.

Address: To the Right hono^rable / Sr Robert Cecill Knight / Principall
    Secretarie to / the Queens Matie
Endorsement: 1598 / vl:^mo Aug: / Do. ffletcher to my M^r.

31 FLETCHER TO SIR WILLIAM DAVISON   6 August 1599
[Bodleian Tanner MS 77, f. 180]

Sir. This niew alarme is from a niew report out of a lettre from Saint
Michaels Island directed to one Maister *Iackson* a marchant to this effect,
That the *King of Spayne* hath sent to the Govenour of the *Terceraes* to send
him with speed all his great Ordinance to furnish his fleet for invasion of
England. Thus much of the lettre (not the lettre it self) is sent to my Lord   5
Maiour, and hath perswaded many that beeleeved not beefore. I can argue
the case no other wise then thus. What if thear bee not any such lettre?
For it seemeth improbable that the King of Spayne would vnarme those
Islands specially at this tyme. What if that part of the lettre wear true, that
hee sent for his Ordinance? Hath hee not need? Ar not all his provisions   10

401

littell inough to deale with the Netherlanders, who have taken the Canaries, as all doo agree? Yet that the King should tell his Governour that it is for England is not after the manner of Spayne, and may seem an addicion, as the manner is. And if hee did so, yet it may bee a fiction, to save his honour with his owne people to seem rather to invade then to bee invaded. I omitt how lykely it is that intending an invasion, hee would have his provisions to seek at this time of the yeer. Wee proceed with our bridge, and other provisions, and must hould this Rule, *that they at the helme discerne a tempest, though it seem to vs to bee fayre weather.* Whether it bee so or no, and what the end is, tyme will discover. How it goeth with vs you shall hear from mee. And so I leave you to the good blessings of God. This 6. of *August.* 1599.

> Your verie own to bee commaunded
> G. FLETCHER.

Address: To the right honourable / Mʳ Davison
Endorsement: From Doctor Fletcher / touching yᵉ Span: Invasion / 6. August 1599 41 Eliz.

32 FLETCHER TO SIR ROBERT CECIL 7 December 1600
[Hatfield, Cecil Papers 181. 45]

Right honourable may it please you to give mee leave to doe the part of a thanckfull man. Beeing muche bound vnto your Honour I desire still I may bee more. I have been a long vnhappy suitor to serve hir Maiestie in the place of Requests. I am now in hand to reniew my suit. Your Honours favourable commendation or no other means wilbee effectuall. I humbly crave it. I desire not to intrude my self into the service of those twoe who attend about hir Highnes person. It shall content mee to bee Assistant in the Court at Westminster as the manner is of the third Man who attends that place. My small desert towards your Honour shall make my Obligation more. The Condition whearof shalbee: If I indevour not to requite your Honour with all Dueties which a thanckfull man ought to doe and shalbee able, then for ever to leese the creditt of an honest man. So humbly I take my leave. From London the 7th of December 1600.

> Your Honours ever to bee commaunded.
>
> G. FLETCHER.

Address: To the right honourable / Sr Robert Cecil Knight / Principall Secretary to hir / Matie

Endorsement: Doctor Fletcher to my M^r.

33 FLETCHER TO SIR WILLIAM RYDER   28 February 1601
[Hatfield, Cecil Papers 77. 3]

My very good Lord. I was committed by your Lordship to Maister Alderman Hampsons by the appointment of soom of the Lords of the Counsell. I have been his prisoner now this fortnight. My libertie restreined, Maister Alderman troubled, my self grieved (though free in conscience) for the least suspition of so wicked a fact, my duety (I thinck) missed by your   5 Lordship, but more at home, whear I have a great familie and many poor children. And thearfore I am humbly to intreat your good Lordship that you wilbee pleased to crave direction from the right honourable Sir Robert Cecill what shalbee doon and whither I may bee discharged or noe. To help the distressed and innocent you know is charitable, and to move thus   10 farre for your own poor Servetour is safe and honourable. Whither this day or toomorrow I refere it to your Lordships good discretion. And so humbly take my leave. The 28th of February. 1600.

> Your Lordships ever to bee commaunded.
>
> G. FLETCHER.

Address: To the right honourable my / very good L. the L. Maior / of London.

34 FLETCHER TO SIR ROBERT CECIL   28 February 1601
[Hatfield, Cecil Papers 77. 4]

Right honourable I beeseach you measure the affliction of a poor faithfull
subiect (in beeing noted by this restraint) by your own most faithfull and
loyall hart. My syncere love and incorrupt hart towards hir Maiestie my
most deer Soveraign and eaven for conscience sake and my reverend affection towards their Lords specially your Honour (to whome I [am] bound
and ever desired to bee most beehoulding) God (that knoweth the secrets of
all harts) and myne own conscience doe witnes with mee. Remember (I
hu[mbly] pray you) my lyfe past, remember your Honours own testimonie
given of mee a few days sithence comparing mee in this point eaven with
your self to bee a true and faithfull subiect. And how should I bee partaker
in the least degree of so wicked a fact? I have erred (I confesse) in my affection towards that Earle, but I have erred with hir Maiestie. I have erred with
your Honour and with many thousands of all degrees, who thought him
woorthy to bee honoured bycause hee was made honoured by hir Maiestie
and to bee loyall and trustie bycause the trust of great affaires was committed
vnto him. But I left him then when hee left his duety towards his Prince,
and will honour none that honour not hir. His late vngodly and seditious
fact I vtterly abhorre with my whole hart, and defye both him and other
and myne own hart, if it should conceive the least disloyall or vnduetiful
thought against hir Maiestie or your Honours. Your Honours good and
grave admonition to take heed of suche as pretend religion and have none,
I will remember and observe with all the care and heed I can. My most
humble suit is, that bycause the citie and my private familie require my
duetyes, (having a wyfe and 12. poor children) you wilbe pleased to give
mee leave to repair home to myne own howse and to enioy the libertie of a
faithfull subiect, which I have ever been, and will continue by the grace of
God, during lyfe. Your Honours iust and honourable favour for my discharge shalbee a bond among many other to bynde mee to you. So humbly
I take my leave. The 28th of February 1600.

Your Honours most humble
G. FLETCHER.

Address: To the right honourable S^r / Robert Cecill Knight Prin- / cipall
  Secretarie to hir Matie

Endorsement: 28 Februar. 1600. / D^r. Fletcher to my M^r.

35 FLETCHER TO THE PRIVY COUNCIL 3 March 1601
[SP 12/279, No. 23]

G. *Fletchers confession.*

On Thursday or Fryday beefore the Earle of Essex his coomming into
London in that tumultuous and seditious manner I mett with Maister
Temple who tould mee that thear wear certein Iesuits and Seminary priests
that lodged in divers places of the Citie, who had vowed to kill the Earle
of Essex, and that they had divised and cast abroad certein Libels to make 5
him odious to the people. Which beeing reported by him (as it seemed) in
good sadnes I did then beelieve, bycause it seemed not improbable, that
beeing so followed by the militarie men and making profession of religion
more then after an ordinary manner, they might suppose that the sayed
Earle stood in their way and might hinder their designes, if they intended 10
any practise against hir Maiestie and the State. The end of his talk was that
if I lighted vpon any of those Libels I would gett a copie and send it to him.
Which (bycause it seemed to bee spoken in no ill meaning) I promised to
doe.

The Saturday following about 10. of the clock in the night when my 15
self and my familie wear all in bed on knocked at my door. Which my servant rising opened to him and brought mee woord that it was Maister
Temple, and that hee desired to speak with mee. Which though it wear
vnseasonable and my self soomwhat offended at it, I thought in good manners I could not refuse, and so willed my servant to light a candell and to 20
call him vp to my beds side. Whear in the heering of my wyfe hee sayed to
mee to this effect: That my Lord of Essex that afternoon about 5. of the
clock had been sent for to coom beefore my Lords of the Counsell, but
beeing in bed and all in a sweat after tennis hee excused himself that hee
could not coom withowt daunger of his health. And beeing sent for the 25

405

second time by Maister Secretarie Harbert (as I remember, who alleadged that hee was to doe the Queen soom present service and that the Spaniards wear on the coast) hee made vnto him the same answear, the rather bycause hee was advertized from a friend at the Court that the way was layed for him by Sir Walter Raleigh and his companie whome hee termed a companie of Ruffians and that if hee went hee should surely be murthered. That hee thought good to acquaint mee with it and soom other of my Lords friends that th[ey] might know in what daunger my Lord stood and how hee was pursued by his enimies naming none but Sir Walter Raleigh and his companie. This was the effect of his talk then.

The next morning hee sent to mee his man, who tould mee that his Maister desired to speak with mee a woord or twoe if I cam that way. Whearvpon having occasion to goe to a Churche in Thames street to heer a Preacher whome I had commended to that parrish beeing that day to bee chosen by them, I went that way by Maister Temples howse. Whear hee tould mee that hee desired to speak with mee to tell mee what had happened that night: vz: That Sir Walter Raleigh and his Companie had sett vpon the Earle of Essex in his own howse to have murthered him in his bed. Whearby I might see that it was true that hee tould mee the night beefore that Sir Walter Raleigh and his companie had layed the way to have murthered the Earle. I answeared him that it was marveil that my Lord of Essex could not make his part good with Sir Walter Raleigh and that it wear good for him to complain. And so not knowing what to make of these reports and pourposing to inquire more of them I went from him to that Church, whear I continued till towards noon, and then coomming foorth to goe home to myne own howse I heard by the way that the Earle of Essex had passed along through the street with a great companie and that hee was gon owt at Algate. Whearupon beeing desirous to know the truthe I diverted to my Lord Maiors and attended him all that day to assist him as any occasion should require my service.

As toutching his coomming into London in that tumultuous and seditious manner or any other his wicked designes the sayed Maister Temple didnot mention nor impart it to mee, neither did the Earle (as I am perswaded) ever thinck so ill of mee as to iudge mee a fitt man or safe for

406

himself to impart with mee any suche vngodly practise knowing mee well　60
that I would not indure to heer suche things, and not reveal them. The
greatest matter I could suspect owt of these reports (which I see now to bee
very fables and divised matters) was that soom great quarrell and open fray
was lyke to break owt beetwixt the Earle and Sir Walter Raleigh.

And as toutching Maister Temple in the reporting of these divises, I　65
doe yet thinck (not knowing the contrary) that having been ever accounted
an honest man hee was deceived and abused by the Earle that he might
deceive and abuse others.

To the Earles own confession, vz, That Maister Temple should say to
him owt of my report that Maister Smythe was in as great daunger as　70
himself I doe truly answear and protest, that I never spake any suche woords
to Maister Temple or any other neither did know that Maister Smyth or
my Lord himself was in any daunger at that time, or had committed any
thing to bring himself into any daunger. Only I remember that Maister
Temple talking with mee soom dayes beefore about the erecting of the　75
Crosse in Cheap. I tould him that my Lord of Canterburies Grace was
offended with Maister Smythe and mee for writing to Oxford for the
opinion of soom learned men toutching the Crosse with the Crucifix &c.

And for the Aldermens disposition towards the Earle though I kniew
that many of them wear well affected towards him (as my self and many　80
others wear whiles hee beehaved himself duetifully towards hir Maiestie)
yet beeing honest and discreet men and faithfull subiects to hir Maiestie and
carefull of their private estates I could and would have tould him (if hee had
asked my opinion of them toutching suche a wicked enterprize) that it had
been a foolish conceipt and mad presumption in the Earle to suppose that　85
they would allow and muche more have ioigned with him in so vngodly
and desperate an attempt. I never spake with any of them about this matter
or any suche vnlawfull practise. And thearfore I could not say hee was sure
of them.

Toutching the Cities suit to the right honourable the Lord Admirall　90
(to move hir Highnes for hir warrant to trayn a certein number of honest
Citizens to make them more fitt for hir Highnes service) it was a suit (as is
well knowen) committed to mee by my Lord Maior and Court of Alder-

men about a yeer and an half sithence, by whome I have been called vpon
95   continually and by the Marchants of this Citie to follow that suit and have
been often blamed by them as if that suit by my negligence had not taken
effect. And for that cause I have been more often with his Lordship about
that suit in a simple meaning to doe my duety (as God knoweth) and to no
other end.

His late practise no lesse mad and foolish then vngodly and seditious I
100   doe vtterly detest and abhorre it with my whole hart and defy both him
and all other and myne own hart if it should conceive the least disloyall or
vnduetifull thought against hir Maiestie my gratious Queen and deer Soveraign or against their Honours whome I reverence in my hart for conscience
105   sake.

G. FLETCHER.

Endorsement: 3. Martij 1600 / Mr D. Fletche[r]

36 FLETCHER TO SIR ROBERT CECIL   14 March 1601
   [Hatfield, Cecil Papers 77. 60]

Right honourable. I humbly thanck you for regarding the humble suit
of my poor wyfe. Hir poor estate and great distresse of so many children
do thus force mee to mone my case and to reveal vnto your Honour my
present state. My great charge and small revenue with the Executorship of
5   my late Brother hath made my debt exceed my estate, beeing vndoon and
woorse then nought by 500^{li}. For discharge whearof I have no means but
the present sale of my poor howse whearin I dwell, and of my Office, if
I can assign it to soom fitt man. At the Quarter day I am to pay 200^{li} vpon
forfeiture of double bonds. I have yet no means, nor now libertie to seek
10   for means for paiment of it, and am infirm through grief of mynd for this
restraint and the affliction of my wyfe and children. How perplexed I am
for them and they for mee. I beeseach your Honour (who ar a Father of so
toward and happy children) to consider.

Toutching my fault what shall I say? I have been abused by those fables
15   and foolish lyes of the Earles daunger and fear of murther by Sir Walter Ra-

leigh. But my hart vntoutched and my hands cleer of his wicked practise which I kniew not of, nor could decern so great a mischief vnder suche a coulour. I will learn wisdoom by this folly. My humble suit is, that you wilbee pleased to bee a mean for my discharge, or if not that, for my en-largement vpon my bond. To relieve a poor distressed familie will please 20 God and bynde vs all (bysides other dueties) to pray to God to blesse you and yours. So humbly I take my leave. 14th of March 1600.

Your Honours most humble Suppliant
G. FLETCHER.

Address: To the right honourable / Sr Robert Cecill Knight Prin- / cipall
Secretarie to hir / Matie
Endorsement: 1600 / March 14. / Dr Fletcher to my M^r

37 FLETCHER TO SIR ROBERT CECIL   21 March 1601
[Hatfield, Cecil Papers 180. 43]

My humble duety to your Honour remembred. Beeing enlarged by your Honours good and speciall means (which I will ever remember with all thanckfullnes and humble duety) I fynd divers suiters for my poor Office towards the Citie. Among other I heer of on who is seen attending in your Honours lodging to procure favour and commendation from your Honour 5 to my Lord Maior and Court of Aldermen. I have been bould to acquaint your Honour with my great charge and poor estate. I have served the Citie in this painfull place now these 15. yeers or thearabouts, and have gott nothing by my great paines but a poor estate. And thearfore desire to give it over vpon condition of soom benefitt towards relief of my great wants. 10 Whiles I hould the place none shalbee found more devoted and ever ready to doe your Honour all faithfull service then my self as so mean a place can make able to requite a person of so honourable sort. My humble suit is that you wilbee pleased not to regard the vncharitable suit of suche as seek to deprive a poor distressed man of that little which God hath given him and 15 vndoe an other to advance them selves. And so most humbly prayeng your Honour in your Christian wisdoom to consider how assured and everlasting

love is procured by clement dealing I humbly take my leave. The 21th of
March 1600.

Your Honours most humble and bounden.
G. FLETCHER.

Address: To the right honourable S^r / Robert Cecill Knight
   Prin- / cipall Secretarie to hir Matie
Endorsement: D^r. Fletcher to my M^r.

38 FLETCHER TO SIR ROBERT CECIL   5 April 1601
   [Hatfield, Cecil Papers 85. 141]

    My humble duety to your Honour remembred. Thear ar in hand to
compound with mee for my Office towards the Citie on Maister Edmonds
and Maister Moor. The former seemeth to bee a man of good discretion
and vnderstanding. Beeing resolved to leave that place I would gladly doe
it in that honest and duetifull sort as might bee pleasing to your Honours
and the Citie to whome I owe this last duety to commend to them for
this service soom honest and sufficient man. Bycause hee sayeth hee is well
knowen vnto my Lords and particularly to your Honour, I humbly pray
you wilbee pleased to signifie your opinion of him, which shall direct mee
to proceed with him or with any other whome your Honour shall iudge
more fitt. So I commend your Honour to the safe protection of Allmighty
God. The 5th of April. 1601.

Your Honours most humble.
G. FLETCHER.

Address: To the right honourable / Sr *Robert Cecyll* Knight, / Principall
   Secretary to the / Queenes most excellent Matie

Endorsement: 1601. / Aprill 5. / Dr Fletcher to my M^r.

39 FLETCHER TO SIR ROBERT CECIL   20 May 1601
   [Hatfield, Cecil Papers 86. 53]

Right honourable. I was enlarged by your Honours meanes (which I
acknowledg with all thanckfulnes) from my late restreint, but continue still
restreyned by Bond to mak apparance beefore your Honours at 2. dayes
warning. Beeing free in conscience, I most humbly pray I may bee freed in
your Honours iudgment, which if it should reteyn the least suspicion, I   5
shall accompt my self a prisoner, though freed otherwise from Bond and
bands. For which cause and for that I have no other meanes to maintein my
self and my poor familie but my Credit and daily travail (which I cannot
follow with any freedoom of mynd or body, standing noted and restreyned
by the said Bond) and for that I have soondry occasions that concern my   10
whole poor estate and my Brothers Orphanes to travail into *Kent, Dorsett*
and *Hampshire* (the Cities service beeing supplied by Maister *Edmonds*) I
humbly pray your Honours favour to discharge that Bond, and to make
mee free that I may remayn your Honours bounden if I bee ever able to
doo you service. And so humbly I take my leave. From *London* the 20th   15
of May. 1601.

                              Your Honours most humble
                                   G. FLETCHER.

Address: To the right honorable / Sr *Robert Cecyll* Knight / Principall
     Secretary to / her Matie
Endorsement: 1601. / 20 May. / Do: ffletcher to my M^r.

40 FLETCHER TO SIR ROBERT CECIL   21 November 1601
   [Hatfield, Cecil Papers 89. 121]

Right honourable. Your greatest gayn by this your Honour, next the
publique good, is to gayn many, and to enable such as you have merited
(in which number my self am one) to doo you service. The experience of
your former favour, and the extremitie of my present state have enforced
mee to this bouldnes. I have been drawn from my profession and practise   5

411

of Law by publique service. Fower tymes I have been employed in her
Highnes service out of the Realm, once Ambassadour, thrice as Agent and
speciall Messenger from her Highnes, without any recompence or allowance from her Maiestie. All which buisines and negotiacions by the blessings of Almightie God wear well effected to her Highnes honour, the publique good and the encrease of her Highnes Coustomes, but the great
hindrance and vndooing of my privat estate, which beeing neglected and
impoverished by these services, is now forced to crave relief. And whear
else but at the ritch and royall hand of my most gracious Prince and Mis-
tresse, in whose service I was employed. Which I assure your Honour I
would not doo, for myne own beehoof (who thinck not much to affoord
gratis all my service and life it self to my Prince and Countrey) but for the
relief of that great charge which God hath given mee, beeing ritch only in
that which maketh a ritch man poor, many Children.

My humble suit to the Queens Maiestie is not great nor ambitious, but
small and reasonable, beestowed vsually vpon other men of least desert, for
her Highnes Graunt of certein Leases in Reversion to the Tenants vse. I
most humbly pray your Honours furtherance. I have no meanes to requite
your Honour but my hartiest thancks, humble service and continuall
prayer to Almightie God, who will not forget your Christian woork in
helping a poor distressed Familie of so many Children, lyke otherwise to
bee vndoon not by negligence of their Father (who hath been a more payn-
full then happy man) but his too much diligence and distraction about
publique buisines. So most humbly I take my leave. This 21th of November.
1601.

Your Honours most humble
G. FLETCHER.

Address: To the right honourable / Sr *Robert Cecill* Knight / Principall
Secretarie to her / Matie
Endorsement: 1601. / November 21. / D^r. Fletcher to my M^r.

41 FLETCHER TO SIR ROBERT CECIL   2 July 1609
[Hatfield, Cecil Papers 127. 89]

Right honourable. God hath brought you to great honour vnder a
great and gratious King that you may bee a dooer and procurer of muche
publique and privat good. Among other my self am one that acknowledg
your Lordships publique merit and private favours towards my self. Which
have made mee bould (though ashamed to speak) to write vnto you my   5
humble suit. Beeing forced vnto it by the vnabillitie of my state to maintein
the charge which God hath given mee I am an humble suiter to his Maiestie
for his gratious help and supportation which at his entrance to this Kingdoom and long beefore hee voutchsafed to promise owt of his own meer
goodnes and Princely grace withowt desert, which bycause I have not nor   10
can not plead (for who can merit of his Soveraign to whome all is due) I
alleage only the true cause of my ege[n]cie which hath happened by no
other means then by relinquishing of my practise of Civil Law for those
emploiments in forrein service never affected nor sued for, but imposed
vpon mee by the State. My humble suit is for your Lordships testimonie to   15
his Maiestie to this effect, that after the meannes of my qualitie I have not
wholy been vnserviceable nor vnprofitable to the State, having fower times
been imployed in publique service and all doon (by Gods blessing) to good
effect, in Scotland, Rusland, Germanie and the Low countries. If your
Lordship please to doe this favour to a man destitute of other help, I shall   20
never fail to shew my thanckfulnes by the readines of my service (for I can
perfourm no other recompence) and by making knowen your Lordships
honourable disposition and Christian pietie in relieving suche as by soom
errour of their own or by malevolence vndeserved of soom other with
whome for their greatnes they can not contest God hath humbled both in   25
their mynds and owtward states. So most humbly I take my leave.

Your Lordships most humble
G. FLETCHER.

Address: To the right honourable / my very good L. the L. high / Treas-
    urer of England.
Endorsement: 1609 / Doctor Fletcher / to my Lord. / rec: 2. July.

413

Explanatory Notes

Licia

Ad Amorem

This poem is by Marullus, *Epigrammaton*, Book III, in *Poetæ Tres Elegantissimi* (Paris, 1582), sigs. e6ʳ–e6ᵛ.

Ad Lectorem

This poem is by Theodore Beza, *Juvenilia*, in *Delitiæ Poetarum Gallorum* 3 vols.; Frankfurt, 1609), III, 597. See note to l. 32, below.

Epistle Dedicatory to Lady Molineux

HL iii–v. *Ladie*...Mollineux. Grosart, in his 1876 edition of *Licia*, pp. 96–97, supplies the following information: Richard Molineux, son of William, and heir to his grandfather, Sir Richard Molineux of Sefton, at his death in 1567, was born about 1560. About 1581 he married Frances, the eldest daughter of Sir Gilbert Gerard [see Charles Henry Cooper and Thompson Cooper (eds.), *Athenae Cantabrigienses* (3 vols.; Cambridge, 1858–1913), II, 141]. They had six sons and seven daughters. It is probable that all the children were born between 1581 and 1600. The twin daughters to whom Fletcher addressed a sonnet are probably the two eldest: Anne and Alice, who became the wives, respectively, of Sir John Byron and of Wil-

417

liam, Lord Dormer. The twins probably were born between 1581 and 1585. Lady Molineux died on 9 February 1621, and Sir Richard on 8 March 1623.

5. *indifferent:* impartial.

12. *æternize:* make eternal.

22. Brownistes. Just before Fletcher wrote this epistle, two of the leaders of the Brownists, Henry Barrow and John Greenwood, had been hanged at Tyburn on 6 April 1593 for "feloniously publishing seditious books and pamphlets tending to the slander of the queen and government." (See *Athenae Cantabrigienses,* II, 151–54.) Robert Browne, the founder of this separatist movement, was a contemporary of Fletcher at Cambridge. For a discussion of "Brownism," see the article in *The Encyclopædia of Religion and Ethics.*

32. *the...pillar:* Theodore Beza (1519–1605). In 1548, before his conversion to Christianity, he published a group of poems now called *Juvenilia.* He later wrote, concerning these poems: "As respects those poems, who is there that either has condemned them more than I, their unhappy author, or that detests them more than I do to-day?" See Henry Martyn Baird, *Theodore Beza* (New York, 1899), pp. 27–31.

41–42. *habilliments:* accoutrements.

43. Sidney...*confesse.* This indicates that Fletcher may have been acquainted with *An Apologie For Poetrie.* Toward the beginning of the essay Sidney says: "And first, truly to al them that professing learning inueigh against Poetry, may iustly be obiected, that they goe very neer to vngratfulnes, to seek to deface that which, in the noblest nations and languages that are knowne, hath been the first light-giuer to ignorance..." (G. Gregory Smith [ed.], *Elizabethan Critical Essays* [2 vols.; Oxford, 1904], I, 151).

43. Haringtons Ariosto. Sir John Harington (1561–1612) was admitted a fellow-commoner of King's on 8 December 1576, proceeded B.A. 1577–78 (1st in the *Ordo*), M.A. 1581. This translation of *Orlando Furioso* was first published in 1591.

68. *affectes:* affection.

69–71. *For...not.* Cf. Angerianus, "Ad Lectorem," *Erotopægnion,* in *Poetæ Tres Elegantissimi* (Paris, 1582), sig. E3ʳ:

418

Si tibi non placeo, placeo mihi; lector, abibis.
Hoc satis, auctori si sua scripta placent.

86–87. *I...blood*. Probably an allusion to Tasso's madness.

To the Reader

23. incrouching: crouching in, fawning.

24–54. And...ought. Professor P. N. Siegel in his article "The Petrarchan Sonneteers and Neo-Platonic Love," *SP*, XLII (1945), 178–79, was the first to point out this passage as a statement of the concept of Neo-Platonic love. In its impassioned tone, one thinks of Bembo's final plea in *The Book of the Courtier* (see the Everyman edition [London, 1928], pp. 316–22).

65. *LEE...HOVGHTON:* Peter Leigh and Richard Houghton. They married two of Sir Gilbert Gerard's daughters, Margaret and Catherine, respectively, and were thus brothers-in-law to Lady Molineux. Leigh was admitted to Caius College on 1 February 1580; M.P. for Wigan, 1586–87, 1588–89; sheriff for Cheshire, 1595; knighted July 1599. He died on 17 February 1636.

To Licia

Source: Gruterus, *Harmosynæ* (Heidelberg, 1587), p. 191.

Sonnet I

Source: Angerianus, "De seipso" *(Poetæ Tres Elegantissimi*, sig. A2ᵛ*)*.

Sonnet II

Source: Angerianus, "De Cælia, et Amore" *(ibid.*, sig. A2ᵛ).

This sonnet is the first of several that demonstrate the Anacreontic concept of love. Others are: IV, V, IX, X, XIII, XIV, XXI, XXX, XXXI. Cf. Sidney's *Astrophel and Stella*, VIII, XI, XVII, XLVI, LXV, LXX, LXXIII, CI (All references are to Sidney Lee's edition of *Astrophel and Stella* in *Elizabethan Sonnets* [2 vols.; Westminster, 1904], Vol. I).

2. *lappe:* the fold of a robe over the breast which served as a pocket or pouch.

4. *sport...happe:* divert himself in his good fortune.

8. *wagge:* mischievous boy.

Sonnet III

Source: Angerianus, "Ad Cæliam" (*Poetæ Tres Elegantissimi*, sig. A4ʳ).

Sonnet IV

Source: Angerianus, "De Cælia, et Amore" (*ibid.*, sig. A5ᵛ).

Sonnet V

Source: Angerianus, "De Cælia, api, et Amore" (*ibid.*, sig. A6ᵛ).
Cf. *Astrophel and Stella*, XII, XLII.

Sonnet VI

Source: Angerianus, "De Cæliæ pictura" (*Poetæ Tres Elegantissimi*, sig. A7ᵛ).

Sonnet VII

Source: Angerianus, "De Cælia" (*ibid.*, sig. A8ʳ).

Sonnet VIII

Source: Angerianus, "De Cæliæ duritie" (*ibid.*, sigs. Bʳ–Bᵛ).

Sonnet IX

Source: Angerianus, "De Cæliæ furto" (*ibid.*, sigs. Bᵛ–B2ʳ).
Cf. *Astrophel and Stella*, XVII.

Sonnet X

Source: Angerianus, "De seipso, et pictore dialogus" (*Poetæ Tres Elegantissimi*, sig. B2ʳ).

Sonnet XI

Source: Angerianus, "De Cæliæ dotibus" (*ibid.*, sig. B3ᵛ).

Sonnet XII

Source: Angerianus, "Ad Cæliam" (*ibid.*, sig. B5^v).

Sonnet XIII

Source: Angerianus, "De Ioue et Cupidine" (*ibid.*, sig. B8^v).
Cf. *Astrophel and Stella*, XII.

Sonnet XIV

Source: Angerianus, "De Cælia, et Cupidine" (*Poetæ Tres Elegantissimi*, sigs. D3^v–D4^r).
Cf. *Astrophel and Stella*, XLII.

Sonnet XV

Source: Angerianus, "De Cælia, et pictore dialogus" (*Poetæ Tres Elegantissimi*, sig. D4^v).
Cf. *Astrophel and Stella*, LXVIII.

Sonnet XVI

Source: Secundus, Basia II, III, and XIII (F. A. Wright [ed.], *The Love Poems of Joannes Secundus* [London, 1930], pp. 40–41, 44–45, 84–85).
Cf. *Astrophel and Stella*, XLII, LXXXI.
9. *propping:* supporting.

Sonnet XVII

Source: Marullus, "Ad Neæram" (*Poetæ Tres Elegantissimi*, sig. b6^r).
Cf. *Astrophel and Stella*, XCV.

Sonnet XVIII

Source: Marullus, "Ad Neæram" (*Poetæ Tres Elegantissimi*, sig. b7^v).

Sonnet XIX

Source: Marullus, "Ad Neæram" (*ibid.*, sig. c2^v).

Sonnet XX

Cf. *Astrophel and Stella*, CI, CII.

9. *Erect:* rouse up, stimulate.

Sonnet XXI

Source: Marullus, "De Amore et Mercurio" (*Poetæ Tres Elegantissimi*, sig. b2ᵛ).

Sonnet XXII

1–4. As has been stated in the Life of Fletcher, p. 4, there is no evidence that Fletcher's father went to Persia.

5–8. These lines refer to Fletcher's daughter Judith, who was born on 1 August 1591. There was a daughter, Sara, who was the first child born after Fletcher returned from Russia, but as she died less than a week after baptism it is highly improbable that she would be the "daughter" of the sonnet.

Sonnet XXIII

Source: Melissus, "De Rosina," in *Delitiæ Poetarum Germanorum* (6 vols.; Frankfurt, 1612), IV, 478–79.

Cf. *Astrophel and Stella*, XXII.

Sonnet XXIV

Source: Angerianus, "De Cælia conualenscente" (*Poetæ Tres Elegantissimi*, sig. D8ᵛ).

Sonnet XXV

Source: Angerianus, "Cælo comparat amicam" (*ibid.*, sigs. C8ᵛ–Dʳ).

Cf. *Astrophel and Stella*, LXVIII.

11. *weildles:* unwieldy.

Sonnet XXVI

Source: Angerianus, "De absentia amicæ" (*Poetæ Tres Elegantissimi*, sig. Dᵛ).

422

3. *Harbour:* Arbor.

6. *enameld:* adorned magnificently.

Sonnet XXVII

Source: Angerianus, "De Cæliæ balneo" (*ibid.*, sig. C3ʳ).

Lee in *Elizabethan Sonnets*, I, lxxxiii, suggests that this sonnet might be the source for Shakespeare's Sonnets 153 and 154.

Sonnet XXVIII

Source: Angerianus, "De suo amore æterno" (*Poetæ Tres Elegantissimi*, sig. D4ʳ).

Sonnet XXIX

Source: Angerianus, "Ad somnum" (*ibid.*, sig. D4ᵛ).

Sonnet XXX

Source: Angerianus, "De Cælia nauigante" (*ibid.*, sigs. D6ʳ–D6ᵛ).

Sonnet XXXI

Source: Angerianus, "Ad eandem [Cæliam]" (*ibid.*, sigs. E3ᵛ–E4ʳ).

Sonnet XXXII

Cf. *Astrophel and Stella*, LX.

Sonnet XXXIII

Source: Angerianus, "De Cælia, et libello" (*Poetæ Tres Elegantissimi*, sig. E2ʳ).

Sonnet XXXIV

Source: Angerianus, "De seipso dialogus [Amore]" (*ibid.*, sig. E3ʳ).

Sonnet XXXV

Source: Muretus, "Margaridi," in *Epigrammes* (4 vols.; [n.p.], 1552), II, 756.

Sonnet XXXVI

 Cf. *Astrophel and Stella*, C.

Sonnet XXXVII

 Source: Muretus, "Margaridi" (*Epigrammes*, II, 755).
 Cf. *Astrophel and Stella*, XIX, XXXIV.

Sonnet XXXVIII

 Cf. *Astrophel and Stella*, LXII.

Sonnet XXXIX

 Cf. *Astrophel and Stella*, XLVIII.

Sonnet XLI

 Source: Gruterus, *Harmosynæ*, pp. 169–70.

Sonnet XLII

 Source: as Sonnet XLI.

Sonnet XLIII

 Source: Gruterus, *Harmosynæ*, pp. 170–71.
 Cf. *Astrophel and Stella*, LXXXIX.

Sonnet XLV

 Source: Bonnefons, "Pancharis," XV, in *Delitiæ Poetarum Gallorum*, I, 668

Sonnet XLVI

 Source: Gruterus, *Harmosynæ*, pp. 178–79.

Sonnet XLVII

 Source: Gruterus, *Harmosynæ*, p. 168.
 Cf. *Astrophel and Stella*, LXX.

Sonnet XLVIII

Source: Gruterus, *Harmosynæ*, pp. 184–85.
3. *feard:* frightened away.

Sonnet LI

Source: Ronsard, *Amours*, I, 32.

Sonnet LII

Source: Ronsard, *Amours*, I, 54.
Cf. *Astrophel and Stella*, LXXVII.
11. *release:* relieve.

An Ode

42. *desave:* deceive.

Doris and Galatea

See Introduction to the Poems, p. 63.
11–16. Secundus has:

> Ne ride: qualis qualis tibi Dori videtur,
> Neptuno tamen est de genitore satus,
> Neptuno, vitreis latè qui præsidet vndis,
> Neptuno, à summo qui Ioue prima tenet.

Ad Lectorem, Distichon

These lines are by Marullus, *Epigrammata et Hymni* (Paris, 1529), sig. A2ᵛ.

Elegie III

16. The reverse of Tilley's Proverb T201. (Morris P. Tilley, *A Dictionary of the Proverbs in England in the Sixteenth and Seventeenth Centuries* [Ann Arbor, Mich., 1950].)

The Rising to the Crowne of Richard the Third

7–12. Probably an allusion to "Shore's Wife" in *A Mirror for Magistrates*. See Lily B. Campbell's edition (Cambridge, 1938), pp. 373–86.

13–18. Probably an allusion to "The Complaint of Rosamond" by Daniel. See Arthur C. Sprague (ed.), *Samuel Daniel, Poems and A Defence of Ryme* (London, 1950), pp. 39–63.

19–24. Probably an allusion to "Elstred" by Lodge. See E. W. Gosse (ed.), *The Complete Works of Thomas Lodge* (4 vols. [Glasgow], 1875–82), Vol. II.

44–47. The reference seems to be to the account in *A Mirror for Magistrates*. See Lily B. Campbell's edition, pp. 182–90.

137. Yorks *Archbishop:* Thomas Rotherham.

155–56. Similar to Tilley's Proverb H305.

174. *another...place:* John Russell, Bishop of Lincoln.

187. *The Cardnall:* Thomas Bourchier, Archbishop of Canterbury.

241. *Nowe...swell:* Cf. Sir Thomas More's lines: "As the sea without wind swelleth of himselfe sometime before a tempest" (Raphael Holinshed, *Chronicles of England, Scotland, and Ireland* [6 vols.; London, 1807–8], III, 379) and Shakespeare's:

> ...as by proof we see
> The water swell before a boist'rous storm.
>
> (*Richard III*, II, iii, 43–44)

245. *despice:* despise.

247. *Londons...Major:* Sir Edmund Shaw.

253. *Doctor:* Ralph Shaw, brother to Sir Edmund. See *DNB sub* Edmund Shaw.

261. The opposite of Tilley's Proverb M794.

The Russe Commonwealth

Preface

5–7. *My...strange.* Herberstein (*Notes on Russia*, I, 1) makes the same comment.

Chapter 1

1–17. *The...Russia.* It seems quite certain that Martin Cromer's *De Origine et Rebus Gestis Polonorum* (Basil, 1568), pp. 16–19, is the basis for the information. An interesting point is that Fletcher cites Strabo as evidence in support of his argument. So does Cromer (p. 16). Fletcher likewise says that some "cosmographers" state that Russia borrowed its name from the "Roxellani." Cromer specifically cites Ptolemy, *Geographia* (Book 3, Ch. 5), Pliny, *Naturalis historia* (Book 4, Ch. 12), and Tacitus, *Historiae* (Book 1, Ch. 79), as writing of the Roxolani in Sarmatia. Richard Eden, "Of the North-East Frostie Seas and Kingdomes Lying That Way" (*Notes on Russia*, II, 194–95), cites these three authors to support the theory that the Russians were the Roxolani.

15–17. *seat...reporteth.* Strabo, *Geography* ([Loeb Classical Library; 8 vols.; London, 1918–32], III, 223).

25–34. *Some...countries.* The source for this is Cromer, *De Origine et*

Rebus Gestis Polonorum, p. 13. The marginal notations are the same in Cromer as in Fletcher, and in the same order. Cf. note to Ch. 1, ll. 1–17.

40–51. Volodemer...Siberia: Most of these provinces were brought under the rule of Moscow between 1463 and 1523. Siberia, however, was not brought under Moscow's control until 1581–84, as a result of the activities of the Stroganovs and Iermak Timofeevich.

43. Nouogrod...*countrey*. "Novogrod velica" means "Novgorod the Great." "Nisnouogrod" or "Nizhni Novgorod" means "Lower Novgorod."

54. Cazan *and* Astracan. Kazan in 1552; Astrakhan in 1556.

56–57. Narue *and* Dorp. Lost to Sweden in 1581.

65–75. *4260...4400*. Seredonin, pp. 112–14, comments: "These figures are much too large and more inaccurate than those given by Herberstein. Therefore Fletcher did not bring the solution of this problem forward, and not only did not make use of his predecessors' figures but did not even know of them. They gave the latitude of Kola as 65°48′ (instead of 68°53′), of Astrakhan as 41°10′ (instead of 46°21′); i.e., the arc between the two parallels of Kola and Astrakhan is equal to 22°32′, or about 2,300 versts, instead of the 4,260 given by Fletcher."

76. *verst...pases*. A verst is 0.68 mile.

77–80. *If...Princes*. Horsey, pp. 206–7, makes a similar comment.

Chapter 2

15. *1700*: 1,100 (Hakluyt, II, 52).

17. *1700*: Moscow to Astrakhan 2,800 (*ibid.*, p. 54).

26–30. *The...bee*. Phineas Fletcher, Piscatorie Eclog II, stanza 13:

> The viny *Rhene*, and *Volgha's* self did passe,
> Who sleds doth suffer on his watry lea,
> And horses trampling on his ycie face:
> (Frederick S. Boas [ed.], *The Poetical Works of Giles and Phineas Fletcher* [2 vols.; Cambridge, 1909], II, 183)

33–37. *So...ground*. Clement Adams, quoting Richard Chancellor (Hakluyt, I, 278–79), says: "The north parts of the Countrey are reported to be so cold, that the very ice or water which distilleth out of the moist wood which they lay upon the fire is presently congealed and frozen."

Beaumont and Fletcher, *The Faithful Shepherdess*, in a prologue speak of King Charles and the queen as welcome:

> As Spring to Birds, or Noon-dayes Sun to th'old
> Poor mountain Muscovite congeal'd with cold.
>
> (Arnold Glover and A. R. Waller [eds.], *The Works of Beaumont and Fletcher* [10 vols.; Cambridge, 1906], II, 448)

Shakespeare, *Love's Labour's Lost*, V, ii, 262:

> Twenty adieus, my frozen Muscovits...

41–48. *When...feete.* Sir Francis Bacon, *Calor et Frigus:* "Cold in Muscovy and the like countries causes those parts which are voidest of blood, as the nose, the ears, the toes, the fingers, to mortify and rot; specially if you come suddenly to fire after you have been in the air abroad, they are sure to moulder and dissolve" (James Spedding [ed.], *The Works of Francis Bacon* [7 vols.; London, 1857], III, 650).

47–48. *Diuers...feete.* Herberstein (*Notes on Russia*, II, 172) records that he almost lost his nose because of the cold.

59. *lightly:* easily, readily.

85. *2800. verst or miles.* When Fletcher uses the phrase "verst or miles" it is difficult to understand whether he means Russian "verst or mile" or English "verst or mile." If Fletcher in this instance means 2,800 Russian versts, it would work out to about 2,100 English miles, which is a great deal closer to the actual length of the Volga—2,325 miles.

90. *Rezan Ozera.* Fletcher was following Jenkinson's map of Russia for this information. Morgan, in *Early Voyages*, I, cxlii, points out that the source is actually the Ivan-ozero. Herberstein (*Notes on Russia*, II, 11) correctly identifies the source as the "Great Lake of Ivan." This would indicate that Fletcher did not know Herberstein's work.

96. *ouerthwart:* in a transverse or cross direction.

106–11. *Onega...Russe.* This offers positive evidence that Fletcher used Jenkinson's map of Russia, as Fletcher's description follows every detail of the map except for the "Volock." Jenkinson's map has "Volgha." Morgan, in *Early Voyages*, I, cxlvi, in discussing the map, says that "the course of the Onega from Lake Ladoga through the Bielo ozero into Lacha is imaginary."

But Seredonin, p. 115, citing Il'insky, says: "Il'insky suggested that Fletcher took Volok to be a river falling into the Gulf of Finland. From Fletcher's indication that this volok meets the river Onega north of Kargopol, Il'insky concluded that the German small volok (portage) [which he found mentioned in a census book of 1582] started on the river Vytegra and ended at the lake Lacha, which was 3 versts from Kargopol. The whole length of this portage (volok) was about 40 versts of that time. This trade route followed the Onega only to the landing stage of Markomusy and from there again by portage to the Shemkov landing on the river Ents, which is a tributary of the Dvina. It is possible that goods were carried both this way and by the Onega up to its mouth. In any case, by his error Fletcher made it possible to determine an important trade route. It is evident that both the search for a waterway and the results of this search were unknown to Fletcher, and he took the word 'volok' (portage) to be the name of a Russian river."

118–19. *There...Volgha.* The river rising in Permia and flowing into the Volga is the Kama. The Vychegda flows into the Dvina. Fletcher's error makes it certain that he used Jenkinson's map, as he shows the "Voichogda" rising in Permia. But it is Fletcher's error in stating that it flows into the Volga.

121–22. *55....10:* 55°45'.

123. *63....50:* 71°10'.

Chapter 3

6. *buckway:* probably buckwheat.

21–23. *The...substantiall.* Richard Chancellor (Hakluyt, I, 254–55) has a very cursory description of the products.

24–45. *First...countrie.* For an account of the subject of furs, see Raymond H. Fisher, *The Russian Fur Trade, 1550–1700* (Berkeley, Calif., 1943).

27. Lusernes: lynx.

28. Martrones: martens.

31–32. *the...winter:* Thomas Dekker, *Brittannia's Honor.* This is a work of several pageants, presented on 29 October 1628, on the inauguration of Richard Deane as Lord Mayor. The third pageant is entitled "*The Glory of Furres,*" in which "a *Russian Prince* and *Princesse;* richly habited in Furres, to the custome of the Country" are enthroned in a chariot (Fredson Bowers [ed.], *The Dramatic Works of Thomas Dekker* [4 vols.; Cambridge, 1952–61], IV, 89–90). In the pageant are these lines (p. 90):

> Th'inuention of warme Furres the Sunne did fret,
> For Russians lap'd in these, slighted his heate,
> Which seene, his fiery Steedes he droue from thence,
> And so the Muss has dwelt in cold ere since.

34–35. *foure...rubbels.* Fisher, *The Russian Fur Trade*, p. 230 n., questions this figure as being somewhat high and suggests that "an amount half as large as that appears more consistent with the facts as we understand them."

67. *Losh:* elk.

80. *Cusconesse...Foxnose.* Fletcher is in error. Cape Kuiski is somewhat south of Cape Kerets; they are not identical.

113. *Cauery:* caviar.

114. *Bellougina:* beluga, the great sturgeon, is found in the Caspian and Black seas and their tributary rivers.

115. *Seueriga:* sevruga, a species of sturgeon.

115. *Sterledey:* sterlet, a small species of sturgeon.

118–20. *The...fiue.* See T. S. Willan, *The Early History of the Russia Company* (Manchester, 1956), pp. 141–43.

136–37. *Vobsko...Vasma.* In 1554 the chief towns for flax and hemp seem to have been Novgorod and Pskov (Richard Chancellor in Hakluyt, I, 254–55).

139. *Stararouse.* In 1554, a chief city for salt seems to have been Kolmogro (*ibid.*, p. 255).

154. *Ribazuba:* walrus ivory.

158. *Morse:* walrus.

161–67. *In...lanthorne.* George Turberville (Hakluyt, II, 103):

They have no English glasse, of slices of a rocke
Hight Sluda they their windowes make, that English glasse doth mocke.
They cut it very thinne, and sow it with a thred
In pretie order like to panes, to serve their present need.
No other glasse, good faith doth give a better light:
And sure the rocke is nothing rich, the cost is very slight.

431

In Marston's *The Malcontent*, I, vii, Passarello says: "...she were an excellent Lady, but that hir face peeleth like Muscovie glasse" (H. Harvey Wood [ed.], *The Plays of John Marston* [3 vols.; Edinburgh, 1934–39], I, 161).

Jonson, *The Devil is an Ass*, Prologue, ll. 16–18:

> *Would wee could stand due* North; *or had no* South
> *If that offend: or were* Muscouy glasse,
> *That you might looke our* Scenes *through as they passe.*
>
> (C. H. Herford and Percy Simpson [eds.], *Ben Jonson* [11 vols.; Oxford, 1925–52], VI, 163)

162. *Slude:* Russian mica.

173. *Ollen:* stag.

192. *Tassel:* tercel.

Chapter 4

4. *The...Mosko.* Webster, *The Dutchess of Malfi*, V, ii, 46–47:

Ferdinand has enough patience:

To drive six Snailes before me, from this towne [Milan] to *Mosco*...

> (F. L. Lucas [ed.], *The Complete Works of John Webster* [4 vols.; London, 1927], II, 107)

5. *founder...vnknowen.* The first mention of Moscow is in 1147, when Yuri Dolgoruki, prince of Suzdal, met Sviatoslav of Seversk and his allies.

7–10. Berosus...Europe: Berosus, *Chaldæi Sacerdotis* (2 vols.; Lyons, 1554), I, sig. K3ʳ: "Eadem tempestate Saturnus rex Babyloniæ misit principes coloniarum Assyrium, Medum, Moscum et Magogum: qui regna condiderunt Assyrium, Medum, et Magogum in Asia, Moscos verò et in Asia simul et Europa."

14–18. *Euan...1246.* Ivan I did not change his title from "Duke" to "King." To his titles of "Grand Duke of Vladimir" and "Grand Duke of Moscow," he added the words "and of all Russia." Semen, Ivan I's son and successor, did adopt this style. There is no evidence for the investiture by a legate of Pope Innocent IV. Fletcher confused this Daniil with Daniel, king of Galicia, who did prevail on the people of Galicia to accept the pope as head of the church in return for papal support. See George Vernadsky,

The Mongols and Russia (New Haven, Conn., 1953), pp. 146–47, 157–59.

23–39. *The...in.* Herberstein's account (*Notes on Russia*, II, 4–5) is very similar. Both accounts state that the number of houses before the firing of the city was 41,500.

23–31. *The...all.* Jenkinson (*Early Voyages*, I, 34–35), speaks mainly of the emperor's castle. Richard Chancellor (Hakluyt, I, 255) has a brief description.

41–66. *where...greatnes.* Herodotus, Book IV, 1–4 ([Loeb Classical Library; 4 vols.; London, 1921–24], II, 201, 203), tells the story as follows: The Scythian men, who had been away fighting the Medes for 28 years, returned home to find that their wives were consorting with their slaves. There were many fights and the Scythians could gain no advantage. At last one of them said: "'Men of Scythia, see what we are about! We are fighting our own slaves; they slay us, and we grow fewer; we slay them, and thereafter shall have fewer slaves. Now therefore my counsel is that we drop our spears and bows, and go to meet them, each with his horse-whip in hand. As long as they saw us armed, they thought themselves to be our peers and the sons of our peers; let them see us with whips and no weapons of war, and they will perceive that they are our slaves; and taking this to heart they will not abide our attack.'" The Scythians acted on this advice, and the slaves, amazed by what they saw, fled. Seredonin, p. 52, points out that the Novgorodians never made such a coin as Fletcher describes (ll. 62–65). Herberstein (*Notes on Russia*, I, 109) describes the coin as having the prince sitting on his throne on one side of the coin and an inscription on the other.

Herberstein (*ibid.*, II, 26–27) records this story but omits the Novgorod coin incident. Instead, he adds that the slaves "betook themselves to a place still called Chloppigrod,—i.e. the Slaves' Fortress,—and defended it." They were conquered, however, and received the merited punishment from their masters.

Raleigh, in *The History of the World*, quotes the story from Fletcher, and says he believes it to be true (William Oldys and Thomas Birch [eds.], *The Works of Sir Walter Raleigh* [8 vols.; Oxford, 1829], IV, 810–11).

Massinger, *The Bondman*, IV, ii, bases the action on this story. See

W[illiam] Gifford (ed.), *The Plays of Philip Massinger* (4 vols.; London, 1813), II, 80–81.

74–76. *Vlademir...1067.* It is possible that Fletcher actually knew this story in Saxo Grammaticus' *Historia Danica* (Paris, 1514), sig. O6ᵛ. But Fletcher might well have gotten it from Hakluyt (see I, 83). This information, it will be remembered, was added in D, and thus after the first edition of Hakluyt's *Voyages* had been published.

81–91. *Their...wood.* In Richard Eden's collection, there is an account of the houses of Moscow: "The Houses are made all of tymber, and are diuided into Parlours, Chambers, and Kychyns, of large roomes.... In maner all the houses haue priuate gardens..." (*Notes on Russia*, II, 244).

Cf. Chancellor, quoted by Clement Adams, in Hakluyt, I, 292.

George Turberville (*ibid.*, II, 102) says:

> No stone worke is in use, their roofes of rafters bee,
> One linked in another fast, their wals are all of tree.
> Of masts both long, and large, with mosse put in betweene,
> To keepe the force of weather out,...

Chapter 5

1. *the...Russia:*

HOUSE OF MOSCOW

Aleksandr Nevsky (d. 1263)

Daniil (1283–1304)

Yuri III (1304–25)	Ivan I (1325–41)
Semen (1341–53)	Ivan II (1353–59)
	Dmitri Donskoi (1359–89)
	Vasili I (1389–1425)
	Vasili II (1425–62)
	Ivan III (1462–1505)
	Vasili III (1505–33)
	Ivan IV (1533–84)
	Fedor I (1584–98)

2–10. *It...name*. The source is Antony Bonfinius, *Rerum Vngaricarum Decades Quatuor cum Dimidia* (Hanover, 1606), pp. 203–4. But Bonfinius does not mention the idea that the Russian House of "Beala" came from the Hungarian people. Indeed, Seredonin points out (p. 55) that this is an example of Fletcher's not having a good understanding of Russian, as he mistook the nickname of "White Tsar" for the surname of the family. Herberstein (*Notes on Russia*, I, 34) says: "Some call the prince of Moscow Albus, or white." He suggests they are so called because of the white garments they wear.

5–9. *For...blinde*. The conversion of Hungary generally dates from King Stephen I (1000–38). Andrew I ruled from 1047 to 1060, and was succeeded by his brother, Bela I (1060–63). Bela II, the Blind, ruled from 1131 to 1141. See Denis Sinor, *History of Hungary* (London, 1959), pp. 35–52, for an account of Hungary during this time.

27–30. *How...them*. Yuri II, duke of Vladimir, died without heirs and the dukedom passed to Yaroslav I. In 1247, Yaroslav died and his sons Aleksandr Nevsky and Andrei presented themselves at Khan Guyuk's court. In late 1247 or early 1248 the khan made Andrei grand duke of Vladimir and Aleksandr prince of Kiev. A new khan, Mongka, was elected in 1251, and all princely patents had to be renewed. Batu (Khan of the Golden Horde) and his son and co-ruler, Sartak, were granted the power to renew the patents of the Russian princes. Andrei refused to go to Sartak, who sent a punitive expedition to Vladimir. Andrei fled to Sweden, and Aleksandr was made grand duke of Vladimir. On his death in 1263, his youngest son was made prince of Moscow, and was thus the founder of the House of Moscow.

38–41. *Wherof...Mosko*. Ivan III was the first to style himself "Emperor," not his son Vasili. Kliuchevsky, II, 21, cites his full style as "Johannes, by the Mercy of God, Emperor of All Rus, and Grand Prince of Vladimir and Moscow and Novgorod and Pskov and Tver and Perm and Ugra and Bolgari and the rest."

51–54. *child...three*. Ivan IV had two children by his wife Anastasia, Ivan (the elder, whom he killed) and Fedor. By his sixth wife, Maria Nagaia, whom he married in 1580, he had a third son, Dmitri (b. 1582). Cf. Ch. 23, ll. 99–102.

53–64. *As...fact.* Horsey, p. 195, also gives the account, and says that Ivan's fury was roused by the son's compassion toward some distressed Christians and by his issuing an order without the tsar's consent.

77–90. *Besides...name.* Horsey, pp. 211–13, comments at length on her and, interestingly, says it was he who persuaded her to return to Russia.

Chapter 6

1–2. *The...manner.* Horsey, p. 209, states that he provided Fletcher with the information for this chapter. In speaking of the coronation of Fedor, he says that he "must referr the relacion therof to Mr. Hackluetts booke of Viages and Dr. Flætchers treatice, with other discourses of the state and government of this commonwælth, procured at my handes longe since..."

Herberstein (*Notes on Russia*, I, 39–42) describes the inauguration of Dmitri, grandson of Ivan III, as grand duke of Moscow and Russia. The ceremony was very similar.

34. *decently:* fittingly.

73. *This...Prouinces.* Seredonin, p. 128, says: "There was no official division into oblasts (provinces) in the sixteenth century, with the exception perhaps of Novgorod and Pskov, which had retained their original unity to a greater extent. However, in the people's mind there still remained a division into provinces, but Fletcher was probably following the enumeration of provinces in the tsar's title, which he knew."

Chapter 7

20. Gauill kinde: gavelkind, the custom of dividing a deceased man's property equally among his sons. Significantly, this was a common practice in Kent, where the Fletchers lived from 1557 on.

71–77. *Wherin...Emperour.* I can find no evidence of this.

77–83. *Some...Emperour.* Although this task was completed during the reign of Ivan IV, the subjugations of the other princes took place during the reigns of Ivan III and Vasili III. See Kliuchevsky, II, 29–36.

Chapter 8

1–10. *Their...concluded.* Fletcher was not exactly correct in his information about the Zemski Sobor. The impression he gives is that the Sobor is a permanent group, but in fact the Sobor met only four times in the sixteenth century—in 1550, 1566, 1584, and 1598. Kliuchevsky comments: "In studying the *Zemskie Sabori* of the sixteenth century we...only see that the *Sobor* was not a permanent institution, that it possessed neither a binding governing authority nor a legally defined jurisdiction, that it was powerless to secure the rights and interests either of the nation as a whole or of its individual classes, and that the elective element in it was either wholly absent or negligible" (II, 313). Fletcher was in error with regard to the representation of the Sobor. There were 374 members of the Sobor of 1566 and 512 of that of 1598. And more significantly, there *were* representatives of the merchant class—75 in 1566. See Kliuchevsky, II, 299–301.

35–73. *Then...homeward.* Fletcher is in error concerning the right of the members to speak their opinions. Kliuchevsky, II, 305–8, gives the discussion of the Sobor of 1566; and the opinion of the clergy was exactly opposite to the view of the emperor. Seredonin, pp. 235–37, says that the formula used by the clergy in addressing the emperor was in fact used, but that it was only "a form of common social courtesy."

Chapter 9

5. *seueral:* separate.

35–71. *Hee...flame.* The institution of the Oprichnina (and Zemshchina) was in 1565; it was suppressed in 1572. For a discussion of it, see Kliuchevsky, II, 74–90. Seredonin, p. 85, points out that in fact the Oprichnina was much smaller in number than the Zemshchina. Horsey, p. 168, only briefly mentions the Oprichnina.

61. *desperate:* despairing.

74. Pomestnoy: "pomestia" (tax on landed property). See Kliuchevsky, II, 134–37.

84–86. *many...them.* Seredonin, p. 183, comments: "Fletcher's remarks that the Russian kniaz families were on the way to extinction proved to be quite correct in respect of five out of the ten families named. Soon the families Staritsky, Mstislavsky, Glinsky, Shuisky, and Vorotinsky died out."

95–98. *These...Realme.* Seredonin, p. 102, says: "Fletcher speaks briefly of Godunov's struggle with his enemies. But he is not quite clear as to the struggle's meaning. He thinks the struggle was bequeathed by Ivan the Terrible, i.e., a struggle with the eminent kniaz families. This struggle had quite a different meaning from the one in Ivan the Terrible's reign; and Fletcher did not quite understand this, because for him Godunov and the Moscow government were already synonymous. He did not emphasize sufficiently that the Mstislavsky and Shuisky had suffered not as enemies of the state but as Godunov's personal enemies, who did not wish to give him a place."

103. Bulgatkoue: Andrei Petrovich Kurakin (d. 1615), governor of Moscow in Tsar Ivan's absence.

104. Gollauni: Petr Golovin. Horsey, pp. 218–19, says he was chief treasurer to Ivan IV, "a man of great birth and courage," that he became "bold and peremptorie" against Godunov, and was sent away in displeasure and "dispatched of his liff upon the waye."

106. Golloohen: Vasili Yur'evich Golitsyn.

106. Suskoy: Andrei Ivanovich Shuisky.

109. Suskoy: Ivan Petrovich Shuisky. He defended Pskov against Stephen Bathory. Fedor gave him all income from Pskov as a reward. He was banished to Belozero for complicity in a plot against Boris Godunov, and died there in 1587.

113. Micheta Romanowich: Nikita Romanovich Yur'ev. Horsey, p. 226, says he was "a stowt, valiant prince, honored and beloved of all men, was now bewitched, his speech and sens taken suddenly from him, yet lived awhiell. But the protector [Godunov] told me it should not be longe."

120. Metheloskey: Ivan Fedorovich Mstislavsky. Horsey, p. 156, says that Mstislavsky was his chief informant about government affairs: "I read in their cronickells, written and kept in secreat by a great priem prince of that country, named Knez Ivan Fedorowich Mistisloskoie, whoe, owt of his love and favour, imparted unto me many secreats, observed in the memorie and procis of his tyme, which was fower score years, of the state, natur, and government of that comonweelth..." His son, Fedor Ivanovich, died in 1622. Cf. Ch. 11, l. 12, and Ch. 15, l. 115.

122. Glimskoy: Ivan Mikhailovich Glinsky. Cf. Ch. 11, l. 12, and Ch. 15, ll. 116–18.

123. Suskoy: Ivan Andreevich Shuisky (d. 1573) had four sons: Vasili Ivanovich, Dmitri Ivanovich, Aleksandr Ivanovich, Ivan Ivanovich.

124. Hubetskoy: Trubetskoi. There were five living at the time of Fletcher's writing: Aleksandr Bogdanovich, Nikita Ivanovich, Nikita Romanovich, Timofei Romanovich, Fedor Mikhailovich.

125. Bulgaloy...Guletchey: Bulgakov-Golitsyn?

126. Vorallinskoy: Vorotinsky.

127. Odgoskey: Odoevsky.

127. Tellerskoy: probably Aleksandr Andreevich Teliatevsky.

128. Taytoue: Petr Ivanovich Tatev (d. 1586).

137–39. *thousand...summe.* Seredonin, p. 190, thinks 1,000 rubles a year is too high for the income of a boyar, and that 400 rubles is probably closer to what the tsar gave in salary.

141. Transendent: one who transcends a classification.

Chapter 10

1–2. *The...Chetfirds.* Seredonin, pp. 267–68, discusses Fletcher's error: "Fletcher's assertion that Russia is divided into four parts and each is managed by a 'Chetvert' is quite wrong. Fletcher was led astray by the meaning of the word 'Chetvert' (a quarter) and therefore gave this meaning." There were a number of departments. See Kliuchevsky, II, 252–58.

7. Shalcaloue: Andrei Shchelkalov (d. 1598). Cf. Ch. 11, l. 29.

12. Shalcaloue: Vasili Shchelkalov (d. 1611). He took part in the Zemski Sobor of 1566, was banished in 1601. Cf. Ch. 11, ll. 29–30.

Chapter 11

13. Scopin: Vasili Fedorovich Skopin-Shuisky (d. 1595), boyar from 1577, governor of Pskov.

18. Trowbetskoy: Nikita Romanovich Trubetskoi.

19. Trowbetskoy: Timofei Romanovich Trubetskoi.

20. Curakine: Grigori Andreevich Kurakin (not Andrei Grigor'evich).

20. Forestine: Dmitri Ivanovich Khvorostinin (d. 1591), outstanding military leader with successes in the Crimea in 1570, 1572, and 1574; led Russian forces against Sweden in 1582 and 1590.

21. Forestine: Fedor Ivanovich Khvorostinin.

21. Sabaroue: Bogdan Yur'evich Saburov (d. 1598). His daughter, Evdokia, was the wife of Ivan, the son of Ivan IV. She died in a nunnery in 1619.

22. Vasilowich: Ivan Vasil'evich Sitsky.

22. Shestinoue: Fedor Dmitrievich Shestunov.

23. Troyconioue: Fedor Mikhailovich Troekurov (d. 1597) was an Astrakhan voevoda.

23. Buterlyney: Ivan Mikhailovich Buturlin.

25. Godonoe: Stepan Vasil'evich Godunov, voevoda in 1573, took part in many campaigns. He was sent to Finland in negotiations in 1592. Cf. Ch. 12, l. 151, and Ch. 27, ll. 13–14.

25. Gregorie...Godonoe: Grigori Vasil'evich Godunov, a boyar from 1584, in charge of Dvortsovy Prikaz. Cf. Ch. 12, ll. 34–35, and Ch. 27, l. 12.

26. Sheremitoue: Fedor Vasil'evich Sheremetev.

27. Cleshenina: Andrei Petrovich Kleshnin (d. 1599) took part in the Crimea war in 1591. Cf. Ch. 27, l. 14.

27. Tatisloue: Ignati Petrovich Tatishchev (d. 1604) was the state treasurer.

28. Peua: Roman Mikhailovich Pivov.

28. Cheremissen: Dementi Ivanovich Cheremisinov accompanied Ivan IV in the Lithuanian campaign of 1579–80. He was taken prisoner and ransomed for 4,457 rubles. He went to Sweden for negotiations in 1589.

29. Alferioue: Roman Vasil'evich Alfer'ev.

30. Wellusgin: Elizar Vyluzgin.

33–37. *These...call.* Seredonin, p. 223, says: "Fletcher knew that Fedor and Boris Godunov first conferred with a few boyars and only thereafter handed their already decided business to the boyars' duma, which generally agreed without question. From this Fletcher concluded that the boyars' duma had no political significance. We cannot reproach Fletcher for this: in the first place, because it is unlikely that this boyars' duma often rejected decisions made by the inner duma, and, secondly, because about two years before Fletcher's arrival Boris had broken the resistance of his more stubborn enemies—members of the boyars' duma. Besides, at this time there were five of Godunov's boyars in the duma itself."

Chapter 12

1–165. *For...rubbels.* One of Seredonin's most valuable discussions is his analysis of Fletcher's discussion of the revenue of the state (pp. 317–35):

"This sum of net revenue [1,430,000 rubles] seemed doubtful to historians, and a suggestion was made that it was gross revenue. But we consider that it cannot even be taken as gross revenue, because it is evident that Fletcher took some figures twice over. If one hundred years later the revenue of the state was about 2,000,000 rubles, it proves that the figure of 1,430,000 for the sixteenth century is impossible, as taxes, population, and the area of the state had increased, and money had fallen in value four times. Could the budget have only increased by a third? The whole history of finance for the seventeenth century, which is now worked out in detail, is a proof of the opposite. An extant document of the year 1611–12 indicates that the whole revenue for that year was 111,584 rubles. Admittedly, this was an exceptionally low yearly income, but it shows how small the reserves of the Moscow treasury were, because certain treasury valuables had to be sold to meet the expenses of the army."

In l. 93, Fletcher says that the income of the Bolshoi Prikhod is 340,000 rubles. It follows, then, that the military prikhod must have paid in no less than 400,000 rubles to make the total of 800,000 rubles. If the military prikhod pays half in, then their total income must have been about 800,000 rubles, which would mean that the military departments were in charge of the greater part of the money of the state, an impossibility. But this does indicate that Fletcher took some sums twice over. Miliukov, says Seredonin, calculates that the army upkeep before the Smolensk war in the seventeenth century did not exceed 275,000 rubles.

Concerning the Bolshoi Dvorets ("the Stewardes office") Fletcher says (l. 33) that in Ivan IV's time the yearly income was 60,000 rubles; but by the good management of Godunov, the income was 230,000 rubles. But even by artificially raising prices and by prohibiting others to sell goods (ll. 266–92), it is highly improbable that grain was sold to the value of

200,000 rubles and timber and hay to 30,000 rubles. Seredonin, p. 326, shows that the expenditures for 1613–14 were 9,762 rubles, and that only 916 rubles were left in the palace treasury. Seredonin adds that the tsar's treasury in 1613–14 was exceptionally low, and that the economy in Fedor's time was much better; nevertheless, such large amounts could not be obtained from the sale of surplus goods, as Fletcher indicates.

Concerning the income received by the Chetverts, Fletcher says that they collect 400,000 rubles yearly. He enumerates thirteen towns and provinces which evidently pay in the largest amounts. The total is 293,000 rubles, and thus 107,000 rubles is the share paid by all the other towns. It should be pointed out that Fletcher probably considered the towns he mentions provinces, which would account for the largeness of the sums. Also, the Ryazan province is shown, when there was practically no town of Ryazan. Only Novgorod Veliki and Pskov can be considered "provincial" towns. Novgorod, according to Fletcher, paid 35,000 rubles to the Chetvert and 6,000 rubles in customs duties. The figure 6,000 is much too large, because from extant records it is evident that the customs duties paid in 1587–88 amounted to 651 rubles. In 1620 Novgorod paid direct taxes of 1,376 rubles and customs of 4,368 rubles; in 1625, direct taxes 2,659 rubles and customs 7,657. Pskov, according to Fletcher, paid 18,000 rubles direct taxes and 12,000 customs duties. For 1677, the total received from Pskov was 13,329 rubles. Ustyug, says Fletcher, paid 30,000 rubles direct taxes, but he does not mention what it paid in customs duties. The total paid in 1677 was 13,052 rubles.

Fletcher's figures for payments to the Chetverts are in all cases higher than the customs payments. A comparison with the seventeenth century indicates that indirect taxation should be higher than direct taxes. The development of direct taxes relates to a later period (Seredonin, p. 330).

Concerning the Bolshoi Prikhod, Fletcher says that the three tables of receipts belonging to this office when the Chetverts receive least amount to 160,000, 90,000, and 70,000 rubles respectively (ll. 87–90). Seredonin, p. 333, says: "What are the three items? Previously two were named, i.e., the customs coming in from large trade towns and the taxes collected by the lower prikazes and handed over to the Bolshoi Prikhod [ll. 65–70].

442

Further, why is the amount shown so short of 340,000 rubles? The total is given as 80,500 rubles, and all the main towns are included in the enumeration, even those paying only 700 rubles. This is all the more strange because Fletcher was more careful about the Chetverts. We have no right to presume that there were considerable payments from the lower prikazes, because the law court duties, the duties on various deeds of purchase, the collections from baths and public houses are counted by Fletcher further in the book [ll. 293–314] over and above the sum of 340,000 rubles."

Seredonin, pp. 334–35, concludes: "Is it possible that Fletcher had grouped all incomes from the three sources—the palace income, the direct taxes, and customs—into one?

"Fletcher continually talks of the sum of 400,000 rubles. It is the amount paid into the Chetvert. About the same amount is paid into the Bolshoi Prikhod (340,000 rubles), and with the addition of incomes from the customs, baths, and public houses, there will be almost 400,000 rubles. Then, Fletcher says, 400,000 is received by the Bolshoi Prikhod from the surplus of the military prikazes. A suspicion arises that the amounts of customs duties from towns had already been included in the amounts shown as received from tiagla and podat', the more so because the latter figure is always higher than the first when this applies to the Chetverts' income from towns and that of Bolshoi Prikhod.

"And therefore is it possible that in the income of the Bolshoi Prikhod, we are shown, after the 80,000 or customs duties are counted, the other income, i.e., direct taxes, etc., under three headings?"

In other words, Seredonin considers the total income, except for the palace income, to be about 400,000 rubles a year.

172–77. *What . . . commodities.* Fisher, in *The Russian Fur Trade*, pp. 108–9, questions whether the furs were really "customs." He suggests that the furs were actually "tributes" which the emperor regularly exacted from the conquered territories.

213. *Diack:* Ivan Mikhailovich Viskovaty. He was ambassador to Denmark, 1563–64, and was in charge of one of the government departments (Posalsky Prikaz). He was executed in 1570.

241–42. *Which . . . dayes.* Fletcher could well have had Horsey's account of Ivan's forcing the monasteries to make an inventory of all their "treasur, moneys, towns and lands" and threatening to dissolve all the monasteries if such accounts were not made (pp. 174–80).

245–65. *He...foote.* Semen's regency lasted from December 1575 to September 1576. When Ivan IV resumed his throne, Semen was made grand prince of Tver, which Ivan subsequently took from him. He was sent to the convent of St. Cyril in 1606, and then to the convent of St. Simeon in Moscow, where he died on 5 January 1616 (Joseph Hamel, *England and Russia* [London, 1854], pp. 224–32).

Horsey, pp. 168–69, was certainly the source for Fletcher's information. Seredonin, p. 80, says that Fletcher's information is incorrect. There is no evidence that the letters patent were annulled by Semen in 1576 and then reinstated by Ivan. If Fletcher's explanation were correct, then there would be extant at least some letters patent that were confirmed in the second half of 1576 and in 1577, but on the contrary, there is a letter patent dated 1578 granted by the tsar to the Suzdal bishop to replace one that had been burnt in a fire two years previously.

293–304. *In...naked.* Jenkinson (*Early Voyages*, I, 38) calls the drinking houses "Cursemay." He omits the financial details, but adds that when a person has drunk away all his goods, "the Tauerner" brings him out in the highway and beats him upon the legs. Then "they that passe by, knowing the cause, and hauing peraduenture compassion vpon him, giueth the monie, and so he is ransomed."

316. *cauillations:* chicaneries.

Chapter 13

21–22. *Wherein...Kolophey.* Seredonin, p. 191, says that it is known that Russians did not have the custom of signing petitions. The petitions known to us were addressed directly to the tsar, but in court the peasants usually addressed themselves to the judge in the following manner: "I have a complaint about the Troetsky abbot Feodosi," or "We have a complaint about the Lopovsk senior men."

23–27. *This...souldiers.* Richard Chancellor (Hakluyt, I, 263): "The poore is very innumerable, and live most miserably..."

444

Robert Best (*Early Voyages*, II, 376): "There is no people in the world, as I suppose, that liue so miserably as do the pouertie in those parts."

Sidney, *Astrophel and Stella*, II:

> ...and now, like slave-born Muscovite,
> I call it praise to suffer tyranny:

Webster, *The Dutchess of Malfi*, III, v, 90–91:

> Must I, like to a slave-born Russian,
> Account it praise to suffer tyranny
> (Lucas ed., II, 87)

32–35. *Secondly...souldiers.* Herberstein (*Notes on Russia*, I, 106) says: "They are, moreover, in a very wretched condition, for their goods are exposed to plunder from the nobility and soldiery, who call them Christians and black rascals by way of insult."

34. *fense:* defense.

35–47. *Besides...inhabitant.* Kliuchevsky, II, 217, says: "The burden of imposts and the lack of means must have deprived him of both the will and the power to extend his small taxable holding, and have forced him to look for support to such extraneous resources and industries as, placed in his way by abundance of water, timber, and waste land, were left untaxed by the State."

58–62. *I...enimie.* Seredonin, p. 204, says: "Fletcher did not know that at that time the sellers and buyers had to pay duty on every article sold. The traders looked at the doors with such fear because a heavy fine threatened them if they were caught in the act of concealed trade."

60. *a liking:* approval.

65. *traine:* something dragged along the ground to make a scent to lure animals into a trap.

74–101. *Yet...Onyka.* The family was the Stroganovs. The founder of the enterprise of trading in Siberia was, as Fletcher says, Anika (1498–1570). For an account of their trade see Fisher, *The Russian Fur Trade*, pp. 23–27.

Seredonin, p. 208, points out that Fletcher's information is incorrect: "In letters patent of Peter the Great to Grigori Dmitrievich Stroganov, it is stated that in the interregnum and in the reign of Mikhail Fedorovich, the Stroganovs paid into the tsar's treasury in money, grain, salt, and precious metals and stones the sum of 423,706 rubles. In the letters patent of the year 7099 (1591), Tsar Fedor favored Nikita Grigor'evich Stroganov, telling him to continue in his possession of ancestral lands and the town of Orel. In six years Grigori Stroganov's ancestral lands were extended still more, and he was given a charter for 15 years. Further, Fletcher asserts that the Stroganovs paid 23,000 rubles podat' per year. In the year 1578–79, the records record that the Stroganovs paid a little over 230 rubles."

121–26. *And...owne.* In a letter to the queen (Letter 18, ll. 114–18), Fletcher speaks of the emperor's desire to remove the English trade to the coast: "To this pourpose the Emperours Counsell consulted at my beeing thear, and conferred with mee abowt the removing of our Marchants trade from Mosko to Archangell, that lyeth 30. miles from the port of Saint Nicolas vpon the river Duyna, to feell how it would bee taken if it wear forced by the Emperour."

133–41. *For...reason.* Fletcher takes this etymology from Cromer, *De Origine et Rebus Gestis Polonorum*, p. 13: "Slauorum autem etymologiam, uel à Slouo, quod uerbum et sermonem: uel à Slaua, quod famam siue gloriam genti significat, omnes deriuant."

Chapter 14

26–28. *Who...good.* Richard Chancellor (Hakluyt, I, 261–62): "For when they attach any man they beate him about the legges, untill such time as he findeth suerties to answere the matter."

35–38. *As...can.* Fletcher, as a lawyer, would not approve of such practice. Cf. Richard Chancellor (*ibid.*, p. 262): "Their order in one point is commendable. They have no man of Lawe to pleade their causes in any court: but every man pleadeth his owne cause...."

54–56. *If...matter.* Seredonin, p. 301, says Fletcher is somewhat confused in this. In this type of case, lots were drawn only to decide who was to kiss the cross. In other cases, the drawing of lots was an independent proof, but this was applied only in cases of minors.

63–66. *This...legges.* Webster, *The White Devil*, IV, ii, 57–58:

> ...I am not in Russia;
> My shinnes must be kept whole.
> (Lucas ed., I, 155)

446

Dekker, *The Seven Deadly Sinnes:* "The *Russians* haue an excellent custome; they beate them on the shinnes, that haue mony, and will not pay their debts" (A. B. Grosart [ed.], *The Non-Dramatic Works of Thomas Dekker* [5 vols. (London), 1884–86], II, 28). Dekker, *Jests to Make You Merrie:* "[the Russians] that beat al debters on the shinnes" (*ibid.*, p. 355).

72. *becudgelled:* cudgeled soundly.

73. *bebasted:* beaten soundly.

93. *the yeare 7096.* This would be A.D. 1588.

137–42. *They...officers.* Fletcher is in error about this. In 1550 Ivan IV promulgated a new code of laws. Karamzin says: "Ivan III issued new civil statutes, and Ivan IV a complete code" (Richard Pipes [ed.], *Karamzin's Memoir on Ancient and Modern Russia* [Cambridge, Mass., 1959], p. 111). Horsey, p. 207, specifically states that Ivan IV did issue a code of laws.

Chapter 15

10–13. *allotteth...foot.* Horsey, p. 181, speaks only briefly of the military forces and the land allotted them: "... the gentilmen and comon synnoboarskes had certaine porcions of lande, corn and mony alowed them yearly, and this ishued owt of certeyn revenues put apart for that purpose, and eschets, robberis and customs, pencions duly paid them whether they goe to warr or noe, without deminucion of any his crown revenues or great standinge treasur."

13–22. *But...people.* Kliuchevsky, II, 143, discusses this problem.

24–72. *First...80000.* Seredonin, pp. 335–46, discusses at length the problem of the size of the military organization. He concludes that Fletcher's estimate of 80,000 men is probably correct, but points out several errors in Fletcher's work. Fletcher considers that all the soldiers are junior boyars (ll. 3–7). Seredonin, pp. 336–39, gives a great deal of evidence from the military lists of 1563, 1577, and 1588 that indicates there were no more than 25,000 junior boyars in Tsar Fedor's time. But he points out that each junior boyar had to appear mounted, armed, and with men. He, in fact, had to bring one man for every 100 chetverts of land he had. Seredonin, pp. 340–42, concludes that the average holding was something less than 200 chetverts, so that, at the most, each junior boyar would be required to bring two men. This would give a total then of about 75,000 men.

Fletcher breaks down the 80,000 men into two groups: one, 15,000 men who are the emperor's regiment; and the other, 65,000 men who comprise the "other troupes." In each group, Seredonin says, Fletcher probably confused the junior boyars and their men and took them as one. Concerning the first group, Fletcher says that when they receive their whole pay, it amounts to 55,000 rubles. This is an oversight on Fletcher's part, as he had just finished saying that none of the 15,000 men received less than 12 rubles, which would total at least 180,000 rubles. Concerning the second group, Fletcher says that the emperor chooses 110 men who are responsible for supplying the 65,000 men. There was never a group of 110 men who had such a responsibility. But from the explanations that Fletcher gives, it is evident that these men were those appointed by the emperor to look after the junior boyars in various towns, to pay them their salaries, and to take on the newcomers.

54–59. *And...place.* But Fletcher says later (Ch. 16, ll. 1–2; Ch. 19, ll. 11–15) that the Tartars, in fact, do invade Russia at least once a year.

129–34. *Euery...bande.* The army was divided into five regiments. Fletcher misses the Bolshoi regiment, as he considers the Bolshoi voevoda to be the commander-in-chief.

Chapter 16

23–40. *Concerning...retire.* Herberstein's account (*Notes on Russia*, I, 96) is much the same. He does add that the wealthier men use lances. There is an engraving of Russian soldiers, fully armed, in Herberstein (*ibid.*, following p. 96).

44. *fowling piece:* a light gun generally used for shooting wild fowl.

61–65. *If...partes.* Richard Chancellor (Hakluyt, I, 259): "But I beleeve they be such men for hard living as are not under the sun: for no cold wil hurt them.... If this Prince had within his countreys such men as could make them to understand ye things aforesaid [the art of warfare], I do beleeve that 2 of the best or greatest princes in Christendome were not wel able to match with him...."

Chapter 17

19. *brauerie:* display of courage, act of bravado.

62–63. *The. . .field.* Herberstein (*Notes on Russia*, I, 97) makes the same comment.

Chapter 18

8–9. *The. . .Lituania.* In 1479 Ivan III conquered Novgorod, and in 1485 he annexed Tver.

12–13. *Basileus. . .Smolensko.* Horsey, p. 206, attributes, incorrectly, these conquests to Ivan IV.

15–18. *These. . .owne.* Fletcher is here referring to the conquests of Ivan III, not his son Vasili III. Soon after Aleksandr (1492–1505) was elected grand duke of Lithuania, Ivan annexed parts of Lithuania along the Ugra and Oka rivers near Dorogobuzh and Mtsensk. To forestall further aggrandizement, Aleksandr concluded a treaty with Ivan in 1494, by which the areas already conquered by Ivan were ceded to him; and in return Ivan agreed to maintain a perpetual peace with Lithuania and to give his daughter, Elena, in marriage to Aleksandr, provided she would remain free to practice her Orthodox religion. In 1499, the Tartars attacked the southern borders of Lithuania; and Ivan invaded Lithuania, alleging that Aleksandr had endeavored to regulate Elena's spiritual life and had persecuted members of the Orthodox church. In 1503, a treaty was signed, by which Aleksandr ceded Kursk, Novgorod-Seversk, Chernigov, Starodub, Bryansk, Dorogobuzh, and Velikie Luki to Ivan. Thomas G. Chase, *The Story of Lithuania* (New York, 1946), p. 74, comments: "In other words, practically one-third of Lithuania's Ruthenian provinces in the East passed to Moscow."

18–26. *But. . .ground.* King Stephen Bathory declared war on Ivan IV on 26 June 1579. Polotsk surrendered to him on 30 August without much struggle, as Ivan IV had stationed his forces at Pskov, Novgorod, and Smolensk in defensive positions and did not venture an offensive attack. Ivan opened negotiations, but he would not yield to renouncing his rights in Livonia. Bathory again attacked—this time Velikie Luki, an important position, as control of this town would give Bathory an excellent base for attacks on the important towns of Moscow, Smolensk, Pskov, and Novgorod. Bathory succeeded in his attack on 4 September 1580. Ivan IV reopened negotiations for peace and sent an envoy, Rezanov, to Vienna and another, Shevrigin, to Rome to enlist the assistance of the emperor and the pope. Pope Gregory XIII sent the Jesuit Antonio Possevino to mediate. On 15 January 1582, a ten years' truce was concluded. Ivan IV surrendered the whole of Livonia and the towns of Polotsk and Velizh, and in return received back Velikie Luki. Sweden, who was in alliance with Poland, took this opportunity to recapture the important town of Narva (6 September 1581), and Ivan IV had to agree to this on 5 August 1582. See F. Nowak, "The Interregna and Stephen Batory," in *The Cambridge History of Poland* (3 vols.; Cambridge, 1950), I, 382–86.

31–35. *And...Russes.* Horsey, pp. 159–61, describes the conquest of Livonia in detail.

43. *Narue.* Horsey, p. 161, says: "He comes to the Narve, robbs and spoiells the town of all their riches, wealth, and merchandizes, kylls and murthers men, weomen, and children, and gives the spoill to his Tartor army."

48. *the Architect.* Horsey, p. 159, says Ivan "caused the eyes of the buylder to be pulled 'bored' owt for his so rare architecture."

64. *naked:* unarmed.

111. *berieueth:* snatches away.

123. *intiernesse:* familiarity.

Chapter 19

3–7. *Secondly...Polanos.* Fletcher follows Cromer's etymology of the word "Polanos" in *De Origine et Rebus Gestis Polonorum*, p. 20. See Introduction to *The Russe Commonwealth*, p. 145.

The people of Poland were called Lachey (Lechs), especially by the Russians, Hungarians, and Lithuanians, but not by the Germans and western Slavs. Most scholars agree that the word is derived from the Slavonic word *L'ada*, meaning a tract of uncultivated land. Some scholars have maintained, however, that the word "Lachy" was the name of one of the old tribes of Poland. See A. P. Goudy, "Racial Origins," in *The Cambridge History of Poland*, I, 10–11.

11–14. *The...yeare.* Horsey, p. 158, says the same thing: "But yet he [the tsar] had continuall warrs with the Crimme Tartor, who did sore anoye him and his subjects with their yearly incourcions."

15–22. *In...Tartar.* Horsey, pp. 164–66, gives a long account of the Tartar invasion. Both Horsey and Fletcher agree that there was treason afoot in the army.

Beaumont and Fletcher, *The Loyal Subject*, IV, v:

> When *Olin* came, grim *Olin*, when his marches,
> His last Incursions made the City [Moscow] sweat,
> And drove before him, as a storm drives Hail,
> Such showrs of frosted fears, shook all your heart-strings;
> Then when the *Volga* trembled at his terrour,
> And hid his seven curl'd heads, afraid of bruising,
> By his arm'd Horses hoofs; had I been false then,
> Or blown a treacherous fire into the Souldier,
> Had but one spark of villany liv'd within me,
> Ye'ad had some shadow for this black about me.
> Where was your Souldiership? why went not you out?
> And all your right honourable valour with ye?
> Why met ye not the *Tartar*, and defi'd him?
> Drew your dead-doing sword, and buckl'd with him?
> Shot through his Squadrons like a fiery Meteor?
> And as we see a dreadful clap of Thunder
> Rend the stiff hearted Oaks, and toss their roots up:
> Why did not you so charge him?
>
> (Glover and Waller ed., III, 149)

23–37. *The...more.* "A letter of Richard Uscombe to M. Henrie Lane, touching the burning of the Citie of Mosco by the Crimme Tartar" (Hakluyt, II, 135–36), mentions the death of about twenty-five Englishmen.

There are two accounts by Englishmen who were in Russia at the time of the Tartar invasion (*Early Voyages*, II, 338–40). Both write of the loss of members of the Russia Company.

Beaumont and Fletcher, *The Loyal Subject*, I, iii:

> Fire and Sword, Gentlemen;

> The *Tartar's* up, and with a mighty force,
> Comes forward, like a tempest, all before him
> Burning and killing.
>
> (Glover and Waller ed., III, 90)

27. *foure.* Horsey, p. 165, says six.

30–35. *but...lower.* Horsey omits this episode. Instead he writes of "the rever and ditches about Musco stopped and filled with the multituds of people" and that afterwards "many from other towns and places, every daie wear occupied within a great circuat to search, dregg, and fish, as it wear, for rings, jewells, plate, baggs of gold and silver, by which many wear inriched ever after" (p. 165).

39–43. *sent...home.* Horsey, pp. 166–67, writes that the Tartar sent an ambassador, who offered the emperor "a fowll rustie kniff to cutt his throate withall." Ivan's answer is interesting: "Tell the miscreant and unbeliver, thy master, yt is not he, it is for my sines and the sines of my people against my God and Christ."

58. *Belschey:* Ivan Dmitrievich Bel'sky (d. 1571), a voevoda in the Ukraine in 1561. He died during the Moscow fire.

61–64. *Hereupon...Haruest.* Spenser, *Faerie Queene*, II, xi, 26, 6–8, describing Prince Arthur's fight with Maleger:

> And in his flight the villein turn'd his face
> (As wonts the *Tartar* by the *Caspian* lake,
> When as the *Russian* him in fight does chace).

Milton, *Paradise Lost*, X, 431–33:

> As when the *Tartar* from his *Russian* Foe
> By *Astracan* over the Snowie Plaines
> Retires,...

67. *list:* limit.

75–76. *bow...sword.* Horsey, p. 166, states that they have "bow and arrowes, with curious rich senetaries [scimitars] by their sieds."

76–77. *They...forward. The Tragedy of Caesar and Pompey,* I, iii, 302–3:

> The sterne *Tartarian*, borne to manage armes,
> Doth feare and tremble at thy Maiesty.
>
> (*Malone Society Reprints* [Oxford, 1911])

80–81. *a...same.* Horsey, p. 166, writes that the Tartars are "cladd but in shepskins coats, gertt to them, with black caps of the same...."

95–119. *As...aware.* The source for this interesting story is Bonfinius, *Rerum Vngaricarum Decades Quatuor cum Dimidia*, p. 296. The invasion took place in 1241. See Sinor, *History of Hungary*, pp. 70–75, for a full account.

125–28. *They...can.* Herberstein (*Notes on Russia*, II, 54–56) discusses at greater length the manner of fighting of the Tartars. He also mentions the pretended flight as a trap for the enemy.

Phineas Fletcher, *Purple Island*, XI, xlviii:

> As when by *Russian Volgha's* frozen banks
> The false-back *Tartars* fear with cunning feigne,
> And poasting fast away in flying ranks,
> Oft backward turn, and from their bowes down rain
> Whole storms of darts; so do they flying fight:
> And what by force they lose, they winne by slight;
> Conquerd by standing out, and conquerours by flight:
>
> (Boas ed., II, 150)

134–45. *They...bondslaue.* Herberstein (*Notes on Russia*, I, 98) makes the same observation.

219–21. *They...body.* Herberstein (*ibid.*, II, 54) says the same thing.

Robert Burton, *Anatomy of Melancholy*: "The *Tartars* eat raw meat, and most commonly horse-flesh, drink milk and blood" (A. R. Shilleto [ed.], *The Anatomy of Melancholy* [3 vols.; London, 1893], I, 265).

Sir Thomas Browne, *Pseudodoxia Epidemica*: "The opinion in Galen's time, which Pliny also followeth, deeply condemned Horse-flesh, and conceived the very blood thereof destructive; but no diet is more common among the Tartars, who also drink their blood" (Geoffrey Keynes [ed.], *The Works of Sir Thomas Browne* [6 vols.; London, 1928–31], II, 285).

230–32. *As...vnpleasant.* Herberstein (*Notes on Russia*, II, 56) makes the same point and adds by way of illustration that when the Tartars are angry with their children, they say "May you abide in one place continually like a Christian, and inhale your own stink!" Richard Johnson (Hakluyt, I, 353) quotes the Tartars as saying the same thing.

251. Darius. Herodotus, Book IV, 120–42. It was only because

Histaeus of Miletus advised the Ionians not to tear down the bridge across the Ister that Darius escaped from the Scythians.

253–63. *For...carriages.* Laonicus Chalcocondylas, *Atheniensis Historiarum. Interprete Conrado Clausero* (Paris, 1650), Book III, p. 73.

264–73. *Pachymerius...no.* Georgius Pachymeres, *Michael Palaeologus* (Rome, 1666), p. 237.

276–80. *For...horsemen.* Cf. Herberstein (*Notes on Russia*, II, 53).

Dekker, *The Honest Whore*, Part 1, II, i, 337–40:

> For gold and sparkling iewels, (if he can)
> Youle let a Iewe get you with christian:
> Be he a Moore, a Tartar, tho his face
> Looke vglier then a dead mans scull,...
>   (Bowers ed., II, 54)

Shakespeare, *Macbeth*, IV, i, 29:

> Nose of Turk and Tartar's lips,...

284. *bandogge:* chained dog.

287. *scantling:* in archery, the distance from the mark within which a shot was not regarded as a miss.

289–356. *Some...Media.* Cf. *The Tartars or Ten Tribes*, ll. 228–49.

290–318. *Of...trueth.* Chalcocondylas, *Atheniensis Historiarum*, Book I, pp. 4–5. Fletcher follows Chalcocondylas' account very closely. Cf. *The Tartars or Ten Tribes*, ll. 253–76.

344–47. *For...be.* In Richard Eden's collection, this religion is attributed to the Lapps (*Notes on Russia*, II, 224).

365. *chrymson:* kermes.

388–89. *Towardes...deede.* Herberstein (*ibid.*, p. 57) says "they have no justice among them."

Chapter 20

8–9. *Samoyt...himselfe.* Herberstein (*Notes on Russia*, II, 39) states this as a fact: "...men who eat one another." Likewise, Richard Johnson (*Early Voyages*, I, 105–6) states that they eat the meat of reindeer, fish, and sometimes of one another.

21. *Slata Baba.* Herberstein (*Notes on Russia*, II, 41, 42) records the story

of Zlata Baba. According to him, "...this idol of the Golden Old Woman is a statue, representing an old woman holding her son in her lap, and that recently another infant has been seen, which is said to be her grandson...." But he does not say what magical powers she is supposed to have. Chancellor, quoted by Clement Adams (Hakluyt, I, 291–92) likewise writes of Zlata Baba.

22. *mappes*. Herberstein in his map of 1549 only shows the figure of Zlata Baba, but Anton Wied's map of 1555 and Jenkinson's map of 1562 have descriptions below the figure.

46–47. *On...Lappia*. In Richard Eden's collection, there is a long discussion of the Lapps (*Notes on Russia*, II, 221–26).

49. Sweetnesse: Sviatoi Nos. Herberstein (*ibid.*, p.106) explains: "Holynose is a huge rock, in the shape of a nose, protruding into the sea, under which is seen a cave which every six hours receives the waters of the ocean, and forms a whirlpool, and alternately discharges them with great uproar, causing a similar whirlpool."

56–57. *Their...simple*. Fletcher's opinion seems to be correct. See Björn Collinder, *The Lapps* (Princeton, N.J., 1949), pp. 77–84.

64. Nowremanskoy. Seredonin, p. 139, says: "The word 'Nowremanskoy' is not at all the same as the word 'Norwegian,' as Fletcher supposes. In Russian memorials, both those of the sixteenth century and earlier ones, we come across a division into the forest Lapp and the wild Lapp, or the Lapps of the mountains and the Lapps of the plains. The first called themselves in their own language, Tre-fennae (the Tersk bank), and the second, Cre-fennae. The wild Lapp lived on the Murmansk bank, and therefore it is possible that it was called the Murmansk Lapp. Fletcher could have easily confused these names and called the Murmansk or wild Lapp 'Nowremanskoy' and called the forest Lapp the wild one."

65. Noruegian...*religion*. According to Collinder (*The Lapps*, p. 19), the Norwegians first attempted to Christianize the Lapps in the thirteenth century. The Russian Lapps were converted to the Christian religion in the sixteenth century.

71–72. *For...world*. Horsey, p. 199, also takes this as a fact, and says: "The King [Ivan IV]...caused many witches magicians presently to be sent for owt of the North, wher ther is store, betwen Collonogorod and Lappia."

72–78. *Though...coast.* In Richard Eden's collection, this ability to control winds is stated as fact (*Notes on Russia*, II, 225).

Webster, *A Cure for a Cockold*, IV, iv, 95–97:

> Trust a woman!
> Never henceforward, I will rather trust
> The winds which *Lapland* Witches sell to men—
> (Lucas ed., III, 76)

88–94. *They...sold.* Stephen Borough (Hakluyt, I, 376) likewise states this, but he saw the market at Kegor.

97. *Olen:* the Russian word for reindeer.

Chapter 21

28–31. *Which...matters.* The beginning of the Christian church in Russia dates from the conversion of Vladimir in 989. George Vernadsky, *The Origins of Russia* (Oxford, 1959), pp. 293–305, has an excellent discussion of Vladimir's conversion.

36–40. *Which...Sarmatia.* Chalcocondylas, *Atheniensis Historiarum*, Book IV, p. 92.

47–48. Nicephorus...*bookes. Nicephori Gregorae, Romanae, hoc est Byzantinæ historiæ Libri XI* (Basil, 1562), Books VIII–IX, pp. 127–210.

50. Polonian...*chapter.* Cromer, *De Origine et Rebus Gestis Polonorum*, pp. 49–50.

51–54. *Vlodomirus...Christ.* Herberstein (*Notes on Russia*, I, 16–17) states this in his account of Vladimir.

74–78. *Ambassadour...Poland.* Archduke Ferdinand came to Moscow to obtain assistance for Maximilian in his war against Sigismund III (1566–1632), the son of John III, king of Sweden, for the right of the Polish crown. Maximilian was first offered the Polish crown, and accepted; but John Zamoyski, the chancellor, placed his strength behind Sigismund, and the crown was then offered to him. In January 1588, Zamoyski defeated and captured Maximilian at Byczyna in Silesia. And on 9 March 1589, Emperor Rudolph II renounced all Hapsburg claims to the Polish crown (F. Nowak, "Sigismund III," in *The Cambridge History of Poland*, I, 451–54).

80–81. *one...Spaine*: Petr Ragon, the tsar's interpreter.

89–94. *reducing...Legate*. Horsey, pp. 207–8, likewise speaks of Ivan's dislike for the Catholics and Antonio Possevino's mission to Ivan.

94. *Anthony*. Antonio Possevino mediated the truce between Stephen Bathory, king of Poland, and Ivan IV. Bathory had decisively defeated Ivan's forces at Polotsk and almost captured Pskov. The Swedes had captured Narva, so Ivan wanted a peace made. He wrote to the pope, Gregory XIII, asking him to mediate; and he sent Possevino. Evidently Ivan IV had hinted that he would consider the reunification of the Russian church with Rome, but nothing came of it, and it seems that Ivan never had any such intention.

98–99. *translation...Mosko*. Horsey, p. 207, only briefly mentions this.

117–21. *So...Sio*. W. K. Medlin, in *Moscow and East Rome* (Geneva, 1952), p. 116, gives succinctly the significance of the transfer of the patriarch from Constantinople to Moscow: "At the ordination of Metropolit Job as Patriarch of Moscow, the Patriarch of Constantinople gave his 'blessing, hereafter, of Patriarchs, in Moscow, with the sanction of the Tsar, according to the election of all the holy Russian synod.' In this statement, there are to be discerned three important factors: the recognition by Constantinople of the Patriarchate of Moscow as permanent; the confirmation of the temporal sovereign's right of sanctioning the patriarchal appointment; and finally the patriarch's election by a council of Russian bishops sitting at Moscow. Patriarch Jeremiah's act constituted a full recognition by Constantinople of the Russian Church's autonomy which had been asserted *de facto* about 120 years before, when Ivan III refused to accept any longer the Patriarch's jurisdiction in Moscow."

127. *hee...Oration*. Medlin (*ibid.*, p. 117) records these words of Jeremiah: "'Since the ancient Rome fell through the Appollinarian heresy, and the second Rome, which is Constantinople, is possessed by the pagan Turks, so then Thy Great Russian Tsardom, pious Tsar, is more pious then all previous kingdoms, is the third Rome,...and thou alone under heaven art called the Christian Tsar in the whole world for all Christians; and therefore the very great act to establish the Patriarchate will be accomplished according to God's will, the prayers of the Russian Saints, thy imperial prayer to God, and according to thy counsel.'"

138–40. *Patriarchship*...Nice. At the Council of Nicaea (325) and at the Council of Constantinople, the Patriarch of Constantinople was granted the place of honor next to the Bishop of Rome.

163. *not*...*Kalender*. Fletcher is correct. Jeremiah prohibited, by a circular letter, the introduction of the Gregorian calendar. See A. N. Mouravieff, *A History of the Church of Russia* (trans. R. W. Blackmore; Oxford, 1842), p. 136.

183. *peculiars:* probably in the ecclesiastical sense, i.e., exempt from other bishops' jurisdictions.

246. *bongrace:* a shade or curtain worn on the front of women's bonnets or caps to protect the complexion from the sun.

247. *listes:* borders, bordering strips.

247. *gardes:* ornamental edgings.

287–93. *Some*...*Cleargy men*. The first printed Slavonic books were published in Cracow, Poland, in 1491. The first printing house in Moscow was founded in 1553. Its work was soon suspended, but started again in 1568. Prior to 1600 only a very few books were printed in Moscow (George Vernadsky, *A History of Russia* [rev. ed.; New Haven, 1942], p. 65).

In Richard Eden's collection (*Notes on Russia*, II, 249–50) it is stated: "Beside the bookes that they haue of the ancient Greeke doctours, they haue also the commentaries and homelies of saynte Ambrose, Augustine, Jerome, & Gregorie, translated into the Illirian or Slauon tongue. . . . Furthermore, besyde the hystories of theyr owne countreys, they haue also bookes, conteyning the facts of great Alexander, and the Romane Emperours, and lykewyse of Marcus Antonius, & Cleopatra."

319–28. *For*...*parish*. Parish priests must be married. By a canon of Feodosi, metropolitan of Moscow (1462–67), a priest who lost his wife could no longer continue in the charge of a parish. This was confirmed by provincial councils of 1509 and 1563. The council in Moscow abolished the prohibition in 1667. See J. M. Neale, *A History of the Holy Eastern Church* (London, 1850), p. 1188.

322. Timothie *1.3.2.* "A bishop then must be blameless, the husband of one wife, viligant, sober, of good behaviour, given to hospitality, apt to teach."

324–26. *If...quondam.* Jenkinson (*Early Voyages*, I, 37) says that if the priest's wife dies, he cannot marry again, and so becomes a monk.

403. Say: a cloth of fine texture resembling serge.

412–15. *Besides...yeere.* Kliuchevsky, II, 185–89, discusses the wealth of the monasteries. The significance of their wealth, he says, is that it enabled them everywhere to raise the purchase price of land, and so to debar other competitors—more particularly servitors of small capital—from bidding for estates offered for sale.

415–16. *Abbey...Troits.* The Troitsky Monastery of St. Sergius was founded about 1340. Kliuchevsky, II, 153, says: "Sergius was a great organiser of monastic establishments, since his humility, his patient consideration for the needs and weaknesses of humanity, and his tireless zeal enabled him not only to elaborate a model system of monastic life in association, but also to foster among the brethren a similar spirit of self-sacrifice and strenuous asceticism to his own."

In a treatise ascribed to Robert Best (*Early Voyages*, II, 369), there is a description of the Troitsky monastery similar to Fletcher's, but without the discussion of land and fees.

425. *80.* The distance is about 30 miles.

451–53. *To...Cloyster-broode.* Sir Thomas Randolph (*Early Voyages*, II, 244) says: "They lie apart, they eate together, and are much giuen to drunkennesse, vnlearned, write they can, preach they doe neuer, ceremonious in their Church and long in their prayers."

457. Gymnosophists: the name given by the Greeks to certain ancient Hindu philosophers who pursued asceticism to the point of regarding food and clothing as detrimental to purity of thought.

499–514. *There...time.* Horsey, pp. 161–62, calls this man "Mickula Sweat" and gives some account of him. Horsey omits the part about "raw flesh," but gives the threats which Mikola made to Ivan. Mikola termed the emperor "bloudsuccer, the devourer and eater of Christian flesh, and swore by his angell that he should not escape deathe of a present thounder boltt, if he or any of his army did touch a hear in displeasur of the least childs head in that cittie, which God, by his good angell, did preserve for better purpose then his rapine...."

516. Pasquils: pasquins.

Chapter 22

1–36. Zautrana...*parish*. J. G. King, *The Rites and Ceremonies of the Greek Church in Russia* (London, 1772), pp. 97–121, gives the complete order of service.

35. *candles...wast*. Robert Best (*Early Voyages*, II, 369) speaks of candles "two yards long and a fathome about in bignesse."

43–57. *Vecherna...seruice*. King (*Rites and Ceremonies*, pp. 59–76) gives the order of service. But Vespers, of all the services, could be celebrated in a number of ways (*ibid.*, p. 82).

68. *baptisme...manner*. King (*ibid.*, pp. 208–20) gives the order of service. Herberstein (*Notes on Russia*, I, 73) gives a very brief description of the baptism rite. Robert Best (*Early Voyages*, II, 372–73) gives an account similar to Fletcher's. He adds that one of the godfathers hangs a cross about the neck of the child.

139. Richard Relph. See Willan, *Early History of the Russia Company*, pp. 190–96.

147–58. *First...religion*. Herberstein (*Notes on Russia*, I, 69) records this, too.

159–60. *The...Easter*. King (*Rites and Ceremonies*, p. 135) says: "In Russia every person is obliged by the civil law to communicate at least once in the year, which is commonly done in the fast before Easter, and they scarcely ever receive it any other time; yet the service of the liturgy or *hearing mass*, as it literally is, is always considered as the principal service of the day."

Herberstein (*Notes on Russia*, I, 78–79) briefly mentions the Communion rite. He omits the details of the service, but adds that (1) the Sacrament is administered to all those over seven years of age; and (2) the Sacrament is administered to those who are ill.

173–81. *Then...Christ*. I can find no authority for the communicants' receiving the Sacrament twice. King (*Rites and Ceremonies*, pp. 151–84) gives the order of service.

Chapter 23

3–7. *bookes...law*. Richard Chancellor (Hakluyt, I, 264) makes the same comment.

44–53. *This...whatsoeuer.* Robert Best (*Early Voyages*, II, 370–71) writes in greater detail of the Russians' use of images.

99. *Emperours...brother.* Dmitri (1582–1591) was the son of Ivan IV and Maria Nagaia. Cf. Ch. 5, ll. 51–52.

116–18. *All...sake.* Richard Chancellor (Hakluyt, I, 266): "As for whoredome and drunkennesse there be none such living: and for extortion, they be the most abhominable under the sunne."

Chapter 24

1–2. *The...countries.* Herberstein (*Notes on Russia*, I, 91–93) does not discuss the details of the ceremony.

Robert Best (*Early Voyages*, II, 373–75) gives only three anecdotes for his discussion of marriage: (1) the man sends a gift of a whip, needle and thread, silk and linen, and figs; (2) after the ceremony they "fall to drinking till they be all drunk"; (3) the man puts silver and gold in one of his boots and if the woman guesses which one, then she does not have to pull off his boots thereafter.

31–38. *On...himselfe.* Seredonin, p. 155, says: "Fletcher erroneously considers that the bride and her mother go to the bridegroom's house on the eve of the wedding. Because Fletcher says that the bride goes there in a cart or in a sled together with the wedding dress and wedding bed, it is evident that he took the dispatch of part of the dowry to the bridegroom's house for the arrival of the bride."

75. *charke:* a small glass or cup.

Chapter 25

36–72. *But...Twelfthday.* King (*Rites and Ceremonies*, pp. 387–93) gives the order of service.

Jenkinson's account (*Early Voyages*, I, 33–34) is like Fletcher's, except that he adds that the blessed water was cast "vpon the Emperours sonne and the Nobilitie." He does not mention the putting of crosses on the doors. Robert Best (*ibid.*, II, 362–63) describes the ceremony much as Fletcher and Jenkinson do. Like Jenkinson, he adds that the blessed water is cast on the emperor and dukes, and he omits the putting of crosses on the doors. King

(*Rites and Ceremonies*, pp. 384–85) records, however, that crosses were put on the doors.

93–98. *They...pension.* Robert Best (*Early Voyages*, II, 363–64) describes this ceremony in greater detail.

113–17. *The...superstition.* The four fasts are Lent, the fast of St. Peter and St. Paul (Monday after Sunday of Whitsunday to 29 June), the fast preceding the Assumption (1–15 August), and the fast of St. Nicholas, St. Philip, and St. Clement (15 November to 26 December).

116. *meere:* sheer.

127–31. *About...Peter.* Richard Chancellor, quoted by Clement Adam (Hakluyt, I, 291) says: "When any man dyeth amongst them, they take the dead body and put it in a coffine or chest, and in the hand of the corps they put a little scroule, and in the same there are these wordes written, that the same man died a Russe of Russes, having received the faith, and died in the same. This writing or letter they say they send to S. Peter, who receiving it (as they affirme) reads it, and by and by admits him into heaven...." Robert Best (*Early Voyages*, II, 375–76) records the same rite.

129. *letter...Nicôlas.* King (*Rites and Ceremonies*, pp. 358–60) gives the prayers that are put into the hand of the dead. They are not, however, addressed to St. Nicholas, but are prayers to God.

132–40. *In...ground.* George Turberville (Hakluyt, II, 101–2):

> The bodies eke that die unburied lie they then,
> Laid up in coffins made of firre, as well the poorest men,
> As those of greater state: the cause is lightly found,
> For that in Winter time, they cannot come to breake the ground.
>
> .   .   .   .
>
> Take this for certeine trothe, as soone as heate is gone,
> The force of colde the body binds as hard as any stone,
> Without offence at all to any living thing:
> And so they lye in perfect state, till next returne of Spring.

137. *billets:* a thick piece of wood cut to a suitable length for fuel.

Chapter 26

59. *He...manner.* Herberstein (*Notes on Russia*, II, 126–31) gives a long account of the banquet at which the tsar entertained him. Robert Best (*Early Voyages*, II, 357–58) describes the tsar's banquet.

74–76. *On...riche.* Jenkinson (*ibid.*, I, 31–33), describes briefly the banquet; but his chief interest is in the cupboard of plate: "There was also a Cupboord of plate, most sumptuous and rich, which was not vsed, among the which was a peece of golde of two yardes long, wrought in the toppe with Towers and Dragons heades; also diuers barrels of golde and siluer, with Castles on the bungs, richly and artifically made."

Richard Chancellor (Hakluyt, I, 257) was also impressed with this plate: "In the middest of the chamber stoode a table or cupbord to set plate on; which stoode full of cuppes of golde: and amongst all the rest there stoode foure marveilous great pottes or crudences as they call them, of golde and silver: I thinke they were a good yarde and a halfe hie."

79. *say*: the act of tasting food or drink before presenting it to a person of high rank.

93–114. *On...pleasure.* Herberstein (*Notes on Russia*, II, 137–38) writes of the bear fights, but states that if the men are wounded they run to the prince crying, "See, my lord, we are wounded." To which the prince replies: "Go, I will show you favour," and then orders them to be taken care of, and clothes and certain measures of corn to be given to them. Cf. Horsey, 178–79, where there is an account of seven "rebellious bigg fatt friers" who were thrown to the bears. Shakespeare, in *Macbeth*, III, iv, 100, writes: "Approach thou like the rugged Russian bear..." and in *Henry V*, III, vii, 141–43: "Foolish curs, that run winking into the mouth of a Russian bear, and have their heads crushed like rotten apples!"

95. *against*: should.

110. *talents*: talons.

111–14. *If...pleasure.* Seredonin, p. 152, points out that Fletcher was wrong, as the tsar rewarded a good fight with either money or cloth.

134. *34.* Fedor was born in 1557.

135. *sixe.* Fedor became tsar in 1584 and died in 1598.

Chapter 27

16. Estoma Bisabroza Pastelnischay: Istoma Osipovich Bezobrazov. "Postelnichy" is the word for chamberlain.

23. *Hagbutters:* harquebusiers—soldiers armed with a portable gun, varying in size from a small cannon to a musket.

Chapter 28

23–24. *To...weeke.* George Turberville (Hakluyt, II, 99):

Drinke is their whole desire, the pot is all their pride,
The sobrest head doth once a day stand needfull of a guide.

Jenkinson (*Early Voyages*, I, 37) says "...their greatest friendship is in drinking."

28–30. *This...weeke.* Robert Best (*ibid.*, II, 376) says the same thing.

28–33. *they...it.* Dekker, *The Dead Tearme:* "...no *Stoues* in *Muscouy* can put a man into more violent sweates" (Grosart ed., *Non-Dramatic Works*, IV, 31–32).

Bacon, *Calor et Frigus:* "...perpetual keeping in in stoves in the winter time as they do in Russia" (Spedding ed., III, 651).

31. Peaches: stoves.

48–53. *The...faces.* Robert Best (*Early Voyages*, II, 375): "...they grease their faces with such coulers, that a man may discerne them hanging on theyr faces almost a flight shoot off."

George Turberville (Hakluyt, II, 100):

Is not the meanest man in all the land but hee,
To buy her painted colours doeth allow his wife a fee,
Wherewith she deckes herselfe, and died her tawnie skinne,
She pranks and paints her smoakie face, both brow, lip,
cheeke, and chinne.

57–58. *The...fashion.* George Turberville (*ibid.*, pp. 104–5) gives a description of the nobleman's attire.

58–86. *First...gold.* Jenkinson (*Early Voyages*, I, 39–40) gives the same information.

61–64. *His...can.* Robert Best (*ibid.*, II, 368) records this practice.

464

George Turberville (Hakluyt, II, 104):

> It is their common use to shave or els to sheare
> Their heads, for none in all the land long lolling locks doth weare,
> Unlesse perhaps he have his sovereigne prince displeas'd.
> For then he never cuts his haire, untill he be appeas'd.

95. *fruntlet*: frontlet.

157–60. *For...them.* Herberstein (*Notes on Russia*, I, 32) says: "It is matter of doubt whether the brutality of the people has made the prince a tyrant, or whether the people themselves have become thus brutal and cruel through the tyranny of their prince." Jenkinson (*Early Voyages*, I, 58) likewise stresses this quality in the people.

177–80. *And...named.* Horsey, pp. 172–73, cites some of the atrocities done by Ivan IV. Having given the examples, Horsey concludes: "I could innumerat many and much more that have felt the like severitie and crueltie of this emperors heavy hand of displeasur, but I forbare to trouble the modest eyrs and Christian pacience of such as shall read it."

183–85. *As...promise.* Jenkinson (*Early Voyages*, I, 37) says: "...they are great talkers, and liers, without any faith or trust in their words, flatterers, and dissemblers."

The Tartars or Ten Tribes

1–2. *subdued*...Assyrians. 2 Kings xvii.6.

27–28. Israel...*Messias*. Romans xi.26–27; Isaiah xxvii.13.

45–50. *A...Judgment*. Romans xi.22.

54. *Apostle...foretold*. Romans xi.26–27.

73–76. ad...*places*. Probably an allusion to Virgil's graphic description of Tartarus (*Aeneid* vi. 548–627).

77–80. *As*...Triballi. I have been unable to identify what "Divines" conjectured that the Ten Tribes were the Alani. Nor can I find an account which equates the Triballi with the Alani or states that the Alani were of Europe (as, in fact, they were Sarmatian in origin).

85–90. *Onely*...Remainders. Du Plessis-Mornay's treatise, *A Woorke Concerning the Trewnesse of the Christian Faith* (London, 1587), was translated into English by Sir Philip Sidney and Arthur Golding. Fletcher's statement indicates that he was not familiar with the volume—perhaps someone had told him what Du Plessis-Mornay had said. He does say, sig. 2G4ᵛ: "And the word Tartars or Totares signifieth *Remnants* or *Leauings* in the Syrian tongue." But Du Plessis-Mornay does not state that the Ten Tribes were the Alani. Speaking of the removal of the Tribes, he says: "For the Israelites were conueyed thence into *Media*, and receiued the vninhabited Countryes to dwell in, and of them came partly the *Cholchians* who in the time of

Herodotus caused themselues to be circumcised; and partly the *Tartarians*, who about the yere of our Lord a thousand and two hundred, ouerwhelmed the earth lyke a waterflud vnder the leading of *Cingi*...."

112. Media...*Cosmographers*. Ptolemy, *Geographia* (Basil, 1540), sig. I6ᵛ; Strabo, *Geography*, Book XI.13.2 ([Loeb Classical Library; 8 vols.; London, 1918–32], V, 302–3).

123–26. Cyrus's...*deportation*. The removal of the Israelites to various parts of Mesopotamia (2 Kings xvii.6) took place about 721 B.C. Cyrus ruled from 559–529 B.C., which would mean that the event occurred about 172 years before his reign began. But Darius (521–485 B.C.) did invade the Scythians about 512 B.C. And it seems rather probable that Fletcher was confused about this and really meant Darius instead of Cyrus. Cf. ll. 287–89.

140–45. So...Esar-haddon. Fletcher was somewhat confused, it seems. Merodach Baladan led revolts against Assyria on the death of Sargon (705 B.C.) but was defeated by Sennacherib in 701 B.C. See Theodore H. Robinson, *A History of Israel* (2 vols.; Oxford, 1932), I, 387–89. Deioces (709–656 B.C.) did unite the Medes; and his son Phraortes marched against the Assyrians. See Herodotus, Book I, 96–102 ([Loeb Classical Library; 4 vols.; London, 1921–24], I, 126–33). The tenth year of Esarhaddon would be 671 B.C.

158–62. *Their*...Bajazet. This is an almost literal translation of the notation on Jenkinson's map of Russia. See Introduction to *The Tartars or Ten Tribes*, p. 310.

180–81. Corazen...*them*. This information is taken from Jenkinson's map of Russia. See Introduction to *The Tartars or Ten Tribes*, p. 310.

183. *univocation*: oneness or identity of name or meaning.

196. Scythian *Shepherds*. Cf. *The Russe Commonwealth*, Ch. 19, ll. 287–89.

197–217. *standing*...*said*. Cf. *The Russe Commonwealth*, Ch. 19, ll. 222–42.

230–49. *Their*...Russe. Cf. *The Russe Commonwealth*, Ch. 19, ll. 289–356.

256–66. "*It*...*People*." Laonicus Chalcocondylas, *Atheniensis Historiarum. Interprete Conrado Clausero* (Paris, 1650), Book I, p. 4. Cf. *The Russe Commonwealth*, Ch. 19, ll. 289–318.

266–76. "*It…Shepherds.*" Chalcocondylas, *Atheniensis Historiarum*, Book I, p. 5. Cf. *The Russe Commonwealth*, Ch. 19, ll. 289–318.

287–89. Israelites…*stories.* Cf. ll. 123–26.

309–10. *16th*…Apocalypse: Revelation xvi.12.

352–55. Morsoy…*Tribes.* Cf. *The Russe Commonwealth*, Ch. 19, ll. 191–97.

360–67. "*That…before.*" 2 Esdras xiii.39–41.

370–73. "*Then…peaceably.*" 2 Esdras xiii.46–47.

389–94. *That…Brightman. Apocalypsis Apocalypseos* (Frankfurt, 1609), sigs. 3I4^v–3K2^r *sub* Revelation xvi.12.

Thomas Brightman was born about 1562. He was admitted a pensioner of Queens' College, Cambridge, on 21 February 1577, and commenced B.A. 1580–81. He died on 24 August 1607. For a biographical account, see Charles Henry and Thompson Cooper, *Athenae Cantabrigienses* (3 vols.; Cambridge, 1858–1913), II, 458–59.

468

The Letters

Letter 1

HL. *LILES*. Robert Liles was admitted to King's College, Cambridge as a scholar on 22 September 1567, and as a fellow on 23 September 1570. He proceeded B.A. in 1571 and commenced M.A. in 1575. In October 1582 he was put out of commons for a fortnight for words against the provost. On 2 October 1583, he was expelled from the university by the sentence of Dr. Bell, the vice-chancellor, and eight other heads of colleges for having sued Thomas Moudeford, M.A., fellow of King's, in a cause of defamation *coram extraniis judicibus*. In 1594 he made an unsuccessful attempt to be restored to his fellowship. He then turned to the medical profession.

JOHNSON. Robert Johnson was admitted to King's College, Cambridge, as a scholar from Eton, on 23 August 1566. He proceeded B.A. in 1571 and commenced M.A. in 1574. He was a fellow from 1569 to 1576. Since his fellowship was terminated in 1576, one may assume that he was expelled or left on his own accord because of his participation in the Goad Rebellion. In June 1576, Johnson wrote a letter to Lord Burghley requesting a position as his chaplain (BM Lansdowne MS 23, No. 44), but there is no evidence that he received the appointment.

Letter 7

HL. *WOTTON.* Thomas Wotton (1521–1587) was a person of great learning, religious devotion, and wealth. He was the son of Sir Edward Wotton (1489–1551), one of Henry VIII's closest advisers. See *DNB.*

3. *Pickarnigus.* William Pickering (1516–1575) was educated at Cambridge. He retired from public service rather early in life and devoted his time to literary pursuits. In his will of 31 December 1574, he willed that his armory and library should remain whole and safe for whoever should marry his daughter, Hester. Thomas Wotton was one of the four executors of this will, and his eldest son, Sir Edward Wotton, married Hester. See *DNB.*

19. *Woottonus patruus tuus:* Nicholas Wotton (1497?–1567).

Letter 8

1. *Lord Ambassadour:* Sir Thomas Randolph (1523–1590).

2. *his negotiation.* See Conyers Read, *Mr. Secretary Walsingham* (3 vols.; Oxford, 1925), II, 240–57, for the details of this mission.

7. *Secretarie:* Sir John Maitland (1545?–1595).

8. *Articles of the Confederation.* Thomas Rymer, *Foedera,* XV (London, 1713), 805–7, prints the agreement.

24. *Bigons:* bygones, denoting what is past, and probably in the sense of offenses against the sovereign or the state. Professor Roland Smith kindly provided the information for this gloss.

29. *French Ambassadour:* Charles de Prunele, Baron d'Esneval.

52. *Maister Gray:* Patrick, Master of Gray (d. 1612).

Letter 9

6. *Lord Ambassadour:* Sir Thomas Randolph.

Letter 10

HL. *SALTONSTALL:* Sir Richard Saltonstall (1521?–1601). He was a governor of the Merchants Adventurers Company.

19. *tolles...vp.* The Merchants Adventurers had complained for some time about this toll, which is also referred to by Fletcher and Saltonstall as

the Beacon and Buoy toll. In a letter from Dr. Schulte of Hamburg to Lord Burghley and Walsingham, dated 19 August 1586, it is stated that it had been the custom of the city of Hamburg to take a small fixed sum of money from all merchandise in compensation for the expenses incurred by the people of Hamburg in making the Elbe River, with its multitude of hidden sandbanks, safe for navigation. The Hamburghers placed and kept in repair a number of buoys and a number of beacons for the warning of sailors (SP 82/2, No. 51).

26. *Alderman...Stilliard:* Maurice Timerman. The Steelyard was the place on the north bank of the Thames, above London Bridge, where the Merchants of the Hanse had their establishment.

33. *Staplers.* The Merchants of the Staple and the Merchants Adventurers had a common origin in the guild of merchants, the Brotherhood of St. Thomas Becket. By 1296 the Merchants of the Staple had a monopoly on the export of wool. Those who were not attached to this particular body were termed Adventurers, since they traded at their own risk. This group formed the Merchants Adventurers and secured a monopoly on cloth trade. By 1500 the export of wool had fallen off considerably, while the export of cloth had greatly increased, which meant that the Merchants Adventurers were replacing the Merchants of the Staple as the most important trading company. Indeed, in 1527 the Staplers had petitioned to the king for relief, asserting that they had the right also to the cloth trade, but their petition was rejected. At this time, consequently, the feelings between the two companies were not at all amicable.

38. *Prince...Parma.* Alexander Farnese. The Earl of Leicester, in a letter to the Privy Council dated 1 August 1587, confirms that the Duke of Parma had agents at Hamburg to disturb the reëstablishment of the Merchants Adventurers there. He concludes that, as the enemy spares no means to deal to Her Majesty's prejudice, it would be good to do something to hinder their practices before it is too late (SP 84/17, ff. 3–4).

Letter 11

3. *Hoy:* a small vessel usually rigged as a sloop.

47. *s. luips:* shilling Lubs or Lubish, the money of Lubeck and Hamburg.

48. *boy...mony:* see note to Letter 10, l. 19.

60. *common subiect.* Sir Walter Raleigh had large and very profitable grants of license to export woolen broadcloths bestowed on him by the queen in 1584, 1585, 1587, and 1589 (SP 12/229, No. 101). Lord Burghley objected that Raleigh's profits were excessive (BM Lansd. MS 41, Nos. 26 and 28; Lansd. MS 42, Nos. 1–6).

63–69. *one...before.* This merchant, Nicholas Warner, wrote the following letter (SP 82/2, No. 61), relating more about this negotiation: "Oure commissioners havinge delyverd her Maiesties lettres vnto the Senate, they appoynted V of the lordes and doctors of the towne to confere with them. And after many metinges, in the ende they concludyd that for the vj ships we shuld discharge them and make sale of our clothes payinge iijs lypse vppon a clothe. So as we made full accompte our ships shuld haue discharged. But sithens (the Senate havinge called the Burghers together) they will not in any wise consent vnto that which was agreed vppon by the V men appoynted by the Senate. But notwithstandinge that agrement passed they will haue a greter tolle then ever we meane to yeild vnto. many foule speches have bene given out by dyverse of this towne, not a litle to the discredit of her Maiesties lettres. But also to the vtter despising of our companie. Many delayes we have had and no ende we cann comme vnto. Yt pleased our commyssioners to appoynt me and Richard Sheparde to goe to Stoade with a lettre of a credytt to conferre with them vppon certen articles. And we fynde them very willinge to receue vs vppon goode and resonable conditions eyther for these vj ships (yf they comme vnto them) or for the next ships that shall comme out of England. We retorned to this towne this evennynge and haue informed our commissioners of their willingnes to receyve vs. So that nowe their meaninge ys with so muche spede as maye be, to vrge them vnto their former agrement, or els to suffer vs to departe with our ships, meaninge to staye any longer their delayes. The tole that we shuld paye at Stoade is ijd vppon a clothe. And all other thinges we shall haue in as goode and reasonable order as we cann requyre. And for myne owne parte I had rather ijd there havinge the goode will of the people then jd here beinge in their hatred and contempt."

472

Letter 12

1–2. *Maister Tirrell:* Antony Tyrrell (1552–1610?), renegade priest and spy.

33. *Maister Beal:* Robert Beale (1541–1601).

71–72. *But...daughter.* Fletcher and Saltonstall were incorrect in assuming that the Danish ships were carrying Frederick's daughter to Scotland. In May 1587, Sir Peter Young and Sir Patrick Vans had been sent as ambassadors to Denmark by James VI, partly to negotiate with Frederick concerning the restitution of the Orkney Islands, which had been pledged as security for the dowry of Margaret by her father, Christian I, on her marriage to James III of Scotland in 1469. They were also commissioned to make searching inquiry regarding the two daughters of Frederick, Elizabeth and Anne, with a view to the marriage of one of them with James VI. The marriage between James VI and Anne was not consummated until 20 August 1589. According to David Moysie (*Memoirs of the Affairs of Scotland, 1577–1603* [Edinburgh, 1830], p. 65), the Scottish ambassadors returned to Scotland in August 1587, which one may assume to be the voyage Fletcher and Saltonstall are here describing.

72. *Kinges daughter:* Princess Anne (1574–1619), the younger daughter of Frederick II (1534–1588), king of Denmark.

74. *Scottish Ambassadour:* Sir Peter Young (1544–1628) and Sir Patrick Vans (d. 1597).

77. *Orcades:* Orkney Islands.

81. *Holy Iland:* Heligsland.

85. *Bishop...Bream:* Duke Johan, the third son of Duke Adolph of Holstein.

Letter 13

12. *guilt:* tax.

13. *Elue:* Elbe.

56. *stivers:* a small coin, usually silver, of the Low Countries. In 1585 the stiver had the value of 3*d.* in English money.

473

Letter 14

18. *Accord of Vtrecht.* April 1473. For a summary of the treaty, see Cornelius Walford, "An Outline History of the Hanseatic League, More Particularly in Its Bearings Upon English Commerce," *Transactions of the Royal Historical Society*, IX (1881), 107–10.

Letter 15

4. *200...Vtrecht.* The Treaty of Utrecht was made in April 1473.

68–69. *Burgher...Captain.* John Wheeler, in his *A Treatise of Commerce*, mentions these men, saying that the Hamburghers had "daily in their Counsell Doctour *Westendorp* of *Groeninghe*, sent thither by *Verdugo*, Gouernor of Westfriseland for the King of Spaine, [who] delayed and dallied with the foresayd Commissioners, so that after much labour spent, nothing in the end was concluded..." (George B. Hotchkiss [ed.], *John Wheeler, A Treatise of Commerce* [New York, 1931], p. 48).

72–73. *losse...Scluse.* July 1587.

Letter 16a

12. *sarpler...wooll:* a bale of wool containing eighty tods.

Letter 16b

6–7. *attendaunce...Hamborough.* See Letters 8 and 9, relating to Scotland, and Letters 10–15, relating to Hamburg.

8–9. *To...reign.* Cf. Letter 20, in which Fletcher proposes the same project to Lord Burghley.

12–15. *If...greater.* Fletcher was admitted and sworn as Remembrancer on 26 January 1586, and at the same time his salary was fixed at £50 per year (Corporation of London, Repertory 21, ff. 384ᵛ–385).

Letter 17

1–4. *My...nation.* See the Life of Fletcher, pp. 25–30, for an account of Fletcher's mission to Russia.

13. *Chauncellour:* Andrei Shchelkalov.

17–26. *When...repeated.* Fletcher records this incident in his *Russe Commonwealth*, together with the full "stile" of the emperor. See Ch. 6, ll. 65–93.

20. *ellnes:* ells.

46. *Diake:* secretary.

67. *loss...Narve.* Captured by Sweden in 1581.

79–80. *they...Nicholas:* Archangel. Cf. Letter 18, ll. 114–18.

102. *Hierom Horsey:* Jerome Horsey (fl. 1573–1627).

114. *League...hand.* See *The Russe Commonwealth*, Ch. 21, ll. 60–86.

128. *Highnes Oration:* The famous oration to the troops at Tilbury in August 1588. See George P. Rice (ed.), *The Public Speaking of Queen Elizabeth* (New York, 1951), pp. 96–97, for the text.

130–40. *Ambassadour...intertainment.* See the notes to Ch. 21, ll. 74–88.

163–64. *Mousickes:* the Russian peasants.

193. *Anthonie Marshe.* See the Life of Fletcher, pp. 26–28.

226. *pudkey.* See *The Russe Commonwealth*, Ch. 14, ll. 99–102.

Letter 18

30–31. *olld...England.* Ivan IV was interested in marriage to Lady Mary Hastings, cousin to Queen Elizabeth. See T. S. Willan, *The Early History of the Russia Company* (Manchester, 1956), pp. 161–63.

135. *peculium:* a private or exclusive possession or property.

Letter 19

HL. *ROKEBY:* Ralph Rokeby (1527?–1596) was educated at Cambridge and Lincoln's Inn. He was appointed chief justice of Connaught in 1570 and became Master of Requests about 1576. See *DNB*.

1–2. *According...lettres.* The letter is found in the Acts of the Privy Council (PC 2/16, p. 466) and is dated 11 January: "A letter to Raphe Rokeby esquier and Doctour Fletcher, in which a peticion exhibited to the Lordes by the legatours of Iohn Northe deceased whoe was one of the factours vnto the Marchauntes trading to Moscovia requiring them to consider of the same and to examine what goodes one Trumbull that was one of the Overseers vnto the Testatour had in anie mens hands or that anie other man here did trade in their owne names for Trumbulls vse, and alsoe what course they should think fyttest to be taken that the same might be stayed yf they should soe advyse for the benefytt of the Legatours to whome Trumbull contrary to an agreement sett downe at his owne request hath and doth refuse to paie the great legacies bequeathed by the Testatour, and for that purpose absenteth him selfe forth of the Realme."

7. *William Trumbull:* Trumbull or Turnbull was chief agent for the Russia Company in Moscow from 1583 to 1584. He used his position as chief agent to engage in private trade, and when he ceased to be agent, he owed the company 3,000 rubles. He was recalled to England to account for his actions, but escaped secretly to Russia, where he remained until his death in 1591. It is highly doubtful that the legatees of the estate of John Norden or Northe ever received the money willed to them.

Letter 20

12. *Maister Mainard:* Lord Burghley's secretary.

30. *Polydor:* Polydore Vergil (1470?–1555?), *Anglicæ Historiæ.*

Letter 21

2. *Graymes.* See the Life of Fletcher, pp. 34–35, for the background to this letter.

3. *Leonard Coast:* Lanarkshire, or perhaps Lanark.

Letter 22

2. *the title.* Cecil had just been made secretary of state.

17. *my suit.* Fletcher's suit was for the position of Master of Requests, which was vacant by the death of Ralph Rokeby. See the Life of Fletcher, p. 25, n. 35, for a discussion of Fletcher's petitions for the position of Master of Requests.

Letter 23

3. *Graimes.* See the Life of Fletcher, pp. 34–35, for the background to this letter.

Letter 24

2. *first fruites*. Under the terms of the statute granting first fruits and tenths to the monarch (26 Henry VIII, c. 3, and renewed 1 Elizabeth I, c. 4), before a person could possess any spiritual office or promotion, he was to pay to the Crown the profits of the spiritual office for one year. Thereafter he was to pay the tenth part of all the profits of the office; however, in the year in which the first fruits were paid, the payment of the tenth was not required.

19–20. *pacefication...displeasure*. Richard Fletcher took a leading part in the conference which drew up the Lambeth Articles, which, because of their extreme Calvinism, angered Elizabeth. In the same year, Fletcher married Lady Baker, widow of Sir Richard Baker, which also offended Elizabeth, who objected to the marriage of any bishop, and thought that this marriage was particularly indecorous, since Fletcher had been a widower for less than two years. Elizabeth forbade Fletcher to attend the court and on 23 February 1595 suspended him from the exercise of all episcopal functions. Through Lord Burghley's mediation, the suspension was relaxed at the end of six months, and the queen became partially reconciled to Fletcher.

24. *prouoke:* invite.

32. *8...children*. See my "Biographical Notes on Richard Fletcher," *N&Q*, n.s. VII (1960), 377–78, for the names of the children.

Letter 27

12. *Reprisall*. The law of reprisal was defined in 27 Edward III, 2 c. xvii. For the text see Danby Pickering (ed.), *The Statutes at Large*, II (Cambridge, 1762), 89.

Letter 28

3–4. *their...affayer*. From the results of the conference, it is known that the two main topics of discussion were (1) the terms issued by Elizabeth to Oldenbarneveldt and Duivenvoorde under which she would continue to help the United Provinces, and (2) the possible terms under which they would submit themselves to Spain.

4. *Grave Maurice:* Graf Maurice, prince of Nassau, was the leader of the military forces of the United Provinces.

11–12. *treatie...Kinges.* The Treaty of Vervins between Henry IV of France and Philip II of Spain was concluded on 2 May 1598.

14–30. *At...buisines.* The dumb show represents the dealings attending the Treaty of Vervins. Acually the cardinal, Archduke Albert of Austria, was not present at the negotiations, nor was Queen Elizabeth, both of whom are represented as being present. The representations of the actions of the respective countries are correct, however. Spain was anxious to make a peace with France so that she could concentrate her forces in conquering the United Provinces. Sir Robert Cecil, who represented the English interests at the conference, urged the French king to accept a peace. The "Boores of *Holland*" who tried to interrupt the negotiations were Admiral Justinus of Nassau and Johan van Oldenbarneveldt.

Letter 29

11–13. *wee...all.* The final treaty was made on 14 July and was more favorable than Fletcher indicates. A translation of the act is extant (SP 84/57, ff. 10–12^v).

14. *soom...twoo.* Oldenbarneveldt was sent as head of a legation to continue negotiations with Elizabeth for the continuation of the war against Spain. She insisted that she would negotiate with the United Provinces only if they would immediately begin payment on their debt. At last, the sum claimed by Elizabeth was reduced from £1,400,000 to £800,000, and it was agreed that the United Provinces should pay £30,000 a year on this debt.

Letter 30

2. *the* Edict. On 6 May, Philip II transferred the possession of the Netherlands to his daughter Isabella and to the Cardinal Archduke Albert of Austria, who was to marry her. On 30 May, Isabella executed a procuration by which she gave absolute authority to Albert to rule over the Netherlands. The Spanish Netherlands agreed to these new arrangements before Albert went to Spain on 14 September.

Letter 31

HL. *DAVISON*: Sir William Davison (1541?–1608), privy councillor and secretary to Queen Elizabeth.

1–2. *Saint...Island*: an island in the Azores.

3. Terceraes: Terceira, an island in the Azores.

Letter 32

4. *Requests.* See the Life of Fletcher, p. 25, n. 35, concerning Fletcher's petitions for the position of Master of Requests.

Letter 33

HL. *RYDER.* Sir William Ryder (1544?–1611) became Lord Mayor in 1600 and was knighted in 1601 for loyalty to Queen Elizabeth during the Essex Rebellion.

1–2. *Maister...Hampsons.* In a manuscript in Hatfield House (Cecil Papers 83.51) it is stated: "Doctor Fletcher, committed to Alderman Lowe," but from Fletcher's statement here and a warrant issued by the Privy Council to Alderman Hampson to allow Fletcher's wife to have a conference with him (see note to ll. 1–2 of Letter 36), it is clear that Alderman Hampson was the person to whom Fletcher was committed.

Letter 34

2. *noted:* indicted.

24. *12....children.* In Letter 26a, Fletcher states that he himself had nine children and had taken in the eight children of his brother, Richard. Probably Fletcher is including in this twelve those children of his brother that are still in his care.

Letter 35

2–3. *Maister Temple.* William Temple, in his examination before Lord Chief Justice Popham and Attorney-General Coke on 1 July, said that on 7 February, the Earl of Essex told him to tell Fletcher that the Jesuits had practised to take away his life (SP 12/281, No. 1).

26. *Secretarie Harbert:* John Herbert.

49. *pourposing:* resolving.

70. *Maister Smythe.* Sir Thomas Smythe, sheriff of London, was, like Fletcher, a friend on whom Essex had counted for aid in the rebellion. Either through fear or a sudden change of mind, Smythe refused to take part in the plot and was subsequently acquitted by the commission.

90. *Lord Admirall:* Thomas Lord Howard, Earl of Suffolk (1561–1626).

Letter 36

1–2. *suit...wyfe.* On 8 March the following warrant was issued by the Privy Council: "A warrant to Alderman *Hampson.* That where Doctor Fletcher was commytted by her Majestys direccion vnto his custody, to remaine close prisoner vntill he hath other order to the contrary. In regard of some importe buisenes that did concerne the said Doctors estate, the Aldermann was required to permytte his wyfe and a servaunte of his acquainted with his buisenes, to haue conference with him about the same in his presence" (PC 2/26, p. 115).

3. *mone:* mention.

8. *Quarter day:* 25 March (Lady Day).

Letter 37

4–5. *on...lodging:* probably Clement Edmondes. See Letter 38. Ann Cecil, Sir Robert's niece, wrote to Cecil in favor of Edmondes about this time (Cecil Papers 78.21).

Letter 38

2. *Maister Edmonds.* Clement Edmondes was sworn assistant to Fletcher as a probationer on 5 May 1601 (Corporation of London, Repertory 25, f. 228ᵛ). On 1 October 1601 the appointment was confirmed and his salary set at half of Fletcher's, or fifty pounds (Corporation of London, Repertory 25, f. 282).

4–7. *Beeing...man.* Although Fletcher is here indicating that he desires to resign his office in the immediate future, the records show that he did not resign until 2 July 1605 (Corporation of London, Repertory 27, f. 41). Edmondes succeeded him as Remembrancer.

Letter 40

7. *once Ambassadour:* to Russia.

7–8. *thrice...Messenger:* to Scotland, Hamburg, and the United Provinces.

Textual Notes

Licia

The corrections indicated by Fletcher in the errata (M4ʳ) have been silently introduced into the text. The errata has the following preface:

> *To the reader.*
> *Courteous Reader) for my owne fault I referre thee to my Preface; but for the Printers, I crave pardon. The excuse is just, if thou knew the cause. I desire thee therefore to correct the greater, thus; the lesse, of thy selfe; and to pardon all.*

The following are the corrections made. The page and line are to this edition:

(Bʳ) Thus] Thue [p. 79, l. 53]
(B2ʳ) gracefull] gracelesse [p. 81, l. 3]
(B3ʳ) such] you [p. 82, l. 6]
(Cᵛ) sonne.] omit [p. 85, l. 14] [But see textual introduction, p. 72.]
(D2ʳ) thy] my [p. 89, l. 12]
(F3ᵛ) make] make make [p. 99, l. 12]
(Gᵛ) hands,] hands hands, [p. 101, l. 7]
(I3ʳ) fingers] singers [p. 114, l. 66]
(K4ᵛ) friend] feiend [p. 122, l. 43]

The Epistle Dedicatory
46   that] thar

47   where,] ~ ;
52   hee] ~ hee
61   this.] ~ :
62   vertues] ~ ;
88–89   Lady-/ship] Lady-ship

To the Reader
4   *favor,*] ~ ;
30   *parte*] ~ ,
37   *themselves,*] ~ , they (Arber)
48   *LICIA.*] ~ :
63   *her.*] ~ :
65   Master] *M.*
65   Master] *M.*

Sonnet I
4   So] ~ to (Grosart 1876)
9   weepe:] ~ ,

Sonnet II
4   happe.] ~ ,

Sonnet III
10   in] ~ all (Arber)

Sonnet V
4   inchain'd] unchained (Arber, Crow)

Sonnet XI
3   sawe] shawe

Sonnet XII
XII] XIII
2   for] *om.* (Crow)
9   thou] though (Crow)

Sonnet XIII
3   heate,] ~ .
7   feare] ~ .

Sonnet XX
14   when] where (Crow)

Sonnet XXI
7   upon thy] ~ the (Crow)

Sonnet XXII
4   But] And (Crow)

Sonnet XXIII
7   Or] And (Arber)
8   mist.] ~ ,

Sonnet XXIV
4   he] she (Crow)
8   let] her (Crow)

Sonnet XXV
3   To] So (Crow)
3   the] ~ ,

Sonnet XXVI
13   thou] then (Crow)

Sonnet XXVIII
8   age] aye (Arber)

Sonnet XXX
XXX] XXI

Sonnet XXXI
14   doe] ~ doe

Sonnet XXXVI
1   of] by (Arber)

Sonnet XXXVII
XXXVII] XXXVIII

Sonnet XXXIX
8   life] live

Sonnet XLI
3   fayle] fall (Crow)

Sonnet XLII
11   thy] my (Crow)

Sonnet XLIII
5   gold,] ~ .

Sonnet XLIV
2   unkind,] ~ .

Sonnet XLVI
4   wound,] ~ .

Sonnet XLVII
3   dunne] dumb (Arber)

Sonnet XLVIII
14   thee] be (Arber)

Sonnet XLIX
3   Then] The (Arber)
6   strive,] ~ .

Sonnet L
6   fame,] ~ .

Sonnet LII
2   shine] shrine (Arber)
14   shew] tell (Arber, Crow)

An Ode
6   hate,] ~ .
35   False] (~)

42 desave,] ~ .
50 ment.] ~ ,
54 end.] ~ ,

Doris and Galatea

8 tell,] ~ .
13 esteeme,] ~ .
32 [marg. note] With one eye.] *om.*
    (Grosart 1876, Crow)
82 to] and (Arber, Crow)

A Lovers Maze

28 Short] Meet (Arber)
28 they] the
28 care.] ~ ,
51 heartlesse] artless (Grosart 1876, Crow)
97 suspect] respect (Crow)

An Elegie

6 she...two] ~ ,... ~ ,
23 A'] A

The Rising to the Crowne of Richard the Third

7 Princes mate] Princesse mate [Arber
    suggests either "Princess made" or
    "Prince's mate." The rhyme re-
    quired is "mate," and the sense
    requires "Prince's."]
55 before,] ~ .
63 no] not (Arber)
70 For] From (Arber)

77 and] or (Arber)
80 up on] on a [Arber]
99 minde,] ~ .
106 beast] sheep (Arber)
130 That] The (Arber)
141 seene,] ~ .
263 despyse,] ~ .

The Russe Commonwealth

Preface

1–25   Most gratious soveraign, beeing employed in your Highnes service in the Countrey of *Russia*, I did what I could to learn the state of that common wealth, and their manner of Government. Whearof having gott soom good and true intelligence, I have reduced the same into order, and presumed to offer it to your Highnes, if it please yow to bee troubled with the sight of it. Their form of Government, as it is heavie to the subiect thear (beeing a most strict and extream tirannie withowt the knowleadge of God, withowt written Law, withowt common iustice) so it may give vs occasion to give thancks vnto God for your Highnes most Princelike and gratious Government: as allso to your Maiestie cawse of reioycing, in that yow are a Prince of subiects not of slaves, that are tied to their obedience with love, not with fear. The Lord allmightie

bless your Highnes with all his good blessinges.

Your Maiesties most humble subiect, and servant.

G. Fletcher. (A)

om. (B, C, E)

Chapter I

3   nor] or (A, B)
5–17   The... *Russia*.] *om.* (A–C)
19   parts... *Sarmatia*] partes, the *White Sarmatia* and the *Black*. The *White* (A, B)
20–21   *Liefland*: as] ~ and (B)
22   &c: whereof] ~ : Whereof (A)
25   *Mosko, Rezan*] Rezan Mosko (A)
25–34   Some... countries.] *om.* (A–C)
34–38   It... *Polonia*.] [Follows l. 62 in A.]
38   lieth] lie (D, E)
38   *Liuonia*] *om.* (A–C)
40   Shires,] ~ . (D)
42–43   *Nisnouogrod*... countrey)] *Nouogrod, Velica*, or *Nouogrod* of the lowe Countrye, *Plesko, Smolensko, Nisnouogrod*, (A)
45   shires perteyning] Provinces or Shires apperteyning (A–C)

488

47–49 The...Twerra] Whereto are added
Twerra (A–C)
49 follow:] ~ (D)
51 the...they] though the people (A, B)
52 yet] ~ they (A, B)
52 of *Russia*] *om.* (A, B)
54 kingdomes] kingdome (B)
55 in] within (A)
56 and...with] or more, within the (A)
57 gone,] ~ , his Townes and Countrey
(A); ~ , theise Townes and Countrey (B, C)
58 and] or (A–C)
59 they call] in the Russ tongue are called
(A–C)
66 verst, or miles.] verse or Myles, as may
appeare by the Iournall sett downe
in the end of this booke. (A); miles
or verse as may appeare by the Iournall sett downe in the end of this
booke. (B); miles or verst. (C)
68 welnie] from (A); *om.* (B, C)
77 mile.] ~ . The countrye hath many
desertes and wast growndes within
yt especiallye beetwixt *Perme* and
Siberia and on the north syde betwixt *Cargapolia* and *Cola.* (A–C)
[The passage "So...partes," Ch. 2,
ll. 7–14, follows this sentence. See
that passage in Ch. 2 for variants.]

Chapter 2

1 sleight] ~ and (A)
6 in] ~ the (A–C)
7–14 So...partes.] [This passage follows l. 77 in Ch. 1 (A–C).]
7 riuer] ~ of (A–C)
9 riuer] *om.* (A–C)
10 the Emperour] he (A, B)
14 those partes] the Countrye (A, B)
15 almost 1700.] about 700. (A, B); almost 700. (C)
15 towardes] ~ the (A, B)
17 1700. verst] 700. verse (A–C)
19 woods] wood (A)
20 is] *om.* (A, B)
21 towards] toward (A)

22 southwest] southwardes (A)
23 fruitful and pleasant] goodly fruitfull
and plentifull (A); fruitfull goodly
and pleasant (B)
24 very] *om.* (A)
24 by reason] by the season (A); by the
reason (B, C)
25 yeare: so] ~ . Soe (A, B)
27 whole] *om.* (A)
30 yarde or] ~ and (A, B)
30–31 they...this] they bee, this (A); it
bee, and this (B); they bee, and
this (C)
31 fiue] six (A)
32 till] *om.* (A, B)
33 melte. So] ~ so (B, C)
37 In...if] If (A–C)
38 or pot] or a pot (A)
38 pot...mettall] pott, or any other
mettall in your hand (A, B)
41 When] In the extremitye of winter,
if (A–C)
41 warme...colde] warme into a cold
roome (A, B)
45–46 many...streates,] *om.* (A–C)
47 sitting...stiffe] dead and stiffe sit-
tinge (A–C)
47 lose their] ~ the (A, B)
49–53 Many...liues.] *om.* (A–C)
49 the...extreame] (~ ... ~) (D)
54 which] that (A–C)
56 the] a (A, B)
61 there,] *om.* (A–C)
74 lakes. Wherein] ~ , whearin (A, B)
75 for] *om.* (A, B)
76 and more] *om.* (A–C)
78–79 sea...are] sea, bysydes their lakes
which are (A, B)
80 proportionate] proporcionable (A)
82 200.] Twentye (A)
84–85 broad...runneth] broad and runneth (A, B); broad, and so runneth on (C)
85–86 of length] *om.* (A–C)
87 is] *om.* (B, C)
89–90 (the...*Asia*)] *om.* (A, B)
91 *Tartar*] *om.* (A–C)

489

93   citie] Citty of (A)
95   their] the (A)
96   ouerthwart. Which] ~ , which (A)
99   thence] soe (A, B)
102   *Nicholas,* and] ~ . It (A–C)
103   bankes] bank (A, B)
105   *Riga*] Liga (A)
106   the...at] the same Bay of Saint
         Nicholas at (A); the same Bay at (B)
107   below...towne] below (A); below
         the River (B); below the Citie (C)
109   *Yama.* So] ~ , so (A, B)
119   of very] of a very (A, B)
121–22   55....minutes] 44. degrees (A);
         55 degrees (B)
123   63....minutes] 72. degrees 35. min-
         utes (A)

Chapter 3

4   rasps,] *Raspes* and (A, B)
4–5   and...bearies in] *om.* (A, B)
8   quantitie, so] ~ . So (C)
9   the] a (A–C)
11   is sowed] they sowe (A, B)
12   time, and] time, (A)
15   sometimes] sometyme (A)
16   tree] *om.* (A, B)
17   13.] xv. (A)
17–18   *alteens...Chetfird*] Alteens a Chet-
         fird (A, B)
27   Their...furres] The Cheife (A); The
         chief furrs (B, C)
27   *Sables,*] *om.* (A)
29   *naturally*] *om.* (A)
30   *Foxe....the*] fox bysydes the furr of
         white *Sea Wolves, White Beares,*
         White Hares &c. Of theise kyndes
         of Furres their store is soe great
         that bysydes the [their (B)] (A, B)
31   clad all] all clad (A)
32   out of] *om.* (B)
35   haue] *om.* (B)
36   countrie] countries (A, B)
37   places] partes (A)
39–40   skin. The] ~ , the (A–C)
40   also] *om.* (A, B)

40   *Perm.* The] ~ , the (A, B)
42   ar] *om.* (A, B)
44   common] *om.* (B)
45   kindes] ~ repeated before (A, B)
46   shipped] carried (A, B)
50–53   whereof...countrie.] wherof ther
         is carried out of the country
         some store besydes an exced-
         inge great quantitye which
         they spend on their ordinarye
         drink which is meade of all
         sortes and their other vses.
         (A, B); whereof...which they
         spend...countrie. (C)
54   *Tartar*] *Tartars* (A–C)
56   great] ~ quantitie or (B, C)
58   also] ~ because they spende not
         much them selues partly (A)
59   fastes: and] fastes, (A, B); fastes.
         And (C)
63   about] *om.* (A–C)
64   parts...territories] Provinces (A, B)
65   *Nouogrod...Vologda,*] *Nouogrod, Vo-*
         logda, (A); *Nouogrod,* and *Vologda*
         with (B)
67–69   Their Losh...There] The Losh
         hide very fair and large, the Ox
         hide but small. Their [small,
         their (B)] (A, B)
70   yeares...Now] yere about one hun-
         dred thowsand. Now (A); yeares,
         a 100 thowsand, now (B); yeares...
         hides, now (C)
70–71   thereabouts...goates]   ther-
         aboutes, besydes Goat (A, C);
         thearabouts. (B)
74   within...*Cazan.*] about *Casan.* (A);
         about *Cazan,* bysides Goates
         skinnes, whearof great numbers
         ar shipped out of the Countrye.
         (B)
76   fish. Where] ~ whear (A)
81   tide] *om.* (A, B)
82   spring,] springe tyme, (A, B)
84   ouer] vppon (A, B)
85   There] They (A, B)
86   which] and (A, B)

87 consort.] ~ . Beinge thus divided they seeke vp and downe for the haunt of the seales [of seales (B)] vppon the Ise. (A, B)

89 nonce. Which] ~ , which (A–C)

90 by] *om.* (A, B)

95 or] ~ the (A, B)

99 plumpe,] ~ so (C)

100 to] *om.* (A–C)

103 sharing] ~ for (A–C)

104–5 from...lard] from them, the body, skyn, and lard (A); from them...lard (B)

105 withall] both together (A, B)

106 behind] ~ them (A, B)

107 an] a (A, B)

108 there about] theraboutes (A–C)

108 taking the] ~ that (A)

110–11 is...vsed] is vsed (A); is vsed and sold (B, C)

114 fish called] *om.* (A, B)

115 *Sterledey.* Wherof] ~ , wherof (A–C)

115 part] *om.* (A, B)

116 *Spaine,*] ~ , and (A)

118 hath] have (A–C)

118 shipped] laden (A, B)

119 of *Narue*] of the *Narve* (A, B)

119–20 of...Now] of 100 shippes yerely small and great, now (A); of 100...Now (B, C)

121 other] ~ Russe (A)

123 now is] is now (A, B)

124–25 stopping...ouerland] former passage (A, B)

127 mainteining...gathering] gatheringe and maynteyninge (A, B)

128 sales...also] sales, partly alsoe (A, B); sales. Partly for (C)

132 sure] *om.* (A, B)

133 for...it] which also (C)

135 but...liues] but of...lyues alsoe (A–C)

136 about] ~ it (A)

138 besides] beside (A)

150 countrie] province (A, B)

154–55 *Persians*...fetch] *Persians, Bougharians,* and other Countries, that fetch (A, B); *Persians*...fetcht (D, E)

156 for] *om.* (A–C)

159–60 are...length] ar of length almost two foot (A); of almost 2. foot leanghte (B)

162 a] ~ kynd of (A)

162–63 *Slude.* This] ~ , which (A–C)

164 for...it] for. This they vse (A, B); for. They vse this (C)

165 inwards and] in or (A); in and (B, C)

166 and for] ~ in (A–C)

166 better] ~ for vse (A)

169 riuer] *om.* (A, B)

171 of...made] is made of yt (A–C)

176 Gurnstale,] *Gurnistall* or Armins (A, B); Gurnestall or Armin, (C)

179 then...any] then haue (A); then anie (B)

181 for] *om.* (A)

182 withall, and] ~ . And (C)

187 horses] horse (A, B)

187 harde. They] ~ , they (D, E)

188 them] *om.* (A)

189 are] *om.* (A, B)

190 diuers...kindes] *om.* (A, B)

190 First,] first (A–C)

191 Hawkes,] ~ and of divers kyndes, as (A, B)

194 foules their] fowle the (A)

199 of] in (A, B)

201 sorts] sort (A)

201 Pikes] *Pike* (A–C)

203 as the] as (A)

203 long, the] ~ . The (A)

205 to the] a (A); to a (B)

206 *Volgha*] River *Volgha* (A)

206 catched] caught (E)

208 kinds] *om.* (A, B)

208 very] *om.* (A)

210 breed] bredeth (A)

211 *Riba bela*] *Beæla Riba* (A, B)

212 salmon] *om.* (A, B)

213 northward, as] Northwardes as (A); Northward, and (B)

214 neere] of (A, B)

215–16 fish...Sea-hearing.] Fishe of the

Fashion and somewhat also of
the tast of a Herringe which
they call the *Selde* [*om.* (B) (a
space for this word left blank)]
or Freshe water Heringe. (A, B)

218   *Cazan*:] ~ &c. (A)
218–19   euery yeere] yeerly (A, B)
220   time] *om.* (A, B)

Chapter 4

[A–C omit Ch. 4, except that ll. 81–94
  follow l. 142 in Ch. 28.]
81   are] ~ all (A–C)
84   or] and (B)
84–85   together. Betwixt] ~ , betwixt (B)
85–86   (whereof…woods)] *om.* (A, B);
      (whearof…gather great…
      woods) (C)
86–88   Euery…manner.] *om.* (A–C)
89   that] other (A, B); the other (C)
89–90   and…more] or brick, that is more
      colld and (A, B); and brick, as
      beeing collder and more (C)
90   their] are the (A); are these (B)
91   that] which (A)
91   wood. Whereof] ~ , whearin (A, B);
      ~ . Whearin (C)
92   God] god may bee noted, that (A–C)
92   that] *om.* (A)
93   rubbels or] ~ and (A, B)
94–98   The…vp.] *om.* (A, B); The incon-
      venience is the aptnes for beeing
      fired which happeneth very
      often. Their chief cities ar Mos-
      ko, Nouograde, Rostove, Volo-
      demer, Plesko, Smolensko, Ya-
      ruslave, Perislave, Vologda, Vs-
      tiug, Colnigroe, Cazan, Astra-
      can. (C)

Chapter 5

[A–C omit Ch. 5.]
25   *Hunnes*, that] ~ . That (D)

Chapter 6

[A–C omit Ch. 6.]
44   *and the*] *and* (E)
52   *Volodemer*,] ~ (D)

Chapter 7

4   to doo] *om.* (B)
5   and] or (A–C)
5   plaine] meare (A, B)
6   Prince,] *Prince* without all regard of
      Nobilitye or Commons (A)
7   by] in (A, B)
13   vnmeasured] vnreasonable (A); vn-
      measurable (B)
23   coffers] Treasury (A); accounts (B)
25   and] ~ other (A)
30   doo] *om.* (A, B)
32   and the] and (A)
35   summoned. Where] ~ , whear (A–C)
36   none] no (B)
37   hand] *om.* (A–C)
38   make] ~ some (A, B)
38   superstitions] superstition (A–C)
39   euen…themselues,] *om.* (A, B)
40   Bishops and] Bishops, (B)
44   seas] *om.* (A–C)
45   false] ~ perswasions of (A); ~ per-
      swasion of (B, C)
49   that countrie] the Realm (A–C)
50   himself. Insomuch] ~ insomuche
      (A, B)
51   for…part] *om.* (A)
52   Notwithstanding,] ~ , that (B)
54   his…the] *om.* (A, B)
57   death. Wherein] ~ wherein (A, B)
59   all] ~ is (B)
60   the iudges] them (A)
61   vpon] in (A)
62   wholly] ~ , (D)
63–68   To…him.] *om.* (A)
67   his head] their heads, (B)
67   off. Which] ~ , which (C)
69   Fourthly, for] 4. As for (A–C)
71   the…also] the Emperour, wherein
      also (A, C); *om.* (B)
72   of] ~ a (B)
73   Realme] State (A, B)
73–74   (the…husband)] *om.* (A–C)
77   any…all] mention (A–C)
80   ouer them,] *om.* (A–C)
80   all] anye (A)

82 wrung cleane] taken quite (A, B); wrung (C)

83 this Emperour] the Emperour that now is (C)

Chapter 8

1 of] for (A)

1 consultation] consultacions (A)

1 for...of] concerning matter of (A); concerning the (B); for matters of (C)

2 *Assembly.*] *Assemblie* or Parliament. (A)

3–4 are...The] are these First the (A); are 1. The (B)

5 being...Councel] *om.* (A, B)

5–6 Certain...&c.] Of the Cleargie (A, B); Of the Cleargie men (C)

9 bond] *om.* (A–C)

9–10 obey...concluded.] knowe nothing of publique matters and to have no parte in makinge but in obeyinge of lawes. (A); knowe nothing of publique matters, but to be vsed at pleasure. (B); obey...doon. (C)

11 The] This (A)

13 meete...said)] meet which for the most parte are (A, B)

14 calleth] summoneth (A, B)

15 Bishops] Bishop (A)

16 them. When] ~ when (A, B)

18 begin. Which] ~ , which (A, B)

21 *Stollie.* And] *Stolloy* or Parliament howse, and (A, B); *Stollye* or Parliament house. And (C)

28 him] the Emperour (A, B)

31 Councel,] Counsell (as was sayed beefore) (A–C)

40 to subiects] *om.* (A, B)

41 his] the (A)

43 poyntes] poynte (A–C)

43 Secretarie. Whereto] ~ , whearto (A)

45 before] *om.* (A, B)

47 propounded. Commonly] ~ , commonly (A–C)

47 it is] *om.* (A, B)

48 *touching*] *in* (A–C)

49 *publike*] *om.* (A–C)

50 *they are*] *are they* (A–C)

50–51 *attend...onlie*] *attend onelie vpon...God* (A)

51 *religion. And*] ~ *and* (A)

53 *dueties...vocations*] *duetie and vocation* (A, B)

53 *doe*] *dothe* (A, B)

56 matter] thing (A, B)

57 Maiestie] Highnes (A, B)

62 *proposed*] *propounded* (A, C)

64 *ar*] *as* (D)

65 *too*] *om.* (A–C)

65–66 *approuing or*] *proouinge and* (A)

67 *freely. And*] ~ , *and* (A)

67–68 *consents, that*] *consents* (A)

73 homeward] *om.* (A, B); home (C)

74–75 or Secretaries] *om.* (A–C)

75 into] in (B)

75 abroad] downe (A, B)

76 of...Realme,] *om.* (A, B)

78 of] or (A)

78 fully] *om.* (A)

79 dinner. And] ~ and (A–C)

Chapter 9

3 sortes. Whereof] ~ whearof (B)

5 priuiledged] absolute (A, B)

5–6 sometime...authoritie] an absolute and severall iurisdiccion (A, B)

6 within] with (A)

7 States or Nobles] Nobles or States (A)

7 But afterwards] Suche as (A, B)

8 they] first (A, B); *om.* (C)

10 ouermatching] ~ of (A–C)

10 neighbours. Onely] ~ , only (B)

12 But...Emperour] *om.* (A)

17 bondslaues. For] ~ , for (A–C)

17 terme and] *om.* (A–C)

23 against...Nobility] *om.* (A, B)

26 dignities. Wherein] ~ , whearein (A, B)

27 or equall] *om.* (A, B)

27 to those] aboue those (A, B)

28 Where] Whearein (A, B)

29 contentions] accusacions (A, B)

29–30 other...of] other, for (A, B); other...for (C)
31 his...state.] himselfe and suche like. (A, B); his person, state &c: (C)
33 at last] *om.* (A, B)
33 rights] right (A–C)
39 called] ~ the (A, B)
39 The] *The* (D)
41 meant...as] *om.* (A, B)
42 him. Wherein] ~ , whearein (A)
47 of] *om.* (A, B)
50 was] wear (A)
52 *Oppressini.*] ~ which he accounted his own parte. (A)
53 or] and (A)
56 practise, viz.] practize (A)
57 misliked: whereof] ~ . Whearof (C)
63 *Tartar.* What] ~ , what (A, B)
69 that] the (A–C)
70 since] ~ that tyme (A)
71 againe] owte (A, B)
75 are] ~ to bee (A–C)
78 not being] beeing not (A)
83 Their] The (A–C)
84 First, many] 1. Many (B, C)
87 else] *om.* (A)
94 Nobilitie] ~ as *Knez Methysthosky* (A, B)
95–96 begunne...still] are (A, B)
102 and...purpose,] *om.* (A–C)
104 The...with] *om.* (A)
104–6 *Gollauni...Andrieu*] *Gollavin* whom they put into a dungeon and thear killed him. *Knez...Gollo-chen. Andrew* (A, B); *Gollavini ...dungeon and thear killed him) ...Andriew* (C)
107 a] *om.* (A, B)
107 wisedome.] ~ &c. (A, B)
107 So] Among other (A, B)
107–8 was...him)] *om.* (A, B); they kill-ed...him) (C)
110 or sixe] *om.* (A–C)
111 *Batore*] *om.* (A, B)
111 100000] 500000 (A)
112–13 and...countrey,] *om.* (A, B)
114 mothers] mother (A, B)

115 poyson...practise.] a violent death by the *Godonoes* meanes. [meanes &c. (B)] (A, B); poison by the *Godonoes* means. (C)
117 is of] *om.* (A, B)
117–18 at this time] *om.* (A, B)
118–19 (mentioned before)] *om.* (A–C)
120 now...nunnery.] *om.* (A, B); now thrust into a Nunnerie. (C)
122 one...house] on left of that howse (A, B); on of this howse left (C)
122 and he] *om.* (A, B)
133 besides] byside (A, B)
134 these...Nobles] these of the chiefest Nobilitie (A, B)
137 a...marks] 2000 Rubbels (A)
137 besides] byside a yearlie (A, B)
139 to] *om.* (A, B)
139 a yeere] *om.* (A, B)
142 rest,] ~ of the Nobilitie (A, B)
143 direction,] ~ but (C)
143 commaund and] *om.* (A–C)
143 *Russia.*] ~ himself, [*om.* (C)] and for riches and revenue farr passing all the rest. (A–C)
145 93700] a hundred fortie and seaven thowsand (A)
147 a yeere] *om.* (A, B)
148 1200] 12000 (D, E)
148 or markes] *om.* (A, B)
150 Landes and Townes] Townes and Landes (A–C)
150 *Mosko.* Besides] ~ bysides (A, B)
154 office] ~ of the horse (C)
154–55 there is] *om.* (A, B)
155 peculiar] ~ and (A, B)
159 without] owt of (A, B)
159 1500] 15000 (A)
163 is] ~ of the Nobilitie (A, B)
163 *Glinskoy*] ~ , which is one of the Nobilitie (C)
164 yeerely. Which] ~ which (B)
165 sister,] ~ and augmenteth well *Boris* his cofers (A–C)
166 The] And so the (A–C)
167 him] himself (A–C)
167 committed] permitted (A, B)

171–72　of...vz.] *om.* (A, B)
172　nor] and (E)
174　*wich*] *vich* (D)
174　vnto] vnder (E)
185　them. So] ~ , so (A, B)
186　are] ~ all (A–C)
188　themselues withall] them (A, B)
189　them] ~ to be verie (A, B)
190　fiue or] *om.* (A–C)
191–92　vpon their] ~ the (A–C)
194　degree] ~ or order (A–C)
194　their] ~ Gentlemen which they call (A, B)
202–3　this...whom] all their Countrey people (A, B); this kynd ar their Countrey people whome (C)
205　forces, and] *om.* (A, B)
206　condition] service (A–C)

Chapter 10

2　or *Tetrarchies*] that is *Tetrarchies* or *Fourthparts* (A, B)
6　the] ~ Chauncellour or (A, B)
7　standing...or] *om.* (A–C)
13　it] *om.* (A–C)
13　an hundred] 100. (A–C)
19　a yeare] *om.* (A)
20　fourth] 4th and last (A, B)
27　or *Vochin*] *om.* (A)
31–32　*Vagha*...like.] *Vaga* and other to Lord *Borise Fedorowich Godonoe.* (A); *Vaga*, and other belonging to Lord *Borise Federowich Godonoe.* (B); *Vagha*...to Lord... like. (C)
39　*Chetfirds*, and] ~ or (A)
39–40　Emperours] *om.* (A–C)
41–42　giuen...Counsell,] *om.* (A, B)
42　done] ~ by them (A, B)
44　particular] ~ shire or (C)
45　these] those (A, B)
52　precinct. To] ~ , to (A, B)
53　as] ~ the (A)
56　all] ~ Civill (A)
58　appeale, and] *om.* (A–C)
60–61　of...Counsell,] *om.* (A, B)
65　receiued] ~ a (A, B)

66　they are] *om.* (A, B)
67　the officer...the] that Office of (A, B)
68–69　annexed...Counsell.] annexed. (A, B)
74　of proclamation] of a proclamacion (A, B)
76　place] places (A)
77　these] this (A, B)
80　special] *om.* (A, B)
84　or...where] or anie whear ells (A–C)
85　an...markes] a hundeth Rubbels or markes (A, B); 100. rubbells or marks (C)
86　thirtie. Which] ~ , which (A–C)
91–92　when...account:] *om.* (A–C)
92　at...seruice,] *om.* (A–C)
93–94　iniustice...people] oppression and iniustice (A, B)
94　There...few] Fiew (A, B)
96　they] *om.* (A, B)
98–99　for both...themselues.] both to pay the other, and to reserve for them selves. (A, B); for... reserve for them selves soom part of the spoil. (C)
100　They] These (A–C)
101　saue...the] save that in (A, C); save in (B)
103　towne. Wherof] ~ , whearof (A, B)
107　of...that] *om.* (A, B)
110–12　borders...Counsell.] borders. (A, B)
114　most: some] ~ . Some (A–C)
115　importance] moment (A–C)
116　clients] ~ and favourers (A–C)
118　Counsell] ~ that reside thear all the year long (A–C)
120　Counsell...long.] Counsell. (A–C)
121　Onely...matters] For their Town matters onelie (A–C)
122　streates] Town (A–C)
125　the] *om.* (B)
126　matter] matters (A, B)
127　him examined vpon] him publiquelie examined by [vpon (C)] (A–C)
128–33　Besides...dispach.] Bysides these, thear is a *Starust* or Alderman

for the ordering of everie severall Companie, bysides *Sotskoies* or Coomstables that have certain *Decetskoyes* or Decurions vnder them. These have the oversight of tenn howshowlds a peece. (A, B); Besides... vnder them...is the sooner... dispach. (C)

139 of...townes,] *om.* (A, B)
143 conteyning] ordering (A, B)
147 vnder] vnto (A, B)
154 make] ~ an (A, B)
155 men...Nobilitie,] *om.* (A–C)
156 Emperour...fauour,] Emperour, (A–C)
157 onely] still (A–C)
157 owne] *om.* (A, B)
160 haue] receive (A–C)
165 (as...sheepe)] *om.* (A, B)
165–66 to...them] *om.* (A–C)
166 Besides the] ~ their (A, B)
167 beare,] have (A, B)
167 small] severall (A, B)
168 besides] byside (A–C)
169–70 nor to] nor (A, B)
170 happily...intended] they should intend (A, B)
172 state and] *om.* (A, B)
175 (besides...means)] by often exactions and (A, B)
177 any...all] all shew (A–C)
180 80000] 8000 (D, E)
183–85 withal...state.] that licence which is permitted vnto them of purpose to make them have a liking of the present State, by wronging and spoiling of the Commons at their pleasure. (A, B); that lycence of...state. (C)
186 and] ~ the (A–C)
186 a...feared] not to bee thought of (A, B); is not to bee feared (C)
187 of] *om.* (A, B)
187 and] ~ of so (A, B)
187 much] the (A–C)

188 desperate...home,] *om.* (A, B); desperate state at home (C)
189 part] ~ of them (A, B)
190 rid] ease (A–C)

Chapter 11

3 they...state] *om.* (A, B)
4 *Boiarens*] ~ or *Counsellours* (A, B)
5 large] ~ or extraordinary (A, B)
6 and] or (A, B)
9 or...Counsell] or the *Lordes of the Privie Counsell* (A, B)
14 then wisedome] then of wisdom and (A–C)
15 that] ~ verie (A–C)
22 *Vasilowich*] ~ *Sytskoy* (A)
32 of these] *om.* (A, B)
32 Lord] Lordes (A, B)
35 vpon] *om.* (A–C)
38 counsel...themselues.] counsail. (A,B)
39 state] ~ and ar (A, B)
39–40 them...sittings] *om* (A–C)
44 seuerall] ~ Office (A–C)
45 the...them] them to the Counsell (A–C)
48 his] their (A, B)
51 determine] ~ vpon (A, B)
51 cause] ~ it self (A, B)
51 can] doth (A, B)
53 Their] The (A)
54 fridayes. Their] ~ , their (A, B)
54 is] *om.* (A, B)
56 consultation] their meeting (A, B)
58 *Roserad*] *Roseradney Dyake* (A–C)
58–59 realme...appointed.] Realm to call them togither. (A); Realm. (B); Realm, to call them togither at the appointment, of the Emperour. (C)

Chapter 12

2 Crowne] *Emperour* (A, B)
5 one] ~ Office (A–C)
6 partes...before.] parts. (A, B)
10 *Vochin.*]~ or *Crownland*.["*Crownland*" is canceled] (A); ~ or *Crownland*. (B)

14 *Chara, Sametska,*] *Charasanetska,*
   (A, B)

15 the] *om.* (A–C)

15 pay some] some pay (A–C)

16 rent] *om.* (A–C)

16 *Obrokey*] Obroke or rent duties (A–C)

21 an] *om.* (A–C)

21 of ground] *om.* (A, C)

25–26 serued...honour,] *om.* (C)

35 this] ~ (as is saied) (A–C)

36–37 specially...*Godonoe,*] ~ *(Borris
   ...Godonoe)*

37 owne] ~ treasure (A–C)

37 runneth] runs (E)

38 treasurie] *om.* (A–C); treasure (D, E)

40 very] *om.* (C)

40 attending] both (A–C)

40 purueying] *om.* (A–C)

42–44 *Chetfirds*...which] *Chetfirds* is divided into fower severall parts,
   which have fower head Officers
   (as was sayed beefore) which
   (A, B); *Chetfird,*...parts (as...
   sayde) have...which (C)

47 *Tagla*] ~ and *podat* (C)

51 or little] more or (C)

53 whole] *om.* (A–C)

54 Offices] Office (A, B)

67 Realme. Besides] ~ , bysides (A, B)

69 moste] greatest (A, B)

70 doe] *om.* (A–C)

70 greatest] most (A, B)

70 custome] customes (E)

74–76 it...If] less they may not pay then
   is sett them down and rated
   preciselie for the Coustoom of
   the year, though they receave
   not so much, if (A, B)

79 8000. rubbels] 8000. (D, E)

84 sometimes...sometimes] soomtime
   more soomtime (A, B)

88 this] that (A, B)

88 of...*Prechod,*] *om.* (A, B)

89 rubbels. The] ~ , the (A, B); marks.
   The (C)

90 The] the (A–C)

91 *Prechod,*] ~ for coustoom only (A)

92 bookes of] ~ for (A)

93 maketh] marketts (A–C)

94 out...trade] of the great Townes
   (A, B)

96–97 Emperour. Which] ~ , which
   (A, B)

103 all] *om.* (A, B)

103 matters] ~ of contract (A, B)

107 these] those (A–C)

107 *Alteens*] alteenes vpon an head (A, B)

107 fiue] iiij (A, B)

109 office] Office of *Pochatney* (A, B)

114 goeth] going (A, B)

114 other] ~ part (B)

116–17 All...income.] *om.* (A, B)

119 called] of the (C)

120 the souldiers] *Boiaren* Souldiours
   (A–C)

121 pay. Which] ~ , which (A, B)

123 the...so] so much so (A, B)

125 the...yeere] for most yeares (A, B)

126 In...sort] The like (A–C)

126 in...surplus] into the *Bulsha Prechod*
   (A–C)

127 offices] Office (A–C)

128 men] *om.* (A–C)

129 pay] *om.* (A, D)

131 *Prechase*...*Nemshoy*] *om.* (A)

133 So] and (A, B)

133 *Pusharskoy*] *Busharskoy* (A, B)

134 *munition*] munition (D, E)

141 amounteth] ~ commonly (A)

141 or] and (B)

142 thereabouts] more (A, B)

145 that lyeth] *om.* (A, B)

149 *Godonoe*] *om.* (A, B)

152 allowed...the] vnder him that serve
   in that (A, B)

157–58 [3rd col.] rubbles cleere,] *Rubbells* (A, B); rubbells or marks
   clear (C)

157 [2nd col.] 230000.] 23000. (D)

166 into] to (D, E)

170 *Turkish,*] ~ (D)

181 officers...&c.] Officers, and Monasteries (A, B)

182 the] *om.* (A, B)

182–83 of will...is,] after a violent and excessive sort, yet after the manner of the *Scythian* pollicie vnder soom (A, B); of...the *Scythian*...is, (C)

185 pollicies] rules of pollicie (A, B)

186 and to] and (A, B)

186 their treasurie] their own treasurie (A, B)

187 was] ~ much (A, B)

188 *were*] ~ *much* (A, B)

189 *a*] *everie* (A, B)

189–90 *at...least:*] *om.* (A, B)

HL iv I] *om.* (D, E)

191 To...no] Not to prevent any (A–C)

192 the] their (A, B)

193 but to] ~ so (A, B)

196 (as...Bee)] *om.* (A–C)

197 commons] ~ beefore (A, B)

201 being chaunged] and for that purpose (it seemeth) they chaunge them (A, B); and for that pourpose partly they ar chaunged (C)

201–2 a...where] everie year, that (A, B)

203 they] *om.* (A, B)

204 inouation. For] ~ , that (A, B)

204–5 vpon...commons,] *om.* (A–C)

205–6 Emperours flies] Emperour his flies (A, B)

206 an] all (D, E)

206 sore. To] ~ , to (A, B)

208 To make] To make soom (A, B); Soomtime to make (C)

208 people] ~ and are spoiled again by the Emperour him self (A, B)

208–9 sometimes...publike] soomtime a publique (A, B); soom publique and notable (C)

210 the Emperour] hee (A–C)

211 transferre] leave (A, B)

211 to...ill] vpon his (A, B)

213 a...Prouinces) one *Ivan Michaelo-wich Visekovatl* (A); one that was a *Diack* or Secretarie on of his provinces (B)

213 besides] beside (A, B)

214 drest] ~ filled (A, B)

215 in] ~ the (A, B)

217–18 asked hee] hee asked (A, B)

220 middes] midst (E)

220 aboue his] ~ the (A, B)

230 stamped some] soom hee stamped (A–C)

231 Whereupon...taxation.] *om.* (A–C)

233 for their] for (A–C)

233 and] ~ soom (A–C)

237 This] And this (A, B)

238 the] their (A, B)

239 is done] they doe though (A, B)

241 once. Which] ~ , which (A–C)

242 were...of] doubted much (A–C)

243 Emperour] ~ to have a larger fliece, (A, B)

243 very] *om.* (A–C)

244–45 in...extremities] *om.* (A, B)

247 from...doings] quite from the trou-bles of his Kingdoom, (A, B); quite from the troubles of the govern-ment, (C)

250 This] That being (A, B)

252 resumed...scepter,] retourned into his seat and resumed his Kingdoom, (A, B)

254 and] ~ to (A, B)

254–55 reseruing...their] taking owt such lands, (A, B); reserving such Lands (C)

257 besides...landes] byside the Land (A, B)

258 money. From] ~ , from (A–C)

261 woorse] ~ government (A, B)

261 man. Wherein] Emperour. Wearin (A); Emperour whearin (B)

262 of] by (A, B)

263 to] and (A, B)

265 walked by] went (A, B)

268 hony, &c.] honney corn &c. (A–C)

269 smal prices] a small price (A, B)

271 their] his (A, B)

272 them,] ~ (as fiew dare to doe) (A); ~ (as fiew dare doe) (B, C)

274 as] ~ of (A–C)

275 receiued into] reserved in (A); re-served into (B)

281 take...and] *om.* (A–C)
288 &c.] and such like. (A, B)
290 maketh] ~ yearlie (A)
290–91 (as...said)] (as was saied beefore) (A, B); *om.* (C)
291 a] everie (A, B)
295 rent...to] *om.* (A, B)
297 yere. Wherein] ~ , whearin (B)
297 besides] byside (A)
298 faultes] errours (A); disorders (B)
299–300 manie...all] spendeth all manie times (A–C)
300 children. Some] ~ , soom (A–C)
312 their] the (A–C)
319 The inhabitants] They (A–C)
320 there. Whereupon] ~ : whearvpon (B)
321 rubbels...purpose.] rubbels. (A–C)
322 citie] town (A, B)
325 leaping] ~ still (A–C)
328 a] on (A–C)
329–30 Hare...it.] hare. (A–C)
330 Which the] ~ his (A, B)
330 praued] ~ or extorted (A, B)
332 extortion,] ~ for a Prince (A, B)
333 poore] *om.* (A, B)
333 in] so in (A, B); in so (C)
334 those Emperours] that Emperour (A, B)
334 subiection] ~ and slaverie (A, B)
335 poore] *om.* (A–C)
335 *like*] *om.* (C)

Chapter 13

1 The] What the state is and (A, B)
1 people] ~ of the Countrey (A–C)
3 their] the (C)
3 of the] ~ their (B)
4 their] the (A, B)
5 land] Realm (A, B)
5 touching] concerning (A–C)
9 vpon. Which] ~ which (A, B)
10 two] *om.* (A, B)
10 vz:] *om.* (A, B)
10 of the] of (A, B)
11 in...though] there (yet (A, B)
11 from that] ~ the (C)

13 their degrees] everie degree (A, B)
15 by...them] so much as they can (A, B)
17 Nobles...Gentlemen] Nobilitie (A, B)
21 Emperours] Emperour (A, B)
22 themselues] them selves their (A, B)
27 his...souldiers.] the Nobilitie and the cheef Officers. (A, B); his Nobilitie and chief Officers. (C)
29 looke] beehold (A, B)
33 the name] their name (A–C)
33 common indeed] open or common (A, B)
34 against] to (A, B)
37 the Emperour] him (A, B)
42 exactions] exaction (C)
47 that...vacant] (~ ... ~) (D)
47 stand] standeth (A, B)
50 The] This (A–C)
56 where...In so much] for fear of soom forreign invasion near at hand, insomuch (A, B)
59 open] ~ soom of (A, B)
60 and...like] *om.* (A–C)
60 still] *om.* (A–C)
62 set...Whereof] invaded. Whereof (A, C); invaded, whearof (B)
64 Emperour] Emperours (A, B)
64 in the] in (D, E)
71 grow] doe grow (A, B)
71 farre] *om.* (A, B)
75 of late] *om.* (A, B)
76 in common] *om.* (A, B)
78–80 Which...more.] *om.* (A–C)
82 wood...like:] wood &c, (A–C)
85 others] other (A–C)
87–88 (for...trade)] *om.* (A, B)
88 the] *om.* (A, B)
90 content] ~ also (C)
90 purse,] ~ and help (A, B)
91 in *Siberia*] of the *Siberians* (A, B)
93 perforce] *om.* (A–C)
94 in...end] *om.* (A, B)
94 disdained,] ~ at the last (A, B)
97 rubbels...more:] Rubbells soomtime more at a time (A, B)

98 their sonnes] his sonns (B)
98 stocke] fliece (A, B)
103 in...aptnesse] soom aptnes in them (A, B)
109 valure] strength (A, B)
109 innouation] innovations (A, B)
109 also] *om.* (A–C)
110 traueling] ~ abroad (A, B)
111 abroad] *om.* (A, B)
111 *Russe*] Russ to be (A, B)
112 be] ~ abroad (A, B)
113 Countrie. Which] ~ , which (A, B)
114 watched] garded (A, B)
115 any...attempt] the attempt of it (A, B)
120 enforce] force (A, B)
122 Marchants] Marchant (A)
124 hereafter] *om.* (A, B)
125–26 of...owne.] growing within their own Countrey. (A, B)
127 degree] degrees (C)
128 *Mousick*,] ~ (D)
128–29 artificer, &c:] *om.* (A, B)
129 aspire...except] aspire. Except (A, B)
130 read,] ~ (as was saied beefore) (A, B)
131–42 Their...distorted.] *om.* (A–C)
147–48 Common-/wealths] Comonwealth (D)
148 rare or] *om.* (A–C)
149 in] ~ the (A–C)
149 farther] further (A)
150 rewarde...preferment] preferments nor other rewards (A, B); preferments nor reward (C)
151 themselues] their good qualities (A,B)
151–53 estate...qualitie.] estate. (A–C)

Chapter 14

2 sort] kinde (A, B)
2 kinds] sortes (A, B)
3 other...way] other that is the superiour by the way (A, B); other, the inferiour Court to the superiour by way (C)
3 seemeth] seems (E)
7 the...These] their Provinces which (A–C)

8 soke, or] villages and (A, B)
8 hundred] Hundreds (A, B)
14 sayd). From] saied) yet at the Emperours appointment. From (A–C)
16 *Mosko*,] ~ , which is the head and cheef Court (A, B)
17 on] *om.* (D, E)
18 *Chetfird*] *Chetfirds* (B)
19 be either] either bee (A, B)
27 day appointed] next day (A–C)
28 by...meanes] *om.* (A–C)
28–29 good. The] ~ , the (B)
29 and excell] ~ doe excell (A–C)
30 dealing towards] beehaviour over (A–C)
30 prysoners. Commonly] ~ , commonly (B, D, E)
31–32 larger fees. Though] a better bribe, though (A, B)
37 order] fashion (A, B)
38 for] *om.* (A, B)
41 plea, or] ~ and (A–C)
42 good,] ~ (C–E); ~ , either (A, B)
44 Crosse] ~ and kisseth it (A–C)
47 the partie] *om.* (A, B)
47 by...officer] *om.* (A, B)
47–48 the...done:] it is offred vnto him, (A, B)
48 in...while] *om.* (A, B)
49 at...feete,] by the Idoll (A, B)
49–50 deliuered...partie,] receaved by him (A, B); receaved (C)
50 before...Idoll] *om.* (A, B)
53 violate...prophane] prophane or abuse (A, B)
57 whatsoeuer,] whatsoever it bee, (A, B)
58–59 fees...noted.] Coustoomes. (A, B)
65 them,] ~ by Law, (A, B)
65 refuse] refused (A)
68 till...payd] *om.* (A, B)
69 Sergeant:] ~ , till the debt bee paied (A, B)
73 bebasted] basted (A, B)
74 will...or] *om.* (A–C)
76 And...price] And if the partie bee

not contented, or the price (C)
79 as] to (A, B)
79 requireth] *om.* (A, B)
80 as] that (A, B)
80 or] and (A, B)
81 circumstances] circumstance (A, B)
83 bill,] ~ of his hand, (A, B)
87 *vntill*] *to* (A, B)
91 *vz.*] *om.* (A–C)
92 *Subscribed.*] *om.* (A–C)
94 backe] other (A); one (B)
99 examination] examinacions (A, B)
101 (called...*Pudkey*)] *om.* (A, B)
102 flesh,] ~ (which is called the *Pudkey*)
     (A, B)
103 fire...by] fire &c. sometimes
     (A, B)
104–5 nayles...like.] nailes &c. (A, B)
107 it is] is it (E)
110 there...matter] by the Emperours
     Counsell, who onlie give iudge-
     ment in matters (A, B)
111 euidence vpon] *om.* (A, B)
112 sawe nor] *om.* (A, B)
112 who] ~ himself (A–C)
112 still] *om.* (A–C)
113–14 committed...tried.] committed.
     (A–C)
115–17 fact...execution.] fact. (A, B);
     fact which is sent down to the
     Duke and Dyack, by them to
     bee executed. (C)
119 on] in (A, B)
121–23 But...yse.] This Sentence is de-
     livered by the Counsell to the
     Lord of the *Chetfird*, and by him
     sent to the Duke and Diake of
     the Shire, whear the fact was
     committed, to execute the
     partie condemned. (A, B); *om.*
     (C)
129 at] to (A–C)
130 verie] *om.* (A–C)
131 all...them.] the greatest punishment.
     (A, B)
132 owne] *om.* (A, B)
132–33 vnto...for] to him. For (A)

135 Emperour,] Emperours treasurie
     (A, B)
135–36 so...iniustice.] they list to make
     a quarrell more to his purse then
     to him. (A, B); so the quarrell is
     made to his purse rather then to
     himself. (C)
139 forms and] *om.* (A, B)
141 his] the (A, B)
142 officers. Which] Officers that are set
     vnder him, which (A, B)
144 extreame oppression] oppressions
     (A–C)
145 good...strong] good (A, B)

Chapter 15

2–4 by...souldiers,] *om.* (A–C)
4 that] and (A–C)
6 borne] allso (A, B)
6 withal] *om.* (A, B)
7 els...matters.] els. In this kinde of
     mainteining his forces by a con-
     tinuall succession, thear is this in-
     convenience. (A, B)
10 certeine] a certain stipend, with (A–C)
10–13 charges...foot.] charges. (A–C)
14 haue] ~ manie and (A, B)
14–15 the...already,] *om.* (A–C)
16 nothing] little (A–C)
16–17 them...two.] them. (A–C)
18 when] whenas (A–C)
19 in] within (A)
21 *Mousick*] Mousicks (A, B)
22–23 This...succession.] *om.* (A, B)
23–25 The...person,] The Emperour
     hath of them in continuall pay
     (A–C)
29–30 company of] *om.* (A, B)
32 of Pensioners] *om.* (A, B)
33 sixty...yere,] 60. 50. and 40....year,
     but (A, B)
34–35 Pensioners. Their] ~ , their (A, B)
35 salarie] salaries (B)
36 haue...and twentie] have 25. (A, B);
     have but 25. (C)
36 twentie,] 20., and (A, B)
41 to] *om.* (A, B)

42 degrees] degree (A, B)
45 being] *om.* (A, B)
49 among them] *om.* (A–C)
55 *Chrim*] *om.* (A, B)
56 *Tartars*] Tartar (A, B)
61–62 manie...all,] manie (A–C)
62 changed] ~ often (A, B)
62 so...he] when him self (A, B)
63 they] these 110 are of the Emperours
     Counsell and (A); these 110 of the
     Emperours Counsell (B); these 110
     being all of the Emperours Coun-
     sell (C)
63 liuings] ~ allso (A–C)
64 but...very] but of (A, B); of very
     (C)
65 rubbels,] ~ to bee delivered vnto
     them, (A, B)
67 Emperours person,] Emperour as
     (A–C)
68 at large.] Generalls. (A, B)
71 himselfe] *om.* (A, B)
74 haue] hath (C)
74 number] ~ then he hath in ordinarie
     pay (A, B)
75 *Sinaboiarskey*] *Sinaboiarskeys* (C)
76 want] wanteth (A, B)
78 a proportionable] such an (A); a (B)
79 their] his (C)
80 to the] vnto the (A, B)
83 that] thear (A–C)
83 he hath] *om.* (A–C)
85 about] at (A–C)
86 *Stremaney*] ~ , (D)
87 owne] *om.* (A–C)
88 himselfe] hee (A, B)
90 receiue] have (A, B)
90 salarie] pay (A, B)
91 measures] ~ , (D)
92 (whom...*Nimschoy*)] *om.* (A, B)
106–7 so...beeyng] of that qualitie other
     wise, as that hee is not chosen for
     his valure or practise in martiall
     matters, but is (A, B)
110 by] *om.* (A, B)
111 and power] and greatnes of power
     and authoritie (A, B)

114 warres,] warre for the most part
     (A, B)
115 commonly] *om.* (A–C)
117 very] *om.* (A, B)
120 as...*Generall*] in Commission, (A, B)
126 *Voiauod...generall*] Generall and the
     other in Commission with him
     (A, B)
131 third is] 3. the (A)
133–34 supply...require.] supplie for the
     rest. (A, B)
141 *Gullauoy*,] *Gollovey* or (A, B)
142 thousands,] thowsands or (A, B)
142 and 100] *om.* (A, B)
147–48 is...the] *om.* (A–C)
150 running] ~ or mooving (A, B)
151 speake of] note (A–C)

Chapter 16

1 When] ~ any (A–C)
3 Lordes] ~ or Secretaries (A–C)
5 Townes] Town (A, B)
7 at] in (A, B)
10 summons] summon (A, B)
12 as] and are (A, B)
20 but] though (A, B); *om.* (C)
20 numbers] nomber (A, B)
22 sayd before] saied in the Chapter going
     beefore. (A, B)
25–26 the...except] his left side, except
     (A, B); the...excepting (C)
27 their] his (A, B)
28 besides] byside (A–C)
30 horse] horses (C)
32 stones] stone (C)
33 very faire] ~ fine (A–C)
40 flie and] ~ or (A)
48 them] anie (A, B)
49 his turne] *om.* (A, B)
51 vnto] to (A, B)
51 his...tilleth] *om.* (A, B)
51 land] lands (A, B)
53 prepared...beforehand.] a souldier.
     (A, B); prepared to bee a souldier.
     (C)
53 Though] Their ordinarie lodging vpon
     benches at home, (when they are

best interteined) prepareth them
well to camp on the grownd, and
their hard fare at home, to live hardlie in the feild, though (A); Their
ordinarie lodging is vpon benches
at home, when they are best interteined, which prepareth them well
to camp on the grownd, and their
hard fare at home, to live hardlie in
the field, though (B)

55–56   prouision...rest.] provision. (A,
      B); provision of victuall. (C)
59   *Tollockno*...eate] *tollockno* and eat it
      (A, B)
60   or...other] and other (A, B)
62–63   out...trauaile,] toile (A, B)
63   apt] fiet (A, B)
64   lodging...dyet] diett and lodging
      (A, B)
64   excell] exceede (D, E)
65   souldiours] souldiour (A, B)
66   seruice. Which] ~ , which (A, B)
68   him.] ~ , though otherwise hee bee of
      a verie strong and fleshie bodye apt
      to bear owt anie labour. (A, B)
68–70   Partly...doe.] *om.* (A, B); Partly
      ...service hee doth. (C)

Chapter 17

4   their] the (C)
10   besides] byside (A, B)
16   which with] bysides (A, B)
16–18   of...they] and noyse of their
      trumpetts drummes and shaw-
      mes, and (A, B)
24   if] when (A–C)
24   be] is (A–C)
25   *Tartar*] *Tartars* (C)
32   sides] ~ both (A, B)
33   thereabouts] thereabout (E)
34   charge and] ~ or (A–C)
35   weapons...is] weapons, (A, B)
36   piece] peeces (C)
39   horse] horses (E)
43   sometimes] sometime (D, E)
44   which] Which (C–E)
46   so] *om.* (A–C)

51   with him] *om.* (A, B)
55   deale] have to doe (A, B)
57   prouisions.] provision both for the
      feild and for battry. (A, B)
60   very faire,] *om.* (A, B)
63   abroad] *om.* (A, B)
63   field. Which] ~ , which (A, B)
64   noted] seen (A, B)
65   hee] they (A, B)
66   men] souldiers (A, B)
68   best] *om.* (A, B)
68   a set] the pitched (A, B)
69   euer...worse] the woorse ever (A, B)
69   and] ~ the (A, B)
72   horsebacke. Which] ~ , which (A, B)

Chapter 18

1   Emperours] Emperour (C)
2–8   Their...1480.] *om.* (A–C)
8–26   The...ground.] But the princi-
      pall part of all his conquests
      was that which hee had in *Litu-*
      ania and *Livonia* whear hee had
      manie goodlie Townes to the
      number of 36 or thearabowts
      with a large territorie belonging
      to everie on. Which he gott
      rather by the advantage of civill
      dissentions and secreat treasons
      then among them selves, then
      by anie force of armes. And so
      lost them again abowt . 7. yeares
      since by a dishonourable com-
      posicion, whearvnto hee was
      forced by the great advantages
      that the Pole had then of him,
      by meanes of the foiles hee had
      given him before, and the dis-
      quiet of his own state at home.
      Onlie hee hath left of that side
      his Countrey the Cities of *Smo-*
      lensko, *Vitobshey*, *Chermigo*, *Be-*
      ælagorod in *Lituania*, in *Livonia*
      not a Town nor on foot of
      grownd. (A, B);

      But the principall part of all
      his conquests was that which

hee had in *Lituania* and *Livonia:*
whear hee had many goodly
Townes with a large territorie
beelonging to every one. Which
hee gott rather by the advantage of civill dissentions and
secreat treasons among themselves then by any force of
armes. And so lost them again
abowt 7. years since by as dishonourable a composition.
Whearvnto hee was forced by
the great advantage that the
Pole had then of them by means
of the foile hee had given him
beefore and the disquiet of his
own state at home. Only hee hath
left of that side his Countrie the
Cities of *Smolensko Vitobskey
Chernigo* and *Beælagorod* in *Lituania.* In *Livonia* not a Town nor
one foot of ground. (C)

27 *Basileus*] hee (A–C)
27 conquered...countries,] wan that
     Countrey (A–C)
29 a] ~ certein (A, B)
29–30 vnder...Captaines.] and being
     governed by certein of his own
     Russ people. (A, B)
31 them. And] ~ , and (A–C)
32 the...time,] again (A–C)
32 with him,] *om.* (A, B)
33 foure,] the people with him, (A, B)
33 or] and (C)
33–34 that...warres,] *om.* (A, B)
35 ouermatch] over maister (A–C)
36 of strength] *om.* (A–C)
36 besides] byside (A–C)
40 afterwards] *om.* (A, B)
42 lying there] thear lyeng (A)
42 in...while] *om.* (A, B)
43–44 his...*Vasilowich*] hee (A–C)
45 (called *Iuangorod*)] *om.* (A–C)
52 againe to] to (A, B); vp to (C)
53–65 On...resist.] [This passage follows
     l. 2 in A.]
53 On] First on (A–C)

53 side,] side whear (A–C)
54 from...*Tartar*] *om.* (A, B)
56 Northward] Northeastward (A, B)
61 are] ~ not naturallie Russ (but of
     (A, B)
62 *Russe,*] Russes) (A, B)
62 and that] *om.* (A, B)
63 and...sword,] *om.* (A, B); and...
     weapon (C)
64 naked] ~ kind of (A, B)
64–65 people...resist.] people. (A, B)
66 the *Russe*] hee (A–C)
67 on] in (A, B)
68 not of] ~ ~ the (A, B)
71 there] *om.* (A, B)
72 of...their] of the ordering his (A, B);
     of ordering his (C)
75 partie] man (A–C)
77 done] ~ beefore (A–C)
83 before hande] *om.* (A, B)
83 foure] *om.* (A, B)
85 are] bee (A–C)
87 easie] ~ a (A, B)
88 got. vz.] gott, that is (A, B)
88 then by] then (A, B)
89 First, hee] 2. Hee (A–C)
90 there some] soom (A–C)
90–91 souldiers...vnder.] souldiers (in-
     ough to keep them vnder) in
     garrison among them. (A–C)
91 Secondly, his] 3. His (A–C)
92 very] *om.* (A–C)
93 often...notwithstanding] often. Not-
     withstanding (A, B); often...
     thrise. Notwithstanding (C)
94–97 Thirdly...one.] *om.* (A, B); 4.
     Hee...broke into...all in on.
     (C)
97 Fourthly, hee] 4. Hee (A, B); 5. Hee
     (C)
99 often] oft (A, B); often and so muche
     (C)
100 to] *om.* (A)
107 *Russe* Emperour] Emperour of *Russia*
     (A, B)
109 well interteyned] *om.* (A–C)
111 First, he] ~ . Hee (A, B)

112   of] ~ all (A–C)
113   Secondly, he] 2. Hee (A–C)
116   Thirdly, he] 3. Hee (A–C)
117   seuerall] speciall (A, B)
119–21   Fourthly...lieth.] *om.* (A, B); 4.
        Hee...small countenance other-
        wise of no...lyeth. (C)
121   Fiftly, he] 4. Hee (A, B); 5. Hee (C)
123   them, nor] ~ or (A, B)
124   enemy...borders.] enimie. (A, B)
124–33   Sixtly...come.] *om.* (A–C)

Chapter 19

2   warre] warrs (A, B)
2–8   are...*Swedens*.] are the *Polonians*
        and *Sweadens* and *Tartars*. (A);
        are the *Polonians*, *Sweadens* and
        Tartars. (B); ar the *Polonian*
        Sweaden and *Tartar*. (C)
9   from vs] *om.* (A, B)
10   and] *om.* (A, B)
11   another] the other (A, B)
15   inland parts.] Countrey. (A, B)
20   aduenture] venture (A–C)
22   *Tartar*.] ~ his enimie. (A, B)
24   building] buildinges (D, E)
26   greatest...the] whole (A–C)
27–28   or...of] *om.* (A, B)
28   you haue] thear have been (A, B)
29   light] *om.* (A, B); a (C)
32   pressing] ~ on (A, B)
36–37   the presse] this meanes (A–C)
37   800000] 600000 (A)
38   thus hauing] having thus (A, B)
40   (as...sayd)] (as is saied) (A, B); *om.* (C)
42   nor] or (A, B)
42   or] and (A, B)
46–47   besides...*Tartar*)] *om.* (A, B)
48   North...Westward,] Northward
        (A, B)
49   to...right] vnto him (A, B)
50   a] *om.* (A, B)
51   was] ~ yearlie (A, B)
51   euery yeare,] him self (A, B)
51–52   to...and] *om.* (A, B)
53   (himselfe...back)] *om.* (A, B)
58   with...vz:] to raunsoom him (A, B)

59   this] his (A, B)
59   furres: which] ~ . Which (C)
60   also was] was allso (A, B)
60   paied] paied anie longer (A, B); any
        longer paied (C)
61   *Russe*] Russe onlie (A, B)
62   that...wonne,] *om.* (A, B)
63   him] his borders (A, B); them (C)
64   Haruest.] the harvest time. (A–C)
67   of the] ~ their (A, B)
73   fight, or] ~ and (A)
75   falcon] *om.* (A, B)
76   sword] ~ made (A, B)
77   readily] ready (C)
78   horsmans] horseman (C)
78   staffe] ~ byside (A, B); ~ bysides (C)
78   speare...weapons.] speare. (A–C)
79–80   The...vz:] Their armour is noth-
        ing els but (A–C)
81   night time] night (A, B)
81–82   same. But] ~ , but (A, B)
82   their...Noblemen] the Noblemen
        or Morseis (A–C)
83   ouer...armie] with their armie over
        a river (A); with their armyes over
        a river (B)
85   horse:] horses, and (A–C)
86   they] *om.* (A–C)
91–131   Yet...greater.] *om.* (A–C)
120   parle] parley (E)
135   rather...die] to dye raither (A, B)
137–45   Wherein...bondslaue.] *om.*
        (A–C)
146   the *Tartars*] they (A–C)
147   and] or (A–C)
148   or] and (A, B)
151   tree] other hard thing (A, B)
152–55   The...praye.] *om.* (A–C)
157   yeere in the] *om.* (A)
157   on...parts] *om.* (A, B)
161   vz.] *om.* (A–C)
164   direction] pleasure (A, B)
167   tributaries] Tributarie (A–C)
168–69   of the] ~ their (A, B)
169–70   whereby...nowe] who hath
        brought it (A, B)
172   against...Christians] *om.* (A, B)

173–90 Herein...againe.] *om.* (A–C)
196 horses] horse (D, E)
197 eaten] eate (D, E)
199 it. So] ~ , so (A, B)
205 wiues, whereof] ~ . Whearof (A, B)
205 widdow. Where] ~ , whear (B)
208 horses] horse (A–C)
210 as] *om.* (A–C)
212 there...brought] they bring (A–C)
213 *Tartar*] *om.* (A–C)
214 also] withall (A, B)
218 and] ~ of (A)
219 sometimes] sometime (A, B)
223 which...*Veij*,] *om.* (A, B)
224 cottage. These] cottage sett vpon a cart, though it bee much larger, which (A, B); cottage though it bee much larger. These (C)
225 they goe] they list to goe (A–C)
225 And] ~ And (D)
226 stage or] *om.* (A, B)
226 place] *om.* (A, B)
230–32 As...vnpleasant.] *om.* (A–C)
233 mooue] remoove with (A, B)
235 parts. And] ~ , and (A, B)
236 part Northwarde,] point, which they mean to goe Northward, (A, B)
237 (where...winter)] *om.* (A, B)
239 to...as] for their vse when (A, B); to serve for their vse when (C)
239–40 From...they] Their Countrey is verie large abowt 2000. verse long from the border of the *Shalcan* to the Russ frontiers. They (A–C)
241 partes,] parts of it, (A, B)
244 before...mettals,] *om.* (A, B)
245 swords,] ~ and (A–C)
245 necessaries...siluer] necessarie vses before golld or [and (B)] silver which (A, B)
247 life,] living (A, B)
248 inuasions.] ~ . Whearin [~ : whearin (C)] they have been happie beefore all other Nations. (A–C)
248–63 Which...carriages.] *om.* (A–C)
264–75 In...serue.] *om.* (A, B); In...the

old)...sickness and death...to measure thinges by...necessitie of them and not by vain shew or pleasure of the eye. (C)
276–87 For...scantling.] *om.* (A–C)
287 very] *om.* (A)
289–318 Some...trueth.] *om.* (A–C)
319 vpon] *vpon* (D)
321 more...other] and in regiment more then (A–C)
322–29 except...rest.] [The order of A–C is the discussion of the Nagay and then the Chircasse Tartar. The marginal notes in D are likewise in that order, but the discussion of the Chircasse Tartar has clearly been revised, and probably Fletcher forgot to interchange the marginal notes.]
322–23 *Tartar*...Southwest] *Tartar*. The *Chirchass* is [are (B, C)] Southward, and soomwhatt on the west (A–C)
323 are] is (A, B)
325 as...*Polonian*] like to the Spanniard (A–C)
328 all] *om.* (A, B)
331 haue] ~ verie (A–C)
332 *Russia*. And] ~ , and (A–C)
333–34 of them...commodities,] *om.* (A–C)
335 tribes. For] ~ , for (A, B)
338 people] *om.* (A–C)
338–39 double...very] false and double in all his doings, and thearfore are (A, B); double and false. And thearfore (C)
340 them] him (A–C)
340 in] within (A–C)
341 for...sake] *om.* (A, B)
346 it] ~ for (A–C)
346 whole] *om.* (C)
347 be. When] ~ when (B)
352 in...hee] that (A, B)
354–91 Next...*them*.] *om.* (A–C)
358 tradeth] ~ , (D)

Chapter 20

[Chapters 19 and 20 in D are developed from one chapter in the MSS.]

1–2   that...Northeast,] *om.* (A–C)

4   flat] fat (B)

4–5   as...haue,] *om.* (A–C)

5   except...*Chirchasses*.] save that the *Chirchasse* is of a better countenance and visage then the rest. (A–C)

6   *Russe*.] Russ and speak the Russ language. (A, B)

8   towardes] to (A, B)

9   times] time (A–C)

10   Cannibals,] cannibals in (A, B)

10   another. Which] ~ , which (A–C)

14   people] ~ that wear (A–C)

15   that neuer] and never (A–C)

16   at...time] *om.* (A, B)

18   I...they] They (A, B)

21–35   As...like.] *om.* (A–C)

37–38   with...same,] *om.* (A–C)

38–44   women...other.] women and live in a manner a wilde and savage life, roving still from on place of their Countery to an other. (A, B); women. They ...berdlesse without any hear growing on their faces. And... look save...and savage...their Countery...other. (C)

44–102   Their...sledde.] *om.* (A–C)

Chapter 21

1   gouernement...Churche,] Ecclesiasticall State within the Countrey of *Russia* (A, B)

3–4   Church...Pope.] Church when it was at the woorst and had corrupted it self as well in doctrine as in discipline. (A, B); Church. (C)

5   their...them] it, then they in the cerimonies and superstitions of their church (A, B)

7   the...practise] the practise (A, B); the practise and vse (C)

8   Secondly...doctrine] 2. What doctrines (A, B); 2. What doctrine (C)

9   Thirdly, what] 3. What (A–C)

10   their] *om.* (A–C)

11   Fourthly, what] 4. What (A–C)

15   Westerne churches] Popish Church (A–C)

19   matter] matters (A, B)

22   (the] (as the (A, B)

24   Emperours,] Emperour (A, B)

26   due...to] vnto him and (A, B)

28   well] *om.* (A, B)

29   storie, or] ~ nor (A, B)

31   countrie...matters.] Countrey. (A, B); Countrie...Common wealth. (C)

34   that] this (A, B)

35   *Greeke*] Constantinopolitan (A); *om.* (B)

37–40   *Laonicus...Sarmatia*.] *Nicephorus* that speaketh of such a marriage with the Kings Daughter of *Sarmatia* abowt the time of *Andronicus* the younger which was abowt the year 1300. (A–C)

42   withall peruerted] perverted withall (A, B)

44   *Greeke* Church] Greeks (C)

45   then] *om.* (C)

45   and] ~ had (A–C)

47   the] ~ saied (A–C)

47–48   *Gregoras...bookes*.] and hath so continued ever since. And that they receaved this form aswell of doctrine as of the Church government from the Greek church, thear are manie evident reasons to induce a man to thinck, which might hear bee sett down, but that it would draw this breif note into over great length. (A, B)

48–59   But...superstition.] *om.* (A–C)

60   At...1588] This last year of 1588 (A–C)

61   called *Hieronomo*] *om.* (A–C)

63   Emperour] ~ of Russia (A, B)

63 giuen altogether] altogether given (A, B)

64–66 intertainment...company.] interteinment. (A, B); intertainment notwithstanding beefore his coomming to Mosko hee had been in Italy with the Pope as was sayed. (C)

66 His] The Patriarches (A, B)

67 points] matters (A, B)

70 Ambassages...passed] wear Ambassages (A, B)

70 *Persian*. Likewise] Persian, and this year (A, B)

71 league] *om.* (A–C)

72 for...dominions:] and so to invade his Dominions on all sides (A, B); for...dominion: (D, E)

74–78 This...*Poland*.] *om.* (A–C)

80 to] ~ the (A–C)

81 for] ~ that (A–C)

81 into *Spaine*] *om.* (A–C)

81 by] ~ the (A–C)

82 *Spanish* king] King of Spain (A–C)

82–83 by...England] by hir Highnes (A, B); by the Queen of England (C)

85 at...time] *om.* (A, B)

86 *Spanish*] Spanish King (A–C)

88 of...and] vpon (A, B)

88 cleargie] ~ his Countreymen (A, B)

89–90 reducing...Rome.] Romish supreamacie over the Russ Cleargie. (A, B)

90–91 that...Rome] *om.* (A–C)

91 Pope,] ~ (from whom hee cam) (A, B); ~ with whome hee had been: (C)

92 times] time (C)

94 belike...meanes] bee a better oportunitie (A, B); bylyke...meane (D, E)

95 treatie...of] *om.* (A, B); the mediation of (C)

96–97 point of] *om.* (A–C)

99 Which] ~ Treatie (A–C)

102 matter was] wear (A, B)

103 reasons] reason (D, E)

103–4 translating...for] equitie of his doings, wear, for (A, B); translating of his Sea to the Citie of Mosko wear. 1. For (C)

107 Secondly, because] 2. Bycawse (A)

111 of...ware,] of his broken commodities (A, B); for his broken wares (C)

113 countrie:] Countrey thearbie, (A, B)

113 Patriarches seat,] seat of the Patriarchshipp (A–C)

115 but] *om.* (A, B)

116 wholy...himselfe] to him (A, B)

119–20 of the...Church,] *om.* (A–C)

124–25 Church...Emperours] *om.* (C)

129 staffe. Which] ~ , which (A–C)

130 other] *om.* (A, B)

132 held] holden (D, E)

134 *Greeke*] great (D, E)

136 with] ~ great and (A–C)

137 giftes more] ritch ghifts (A, B)

140 *Nice*) is] Niece (though subiect to the Turk for a 100. yeares and more) is (A, B); Niece subiect to the Turk for these 140 years or more) is (C)

142 subtil] *om.* (A, B)

142 good] his (C)

143 away] *om.* (A, B); his way (C)

143–44 into *Poland*] *om.* (A, B)

144 not] noe (A, B); counterfaict (C)

145–46 betwixt...*Russe*] in the Greek (A, B)

146 this] the (A, B)

147 so...payed] paied well (A, B)

147 elect...withall] byside have elected an other (A, B)

148 they will] it is (A, B)

148 man] late (A, B)

151 to...Rome] vnto him (A–C)

151–52 peraduenture...them] it may seem hee devised to cast in this matter of schisme (A, B); peradventure...this practice to cast...them (C)

153–55 know...sea.] have learned the inconvenience that would grow to their state, by letting in that Beast. (A,B); know well inough by the example of other Christian Princes what inconvenience would growe hearby to their state. (C)

155 To] For (A–C)

156–57 was...of] inquired verie much, concerning (A, B); was very inquisitive concerning (C)

157 of christendome] Christian (A)

158 very] *om.* (A, B)

159 his court.] the Pope. (A, B)

160–76 With...decree.] *om.* (A–C)

177 now...to] of (A, B)

181–82 at...authoritie.] at the least they must suppose it to be soe, except they will graunt that they have made a badd bargain, and bought that of the Greek, that him self had not right to sell. (A, B); at least this niew Russe ...authoritie. (C)

184 the] *om.* (A, B)

186 called...*Metropolite*] *om.* (A, B)

187 and] ~ this (A–C)

195 are the] ~ their (A, B)

196 *Crutitska*] Volodemer (A–C)

197 *Volodemer*] Crutitska (A–C)

198–99 diocesse...them.] dioces. (A, B)

200 iurisdiction, of] ~ first of the Patriarch, (A–C)

202 vsed] claimed (A–C)

202 Christendome. For] Christendoom by the Canon Law. For (A, C); Christendoom by the Canon Law, for (B)

204 their...to] they vsurp manie things that belong to the Civill magistracie as (A–C)

206 also...haue] they have allso (A–C)

207 Commissaries] ~ &c. (A, B)

210 the Priestes:] the pore Priests, (A–C)

211 poore] other (A–C)

212–13 beareth...those] hath not to deal with them (A, B)

213 Court. But] ~ , but (A–C)

218 intreat] gett favour (A, B)

220 speciall...fauour] verie speciall grace (A, B)

227 a piece.] a piece, to whom thear is allotted owt of their livings the summe of fortie Rubbells. (A, B); a piece that resemble the elders in the primitive Church to whome their is allotted owt of the Bishops livings the summ of 30. Rubbells a year. (C)

227 with] *om.* (A, B)

228 the...necessarie] manie speciall or necessarie (A, B); the speciall and necessariest (C)

232 rubbels, or markes.] Rubbells. (A–C)

236 *Nouograde.*] ~ . But the Emperours of late have well abated their revenues, which notwithstanding wear large [wear very large still (C)] if they received it clear, and had it all at their own disposicion to spend as they listed. But their Steward is ever [ever *om.* (C)] of the Emperours appointing, and hath a Commission both to receive all their rents, and to expend what is necessarie abowt their howshold provision. If anie thing bee left at the yeares end, hee giveth account [account of it (C)] to the Emperours Officers. The *Patriarch*, *Metropolits*, *Arch Bishopps*, and *Bishopps* are allowed onlie to their privat purse, for the expenses of their persons abowt 200. or 300. Rubbells a piece by the year. (A–C)

238 solemnest] soleime and formall (A, B); solemnest and formallst (C)

251 marueilous] great (A, B)

253 himselfe. They] himself, and they (A, B)

254 nor] and (A, B)

255–56 by...reason] thearfore (A, B)

256 for] by reason of (A, B)

260 inauguration] inaugurations (B)

260–61 They...Archdeacons.] To this

purpose they have their deanes,
and Archdeacons, after the
order of the Popish Churches.
And if it bee asked, what vse
they have in their Churches
[they...Churches] their Church
hath (C)] of their Patriarch,
Metropolites, Archbishopps &c.
I can note nothing save that
among so manie dead Idolls as
they woorshipp, they may have
soom a live [a live] live ons (C)]
to furnish their Church withall.
(A–C)

266 day] *om.* (A, B)
268 his] their (A, B)
269 or like] *om.* (A–C)
269 effect:] ~ . (A–C)
269 anie] ~ thear (A, B)
271 against...Prince] *om.* (A, B)
271 he] ~ shall (A, B)
271 practise:] practises against his Prince,
    (A, B); practises (C)
272 he haue] anie have (A,B); hee hath(C)
275 haue...set] have set it (A, B)
276 that...and] with great solemnitie
    (A, B)
277–78 Acte...diuinitie.] act. (A, B)
278 At the] At (A–C)
280 maner of] *om.* (A, B)
280 are they] they are (A)
281 keepe] shutt (A, B)
281 in] learning into their Countrey
    (A, B)
283 haue perswaded] perswade (A); per-
    swaded (B)
284 innouation] innovations (A–C)
285 the] their (A–C)
285 but] ~ the very (C)
286–87 a...hardly] sound learning and
    wisdoom speciallie godlie wis-
    doom will not well (A, B);
    good and sound wisdoom that
    is helped by learning and liber-
    all education will not (C)
291 himselfe] *om.* (A, B)
291–92 in...time] *om.* (A, B)

292 quite...vp,] burned in the night
    time (A, B)
292 as] ~ it (A, B)
292–93 by the] by (A–C)
293 Cleargy men] Bishopps and other of
    the Cleargie (A, B); Bishops and
    other the Cleargie men. (C)
294 *Papaes*] *Pape* (A, B)
297 for...not] *om.* (A–C)
299 first] *om.* (A–C)
300 then] *om.* (A–C)
301 some] *om.* (A, B)
305 their] ~ Maisters and (A–C)
306 farther] *om.* (A–C)
307 learning] ~ or knowleadge (A, B)
310 deck their] ~ the (A, B)
310 the] *om.* (A, B)
311 Churches] Church (A–C)
311 Their...great] Thear are manie of
    them (A, B)
312 descretion] regard or discretion (A–C)
312 for deuiding] to divide (A, B); in
    dividing (C)
314 as] ~ is (A–C)
314–16 where...Which] whear thear is
    an idolatrous or ignorant minis-
    terie, whear [ministerie. Whear
    (C)] the people are content to
    want the preaching of the
    woord which (A–C)
316 well be] bee well (A, B)
317 the...and] people into (A, B)
321 make] ~ is (A, B)
322 1. 3. 2.] 1 cap. 3. vers. 2 (A, B)
322 not well] corruptly (A–C)
327 accounted] counted (A, B)
328 and of] ~ in (A, B)
329 him] *om.* (A, B)
330 els] ~ to him (A, B)
330 must stand] standeth (A, B)
331 of...make] of his people, and mak-
    eth (A, B)
332 as] *om.* (A)
333 and the] and for the (A, B)
334 *Molitua*] *Molytva* or praier for remis-
    sion of sinnes (A, B)
334 besides] byside (A, B)

335 priuate] *om.* (A, B)

335–36 a...Priest,] the priest to say a privat prayer (A, B)

337 goe] ~ by land (A, B)

337 saile] ~ by water (A, B)

337–38 doeth. Which] ~ , which (A, B)

339 at randome,] *om.* (A, B)

339 being] is (A, B)

339–40 Church-/prayers] Church-prayers (D)

340 And this] It (A, B)

340 holy, and] *om.* (A, B)

341 be] ~ but (A, B)

341 mouth...owne.] mouth. (A, B)

343 to] of (A, B)

343 yeere. What] ~ , what (A, B)

344 their countrey,] their Town and Countrey (A, B); the Countrey (C)

344 and...about,] of other parishes, (A, B)

345 make] give (A, B)

348 among them] *om.* (A, B)

351 dishes] ~ of praiers (A–C)

351 for the] and to offer vpp to the (A, B); for his (C)

351 wel] *om.* (A, B)

352 besides] byside (C)

355 their] the (C)

355–56 they...deuotion] doe receive their devotions (A, B)

356 the...is] they are (A, B)

358 thirtie...rubbels] xx or xxx Rubbells or marks (A–C)

358 yere: whereof] ~ . Whearof (A)

360 knowen] not so much knowen by anie good qualitie above the rest, but (A, B); not so much knowen by any good qualitie that is in him above the rest but (C)

361 eares,] ears, and (A–C)

361–62 broad...hand.] cape. (A, B); broad cape. (C)

364 him] *om.* (A–C)

365 besides] byside (A, B)

368 verie] *om.* (A, B)

372 be their] ~ the (A–C)

373 the] their (A–C)

374 an...greater] a greater number (A–C)

375 other] *om.* (A–C)

376 them. For] ~ , for (A–C)

378 and sweeter] *om.* (A–C)

379 Saint.] ~ or other. (C)

383 Commons...causeth] Commons, which cawseth (A, B); Commons. Which commonly cawseth (C)

384 blowes.] ~ that light vpon others. (A, B)

386 displeasure. These] ~ , which (A–C)

389 lawes] Law (A, B)

391 a...to] his protection to (A, B); a protection for (C)

394 to...receiued] *om.* (A–C)

394 hee] *om.* (A–C)

396 rubbels, and] Robbells (A, B)

399 apparell. Then] ~ , then (A, B)

401 ground, girded] grownd, and girt (A, B); ground girt (C)

402 vppermost] vpper (C)

402 weede] garment (A, B)

405 skinne...these] skinne (for shaving they like not) and this (A–C)

405–6 pronounced...haire:] pronounced in the mean time by the Abbott him self. (A, B); pronounced... whilest...hear. (C)

407 *now*] *om.* (A, B)

408 *cleane*] *quite* (A, B)

414–15 one...thousande] 10000 soom 20000 (A, B)

416 the] to the (A, B)

417 rubbels...yeere.] Rubbells a year. This is manie times visited by the Emperours for devotion, soomtimes allso they visitt their purse withowt anie devotion. (A, B); rubbells a year. (C)

423–24 fruitful...husband.] fruitfull for children. (A, B); fruitfull. (C)

424 Lightly...goeth] A year or two since shee went (A, B)

426 thousand] hundreth (A, B)

427 But] ~ as yet (A–C)

428–29 prayers...way.] praier. (A, B)

430 Fryers,] ~ , it (A, B)
431 the] their (A, B)
432–33 *Vologda*...offered] *Vologda* by an interpreter. Thear was brought vnto (A, B)
433 Testament...him] testament whear hee tourned (A, B)
434 Gospel. Where] ~ , whear (A, B)
435 first] *om.* (A, B)
436 answered, that] answeared (A, B)
436 well] *om.* (A, B)
437 in] of (A–C)
438 not.] ~ well. (A, B)
439 saued? Whereunto] ~ : whearvnto (B)
445 bread] meat (A, B)
445 Friers of] ~ in (A–C)
446 partly] *om.* (A, B)
447 man] Friar (A–C)
448 whereof...admitte] soom of great account, that admitteth (A, B)
452 their] the (C)
452 needes] needeth (A, B)
453 vncleannesse] wicked life (A, B)
454 superstition] superstitions (C)
455 man] mouth (A, B)
457 those] the (A–C)
458 their...and] any knowledg or (C)
459 middle,] middes, eaven in the streets, in the extreamitie of winter, (A–C)
460 hanging] growing (A, B)
462 middes...winter.] middes. (A–C)
462 they take] take they (C)
464 what...list] or doe what they thinck good (A, B)
465 very] *om.* (A–C)
467 that is,] *om.* (A, B)
467 sinnes. And] ~ , and (A, B)
467 anie] one (A)
470 the...taking] him to take (A–C)
470 sort] manner (A, B)
471 kinde] sort (A, B)
471 it is] *om.* (C)
471 very] *om.* (A, B)
472 in] ~ the (A–C)
473 at...time] *om.* (A, B)
473 they...one] on they have (A, B)

474 naked] *om.* (A, B)
476 Common wealth] Countrey (A, B)
479–80 Emperour...people.] Emperour. (A, B); Emperour...oppressions towards...people. (C)
482 he...there] (they say) hee doth (A, B)
483 to] *om.* (A, B)
485 themselues, which] ~ . Which (A)
486 at *Mosko*] at the *Mosko* (A, B)
486–87 this...in] hee had but ill success in the (A, B); hee had but ill luck in (C)
488 by him] *om.* (A–C)
490 merily] nimblie (A, B)
491 night. And] ~ , and (A, B)
493 haue] take vpon him (A, B)
494 miracle...him] miracle. (A, B)
494–95 Besides...thence] Again a fiew dayes beefore I cam owt of the Countrey (A, B)
498 their Saint] *om.* (A–C)
499 no...Miracle-worker.] him soom discreditt. (A, B)
500 account] ~ not long since (A, B)
501 much good] soom good thear (A, B)
504 a...And] rewards, and (A, B); rewards. And (C)
504 the Emperour] him again, (A–C)
505 rawe] *om.* (A, B)
505 Which] ~ when (A–C)
506 seeing, bid] saw, hee badd (A, B); saw he bid (C)
507 in the] ~ their (A, B)
508 forbidden...Church.] forbidden. (A, B); forbidden by the...Church. (C)
508–9 (which...*Iacke*)] *om.* (A, B); or *Iack* (C)
509 quoth] saith (A, B)
510 in] ~ the (A, B)
512 vpon him] on him shortlie (A, B)
519 as] ~ thear (A–C)
519–20 of them,] *om.* (A–C)
520 beyng...in] *om.* (A, B)
521 his gouernment] him (A–C)

Chapter 22

1 *Zautrana*...It] *Sautrana*, and (A–C)
10 or] ~ the (A, B)
12 enter] coom (A, B)
12 only. Where], ~ , whear (A, B)
15 *&c*:] *om*. (A, B)
16 *praysed... the*] praysed be the (D)
16 *the Sonne*] Soon (A–C)
18 that] the (A–C)
21 or] and (A–C)
21 Images] Image (B)
24 the] his (A, B); their (C)
25 This] Which (A–C)
25 that] *om*. (A, B)
25–26 heauenly...chauncel,] the Chauncell, and (A, B); the Chauncell or heavenly door and (C)
28 This] that (A, B)
28–29 yeere,...them] year. This they read (A, B)
34 their] the (A, B)
35 the] *om*. (A–C)
37 of the] a (A–C)
38 (or Compline)] that is *Complin* (A, B)
46 *&c*. And] ~ and (A, B)
50 vp so] togither, as (A–C)
51 *Prayse...Prayse*] Praise, praise (A, B)
51 together...very] which maketh a (A, B)
53 *&c*. And] &c. and (A–C)
58 high] *om*. (A, B)
63 their...to] they keep it and (A, B)
64 Idols.] Idolls &c. (A–C)
66 church] *om*. (A, B)
66–67 they...churches.] thear is none allowed them. (A, B)
69–70 Church...if] Church. And...be ...bee born. If (A); Church, and...must be...be born. If (B); Church and...is...borne. If (C)
75 him. And] ~ , and (A–C)
76 Christian, &c.] Christian. (A, B)
77 This ended,] Then (A–C)
86–87 he...thrise] plungeth him thrise

in (A, B); plungeth the child thrise (C)
87–88 point necessary] necessarie point (A–C)
88 in] into (A, B)
91 vz:] that is (A–C)
92 *Ghost*. For] ~ , for (C)
93 the words] baptisme (A–C)
95 by] ~ the (C)
97 precisely...downe.] prescribed to the Priest. (A–C)
99 forehead] ~ of the child (A–C)
102 this] that (A, B)
102–3 Christian, &c. All] Christian. All (A, B); Christian &c: All (C); Christian, &c: all (D, E)
104–5 Christian...dore)] Christian(A–C)
107 (as...mediatour)] *om*. (A, B)
108–12 If...church.] *om*. (A–C)
114 form. As] ~ , as (A, B)
120 baptized. And] ~ ; and (A–C)
120 they] *om*. (A–C)
121 hatred] ~ that (B)
123 after] ~ the (A–C)
127 reproches against] reveilings vpon (A–C)
131 for...purpose] *om*. (A–C)
133 more libertie,] favour (A, B)
138 onely] on (A, B)
140–41 put...and] *om*. (A, B)
142 had,] ~ gott by vnlawfull meanes (A–C)
144 rioter...person.] rioter. (A–C)
145 baptisme] doctrine (A, B)
147–55 the...himselfe] their church, whear [Church. Whear (C)] the Friars take them privatlie into the [their (C)] monasterie church, and thear teach them how to beehave them selves (A–C)
156–57 crossing himself,] signing them selves with the Cross, (A–C)
158 religion.] ~ . Soomtimes they baptize within privat howses. (A, B)
161 The] Their (B)
162 thus] this (A, B)

163 Priest...Then] Priest (whom... fa-
     ther) then (A–C)
164 Communion] Common (C)
169 table. Where] ∼ , whear (A–C)
173 claret...he] claret or redd wine, the
     (A, B); claret or redd wine. Then
     (C)
175 deliuereth] ∼ vnto (A, B)
179 together] *om.* (A, B)
181 in] *om.* (A, B)
182 armes. And] ∼ , and (A–C)
182 againe,] ∼ , and (A, B)
183 so] *om.* (A, B)
184 places...Where] standing again,
     whear (A, B)
187–88 after. Which] ∼ , which (B)
189 cabbage, and] ∼ or (A, B)

Chapter 23

2   they...publiquely] refuse (A–C)
3   of...as] *om.* (B)
3   the bookes] *om.* (A, B)
12 dayly] *om.* (A, B)
13 *Reuelation*: which] ∼ . Which (C)
15–16 conteyned within] of (A–C)
16–17 especially...Church] Antichriste
     and the rest (A, B)
17 Churches. Notwithstanding] ∼ , not-
     withstanding (A, B)
19 and the] and (A, B)
19–20 by...inuasion] foretolld them by
     God, (A, B)
20 prophecies] prophecie (C)
24 God. Wherein] ∼ , whearin (A, B)
26 church] churches (A–C)
27 3. That] Thirdly that (C)
31 4. Concerning] Fourthly concerning
     (C)
31 in the] in (A, B)
32 of God] *om.* (A, B)
32–33 that...Sonne.] they are free from
     the errours of *Arrius Macedo-*
     nius, *Marichie* and the rest.
     (A–C)
34 5. About] But abowt (A–C)
39 this] the (A–C)
47 offerings, and] offerings, (A, B)

51 not] no (C)
53 very] *om.* (A, B)
54 forth] *om.* (A, B)
55 table. Though] ∼ , though (A, B)
55 that stick] so that they sticke owt
     (B)
56 outwards] owtward (A, B)
57 to...in] for (A, B)
60 6. For] 5. For (A, B); Fiftly for (C)
61–62 works...that] woorks. And (A);
     workes, and that (B)
63 God. And] ∼ , and (A)
69 courts,] ∼ and (A, B)
71 7.] 6. (A–C)
74 8.] 7. (A–C)
75 the] that (A, B)
77 9.] 8. (A–C)
77 *Lords*] *Lord* (A)
78–81 Yet...it.] [This passage follows l.
     87 in A and B.]
78 Yet concerning] 11. Concerning
     (A, B)
79 so] as (A, B)
82 10.] 9. (A, B)
84 11.] 10. (A–C)
88 12.] 11. (C)
89 then] ∼ the vse (C)
93 one] anie (A, B)
95 13.] 12. (C)
95 vnlawfull] ∼ , as (A)
95–96 the...men] the Cleargie (A);
     their Cleargie men (B, C)
96 priests only] priests (A, B); priest
     only (C)
98 marriage. Which] ∼ , which (A–C)
99 old. Who] ∼ , who (A–C)
102 to...priests] *om.* (A, B)
106 false] ∼ and vain (A–C)
107 holde] ∼ and ar fallen into, (A, B)
114 the] their (A, B)
118–22 sake...it.] sake. (A, B); sake
     partly...any innovation of that
     relligion that...it. (C)
119 them:] *om.* (E)
123 sort] ∼ among them (A–C)
124 sense] knowleadge (A, B)
127 images...superstitions:] idolatrie.

(A, B); images and woorshipping
of them. (C)
128 vnto] to (A)
128–29 to morrow...them.] to them to-
morrow. (A, B); to them to-
morrow if hee pleased. (C)
131 none: saue] ~ , Save (C)
133 28.] xviij (A–C)
134 of] ~ their (A, B)
134 and...like,] *om.* (A–C)
135 at] ~ the (A, B)
135 house...fire.] howse, whearinto they
wear shutt fast and the howse sett
on fier. (A–C)
136 like] likelie (A)

Chapter 24

1 solemnizing] ~ of (A, B)
4 woing: which] ~ . Which (A, B)
5–6 kin...taken] *om.* (E) [The compos-
itor skipped one line in D.]
9 of] ~ their (A, B)
9 their] *om.* (A–C)
18 more,] ~ , but (A, B)
19 home] ~ again (A, B)
22 one...other] the on to the other
(A, B); one to another (C)
24 If] And if (A, B)
26 breedeth] maketh (A, B)
30 other,] ~ , but (A)
32 eaue] daye (A, B)
35 in. For] ~ , for (A–C)
40 put] ~ vp (B)
42 middle. And] middes, and (A–C)
43–44 the...themselues] though they
bee (A, B)
45 of] ~ the (A, B)
47 Bride. Which] ~ which (A, B)
56–57 protect...cherish] cherish and
defend (A, B)
59 ende,] ~ thear (B)
61 likewise] in order (A, B)
61 themselues] them selves likewise
(A, B)
62 kinreds. And] ~ , and (A, B)
69–70 thenceforth...become] that they
are all (A, B)

74–75 wine. Whereof] ~ , whearof (B)
75 full] *om.* (A, B)
77 below,] *om.* (A, B)
81 hers, where] ~ . Whear (A)
87–89 head...that] head, and a great
charge by hir friends not to
speak all that night, so that
(A, B); head...friendes) so
that (C)
90 marriage. Neither] ~ , nor (A, B)
93 reuerence] humilitie (A, B)
93–95 If...himselfe.] *om.* (A, B)
97–98 the...festiuall] so long as they
feast togither (A, B)
99 called] ~ the (A, B)
102 a] *om.* (A–C)
102–3 wiues. Except] ~ , except (A, B)
104 sort.] degrees. (A, B)
107–9 Frier...can.] friar if hee pretend
devotion. (A, B)

Chapter 25

1 The] Their (A, B)
1–2 number: especially] number, and
fowl for superstition. That which
a man shalbee forced most to
see is (A, B); number and fowl
for superstition. That which a
man shall bee forced to see more
often then hee would is (C)
6 gesture. Which] ~ , which (A, B)
7 reuerence...woorship] woorshipp
and reverence (C)
11 in] to (A–C)
13 brests. And] ~ , and (A–C)
14 their...rest,] the night past (A, B)
15 or,] *om.* (A–C)
16 When] when (D, E)
17–18 brests. Except] ~ , except (A, B)
24–27 crosse...And] cross, and bow
them selves to it. When...
great or small...Crose, and
(A); crosse, and (B)
29 maner:] ~ indeed, (A)
49 after...Patriarch] after that the Patriarch (B); after, the Patriarches
(D, E)

55 and] ~ those beeing ended, hee
      (A, B)
57–58 maketh...water.] and manie
      other circumstances, maketh
      the River as holie water as that
      within the Church. (A); (with
      many other circumstances)
      maketh the River all holy
      water. (B)
61 houses] howse (A, B)
62 you...see] first coom (A, B)
65 also] *om.* (A, B)
68 finger] fingers (A, B)
68–69 into...water] in (A, B)
69 When...done,] Last (A, B)
69–70 to...riuer] *om.* (A, B)
70 of...water:] their fill of it, (A, B);
      of this sanctified water, (C)
71 a horse.] a horse, and them selves not
      much holier. The like is doon by
      other Bishopps in all parts of the
      Realm. (A); horse, them selves not
      much holier. The like is doon by
      other Bishopps in all parts of the
      Realm. (B); a horse themselves not
      much holier. (C)
71 Their] The (A)
72–73 The...Realme.] *om.* (A, B)
75 extremitie:] ~ , whearby they kill
      manie through their vnreasonable
      superstition, (A, B)
76–78 God...killed] God, as *Borise*, chief
      man next the Emperour, at my
      beeing at the Mosko, that
      having but on soon killed him
      (A, B); God whearby...killed
      (C)
82–87 They...mysterie.] *om.* (A–C)
88 likewise] *om.* (A–C)
89 their] the (A)
89–90 which...into] who having hal-
      lowed the dishfull they power
      it (A); who having hallowed
      the dishfull, hee powereth it (B)
90 giueth] give (A, B)
91 sober.] ~ . Which is no dispraise after
      the Russe Diett. (A)

95 horse] *om.* (A–C)
99 of Christ] *om.* (A–C)
103–4 are...gun-powder] with rosen and
      gunpowder are made (A, B)
104 that] who (A, B)
106–7 Bishops pageant] Bishoppe (A–C)
107 himselfe,] *om.* (A–C)
108 plaid] *om.* (A, B)
109 at all] *om.* (A, B)
113 Lentes euery] ~ , through (A, B)
114 ours...second] ours, the 2. (A, B)
115 Midsommer...third] midsommer,
      the 3. (A, B)
115 Haruest time...fourth] harvest, the
      4. (A, B)
116–17 superstition] devotion (A, B)
118 and...but] with (A, B)
118 neither] nor (A, B)
125 their] the (C)
128 the] ~ little (A, B)
132–40 In...ground.] *om.* (A–C)
133 enter,] ~ (D)
142 departed. What] ~ , what (A, B)
143 paines.] ~ , and to stick vpp candells
      abowt the grave. (A, B)
146 prophane, and] *om.* (A, B)
147–48 backside...die.] backside. (A, B)
151 long and] *om.* (A, B)
153 their] these (A, B)
155 God] ~ chieflie (A, B)

Chapter 26

3 washing,] ~ his hands (A, B)
10 day. For] ~ , for (A, B)
16 before him] *om.* (A, B)
17 manner, first] ~ . First (B)
18 breaste] breastes (B, C)
19 *Syhodestua:* which] ~ . Which (B)
20 *God, Lorde*] God (C)
21 image, or] ~ of the (A)
23 or] and (A, B)
29 (as...it)] *om.* (A–C)
29 in...hand:] *om.* (A, B)
36 hath] have (A, B)
36 &c. And] ~ , and (A–C)
37 roome] Chamber (A–C)
38 chambers.] lodgings. (A, B)

44 long] *om.* (C)
46 fauour] ~ with him, and (A, B); ~ and (C)
48 ordinarie] ordinarilie (A)
53 time] while (A)
54 some of] *om.* (A–C)
54 Councell] ~ , or soom of his (A–C)
55 them. And] ~ , and (B)
55 conferre] conferring (A–C)
57 and] *om.* (B)
57 vntill...be] till (A, B)
64 before. There] ~) whear (A, B)
72 rost] roasted (A, B)
80 on] down vpon (A, B)
82 counted] accounted (A–C)
84 reste] ~ and sleep (A–C)
85 sleepe,] *om.* (A–C)
89 himself] ~ again (A–C)
91 manner. This] ~ , which (A, B)
93–117 On...daies.] *om.* (A–C)
117 Somtimes] Sometyme (B)
128 a] the (A)
128 laughter. For] ~ , for (A, B)
129 simple and] simple. (A, B)
129 gentle, and] gentle (A, B)
132 way. Besides] ~ , bysides (A)
134 of] *om.* (B)
135 sixe] 5. (A–C)

Chapter 27

1 these] ~ 7. (A–C)
3 Horse...more] *Horse*, which goeth no farther (A, B); horse which conteineth no more (C)
4 be ouerseer] the oversight (A, B)
4 not] ~ to bee (A, B)
5 the] his (A)
11 houshold at] ~ . At (A, B)
12 is] *om.* (A, B)
13 monies] money (B)
20 officers...offices] offices and officers (B)
20 chiefest] greatest (A)
21 beside] bysides (C)
24 lighted] light (A–C)
27 his] the Emperours (A, B)
33 that] to (A)
36 watch] ~ withowt, (A, B)

40 faire] *om.* (A, B)
42 houses. Which] ~ , which (A–C)

Chapter 28

1 The] What the (A, B)
1 people,] ~ is, (A, B)
2 partly be] bee partlie (A)
2 said] ~ beefore, (A, B)
3 and vsage] *om.* (A, B)
4 bodies,] ~ , with their diett, apparrell, [apparellinge, (B)] and such like, (A–C)
5 fleshly] fleshie (A)
5–12 bodies...humors,] bodies (as dwelling vnder a northern climat) but verie vnweildie, and vnactive withall, as being full of gross humors, which coommeth partlie by the numnes, which they gett by the colld, but speciallie of their diet, that standeth most of roots, onnyons, garlike, cabbage, and such like, (A, B); bodies: counting ...burley. But...withall which ...humours, (C)
14–24 Their...weeke.] When they exceed and have varietie of dishes, the first are their baked meates (for rost meat they eat [vse (B)] little) and then their brothes or porrage. They beginn commonlie with a Charke or small cupp of aquavite (which they call Russ wine) and then drinck not, till towards the end of their meales, taking it in largelie and all togither, with kissing on an other at everie pleadge. To drinck drunck, is an ordinarie matter with them, everie day in the week. And thearfore after dinner, thear is no talking with them, but everie mann goeth to his bench, to take his afternoones sleep, which is as ordinarie with them, as their nights

rest. **[**And...rest. To...week.
(B)**]** (A, B)

24 common] *om.* (A, B)
25 a] *om.* (D, E)
27 meashed with] ~ in (A, B)
28 would breede] breedeth (A, B)
28 many] ~ gross humors, and would
fill them full of (A, B)
30 twise...euery] twise, thrise, or fower
times a (A, B)
31–32 *Peaches...like*] peaches and potlads, which are made like open
and close (A, B)
36 darke, and] *om.* (A)
38 that] which (A, B)
39 men. Whereof] ~ , whearof (B)
39 I...bee] is (as it seemeth) (A, B)
42 because] by reason (A, B)
43 of] *om.* (A)
43 both...patiently,] and with a great
deal more patience (A, B)
46 as...almost] allmost as hott (A)
46 at a] ~ the (A, B)
48 that] *om.* (C)
48 mende] amend (A)
51 made...matter,] no matter with
them (A, B)
51–52 their husbandes:] the husbands
them selves (A); their husbandes themselves (B)
52 make] give (A, B)
54 them...fowle] theyr wives of such
foule skinned (B)
54 to become] to bee made (A); made (B)
55–56 This...of.] *om.* (A, B)
59 little...then] but (A–C)
62 Emperour. Then] Emperour what
time (A, B)
65 for] *om.* (A, B)
68 pearle...stone,] pretious stone and
pearle (A)
70 vnto] into (D, E)
70 while] whiles (A–C)
72–73 close coat] cote close (B)
78 low, and] low, (A)
79 all] *om.* (A–C)
84 folles] cloutes (A); cloth (B)

84–85 in steed...hose] *om.* (A, B)
89 Gentlemen.] gentlemen. This is the
Noblemans attire. (A, B)
90 attire] apparrell (A–C)
92 cloth, or] ~ of (C)
103 stone] stones (A, B)
105 pendent. The] ~ , the (A–C)
108 set] ~ thick (A, B)
109 stone] ~ very thick (C)
112 or...guilt] *om.* (A, B)
112–13 walnut. Which] ~ , which (B)
115 their backes] the back (C)
117 elbowes] elbow (A, B)
119 On] Of (A)
124 shew...selfe] shew (A, B)
127 of the] ~ his (B)
128 a] *om.* (A, B)
129 sheepskinne] sheepes skyn (B)
132 their...habite] in the winter (A, B)
132 time] *om.* (A)
133 they weare] hee weareth (A, B)
133 their shirts] his shirt (A, B)
133 their backes] his back (A, B)
134 their legges] his leggs (A, B)
134 redde or blew] blew or red (A, B)
136 the Sommer] sommer (A, B)
136 her] their (A, B)
137 for so] as (A, B)
142 shee] it (A–C)
143–96 As...profession.] [This passage
follows l. 13 in C.]
147 a...pride,] verie pride and disdain,
(A, B)
149 their] this (A–C)
149 vp] ~ among the Russ people
(A–C)
150–51 by...State,] most agreable to the
State that now is, (A–C)
151 gouernment. Which] ~ , which (A)
154–55 to be...of] *om.* (A, B)
156 print into] woorse print vpon (A, B)
157 mindes] ~ and qualitie (A, B)
157 his] the (A, B)
157 verie] *om.* (A, B)
158 chiefe...other] *om.* (A, B)
159 are...as] they ar (A, B)
159 one...specially] *om.* (A, B)

162 to the] ~ a (B)
162 dust...lieth] verie dust (A)
163 the] an (A–C)
164–65 By...You] They...man. By...
  murder. You (A); They...
  man. By...murther, yow (B)
166 sometime] sometimes (A); many
  tymes (B)
166 very] *om.* (B)
166 townes,] Townes and Cities, (A, B)
166 hee] they (A)
167 out] *om.* (A, B)
168 rescue him] ~ the partie (A)
169 cruelties] ~ that are (A, B)

171 such as] them that (B)
174 violent...desperate] desperate and
  violent (B)
174 manner, with] ~ . With (A)
177 so...and] *om.* (A, B)
183 for the most part] *om.* (A)
185 may be] may partly bee (C)
185–86 haue traded] trade (A)
190 odious] much hated (A–C)
190 to all] of all (A, C); of (B)
190 to] *om.* (A–C)
191 honest...iust] of honest and iust
  beehaviour (A–C)
195 Heathenish] heathen (A, B)

The Tartars or Ten Tribes

65 of] in (W)
67 mercy...vouchsafed] Mercy which God vouchsafed (W)
69 in] of (W)
69 World; as] ~ ! As (W)
72 he] ~ had (W)
73 of] ~ all (W)
73–74 you know,] *om.* (W)
75 in] ~ a (W)
76 of...the] in both (W)
77 for the] ~ that (W)
78 an] a very (W)
80–81 this their] this (L)
81 through] ~ the (W)
81 into another] to the other (W)
86 as] both (W)
88 which] *om.* (W)
89–90 *Tartar...Remnants* or *Remainders*] [Each enclosed in brackets in L.]
89 signifies] signifyeth (W)
91 who] which (W)
95 I] *om.* (W)
100–105 planted; as...parts.] planted (as... Parts,) (W)
101 great] *om.* (W)
103 States] State (W)
103 make] ~ a (W)
104 foreign] firm (L)
105–6 parts....Cities] Parts,) were the Cities (W)
109–10 *Haborus,* whereof] *Habor.* Of which (W)
113 who] which (W)
114 Sea] Seas (L)
114 calls the] calleth (W)
117 Country] Countries (W)
117 or] and (W)
118 and *Chualensky*] or ~ (W)
118 *Siberian*] *Hibernian* (L)
123 Monarchies] Monarchy (L)
123 have] hath (W)
125 thereabouts] thereabout (W)
126 into a] a very (W)
132 part] Parts (W)
132 by the] by (W)
133 who] which (W)

135 but] ~ rather (W)
138 habitations] Habitation (W)
141–42 serves...turns] served their Turn (W)
142 unto] to (W)
142 these] those (W)
143 and] *om.* (W)
146 Tribes...reunite] Tribes not long after did reunite (W)
148 desires...ever] Desire...ever disdaining (W)
151 followeth] follows (W)
153 greater] great (W)
153 scituated] situate (W)
159 with] by (W)
163 differing] *om.* (W)
164 and their] the (W)
172–73 that...*Hebrews*?] that of *Miriam* among the *Hebrews* (W)
173 *James,* with] ~ , or (W)
175 besides, the] also (W)
176 upon a] ~ an (W)
177 the Mount] that *Mount* (W)
180 and the] and (W)
181 agoe,...them,] ago (—*deest nonnihil,* I guess by the *Russe*) (W)
182 sometimes] sometime (W)
184 or] and (W)
187 for the] for (W)
188 dwelling places] Dwellings (W)
191 is] ~ now (W
192 *Nova Britannica*] *om.* (W)
194 *Persians*] Persian (W)
197 unless] except (W)
202 all the] all (W)
206 as] *om.* (W)
207 the] their (W)
208 make a] ~ the (W)
209 there continuing] continuing there (W)
212 parts] ~ by (W)
214 into] in (W)
221 nor] or (W)
221–22 to...Kinreds] and...Kinreds (L); to avoid the Confusion of their Kinred (W)
222 for] ~ the (W)

521

223–24 whole, they...People.] whole.
    (W)
224 and] *om.* (W)
225 else] *om.* (W)
231 *Chrime-Tartars*, which] *Chrime Tar-*
    tar; who (W)
233 pension] Pensions (W)
234 The Second is] *om.* (W)
235 The Third is] *om.* (W)
235 The Fourth is] *om.* (W)
236 other is] other (W)
237 barbarous] laborious (L)
237 The Fifth is] *om.* (W)
237 whence] from ~ (W)
238 who] which (W)
240 The sixth is] *om.* (W)
240 The seventh is] *om.* (W)
241 The eighth is] *om.* (W)
242 affected] affecting (W)
245 The ninth is] *om.* (W)
245 10.] *om.* (W)
246 *Herdman Tartar*] [Enclosed in brack-
    ets in L.]
246 by an ἐξοχῇ] *om.* (W)
248 above] of (W)
249 besides] beside (W)
250 who] which (W)
251 the Historians, who] Historians which
    (W)
252 Nation] ~ first (W)
254 nor] or (W)
256 said] saith (W)
257 derive] derives (W)
258 who] which (W)
258 probably] probable (L)
259 manners. That] ~ ; that (L)
260 at] *om.* (W)
263 number] great ~ (W)
264 throughout] through (W)
266 It...manifest,] it is a very manifest
    Truth, (W)
267 who] which (W)
268 means] meaneth (W)
270 like] agreeing with (W)
272 higher] the ~ (W)
273 *Turk*] [Enclosed in brackets in L.]
273 a Herd-man] an *Herdman* (W)

275 have] hath (W)
277 begins] beginneth (W)
280 doth] may (W)
284 with] to (W)
285 but] ~ that (W)
286 *Tartar*] *Tartars* (W)
287 *Israelites*] Israelite (W)
288 *Cyrus*...may] *Cyrus's* Time, may (W)
288 from] out of (W)
290 Fifthly...affirm] 5. Themselves af-
    firm (W)
290 receive] have received (W)
293 it...that] is reported (W)
298–99 reported and] *om.* (W)
299 some] certain (W)
300 *Russes*] *Russe* (W)
306 *Israelitish*] Israelite (W)
309 that] this (W)
313 their] the (W)
314 dwelling-place] Dwelling (W)
314 Country] Countries (W)
321 towards] toward (W)
322 lyes] lyeth (W)
325 or...lyes] and *Palestine* lieth (W)
326 towards] toward (W)
326 East] North (W)
327 who] which (W)
328 the River] *om.* (L)
331 speaks] speaketh (W)
334 way] ways (W)
334 have] hath (W)
334 are] is (W)
336 literally] ~ to be (W)
337 *Tartars*] *Tartar* (W)
339 Oriental] Orient (W)
342 higher] hither (W)
342 and] or (W)
346 lyes] lieth (W)
348 lyes] lieth (W)
348 betwixt] between (W)
351 agrees] agreeth (W)
352 10 in all] *om.* (W)
353 beside] besides (W)
355 all...Tribes.] his Tribe. (W)
355 famed] feigned (W)
357–58 more...here] here more ob-
    scurely (L)

359 latter time.] later Times. 2 Esdras, 13.
    cap. (W)
360 is...called] there is called (W)
361 gather to] ~ unto (W)
362 who] which (W)
362 Captives] captive (W)
365 to] into (W)
367 man] Men (W)
368 that...means] he meant (W)
368 lyes] lieth (W)
370 46] 26 (L)
373 peaceably] peaceable (W)
374 tells] telleth (W)

376 who] which (W)
376 Captive] Captives (W)
381 Tribes, who] Tribe, which (W)
382 those] these (W)
385 their] *om.* (W)
386 be] ~ an (W)
386 River] Water (W)
387 removing] Removal (W)
389 not] ~ now (W)
390 the] that (W)
390 then] than (W)
391 or] ~ the (W)

The Letters

The following letters have been printed:

1. James Heywood and Thomas Wright (eds.), *The Ancient Laws...for King's College, Cambridge, and for...Eton College* (London, 1850), p. 239; Grosart 1876, p. xvi.

2. Heywood and Wright, *Ancient Laws for King's College*, p. 241; Grosart 1876, p. xvii.

3. Heywood and Wright, *Ancient Laws for King's College*, p. 240

4. *Ibid.*, pp. 245–46.

6. *Ibid.*, pp. 248–49.

9. Grosart 1876, p. xxvii.

17. Edward A. Bond (ed.), *Russia at the Close of the Sixteenth Century* (London, 1856), pp. 342–51; Sir Henry Ellis (ed.), *Original Letters of Eminent Literary Men...* (London, 1843), pp. 79–85.

18. *Early Voyages*, I, cviii–cxiii.

20. Grosart 1876, pp. xxxv–xxxvi.

24. Alexander Dyce (ed.), *The Works of Beaumont and Fletcher* (11 vols.; London, 1843–46), I, xiv–xv; Thomas Birch, *Memoirs of the Reign of Queen Elizabeth* (2 vols.; London, 1754), II, 113–14.

36. The late MS copy in the British Museum has been printed in Grosart 1876, pp. xxx–xxxi; Charles Henry Cooper and Thompson Cooper, *Athenae Cantabrigienses* (3 vols.; Cambridge, 1858–1913), III, 36.

Letter 1
FLETCHER, LILES AND JOHNSON TO LORD BURGHLEY] [From the contents it is clear the person to whom the letter is addressed is the Chancellor, Lord Burghley.]
7 Authoritie;] ~

Leer 2
FLETCHER TO LORD BURGHLEY] [From the contents it is clear the letter is to Lord Burghley.]
6 matter.] ~

Letter 3
FLETCHER TO LORD BURGHLEY] [From the contents it is clear the letter is to Lord Burghley.]

Letter 4
26 quod] Quod
30 Rei publicæ] Reip. [I have in each case expanded this as two words.]

Letter 5

1   Domine,] ~

Letter 7

58–59   Tuæ . . . Cantabrigiensis.] [The
words in brackets are illegible,
but this closing is used frequently
in the volume of letters.]

Letter 8

FLETCHER TO SIR FRANCIS WAL-
SINGHAM] [The only evidence that
this letter is to Walsingham is that most
of the correspondence in Cott. Calig. C.
viii is to Walsingham. Also, Letter 9 is to
Walsingham and indicates that Fletcher
was under his patronage.]

1   Honourable.] ~

19   glory,] ~

19   Church,] ~

21   twoe,] ~.

30   League,] ~

48   resist,] ~.

58   other,] ~ .

Letter 9

FLETCHER TO SIR FRANCIS WAL-
SINGHAM [The endorsement is in
Walsingham's hand.]

Letter 10

HL   A true copie of the letter sent fro
Mr Gov̄nor and Mr / Doctor ffletcher from Hambrough
[Letters 10, 11, and 13 are all copies
in the same hand.]

30   it.] ~

47   England.] ~ ,

52   England.] ~,

60   same.] ~

64   almightie.] ~

Letter 11

HL   A true copie of a lr̄e sent from Ham-
brough by Mr / Gov̄nor and Mr /
Doctor ffletcher dated the xxixth
Iune 1587.

3   Flint] flint

43   departed;] ~

52   it.] ~

69   before.] ~ ,

74   hand,] ~

Letter 12

6   lyfe and] ~ as

Letter 13

4   effect.] ~

4   pointes.] ~

38   there,] ~

38   hope of] of hope

41   last.] ~

Letter 14

FLETCHER AND SALTONSTALL TO
THE PRIVY COUNCIL] [There is no
address to either Letter 14 or Letter
15; however, from the contents it is
clear that the writers are those who had
the commission to deal with Hamburg
(Fletcher and Saltonstall). In line 10, a
reference is made to "your Honours
Letters written to the Senat." The Privy
Council did write letters on behalf of the
Merchants Adventurers (see Letter 10,
l. 9).]

41   Nonsuch. Which] Nonsuch / the /
Which [Although "the" is not canceled, it seems that this was Fletcher's intention, as he starts a new
sentence in the following line.]

49   1586] 86

Letter 15

FLETCHER AND SALTONSTALL TO
THE PRIVY COUNCIL] [See textual
note to heading of Letter 14.]

60   proofes.] ~

64   communicated] [two canceled lower-
case d's — dederunt]

78   men, vittail,] ~ ~

79   Stoad,] ~

525

Letter 16a

1587] [The date assigned by the Historical
Manuscripts Commission is 1598, which
is much too late. In Reason 2, Fletcher
asks the queen to remember his present
employment to Hamburg, and the only
time Fletcher went to Hamburg was in
1587.]

Letter 17

FLETCHER TO LORD BURGHLEY]
[There is no address, but the endorsement is in Burghley's hand.]
71–72 intended.] ~
141 them that] ~ , That
164 but] by

Letter 18

FLETCHER TO THE QUEEN] [E. S.
Vilenskaya in "K Istorii Russko-Anglii-
skikh Otnoshenii v XVI v." ("A Contri-
bution to the History of Russo-English
Relations in the Sixteenth Century"),
Istoricheskie Zapiski, XXIX (1949), 123–
34, argues that this letter is by Fletcher
and is addressed to the queen. T. S.
Willan has briefly summarized her arguments in *The Early History of the Russia
Company* (Manchester, 1956), pp. 205–6,
n. 2, and accepts her conclusions. I agree
that they should be accepted.]
7 French,] ~
124–25 Bougharians, Medians,] ~ ~

Letter 20

3 tale,] ~ .
12 need.] ~
22 discourse.] ~
30 endeth,] ~
32 death,] ~ .
33 Anne,] ~ .
35 deserts,] ~ .
36 iudiciall,] ~ .
38 time,] ~ .
Matters to bee instructed in King Edwards time
2 Bolloign.] ~
6 vpon.] ~

7 Spain,] ~
7 Scotts,] ~
8 &c.] ~
15 matter.] ~
17 Marie.] ~
19 reign,] ~
21 Marie.] ~

Letter 21

15–21 [The enclosures have not been included, as they are summarized
in the *Calendar of Border Papers*,
II, No. 291.]

Letter 22

8 experience,] ~ .
20 shalbee,] ~ .

Letter 23

1–3 [The enclosures have not been included, as they are summarized in
the *Calendar of Border Papers*, II,
No. 304.]

Letter 24

[This letter is a scribal copy. For its relation
to Letter 25a, see the textual note to that
letter.]
6 fruites,] ~
15–16 Wickham, Hadham,] ~ ~
35 thirds,] ~
35 400^{li},] ~

Letter 25a

1596 or 1597 [This letter is endorsed 1597,
but because of its similarity to Letter 24,
I would prefer to date it sometime toward the end of 1596. Although the
two letters are very similar, this petition
seems to be an amplification of Letter 24.
The suit is more definite (ll. 40–41), and
a schedule for payment of the debt is
attached (Letter 25b).]
6 fruits,] ~
35 400^{li},] ~

Letter 25b

7   Year.] ~
8   payment.] ~

Letter 26a

1596 or 1597] [CSP Dom. (1595–97), p. 247,
    dates the letter: "June?, 1596." From
    Reason 3 one can infer that the suit for
    remission of part of the debt had been
    submitted, and thus this letter would
    follow Letters 25a and 25b. As Queen
    Elizabeth cites Reason 1 of this letter in
    her discharge of the debt on 27 April
    1597, it would further indicate that this
    petition was the last of the three.]

Letter 35

FLETCHER TO THE PRIVY COUN-
    CIL] [There is no address, and nothing in
    the letter indicates to whom the confes-
sion was sent. The Lords of the Privy
Council had committed Fletcher to
custody (Letter 33, ll. 1–3) and had also
issued a warrant to Alderman Hampson
to permit Fletcher's wife to see him on
business (PC 2/26, p. 115). It would also
seem likely that Fletcher would address
his confession to the group who had the
power to release him.]

76   Cheap.] ~
76   Canterburies] Cant.
97   effect.] ~

Letter 36

[There is a late MS copy of this letter: BM
    Add. MS 6177, f. 151.]

9   bonds.] ~

Letter 41

19   Scotland, Rusland,] ~ ~

Index

Index

[Page references to primary material are italicized;
page references to secondary material are in roman type.]

531

Index

Berosus: cited by Giles F., *185*; source for *Russe Commonwealth*, 144, 432

Best, Robert: quoted, 445, 459, 460, 461, 462, 463, 464

Beza, Theodore: source for *Licia*, 417, 418

Bezobrazov, Istoma Osipovich, *299*, 464

Bishop of Lincoln, visitor of King's College: petitioned by fellows of the college, 10; writes Lord Burghley, 10

Bodyansky, O. M.: his translation of *Russe Commonwealth* confiscated, 167

Bolshoi Dvorets, *213–14*, 441–42

Bolshoi Prikhod, *215–17*, 441–43

Bond, Edward A.: editor of *Russe Commonwealth*, 167

Bond, Thomas, 7

Bonfinius, Anthony: cited by Giles F., *188*; source for *Russe Commonwealth*, 144, 145, 435, 453

Bonnefons, Jean: source for *Licia*, 57, 424

Bonner, Edmund: Giles F. writes poem on death of, 8

Boristhenes River, *172*, *177*

Borough, Stephen: cited, 456

Botero, Giovanni: source for *The Tartars or Ten Tribes*, 310

Bourchier, Thomas, Archbishop of Canterbury, 426

Bowes, Sir William: appointed commissioner, 35

Boyars, *203*, 439, 440–41

Brand, John, *350*

Brerewood, Edward: rejects theory that the Tartars are the ten lost tribes of Israel, 312

Bridgewater, Richard, Chancellor of Ely, 15

Brightman, Thomas: cited by Giles F., *330–331*; source for *The Tartars or Ten Tribes*, 309, 468

Brooke, Maximilian: Giles F. writes poem on coat-of-arms of, 14, 17

Brooke, William: William Trumbull owes money to, 27

Browne, Sir Thomas: possible use of *Russe Commonwealth* by, 150; *Pseudodoxia Epidemica* quoted, 453

Brownists, 75, 418

Buccleuch, Duke of: rescues Kinmont Willie, 33–34

Buck, Thomas, printer, 159

Buckhurst, Lord, Thomas Sackville: urges United Provinces to negotiate with Spain, 41

Bulgakov-Golitsyn, *202*, 439

Burghley, Lord, William Cecil: Giles F. proposes a Latin history of Queen Elizabeth's reign to, *383–88*; Giles F. reports his negotiations in Russia to, 27, 135; Giles F. seeks patronage of, 31; ignores Giles F.'s request for patronage, 36; letter from Bishop of Lincoln to, 10; letter from Giles F., Robert Liles, and Robert Johnson to, *337*; letters from Giles F. to, *338*, *338–39*, *341–42*, *343–44*, *367–75*, *383–88*, *389–90*, *391–92*; mediates in Grame affair, 34; note by Roger Goad to, 11; objects to Sir Walter Raleigh's grant of license to export wool, 472; petitioned by Russia Company to suppress *Russe Commonwealth*, 150–54; recommends clemency in dealing with the Grames, *391–92*; suppresses *Russe Commonwealth*, 153–54; takes action against fellows of King's College, 11–13; urges United Provinces to negotiate with Spain, 41

Burton, Robert: possible use of *Russe Commonwealth* by, 150; *Anatomy of Melancholy* quoted, 453

Burton, Thomas: admitted freeman of City of London, 43

Butts, Bridget: Giles F. writes three epitaphs on, 8–9

Buturlin, Ivan Mikhailovich, *211*, 440

Byron, Sir John, 417

Caesar, Julius: writes letter to Sir Robert Cecil, *396–97*; mentioned, 35, 40

Carr, Nicholas: Giles F. writes two poems for, 9

Caviar: chief product of Russia, *181–82*, *184*

Cawley, Robert R.: cited, 149

Cecil, Ann: poem by Giles F. on marriage of, 9

Cecil, Sir Robert: congratulated by Giles F. on being made secretary of state, *390–91*; Giles F. petitions, for position of Master of Requests, *390–91*; Giles F. seeks favor of, 46; letter from Giles F., Julius Caesar, Daniel Dunn, and John Lloyd to, *396–97*; letters from Giles F. to, *390–91, 401, 402–3, 404–5, 408–9, 409–10, 410, 411, 411–12, 413*; negotiates with United Provinces, 41

Chalcocondylas, Laonicus: cited by Giles F., *254, 255, 262, 326–27*; source for *Russe Commonwealth*, 137, 138, 144, 454, 456; source for *The Tartars or Ten Tribes*, 310, 467, 468

Chancellor, Richard: quoted, 428–29, 430, 431, 433, 434, 444, 448, 455, 460, 461, 462, 463

Chandler, M. J., 33 (n. 72)

Charde, Thomas: in debt, 21

Charisius, Jonas, ambassador from Denmark, 47

Cheremisinov, Dementi Ivanovich, *211*, 440

Chetverts: description of jurisdictions, 205–206; income, *214, 216, 217*, 442–43; Russia divided into, *174, 205*, 439

Christianeis: country people of Russia called, *205*

Christianity: introduced into Russia in A.D. 990, *262–63*

Churchyard, Thomas: "Shore's Wife" alluded to, 426

Clesinine, Andreas, *299*

Cobham, Lady, *336*

Cobham, Lord, 17

Coke, Sir Edward: orders examination of Giles F., 44

Collinder, Björn: cited, 455

Colmer, Clement: appointed commissioner, 35

Common Council, City of London. *See* London, City of

Cooper, Charles Henry: cited, 9

Court of Aldermen, City of London. *See* London, City of

Crim tartar: burning of Moscow by, *247*;

homage done to, by the Russian tsar, *247–48*; invasion of Russia by, *246–47, 248*, 451–52; Turks descendants of, *255*; mentioned, 326

Cromer, Martin: Giles F. alludes to, *262*; source for *Russe Commonwealth*, 144, 145, 146, 427, 427–28, 446, 450, 456

Crow, Martha: editor of *Licia*, 71–72

Dacres, Christopher, *389*

Dallye, W., 153

Daniel, Roger, printer, 159, 160

Daniel, Samuel: "Complaint of Rosamond" alluded to, 426

Daniil, Duke of Moscow, *185*, 432

Darcie, Edward, 32

Davison, Sir William: letter from Giles F. to, *401–2*; mentioned, 479

Daye, John, printer, 70

Dekker, Thomas: probable use of *Russe Commonwealth* by, 150; *Brittannia's Honor* quoted, 430–31; *The Dead Tearme* quoted, 464; *The Honest Whore* quoted, 454; *Jests to Make You Merry* quoted, 447; *The Seven Deadly Sins* quoted, 447

Denny, Sir Edward, 396

De Vere, Edward, Earl of Oxford: poem by Giles F. on marriage of, 9

Dingoe Novogrodskoy: coin commemorating victory of Novgorodians over Scythians, *186–87*, 433

Dormer, William, Lord, 417–18

Dorrington, William: admitted to King's College, 7; co-author of memoir of Nicholas Carr, 9

Drake, Sir Francis, *365, 371*

Du Bouzet, Charles: translator of *Russe Commonwealth*, 167

Duivenvoorde, Admiral, 40, 41, 477

Dunn, Daniel: letter to Sir Robert Cecil by, *396–97*; Master of Requests, 25 (n. 35); mentioned, 35, 40

Dunning, Robert: participant in college dispute, 10–13

Du Plessis-Mornay, Philippe: mentioned by Giles F., 310, *321–22*; *A Woorke*

Index

Index

Index

Index

Index

Index

Wheeler, John: quoted, 474

Whiston, William: advances theory that Tartars are the lost tribes of Israel, 312; editor of *The Tartars or Ten Tribes*, 314–315

Whyte, Eustace, a seminary priest, 32

Willan, T. S.: cited, 431, 460, 475

Wotton, Edward: sent to Scotland, 20–21, 470

Wotton, Nicholas, *344*, 470

Wotton, Thomas, 13, *344–46*, 470

Young, Sir Peter, *357*, 473

Yur'ev, Nikita Romanovich, *202*, 438

Zemsky Sobor: institution of, *200–201*, 437

Zlata Baba: the myth of, *258–59*, *454–55*; mentioned, 146